Reviews for *A Nation in Waiting*

'For those who seek an understanding of the political and social dynamics of contemporary Indonesia, there is no better starting point.'

Jamie Mackie, *Asian Wall Street Journal*

' ...one of the most important books on Asia in many years. Schwarz has peeled back the covers that normally cloak the workings of the Indonesian political and business system... His book is measured, thoughtful and intensely readable.

David Jenkins, *Sydney Morning Herald*

'This fascinating work on policy making in Indonesia is essential reading for all serious students of this subject.'

John MacDougall, *Journal of Developing Areas*

'As thoughtful an account of the Suharto era in Indonesian politics as one could hope for.'

Foreign Affairs

'...beautifully written, evocative and wide-ranging. It is truly an outstanding work which will greatly influence our understanding of Indonesia.'

Merle Ricklefs, *The Australian*

' ... the best overview of the dynamics of modern-day Indonesia so far.'

Andrew MacIntyre, *The Australian*

'... an invaluable guide to the forces at work within the country that will shape the future. This is a well-informed, easy-to-read and badly needed book.'

Philip Bowring, *International Herald Tribune*

' ... a balanced, incisive, and knowing analysis of this complex country... No other author comes close to blending his scope, detail, vividness, and even-handedness.'

David Dapice, Tufts University

'Anyone who knows Indonesia well will read [this book] with interest, and anyone who wants to know modern Indonesia better, or at all, will do well to read [it] soon.'

Journal of Asian Studies

A Nation in Waiting

A Nation in Waiting

Indonesia's search for stability

ADAM SCHWARZ

TALISMAN

Third impression published 2004

First published in 2004
Reprinted @ 2005 (Text Correction)
Talisman Publishing Pte Ltd
52, Genting Lane #06-05
Ruby Land Complex 1
Singapore 349560
Phone:(65) 67493551
Fax: (65) 67493552
Email: customersvc@apdsing.com

ISBN 981-05-0506-X

Map by Valda Brook

Set in 10/11 pt Times
Printed by Saik Wah Press Pte Ltd

To my wife, Stacey,
and my two sons, Jackson and William

About the author

Adam Schwarz has spent nearly two decades professionally engaged in Southeast Asia. For ten years he was a correspondent for the *Far Eastern Economic Review* in Jakarta, Hong Kong, Bangkok and Hanoi, covering political, economic, corporate, military and environmental affairs. He ran his own consulting firm, Nusantara Consulting, based in Washington, providing political and economic risk analysis for private, public and multilateral clients. While in Washington, he was an adjunct professor at the School of Advanced International Studies, Johns Hopkins University and the School of Foreign Service, Georgetown University. He joined McKinsey & Company, a leading global management consultancy, in 2001 and is currently a Senior Fellow at the Mckinsey Global Institute, McKinsey's in-house economics think-tank. A widely published writer on Indonesia and the region, he is a member of the Council on Foreign Relations in the United States and a Research Fellow at Murdoch University's Asia Studies Centre in Australia. He is currently based in Singapore.

Contents

Introduction to the Third Impression

"One of the things that everyone knows but no one can quite think how to demonstrate is that a country's politics reflect the design of its culture. At one level, the proposition is indubitable – where else could French politics exist but France? Yet, merely to state it is to raise doubts. Since 1945, Indonesia has seen revolution, parliamentary democracy, civil war, presidential autocracy, mass murder, and military rule. Where is the design on that?"

Clifford Geertz[1]

Indonesia's five years of democracy since the fall of Soeharto have been a roller-coaster of emotions and expectations. Exhilaration and a sense of liberation have been whiplashed by disillusionment and a yearning for the predictability embedded in 32 years of authoritarian rule. More than half a decade out of the presidential palace, Soeharto's legacy remains powerful: how he exercised power, dealt with social conflicts, understood economic development and distributed the spoils of growth have all profoundly influenced the leaders that followed him, some in positive ways, others not. Deciphering Indonesia today still hinges on understanding the Soeharto record.

Democracy and *reformasi* have released Indonesia from the shackles of Soeharto's New Order government. Political freedoms have expanded across the board. Indonesians now take for granted the right to assemble, speak their minds, and form organisations, political parties and even new provinces. The media have been transformed, both in terms of numbers and in the breadth of opinions expressed. Decentralisation has significantly weakened Jakarta's economic and political hold over the archipelago's far-flung regions. The military has lost both its reserved seats in the national parliament and its control over the police force . Changes to the constitution – up to and including permitting direct elections for president – underpin the country's democratic foundations and have made political institutions more representative. In 2004, one democratically elected, civilian government is scheduled to transfer power to another – a first for Indonesia.

Still, future voters are unlikely again to wallow in the euphoria that enveloped the 1999 elections. Then, more than 100 million people went to the polls in an atmosphere akin to a nationwide street party. Many older Indonesians were reminded of the heady days of the early 1950s after independence at last had been wrested from the Dutch. But gaining democracy, like gaining independence, represents a beginning, not an end. For many Indonesians, the new political contract has not made them any less poor or less concerned for their future. Democracy has not been a panacea. Not even a palliative.

Transitions from authoritarian rule are rarely linear and are never easy. Countries that underwent similar transitions in Latin America and Eastern Europe often required a decade or more to achieve real traction. Indonesia's transition was particularly challenging, as it began abruptly, without preparation and amidst a severe economic crisis.Indonesians' innate pragmatism, patience and pluralism may well provide the country's leadership with enough time to learn how to operate effectively within a democratic context. But that patience, as Soeharto discovered in 1998, is not limitless. Indeed, tensions are inarguably on the rise between a desire for continued *reformasi* and a demand for more effective governance.

Disillusionment with political leaders is deepening. The economy has yet to recover from the financial crisis that began in 1997. New investment is scarce, and unemployment is rising. Per-capita income is still some 10% lower than when the crisis first struck six years ago. Vigilante gangs are on the prowl and paramilitary outfits flex their muscles , testimony to the inadequacies of the newly independent police force. Corruption remains a national scourge, wreaking economic damage even worse than under Soeharto's rule in the view of many business executives.[2] On balance, party politics continues to strike most Indonesians as irrelevant if not an impediment to effective governance, while the executive branch is seen as weak and rudderless. In a recent national poll, fewer than half of Indonesians believed their country was going in the right direction, compared with more than 70% at the time of the 1999 elections.[3]

Such a disturbing lack of optimism is at least partly rooted in the records of the three politicians who have claimed the title of President in the past five years. B. J. Habibie, having spent his entire political career happily in Soeharto's shadow, assumed the presidency when Soeharto stepped down in May, 1998 (having been vice-president in the prior two months). Indelibly tied to the New Order government, Habibie faced the near-impossible task of remaking himself as a reformist charting a new course for Indonesia. Although a brilliant engineer and tireless worker, Habibie had no experience of operating within a democracy, and had few constituencies of support with his patron having faded out of the picture. Inevitably, perhaps, he was tarred by an investigation into a messy banking scandal, which further eroded his chances in the 1999 elections.

History may well accord Habibie a reputation as a reformer, even a liberal, but not as a successful President. Two initiatives are his principal political bequests, both of which weakened the nation in the eyes of many Indonesians, even if laudable in concept. Impetuously, he called for an independence referendum in East Timor, the former Portuguese colony annexed by Indonesia in 1976. Habibie did not understand the nuances of the political dynamics within East Timor or within Indonesia (and the Indonesian military). Unsurprisingly, the East Timorese voted overwhelmingly for independence in a snap referendum in August 1999, triggering an orgy of violence by paramilitary thugs, with the tacit support of the Indonesian military. Habibie's second failure was to decentralise political and economic power away from Jakarta on a timetable that was almost absurdly short. Moreover, Habibie, fairly or not, was tainted as an opportunist trying to curry political favor with the outer regions prior to the 1999 elections. Decentralisation has not been the disaster that some feared, but its rushed implementation has created a litany of woes, among them rampant corruption at the local level and a drop-off in investment.

Habibie was followed as president by Abdurrahman Wahid, the charismatic leader of Indonesia's largest Muslim group, the Nahdlatul Ulama (NU). A savvy backroom political player, Wahid outmanoeuvred the current president, Megawati Sukarnoputri, to seize victory at the October 1999 meeting of Indonesia's super parliament, the *Majelis*

Permusyawaratan Rakyat, a relic of Soeharto's political apparatus. Megawati's party, the Indonesia Democratic Party of Struggle (PDI-P), had been clear winners in parliamentary elections held earlier in 1999. But Megawati was not a politician in the same league as her flamboyant father, Sukarno, Indonesia's nationalist hero and first president. She spurned numerous opportunities to put together a winning coalition, and eventually had to settle for the vice-presidency.

Wahid had been a popular and daring opposition figure during the Soeharto era. A liberal at heart, he was beloved not only by Muslims but also by ethnic minorities and non-Muslims. But although Wahid had enormous symbolic appeal, he had neither a talent for nor interest in the nitty-gritty details of managing Indonesia's transition from authoritarian rule. Hobbled by a stroke that left him nearly blind, Wahid was further constrained by a lack of parliamentary support. His party, the National Awakening Party, or PKB, won only 12% of the seats in the 1999 legislative elections.

An eccentric intellectual as a Soeharto-era dissident, Wahid as president resisted all attempts at imposing bureaucratic discipline on his administration. Within six months, Wahid's government had degenerated into farce, with ministers openly contradicting each other and some overtly undermining the president. His erratic and sometimes provocative behavior turned off the elite, scared off investors and alienated one mass-based constituency after another. Wahid's presidency lasted only 21 months; his impeachment was given critical support by a still-bitter Megawati, who would succeed him as president in August 2001.

Just weeks after Megawati had assumed office, Al Qaeda attacked the World Trade Center. The new president's reaction to the outrages of September 11 was achingly slow and inadequate. Initially, she abdicated public discourse to Islamic radicals who sullied Indonesia's international image and alarmed potential investors. Unlike Wahid, an articulate advocate of Indonesia's religious pluralism, Megawati was unwilling and perhaps unable to give voice to Indonesia's religiously tolerant majority.

Yet Megawati brought a welcome calmness to the presidential palace after the eccentricities of its two previous incumbents. She was only too happy to be low profile. Her demeanour soothed the financial markets and partly redressed the view among international investors that Indonesia was too risky. However, like her two predecessors, Megawati lacked the managerial skills essential to getting things done. She also was uninterested in day-to-day policy and lacked a vision for Indonesia's future that ventured beyond a few general principles. An indifferent and uncomfortable public speaker, Megawati comes across to many as aloof, even elitist. By the end of 2003, her earlier high standing among the PDI-P faithful had been considerably weakened.

Although each quite different personalities, all three of Indonesia's post-Soeharto presidents have done little to build the foundations for the future. None has paid sufficient attention to the crucial task of restoring economic growth. None has warmed to the role of Educator-in-Chief, explaining to the Indonesian people the essential requirements for building a successful democracy. None has tackled the corruption that ensnares Indonesia's economy and erodes social trust. Perhaps most damagingly, none has evinced a burning commitment to creating and nurturing the strong institutions and rule of law so critical to successful democracies.

Of course, Indonesians' rising dissatisfaction cannot be blamed solely on the leadership capabilities of Habibie, Wahid and Megawati. Three decades of Soeharto's one-man rule left Indonesia poorly equipped for representative democracy and the manner of its ending immeasurably exacerbated the transition from his authoritarian rule. Soeharto's weakening of all governmental institutions other than the executive branch ultimately left Indonesia the country most ravaged by the 1997-98 financial crisis. Unlike other crisis-hit countries, Indonesia had neither a functional political process for achieving consensus on a crisis management strategy not a functioning legal system to restructure the economy.[4] Once the crisis began, investors (belatedly) focused on Indonesia's governance shortcomings and bolted for the exits. With this as backdrop, no leader, no matter how skilled, would have found it easy to shepherd Indonesia in the immediate post-Soeharto era.

Ethnic, religious, territorial and societal tensions were bottled up during Soeharto's tenure, and predictably burst into the open once he had departed the scene. Following the granting of independence to East Timor in 1999, separatist threats in Aceh and West Papua (renamed from Irian Jaya) drained precious resources from the center and complicated the task of redefining the military's political role. Brutal clashes between Muslim and non-Muslim communities in Sulawesi and the Moluccas sorely tested Indonesia's cherished self-image as a nation of diversities able to live in harmony. And the horrific bombings in Bali in October 2002 and in Jakarta in August 2003 punctured the illusion that Islamic radicalism could not grow roots in Indonesian soil. The bombings, and the trials that followed them, revealed Islamic extremists to be more numerous in Indonesia than commonly thought, and that they enjoyed considerable support from and linkages with foreign radical groups, including Al Qaeda.[5] Perhaps the only positive outcome of the bombings was to shatter the widely held belief that Indonesia was unaffected by the war on terrorism. Although the government remained largely unwilling to concede the presence of Al Qaeda-linked operatives and networks in Indonesia, the country's various law enforcement agencies received generally high marks for tracking down the perpetrators of the Bali and Jakarta bombings.

Gaining ground in the battles against terrorism, separatism and political disillusionment would be immeasurably helped by some vigour being restored to Indonesia's economy. Again, the causes of Indonesia's post-crisis economic struggles are a mixture of the difficult conditions inherited from Soeharto and weak leadership by his successors. Progress has been made in some areas, especially over the past two years. Inflation is down to mid-single digits, the rupiah is stronger against major currencies, and interest rates are no longer punishingly high. Government debt is now more manageable, having exceeded 100% of GDP in 2001. Privatisation has proceeded fitfully, but at least has not ground to a halt.

Necessary institutions are slowly emerging. A new law ensuring the independence of the Central Bank should help avoid a repeat of the negligent, irresponsible use of the country's financial assets seen in 1997-98. An anti-corruption commission and new commercial court have been established, as have quasi-independent regulatory bodies for the telecommunications and oil and gas industries. The Indonesian Bank Restructuring Agency (IBRA) has largely completed its mission of selling off the assets seized by the government during the financial crisis.

Yet Indonesia's economy remains in a parlous state, being the slowest to get back on track of all the crisis-ravaged Asian countries. Although the large and resilient informal sector has lessened the pain, recent annual growth of 3-4% is not nearly sufficient to absorb the more than 2 million job seekers who enter the workforce each year. With unemployment rising, little headway is being made in reducing the incidence of poverty: more than half of all Indonesians get by on less than two dollars a day. Not surprisingly, survey after survey shows that most Indonesians regard the economy as the biggest crisis facing the country.

At the industry level, much-needed reforms are still awaited. Banks, for example, have stabilized their balance sheets but they are not yet acting as financial intermediaries to the Indonesian economy. Weak governance at the bigger state-owned banks practically ensures more scandals lie ahead. Trade protectionism is on the rise, shielding Indonesia's least productive firms and thus eroding the country's general level of competitiveness, even while competition from China and India steadily rises.[6] Investors have fled from cost-sensitive industries such as textiles and electronics. Few of Indonesia's large corporations have been significantly restructured, as has been the case in other crisis-hit countries.

Perhaps most worryingly, Indonesia is signally failing to attract new investment. Both foreign and domestic flows are far below pre-crisis levels. The country's physical infrastructure (eg, roads, power plants, water treatment facilities) is increasingly dilapidated, further discouraging new investment. Shockingly, Indonesia has experienced a net negative outflow of capital every year between 1998 and 2002. For no other country in Southeast Asia was that true, not even for a single year in that period.[7] Decentralisation has contributed to the dismal investment record, particularly off-Java. Although a number of promising local leaders have emerged, many newly empowered district administrations have introduced a bevy of new taxes and investor-unfriendly regulations. Nationally, the political leadership is unsophisticated in – and in some case indifferent to – global economic realities and the dynamics of capital flows. Although they have achieved some notable successes in consolidating democratic reforms, the main political parties have a less stellar record on economic issues. Indeed, the parties by and large remain immature and insular, which has done little to improve the confidence level of the business community. Most worryingly for foreign investors, little progress is observable in ensuring the rule of law holds sway and in creating well-functioning, market-regulating institutions.[8] Without them, Indonesia's investment risk remains high.

Indeed, a half-decade of ineffective government and middling economic growth have left Indonesians increasingly nostalgic for Soeharto's strong-armed, corrupt but effective rule. "Is it surprising," asked *The Jakarta Post* at the end of 2003, "that in less than six years since the fall of Soeharto, democracy is equated with chaos, and dictatorship with leadership and stability?"[9] There is more than elite angst at work here. In a wide-ranging, countrywide survey carried out in mid-2003 by the Asia Foundation, a majority of Indonesians said they were ready to forego some political rights and freedoms in exchange for an authoritarian leader capable of maintaining law and order.[10] Soeharto nostalgia is now captured in the acronym SARS, which in Indonesia now also stands for '*sindrom aku rindu Soeharto*', roughly translated as the "The I Miss Soeharto syndrome". (No social phenomenon is allowed to pass in Indonesia without being accorded its own acronym.)

Interesting parallels can be found in Eastern Europe where, a few years after the fall of the Berlin Wall, several (mildly reformed) communist parties were voted back into power. In times of rapid change, people naturally reach out for the familiar, flaws and all. So it is in today's Indonesia, where Soeharto's old party, Golkar, is resurgent and retired military figures are emerging as presidential candidates.

Post-Soeharto governments have been inadvertently complicit in fuelling this phenomenon. For example, their refusal to prosecute corruption cases involving Soeharto's family and associates has obscured the damage inflicted on the economic and social fabric by decades of state-sanctioned corruption.

Posterity's account of Soeharto, the main character in this volume and the man who styled himself Indonesia's Father of Development, remains uncertain a half-decade since he was forced from power. In the long view of history, Indonesia's transition from Soeharto's politically repressive but economically effective rule is still in its early stages, and it is uncertain which side of the ledger historians will remember most clearly. What is clear is that the challenges of nation-building abound in Indonesia, none more so than the urgent task of rebuilding governmental institutions and the rule of law. This is the challenge that must be met if Indonesian democracy is to settle firm roots in this volatile land.

❖

This new printing of *A Nation in Waiting* contains the ten chapters included in the original edition, which was published in 1994, plus the two chapters written for an updated edition published in 1999, about a year after Soeharto had stepped down. The ten chapters of the original edition, which have not been modified, are primarily concerned with Indonesia of the late 1980s and early 1990s. The book begins with a look at the origins of the Indonesian nation (Chapter 1), Soeharto's rise to power (Chapter 2), and the successes and failures of Soeharto's economic policies up through the early 1990s (Chapter 3), three topics that remain relevant in understanding the background to the contemporary political debate.

The book then turns to a discussion of specific challenges facing Indonesia in the middle part of the decade: reconciling economic nationalism with the demands of globalisation (Chapter 3); reducing resentment of the ethnic Chinese minority (Chapter 5); curbing corruption and nepotism (Chapter 6); accommodating Islamic political aspirations (Chapter 7); finding a solution to the East Timor problem (Chapter 8); establishing a legal framework for individual rights (Chapter 9); and coping with the pressures for political reform (Chapter 10).

The two chapters added to the current edition were written in early 1999. Chapter 11 picks up Indonesia's story in the mid-1990s, about where the first edition left off, and carries through to Soeharto's resignation. It describes Soeharto's ever-decreasing tolerance of criticism, his use of Islam as a political tool, his fostering of military disunity and his unwillingness to rein in his increasingly rapacious children. The chapter continues with a detailed account of Soeharto's responses to the financial crisis beginning in 1997 and a day-by-day recounting of Soeharto's last weeks in office.

Chapter 12 covers the period form President Habibie's inauguration in late May 1998 through March 1999. It discusses Habibie's only partly successful efforts to build a constituency of political support and the re-emergence of Islam as an important political actor. The chapter explains the dilemma facing the Indonesian military as it struggles to redefine its political role in post-Soeharto Indonesia and it describes the important obstacles still to be overcome in restoring economic health. The chapter concludes with a look at the major political challenges facing Indonesia as it entered the new millennium.

As is often the case with projects such as these, there are far more people to thank than space allows. My greatest debt is to the many Indonesians who have generously taken the time to share with me their insights, aspirations and beliefs. It is through their voices that I have tried to tell Indonesia's story. I also thank Penny Burtt, William Daniel, Greg Fealy, Bert Hofman, Sydney Jones, Catherine Lugrin and Steve Proctor for their helpful comments on earlier drafts of this introductory essay. Of course, all the usual disclaimers apply: the responsibility for the opinions and judgments expressed in the following pages is solely mine.

Adam Schwarz

Singapore, February 2004

1. Clifford Geertz, 'Afterword: The Politics of Meaning', in *Culture and Politics in Indonesia*, ed. Claire Holt, Cornell University Press, Ithaca, 1972, p. 319.

[2] For a full treatment of the corruption phenomenon in Indonesia, see World Bank, "Corruption in Indonesia: A Development Perspective", Draft World Bank Report, Jakarta, September 2003. In surveys conducted by Transparency International, Indonesia is perennially ranked as one of the most corrupt nations in the world.

[3] Asia Foundation, "Democracy in Indonesia – A Survey of the Indonesian Electorate in 2003," Jakarta, 2003.

[4] The point is well covered in Bert Hofman and Ella Rodrick-Jones, "Indonesia: Rapid Growth, Weak Institutions," (forthcoming).

[5] The Brussels-based International Crisis Group has published a series of authoritative reports on radical Islamic groups in Indonesia. See for example, "Jemaah Islamiyah In Southeast Asia: Damaged But Still Dangerous", August 26, 2003; and "Indonesia Backgrounder: How The Jemaah Islamiyah Terrorist Network Operates", December 11, 2002.

[6] Indonesia ranked 72 out of 102 countries surveyed in the 2003 Global Competitiveness Index published by the World Economic Forum. Indonesia ranked 69 out of 80 countries in the 2002 survey. In each year, Indonesia ranked lower than all other surveyed countries belonging to the Association of Southeast Asian Nations. For more details, see *The Global Competitiveness Report, 2003-2004*, World Economic Forum

[7] UNCTAD World Investment Report, 2003. There is some doubt about the comparability of the capital flows in different countries. Indonesia, for example,

includes loan repayments in its calculations of foreign investment, while other countries do not. Nevertheless, Indonesia's record in restoring vigorous investment flows in the past five years has been exceedingly poor.

[8] An excellent recent analysis of the linkage between institutions and economic growth is in Dani Rodrik, Arvind Subramanian and Francesco Trebbi, "Institutions Rule: The Primacy of Institutions over Geography and Integration in Economic Development," CID Working Paper No. 97, Center for International Development, Harvard University, Cambridge, MA, October, 2002. An investor survey carried out by the World Bank and the Asian Development Bank in 2003 showed that the top three obstacles to new investment were macroeconomic instability, policy uncertainty, and corruption. For more details, see World Bank, "Indonesia: Beyond Macroeconomic Stability," December, 2003, pp. 28-29.

[9] Quoted in "The 2004 Elections: The Enemy Within", *Jakarta Post*, December 30, 2003

[10] Asia Foundation, "Democracy in Indonesia – A Survey of the Indonesian Electorate in 2003," Jakarta, 2003.

Introduction to the Second Edition (1999)

"When Soeharto goes, everything will have to be reinvented."

Goenawan Mohamad[1]

On 21 May 1998, Indonesia's President Soeharto[2] resigned his office, bringing to a close 32 years astride the world's fourth largest country. Buffeted by the financial crisis that swept through Asia in the second half of 1997, the autocrat's political support crumbled in tandem with the Indonesian economy.

In the weeks leading up to Soeharto's fall from power, thousands of students had taken to the streets of Indonesia's main cities, clamouring for the president's ouster and an end to his corrupt rule. Religious leaders and long-time political allies refused Soeharto's pleas for support, shattering the elite consensus that had underpinned his power for so long. It was an abrupt and humiliating end for Soeharto, coming just ten weeks after he had been sworn in for his seventh five-year term in office.

Three decades earlier, before most of today's Indonesians were born, Soeharto had assumed power with significant public goodwill. He promised an end to the political ferment that marked the rule of his predecessor, Soekarno, and pledged to focus the nation's energy on economic development.

But by the end of his long tenure, Soeharto stood virtually alone, surrounded only by palace loyalists and a handful of relatives. His claims to political legitimacy had come to rest solely on his economic achievements, and when the economic crisis arrived, Soeharto's main pillar of legitimacy was knocked out from under him.

The story of how Soeharto alienated his erstwhile supporters is a complex one. To a certain extent, Soeharto fell victim to his own success: years of economic development and greater educational opportunities produced a populace no longer willing to be treated like political adolescents.

Twenty years into his rule, as I noted in the introduction to the first edition of this volume, many if not most educated Indonesians had already grown tired of Soeharto's alternately paternalistic and repressive regime. They were no longer willing to accept the negative aspects of his rule – the general unresponsiveness of the political process, the weakness of the legislative and judicial branches of government, the prevalence of officially sanctioned corruption, and the very unpredictability of Soeharto's eventual departure from power – as the necessary and unavoidable costs of economic progress.

As the 1990s progressed, a swelling tide of Indonesians yearned for a more modern nation governed by men and women with at least some appreciation for the ideals of efficiency, accountability and fair play. It is Indonesia's misfortune that a change in this direction could not and did not begin until the country had plummeted into the depths of economic despair.

It is still not clear how history will remember Soeharto's rule. As a major-general in the Indonesian army, Soeharto came to power amidst extraordinarily adverse conditions. In the mid-1960s, Indonesian society was convulsed with hatred and violence and its economy was nearly dysfunctional. In the three decades that followed, Soeharto's government oversaw rates of economic growth that were the envy of much of the developing world. He took an impoverished, agrarian nation unable to feed itself and brought it into the ranks of middle-income countries with a per capita income of over US$1000. Soeharto's New Order government dramatically reduced the incidence of poverty while steadily raising education, literacy and health standards.

But the negative side of the ledger is also full. Corruption, mismanagement and brutality were as much a part of Soeharto's government as economic development. By the 1990s, Soeharto had become increasingly aloof and distanced from the everyday realities of ordinary Indonesians, unable or unwilling to recognise the damage he was inflicting by retarding Indonesia's political development. A groundswell of demands for a different sort of politics went unheeded and perhaps unheard. Surrounded by sycophants, Soeharto became the last casualty of his own three-decade-long effort to weaken Indonesia's political feedback mechanisms.

Soeharto's refusal to plan for his own succession put an enormous strain on the Indonesian body politic and ultimately diminished what he had achieved both in terms of economic development and restoring social harmony. In the end, he was removed from power only after a sudden economic decline led to a paroxysm of violence that deeply rent Indonesia's social fabric. Soeharto's historical legacy will depend to some extent on how well and how quickly his successors are able to right the Indonesian ship of state.

At the time of this writing, Indonesia's transition cannot yet be called a transformation. Indonesia's reformist leaders enjoy wide popular support, but their task is an enormous one. Long-buried grievances quickly rose to the surface once Soeharto had left the scene. Disturbing and often unexplainable bouts of ethnic and religious violence occurred with dismaying regularity in the twelve months after Soeharto stepped down. Outer-island resentment at Jakarta's dominance of political and economic decision-making fuelled separatist sentiment in several provinces, calling into question Indonesia's ability to maintain its current borders. Influential officials groomed by Soeharto, among them President Habibie, resisted public demands for an investigation into Soeharto family corruption and an accounting of human rights violations by the military. The collapse of the financial system and the millions of Indonesians who have again fallen into poverty will haunt economic policymakers for years to come. Only time will tell if Indonesia's future leaders, saddled with a badly damaged economy and discredited political institutions, can overcome these challenges while sustaining a democratic form of government and upholding Indonesia's pluralistic traditions.

I am indebted to many people without whom my professional and personal experiences in Indonesia, much less this book, would have been the poorer. My initial arrival in Indonesia in 1987 came courtesy of the Henry Luce Foundation, which provided me with a generous grant to spend ten months working at the *Jakarta Post*. I would like to thank the Foundation's former president Bob Armstrong, two of his staff, Helene Redell and Terry Lautz, and the indefatigable Elizabeth Luce Moore for their unfailing support and helpful advice. For showing me the ropes early on in Jakarta, I am grateful to Cinnamon Dornsife and Gordon Hein of the Asia Foundation. Sabam Siagian, the *Post*'s former editor and a profound student of Indonesian politics, was also a fine teacher.

From 1988 to 1992, I reported on Indonesia for the *Far Eastern Economic Review*, and I should like to thank the *Review*'s former editor Philip Bowring for giving me the leeway to pursue stories that other editors would have shied away from. Fanny Lioe at the Review's Jakarta bureau, a fount of useful information and good cheer, helped me more than she knew.

My greatest debt is to the many Indonesians who, for the journalist, fall under the rubric "sources". They differed by occupation – diplomats, business executives, economists, non-governmental activists, students, academics, lawyers, politicians, government officials, religious leaders, and military officers, to cite the most important – but they all had certain traits in common: most especially, courtesy, patience and the willingness to point me in the right direction. The information I gleaned from them forms the raw material of this book. They are too numerous to mention here but I would be remiss in not singling out a few people for a word of thanks: Arief Budiman, Marzuki Darusman, Kwik Kian Gie, Hasnan Habib, Manggi Habir, Fikri Jufri, Gunawan Mohamad, Rosita Noer, H.J.C. Princen, Rizal Ramli, Emil Salim, Marsillam Simanjuntak, Sjahrir, Laksamana Sukardi, Abdurrahman Wahid, and Sucipto Wirosardjono.

The staff at the Center for Strategic and International Studies provided insightful analysis on a variety of topics. Many of the senior business executives grouped under the Chamber of Commerce and Industry and those affiliated with the Prasetya Mulya group generously spent many hours explaining the fine points of Indonesia's political economy to me. And in the non-profit field, I would like to thank the many staffers at the

Legal Aid Institute and Walhi who always found time to return calls and answer any and all questions. I am equally grateful for the help provided by many of my colleagues in the domestic and foreign press, with whom I shared the frustrations, challenges, and satisfactions of covering the Indonesian story. Lastly, I must thank Jeffrey Ballinger, David Dredge, Catherine Lugrin and Elizabeth Pisani whose curiosity, boundless energy and unstinting friendship made my time in Indonesia all the more enjoyable.

The Asia Research Centre and Murdoch University provided generous financial assistance and superb facilities in the course of writing this book. I am extremely grateful to the Centre's director, Dick Robison, for his support of this project and his innumerable useful suggestions during the writing process. A number of others read parts of the book in draft from and offered many helpful comments, including Greg Barton, Claire Bolderson, Harold Crouch, Greg Fealy, Herb Feith, Jonathan Friedland, Gene Galbraith, Vedi Hadiz, Alec Hansen, Hal Hill, Tom Hyland, David Jenkins, Aristides Katoppo, Bill Liddle, Jamie Mackie, Andrew MacIntyre, Adnan Buyung Nasution, Pierre Pont, Margaret Scott and Marianne Vysma. Steve Proctor applied a deft editing touch to the final draft. I absolve them all of responsibility for the views and judgments expressed in the following pages, which is solely mine.

Adam Schwarz
Washington, June 1999

[1] Interview, Goenawan Mohamad, 23 July 1996.

[2] Soeharto, like many Javanese, has only one name. In this book, his name is written using the older spelling system. In 1972, the Indonesian and Malaysian governments established a common system of spelling, under which the main changes were that the old *dj* becomes *j*; *j* becomes *y*; *tj* becomes *c*; and *oe* becomes *u*. In most instances, this book uses the modern spelling system for the names of people and places. Some exceptions are made for names like Soeharto, which are commonly spelled in the Indonesian press using the old system. A further confusion arises in references to individuals with a first and a family name. In the Indonesian press, some individuals are always referred to by their first name, others by their surname. I have endeavoured to follow the system of references employed by the Indonesian media.

1
Growing pains

I have made myself the meeting place of all trends and ideologies. I have blended, blended, and blended them until finally they became the present Sukarno.

Sukarno[1]

Civil society is a fine place, but it is not a place of peace.

Leon Wieseltier[2]

In January 1966, amidst the darkest days of the Indonesian Republic, the two men who above all others deserve credit for fashioning a nation out of a sprawling hodgepodge of islands and peoples, came together for an awkward meeting in the Merdeka Palace, the presidential office.

For the past ninety days Indonesia had been convulsed with violence and unbridled rage. Hundreds of thousands of Javanese, Sumatrans and Balinese had been slaughtered, cut down in their homes, in village pathways, in congested city alleys and in the twinkling green rice paddies that give Indonesia its astonishing beauty. The killings carried an emphatic, horrific and incontrovertible message: Sukarno's dream of unifying a fractious populace by the force of his own personality, of creating a harmonious 'big tent' of suspicious soldiers, restless Muslims, strident communists and fire-breathing nationalists had been a mirage, a colossal miscalculation by a man who had put far too much faith in his own powers of persuasion.

By the time the crisply uniformed Soeharto strode into the Merdeka Palace, Sukarno was an embittered angry man. Just four months earlier Sukarno had been near the peak of his powers, the armed forces under his control, the communists at bay and the Muslims in retreat. Neither a

1

neglected economy, ruinous foreign adventurism nor a raucous love life had seemed a real threat to his hold on power. By January, though, Sukarno's strongest pillar of support, the communists, had been all but eliminated as a political force, mostly at the hands of his other two pillars of support: the Muslims and the army. Worse, the military, anxious to occupy what it perceived as its rightful place at the apex of government, was rapidly closing off Sukarno's room for manoeuvre. Led by Soeharto, a relatively obscure major general, the army had seen its opening and was about to take it.

Students, egged on by the army, were parading through the streets calling for Sukarno's head. When Soeharto arrived, Sukarno launched into a tirade against the student demonstrators, demanding that the army bring them into line. He denied Soeharto's charge that the Indonesian Communist Party had been responsible for an abortive coup on 30 September 1965, the event that sparked off the wave of killings that would follow. His rantings turned into pleadings. All fell on deaf ears. In a remarkable turn of fortunes, it was now the unknown Major General Soeharto who held all the cards and, as it turned out, he was to play them masterfully. Near the end of their meeting, a dispirited Sukarno, President for Life, Supreme Commander, Mouthpiece of the Indonesian People, and Great Leader of the Revolution, asked plaintively: 'Soeharto, what are you going to do with me? I am your leader.'

'I have always respected you as I have my parents,' Soeharto replied. 'To me you are not only our national leader, but I consider you as a parent. I'd like to regard you highly but, unfortunately, you do not wish this.' It was, though clouded with typical Javanese indirection, a readily understood message that Sukarno's days were numbered. 'I was sure,' Soeharto said in a later recounting of the story, 'that Sukarno knew what I meant.'

He was right. Sukarno, finally beginning to decipher the writing on the wall, asked one more time, just to be sure: 'Is this true, Soeharto?'

'Yes, it's true,' Soeharto replied. And so began the transition between Indonesia's first two presidents. Within two months Soeharto would wrest executive power away from Sukarno. Within two years, he had been officially declared president. One of his first acts was to place Sukarno under house arrest from where little more was heard of him until he died in June 1970. In a parting shot, Soeharto instructed that Sukarno be buried in a remote village in East Java and not, as his family wished, near his home in Bogor, 60 kilometres from Jakarta.[3]

Early in his tenure Soeharto described his regime as the New Order and in many ways it was. It replaced Sukarno's revolutionary rhetoric with the pragmatic use of power. Far from the liberal parliamentary democracy of the 1950s, Soeharto has headed an authoritarian, military-dominated government. The New Order's driving feature has been economic development and building strong political institutions. What made Sukarno tick, and what he is remembered for despite all his faults, was bringing to Indonesia a political identity. Above all the New Order is notable for a powerful government and a weak civil society. The opposite was true for the Old Order.

But the writing of history that paints the New Order as the antithesis of the Old Order, as if the first twenty years of Indonesia's nationhood bears scant relation to what was to emerge from the convulsions of 1965–66—as some New Orderists are wont to do—is deeply flawed. There were some important continuities from the Old Order, and especially from the 1959–65 Guided Democracy period, to the New Order: the army's view of its place in society and in government; the president's belief in a powerful presidency; a broadly shared sense of nation; a domineering Java; a divided Muslim community; a resented ethnic Chinese business class; a weak legal system and, closely related, a rich tradition of corruption, nepotism, smuggling and patronage.

In assessing Indonesia in the early 1990s and speculating on its future direction, the continuities are at least as important as the changes. They illustrate some of the stronger strands in the societal fabric. Whether they are useful as tools of prediction is another and more complex question, for nothing is immutable. Indeed, in the 1990s, the official view that there is nothing worth rescuing from the 1950s' experience with parliamentary democracy is likely to come under increasing scrutiny. In any case, it would be foolish to ignore the Old Order and what came before. The New Order, and Soeharto especially, have their roots there.

Before the Old Order was New

Like many countries emerging from colonial rule, the Indonesian nation owes its geographical contours to its former colonial power, the Netherlands. The Dutch first arrived more than three hundred years before independence in 1945, seeking spices and wealth for an expanding empire. In 1605, the Dutch East Indies Company (VOC) uprooted the Portuguese from their stronghold in the Spice Islands, now called the Moluccas, in eastern Indonesia, and gradually expanded its hold over the archipelago.

The Dutch, like the Javanese dynasts who preceded them, operated on a tribute system with taxes being paid in kind, either in crops like rice or pepper or in labour for building roads or palaces, personal services to the king and officials, and military service.[4] The common language was Malay, brought to the coastal regions of Java and Sumatra centuries before by Islamic traders.

For most of the colonial period, the Dutch had at best a tenuous hold on their territories. On Java, for example, the VOC controlled little more than the port city of Batavia until well into the eighteenth century when the Mataram dynasty in Central Java began to crumble under its own weight. Dutch troops were engaged constantly in quelling one rebellion or another on and off Java. Local leaders like Prince Diponegoro in Central Java, Imam Bonjol in West Sumatra and Pattimura in the Moluccas weakened the Dutch and tied up the colonial military forces. In the late 1800s, the Dutch waged a bloody, thirty-year war with the fiercely Muslim Sultanate of Aceh on the western tip of Sumatra.[5]

The advent of the twentieth century saw the first stirrings of nationalist sentiment on Java. Reformist Islamic groups like the Sarekat Islam (Islamic Union) and the Muhammadiyah (Followers of Muhammad), both established in 1912, represented the first attempts at mass-based movements in the Indies. In 1927, a group of Dutch-educated nationalists led by the 26-year-old Sukarno founded the Indonesian Nationalist Party, the PNI. 'The PNI stood for a new political identity that . . . transcended and encompassed the many societies of the Indies . . . In October, 1928, a congress of youth organisations brought the idea forth in one echoing phrase, "one nation-Indonesia, one people-Indonesian, one language-Indonesian".'[6] The PNI successfully promoted the adoption of the trading language Malay as the national language, *bahasa Indonesia*. The party also conceived the national flag and anthem that survive today.

Needless to say, the Dutch were unenthusiastic about the nascent Indonesian nationalism. The Sarekat Islam was effectively suppressed in 1926 and the principal nationalist leaders Sukarno, Mohammad Hatta and Sutan Sjahrir were hounded, exiled and imprisoned for a good part of the fifteen years preceding the Second World War. Sukarno, the most well known of the early nationalist leaders, was born in 1901 in the East Java city Surabaya and later went on to study engineering in Bandung. He was arrested by the Dutch in late 1929 and a few months later sentenced to four years in jail. Released in late 1931, Sukarno was arrested again in 1933 and exiled without trial, first to Flores in eastern Indonesia and then to Bengkulu in southern Sumatra.[7] In 1934, Hatta and Sjahrir were also arrested and exiled without trial to Upper Digul in West Irian. Later, ironically, they were moved to one of the Spice Islands, the original conquest of the Dutch traders but by the early twentieth century a forgotten backwater.

Revolution and nationalism

Without much fanfare or resistance, the Dutch surrendered to the invading Japanese army in March 1942. For displacing their colonial masters, the Japanese were at first hailed by Indonesians as liberators, but it was to be a short-lived romance. Indonesians by the hundreds of thousands were conscripted by the Japanese for military duty elsewhere in Southeast Asia, many never to return. 'The wages of Indonesians who stayed were taxed to support the Japanese war effort. Export industries collapsed, unbacked occupation currency sparked rampant inflation, and rationing led to black markets and widespread corruption.'[8] After initially taking a benevolent view of Indonesia's embryonic independence movement, the Japanese soon banned the flying of the Indonesian flag and playing of the national anthem. As one Indonesian official later commented, 'Most Indonesians wished the Japanese had never come in the first place. Theirs was indeed the most terrible rule twentieth century Indonesians were made to suffer.'[9]

The Japanese maintained the basic Dutch administrative system, continuing to rule through the established elite. But their political style was completely different. 'Where the Dutch were conservative and aimed to keep their subjects quiet, the Japanese were totalitarian and sought to stir them up.'[10] As an unintended consequence of their own war-promoting propaganda campaign, the Japanese created a small opening for Indonesian nationalist leaders to establish for themselves a broad-based network of support.

By the time Japanese rule ended in August 1945, the fire of nationalism was burning brightly. On 17 August 1945, two days after the Japanese surrendered to the Allied Forces, Sukarno and Hatta proclaimed independence. A constitution was drawn up and a cabinet formed.

With the Japanese in retreat, the Dutch attempted to reclaim their colonial territory and over the next four years the battle for Indonesia was waged. Ultimately, however, the Dutch reconquest was a lost cause. The former colonial power was on the wrong side of the wave of history and came under increasing international pressure to relinquish its claims. The Hague Agreement of 2 November 1949 ceded Dutch control of all Indonesian territories except the western half of the island of New Guinea and, in December 1949, the Dutch flag came down for the last time. Indonesia was on its own.

The struggle for political independence was the all-encompassing Indonesian preoccupation prior to 1950, a struggle which could not have prevailed without a widely-shared commitment to the nationalist cause. Indeed, success in having held together such a large and disparate congregation of islands in the face of a determined assault by an established European power remains until today a source of intense pride to all Indonesians. But having achieved independence the difficult task of government and nation-building began. In marked contrast to the broadly supported goal of independence, it soon became clear that there were varied and contradictory ideas of how to govern. And governing a nation like Indonesia must have seemed an almost overwhelming challenge to the young politicians emerging from the war of independence.

Indonesia consists of over 13 000 islands stretching more than 5000 kilometres from east to west, or roughly the distance from London to Baghdad. The country's land mass is just short of two million square kilometres, about the size of Mexico, and possesses territorial waters nearly four times that size. Only about half of Indonesia's islands are inhabited and less than thirty have more than a token population. The most populous—and home to 60 per cent of Indonesians—is the volcano-strewn island of Java, which is about the same size as England or Arkansas. Blessed with fertile soil and frequent rainfall, it is otherwise poor in natural resources.

The three biggest Indonesian islands, Irian Jaya, Kalimantan and Sumatra, are among the five largest in the world and possess abundant natural resources, not the least of which is the second largest—next to Brazil's—tropical rainforest in the world. These islands and the waters near them are also rich in oil and gas. But Sumatra excepted, Indonesia's large islands are sparsely populated. Kalimantan, for example, is the same size as France but has fewer than ten million inhabitants. Spread out over these many islands are literally hundreds of spoken dialects and cultural sub-groups. Little wonder, then, that maintaining national unity has been the one constant preoccupation of all of Indonesia's leaders throughout its short history.

The Old Order

Indonesian history prior to Soeharto's arrival can be broken into two periods: the parliamentary democracy period from 1945–59; and Sukarno's Guided Democracy of 1959–65. While a full treatment of this twenty-year period is well beyond the scope of this book, several aspects of what is now known as the Old Order are worth a brief perusal. The most important of these are the struggle to establish an ideological basis for the Indonesian state, and the military's evolving role within the leadership of that state.

The official New Order version of Indonesia's political history from 1945 to 1965 is, to put it mildly, selective and one-sided. Current history textbooks portray authoritarianism as the form of government most suitable to Indonesian culture, and liberal democracy as a culturally inappropriate form of government recklessly imported from the West. They glorify the military's role in securing independence and safeguarding national stability and denigrate the contributions of civilian politicians. They portray the period of parliamentary democracy as an unvarnished failure, an aberrant political experiment best forgotten.

Dissatisfaction with Soeharto's brand of authoritarianism in the 1990s, however, is leading many Indonesian and foreign scholars to re-examine the 1950s. Few would deny that parliamentary democracy had many flaws. Government in the 1950s, as might be expected in a young nation led necessarily by inexperienced politicians, was often chaotic and not especially effective.

But to many in the Indonesian elite in the 1990s, there are several features from the parliamentary democracy period well worth salvaging, in particular constitutional safeguards against dictatorship and for the protection of human rights, an independent judiciary and a sense that government ought to be accountable to the people, a conviction notably lacking in the 1990s.

The current powerholders, naturally, are adamantly opposed to any new look at the 1950s which portrays parliamentary democracy in a favourable light, a view which strikes directly at the New Order's very legitimacy. But since many of the demands for government reform in the 1990s refer not to 'foreign' systems of government but to a mode of government already tried in Indonesia, a quick review of the '1950s' experience' is warranted.

The constitutional debates

Indonesia has had three constitutions. The 1945 Constitution was announced on 18 August 1945, a day after Sukarno and Hatta had proclaimed independence. It is short (37 Articles), vague and provides for a powerful presidency. (Several months after this constitution came into being, the government was changed by decree to a parliamentary system.) In 1949, following negotiations with the Dutch over a cease-fire, a 'Federal Constitution' was drawn up for the 'Republic of the United States of Indonesia'. This constitution was considered unduly influenced by the Dutch and, a year later, a new constitution freely drafted by Indonesians came into being. The 1950 Constitution was lengthier (146 Articles), provided detailed guarantees for individual freedoms, and stipulated a parliamentary system of government with the president holding a largely ceremonial role. It survived until 1959 when Sukarno decreed that the 1945 Constitution would return to force.

All three constitutions were meant to be provisional; all were drawn up relatively quickly and by a relatively small group of Indonesians. Even while the 1945 Constitution was still in the drafting stage, Sukarno was stressing the need for a permanent constitution to be drawn up by a more representative body. '[T]he constitution we are now drafting is a provisional one,' Sukarno said in mid-1945. 'If I may say: this is a constitution made in a flash of lightning. Later if we have already established a state and are in a peaceful situation, we will certainly call the People's Consultative Assembly which will frame a complete and perfect constitution.'[11]

Article 134 of the 1950 Constitution called for a constitutional assembly to be convened as soon as possible to enact a permanent constitution. Elections to that assembly, known as the *Konstituante*, were held in late

1955 and its deliberations lasted until it was put out of business by
Sukarno in 1959.

The two most important periods of constitutional debates took place
in mid-1945 and during the *Konstituante*. The debates ranged from the
specific—the national flag—to the broad—the proper relationship between
the organs of state. By far the most contentious issue running through all
the debates concerned ideology or, more concretely, the ideological basis
of the state. There were three main schools of thought which can be called
integralists (also known as authoritarians, traditionalists or, to some,
Pancasila-ists), Islamists and, for want of a better term, constitutionalists.[12]

In the mid-1940s, the notion of the integralist state was pushed most
strongly by Supomo, then a senior judge in the Japanese occupation
government. Borrowing from European philosophers Hegel and Spinoza
and admiring of governments in Nazi Germany and wartime Japan, the
integralists rejected the idea of a separation between rulers and ruled.
They specifically rejected the individual-oriented systems of government
current in Europe and the United States. 'The traditionalists rejected
individualism as the root of colonialism and imperialism. They preferred
instead the stylised collectivism of the ancient Javanese kingdom, the
mystical sublimation of subject, ruler and realm.'[13]

Supomo likened the state to a large family in which the members of
the society were integrated into the whole. In a 31 May 1945 speech to
a committee set up in Jakarta to prepare a constitution, Supomo said 'the
individual cannot be segregated from the others. Nor can he be separated
from the outside world, from groups of humans, not even from other
creatures. Everything mixes with other things, every living thing depends
on all other forms of life. This is the totalitarian idea, the integralist idea
of the Indonesian nation.'[14]

For the integralists, sovereignty was to be held by 'the people', not
by individuals. Individualism was seen as the source of conflict between
the government and the people. In an integral state, there was no need
for specific guarantees for human rights, as these would imply separation
between the state and individuals. In an ideal family, Supomo maintained,
children are taken care of and are protected by loving parents: they do
not need their 'human rights' protected from the whims of their parents.
'It could not be envisaged,' said lawyer Adnan Buyung Nasution of the
integralists, 'that state power wielded by the state's functionaries might
also be used to serve the particularistic interests of the rulers, that it might
be used against the interests of the people and that it might take the form
of repression.'[15]

Two practical consequences of the integralist view were a large role
for the state in the economy, particularly as it concerns ownership of land
and natural resources, and a strong commitment to cooperatives as a

primary pillar of the economy. The integralist state, said its proponents, was concerned primarily with 'social justice' whereas individualism led to capitalism which in turn was linked with colonialism and this, of course, was to be rejected. Consequently, Supomo's views proved popular with advocates of economic socialism.

In contrast, for many Muslim representatives to the constitutional talks, the overriding goal was to ensure that Indonesia would become an Islamic state. Of all the world's great religions, Islam is most committed to the idea of unity between government and religion[16] and Indonesian Muslims, represented by the umbrella party Masyumi, wanted the new republic to formally espouse Islam as the state religion. With some 85 per cent of Indonesians professing Islam as their faith, Muslim constitutional delegates claimed that an Islamic state was a necessary political embodiment of the nation's Islamic community.

On many other constitutional issues—like, for example, human rights—Indonesia's Islamic parties would prove to hold strikingly different opinions. But on the issue of an Islamic state, all Islamic parties responded to the 'call of the Faith'[17] and maintained a unified bloc. (The diversity of opinion within Indonesia's Islamic community is described in more detail in Chapter 7.)

The constitutionalists formed a third lobbying group, but one concerned less with ideology per se than with the proper forms of the state. The essence of the constitutional state, says Nasution, includes 'procedures for the effective participation of the people in government, limitation of the government power, and accountability of the government to the people'. A constitutional government, he says, is based on 'an ethic of means rather than of ends, however noble and just these may be'.[18] Leading the constitutionalist camp in the mid-1940s were several prominent nationalist leaders: Mohammad Hatta, Sutan Sjahrir and Mohammad Yamin.

A chief concern of the constitutionalists was what Nasution calls the 'problem of power'. Hatta, for example, while vigorously defending himself against the charge of individualism, maintained that individual rights needed protection to prevent the new Indonesian state from becoming a state based merely on power. Even in a family, Hatta said, the members still must have the right to express their feelings in order to take good care of the collectivity.[19]

In the constitutional debates preceding independence, the arguments of the constitutionalist lobby fell mostly on deaf ears. In the heady days of mid-1945, flush with the revolutionary spirit, most participants in the constitutional debates were prepared to assume the best of Indonesians as leaders, and consequently focused more on ideological issues than on the relationship between the government's controlling institutions.

Constitutional delegates from the non-Muslim parties viewed the prospect of an Islamic state with horror. In their view, a victory by the Muslims would destroy their hopes for a unified Indonesia. They felt, and probably rightly, that an overly Islamic constitution would lead to immediate revolts by Indonesia's non-Islamic communities, especially those located on the more remote islands.

Sukarno, sympathetic to the integralist view as an ideology but above all a nationalist, offered a way out. On 1 June 1945, Sukarno spelled out his views on Indonesian nationhood. He called for a nation based on Pancasila, or five principles. They are: belief in one supreme God; justice and civility among peoples; the unity of Indonesia; democracy through deliberation and consensus among representatives; social justice for all.[20] The primary objective of this fuzzy doctrine is rooted in its first principle which aimed to undercut demands from the Muslim community for an Islamic state.

'More generally,' says American political scientist Bill Liddle, 'they represent a search . . . for broadly inclusive principles to bind together the diverse groups of an extremely pluralistic society.'[21] Pancasila has proven to be an ideology of remarkable longevity and flexibility. It has been at times—and often at the same time—both a forceful binding agent for a young nation and a powerful tool of repression.

When first announced, says Nasution, Pancasila was seen as 'a meeting point for all the different parties and groups, a common denominator of all ideologies and streams of thought existing in Indonesia.' The principles it espoused were not seen as favouring any particular political system over another. But later, as the nature of Indonesia's government changed, Pancasila began to take on a more specifically political connotation. As the parliamentary democracy period came to an end, it was put forward as the 'only political ideology guaranteeing national unity and suitable to the Indonesian personality and, therefore, the only appropriate basis of state for Indonesia'.[22] Under Soeharto's New Order rule, Pancasila has been seen as synonymous with and justification for an integralist view of the state.

In its original formulation, however, Pancasila did not quite succeed in overcoming Muslim demands for an Islamic state. Pancasila was distrusted by Muslim parties who saw in its religious tolerance a loophole for the atheist Indonesian Communist Party to exploit. Consequently, a few weeks after Sukarno's speech, a constitutional committee agreed to a short addition to the Pancasila doctrine. The first principle became: 'Belief in One God, with the obligation for adherents of Islam to implement the Islamic law (*Shariah*).'

Known as the Jakarta Charter, it was meant to be included in the preamble of the 1945 Constitution but, after a change of heart by the nationalist and non-Muslim parties, the passage was dropped just before the constitution was proclaimed on 18 August 1945. Its omission engendered deep distrust in parts of the Islamic community against the secular nationalists who would emerge from the revolutionary struggle in charge of the government. Isa Anshary, a Masyumi firebrand, called the omission a 'magic trick . . . an embezzlement against the Muslim stance'.[23] Islamic resentment over the exclusion of the Jakarta Charter would colour the political debate almost continuously for the next fifteen years.

The roaring fifties

Having finally secured full independence in 1950, Indonesians were at last free to govern themselves. The 1950 Constitution, markedly different from the 1945 Constitution in many respects, was in force. It mandated a parliamentary system of government and spelled out at length constitutional guarantees for human rights, drawing heavily on the United Nations Universal Declaration of Human Rights drawn up in 1948. It also provided for a number of safeguards against the misuse of power by putting in place a system of checks and balances for political institutions and by making the military subordinate to the nation's civilian leadership.[24]

The task of governing proved to be far more difficult than the constitutional framers imagined. The Indonesian citizenry had been politicised to a exceptional extent in the 1940s, first under the Japanese from 1942–45 and then during the four-year struggle for independence which followed. Unfortunately for Indonesia's new leaders, there was as yet no consensus on what sort of nation Indonesian would be, and this confusion, plus the weakness of new political institutions, injected a great deal of instability into the political process. It was, in Ben Anderson's phrase, 'a kind of permanent round-the-clock politics in which mass organisations competed with each other at every conceivable kind of level without there being any real resolution'. In such a climate, pragmatic governance became almost impossible. 'Politics in universities, in factories, in schools, in plantations and so forth, never could come to real resolution precisely because the electoral mechanism was not in place,' Anderson says.[25]

One of the most serious problems facing the young nation was establishing a sense of national unity. On the Outer Islands, home to many of the nation's most valuable economic resources, there was in places substantial resentment at Java's political domination. A number of regional rebellions emerged in the early 1950s, with the most serious being the West Java-based Darul Islam campaign promoting an Islamic state and a secessionist movement based in the south Moluccas.

The government also fell far short of the revolutionary ideal of eradicating poverty. Most of Indonesia's new leaders, seeing free market capitalism as the driving force behind colonialism, favoured a socialist economic path but had few ideas on how to manage such an economy.

Many of the nation's major plantations and industrial enterprises remained in the hands of the Dutch.

In addition, the government had no coherent plan to deal with the resentment many Indonesians felt for the small ethnic Chinese community. The Chinese had done relatively well under Dutch rule, acting as merchants, traders and tax-collectors for the colonial regime. Although numerically small, less than four per cent of the population, they wielded considerable clout in the economy and their existence generated much enmity amongst indigenous Indonesians.

It wasn't until 1953 that the government announced plans for the country's first general elections, which did not take place for another two years. The 1955 elections are considered Indonesia's only brush with free and fair elections, with more than 90 per cent of registered voters casting a ballot. Unfortunately, the election results contributed little to political stability. The two big Muslim parties Masyumi and Nahdlatul Ulama (Revival of the Religious Scholars) received 20.9 per cent and 18.4 per cent respectively of the vote. Sukarno's Indonesian Nationalist Party pulled in 22.3 per cent of the vote, while the Indonesian Communist Party obtained a 16.4 per cent share, with the smaller Socialist Party collecting an unexpectedly low two per cent of the vote. With no one party obtaining a workable majority, parties were obliged to continue the difficult and unstable practice of forming coalitions in order to govern.

The Konstituante

A second election took place in 1955. In December of that year, 90 per cent of registered Indonesian voters turned out again to cast a ballot for the *Konstituante*, or Constitutional Assembly, the body set up to draft a permanent constitution. As with the general elections three months earlier, the *Konstituante* elections were considered clean and fair and the results representative of the spectrum of Indonesian opinion. Five hundred and fourteen delegates were elected to the *Konstituante*, with the four main parties—the Nationalists, Masyumi, Nahdlatul Ulama and the Communists—contributing the most members.

In official Indonesian history, it is the failure of the *Konstituante* to arrive at a consensus on a new constitution that obliged Sukarno and the military to reassert control over the political process, return to force the 1945 Constitution and introduce Guided Democracy. In the 1990s, this accepted history has come under attack by scholars who claim that the *Konstituante*'s accomplishments were much more significant than is generally recognised.

Just as Indonesia's leaders were split by ideological differences in the mid-1940s, so too were delegates to the *Konstituante*. Representatives of the Muslim parties, determined not to be out-manoeuvred still again, took a hardline stance in debates on the ideological basis of the state. Their primary objective was to resurrect the Jakarta Charter and see it inserted in a permanent constitution. Their opponents, led by the Nationalist and Communist Parties, were just as adamant in resisting moves for an Islamic state.

Whether the *Konstituante* would have forced a compromise on the issue of state ideology will never be known. The *Konstituante*'s proceedings were stopped by Sukarno's order in mid-1959, nine months before the *Konstituante* was scheduled to finish its work. More relevant to the present discussion, however, is that on other issues *Konstituante* delegates had much more success in reaching a consensus, especially in the field of human rights and in recognising the need to provide safeguards against the arbitrary use of power. In Nasution's opinion, 'fundamental agreement on human rights may be considered as the most unequivocal outcome of the whole work of the *Konstituante*.'[26]

Outside the *Konstituante*'s meeting hall, however, a crisis atmosphere was building. The failure of the 1955 general elections to interject more predictability into the political process and the gradual deterioration of the economy had increased dissatisfaction with the Indonesian parliament. Meanwhile, constant regional rumblings had persuaded many military leaders that the nation's civilian leadership was unable to hold the country together.

National unity was dealt a blow in 1958 when an intra-military dispute led to a group of officers setting up a rebel government based in West Sumatra. The Revolutionary Government of the Republic of Indonesia (PRRI), supported by several leading members of the Islamic party Masyumi and some other civilian intellectuals, did not seek to break up the Indonesian nation. Rather, its formation reflected the frustration of regional military commanders with the armed forces headquarters and the civilian political leadership in Jakarta, and their desire to see a new national government.[27]

But in Jakarta the PRRI rebellion was seen as a real threat to national unity, especially when it was learned the rebel government was receiving logistic and military support from the US Central Intelligence Agency (CIA). Convinced Sukarno was falling under the influence of the Indonesian Communist Party, the CIA, against the advice of the US embassy in Jakarta, chose to prop up the rebel PRRI army as a way of placing pressure on Sukarno. The plan backfired. The exposure of the CIA's involvement strengthened Sukarno's hand as he was able to rally new support in the face of foreign aggression. In addition, by weakening the Indonesian Communist Party's strongest parliamentary foe, the Masyumi—Sukarno banned the Masyumi in 1960 for its support of PRRI leaders—the rebellion in the short run strengthened the Communist Party's position.

Other factors contributing to the crisis atmosphere included an attempted assassination of Sukarno in late 1957—also blamed on regional rebels, though never proved—and the UN failure to vote favourably on an Indonesian motion to force the Dutch to accelerate negotiations on the transfer of what was then called West Irian to Indonesian control.[28] (Occupying the western half of the island of New Guinea, the territory was incorporated into Indonesia in the 1960s and renamed Irian Jaya.)

With central government control increasingly under strain, in late 1958 Sukarno began pushing for a return to the 1945 Constitution and for his notion of 'Guided Democracy', a form of government which would prove to be increasingly undemocratic. Although keen to gain the approval of the *Konstituante* for his plan, he was ultimately unsuccessful. There was some support in the *Konstituante* for Sukarno's proposal but most delegates were opposed to an unconditional return to the 1945 Constitution. Delegates from all the major parties, including the Islamic parties, voiced concern about, as one delegate put it, the 'inherent potential for dictatorship' in the 1945 Constitution.[29]

In mid-1959, Sukarno offered a compromise to the *Konstituante*. In exchange for the constitutional assembly suspending its deliberations and accepting the return to force of the 'spirit of 1945', Sukarno offered to make binding on the government many of the provisions already agreed to by the *Konstituante*, including those on human rights.

Sukarno was not, however, willing to accept the Jakarta Charter as binding on the future government and on this point the negotiations with the *Konstituante* collapsed. After the *Konstituante* voted on—and rejected—the acceptance of the Jakarta Charter in May 1959, the Islamic parties refused to vote in favour of Sukarno's proposal for Guided Democracy.

Failing to bend the *Konstituante* to his will, on 5 July 1959 Sukarno dissolved the assembly, abrogated the 1950 Constitution and called for the re-establishment of the 1945 Constitution. The *Konstituante*'s agreed-on provisions concerning human rights and the division of government powers—provisions Sukarno had been prepared to accept six weeks earlier—were forgotten.

The army weighs in

The crisis atmosphere of the late 1950s combined to strengthen support, within the parliament, the *Konstituante* and society at large, for a reassertion of control over the political process by a strong leader. But perhaps the greatest push came from the armed forces. One of the main stories of the 1950s was the military's increasing frustration with its limited political role.

The Indonesian army was born amidst a political struggle for independence and members of the army have always seen their mission in political terms. As early as 1947, the military under the leadership of General Sudirman had begun setting up its own, parallel system of government so that each civilian official, from provincial governors down to district supervisors, would be matched with a corresponding figure from the military. Although the two systems were parallel in structure, at each level of the bureaucracy the military counterpart wielded more power, a relationship for which the military became increasingly nostalgic during the 1950s.[30]

The army views its own role in history as the institution which first forged the nation and then saved it from itself time and again. Official armed forces (Abri) doctrine contends that during the 1945–49 campaign against the Dutch, civilian leaders were far too willing to compromise and negotiate with the Dutch and not willing enough to fight the war of independence on the military battlefield. This fundamental disagreement lay behind many of the cabinet changes during this period.

The military was acutely unhappy operating under the rules of parliamentary democracy, a system of government which accorded the army a political role far less than what it thought it deserved. For almost the entire period of parliamentary democracy, for example, the Defence Ministry portfolio was held by a civilian, and military leaders often felt themselves victimised by civilian politicking.

When the 1955 general elections failed to resolve the causes of political deadlock, Abri began exerting more and more pressure on Sukarno to force changes in the system. In March 1957, the army successfully persuaded Sukarno to impose martial law to counter threats to national unity. In the following year the army threw its full support behind Sukarno's Guided Democracy proposal and for the return to the 1945 Constitution.

The 1945 Constitution held an obvious appeal for the military. Unlike the 1950 Constitution, which had no political role for the army, the 1945 Constitution provided for parliamentary representation for 'groups prescribed by statute'.[31] And, in late 1958, just before the Cabinet obligingly agreed to extend martial law for another year, Sukarno's National Council recognised the military as a 'functional group'. With the 1945 Constitution back in force, the military would be able to count on a sustained political role without having to resort to martial law.

By the late 1950s, the military's suspicions of civilian political parties had reached the breaking point. The debates over an Islamic state in the mid-1940s and subsequent efforts to re-open these discussions in the *Konstituante* created in the army a widespread impression that crusading Muslims represented the single biggest threat to Indonesia's national integrity, a suspicion which remains widely held today. Hatred for the Indonesian Communist Party also ran deep. The party was the army's only rival as a mass-based institution and, at least at the peasant level, the communists had the better political machine.

Earlier in 1958, the army's political ambitions began to take concrete shape with the unveiling by Major General Abdul Haris Nasution, then the army chief of staff, of a new doctrine called the 'Middle Way'. The doctrine was announced in a speech at the National Military Academy in the Central Java city Magelang. It described the Indonesian military's purpose as two-fold: a military force as well as a social-political force.

The doctrine articulated the military's view that it deserved a larger role in the running of government and, over time, opened the door to military involvement in virtually every nook and cranny of society. Nasution attempted to allay concerns that the 'Middle Way' would inexorably lead to military dictatorship. 'We do not and we will not copy the situation as it exists in several Latin American states, where the army acts as a direct political force. Nor,' he continued, 'will we emulate the Western European model, where armies are the dead tool [of the government].'[32] At the time, notes political scientist Salim Said, 'the "Middle Way" speech was looked upon by many as a lesser evil compared to [the prospect of] a total military takeover' and therefore elicited only lukewarm opposition from civilian politicians.[33]

Once Guided Democracy had come into force, the army would gradually expand the limits of the 'Middle Way'. The army demanded and received representation in the cabinet, civil service and the parliament. Once Sukarno was removed from power in 1966, one of the army's first moves was to expand Nasution's 'Middle Way' into a doctrine which came to be called *dwifungsi*, or dual function. By the 1990s, the army had used *dwifungsi* to push its way into the societal fabric to an extent that would have been the envy of 'several Latin American states'.

Sukarno: A (mis)guided democrat

The debate on Indonesia's brush with parliamentary democracy in the 1950s has a long life yet to live. The New Order's contention that it failed because of its own inherent weaknesses is sure to come under increasing scrutiny by activists and scholars outside the government who contend that other factors—such as a desire by Sukarno and the army for more power—also need to be taken into account.[34] But whatever the reasons, the disbanding of the *Konstituante* in July 1959 ended Indonesia's democratic experiment and ushered in Sukarno's 'Guided Democracy'.

Guided Democracy, its title notwithstanding, meant in practice a return to a system of personal rule more reminiscent of Javanese feudalism than the chaotic democratic experiment of the 1950s. 'In Guided Democracy,' Sukarno once said, with typical flair, 'the key ingredient is leadership. The Guider . . . incorporates a spoonful of so-and-so's opinions with a dash of such-and-such, always taking care to incorporate a *soupçon* of the opposition. Then he cooks it and serves his final summation with "OK, now my dear brothers, it is like this and I hope you agree . . ." It's still democratic because everybody has given his comment.'[35]

Draping himself in nationalist clothes, Sukarno used strident rhetoric and nimble politicking to strengthen the executive branch and keep actual and potential opponents off balance. Foreign policy took a decidedly anti-Western tone. Sukarno intensified efforts to wrest control of Irian Jaya from the Dutch and launched an ill-fated military campaign against Malaysia to protest the establishment of the Malaysian states of Sabah and Sarawak on the island of Borneo.[36] Relations with Beijing and Moscow improved while ties with the USA became increasingly strained, not least because of CIA support for the PRRI rebellion in West Sumatra.

Sukarno fashioned a supporting coalition of forces which he called Nasakom, an abbreviation for nationalists, religious groups and communists. It was an inherently unstable coalition and the fact that it lasted as long as it did reflected more on Sukarno's political skills than on any shared beliefs among the three groups.

Islam as a political force was in disarray in the early 1960s: the Masyumi party had been banned and many of its leaders imprisoned or driven into exile. The less radical Nahdlatul Ulama (NU) remained a political force, but one far less threatening to the army and non-Muslims. Unlike the Masyumi, the NU was prepared to work with Sukarno and tone down demands for a return of the Jakarta Charter. But for all the major Muslim groups, the rising influence of the Communist Party became a source of serious concern. The party's work in rural areas, and especially its support for land redistribution, was blamed for drawing support away from Islamic preachers. Sukarno's protection of the party, then the largest communist party outside China and the Soviet Union, left Muslims increasingly disillusioned with his leadership. The same dynamic was at work within the military. Although far happier with Guided Democracy than the system it replaced, the military chafed at being only one of the 'functional groups' jockeying for power beneath Sukarno.

Sukarno's brand of economic nationalism did little to improve Indonesia's economic development. He oversaw a steadily larger role for the state in the economy and seriously strained relations with foreign businesses and overseas donors. Sukarno followed up the 1958 nationalisations of Dutch property—a consequence of the dispute over Irian Jaya—by expropriating British and American firms as part of his *Konfrontasi* (confrontation policy) against Malaysia. Together, the two-phase nationalisation policy brought about eight hundred enterprises under Indonesian government control.[37]

For Sukarno, still imbued with notions of revolutionary grandeur, economics took a back seat to the political struggle. In a famous speech on 25 March 1964 Sukarno told the United States to 'go to hell with your aid', a popular piece of political grandstanding that would be used by Soeharto against the Dutch exactly 28 years later. And in January 1965 Sukarno pulled Indonesia out of the United Nations in a pique against the UN's admission of Malaysia as a member state.

Meanwhile, debt and inflation soared and exports suffered. Foreign exchange receipts from the plantation sector, for example, one of Indonesia's most important source of exports, declined from US$442 million in 1958 to US$330 million in 1966. Smuggling, a chronic problem in an archipelagic state like Indonesia, was rampant. A present day legacy of Old Order smuggling is that Singapore, afraid to embarrass its giant neighbour, still doesn't officially report the extent of its trade with Indonesia.[38]

With the masses all but removed from the political equation, Indonesian politics increasingly came to revolve around Sukarno's palace. And as the 1960s wore on, Sukarno had to work harder and harder to keep his Nasakom coalition together. The tension between the main players of the inner circle—communists, Muslims and the military—rose steadily.

The Communist Party began a campaign to force the military to represent more closely the components of Sukarno's Nasakom grouping. This meant, in practice, more orthodox Muslims and communists in the top reaches of the military. The army was also rattled by communists' efforts to fashion their own armed fighting force.

The intellectual class was another target of the communists. The Communist Party-affiliated People's Cultural Institute, known as Lekra, railed at artists, journalists, poets and playwrights deemed insufficiently committed to the cause. Its motto was: Politics is the Commander.[39] In its rural strongholds, the party launched 'unilateral actions' against large plantations and farms to force compliance with a 1960 land reform law, further aggravating tensions with local Muslim landlords.

In August 1965 Sukarno's health worsened, an event which seems to have sparked the last fatal crack in his governing coalition. Less than two months later came the abortive coup which marked the beginning of the end of the Old Order.

Why did Guided Democracy follow parliamentary democracy into the dustbin of history? The short explanation is that Sukarno was simply not strong enough to keep in check the irreconcilable political and social forces he had mashed together to support his personal rule.[40] Soeharto has avoided this pitfall, at least so far. Rather than juggling together what he perceived as incompatible social forces under civilian leadership, Soeharto enormously strengthened the power of the state, made the military the pre-eminent political institution and distanced from power those not willing to play along with the new rules of the game.

The mysterious coup

Two dates stand out in modern Indonesian history: Sukarno's declaration of independence on 17 August 1945 and the end of two decades of civilian control on 30 September 1965. Given the profound and lasting changes in Indonesia's economic and political management which occurred after 1965, it is surprising that some important facts about that fateful September day and its immediate aftermath remain shrouded in mystery, even after the passage of almost thirty years.

After darkness fell on 30 September, six generals and a lieutenant were kidnapped by a group of leftist officers, led by Lieutenant Colonel Untung, who called themselves the Thirtieth of September Movement. General Nasution, the armed forces chief of staff, was on the kidnappers' target list but managed to escape.

Before the night was out, the seven officers had been killed and their bodies dumped into an unused well at the Halim Air Force base on the eastern outskirts of Jakarta, from where the coup plotters based themselves. The pro-Sukarno Thirtieth of September Movement claimed the coup was a pre-emptive strike aimed at preventing an imminent coup by a Council of Generals. Whether a Council of Generals ever existed is unclear, but little credible evidence has come to light suggesting the army had plans to launch a coup to topple Sukarno. From the very beginning, Sukarno vehemently denied any prior knowledge of Untung's coup or involvement with the coup plotters.[41]

The army's response to the coup was led by Major General Soeharto, who headed the strategic reserve command, Kostrad. Upon learning that army commander Lieutenant General Achmad Yani had been kidnapped, Soeharto assumed control of the army early on the morning of 1 October.[42] Navy and police were put under his command. In a speech broadcast on radio at 9:00 pm on 1 October, Soeharto described the coup as a counter-revolutionary movement and told the nation that the army was back in charge. During that night, troops from the elite Army Paracommando Regiment overran the Halim Air Force base with minimal resistance. The coup was effectively over, little more than thirty hours after it had begun.

From the very beginning, the army has maintained that the coup was plotted and carried out solely by the Communist Party.[43] The evidence for this is sketchy. The army version rests heavily on the presence at Halim of the party's leader D. N. Aidit and elements of communist women and youth groups, as well as on later confessions by coup plotters and Communist Party members which seemed to suggest that parts of the party's leadership did have prior knowledge of the coup and that Untung had been influenced by the communists. Aidit himself was shot in Central Java a few weeks after the coup although his 'confession' was submitted in later court hearings to support the army version.

Two scholars connected to Cornell University, Benedict Anderson and Ruth McVey, presented an alternate theory in a 1966 essay. The 'Cornell Paper'[44] as it came to be known, concluded that the coup was primarily the result of internal army divisions, in which younger Javanese officers had acted against an older Jakarta leadership viewed as decadent and corrupt. The authors argue that the Communist Party, having done reasonably well under Sukarno, had little motive to launch a coup and that its role was incidental. The Cornell Paper notes that Aidit appeared to be reacting to events rather than leading them, and, intriguingly, that his party made no effort to rouse its mass membership in support of the coup.

Although not without its flaws—in particular its view that the Communist Party was not involved at all in the coup—on balance the Cornell Paper seems to offer a more credible interpretation of events than the army's contention that the communists were solely responsible. The Cornell version, however, is akin to heresy in New Order annals which not only hold the Communist Party responsible for the coup, but have made communism an enduring bogeyman to be dredged up regularly to dismiss and delegitimise criticism of the ruling regime. Not even the end of the Cold War has cooled the enthusiasm of New Order leaders for stamping the communist label on unwanted political activity.[45]

The bottled-up tensions that had been building for years exploded into the open in the weeks and months following the coup. As Sukarno's Nasakom coalition crumbled and its constituent parts turned on each other, a bloodbath ensued with few historical parallels. The Communist Party, containing some 300 000 cadres and a full membership of around two million,[46] was liquidated as a political force and hundreds of thousands of its members slaughtered.

The worst affected areas were the Communist Party strongholds of Central and East Java, although large numbers of deaths were reported in Bali and North Sumatra. The massacre began with little warning, raged unabated for the remainder of 1965, sputtered on through 1966 and then stopped. Estimates of deaths range from under 100 000 to more than one million. The most common and credible estimates are 300 000–400 000 killed. The US Central Intelligence Agency described the killing spree like this: 'In terms of numbers killed, the anti-PKI [Indonesian Communist Party] massacres in Indonesia rank as one of the worst mass murders of the twentieth century, along with the Soviet purges of the 1930s, the Nazi mass murders during the Second World War, and the Maoist bloodbath of the early 1950s. In this regard, the Indonesian coup is certainly one of the most significant events of the 20th century, far more significant than many other events that have received much greater publicity.'[47]

Real and suspected Communist Party members were killed by the thousands by local vigilantes and army units throughout the two densely populated Javanese provinces and elsewhere in the republic. The party put up little organised resistance which for some acted as proof of its complicity in the coup and for others as proof of its innocence. Many party members were killed by knife or bayonet. Bodies were often maimed and decapitated and dumped in rivers. At one point officials in Surabaya in East Java complained to army officials that the rivers running into Surabaya were choked with bodies.

What role the army played in the killings has never been satisfactorily explained. According to Robert Cribb, 'in some cases the army took direct part in the killings; often, however, they simply supplied weapons, rudimentary training and strong encouragement to the civilian gangs who carried out the bulk of the killings. In most cases, the killings did not begin until elite military units had arrived in a locality and had sanctioned violence by instruction or example.'[48] Many jailed or detained Indonesians were handed over to vigilantes for killing. Among the rampaging civilian vigilantes, Muslim groups were well represented, especially the militant Ansor youth wing of the Nahdlatul Ulama, and at times the killings took on the fervour of a Jihad, or Islamic holy war.

Explaining the explosion of rage and violence has taxed scholars from all ideological corners. Cribb emphasises the importance of local factors. In East and Central Java, Communist Party efforts to accelerate land reform deeply antagonised existing landholders and threatened the social dominance of Islamic preachers. In Lampung province in southern Sumatra, Javanese immigration seems to have been one contributing factor behind the killings. Christian clergy and teachers suffered at the hands of local Muslim youths in some of the predominantly Christian islands of Nusa Tenggara. 'On the island of Bali, Indonesia's only overtly Hindu province,' journalist Hamish McDonald writes, 'the killings developed just as fervently, with priests calling for fresh sacrifices to satisfy vengeful spirits over past sacrileges and social disruptions.'[49] In West Kalimantan, eighteen months after the killings had peaked in Java, indigenous Dayak tribesmen drove some 45 000 Chinese out of rural areas, killing hundreds, perhaps thousands, in the process.[50]

Given the massive dislocation brought on by the massacre, it is surprising, as Cribb notes, that the killings appear to have engendered little introspection by Indonesians and little more than casual notice by the international community. There has been no national soul-searching as was the case in post Second World War Germany. Many Indonesian histories, in fact, skip over the event as if, by being largely unexplainable, it was largely insignificant.

Supporters of the integral view of the state suggest that the disruptive effect of forcing a culturally unsuitable form of government onto Indonesian society in the early post-independence years bears some responsibility for creating the communal hatreds which underlay the bloodbath. Those on the other side of the political battlefield pin the blame on Sukarno and the military for rejecting the democratic process—in which competing interests can be debated openly—and replacing it with a form of authoritarianism in which these interests are bottled up and can be expressed only through violence.

In the prevailing climate of 'ideological absolutism', in Buyung Nasution's words,[51] in which the mechanisms for resolving disputes had all but withered away, Muslim groups and the military came to adopt an uncompromising 'us or them' attitude toward the Communist Party. And after the killing was over, many Indonesians seemed to shrug off the massacre as something 'the communists had coming to them'.

Abroad, the massacre was acknowledged as a Cold War victory over communism. With stunning insensitivity, *Time* magazine described the eradication of the Communist Party as 'The West's best news for years in Asia'.[52] Despite the absence of a public debate over the meaning of the slaughter, or perhaps because of it, the massacre hangs like a cloud over the New Order, its memory relegated to a musty corner of history but not, by any means, expunged. No one knows exactly why the beast emerged and the possibility of its return has inculcated in the New Order regime a deep streak of political caution.

The last days of Sukarno

The army, convinced of the Communist Party's culpability, set out to identify and remove from power civilian and military officials suspected of harbouring sympathies for the party, while Soeharto adroitly gathered support for himself as the army's leader. With the communists being systematically eliminated and the other political parties in disrepute, Indonesia's power centres had been reduced to two: the army and Sukarno. And Sukarno, without the backing of the Communist Party and having lost the trust of the Muslims, quickly found himself outflanked.

By the beginning of 1966, Soeharto was prepared to openly defy Sukarno, a step previous army leaders had shied away from. In the months following the bungled coup, Sukarno desperately sought a political solution which would mollify the army and keep himself in power. One non-negotiable demand by Soeharto, however, was that Sukarno blame the Communist Party for the coup and forever remove it from politics, a step the proud Sukarno could not bring himself to make.[53]

Even if Sukarno had turned his back on the communists, the likely result would have been simply a postponing of Sukarno's removal from power rather than a continuation of Guided Democracy. Once the bodies of the generals were found in the Halim well, the die was cast. Having long sought more control of the political system, the army had its opening with the bungled coup and was unlikely to be denied for long. Guided

Democracy provided a sufficiently serviceable political vehicle for Soeharto: all that was lacking was to replace its civilian leadership with one drawn from military ranks.

2
Soeharto takes charge

The democracy that we practice is Pancasila. Briefly its major characteristics are its rejection of poverty, backwardness, conflicts, exploitation, capitalism, feudalism, dictatorship, colonialism and imperialism. This is the policy I have chosen with confidence.

Soeharto[1]

We're very happy with the status quo. It's not time yet for a different system.

Rachmat Witoelar[2]

Everyone, without exception, does the bidding of Suharto, and he is suspicious of anyone who acts without his permission. He can't take criticism. He wants everyone to follow his line 100 per cent. But with what consequences for the country? Just look around. You never hear a minister make a major pronouncement without it being noted that he just emerged from a meeting with Suharto, or that it was the President's wish that it be so. Suharto has no interest in creative and independent actions. Look at the people around him now. Even when they know big mistakes are being made, they remain silent and agree. No one has any guts.

Ibnu Sutowo[3]

In January and February, 1966, the test of wills between Sukarno and Soeharto picked up steam. Desperately seeking to shore up his fading authority, Sukarno sought clear expressions of support from civilian politicians and friendly military officers. For his part, not wanting the military to be seen to be usurping power from the constitutional head of state, Soeharto preferred to move cautiously. He kept waiting for Sukarno to adjust to the changed circumstances in Indonesia. Sooner or later, Soeharto figured, Sukarno would act to save his own position by distancing himself from the communists and recognising the greater powers now held by the military. The anti-Sukarno student demonstrations which Soeharto had encouraged since the beginning of the year were intended to help Sukarno in this adjustment process.

But time was running out. Sukarno obviously had chosen a different path from the one to which he was being led by Soeharto. Elements of the military leadership, antagonised by Sukarno's impassioned defence of the communists, were pushing for more pressure to be applied to Sukarno.

The final straw for the rightist officers was a cabinet reshuffle unveiled by Sukarno on 21 February. Ten members of the previous cabinet were dismissed, including several high-ranking military personnel such as General Nasution, then Coordinating Minister for Defence and Security. Even worse from Soeharto's perspective, a number of ministers considered pro-communist were retained, including Deputy Prime Minister Subandrio.

The new cabinet was, in effect, a direct challenge to Soeharto. If he didn't respond, he would allow Sukarno a good chance of rebuilding his power base and the military's aspirations for political supremacy would be set back, perhaps permanently. But at the same time, pro-Sukarno officers were still numerous enough to make Soeharto hesitate over an open challenge to the president.

He needed, in other words, a 'way to reject the cabinet without taking action that would force members of the armed forces to choose between Sukarno and Suharto', writes Harold Crouch. The means he chose, 'was to give covert approval to a group of strongly anti-Sukarnoist officers who encouraged students to create an atmosphere of chaos in the capital.'[4] The idea was to force Sukarno to turn for help to the 'moderate' Soeharto to prevent a takeover by army extremists.

A meeting of the full cabinet took place on 11 March. With students stridently demonstrating outside, the climate was extremely tense. The only notable absentee was Soeharto who was home with what he said was a throat ailment. Shortly after the cabinet meeting began, Sukarno was handed a note informing him that unidentified troops had begun to assemble outside. Along with Subandrio and one other minister, Sukarno immediately left the meeting and flew by helicopter to his palace cum retreat in Bogor. Once Sukarno had fled, Major General Amir Machmud left to tell Soeharto what had happened.

Exactly what transpired in that meeting is another matter under contention. Machmud said Soeharto instructed him and two other generals to reassure Sukarno 'that the army could keep the situation under control if given the full confidence of the president'.[5] Whatever their instructions, the outcome of a subsequent meeting between the three generals and Sukarno was the 'Letter of 11 March', later referred to as Supersemar. In it, Sukarno assigned Soeharto 'to take all measures considered necessary to guarantee security, calm and stability of the government and the revolution and to guarantee the personal safety and authority [of Sukarno]'.

Did Soeharto and his aides draw up Supersemar before the three messenger generals left to visit Sukarno? It is a scenario which the army, anxious to dispel any accusations of a military coup, firmly denies. Machmud goes so far as to claim that Sukarno, persuaded that only the army could restore order in Jakarta, proposed that Supersemar be drafted. The more common view is that the three generals had a good idea of what Soeharto wanted from Sukarno though not in the form of a finished document. The actual wording of Supersemar, in this view, took shape in the discussions with Sukarno and Subandrio in Bogor.

Authorship aside, the document marked the effective end of Sukarno's rule. In a widely quoted comment, Crouch described the day's events as 'the disguised coup of 11 March'.[6] It is a description which Soeharto, who depends on constitutional legitimacy to maintain his own hold on power, vigorously disputes. 'I have never thought of Supersemar as a means to gain power. Neither was the written Instruction of 11 March an instrument to stage a disguised coup. Supersemar was the beginning of the struggle of the New Order.'[7]

The mechanics of Supersemar remain a morsel for future historians to paw over. But despite Soeharto's protestations, Supersemar was very much a means to power, and Soeharto didn't wait long before flexing his muscles. On 12 March he banned the Indonesian Communist Party and dissolved all its affiliated organisations. Four days later, when Sukarno refused to dismiss cabinet ministers distrusted by the army, the army simply arrested them.

The emergence of Supersemar knocked the wind out of the sails of pro-Sukarno loyalists in the armed forces. Despite their unhappiness with Soeharto's new powers, few felt able to defend the Communist Party. The party itself, having been all but destroyed, was even less able to offer resistance. Sukarno, belatedly realising how Supersemar was going to be used, scrambled to repudiate it. But what he had signed he was unable to revoke. In his confrontation with Soeharto, Sukarno had lost.

The smiling general

When Soeharto burst upon the scene in 1965, little was known about him. While he was the most senior general not kidnapped by the coup plotters, there were other generals of similar stature and it startled virtually everyone that Soeharto would move to the fore as authoritatively as he did. He was not considered to be especially politically minded. And historians scouring Soeharto's past for signs of a budding politician have little to show for their efforts.

Soeharto was born on 8 June 1921 in a small, poor and unremarkable Central Javanese village called Kemusuk and grew up in a sprawling family heaped with stepbrothers, stepsisters and cousins. He was the only child of his natural parents who divorced shortly after he was born. From an earlier marriage his father, a village irrigation official, had two children and a later wife bore him four more. His mother Sukirah also remarried and had seven more children.[8]

Shortly after his birth, Soeharto was taken to live with the younger sister of his grandfather because his mother was ill. In his first ten years, he moved from one household to another: for a while with his mother, then a stint with his father, then his father's sister, and then his own stepsister, then a relation of his father. Even by the standards of Java's flexible family structures, Soeharto's childhood was an unsettled one.

But Soeharto speaks lovingly of his family upbringing and betrays no resentment at being passed from house to house. He remains close to his agricultural roots and his presidency has paid special attention to the concerns of farmers. In his autobiography, he makes little effort to hide the depth of his family's poverty: 'In my childhood I had to endure such suffering which perhaps others could not imagine. But if I draw a lesson from my past, then I would say it is because of this suffering that I have become who I am. I have become a person who can really think about and feel what hardship means.'[9]

While in junior high school, Soeharto's family could not afford to buy him the stipulated pair of short pants and shoes and he was forced to leave. At the age of eighteen, he finished his studies in Yogyakarta at a school run by the Muhammadiyah, the large Islamic organisation.

He struggled to find a job before finally being employed as a bank clerk. One day while riding his bicycle he tore the traditional Javanese sarong he was required to wear to work. As he was too poor to buy a new one, 'that ended my work at the bank', he says. He discovered his true calling some months later when he enlisted in the Royal Netherlands Indies Army (KNIL). Again, the job was short-lived as the Dutch surrendered to the Japanese in early 1942. Soeharto then joined the local militia organised by the Japanese, rulers he later described as deeply oppressive. When the Japanese left, Soeharto joined the fight against the Dutch and rose quickly through the ranks in the newly formed Indonesian army.

Soeharto took part in the March 1949 offensive to retake Yogyakarta from the Dutch and, shortly after the Dutch had left for good, he was dispatched to Sulawesi to help put down a revolt there. Soeharto went on to serve in the Diponegoro regional divisional command in Central Java in the mid-1950s and became involved in combating the Darul Islam rebellion. In 1957 he was promoted to Diponegoro commander with the rank of colonel. On the home front, Soeharto's family arranged for him to marry a local girl, Siti Hartinah, in December 1947. They would have six children, three boys and three girls.

After marriage, Soeharto quickly learned how to provide for the family, and not just his own. In the early years of the republic the army was forced to supplement its budgetary allotments with independent financing. It was common for regional military officers to hook up with local merchants to generate additional revenue or, more simply, to impose a tax on economic activities in their area. Soeharto proved to be a particularly able businessman.

In the mid-1950s Soeharto first encountered Chinese entrepreneurs like Liem Sioe Liong and Bob Hasan who, in the New Order, would become two of the most powerful businessmen in the land. Although the details are sketchy, it appears Soeharto was a shade too energetic in his business dealings on behalf of the Diponegoro division and at times crossed the line into outright smuggling. He was shifted prematurely from his post in 1959 by General Nasution, then the Minister for Defence and Security, and sent to the army staff college, Seskoad.[10]

Soeharto managed to rehabilitate himself in the eyes of his superiors while studying at Seskoad and, upon finishing, he was promoted to brigadier general. Shortly after, he was put in charge of the Mandala campaign to wrest control of West Irian from the Dutch. (Soeharto gave his youngest son Tommy, born in 1962, the middle name of Mandala after the campaign.)

Based in Makassar, later renamed Ujungpandang, Soeharto drew up plans for an invasion of Irian Jaya. But before the plans could be put into effect, Indonesia's diplomatic offensive at the United Nations bore fruit and the Dutch, under pressure from the United States, agreed to withdraw from West Irian. Upon his return to Jakarta, Soeharto, then a major general, was made commander of Kostrad, the army's elite strategic reserve command, where he remained until the abortive coup of 30 September 1965.

The New Order

The architects of Soeharto's New Order government defined their main mission as the need to re-establish order in Indonesian society. The upheavals which followed the September 1965 coup provided the immediate pretext for a new approach to governance, but the pressure for change had been building for some time. The experience with parliamentary democracy in the 1950s and with Sukarno's Guided Democracy in the first half of the decade had convinced many in the military of the need for a much stronger government.

In their view, a strong state—relatively insulated from the interests of any particular social group and capable of suppressing antagonisms based on ethnicity, religion or geography—was the 'essential condition of present-day industrialisation'. The core beliefs of this group, writes Ruth McVey, were that 'popular participation in politics must be strictly limited, the country must accede to the realities of world power and economic relationships, and that what mattered was material accomplishment of "development" rather than the realisation of a national essence or an international ideal.'[11]

Political 'order' and economic development, in other words, were seen as two sides of the same coin. Order, as Soeharto's government conceived it, was not a condition resulting from the use of force; it followed, rather, from the enforcement—however selective—of the government's rules. 'However arbitrarily its minions may act, the New Order seeks to portray itself [as] the defender of "normality" and the "rule of law", the umpire enforcing the ground rules for interaction between Indonesia's social forces.'[12]

In the early years of the New Order these views found support from a broad swath of society. With ex-Communist Party members as notable exceptions, many groups felt the new rules of the game could only be an improvement: these groups included civilian politicians happy to see the demise of Guided Democracy, government economists (later to be called technocrats), liberals hoping for a restoration of constitutional democracy, journalists and intellectuals happy to be freed from the ideological strictures of the communist-linked People's Cultural Institute, Muslims pleased with the elimination of the communists as a political force, businessmen excited about the prospect of an economic resurgence, and many others tired of ceaseless political ferment. Some of these groups were to see their hopes fulfilled, others were to become gradually and then deeply disappointed.

1966–1974: Order begins

With the Supersemar decree in hand and Sukarnoist officers in disarray, Soeharto went to work purging the military and civil service of leftist elements. Thousands of arrests were made. Major General Soemitro and his successor Major General Mohammad Jasin, commanders of the Brawijaya army division in East Java, finished off what was left of the Communist Party. In the navy, Admiral Sudomo, an assistant to Soeharto in the Mandala campaign, cleansed the force of leftist officers in the late 1960s. The pro-Sukarno air force chief Omar Dhani was tried and sentenced to life imprisonment.

In hindsight, it is easy to forget that Soeharto's success in securing support from within the military came as a surprise to many. 'We certainly didn't expect Soeharto to become the successor to Sukarno,' said General (ret.) Soemitro in an interview in 1989. 'At that time, our hope was on [then armed forces chief of staff] General Nasution but he didn't have the guts to face Sukarno man to man.'[13] But Soeharto proved his doubters wrong. Working methodically, never overplaying his hand, he masterfully consolidated his hold over the armed forces. He curbed the power of regional commanders and made them answerable to him. A critical General Nasution was deftly shunted off centre stage. Through persuasion and more forceful means, Soeharto stemmed the zealousness of militantly anti-communist officers such as Kemal Idris, Sarwo Edhie and Dharsono who wanted a quicker transformation of the political system. By the end of the 1960s, Soeharto's military base was secure.

Meanwhile, military officers in Soeharto's camp developed and expanded on General Nasution's 'Middle Way' concept. *Dwifungsi*, or dual function, as the concept was renamed, provided the theoretical backing for the military to expand its influence throughout the government apparatus, including reserved allocations of seats in the parliament and top posts in the civil service. In contrast to military takeovers in Latin America and elsewhere, the Indonesian military never defended its expanded political role as a temporary phase that would pass once an immediate crisis was over. On the contrary, the message of *dwifungsi* was that the military's role in politics was to become permanent.

In March 1967 Soeharto was formally named acting president, and, a year later, president. Sukarno, defiant to the end, was by then marginalised as a political actor. Indonesia patched up its rogue image overseas by lowering the temperature in its dispute with Malaysia and by beginning the long process of putting its economic house in order.

By the mid-1960s, Indonesia's economy was in such dire straits that immediate attention was required. Soeharto turned for advice to a team of Western-trained economists henceforth known as the technocrats. Their immediate objectives were to rein in inflation, stabilise the rupiah, get a handle on foreign debt, attract foreign aid and encourage foreign investment. They succeeded on all fronts, and the details of how they did so are covered in the following chapter.

After placing economic policy in the hands of the technocrats, Soeharto set about creating a more pliant political system. The New Order began with civilian political leaders under a cloud. But Soeharto was not of a mind—and probably unable—to ban all civilian political activity. Instead, the idea was to restructure the political system in such a way that it could no longer compete with the executive office for power. The forms of government would stay, but those outside the executive branch would be steadily drained of influence.

Soeharto gathered around him a corps of personal assistants, known as *staf pribadi*, or *spri*, of which the most powerful were Ali Murtopo, assistant for political affairs, and Sudjono Humardhani, assistant for economic affairs. Unlike under Sukarno, cabinet ministers would no longer be political operatives in their own right; instead, they would implement the policies of the government.

In the immediate aftermath of Sukarno's overthrow, political parties still held a commanding majority in the People's Consultative Assembly, or MPR, the body authorised by the constitution to select a president and to which the president is nominally accountable. That was soon to change. In 1967, the government gave itself the right to appoint one-third of the representatives to the People's Assembly and more than one-fifth of the sitting parliament, known as the DPR. In addition, elections scheduled for 1968 were postponed until a non-hostile parliament could be assured.

Meanwhile, the new regime wasted little time in meddling in civilian politics. In April 1966, the Nationalist Party came under heavy pressure from the government to dismiss its pre-New Order leaders and replace them with officials more to the liking of the new powers.

Muslim groups were also to be disappointed. Having played a central role in the anti-communist purges of 1965–66, Muslims expected a commensurate political role in the New Order. Leaders of the banned Masyumi party petitioned unsuccessfully for its reinstatement. What soon became clear was that the military–Muslim partnership in the anti-Communist Party crusade was a short-term marriage of convenience. On longer term strategic matters, the two groups remained as far apart as ever. In 1968, Soeharto authorised the formation of a new Partai Muslimin Indonesia, Parmusi, but the former Masyumi leaders were banned from playing any part and a government nominee, Djaelani Naro, was subsequently elevated to chairman.

In 1967, the army introduced a new player on to the political stage. Building on an army-organised association of anti-communist groups started in 1964, Soeharto and his assistants announced that Golkar (from *golongan karya*, or functional groups) would be the regime's parliamentary vehicle. In keeping with the army's distaste for party politics, the new association was to be referred to not as a party but as a Functional Group. Golkar housed several hundred smaller 'functional groups' of peasants, labour unions and businesses and so on. Later, Golkar would be dominated by three currents: the army, bureaucracy and its own civilian wing, with the army remaining very much the senior partner. The mass-based groups present at Golkar's birth quickly faded into insignificance, just as the masses disappeared from the political scene more generally.

For the same reasons a return to the 1945 Constitution appealed to the army in 1959, so too did Golkar hold its attractions for a military striving to find a constitutionally-justified vehicle for greater political influence. 'The Golkar concept was immensely useful to the Army,' writes David Reeve. 'If the nation were conceived of as made up of golkar [functional groups], and the Armed Forces were included among them, then the military were entitled to play a role in all fields, political and economic, as other golkar did. Thus the concept of the Armed Forces as a golkar is the core of what was . . . called the "dual-function" of the Indonesian military.'[14]

Elections were rescheduled for 1971, a postponement considered long enough to enable Golkar to assemble the necessary electoral machinery to produce a majority for the government. Given the continuing strength of the longer established parties, this appeared an overwhelming challenge but Ali Murtopo and his all-purpose Opsus (special operations) unit proved to be up to the task.[15] Massive intervention followed. Civil servants were in effect obliged to support Golkar. District leaders and village heads were given 'quotas' of Golkar votes to fill and development funds were promised to pro-Golkar regions.

Meanwhile, the two top vote-getters in the 1955 elections, the Nationalist Party and Parmusi (the Masyumi's heir), had been manipulated so blatantly by the government that they lost all credibility with their pre-1966 supporters. In the elections, Golkar won a stunning 63 per cent of the vote. The Nahdlatul Ulama held its 1955 share of about 18 per cent, but both the Nationalist Party and Parmusi–Masyumi collected less than seven per cent, a far cry from their 1955 performance. Even the victors didn't consider the victory particularly genuine. 'If you had left it to Golkar in 1971, without any interference from Abri [the armed forces], the Muslim parties would have won. I can assure you of that!' was the view of General Soemitro, who in the early 1970s headed the potent Kopkamtib internal security agency.[16]

In the following three years, two developments added to the sophistication of the Golkar machinery and made the 1971 brand of intervention less necessary for the future. In 1973 the nine political parties (not including Golkar) were 'encouraged' to dissolve themselves voluntarily. In their place, two new parties were created: the United Development Party, to which the former Muslim parties gravitated, and the Indonesian Democratic Party, which attracted adherents of the former nationalist and Christian parties.

The idea, which appeared to have come from Murtopo, had the effect of further weakening the parties by fostering internal disunities, a problem which has plagued them to the present day. This, however, was not Soeharto's concern. He wanted a parliament that would endorse his policies, not offer differing ones. 'With one and only one road already mapped out, why should we then have nine different cars?' he asked. 'The General Elections must serve the very purpose for which they are held, that is, to create political stability,' he added. 'Only these kinds of elections are of value to us.'[17]

The second development was a political notion advanced by Murtopo called the "floating mass" concept. The idea was that the populace would become a floating mass allowed to vote once every five years but otherwise refrain from political activity. This was accompanied by restrictions on party activity in rural areas. Golkar, too, was affected by these restrictions but it was much better able to maintain links with rural areas via the army which had a presence in virtually every village.

Despite the circumscribing of civilian politics, the early New Order period is remembered for a brisk social and cultural life. Authors and playwrights enjoyed a brief season of fertile activity and the press was lively and relatively unrestrained. Students held high hopes that the new military overseers would put an end to the pervasive corruption and patronage of Sukarno's Guided Democracy. Slamet Bratanata, a minister in Soeharto's first cabinet and later a strident critic of the regime, likened the 1967–74 interval to the Prague Spring of 1968.[18]

1974: The balance shifts

By 1974, disillusionment among some of Soeharto's erstwhile supporters was on the rise. Contrary to early student hopes, it soon became clear that the elimination of corruption was not a central priority of the government. Corruption merely became more institutionalised, with army officers and their (usually Chinese) business cohorts being the chief beneficiaries. The army had seen its economic role multiply in the 1950s though the nationalisation of foreign companies and it was loath to relinquish its hold on extra-budgetary sources of revenue. For his part, Soeharto had sealed his hold over the armed forces by bringing the art of patronage to new levels and wasn't about to dispense with the tools of the trade.

Critics, inside and outside the armed forces, deplored the increasingly cosy relationship between the 'financial generals', of whom Soeharto was only the most senior, and a small group of ethnic Chinese businessmen. Soeharto's top two assistants, Ali Murtopo and Sudjono Humardhani, were considered the leaders of the 'financial generals' and became prime targets of press criticism. A group of so-called 'professional soldiers' looked to General Soemitro, deputy commander of the armed forces and head of the Kopkamtib internal security agency, and Major General Sayidiman Suryohadiproyo, deputy chief of staff of the army, to advance their views. Their chief concern was that the activities of the 'financial generals' were bringing the army into disrepute and detracting from efforts to modernise the armed forces.[19] It was an old schism, begun in the 1950s and one which continues today.

On the economic front, an influx of foreign investment had led to serious dislocations in the workforce. Labour-intensive factories run by indigenous Indonesian entrepreneurs suffered in competition with capital-intensive plants set up by foreign investors. The Japanese, responding to the generous investment inducements offered by the technocrats, had moved into Indonesia in a big way and were involved in a wide variety of manufacturing industries. Many overseas investors came in as 100 per cent owners, though when they did take on a local partner, they tended to favour well-connected military officers or leading Indonesian-Chinese businessmen.

The influx of foreign investment, combined with a surge in oil revenues, had given the 'financial generals' vastly larger pools of funds with which to grease the wheels of their patronage machine. Humardhani was doubly targeted as he was also closely identified with luring Japanese investment into Indonesia. He, along with Murtopo, founded a think tank in the early 1970s, the Centre for Strategic and International Studies, which at its inception was seen as the intellectual incubator for the New Order's principal political operatives.

In late 1973, resentment began seeping to the surface. Anti-Chinese riots in Bandung, a quiet city in the hills of West Java, damaged about 1500 shops and houses. A striking feature of the demonstrations was the lateness of the army in responding. The delay in acting, it seemed, was explained by the soldiers' sympathy with the rioters. Soemitro courted the support of students and did little to dampen criticism of Murtopo and the other 'financial generals'.

The situation came to a head in January 1974 when the Japanese prime minister, Kakuei Tanaka, arrived for a state visit. In the morning after his arrival, thousands of students demonstrated in the streets of Jakarta, calling for a reduction of prices, an end to corruption and the disbanding of Soeharto's club of private assistants.[20] It seemed to many that Soemitro had given the green light to students as a way of putting pressure on Soeharto to distance himself from his two most influential advisers, Murtopo and Humardhani, a tactic Soeharto had used to great effect in 1966 against Sukarno.

By the afternoon of the same day, though, the demonstrations had turned into a riot in which hundreds of cars were burned and shops looted. The most visible symbol of the Japanese presence in Indonesia, the showroom of Astra, the local firm which imported Toyota automobiles, was burned to the ground. Astra, not coincidentally, was owned by an Indonesian-Chinese family. Only a day later, when troops fired on looters, killing about a dozen, was the riot brought under control.

The Malari incident, as the anti-Japanese riots came to be known, marked a turning point for Indonesia. 'The government had been shocked to its very roots by its inability to maintain law and order during the visit of an extremely important guest,' says American scholar John Bresnan.[21] Although the government blamed the riots on malcontents from the banned Socialist and Masyumi parties, an important contributing factor was the divisions within the armed forces. Malari, by being a clear victory for the 'financial generals', dampened the disunity. Soemitro was blamed for inciting the students and relieved of his post as Kopkamtib chief. He soon 'resigned' from his post as deputy chief of the armed forces. Sayidiman was shunted into a less powerful staff job and other Soemitro supporters were made ambassadors or otherwise removed from direct troop command. Although it was becoming clear before 1974, after Malari the army more clearly understood that personal loyalty to Soeharto counted for a great deal more than the army's institutional clout.

A second lesson from Malari was the danger of allowing factional disputes within the nation's leadership to spill over into—and possibly exacerbate existing tensions within—societal groups, be they civilian parties, the press, Muslims or student groups. 'Intra-elite politics was henceforth to be quarantined from the masses. In that sense, Malari marked a decisive shift from the relatively open, pluralistic phase of political life under the New Order towards one in which society-based forces were to be largely excluded and rendered almost powerless to influence state policies or the distribution of power at the top,' according to Australian political scientists Jamie Mackie and Andrew MacIntyre.[22]

In the months following Malari, twelve newspapers were closed and hundreds of Indonesians were put on trial for their role in the disturbance. Campus life grew more subdued and the press became more cautious. Malari had its economic implications as well. The investment laws were modified to prevent 100 per cent foreign ownership, obliging new foreign investors to form joint ventures. After Malari, the tone of the New Order was largely set. To be sure, some leaders within the armed forces continued to be dissatisfied with Soeharto's rule but there were to be no more public challenges to Soeharto's authority from within active duty ranks.

1975–1985: Soeharto consolidates

In the middle decade of his rule, Soeharto gradually moved to strengthen his control over the political process and prevent expressions of dissatisfaction from bubbling to the surface. The treasury, flush with oil revenues, was able to accelerate its spendings on infrastructure and nudge economic growth higher.

Nonetheless, the late 1970s held some difficult moments for Soeharto. A calamitous mishandling of the affairs of the state oil company Pertamina threatened, for a time, to undo much of the work carried out since the mid-1960s to rehabilitate the economy. A badly handled invasion of East Timor in 1975 weakened Indonesia's international standing and revived internal army divisions. Several consecutive years of poor rice harvests added to the tension in rural areas.

Muslims, angered by Soeharto's sponsorship of a Christian-supported marriage bill and his efforts to make *kebatinan*, or traditional Javanese beliefs, into one of Indonesia's officially acceptable religions, posed a real threat to Golkar's hegemony in the 1977 elections. University students continued to agitate against corruption and the increasingly authoritarian nature of Soeharto's government.

The government responded with another burst of voter coercion and intimidation, including the 1978 Campus Normalisation Law which squelched political activity at the universities. The government's efforts resulted in another comfortable Golkar victory and Soeharto was duly given another five-year term as president by the People's Assembly session in March 1978.

In 1979–80, a collection of retired officers and outspoken civilians— known alternately as the Group of Fifty and the Petition of Fifty— launched a series of broadsides at Soeharto complaining of the way the army was being used as Golkar's political fixer and demanding political reforms. After a time, Soeharto struck back, revoking the critics' travel privileges and forbidding newspapers from printing their pictures or quoting their comments. 'I didn't like what the so-called Petition of 50 did. I didn't like their methods, even more so because they called them-selves patriots,' Soeharto said.[23]

By the early 1980s, the situation had turned around for Soeharto. Bumper harvests of rice in 1979–81 had eased food shortages in rural Java and a major rise in oil prices in 1979 pumped still more funds into the treasury. More curbs were placed on student protests, new laws permitting greater censorship of the press were enacted, and a wide-rang-ing indoctrination program was undertaken to spread the word of Pancasila. Soldiers, teachers, politicians, doctors, even overseas students were required to attend classes to better understand the meaning of Pancasila in Soeharto's Indonesia. The 1982 elections went far smoother for Soeharto than the previous two polls. Allegations of vote-rigging were less pronounced and Golkar's share of the ballot rose to 64 per cent. The following year, Soeharto was appointed to a fourth term by an ever more quiescent People's Assembly.

In 1984, Soeharto decreed that all social-political organisations, includ-ing the civilian political parties, must declare Pancasila as their sole ideology, or *asas tunggal*. It was a particularly unwelcome development for the Muslim-linked United Development Party representing, as it did, an exclamation point to the defeat suffered by Muslim groups in the ideological battles of the 1950s. Shortly after, the party ceased to be a credible opposition threat when the Nahdlatul Ulama pulled out to con-centrate on social and religious activities.

As the 1980s unfolded, the main story on the political front was the ever-increasing stature of Soeharto and the fading away of potential opposition to him, either from the civilian arena or from within the army. Critical officers were removed and replaced with loyalists. Organisations of all kinds existed under the constant threat of being accused of anti-Pancasila activities. The obligation of swearing allegiance to Pancasila was extended to non-governmental organisations and other social groups. The New Order's aversion to public politics grew progressively more severe to the point that even the term 'politics' itself, says sociologist Arief Budiman, became a bad word.[24] David Jenkins, writing in 1984, describes the degree of control Soeharto had achieved almost two decades after taking power:

> Suharto stood at the apex of the pyramid; his appointees sat in each of the key executive, legislative, and judicial branches of government . . . His writ extended into every department and into every state-run corporation; it reached down, if he chose, to every village . . . In short, he had established himself as the paramount figure in a society in which deference to authority is deeply rooted.[25]

1986–1993: Order secured

Jenkins' description has stood the test of time. The only comment that might be added is to note that in the nine intervening years, Soeharto has, if anything, made himself still more unassailable. The mid-1980s collapse of oil prices slowed Indonesia's economy for a time but a comprehensive program to wean the nation off its dependence on oil revenues had put the economy back on track by the end of the decade.

In the 1987 general elections, Golkar, benefiting from the Nahdlatul Ulama's withdrawal from the United Development Party, saw its share of the votes rise to 73 per cent. The People's Assembly meeting dutifully appointed Soeharto to another term as president in early 1988, although not without some minor disturbances. Military leaders, unhappy at the prospect of Golkar chairman Sudharmono being appointed vice-president, attempted until the last minute to persuade Soeharto to change his mind.

After failing to do so, the army went to work strengthening its influence in Golkar but, though successful, the move tended to highlight the military's political weakness vis-a-vis Soeharto, rather than its strength. As army officers should have known better than anyone, political power did not rest with Golkar, but with Soeharto.

With civilian society in check, Soeharto in the late 1980s no longer needed—nor cared—to share the political limelight with the armed forces. Like the political parties and the civil service, the military was expected to endorse and implement the executive's policies, not share in the formulation of those policies.

It seemed for a time in the late 1980s that Soeharto would step down as president in 1993. He even hinted as much in his autobiography. Soemitro, a retired general and political analyst, was among those who took Soeharto at his word: 'I am completely sure Soeharto will not be president after 1993,' he said in an interview in mid-1989.[26] But by the early 1990s it was generally understood that Soeharto had no intention of moving aside. He responded to criticism of his authoritarian rule by promising to widen the space for public debate, though little of substance came from these promises.

Soeharto was by now well versed in the tactics of divide and conquer. In response to what he perceived as flagging support from the military, Soeharto in the early 1990s courted support from the Muslim community, a move which had the added benefit of convincing some prominent Muslim leaders to temper their criticisms of the government. In 1992, the Golkar machine cruised to another comfortable victory, collecting 68 per cent of the votes.

In March 1993, after another uneventful People's Assembly session, Soeharto began his sixth five-year presidential term. His former aide, General Try Sutrisno, was his new vice-president, his brother-in-law General Wismoyo Arismunandar, was the new army chief and other former aides were sprinkled throughout the military leadership. The cabinet Soeharto formed in mid-March 1993 seems tame even by the deferential standards of modern Indonesian politics. And, despite opposition from several leading military officers, he succeeded in elevating a longtime loyalist, Information Minister Harmoko, to the chairmanship of Golkar in October 1993 and in placing two of his children in senior slots on Golkar's executive board.

But not all the signs were auspicious for Soeharto in 1993. On a string of issues in the latter half of the year, his government performed ineptly and found itself out of sync with an increasingly assertive society. Near the end of the year, a series of protests and street demonstrations by students and Muslim groups forced the government to withdraw its support for a state-sponsored lottery. On one occasion, the protesters made it to the gates of the presidential palace, the first time that had happened since the anti-Sukarno rallies in early 1966. Emboldened by their success with the lottery issue, students stepped up the pace of protest in late 1993 and early 1994; some groups demanded, in strikingly personal terms, a special session of the People's Assembly to call Soeharto to account for the failings of his administration. Others criticised the business dealings of Soeharto's children, several of which have built up enormous business empires in the space of less than ten years.

Also in 1993, the government's repeated attempts to meddle in the election for a new chairman of the Indonesian Democratic Party not only backfired but left the government looking badly out of touch with grass-roots pressure for more democratisation. When voters in Central Kalimantan rejected the government's imposed choice for provincial governor in December 1993, the Home Affairs Ministry in Jakarta had no choice but to back down and acquiesce to demands for a new election.

The government suffered a similar rebuff when the members of the Indonesian Chamber of Commerce and Industry met to elect a new chairman in early 1994: the candidate said to be backed by Soeharto was roundly defeated.

Taken together, these events tended to take the shine off Soeharto's image of invincibility. Even some of the president's supporters have begun to wonder whether Soeharto's famed political acumen is beginning to slip away; his critics now talk frequently about a crisis of authority afflicting the Indonesian nation. But it is far too early to prepare Soeharto's political obituary. While criticism of his rule has clearly begun to rise and is unlikely to abate, Soeharto remains very much the predominant political actor in Indonesia. His control of the armed forces leadership, the parliament, Golkar and, by extension, the People's Assembly, leave him holding most of the cards in the political deck. While the next five years could well prove to be rocky ones for Soeharto, he will remain a formidable adversary to any challengers to his throne.

The soldier's politician

How did it happen? How did an obscure, seemingly apolitical major general outflank the nationalist hero and master politician Sukarno, domesticate civilian politics, bend a fractious military to his will and survive one challenge after another during almost three decades in power?

A description of Soeharto's political prowess must begin with a reference to his military roots. Soeharto came to power on the army's coattails and the repressive might of the army has been the single most important factor in undermining potential opponents throughout his tenure. The army has forcefully suppressed any number of demonstrations, from the Malari incident in 1974, to a series of anti-Chinese outbreaks, to Muslim-associated protests in Jakarta in 1984 and in Lampung province in 1989. And it is engaged in ongoing campaigns in East Timor, Aceh and Irian Jaya.

But open shows of force are not really the New Order's style. Soeharto's—and the armed forces's—objective is social control, not military control. Pursuing what it calls a 'security approach' to actual and potential sources of dissent, the military has tried to prevent unwanted political activity rather than rely on repression once that activity has appeared. To carry out this mission, the military has attempted to insinuate itself into all-important social and political movements. One practical effect has been the creation of an enormous intelligence network.[27]

The 'security approach' and the army's might have enabled the New Order government to repel direct challenges to Soeharto's rule. But a more important component of the president's success is that he has made it very difficult for challenges to be mounted in the first place. By 'depoliticising' Indonesia or, more accurately, by setting stringent curbs on what political activity can take place, it is virtually impossible for any dissatisfied group to pose a credible challenge to Soeharto using the existing political institutions.

Soeharto, for example, has been rigorously attentive to the constitutionally prescribed norms of behaviour for presidential elections. When asked about his succession, he invariably replies that it is a matter for the People's Consultative Assembly to decide, as stipulated by the constitution. Every five years, Soeharto dutifully submits a 'statement of account' to the Assembly explaining his actions of the previous five years.

Of course, while the form of the constitution is adhered to, the same cannot be said of its 'spirit'. A large majority of the 1000-member Assembly is appointed or approved by the sitting executive. Members are usually given no more than one or two days to read and accept the 'statement of account', which runs to several hundred pages. Critics and opponents come under tremendous pressure not to disrupt the 'national consensus'; in practice, this means voting is taboo. The Assembly, in fact, has not held a formal vote since Soeharto came to power.[28] Every five years, all 1000 members 'vote' by acclamation for Soeharto's re-election.

Any unwanted political activity outside the constitutional bodies risks being labelled anti-Pancasila by those in power. These parameters on political behaviour extend far beyond the constraints on civilian political parties. Virtually all trades and businesses are grouped into associations which are then folded into larger and larger associations, each more removed from the concerns at the bottom. The same dynamic affects labour unions, which in 1985 were obliged to join an umbrella and largely ineffectual labour organisation. The Ministry of Information keeps close tabs on the Association of Indonesian Journalists. Artists must obtain a bewildering variety of permission letters and licences from several branches of the military before a performance can be held. Non-governmental organisations have some leeway of movement but they, too, operate under a constant threat of government harassment. If they fail to report sources of funding, for example, they risk being dissolved by the government.

A second important feature of Soeharto's rule is his frequent and shrewd use of patronage to buy off critics, particularly from within Abri. In the early New Order years, Soeharto defused dissent by giving troublesome officers prestigious ambassadorial posts or setting them up in business. Many retired officers have benefited handsomely from equity stakes in timber companies.

Harold Crouch, who calls this style of rule 'patrimonialism',[29] notes that the uses of patronage are just as potent when applied to active-duty officers, many of whom are linked to private businesses on the side. As the New Order progressed, so did the art of patronage. Revenues collected from Soeharto's close business associates in sectors such as oil, construc-

tion and agro-business—often washed through non-profit foundations—
have enabled Soeharto to expand the distribution of patronage to potential
critics in political, religious and social circles.

But even when patronage is not enough to silence critics, Soeharto
has been careful not to make enemies recklessly. In dealing with the
dissident officers of the Group of Fifty, for example, Soeharto made their
lives difficult but he stopped short of throwing them in jail. Others, it
should be added, have not been so lucky.

More positively, Soeharto draws strength from what Liddle calls
'performance legitimacy'.[30] Indonesia, though still poor, has come a long
way since Soeharto assumed power. His economic policies have been, by
and large, pragmatic and rational compared with the ad hoc and often
illogical course set by Sukarno. Unquestionably, the standard of living of
the average Indonesian has improved since Soeharto took power.

Indonesia's political stability has been a magnet for foreign investors
looking for a safe, low-wage home for their capital. Oil, of course, has
been an unexpected boon for Soeharto but he has spent the windfall
wisely, at least in comparison with leaders of other oil-rich countries. And
Indonesia deserves credit for responding quickly to the oil price collapse
in 1986 and promoting its non-oil, export-oriented industries. A family
planning program has checked the growth of a population which once
threatened to spiral out of control and a successful rice planting strategy
has kept hunger to a minimum.

Performance legitimacy carries over to the political realm. Leaving
aside the appropriateness of Soeharto's brand of rule for the 1990s, the
New Order government has injected a sense of purpose and order into a
political system which under Sukarno was chaotic and ineffective. Most
Indonesians would agree that national unity—and, more broadly, a sense
of nationhood—has strengthened under Soeharto. Many would say that
an extended period of restricted political activity and circumscribed press
freedom—in which public expressions of ethnic and religious animosities
are not welcome—has helped lower the temperature in sensitive areas.

Ideology has played a key role in the Soeharto era. While not openly
saying so, the New Order's main architects hold to a view of society very
similar to that held by the 'integralists' of the 1940s and 1950s. The sole
national 'ideology', Pancasila, has been appropriated by the New Order
to reflect this view of state and society. And by obliging all social groups
to swear allegiance to Pancasila, Soeharto has tried to make all
Indonesians endorse the same view. This approach has been useful to New
Order leaders in a number of ways. One is that it has made any calls for
political change seem perverse and contrary to Indonesia's national character.

By equating Pancasila with Indonesia's 'national essence', and by
using it as an ideological justification for authoritarian rule, Soeharto is

able to give his brand of rule a flavour of permanence. Frequent and ominous warnings about the ever-present threats to national unity—from, among others, communists, radical Muslims, and Westernised liberals— are meant to ward off moves for political change. In a society which is culturally comfortable with strong rule and deeply concerned with national unity, these warnings act as powerful disincentives to political reformation. The political choice available to Indonesia, Soeharto argues, is not between authoritarianism and democracy; it is between 'Pancasila democracy'—that is, the status quo—and chaos.

As noted earlier, history plays an important role in this argument. The New Order's representation of the 1950s reinforces its basic message that political liberalism in out of tune with Indonesia's *kepribadian bangsa*, or national personality. In the language of the New Order, David Bourchier writes,

> the fifties stand for Westernism, national disintegration, economic backwardness and chronic political instability, the mirror image of the New Order's accent on indigenism, national unity, development and political stability. In practical terms, the fifties serve as a stick with which to beat those calling for the separation of powers, regional autonomy, parliamentarism, an expansion of political rights or press freedom.[31]

And if the 1950s are used to argue against parliamentary democracy, the 1960s are used to argue *for* authoritarian rule. The September 1965 coup and the bloodbath which followed are considered to be the unfortunate but almost inevitable consequences of having experimented with an alien political system in the early years of independence.

Lastly, foreign policy has been carefully directed so as not to detract from Soeharto's domestic agenda. Shunning Sukarno's confrontational approach to external affairs, Soeharto has kept Indonesia largely out of the international spotlight. This is partly a reflection of his style and partly a consequence of the priority given by the New Order to economic development. Upon taking power Soeharto quickly extricated Indonesia from its *Konfrontasi* with Malaysia. And for the rest of his tenure he successfully kept the nation from becoming embroiled in superpower politics.

Beginning in the late 1980s, however, with the Cold War winding down and the domestic political situation well in hand, Soeharto has begun to seek a higher profile overseas. Indonesia played a key role in getting the warring factions in Cambodia to agree to UN-sponsored elections in 1993. Further burnishing its credentials as a regional leader, Indonesia hosted a series of workshops in 1991–93 aimed at settling the conflicting claims to the Spratly Islands in the South China Sea and at finding a political solution to the Muslim insurgency plaguing southern Philippines. In 1992, Indonesia was elected to chair the 108-nation Non-Aligned

Movement (NAM) for a three year term. (By early 1994, some Indonesian officials were already talking about the possibility of securing re-election to the NAM chairmanship for the 1995–98 period.) Finally, Indonesia and its fellow members of the Association of Southeast Asian Nations (ASEAN) have helped establish the 17-nation Asia–Pacific Economic Cooperation forum as an influential trade grouping. Indonesia was chosen to hold APEC's rotating chairmanship for 1994. Looking to the future, Indonesia has announced its intention to seek election to a non-permanent seat on the UN Security Council for the 1995–96 term.[32]

There would appear to be several reasons behind Soeharto's newly discovered appetite for a more ambitious foreign policy. Undoubtedly, he is motivated by a desire to bolster his prestige at home and to defuse the nostalgia some Indonesians have for the high-profile approach of his predecessor Sukarno.[33] A second reason is the need to counter the negative publicity which Indonesia has attracted in recent years from the United States and other industrialised nations. Since the early 1990s foreign criticism of Indonesia's handling of East Timor and of its labour, environmental and human rights record has picked up markedly. Indonesian officials hope that the country's emerging role as a 'moderate' voice of the developing world will help blunt this criticism over time.

What about society at large? What do Indonesians feel about Soeharto? Conversations with Indonesians about their two presidents throw up a melange of emotions. Sukarno is a hero to some and a bumbling megalomaniac to others. Soeharto stirs different responses, ranging from respect and admiration to fear and antipathy. It is difficult to get beyond anecdotal evidence as the curbing of civilian politics has made the Indonesian voice difficult to hear. The five-yearly elections, carefully arranged to produce a Golkar victory and, by extension, an endorsement of Soeharto, are of little help.

We know that Soeharto came to power with considerable support from society. Much of the Indonesian elite was grateful for a return to some degree of normalcy in public affairs, and Indonesians from all social layers take pride in the country's obvious economic development. Over nearly three decades, however, Soeharto has squandered some of that support. Students, some Muslim groups, intellectuals and others chafe at the restrictions placed on open communication and their exclusion from the political process. For all Indonesians, the overwhelming power of Soeharto's government has meant an erosion of civil liberties. Many Indonesians, rural and urban-based alike, feel they have little control over their own destinies.

Other societal groups remain overt Soeharto supporters. They share a belief that the army must keep its dominant role to maintain national unity, to prevent ethnic or religious divisions from sundering the country, and to provide the political stability conducive to economic development.

A common view from these quarters is that 'Indonesia is not ready for democracy'. The downside of Soeharto's authoritarian rule—among others, corruption, a politically-controlled judicial system, and a largely contentless public debate—are accepted as unfortunate but tolerable costs.

Soeharto: president, general and king

The final piece of the Soeharto puzzle is the man himself. For somebody who has been atop one of the world's largest countries for so long, Soeharto remains in many ways a mysterious figure. He does not relish the limelight and seems uncomfortable in public. His annual Independence Day speeches are more often than not wooden and bereft of emotion.

Soeharto's forays outside Jakarta, however, allow him to present a more relaxed figure. He travels frequently to inaugurate new factories or plantations around the country and usually makes time to meet with small groups of farmers and peasants. Soeharto comes alive in these meetings, displaying an easy rapport with the rural poor and an obvious empathy with their concerns. By contrast, he keeps his contact with journalists to an absolute minimum. Those who meet him regularly find him hard to read and, more so since the mid-1980s, aloof. 'I find him kind of scary,' one cabinet minister told me, 'cold, hard eyes that look right through you.'[34]

Soeharto is known to be a diligent worker, often rising before dawn and receiving guests at home well into the evening. He lives unostentatiously in a modest if well-guarded house in central Jakarta. He puts great stock in personal relationships, and a number of Indonesia's most famous citizens owe their prominence to long associations with him. Businessmen such as Liem Sioe Liong and Bob Hasan came to know Soeharto in the 1950s. Soeharto first met the current Minister for Research and Technology B. J. Habibie when the latter was but thirteen years old. Admiral Sudomo, the Coordinating Minister for Political Affairs and Security from 1988 to 1993 was Soeharto's naval assistant in the 1961 Mandala campaign to seize Irian Jaya. Wahono, the Golkar chairman from 1988 to 1993, was Soeharto's assistant in Kostrad in 1965. Only Soeharto's personal loyalty to Ibnu Sutowo saved the former Pertamina czar from being prosecuted for mismanagement of public funds.[35]

As Soeharto has grown older, however, his clique of trusted advisers has dwindled. Many of the peers that Soeharto once turned to for advice have died or fallen out of favour and, as a result, the president has come to depend more heavily on input from members of his family, of whom he remains deeply protective. It is a characteristic which has occasioned much heartburn and frustration among many of the other members of the 'inner circle'.

Soeharto's 1988 autobiography sheds some light but not a great deal.

He speaks movingly about his youth and his early military career. But mostly the tone is detached and there are, to put it mildly, some surprising omissions. There is virtually no mention of the anti-communist purge of 1965–66 and no mention at all of the Malari incident. The book also displays a degree of insecurity rarely seen in Soeharto's public persona, especially in the parts where he disparages the contributions of some his most important assistants. This suggests that loyalty is largely a one-way street for Soeharto, and that he feels a need to claim all the credit for Indonesia's successes for himself. 'When he was alive, some people thought Ali Murtopo [who died in 1984] was the man who decided everything . . . This just wasn't true. The proof? After Ali Murtopo died, the government went on as usual,' Soeharto says.

He is equally scornful of Sudjono Humardhani who, when alive, was widely viewed as Soeharto's mystical adviser. 'I had heard people say that he knew more about mysticism than I did but Sudjono himself used to do the *sungkem* (pay his respects) to me. So those who thought that Sudjono was my guru in mysticism had it wrong. He would ask me about it, not the other way around. He himself once said, "I learn from Soeharto".'[36]

This attitude extends to the treatment of ministers and top aides who are still alive. In March 1993, Soeharto reshuffled his cabinet. Radius Prawiro, Johannes Sumarlin and Adrianus Mooy—technocrats who had put in decades of service to Soeharto's government—were dropped without any public mention of, much less a word of gratitude for, their past service. Their removal had several causes—discussed in later chapters— but one reason put forward by some cabinet insiders was that Soeharto resented the amount of credit attributed to the technocrats for Indonesia's economic accomplishments.

Soeharto's style, as far as it goes, is deeply rooted in Javanese culture. Benedict Anderson, in his pioneering work on the subject,[37] explains that in Java power is accorded to a ruler, rather than earned per se. Power descends on one who rules. It is a static, fixed and all-encompassing commodity. The Javanese ruler does not have some of the power, he has all of it. Power is a zero-sum game: to get it, you have to take it from someone else. There is no sense of broadening your scope of power by seeking a mandate from your subjects. 'Power is neither legitimate or illegitimate. Power is,' Anderson says.[38]

Implicit in this formulation are deeply-held notions of harmony and unity, concepts which help explain Indonesians' strong sense of national-ism and an acceptance of strong rule. The integralist view of the nation-state, obviously, accords nicely with the notion of Javanese power. This notion also underlines Soeharto's devoted attachment to Pancasila which, again, in his eyes accurately reflects the Javanese ideals of harmony and unity. The principles of Pancasila alone provide a sufficient set of 'ethical' values for leaders, obviating the need to adopt, say, new or modern 'ethical' values put forward by Islamic groups.[39]

The Javanese conception of power sheds light on other features of New Order rule. It helps explain, for example, the pressure for consensus in the political sphere. If 'only' nine hundred members of the People's Assembly voted for Soeharto, for example, that would imply the existence of another 'power' to whom one hundred members owed their loyalty. This would be seen by Soeharto as a serious blow to his ruling mandate.

The view of power as indivisible rules out an independent judicial system. The law, like politics or the press to give two other examples, does not stand outside the purview of the ruler. Instead, it answers to him. It exists very much inside the pyramid with Soeharto at the peak. The extent of Soeharto's involvement in the collecting and spending of state funds fits in here as well.

That Soeharto feels more accountable to a higher authority—from where he perceives his power is sourced—rather than to the people he rules is evident in his own statements.

> I have always asked God to guide me in each of my tasks. And thank God, to this day . . . I have never felt that I have failed. And if people think I have been wrong, I think: 'Who is it who can rightfully gauge my mistakes? Who decides if something is wrong?' I believe that whatever I do, after I've asked for guidance and direction from God, that whatever the results, these are the results of His Guidance.[40]

Cultural factors also help explain Soeharto's personal behaviour. The Javanese ruler, it is said, exerts power without seeming to. The goal is to present a picture of tranquillity bordering on inertia, to rule without really trying to. 'Excessive activity and exertion are scorned in Javanese culture,' says Karl Jackson, borrowing from Anderson. 'The truly powerful man is the one who sits motionless while his enemies energetically posture and exercise their power, giving the evidence that they are so weak that they are forced to make the first move, dissipating their power rather than concentrating it.'[41]

Put another way, it is considered bad form to exercise power crudely, to impose a public defeat on an opponent. These notions of Javanese power square nicely with Soeharto's actual behaviour. Apart from the occasional outburst of pique, he keeps his cards close to the chest. For the most part his approach to critics is cautious and subtle. He prefers to dispose of opponents harmoniously, to co-opt rather than repress, to win without inflicting defeat. His 'life's guidelines' are summed up in a favoured Javanese maxim: 'Don't be easily surprised, don't be overwhelmed by anything, and don't overestimate your own position.'

Soeharto and the 1990s

How this leadership 'style' will serve Soeharto and Indonesia in the years ahead is another question and one which the remainder of this book will attempt to explore. One problem with Soeharto's view of the state and his understanding of power is that they tend to negate the pluralism of Indonesian society. What a Javanese farmer may feel is culturally acceptable in a ruler is not the same as what a hotel clerk in Bali may feel. A banker in Surabaya has a different view of society than a Sumatran plantation worker.

It has been, of course, one of Soeharto's main convictions that these sorts of differences need to be subordinated to the common good and that, secondly, the common good can be best divined by an authoritarian state unbeholden to the interests of any one social group. But this approach to governance, although not without its benefits, has its costs. The economy is being held back by corruption and the absence of a modern legal framework. In social terms, a government obsessed with control squashes initiative and makes individuals afraid to speak their minds.

The ideological blanket over political activity has left political structures still standing but only over weak foundations. In their relentless invoking of Pancasila, the New Order's defenders seem to believe Sukarno's makeshift doctrine possesses something akin to incantatory powers, able to do away with anything not to their liking. There is nothing inherently wrong with Pancasila, of course. Its five principles are well-meaning and unobjectionable and its message of religious and ethnic tolerance no doubt has helped moderate communal tensions.

The danger arises from the habit of some New Order leaders in treating Pancasila as the answer to all public policy disputes. Used in this way, Pancasila acts simply to prevent any meaningful communication between rulers and the ruled. Moreover, decision-making by consensus, practical at the village level, becomes something else when applied to a multicultural, multi-ethnic nation of 180 million people and a US$130 billion economy. At this level, consensus comes to be seen more as obligatory agreement with the powerholders, rather than a process of compromise and give-and-take.

Differently expressed, the danger is that the inability to articulate interests through formal political mechanisms reduces tolerance for competing interest groups, encourages sectarianism and favours those advocating more radical and disruptive solutions.

Some of the problems Soeharto came in to 'solve'—regional resentment of Java, 'excessive' political demands by Muslims, and ethnic tensions, especially those directed at the Chinese—have been merely placed out of sight, not resolved. Such a cooling off period may have been necessary in the process of nation-building. But these problems still exist and need to be dealt with in a more concrete way. 'Pancasila Democracy', static and exclusivist, does not appear to be up to the task. In fact, it may be making some of the problems worse.

No one in Indonesia disputes the benefits of stability and social harmony. And, with income and education levels still low and latent ethnic and religious rivalries still a real concern, many Indonesians accept the argument that a 'strong state' is suitable at the country's current stage of development. But not all 'strong states' are the same, and there is a growing body of thought in Indonesia which says that Soeharto's 'strong state' is in need of an overhaul.

These Indonesians believe that the battened-down environment of the New Order has outlived its purpose, and that a weak judiciary, an impotent parliament and a pervasive military presence can no longer be accepted as the unavoidable costs of development. This view holds that a freer, more dynamic public discourse is both non-threatening and necessary if Indonesia is to come to a lasting accommodation with its most fundamental challenges: creating a modern and efficient economy; accommodating the political aspirations of Muslims; overcoming ethnic rivalries and regional divisions; and putting in place the mechanisms for a predictable and non-violent leadership transition. Whether Soeharto is up to the task of overseeing such a shift in approach remains to be seen.

3
The emerging tiger

We can't slow down. We have to keep moving forward, always forward.
Once we reach deregulation fatigue, it's going to be very hard to reverse.

Johannes Sumarlin[1]

Everyone keeps saying deregulation is some kind of panacea, that it will
solve all our problems. It might be good for Jakarta and the modern
factories but it's destroying the farmers and it's killing the cooperatives.

Mubyarto[2]

Little else is requisite to carry a state to the highest degree of opulence
from the lowest barbarism, but peace, easy taxes, and tolerable
administration of justice; all the rest being brought about by the natural
course of things.

Adam Smith[3]

Invitations sent out to Jakarta-based journalists in late November 1988
had no trouble capturing the interest of the normally sceptical press corps.
A news conference was to be held by all of Indonesia's top economic
ministers and presided over by Radius Prawiro, then Coordinating Minister for Economy, Finance, Industry and Development Supervision.

Just a month earlier Indonesia's technocrats—as the economic ministers are called—had announced far-ranging reforms to the financial sector,
removing restrictions on bank licences and branch openings, giving banks
more control over their deposits and unshackling the Jakarta Stock
Exchange. After several years of incremental reform of a highly regulated
economy, Pakto, as the October 1988 package was referred to, came like
a bolt of lightning. It went much further than most analysts expected. It

49

was to begin the rejuvenation of Indonesia's economy from the rut it had slipped into in the mid-1980s.

Before the unveiling of the November package, expectations ran high. Indonesia was not short of businesses and industries for the reformers to seize on as potential targets. During the previous decade, the government had regulated the private sector into near paralysis, raising costs to consumers and making many Indonesian products uncompetitive on world markets. Worse, the economy was riddled with politically protected trading and distribution monopolies, many in the hands of Soeharto relatives or close associates.

With the collapse of oil prices in the mid-1980s, Indonesia faced some hard choices. No longer able to depend on oil revenues to subsidise inefficient domestic producers, Indonesia desperately needed to lower production costs across the economy, encourage private enterprise and develop industries which could compete in export markets. To get there, economic reformers had to tackle the root causes of their 'high-cost' economy, no matter how politically awkward these moves would be.

A good example of the obstacles they faced was a monopoly on the import of plastics. In 1984, three state-owned trading companies had been given an exclusive licence to import the raw materials necessary for plastics production. Less than six months later, the three firms appointed a Hong Kong-registered company, Panca Holding, as the sole importing agent for plastics.[4] Businessmen claimed Panca Holding's role as middleman had added 15–20 per cent to the cost of imported plastics materials, some 30–40 per cent to the cost of finished products which use plastics, and, in the process, had stuffed tens of millions of US dollars annually into its own till. Behind Panca Holding's corporate veil were its main beneficiaries: Sudwikatmono, President Soeharto's cousin, and two of the president's sons: Sigit Haryoyudanto and Bambang Trihatmodjo.

This sort of operation was at the heart of the technocrats' concerns and one which the November reforms were designed to chip away at. Prawiro opened the press conference by announcing simplifications to the foreign investment rules, making it easier and more attractive for foreigners to invest in Indonesia. Next on the list was a freeing up of the heavily regulated inter-island shipping industry. The third item was trade reform. Some steel imports were liberated from the grasp of Krakatau Steel, the giant government-owned steel company, and opened to general traders. Lastly, almost as an afterthought, Prawiro mentioned that the import of plastics would be opened up to private traders. The announcement set off a vigorous rustling of paper and quizzical glances. Journalists clamoured for clarification. Yes, Prawiro confirmed, Panca Holding no longer had a monopoly on plastics. One of the most glaring examples of government-sponsored cronyism was no more.

A month later, a third package of reforms was announced, this time focused on the capital markets. Taken together, the three liberalisation packages rushed through in the closing months of 1988 can be seen as a high-water mark for Indonesia's technocrats. The sceptics were quieted. The reformers had taken on some of the 'sacred cows' of crony capitalism and had won. But having regained the commanding heights of economic policy, they had to begin the gritty work of protecting their turf. In the ensuing years economic reform continued although at a slower and less dramatic pace. A concerted focus on exports generated new sources of foreign exchange revenues, reduced Indonesia's dependency on oil revenues and helped boost economic growth.

But by the early 1990s a failure to lower interest rates and a few celebrated bank failures combined to tarnish the technocrats' star. They also encountered fierce resistance from those accustomed to benefiting from Soeharto's political patronage. Lastly, the technocrats suffered to some extent from their own successes. With the economy rescued from its troubled state of the mid-1980s, the technocrats lost some leverage to push through difficult and fundamental reforms. One technocrat, only half joking, described Indonesia's vigorous growth in the period 1989 to 1991 as a 'curse in disguise'.[5]

In a March 1993 cabinet reshuffle, the abrupt dismissal of three leading technocrats clouded the prospects for further reform of the economy. The new cabinet contains ministers in the technocratic mould but also officials who contend Indonesia needs a dramatic shift in its economic priorities.

The key, as always, lies with Soeharto. The apparent diminishment of the technocrats' influence should perhaps be seen merely as Soeharto trying to defuse political criticism aimed at him rather than as an attempt to alter the country's basic economic direction. Or it may be that Soeharto no longer believes the technocrats' economic prescriptions are the right ones for Indonesia.

The distinction is an important one. Soeharto's legitimacy as ruler rests above all on his ability to bring economic development and prosperity to Indonesia. A weakening of the economy would undermine this legitimacy and strengthen the hand of those demanding political change. Since Soeharto came to power, millions of Indonesians have been lifted out of the sink of poverty. But the technocrats' efforts to fashion a modern, efficient economy are far from complete. A sluggish, unresponsive bureaucracy, an antiquated and unpredictable legal system, and widespread nepotism, corruption and political patronage are powerful countervailing forces.

It is too early to say whether the latter characteristics are indelibly a part of Soeharto's leadership style. He has at times adjusted effectively to pressures for change in the past. But there is a limit to how much ground Soeharto can cede to economic reformers without weakening his control over the political process, something he has shown little inclination to do in the past. Will Soeharto continue adjusting his political style to keep Indonesia's economy on track and bend to international economic realities? Or will the need to preserve the political edifice he has created take precedence over the demands of a market-driven economy? The answers will determine whether 'economic development' will be remembered as Soeharto's crowning achievement or the factor that ultimately loosened his hold on power.

The makers of policy

The New Order began on the edge of an economic abyss. Export revenues were stagnant or sliding, investment had trickled almost to a stop, factories were operating at a fraction of capacity and with outdated equipment, inflation had topped 1000 per cent a year, relations with foreign donor institutions were in tatters, and infrastructure was crumbling. The government was running a massive budget deficit, the foreign debt had reached more than US$2 billion and interest on this debt exceeded Indonesia's total export revenues. Sukarno's economic legacy was not a bountiful one.

Soeharto entrusted economic policy to a handful of mostly US-trained economists who had little choice but to turn to the outside world for help. Relations with multilateral and country donors were patched up and an investment code was hastily drafted to lure overseas capital. Within a few years the technocrats had stabilised the economy and laid the seeds for growth. Inflation came down reasonably quickly and foreign debts were rescheduled.

The original crew of technocrats was led by Professors Widjoyo Nitisastro and Ali Wardhana. These two men have remained at the forefront of Indonesian policymaking for a remarkably long period of time, even if their influence with Soeharto has waxed and waned. Widjoyo based himself at Bappenas, the national planning board, from where he drew up the basic guidelines for economic policy and nurtured a generation of economists. Wardhana served as finance minister for three terms, and then as coordinating minister for the economy in Soeharto's fourth term. Since 1988 both men have been retained by Soeharto as advisers on economic policy.

In times of economic distress, like the late 1960s and mid-1980s, Widjoyo, Wardhana and the other technocrats have enjoyed a broad mandate to determine economic policies. At other times their influence has been more restricted. But during Soeharto's entire tenure, the technocrats have retained control over the finance and monetary portfolios. Schooled in neo-classical economic theory, they have committed themselves to monetary policies which have kept inflation in check and currency volatility to a minimum. The technocrats tend to trust the market to determine how capital should be allocated.

At least two other powerful groups have competed with the technocrats for Soeharto's ear. One we can call economic nationalists whose most common characteristic is a belief that the government should maintain a large role in the economy. A key nationalist plank is that the government must help indigenous, or *pribumi*, businessmen catch up with their ethnic-Chinese counterparts.

A forceful exponent of this view was Ibnu Sutowo, who in the early 1970s turned the national oil company Pertamina into a vast fiefdom active in dozens of industries. At present, Minister for Research and Technology B. J. Habibie, who began his government service working for Sutowo and who in many respects resembles the oil baron, is counted as the strongest cabinet-level nationalist. Habibie's point of departure is that Indonesia can never hope to catch up with the world's industrialised nations without a concerted, government-led push to speed up the natural pace at which technology is transferred among nations.

The second group arrayed against the technocrats is motivated less by ideology or policy considerations than by the more prosaic quest for profit and wealth. The characteristic which this group shares is easy access to Soeharto. Timber king Bob Hasan would fit into this group, as would Liem Sioe Liong who, during Soeharto's rule, has become the wealthiest businessman in Southeast Asia. Relatives of Soeharto, particularly four of his children, fill out the rest of the group which, for want of a better term, we can call crony businessmen.

They have amassed wealth through government-granted import and trading monopolies, privileged access to government contracts and state bank credit, and the ability to bend government policies in their favour. In return, they bankroll a good measure of Soeharto's patronage activities and stand ready to provide emergency funds in crisis situations. Collectively, they form a powerful adversary to the technocrats (and to the nationalists) thanks to their clout with Soeharto, and on many occasions they have succeeded in delaying or undermining the technocrats' efforts to simplify the bureaucracy and make the economy operate more transparently.

Soeharto's allegiance to each of these actors—economists/technocrats, nationalists, cronies—fluctuates over time, adjusting to a variety of economic and political variables, both domestic and international. Each group, in its own way, serves a purpose for Soeharto. As Bill Liddle puts it, using slightly different terms: 'the economists are the producers of wealth, the patrimonialists are the distributors of a large portion of it for political purposes, and the nationalists are the embodiment of his ·dream for more rapid progress toward an industrialised, internationally powerful Indonesia.'[6]

A random walk through the New Order

The battle for ideological supremacy between the technocrats and the nationalists can be divided into three phases. From 1966 to 1974, the technocrats succeeded in imposing a fair degree of discipline over the economic policymaking process. One of their earliest steps was to adopt the principle of a balanced budget. In practical terms, this is more fable than fact as foreign borrowings and external aid are counted as government 'revenues' in the annual budget. Nevertheless, the provision has served a useful purpose in setting at least some kind of limit on the demand for state funds. A second innovation was to remove foreign exchange controls. Ever since, the prospect of easy capital flight has tended to discourage inflationary or otherwise destabilising economic policies.

The technocrats also proved to be able political operators. The dean of the technocrats, Widjoyo Nitisastro, is renowned for his skill in persuading Soeharto of the merits of technocrat-supported measures. It is a skill which nettles the nationalists. A prominent nationalist, former Minister of Industry A. R. Suhud, once described the technocrats' approach like this: 'The technocrats are very good at scaring the Old Man. They keep him on the razor's edge, and that's how they get their way. They tell him that if he doesn't follow their suggestions the people will go without food and clothes, or the economy won't grow.'[7]

But two developments in the mid-1970s undermined the influence of the technocrats, and ushered in the second phase of the technocrat–nationalist rivalry. The first was the Arab-led boost in oil prices in 1973, which put massive additional resources at the disposal of the government. Second, the Malari riots in January 1974 highlighted for Soeharto the degree of public unhappiness with the rising economic dominance of foreign investors and ethnic-Chinese businessmen. The wealth provided by the higher oil prices enabled Soeharto to try a new approach to deal with public restiveness.

Indonesia scholar Heinz Arndt, writing in 1974, described the scope for change made possible by cascading oil revenues: 'Indonesia in 1974 is like a man who has won first prize in a lottery. The opportunities are immense, almost unimaginable. But so are the pressures and temptations to spend too much too fast, and the difficulties in making wise and effective use of the windfall.'[8] For the next decade, Indonesia, as Asia's only member of the Organisation of Petroleum Exporting Countries (OPEC), availed itself of many of the opportunities and succumbed to many of the temptations that Arndt predicted.

The surge in oil prices in 1974 produced for Indonesia a revenue windfall of US$4.2 billion that year, then equivalent to about one-sixth of gross domestic product. Ibnu Sutowo used some of this windfall to complete the transformation of the state oil monopoly, which he headed, into a business empire that went far beyond oil production. His investments ranged from oil tankers to steel to construction. He also spent lavishly on the accoutrements of his office and all but dispensed with internal accounting rules. He departed from the scene in 1976 after it was revealed that Pertamina had run up debts of US$10.5 billion—approximately 30 per cent of Indonesia's gross domestic product at the time—and was unable to meet its obligations.[9]

Pertamina's debt problems were eventually solved, but only after a mammoth government bail-out that nearly doubled the country's foreign debt.[10] Oil continued to be a massive money-spinner for Indonesia for the rest of the decade. But a second surge in oil prices in 1979–80, which pushed up the government's oil revenues in 1981 to US$13.4 billion, left the nation dangerously dependent on a single commodity. In fiscal 1981, exports of oil and gas made up more than 80 per cent of total merchandise exports, and oil and gas-related revenues accounted for 71 per cent of the government's budget receipts.

The nationalists used part of the oil wealth to subsidise new industries like steel, cement, chemicals, fertilisers, aluminium and machine tools. Early beneficiaries were big-ticket industrial projects like the Krakatau Steel plant, the Dumai oil refinery and the Asahan aluminium smelter.

Meanwhile, Indonesia's ardour for foreign capital cooled. A profusion of new regulations and credit subsidies attempted to help *pribumi* businessmen close the gap with the more affluent ethnic-Chinese business community. 'We were drawn into a sustained period of inward-looking economic development,' said Prawiro in a late 1980s speech, 'and [we] placed an over-emphasis on strategies of import-substitution. To make the strategies work, we engaged in extensive intervention in the allocation of capital, pricing, and other aspects of production. Over time, this generated inefficiencies and added costs to our productive process, in turn prompting further government intervention. This was in danger of becoming a "vicious circle" of market distortions.'[11]

While many private enterprises with strong political pull did well in this period, smaller firms, buried under an avalanche of credit ceilings and regulations covering production, investment and distribution, suffered at the hands of the nationalists. A temporary defusing of *pribumi* resentment had been bought at the expense of economic virtue. A scathing World Bank report on the Indonesian economy in 1981 said that the prevailing economic policies were hindering rather than helping two of the government's major objectives: job creation and the fostering of *pribumi* businessmen.[12] The report seized on the cement industry as an example, noting that a minimum of 24 separate licences had to be obtained by potential investors.

The nationalist star declined with the price of oil. When the commodity dropped to US$10 a barrel in 1986[13]—from US$30 a barrel just two years before—Indonesia was left to play catch-up to countries such as Thailand, which had been forced to restructure its economy earlier. 'In hindsight,' Prawiro says, '. . . our sheer riches also made us spoiled. We felt cushioned from the need to diversify our export economy. In [a] way, oil and gas had an almost "opiating" effect on our national vision of economic development throughout the 1970s and into the early 1980s.'[14] But bad times, as the saying goes, often create good policies.

In the mid-1980s the contest between the technocrats and nationalists entered a third phase. Faced with the imperative of generating more foreign exchange, the technocrats worked assiduously to undo much of what the nationalists had done. Import-substituting industrialisation was gradually transformed into an export-oriented pattern of development. The welcome mat for foreign investors reappeared and subsidised credit programs toppled down the agenda. 'We . . . abandoned our own earlier vision of mercantilism,' said an almost giddy Prawiro at the height of the technocrats' power in 1989, 'and, instead, discovered the "wisdom of the market economy".'[15]

'A simple chain of economic reasoning makes it clear why economic policy makers were drawn inexorably down the path of structural adjustment,' explained Ali Wardhana in a 1989 speech. The 'chain' works like this:

> Economic growth and development require export growth to pay for imports and to service debt. Reliable export growth requires non-oil exports from agriculture and manufacturing. Non-oil export growth requires an efficient, productive economy, which needs a competitive domestic market. [Since] protectionist policies and government controls [are] inimical to the competitive domestic market, creating instead the present high-cost economy, they need to be dismantled, i.e., the economy deregulated.[16]

In 1984, the tax code was overhauled and the structure of taxation rates simplified. The year before, the technocrats had taken a first crack at opening up the banking system by removing government-imposed ceilings on interest rates. And a year later, the corruption-ridden customs office was disbanded overnight and import inspection duties were contracted out to a Swiss surveyor company, Societe Generale de Surveillance. In 1986, the rupiah was devalued to boost the competitiveness of Indonesian exports and non-tariff barriers on several hundred items were replaced by tariffs. Foreign investors responded by pouring billions of dollars into new factories and manufacturing plants. Interest was especially strong from South Korea, Taiwan and Hong Kong where appreciating currencies and rising land and labour costs were eroding the competitiveness of manufacturing operations at home.

Without doubt, the financial sector has undergone the most radical change in recent years.[17] Indonesia's investment targets required a vigorous mobilisation of domestic resources, a task beyond the seven stodgy state banks. Secondly, the reforming technocrats could go further and faster with the financial system than with other areas of the economy because it fell under their direct management.

The landmark financial sector reforms in October 1988 took the lid off what was a closely regulated industry. In 1988–91, the number of private banks more than doubled to 135, eighteen new foreign banks were licensed and several thousand new bank branches were opened. In the four years from January 1988, total deposits in the Indonesian banking system more than trebled to US$48 billion. Over the same period, loans rose 250 per cent. Private banks provided most of the action, stealing market share from the state institutions. In 1991, for the first time ever, private banks' share of total deposits surpassed that of the state banks, although the latter retained a comfortable lead in outstanding loans.

The long-dormant equity market experienced an even more radical shake-up. Following the October 1988 reforms, dozens of firms rushed to list shares on the Jakarta Stock Exchange which, in 1989, was the fastest-growing bourse in the world. Foreign brokers flocked to Jakarta to set up offices and new portfolio investment flooded in. Perhaps more than any other factor, Indonesia's emerging capital market brought the nation's economic resurgence to the attention of the outside world.

Whether the deregulating momentum maintains its force as the 1990s unfold remains to be seen. Economic reformers have plenty of work to do, but they will be up against powerful political forces. But before turning to the remaining agenda, it is worthwhile perusing Indonesia's economic record so far.

Successes and failures

By most measures, Indonesia's economy has performed well since Soeharto took power.[18] Pragmatic and effective monetary management, increases in investment and labour productivity and the oil bonanza combined to give Indonesia an average annual rate of growth of more than 7 per cent from 1968 to 1981. From 1981 to 1988, annual growth slowed to an average of 4.3 per cent, a result of the fall-off in oil revenues and the accumulated effect of overzealous government intervention and regulations in the late 1970s and early 1980s. From 1989 to 1993 the economy again grew by almost 7 per cent a year.

From 1965 to 1988, macroeconomic growth plus a successful family planning program combined to raise Indonesia's per capita gross national product by 4.3 per cent a year, a better performance than most of Indonesia's neighbours in Southeast Asia and almost all oil-exporting economies.[19] The New Order has significantly upgraded the nation's

physical infrastructure. From 1975 to 1990, the installed capacity of the
state electricity company increased eighteen-fold, the number of telephone
lines rose seven-fold and the length of paved roads increased nearly
six-fold. A successful satellite transmission system was established, providing a communications link between Jakarta and the country's remoter
areas. Oil wealth funded the construction of thousands of schools, health
centres and mosques. A primary level education has been provided to
virtually all Indonesians, both male and female.

Lastly, agriculture was a big winner. The government has spent heavily
on fertiliser subsidies, crop intensification programs and farmer training.
The decision to focus so strongly on agriculture is probably best explained
by Soeharto's rural upbringing and his memory of how rice shortages
destabilised Sukarno's regime. Although farmers had no political voice to
speak of, they did comparatively well in obtaining subsidised credit.[20]
Within a decade, 1974–1984, Indonesia moved from being the world's
largest rice importer to self-sufficiency.

Using social indicators as a yardstick, Indonesia has done reasonably
well but, on a comparative basis, less impressively than in its macroeconomic performance. Employing an eight-country sample (Indonesia,
Malaysia, Philippines, Thailand, China, India, Mexico and Nigeria), Australian economist Hal Hill notes that Indonesians' life expectancy—61
years in 1988—is lower than all but India and Nigeria. In the categories
of adult illiteracy (26 per cent in 1985) and infant mortality (68 per 1000
in 1988) Indonesia lags behind its Southeast Asian neighbours and
Mexico, is about the same as China and has done better than India and
Nigeria.[21] Indonesia's population per physician was almost twice the
average of all developing countries in the mid-1980s, according to the
World Bank.[22]

Poverty alleviation stands as one of the New Order's most significant
achievements. While the data is sketchy, some estimates suggest that
almost 60 per cent of Indonesians in 1970 were living below the poverty
line. By 1990, the figure had dropped to 15 per cent. A 1990 World Bank
report found that in the previous two decades, 'Indonesia had the highest
annual reduction in the incidence of poverty among all countries stud-
ied.'[23]

Several important qualifications have to be made when analysing the
New Order's economic track record. One is that all growth figures start
from a very low base. 'Conditions were so disastrous in 1965 that any
return to normalcy would have resulted in significant improvements,' says
Hill.[24] A second is that poverty indicators are notoriously unreliable. Some
private economists estimate that significantly more than 15 per cent of
Indonesians continue to live at or under the poverty line.

And a third is that growth has come at the expense of the environment.
Using a concept called 'natural resource accounting', researchers at the

Washington-based World Resources Institute attempted to recalculate Indonesia's economic growth by taking into account the depreciation of natural resources, a 'loss' that traditional economic statistics ignore. After subtracting for the loss of forests, oil and soil on Java, they estimated that Indonesia's real growth—net domestic product—from 1971 to 1984 was only 4 per cent a year, not the 7.1 per cent annual growth suggested by traditional economic measures.[25]

The remaining agenda

As the statistics listed above show, Soeharto can justifiably claim he has brought a good measure of economic development to Indonesia. But the modernisation of Indonesia's economy is a process only just begun. Despite considerable progess in diversifying its resources of foreign exchange, for example, Indonesia remains dependent on a few key commodities such as oil and timber. Efforts to boost tax revenues have been blunted by bureaucratic inefficiency and corruption. And finding jobs for the millions of Indonesians who join the workforce each year remains a daunting task. According to estimates by the manpower ministry, some 38 per cent of Indonesian workers are unemployed or can only find work less than 35 hours a week. 'Viewed from a 1965 perspective Indonesia's performance has been better than most observers would have dared hoped for,' says Hill. 'But the record provides no grounds for complacency. While economic circumstances are no longer as desperate as they were in the 1960s, the challenges to policymakers in the 1990s are in many respects just as formidable.'[26]

But at the risk of oversimplifying, the challenge is not so much identifying what needs to be done but finding the political will to do it. The reformers have achieved a great deal in deregulating economic activity, but broader attempts to change the way business is conducted and the economy is managed have failed to make much progress, mainly, it seems, because Soeharto does not consider them necessary.

From Soeharto's perspective, says Jamie Mackie, 'considerations of rapid growth, efficiency and productivity constantly have to be balanced against [the] political considerations of maintaining order and control.'[27] And, as we have seen, Soeharto's notions of 'maintaining order and control' require an all-powerful chief executive whose management style includes the frequent use of patronage, the cultivation of personal relationships with leading economic actors and the maintenance of a large centralised bureaucracy to carry out his orders. These are some of the economic costs of political stability.

Over the past 28 years, Indonesia has shown that a patrimonial political structure is not fatal to capitalist economic development, at least at the early stages of industrialisation. When flagging economic growth demanded changes in policy, Soeharto has been able to adjust. He has had little difficulty in, as Liddle puts it, 'assimilating economic liberalisation and political patrimonialism into his more general cultural commitments'.[28] But if the modernisation of Indonesia's economy is to continue, this assimilation process is certain to become increasingly difficult. At some stage, for example, the patrimonial state will come into conflict with the need for a trustworthy and objective legal system, for a more efficient government bureaucracy and for a more rational, less personal relationship between the government and business.

The areas discussed below—reforming the state economic sector; providing for balanced regional growth; and strengthening the legal system and making the government function in a more transparent manner—all illustrate the limits to economic reform in Soeharto's Indonesia.

Privatisation

A major plank in the technocrats' reform drive which began in the mid-1980s was to make the private sector the engine of Indonesia's economic growth. To do so, they needed to make the bureaucracy less hostile to private business and to rationalise the government's direct role in the economy. It was—and is—a formidable task.

Picking up where Sukarno left off, Soeharto has overseen a steady increase in the percentage of economic activity accounted for by state-owned enterprises. The government's share of total expenditures as a percentage of gross domestic product tripled from 1966 to 1980 and, despite some levelling off in the 1980s, remained twice as large in 1990 as it was when Soeharto took over.[29] As the 1990s opened, state enterprises were the dominant players in banking, plantations, the transport and mining sectors and a host of manufacturing industries. They accounted for about 30 per cent of gross domestic product or almost 40 per cent if agriculture is excluded,[30] a significantly larger role than state enterprises play in most developing countries.

In June 1989 Finance Minister Johannes Sumarlin ordered an audit of the 189 state enterprises plus a further 28 firms in which the government held a minority share. After two-thirds were deemed financially unsound, Sumarlin unveiled a plan to slash the government's direct business role by merging state enterprises, floating their shares on the stock exchange, splitting off subsidiaries to the private sector, subcontracting private management or outright liquidation.

The plan barely got off the drawing board.[31] Economic considerations were partly responsible: without a stronger stock market, the chances of privatising state enterprises by 'going public' were slim. When the stock market weakened in 1990, the option of floating state enterprise shares on the exchange became even less attractive. At a more practical level, the accounts of many of the enterprises were so poorly kept that it will take several years of diligent auditing before accurate financial statements can be shown to potential investors.

But the real hurdle is political. The bureaucracy has led a determined rearguard action defending its turf. The Ministry of Mines and Energy oversees eight enterprises, seven of which, including the oil giant Pertamina, landed in the financially unhealthy category. But Ginanjar Kartasasmita, then the Minister of Mines and Energy, predictably blamed the messenger. If the audit showed his firms in a bad light, he said, then there must be something wrong with the audit. 'There should be additional bases for evaluating the health of the firms,' he told a parliamentary commission in September 1989. The Ministries of Research and Technology, Public Works, Transportation, Trade and Industry took a similar stance.

This attitude partly reflects an ideological preference by economic nationalists like Ginanjar for a large economic role for the state. Minister Habibie, as mentioned above, argues more specifically that Indonesia needs large state enterprises to lead the way into a high-tech future. And partly it reflects a fear of exacerbating the already serious tensions between *pribumi* and ethnic-Chinese businessmen. State-owned enterprises are viewed by some as a needed counterweight to the large Chinese-controlled and privately-owned conglomerates.

But mostly it reflects Soeharto's lack of enthusiasm for privatisation. He, too, is ideologically partial to big government. But a more strictly political reason for Soeharto's distaste of privatisation is that state enterprises are his principal providers of patronage funds. Soeharto is always consulted when major contracts are to be awarded by the largest of the state enterprises: Pertamina, the state electricity utility PLN, the telephone company Telkom, the national logistics board Bulog, the state tin-mining company PT Timah, the national flag carrier Garuda Indonesia, the state road agency Jasa Marga, and leading companies controlled by the Ministries of Transportation, Forestry and others. Not uncommonly, contracts are steered to cronies or are doled out to mollify critics. The allocation of credit by the large state-owned banks is subject to the same process. Privatisation would mean, in effect, that Soeharto would relinquish one of his most important tools for maintaining his hold on power.

Despite these political hurdles, economic realities are pushing Indonesia inexorably down the path of privatisation. A fall-off in the price of oil and heightened competition in the region for new foreign investment are making it harder for the government to subsidise money-losing enterprises under its control. Some state-owned firms will have to be set loose. How many and when will be up to Soeharto to decide. 'Economic necessity is forcing the government to consider privatisation more seriously,' concedes Sjahrir, an economist at the Institute for Economic and Financial Research. 'But nobody knows whether Soeharto will support it.'[32]

Problems at the periphery

Widening regional inequalities pose another severe challenge to the technocrats and, for that matter, to the government as a whole. If one effect of the New Order has been the creation of a highly centralised political system, a similar process has occurred in economic affairs. The responsibility for setting regional spending priorities was given to the national planning board and other Jakarta-based ministries. The oil boom further centralised the process of economic policymaking as more money became available to bureaucrats in the capital. With regional military commanders firmly under the watch of the armed forces headquarters in Jakarta, provincial governors hand-picked by the home affairs minister, and provincial legislatures as impotent as their national equivalent, the regions had few means with which to contest this state of affairs.

For most of the New Order period, though, this arrangement made sense. With much of Indonesia's resource wealth located in a few provinces, a strong central body was needed if the gains of development were to be distributed equitably across the country. But the rapid growth of the manufacturing sector, the declining importance of oil taxes in the government's menu of budget revenues and the persistence of uneven regional development have combined to make this argument less compelling.[33]

The resurgence of Indonesian manufacturing since the late 1980s has brought benefits mostly to the western provinces of Java, Bali and Sumatra. Infrastructure—roads, electricity, ports, etc.—are much better in these provinces than in the poorer East and as a result they have received the bulk of new private investment. 'Under these circumstances it is probable that a widening gap will open up in income and living standards between Java and many parts of the Outer Islands,' writes economist Anne Booth.[34]

Although sound economic and political reasons now exist for giving the provinces more say in their own development, the pressures for decentralisation are making little headway against the concentration of power in Jakarta. On the one hand, there is a built-in bureaucratic reluctance to devolve power away from the centre. As sociologist Taufik Abdullah puts it: 'The bureaucrats in Jakarta want to push a button and see things happen all over the country.'[35] Cultural snobbery also plays a role. Many Javanese, Indonesia's most numerous ethnic group, see no reason why their political and bureaucratic norms shouldn't be adopted nationwide.

But, as with the case for privatisation, the main obstacles to greater autonomy for the provinces are mostly political. Philosophically, as we have seen, Soeharto's notions of governance include the idea that power should be centralised. Many politicians and army officers fear that giving the regions more control over their resources will worsen, not alleviate, separatist tendencies. Economic decentralisation, in their view, is but the first step to political disintegration. 'I think if we decentralised we would have a lot of political troubles,' said former Golkar secretary–general Rachmat Witoelar in an interview in 1990. 'We can entertain the idea of decentralisation but it can't happen, at least not for the next ten years. It would risk the dissolution of the unified nation. History shows that we are easily influenced by parochial tendencies.'[36]

The view from outside the government, though, is that the do-nothing approach favoured by Witoelar and others will bring about exactly the situation they fear. Indonesia is not threatened by widespread secessionist sentiment at present, notes Booth, but 'there is . . . a very real danger that by refusing to concede any economic or political devolution, and by insisting on maintaining the status quo, the centre could create just such a situation in fifteen or twenty years time.' University of Indonesia economist Dorodjatun Kuntjorojakti takes the same line: 'Social upheaval [in the regions] is rooted in a *relative* sense of deprivation,' he warned in a 1990 interview.[37]

In some areas, resentment and unrest arrived a long time ago. A lesson that is often missed about the 1950s is that the regional rebellions which plagued the young Indonesian state were almost always driven by resentment of Jakarta's control over the nation's wealth. The rebels' primary objective was not secession from Indonesia, but a change of government in Jakarta, or at the very least, a change in Jakarta's policies towards wealth distribution.

That same dynamic is at work today. From the perspective of resource-rich provinces like Aceh (natural gas), Riau (oil), East Kalimantan (oil and timber) and Irian Jaya (copper, gold and timber), the current system seems like a replay of colonial times. Their natural resources, according to their leaders, are being exploited primarily to improve living standards at the centre. Economic jealousies are helping keep alive armed insurgencies in Aceh and Irian Jaya. In both provinces, the wealth produced per inhabitant (as measured by per capita gross domestic product) is among the highest in Indonesia. But in both provinces income and consumption per person—which more accurately reflect the quality of living—fall much lower in the national rankings.

For many provinces, the presence of abundant natural resources is only poorly correlated with the absence of poverty. Consequently, while most of Indonesia's poor live on Java, the incidence of poverty is much higher on some of the Outer Islands than it is on Java. Almost half of the inhabitants of East Nusa Tenggara province, for example, and about a third of the inhabitants of East Kalimantan and the Moluccas live below the poverty line.[38] Indeed, despite the national success in raising living standards in recent decades, some economists believe that the number of Indonesians living below the poverty line in some eastern provinces actually increased during the 1980s.

Irian Jaya is the most extreme case. In 1985 it had the sixth highest per capita gross domestic product among Indonesia's 27 provinces but also had the highest incidence of rural poverty.[39] Infant mortality in Irian Jaya is 133 per thousand, 85 per cent above the national average; life expectancy is just 48 years. 'The people in the house called Irian Jaya feed those in other houses but are themselves starving. Do you think this is fair?' asked Irian Jaya's highly regarded governor Barnabas Suebu in a 1991 interview. 'The government must do more to make the investment climate in Irian Jaya more attractive. I've asked for tax holidays, new credits etc. but I'm still waiting for an answer,' he said.[40]

How can these trends be reversed? A growing number of economists and political scientists believe that provincial wealth differentials can only be dealt with by decentralising economic policymaking. The current system—in which development funds are doled out by Jakarta in equal lump-sum payments to the provinces—has failed to exploit regional comparative advantages and, says Abdullah, 'has destroyed local ingenuity and initiative'.[41]

Policy making power begins with access to revenue. With non-oil taxes again comprising well over half of the government's budgetary revenues, says Booth, there is 'a strong case for turning over at least a proportion of the revenues from both income and value added taxes to the regional governments'. And, she adds, 'as the root causes of poverty differ by province, individual provinces should be given the primary responsibility for designing and implementing poverty alleviation strategies, and be given first call on all income accruing within their boundaries in order to fund such strategies'.[42]

But to return to the point made above, the difficulty with this approach is that it addresses only one part of the problem. Economic decentralisation cannot be separated from the issue of devolving political power to the provinces. There is, observes Booth, 'little reason to expect that provinces and sub-provincial levels of government will use additional revenues responsibly unless control can be exercised over their behaviour through the ballot box'.[43]

This, then, is the quandary facing Soeharto. Ever since taking power, he has viewed economic development and strong centralised political control as flip sides of the same coin. But that equation is no longer valid. A regionally balanced process of economic development demands a decentralisation of economic decision making which in turn requires some measure of political decentralisation as well. Which side of the equation will give ground in the 1990s is yet to be seen.

The business climate

Another weakness in the Indonesian economy is that the supporting services for a modern business sector—accounting and law firms especially—have not kept pace with the growth of the broader economy. Consequently, a great deal of business activity in the private and state sectors remains clouded by ambiguity and uncertainty. For some firms, of course, and especially for the politically well-connected, these conditions can be a distinct advantage. But for most enterprises, their owners and the banks that lend to them, the lack of transparency makes doing business in Indonesia more expensive. More generally, the lack of clearly defined and widely understood 'rules of the game' has retarded the country's economic development.

The revitalisation in 1989 of the Jakarta Stock Exchange, which requires listed companies to disclose financial statements, has improved matters somewhat with regard to financial transparency. But it also highlighted the unreliability of Indonesian accounting practices. Indeed, the last few years are full of examples of bankers, brokers and investors discovering that reliance on the audited statements of Indonesian companies—public and private—can be a costly affair.

The costs of 'creative' and often fraudulent accounting practices are also borne by the government, particularly when it comes to tax collection. In 1992, tax collected by the Indonesian government was equal to about twelve per cent of gross domestic product, a sharp improvement over a decade ago but still well below that achieved by neighbouring countries. (The equivalent ratio in Thailand and South Korea, for example, was seventeen per cent.) Indonesia's low tax compliance, in turn, contributes to other problems, among them a need to borrow more from overseas and a rise in social jealousy directed at the rich.

The problem for the technocrats is that efforts to increase tax compliance can only go so far if they are limited to administrative reforms. A political commitment is also required to enforce accounting rules and apply the tax code fairly and objectively, a commitment which does not appear to dovetail with Soeharto's political philosophy. Indeed, protection from the tax office is one form of patronage that Soeharto uses to secure the loyalty of influential members of the Indonesian elite. As one analyst of the tax system diplomatically put it in 1993: '[E]ven if the will and capacity is present within the tax administration to increase tax compliance by tax evaders, it will not be possible to investigate as long as there is no serious political will to improve the tax revenues of certain people and groups of peoples.'[44]

The same sorts of problems plague the legal system which often is more an obstacle to the business community than an independent arbiter of business practices. The legal code is 'ill-defined, antiquated and opaque', says Hal Hill, noting that many laws date well back into colonial times.[45] It certainly does not provide much guidance for many aspects of modern corporate life. Securities law is particularly weak. A still more serious problem is that the judicial system is at the same time deeply politicised and hugely inefficient; as a result, enforcement of the law is unpredictable and uneven.

Like the tax system, the legal system cannot be viewed in isolation from the social and political milieu in which it exists. Just as tax collectors are poorly paid, so too are judges and as a result bribery is widespread. Likewise, there appears to be little appetite for bolstering the independence and integrity of the legal system. On the contrary, the law remains very much under the influence of the nation's political powerholders for whom a clearer legal framework is not necessarily in their best interests.

All of this raises costs in the economy, even if these costs are hard to quantify. Banks, to give a specific example, have little legal recourse if a borrower fails to repay. If a bad debtor is brought to court, Indonesian and foreign bankers complain, more often than not the judge is paid off and the case gets thrown out. Unable to pursue bad debtors through the courts or to foreclose on collateralised assets, banks simply charge higher interest rates to Indonesian borrowers, costs which are then paid by consumers or tacked on to the price of Indonesian products sold abroad.

The following case study—which details the rise and fall of cigarette maker Bentoel—illustrates both the deficiencies in the legal and accounting professions and how business–government relationships can complicate life in the world of commerce.

Case Study: Bentoel [46]

A Chinese merchant named Ong Hok Liong stumbled onto a promising business sixty years ago near the East Java city Malang. For the previous ten years Hok Liong had been scrabbling along selling rice, nuts and tobacco door to door but in 1930 he hit upon an idea that would bring him great riches. He mixed tobacco with a sprinkling of cloves and wrapped it all up with bits of corn husks. Known as *klobot*, the cigarettes proved immensely popular. Later, paper was substituted for corn husks and the cigarettes renamed *kreteks*. *Kretek* manufacturing became and remains one of Indonesia's largest industries. By the end of the 1980s, Bentoel was the country's third largest *kretek* manufacturer, employed 12 000 workers and held an exclusive licence to make Marlboro cigarettes in Indonesia.

Like many Chinese-run businesses, Bentoel was a family enterprise.

And like many family enterprises, Bentoel's family expanded, became divided and eventually disintegrated into competing factions. Professional management took a back seat to family squabbles and shareholder indifference. Budiwijaya Kusumanegara (Tjioe Jan Hwie), a second-generation descendant of Hok Liong, became Bentoel's chief executive in 1967 and survived until December 1990 when the other shareholders threw him out of office.

The reasons became clear a few months later. The new Bentoel president Suharyo Adisasmito hired the Jakarta-based consulting firm Business Advisory Group to have a look at the company's books. When the consultants gave Bentoel's creditors a glimpse of the company's true financial state, the banks panicked. In June 1991, Citicorp withdrew a planned US$50 million refinancing facility for Bentoel and the firm subsequently declared itself insolvent. It emerged that Bentoel had debts totalling some US$350 million, giving the firm a negative net worth of around US$200 million.

Foreign creditors were horrified. For many of them Bentoel had been a good customer for years and its financial statements had given no indication of impending liquidity problems. Banks quickly reassessed their Indonesian loans and, worried that Bentoel's accounting standards were typical of Indonesian companies, began pushing up the interest rates charged to all Indonesian borrowers. Although it was obvious from the start that banks would be forced to accept some writedowns on their Bentoel loans, they insisted they be repaid in full. Unfortunately for them, they would soon realise they had little leverage.

Bentoel's debts were divided almost equally between Indonesian and foreign banks. Two state-owned banks, Bank Rakyat Indonesia and Bank Bumi Daya, had lent Bentoel more than US$150 million between them. Some 27 foreign banks formed a creditors' coordinating committee to represent them, but the state banks, which were better collateralised than the foreign institutions, refused to join.

Between June and October 1991 Indonesian investors circled Bentoel looking for a way in. Soeharto's youngest son, Hutomo Mandala Putra, offered to take over Bentoel but then withdrew. In September, Peter Sondakh, chairman of the diversified trading conglomerate Rajawali, made his pitch. He had looked into buying a stake in Bentoel in late 1990 but backed off when he realised the extent of the company's troubles. Less than a year later, he was back in the hunt. Sondakh enlisted the support of Bank Rakyat, the internal security agency Bakorstanas and several top officials in the economic ministries. Foreign banks were not consulted.

The last piece of Sondakh's puzzle involved Budiwijaya. At Budiwijaya's urging, most of Bentoel's loans had been personally guaranteed by Bentoel shareholders although, notably, Budiwijaya was careful not give any personal guarantees of his own. Sondakh offered to release the other Bentoel shareholders from their personal guarantees in return for their support of his takeover bid. Sondakh also promised not to pursue legal action against Budiwijaya if the former Bentoel head convinced the other Bentoel shareholders to vote in favour of Sondakh's plan. Budiwijaya was only too happy to accept.

On 5 November 1991, a majority of Bentoel shareholders voted to transfer 70 per cent of the company's equity to Rajawali. Except for being relieved of personal guarantees—a legally suspect manoeuvre in the eyes of foreign creditors—Bentoel shareholders received no other compensation in return for relinquishing control of the company. When some shareholders objected to the deal, Bank Rakyat threatened to put Bentoel into liquidation if they didn't support Rajawali.

Having obtained majority control of the company, Rajawali removed Bentoel's top management, cancelled Business Advisory Group's contract and sent in a team of auditors from Klynveld Peat Marwick Goerdeler (KPMG). It also retained merchant bank Jardine Fleming Nusantara, of which it owned fifteen per cent, as financial adviser. Before KPMG auditors arrived at Bentoel headquarters, however, the military had a good look through Bentoel files, apparently in search of politically incriminating documents. It was suggested at the time that Budiwijaya's illicit dealings had involved senior government officials. Rajawali officials concede that some files were removed prior to KPMG's arrival, though they claim not to know what was in them.

KPMG found enough, though, to put together a reasonably complete picture.[47] The exact sequence of events isn't known—and may never be known—but it is clear that Bentoel's descent into insolvency was due both to widespread fraud and gross incompetence, ably assisted by negligent and haphazard credit analysis by its lenders. It appears that Budiwijaya had been siphoning off Bentoel funds by procuring the company's supplies through local and offshore trading agencies—which he owned—and paying sizeable commissions to the agencies. Records were found showing Bentoel had some US$130 million stashed in bank accounts around the world and detailing Budiwijaya's considerable investments in real estate in Australia, Canada and the United States. (In 1988 an Australian business magazine included Budiwijaya in its list of the wealthiest three hundred Australians.) Almost a half million US dollars was found in cash in Budiwijaya's office, wrapped up in neat bundles of Rp. 10 000 (US$5) notes.

Untold funds were lost through inefficiency and lax management. Internal accounts bore little relation to reality, and financial statements were intentionally doctored to mislead creditors and the tax authorities. It turned out that the same Bentoel assets had been pledged to two, three and sometimes more creditors. Millions of US dollars had been distributed to top shareholders, directors and managers in commissions, dividends and interest-free loans, even though the firm had been technically insolvent since at least 1985. Fiduciary responsibility was not a top priority for the Bentoel family.

Surprisingly, banks failed to notice even the most glaring discrepancies. The fact that Bentoel's market share declined from twenty per cent in 1978 to nine per cent in 1991 should have alerted at least some credit officers that something was amiss. In Bentoel's English-language statements given to foreign creditors, Bentoel's US dollar debts were converted into rupiah at the exchange rate prevailing when the loans were first taken out. There was no adjustment to account for subsequent devaluations of the rupiah. As a result the listed loans were grossly understated. The English-language statements also carried the usual reminder that the accounts should be read in conjunction with the accompanying notes. With Bentoel's statements, however, there were no accompanying notes.

By early 1992, tensions were rising. Among the foreign creditors, the smaller, offshore banks plus the Bank of Tokyo maintained a hard line. They insisted on full repayment and wanted criminal action begun against Budiwijaya and Bentoel's accountants. There was also some talk by the smaller correspondent banks of suing Citibank and Bank of Tokyo for failing to analyse Bentoel's books properly.

Most of the foreign creditors based in Indonesia, however, realised that there was little relief to be had through the judicial system and that, even if they tried, they would only be putting their future business in Indonesia at risk. Meanwhile, the rift grew between the foreign banks and the state banks. Bank Rakyat and Bank Bumi Daya, apparently on instructions from the government, resumed lending to Bentoel. Failing to find common cause with the state banks, the foreign banks' negotiating options dwindled.

By February 1992 the KPMG report on Bentoel had been completed. The only snag was that the auditors didn't want to give it to the creditors. On the one hand, the report had to be frank enough so that KPMG would not later be accused of misrepresentation. On the other hand, aware that the truth sometimes plays second fiddle to political expediency in the Indonesian legal system, they didn't really want to say what they knew for fear of being sued for libel. The original solution was to let creditors read the report in Rajawali's offices but not be allowed to take away a copy. Later, but only after still more delay, banks were given a copy after signing confidentiality agreements.

Keeping a lid on what had happened at Bentoel served another purpose. The KPMG report detailed widespread tax fraud on the part of Bentoel. Rajawali was afraid that if the tax office would hear of the report's contents, it would push to the front of the creditor queue and, if it did so, a deal with foreign banks would become much harder, if not impossible, to reach. By law, tax claims of the government take priority over all other creditors. Meanwhile, the tax office appeared to have received instructions from high levels of the government not to investigate Bentoel unilaterally.

The foreign creditors continued to actively but unsuccessfully search for friends. The creditors group went to see Indonesia's senior economics minister, Radius Prawiro, but no help was forthcoming. 'It's a private matter,' Prawiro demurred. The creditors then asked the attorney general to press criminal charges against Budiwijaya but he declined.

The banks were left with few good choices. Liquidation wasn't much of an option since the two state banks had the better collateral and would therefore have first claim on what remained of Bentoel assets. And although they suspected fraud by Budiwijaya, there was little they could do independently of Rajawali. If anyone was going to sue Budiwijaya, it would have to be Rajawali as the new majority shareholder. But Sondakh had promised not to take that step in exchange for Budiwijaya's support for his takeover bid. Budiwijaya therefore remained a free man in Malang; Bentoel's former accountants continued to do business unperturbed.

In June 1992, Rajawali offered a deal to Bentoel's creditors. Banks could cash out immediately if they were willing to write off 90 per cent of their exposure. Or they could accept a combination of senior Bentoel debt and ten-year, low-interest convertible bonds. The better a bank's collateral, the higher the proportion of senior debt in its offer sheet. On average, banks were being asked to accept writedowns of almost 50 per cent.

The foreign banks, without the support of the state bank creditors, responded by filing a bankruptcy petition in the Malang city court against a Bentoel shareholder who had personally guaranteed some of Bentoel's corporate debts. In November 1992, the Malang court ruled that the banks had no grounds for enforcing a personal guarantee until Bentoel itself had entered liquidation proceedings. Later, the court ruled that there were no grounds for putting Bentoel into liquidation. The banks were stymied again.

In all likelihood the Bentoel case will drag on for some years. And the foreign banks probably will end up agreeing to reschedule Bentoel's debts. But the memory will remain. In early 1993 I asked one American banker in Jakarta what lessons he learned from Bentoel:

> Bentoel was a painful reminder that we operate here on slippery ground. If borrowers repay, there's no problem and, in fact, we make pretty good money. But if something goes wrong, we're screwed. The courts aren't going to help. The government is not going to help. And whatever deal gets made, Indonesians with the right connections are going to get the best part of it. So you tell me, how do you assess the risk of lending into a climate like that?[48]

4
The politics of making policy

Supported by heavy protection, and in some cases sizeable public investment, [Indonesia's] domestic producers in the targeted high-technology industries, such as steel, engineering, ship-building, aerospace and telecommunications, supply small, protected domestic markets at high cost. . .They absorb scarce technical and professional manpower that could serve more productive purposes if redeployed in the private sector.

World Bank[1]

In my opinion, the root of Indonesia's economic problems, from the problem of poverty to the foreign debt to the balance of payments, is that Indonesia's industrialisation process is too little concerned with high technology.

Sri Bintang Pamungkas[2]

What does Soeharto really want? No one knows. Even those on the inside don't have any idea.

Ali Wardhana[3]

In late 1990, the Indonesian tax office did an audit on PT PAL, a shipbuilding firm based in East Java and one of the ten state-owned enterprises classified as 'strategic industries'. All are under the control of B. J. Habibie, State Minister for Research and Technology. The strategic industries—which also include a steel mill, an aircraft manufacturer and a number of defence-related operations—form the core of Habibie's power base and are the concrete embodiment of his dream to see Indonesia become a technologically advanced nation. They are also a source of

71

constant controversy. The Indonesian military resents Habibie's encroach-
ment on areas it considers its own turf while government economists
regard Habibie's empire as a profligate waste of state resources.

But Habibie is untroubled by his critics. He has in his arsenal the best
form of protection available in Indonesia: the friendship and trust of
President Soeharto. Like many of the most powerful personalities in
Indonesia, Habibie's links with Soeharto stretch back a long way. As a
young officer in the early 1950s, Soeharto was dispatched to Sulawesi to
help put down a revolt there. Across the road from where Soeharto's unit
was stationed lived the Habibie family. Habibie's mother was a native of
Yogyakarta and Soeharto enjoyed 'listening to her stories in Javanese'.[4]
He was present when the 13-year-old Habibie's father passed away. Later,
one of his subordinates married an older sister of Habibie and Soeharto,
as commander of the brigade, stood in as the bride's father-in-law. For
the remainder of his time in Sulawesi, Soeharto kept an avuncular eye on
the Habibie family's precocious son.

Four decades later, Soeharto continues to blanket Habibie in a protective cocoon. The tax audit discovered that PT PAL had under-reported
income for a three-year period, 1985 to 1987. In a letter dated 10 October
1990, then Finance Minister Sumarlin informed Habibie that PT PAL was
liable for past tax payments plus fines, which together amounted to about
US$80 million. On 25 March 1991, Habibie wrote back refuting the audit
and saying that payment of past taxes 'would be a burden for PT PAL
and damage its future prospects'. He sent a copy of the letter to Soeharto.
Two days later, State Secretary Murdiono passed on a terse, very un-
Javanese message from Soeharto to Sumarlin: 'If the Minister of Finance
has a problem with waiving PT PAL's tax payments, then the President
will do it. PT PAL is a state-owned company, not a private Habibie
enterprise, and it doesn't need to be squeezed of tax.' The subject was
dropped.[5]

Politics and policy

The link between economic policy and politics is a complicated one in
any society. So it is in Indonesia. Soeharto came to power determined to
restrict the political process to a small elite in the belief that less politics
was a necessary precondition for a prolonged period of economic development. And, indeed, throughout the New Order economic policy has
been formulated within a government progressively more insulated from
social and political forces. Soeharto has relied at different times on
different policy advisers, but they have come always from within a limited
circle.

But as the president moves toward the end of what probably will be
his last term, the political sphere is likely to widen again. There is a very

real possibility that economic policymaking in the 1990s will have to accommodate the political considerations of a government preparing for a rare change at the top.

Exactly how the twin processes of economic and political development will interact as the decade unfolds is impossible to say. It is easier to recognise that the Indonesian economy is at a turning point and choices have to be made. The choice favoured by the technocrats is for Indonesia to continue down the path of export-led industrialisation, utilising its comparative advantages of plentiful labour and abundant natural resources, acknowledging a leading role for the private sector, and relying on the market to determine how capital is to be allocated.

For it to succeed, though, the process of economic reform must be accelerated. There must be renewed efforts to push down costs in the economy so that an increasing number of Indonesian products can compete in overseas markets. There must be further efforts to deregulate economic activity, reduce corruption, winnow the government's direct role in the economy, collect more taxes and improve the legal framework for business. Finally, more efforts must be made to improve Indonesia's attractiveness as a destination for foreign capital.

The alternative is for Indonesia to change tack, reassert the government's primary role in setting national economic priorities and commit more government resources to supporting the industries and firms favoured by the group known as economic nationalists. This approach, for which Habibie is the most forceful advocate, has certain immediate political benefits for Soeharto, benefits which are discussed more fully below. Whether it can also keep Indonesia's economic development on track is unclear, but the evidence submitted so far is unconvincing.

A cabinet reshuffle announced by Soeharto in March 1993 appeared to signal some shifts in economic priorities, although it may take several years to know how significant the shifts will be, or indeed whether there will be any shift at all. But on paper at least, the technocrats appear to have lost ground to the nationalists or, as some call them, the technologists.

Technocrats heading the three main monetary portfolios—the Coordinating Minister for the Economy, Radius Prawiro; the Finance Minister, Johannes Sumarlin; and the Governor of the central bank, Adrianus Mooy—were dropped from the cabinet. Although they were replaced with ministers considered to be in the technocrat camp—Saleh Afiff, Mar'ie Muhammad and Soedradjad Djiwandono, respectively—other portfolios fell from the technocrats' grasp.

The biggest shock for the technocrats was the appointment of Ginanjar Kartasasmita to head the national planning board, a central technocrat portfolio since the beginning of the New Order. Ginanjar, educated in Japan and trained as an engineer, belongs to the nationalist camp. Habibie, who kept his post as minister for research and technology, successfully lobbied to have a handful of his aides appointed to the cabinet, including the new ministers for education and culture, transportation, and trade. Another of Habibie's assistants was named as Ginanjar's top deputy at the planning board.

In Soeharto's Indonesia, titles and positions do not necessarily imply political power. What counts is access to Soeharto. For many years, for example, the two senior technocrats, Widjoyo Nitisastro and Ali Wardhana, have been able to exert considerable influence over economic policy even though they did not hold any official cabinet slots. What they did have was Soeharto's trust. One message of the March 1993 cabinet shake-up, however, was that the trust between Soeharto and his long-serving technocrats seems to have waned.

In recent years, the technocrats have been buffeted by broadsides from a wide range of critics. Soeharto's reshuffling of economic portfolios in 1993 can be at least partly explained by a desire to distance himself from this criticism. The early 1990s have also seen Habibie extend his mandate from the economic field into the political and religious arenas, and in the process lift the profile of his technology-driven economic vision. Whether Habibie can translate this higher profile into a change of economic policy remains to be seen. There are both powerful arguments in favour of continued adherence to the technocratic policy menu, as well as persuasive reasons to believe that Habibie's economic ideas will become more fashionable as time goes on. Between these two opposing poles stands Soeharto, and no one claims to have a firm idea of his views on economic policy. The best that can be done is to survey the dynamics working for and against both the technocrats and Habibie.

Limitations of the technocratic approach: real and perceived

Policy failures

The most justifiable criticism aimed at the technocrats is that their reforms of the financial sector were a case of too much too fast. Needing to mobilise new sources of domestic revenues to replace the loss of oil-related income, the technocrats swept away barriers to new banks and bank branches and took other steps to create a more competitive banking climate. They lowered the initial capital requirement for a new bank to about US$6 million, a sum which in hindsight was far too low.

Money flowed into the system. By one measure, Indonesia's money supply increased more than two and half times in the three-year period beginning in early 1989. But since the rapid rise of money in circulation contributed to an upsurge in inflation, Bank Indonesia (the central bank) was forced to take drastic steps to bring the money supply under control. The result was a sharp run-up in interest rates and higher costs for Indonesian businesses.

The same process was at work on the asset side of the banks' balance sheets. Freed from a regulatory straitjacket, some banks doubled the size of their outstanding loans several years in a row. Much of this lending went into retail banking products like credit cards, car loans and mortgages. Some were so anxious to expand market share that they simply ignored credit analysis. Government supervision was lax. Bank Indonesia was late in imposing prudential lending requirements and minimum capital provisions. Other regulations, like rules limiting a bank's exposure to companies owned by the same shareholders, were poorly enforced. The spectacular collapse of Bank Summa in late 1992 brought these failings into full view.

By the early 1990s the volume of bad debts had started to rise and banks responded by making fewer loans. Lending rates in 1991–92 stayed stubbornly high at about 25 per cent despite repeated entreaties to bring them down by Bank Indonesia Governor Mooy. Some banks became insolvent and were subsumed into healthier institutions. Many bankers predict the consolidation of the banking industry is likely to continue for several years. In that time, the painful process of writing down uncollectible loans is likely to act as a brake on credit growth.[6]

The extent of the debt problem became apparent in June 1993 when a list of bad debtors allegedly compiled by the central bank was leaked to the press. The list, which showed the debts owed to the seven state banks which were not being serviced, was described by a senior government economist as 'substantially accurate'.[7] Several of Soeharto's children and close business associates featured prominently on the list, which revealed that eight of the top 22 borrowers from the state banks were behind in payments on more than 40 per cent of their outstanding loans. For the banking system as a whole, bad and doubtful debts accounted for an estimated 15 per cent of all bank loans in December 1993, more than double the level of five years earlier.

The stock market's fall from grace was even more abrupt. From April 1990 to the end of 1991, the stock market index lost almost two-thirds of its value, finishing a three-year roller-coaster ride not far from where it started. The index dropped 40 per cent in 1991 alone, turning in one of the world's worst performances. A big part of the problem was the failure of the market's supervisory board, Bapepam, to set out rules of behaviour and enforce them. Companies went public at absurdly inflated prices, insider trading was rife and disclosure was minimal. In 1992–93 the technocrats began making efforts to impose a modicum of professionalism to the exchange and were rewarded by a second bull run in late

1993. But even so, it will be some time before the faith of overseas investors is fully restored.

In their defence, the technocrats say they had little choice but to rush forward when they had the chance. 'We had a window of opportunity when oil prices fell,' Finance Minister Sumarlin said in a 1989 interview, 'and we couldn't let it pass by. If we had waited to dot every "i" and cross every "t" nothing ever would have gotten done. We thought it was better to just issue the deregulation measures and then correct them later.' Bank Indonesia Governor Mooy added that part of the problem was lack of experience. 'Listen, everyone is a student here,' he said. 'This process is like cooking: you have to try a few things before you get it right. We are,' he admitted, 'still in the trial and error phase.'[8]

These defences garner little sympathy from the technocrats' critics who contend that the benefits of financial deregulation—a rise in funds available for investment, better customer service by banks, and revitalisation of the equity market—are outweighed by the costs—higher lending rates, higher risk for bank depositors, and inadequate protection for investors in the stock market. 'The way the technocrats deregulated the banking sector was wrong and irresponsible,' said Nasir Tamara, the deputy publisher of *Republika* newspaper and an unabashed Habibie admirer.[9]

Lack of coordination

A second criticism of economic policy in recent years is that it lacks focus. The technocrats' basic strategy was to get the ball rolling in the areas in which they had the most influence—such as the banking sector and stock market—and hope that the reform ethic would prove contagious. If the strategy was going to work, the technocrats' counterparts elsewhere in the government had to play along. Fiscal policies had to support, not work against, monetary policy. Costs had to be lowered along the entire production and distribution process and the economy had to be made more efficient.

As it turned out, the reform spirit did catch on in the non-economic ministries but not nearly as fast as the technocrats hoped. 'We've done a lot in the financial sector which was necessary, but it is not enough. I'm not happy with how far deregulation has proceeded in the "real" sectors of the economy. We now have an imbalance between strong monetary expansion and slower growth in the productive sectors,' Sumarlin complained in 1991.[10] Another technocrat put it like this: 'We set the banks free and told them to mobilise resources and they did. But if we—the whole government—don't act in concert to bring costs down and remove the distortions, then there are going to be a lot of bankers chasing not too many good borrowers. And that's a problem.'[11]

The root of the problem is that Soeharto has given the technocrats only a limited mandate to carry out economic reform. They have had enough leeway to open up the financial sector, lower import tariffs and remove some non-tariff barriers and take other steps to improve Indonesia's investment climate. But they have not had enough power to make fundamental reforms in the way the government bureaucracy operates, for example, or to compel cooperation from the likes of the minister of justice. Often it has seemed that different parts of the government are working at cross-purposes. 'Our frustration,' said Wardhana, 'is that we have control over part of the game but we can't win the game unless other parts play along.'[12]

This lack of coordination takes other forms as well. The technocrats have been frustrated by the difficulty of codifying deregulation measures into law. Supporting legislation for the financial sector in particular has been slow in coming. A major contributor to these delays is the lack of interest by top officials at the justice ministry.

Lastly, many of the reforms that have been agreed on at the top levels of government are not being implemented by the unwieldy and poorly-disciplined bureaucracy. The problem is even more acute in the outer provinces, where the bureaucracy in many cases actively discourages new investment. 'The problem with the bureaucrats in the regions is that they are a long way removed from the deregulatory impetus which starts in Jakarta,' observes University of Indonesia economist Iwan Jaya Aziz. 'Out there they still have the 1970s attitude toward business. The result is that they scare off a lot of potential investors.'[13]

Corruption

The corruption issue has been damaging to the technocrats in several ways. They have come under severe criticism for not doing more to reduce the level of corruption in government and in some cases they have been accused of being corrupt themselves. From the other side, their policies have been resisted by past and present beneficiaries of Soeharto's patronage. The ending of the import monopoly for plastics which was discussed at the opening of Chapter 3 is one example of how the deregulation drive has cut into the revenues of politically influential businesses.

Critics complain that the technocrats have helped favoured businessmen by giving them the inside track on government contracts and providing them with credit from state banks. Sumarlin, for example, was accused in 1991 of using money from the government pension fund to help shore up the sagging balance sheet of Bank Danamon, which is owned by Usman Atmadjaya, an Indonesian-Chinese businessman. Prawiro has been criticised for steering several large government contracts to relatives of Soeharto and to his own family members.

To what extent individual technocrats have benefited personally while in office is hard to say. To be sure, personal links between leading government officials and the top ranks of the business community are pervasive in Indonesia. And economics ministers are not immune from these pressures. But more generally, pinning the blame for corruption on the technocrats misses the mark. The patrimonial nature of Indonesia's government, its lack of accountability, the weakness of the legal system and Soeharto's cultivation of selected businessmen and women are what lie behind the prevalence of corruption in Indonesia. In many cases opposition by the technocrats to government favouritism has been ignored by Soeharto. A case in point is the awarding in 1990 of a monopoly on the trade in cloves to Soeharto's youngest son Tommy.

This defence holds little water with the likes of Habibie disciple Tamara. 'The technocrats have no guts, no integrity. It is their responsibility to stand up to Soeharto,' he said.[14] If the technocrats object to implementing Soeharto's decisions, the critics say, they should have the courage to resign. It is a good point. But it begs a larger question. Would resigning change the way Soeharto runs the government? Even the technocrats' most ardent critics doubt that it would.

Foreign debt

Another strike against the deregulation campaign is that it has increased Indonesia's indebtedness to the outside world. Nationalists complain that the mounting foreign debt has made Indonesia excessively vulnerable to pressure from foreign bankers and aid donors.

Between 1988 and 1992 Indonesia's total foreign debt rose sharply to almost US$80 billion. The fastest-growing segment was in private commercial loans which at end-1992 reached some US$23 billion, or about 30 per cent of the total. The run-up in new borrowings by private companies is closely linked to the deregulation measures introduced in the late 1980s. With more areas of the economy opened up to private business, companies began investing in new factories and these investments in turn pushed up demand for imported machinery and capital goods. A commercial real estate boom in Jakarta and other major cities also added to the debt bill.

In 1992, Indonesia's debt service ratio—which measures debt servicing payments against exports—amounted to a worrying 32 per cent. The technocrats consider a ratio in excess of 25 per cent to be unsustainable. Other figures also suggest that Indonesia's foreign debt has risen to dangerous levels. The country's total foreign debt, equal to 29 per cent of gross national product (GNP) in 1982, had by 1991 risen to a level equivalent to 72 per cent of GNP, according to economist Rizal Ramli. In contrast, before the Latin American debt crisis exploded in 1981–82, the total foreign debt of Mexico and Brazil relative to their gross national product was only 52 per cent and 36 per cent, respectively.[15] 'In maintaining a stable macroeconomic environment,' the World Bank said in a 1993 report, 'the main challenge stems from Indonesia's large external debt.'[16]

But debt, the government economists point out in their defence, is not the problem. What matters is how the borrowed funds are used. Provided the foreign borrowings were used productively—that is, in ways that boost export revenues—higher levels of foreign debt are acceptable. But there is no doubt that at least a portion of the new borrowings were used unproductively on account of widespread corruption, political favouritism and other economic inefficiencies. In addition, the government has been forced to borrow offshore to supplement its domestic sources of revenue because political obstacles have prevented tax collection from picking up as fast as the technocrats had planned.

Having removed foreign exchange restrictions early in the New Order, there was little the technocrats could do to slow foreign borrowings. Finally, in September 1991, they were forced to act. A commercial offshore loan team was established from which all projects with a government connection had to obtain approval before borrowing abroad. The move was aimed at stopping billions of dollars' worth of infrastructure projects that were in the planning stage at the time, many of them sponsored by crony businessmen and financed by state banks.

The technocrats, under intense pressure from the most powerful of the cronies, have since had to waive these borrowing restrictions in several celebrated cases. If the leakage becomes more widespread, Indonesia's debt problem, still manageable at current levels, could well become a burden only too familiar to Latin American governments.

Wealth inequalities

Perhaps no issue of recent years has been more contentious—and more damaging to the technocrats' standing—than the debate over the distribution of wealth. Economics is only a small part of the debate; politics and culture play the major roles.

There are two aspects to the 'wealth gap' debate: poverty and equity. By international standards, Indonesia has done well in reducing the incidence of poverty during the past 25 years. How well is a matter of dispute. Some economists contend that the government has set the poverty line artificially low, and therefore poverty is still more widespread than officially admitted. But while some alternative measures produce higher poverty rates than the official government data, all of the measures show that poverty has declined markedly under Soeharto's rule.

Equity is a more complicated issue. Critics say that even if poverty has declined, the pattern of economic growth in Indonesia has created more inequalities in wealth distribution. What empirical evidence exists, however, suggests the opposite. Analyses which use the government's data on income and expenditure patterns show that the distribution of wealth has hardly changed at all during the New Order and, further, that it is reasonably 'equal' by international standards.[17] The relatively even distribution of wealth in Indonesia is due to factors such as well-targeted government programs for agricultural development, and heavy government spending on primary education, health and subsidies for rice growers.

Nevertheless, criticism of wealth inequalities has become increasingly strident in recent years. Critics of the technocrats contend that the economic deregulation campaign begun in the mid-1980s has helped large corporations and wealthy individuals far more than small traders and businesses. There is some truth in this argument. Large corporations were able to move quickly to take advantage of new business opportunities because they had management systems already in place and found it relatively easier to obtain bank financing for new investments. It is also true, as noted earlier, that rapid private sector growth in recent years has exacerbated wealth differentials between Java and many of the Outer Islands.

Economist Rizal Ramli says that deregulation has effectively reduced bureaucratic hurdles for big corporations but not for small firms. 'The government has not taken steps to ensure opportunities are available for all companies. Nothing has been done for small companies.' The root of the problem, he says, is 'that the technocrats have been in power too long and are insensitive to societal concerns.'[18]

This charge is vigorously disputed by the technocrats and other economists. They argue that the rapid growth of the private sector in recent years has been remarkable for *not* increasing wealth inequalities. They point out that the private sector has created millions of jobs and contend that, on an aggregate basis, the whole nation has benefited from their reform program. 'There is no proof that the wealth gap has gotten wider in the last three years,' bristled Mooy in a 1991 interview. 'Even if it had, could you blame it on the deregulation drive? No! The inequalities were created by the policies in place before the reforms started.'[19]

Critics of the technocrats are often guilty of confusing wealth distribution for the nation as a whole and wealth distribution within the modern, largely urban-based business sector. In this community there is another dynamic at work: ethnicity. And here the problem is not so much that there are rich people, but rather who those rich people are.

Indonesia's small, ethnic-Chinese business community dominates the private sector. Probably more than any other group, Indonesian-Chinese were the first to benefit from the deregulation drive. The growth of their companies was particularly noticeable in the big cities. Many of them built new office blocks and put their corporate logos on display for all to see. Their banks expanded the most rapidly, bringing their corporate presence to every corner of the archipelago. They were the first to raise funds through the stock market, taking advantage of the bourse's boom in 1989.

On the surface, then, it *did* seem that ethnic-Chinese were the prime beneficiaries of the deregulation campaign. At one level, this development was unavoidable. If the point of deregulation was to promote more private sector business activity, then it was natural that companies owned by ethnic-Chinese would do well. But many didn't see it that way. Many leading *pribumi* businessmen concluded that the technocrats' deregulation measures were specifically aimed at helping the ethnic-Chinese increase their dominance of the business world. The fact that many of these same *pribumi* businessmen also benefited from the deregulations didn't blunt their resentment. As Hill puts it: '[T]he politics of envy often overrides careful economic analysis.'[20] Soeharto's habit of doling out favours to some of the biggest Chinese businessmen and the widespread perception that the Chinese don't pay their fair share of tax have fuelled the 'ethnic argument' against deregulation.

If ethnicity lay close to the surface of the wealth gap debate, so too did religion. Although almost 90 per cent of Indonesians are Muslims, the three leading technocrats of the 1988–93 cabinet—Prawiro, Sumarlin and Mooy—were all Christians. A number of prominent Muslim leaders accused the technocrats of formulating policies in such a way as to help Christians at the expense of Muslims. Since most ethnic-Chinese Indonesians are not Muslim, the combination of religious and ethnic-based opposition to the technocrats' policies became a potent mix. 'The economic ministries are to blame for the wealth discrepancies in Indonesia today,' says parliamentarian and Muslim leader Sri Bintang Pamungkas. 'The status quo in Indonesia is wrong, politically, economically and culturally. What has the government done for the poor? It has done nothing!'[21]

In the cabinet Soeharto formed in March 1993, two of the three leading technocrats were replaced by Muslim economists and, for the cabinet as a whole, only three of the 41 ministers were Christians compared with six in the former cabinet. The changes were applauded by many Muslim leaders. 'Soeharto's new cabinet has fulfilled our hopes,' said the Muslim critic Imaduddin Abdulrahim. 'Their programs are what are needed by Muslims [because] for the first time 90 per cent of this cabinet is composed of Muslims.'[22]

Cultural norms

One of the less appreciated explanations for the resistance to the tech-nocrats' policies concerns the cultural acceptability of the kind of economy the technocrats are trying to create. Born from the ashes of colonialism, Indonesia entered independence with a strong predisposition against cap-italism because it was associated with the exploitative aspects of colonial rule. Many of Indonesia's early leaders, including Sukarno, favoured a socialist economic path with the government playing an important role in the economy in order to safeguard the interests of the poor. This idea, of course, fit in well with Sukarno's broader belief in a corporatist, paternal form of government.

Article 33 of the 1945 Constitution sets out the government's economic responsibilities. It states, in part: 'Branches of production . . . which affect the life of most people shall be controlled by the State.'[23] The constitution also states that cooperatives, the private sector and the government shall be three equal partners in economic development.

Sukarno's management of the economy, as described in Chapter 1, was a long way short of successful. Nonetheless, the socialist ideas popular in the 1950s continue to hold sway within certain intellectual circles. More broadly, the notion that the government exists to protect the poor against 'greedy capitalists' is one which both Sukarno and Soeharto have sup-ported.

Consequently, the technocrats' attempts to reduce the government's direct role in the economy have been assailed by some as being 'anti-social justice' and in favour of pushing Indonesia toward 'liberal' capital-ism. 'Capitalist notions of private self-interest as the basic building blocks of the public interest', to borrow Jamie Mackie's phrase,[24] is seen by this camp as alien to Indonesia's national character. The technocrats' deregu-lation policies have 'removed protection for the poor and given advantage to the strong', says Mubyarto, a populist-leaning academic at Yogyakarta's Gadjah Mada University.[25]

Soeharto, notwithstanding the fact that he has presided over what can only be called a capitalist revolution, appears to share this unease. 'Our goal,' he says in his autobiography, '[is] the greatest possible prosperity for the most number of people, not like what is the case in liberal countries.' In other parts of the book, Soeharto, using language with curious Marxist echoes, speaks of private sector-led growth as the 'first phase' of Indonesia's economic development. 'Ultimately,' he continues, 'cooperatives must be the main pillar of our economy.'[26]

Anecdotal evidence suggests that a distaste for a market-driven capi-talist economy is widely-held, even by many who have benefited from the reform drive. In 1989, economist Bruce Glassburner asked 36 members of Indonesia's political elite to describe their views of the economy.

He deliberately chose the same people interviewed in the late 1960s by political scientist, Frank Weinstein, who found his subjects hostile to free enterprise and in favour of a strong state role in the economy. The interviewees told Glassburner their views hadn't changed from when they talked to Weinstein.[27]

The Muslim leader Imaduddin, when asked his opinion of why some leading technocrats were dropped from the cabinet announced in March 1993, said: 'They were directing a capitalist economy which is not in line with the 1945 Constitution, thus it is only natural if they were replaced.'[28] Two other prominent critics who object to the capitalist overtones of the technocrats' policies are Sri Edy Swasono, the firebrand head of the Council of Indonesian Cooperatives, and his brother, Sri Bintang Pamungkas, an outspoken legislator with the Muslim-oriented United Development Party.[29]

Swasono is deeply critical of the lack of technocrat support for cooperatives, while his brother has a more general objection to the way the government has lost ground to the private sector in economic matters. Pamungkas believes equity would be best served by disbanding business conglomerates and placing less priority on growth and more on wealth distribution. 'The problem with the central bank now is that it isn't able to control who the banks lend to. It should be one of the missions of the Indonesian banking system to close the wealth gap,' he said.[30]

Part of the blame for the failure to sell 'economic reform' to the Indonesian elite rests with the technocrats or, more generally, with the political system in which they operate. Because they have been cushioned inside an authoritarian regime, the technocrats have not been required to solicit political support for their policies. Consequently, although the technocrats' view of the 'market' as the central feature of a modern economy has spread to much of the Indonesian elite, there has been a distinct lack of success in 'socialising' this concept in the broader Indonesian populace. It is a failure which could haunt the technocrats as Indonesia moves, however slowly, towards a more pluralistic political process.

Political frustration

Although their economic prescriptions vary, non-governmental actors as diverse as liberal economists, orthodox Muslim leaders, nationalist politicians and leftist academics share a resentment at being excluded from the political process. Even those who agree with the technocrats' basic approach have been slow to publicly say so because they don't want to be seen as endorsing the status quo.

This complaint has little direct bearing on the technocrats, of course; it is directed at the political system created by Soeharto. But while this sense of frustration might be a case of misdirected animosity writ large, it nonetheless represents a serious political problem for the technocrats.

Since it is a hazardous business to criticise Soeharto, it is a common practice in Indonesia to take the indirect approach. And the technocrats make an inviting target. They are closely associated in the public mind with the New Order government, having held influential positions since Soeharto first came to power. And outside their support from Soeharto, they have little political constituency of their own and have shown little inclination to build one. Even if they were so inclined, justifying their record would be complicated by constraints on free expression which make it difficult to conduct an honest, public discussion of several important topics, such as the role of the Chinese and the extent of corruption.

Thus, attacking the technocrats' record serves as a useful outlet for expressing frustration with the exclusive nature of Indonesia's government. The pervasiveness of corruption, regional inequalities, money-losing state-owned enterprises, the so-called wealth gap and a lack of policy coordination can all be blamed on the technocrats, not Soeharto. 'Frustration is rising because the technocrats monopolise the economic discourse,' asserts Habibie cheerleader Tamara.[31]

Some of the Muslim leaders who have attached themselves to Habibie's coattails have become particularly able practitioners in the art of proxy politics. Their primary objective is greater political power, a desire they feel, probably misguidedly, that Habibie can help them to fulfil. The stronger Habibie is, they believe, the better off they will be. And since the technocrats are considered rivals to Habibie for Soeharto's ear, the strategy of the Muslims, explains Umar Juoro, a researcher with the Habibie-linked Centre for Information and Development Studies (CIDES), 'is to attack the technocrats because they are close to Soeharto and, by weakening the technocrats influence, Habibie will gain influence with Soeharto.'[32] One frequently used tactic is to accuse the technocrats of relying on foreign advisers and consultants to draw up their policies. A second, as noted above, is to suggest that the technocrats, and by implication Soeharto, are deviating from the 1945 Constitution.

Proxy politics, of course, is a game Soeharto can play as well as anyone. If public criticism mounts against the technocrats—even if the real criticism is intended elsewhere—it can be defused simply by making it appear that their influence has declined. And that is exactly the impression created by the cabinet changes announced in March 1993.

Soeharto

The final component of the anti-technocrat coalition is—or may be— Soeharto. Neither the technocrats nor the Habibie camp seem to have a clear idea of what changes, if any, Soeharto feels should be made to Indonesia's economic policies. For the general public, the near impossibility of divining how policies are formulated is old hat. What is new at present is that even his top aides are mystified. But there are at least some signs that Soeharto is uncomfortable with the political implications of economic reform.

For one, the technocrats' preference for relying on the market to determine industrial winners and losers implies a loss of government control over the economy, a trend that poses obvious conflicts with Soeharto's nurturing of an all-powerful, quasi-feudal state. Soeharto, it appears, has also grown tired of constantly being pressured by the technocrats to push through new reforms, pressure which is often portrayed as having come from foreign investors or aid donors.[33] One of the easiest ways to avoid this pressure is to avoid the technocrats.

Habibie: the case for technology

Many of the factors that are working against the technocrats are working for Minister Habibie. As a consequence, it is quite possible that Habibie will become even more influential as Soeharto moves toward the end of his current term.

Habibie's views on the economy first brought him to national attention two decades ago. Those views and the criticism they have elicited are laid out below. But Habibie cannot be considered only in the light of his economic convictions because in recent years his influence has spread into the political and religious arenas. Habibie was thought to be a leading contender to replace Sudharmono as Indonesia's vice-president in 1993. And although he was passed over for retiring armed forces commander Try Sutrisno, his political standing increased with the appointment of several of his acolytes to the cabinet.

He is given credit for successfully organising the People's Consultative Assembly in March 1993 which re-elected Soeharto and he played a crucial behind-the-scenes role in organising the Golkar congress in October 1993 that chose Information Minister Harmoko as the party's new chairman. It appears that Habibie is one of the aides Soeharto will count on to ensure that the president's transition, when it comes, will be a smooth one. To be in a position to do that, Habibie is likely to entrench himself and his aides in the leadership of the ruling party Golkar in the years ahead. Some Habibie supporters are already talking up the possibility of Habibie becoming Indonesia's next president.

The Habibie phenomenon gained a religious component in 1990 when Soeharto placed Habibie atop a newly created grouping of leading Muslim figures, the Indonesian Association of Muslim Intellectuals, abbreviated as ICMI. ICMI's formation and political ramifications are reviewed in

Chapter 7. For the purposes of this chapter, the relevance of Habibie's links with the ICMI Muslims is that they have considerably broadened the political support for his economic ideas.

The core of Habibie's economic ideas is that high value-added technology is the key to future economic success. He believes Indonesia must reorient its economic policies to focus on the 'competitive advantages' that only technology can provide, rather than relying on the nation's 'comparative advantages' of abundant labour and natural resources. A focus on technology will add value to domestic production, Habibie argues, and increase the productivity of Indonesian workers. The technology acquired and applied in specific areas is expected to have a multiplying effect throughout the economy. Habibie argues that engineers and technicians trained in selected areas—like aircraft manufacturing—will then spread their knowledge to other areas. In this way, the entire economy will become more technologically proficient.

Since Habibie believes that private firms will not on their own invest sufficiently in research and development or attach sufficient importance to the transfer of technology from foreign firms, the government must play a leading role in these areas. Up to now, the government has concentrated its development expenditures on basic infrastructure like roads, bridges and power stations. In the future, Habibie contends, technology should be regarded as a crucial component of the nation's 'infrastructure' and be invested in accordingly. In a policy speech delivered in early 1993, he spelled out his views in more detail:

> In national interest terms, the comparative advantage approach doesn't promise much except high economic growth in the short term through integration with the international marketplace . . . But it is difficult to argue that this growth can continue [in the future] because of the ease with which labour-intensive industries can relocate to countries with even lower labour costs . . . Promoting value added manufacturing and high technology industries won't bring high growth in the short run—it might even lower growth for a time—but in the long run national interest will have been well served because national economic development will no longer be determined by the international division of labour . . . [In the future] trade policy should not be based purely on free trade but should promote priority industries through government subsidies and protection. Deregulation policies should be directed at non-priority sectors and formulated in ways that help the priority industries.[34]

Habibie argues that his approach will accelerate Indonesia's industrialisation process. One of the main problems with the technocrats' market-based approach, he says, is that it lacks a well-defined industrial policy and pays far too little attention to the development of human resources. Habibie would like to create in Indonesia a government coordinating agency for national business development similar to the Ministry of International Trade and Industry in Japan. He commonly cites the example of Airbus Industries—sponsored by a consortium of four European governments—as a model for government–business interaction in Indonesia.

Habibie's industrial development efforts are centred on ten state-owned enterprises grouped under the Coordinating Agency for Strategic Industries.[35] The biggest of the strategic industries are the aircraft manufacturer IPTN, the West Java steel complex Krakatau Steel and the shipbuilder PT PAL, all of which benefit substantially from direct and indirect government subsidies. Habibie generates business for these firms by selling their products to other government agencies and through 'offset' arrangements with foreign companies supplying technologically sophisticated equipment to Indonesia. When the national airline Garuda Indonesia buys aircraft from Boeing of the United States, for example, a portion of the contract will be spent at IPTN, mostly for the manufacture of aircraft components. Similar deals have been arranged with suppliers of fighter jets for the air force, warships for the navy and satellites for the telecommunications ministry.[36] (Using the armed forces as a vehicle to build up his strategic industries is a particularly attractive option for Habibie as the military is the only Indonesian institution able to import equipment duty-free). In late 1993, Habibie struck a deal with the Malaysian Prime Minister Mahathir Mohamad under which Indonesia agreed to import Malaysia's Proton car in exchange for Malaysia buying an unspecified number of 40-seat aircraft manufactured by IPTN.

The cost effectiveness of these offset deals, and of Habibie's empire more generally, is impossible to discern. Financial information on the so-called strategic companies is sparse and generally considered unreliable. All are thought to be unprofitable, although they have absorbed many billions of dollars of government investment. In 1991, the ten firms considered 'strategic industries' accounted for almost half of all losses reported by Indonesia's state-owned enterprises.[37]

American business school professor David McKendrick is one of few outside analysts who have taken an in-depth look at Habibie's showcase project, the aircraft manufacturer IPTN. After studying IPTN's performance since 1976, McKendrick concluded that through 1988 'one can say with confidence that IPTN's financial performance has been altogether unimpressive.' McKendrick argues that 'while [IPTN] suffers from inexperience at all levels, its most critical deficiency was its managerial capability: weak management was primarily responsible for bottlenecks in production, and such delays discouraged potential buyers.' Finally, McKendrick convincingly rebuts Habibie's contention that high-tech showpieces such as IPTN have spread technological competence into the broader business community. On the contrary, he says, 'no such inter-firm links have been spawned [by IPTN]. Not only is IPTN insulated from public scrutiny, it is insulated from the greater Indonesian economy because of an unwillingness or inability to draw other firms into its circle of activities.'[38]

Predictably, perhaps, Habibie's supporters reject the validity of analysing the strategic industries on a profit and loss basis. 'It all depends on how you look at the money that has been spent,' says Tamara. 'If you look at it as a cost, yes, it is expensive. But we should look at it as an investment in the future.'[39]

Habibie passionately believes in his high-tech vision. A man of extraordinary energy and considerable charm, he tirelessly campaigns to attract new converts to his views. He travels extensively and, by Indonesian standards, is relatively accessible to the press. In interviews, Habibie animatedly holds forth behind a mammoth desk covered from end to end with model airplanes and helicopters. But enthusiasm alone does not explain Habibie's insulation from the usual budgetary procedures. This he owes to his close relationship with Soeharto.

Habibie had risen to the post of vice-president for applied technology at the German aircraft manufacturer Messerschmitt Bulkow Blohm in the mid-1970s when Soeharto asked him to return to Indonesia. Soeharto told him at the time: 'Habibie, you can do whatever you want [in Indonesia] short of fomenting a revolution.'[40] Habibie has made full use of the carte blanche. Today, Habibie's access to the president is said to be better than any other cabinet minister. (Habibie has been known to make this point himself when marketing his products overseas.)

Habibie's vision of Indonesia as a technologically advanced industrial powerhouse is carefully crafted to appeal to Soeharto. Habibie portrays the technocrats' economic policies as turning Indonesia into a mere pawn of international capital, a nation to be exploited for its natural resources just like the Dutch did for centuries before independence. His approach, on the other hand, promises to make Indonesia a more independent and powerful actor on the world stage. The technocrats' polices were appropriate to the first 25 years of the New Order when economic stabilisation was the primary concern, Habibie believes, but for the next 25 years—the 'take-off' period—a new 'vision' is needed. The argument has found a sympathetic listener in Soeharto.

'We cannot be dependent on other people,' Soeharto said in his autobiography. 'That is why I have decided on the policy: Buy the CN-235 [a small passenger plane produced by IPTN]. This is to protect our industry. It is our duty to buy our own products, even though they may not be perfect.'[41] In addition to its nationalist appeal, Habibie's approach is alluring on other grounds. A large interventionist government which Habibie favours coincides well with Soeharto's own view of government. And by providing a rationale for government subsidies and tariff protection, Habibie gives Soeharto an excuse to resist the technocrats' constant pushing for more deregulation.

A crucial factor behind Habibie's rising popularity is the man himself. Like leading technocrat Widjoyo did many years before, Habibie has learned what approach works best with Soeharto: humility mixed with a dose of obeisance. '[Some] people seemed to think that Habibie might use his ingenuity to influence [me],' Soeharto mentions in his autobiography. 'They didn't know that Habibie always asked for my advice. [Habibie] is not a man who thinks he knows best. Whenever he reports to me, he spends hours with me only because he wants to understand what I think of the matters he puts forward, what my philosophy is . . . He always seeks my advice on the principles of life. He asked for my photo and I let him have his choice, one of me in Javanese dress . . . He put the photo in his office and later made a copy of it for publication in his book. He regards me as his own parent.'[42]

But if any single factor can be credited for tilting the balance in Habibie's favour in recent years, it is probably the political backing of the Muslim leaders grouped in ICMI. The marriage of the ICMI Muslims, a group traditionally focused on concerns of social justice, with the high-tech visionary Habibie is a strange one and, as described above, has more to do with politics than economics. Habibie's value to this group is that he represents something other than the status quo. The fact that Habibie is prepared to debate his ideas publicly and, indeed, to court support for them from the Indonesian elite—a skill the technocrats have never mastered—adds to his appeal. 'He allows us to disagree,' says researcher Umar Juoro, plaintively.[43]

Whatever their motivation, the speed at which some ICMI Muslims have become converts to Habibienomics is nothing less than astonishing. In the space of just two or three years, they have come to believe that in Habibie's vision lies the promise of a brighter future. '[Aircraft manufacturer] IPTN is great,' gushed Tamara, who also heads ICMI's department of international relations and communications. 'I'm so happy to see so many technicians.'[44]

Habibienomics: a critique

Some of Habibie's basic assumptions are shared by the technocrats. There is common ground, for instance, on the need to develop human resources and on the value of putting more 'hard sciences' into the national curriculum and supporting vocational training programs. The differences lie in how to reach these objectives. 'We've done a lot in terms of human resource development in the New Order,' says technocrat Ali Wardhana. 'The problem is Habibie wants to jump from where we are to very highly skilled industries. But there are no shortcuts; you can't simply produce a class of instant engineers. It took us 25 years just to make primary education available to all Indonesians.'[45]

Hartarto, the Coordinating Minister for Industry and Trade, a post created in March 1993, fits in somewhere between the technocrats and Habibie. An engineer by training, he supports rapid industrialisation but only within the limits of Indonesia's resource capacities. 'We know we can't continue relying only on products which depend on natural resources or plentiful labour,' he concedes. 'But we have to raise our comparative advantages so that they become competitive advantages. We have to move towards high technology incrementally. We are already capable of making and exporting many sophisticated products, including electronics, steel, chemicals, machine tools, heavy equipment as well as others.'[46]

Criticism of Habibienomics tends to fall into two camps. The first asks whether Soeharto's government can play the role designed for it under Habibie's vision. The second focuses on the difficulties of financing Habibie's ambitious plans and to what extent this financing will come at the expense of currently funded government programs. The first asks of Habibie's approach: will it work? The second asks: should it work?

The government–business relationship

The government plays a crucial role in Habibie's plans for industrial transformation. Its tasks will be to pick which industries and business sectors are deserving of special support from the public purse. Industrial 'winners' will be selected based on their potential for increasing Indonesia's technological capabilities. To achieve this goal, industrial 'winners' will need to be protected for an indeterminate period from foreign competition through the use of government subsidies and tariff and non-tariff barriers. Habibie and his supporters enthusiastically point to South Korea and Taiwan as examples of how this kind of government intervention can produce successful industrialisation *and* rapid economic growth.

Many economists including those at the World Bank say Habibie has his economics all wrong. '[Only] as local firms gradually acquire technological capabilities commensurate with a rise in a country's level of development, does it become feasible for governments to encourage industry to move up the technological ladder through limited, well-designed interventions,' the World Bank said in a 1993 report. 'Policies centred on a "technological leapfrogging" strategy, involving the development of targeted high-technology industries supported by direct public investment or subsidies and high levels of protection, have proven costly and ineffective in most countries.' South Korea, the Bank notes, which has a per capita income ten times that of Indonesia, 'did not build a steel industry until the late 1970s, and other heavy industries until the 1980s.' It is only now preparing to enter the aircraft assembly field.[47]

Even economists and other observers who sympathise with Habibie's aims argue that his strategy has little chance of success in the current political environment. For Habibie to deliver on his promises, they say, the government has to pick the right 'winners'. Clear and rational criteria have to be spelled out and adhered to. Those picking the 'winners' have to be isolated from those benefiting from government protection. The 'winners'—government or private—will have to be able to meet clearly understood and objectively applied standards of performance. Government protection should not be continued for those who fail to meet these objectives.

Indonesia, they add, has already experimented with heavy government intervention in the economy, and the lessons from that period should not be forgotten. In the late 1970s and early 1980s, economic nationalists in the government, with pools of oil wealth at their disposal, intervened extensively in the economy. Among their stated goals were to promote domestic production—'the campaign to use domestic products is important in strengthening our sovereignty as a nation,' explained Ginanjar[48]—and to strengthen the business capabilities of *pribumis*.

But the criteria for these goals were never adequately explained. Those benefiting from government help were, by and large, those with sufficient political clout to demand such help. Government intervention became an excuse to bestow patronage on politically powerful businessmen and other assorted economic free-riders. In the end, import-substituting industrialisation turned out to be an expensive fiasco and provided the immediate context for the technocrats' radical reform measures introduced in the late 1980s.

Explanations of why this happened return ultimately to the patrimonial style of Soeharto's rule. Indonesia's government is noted for the extreme concentration of power at the very top and the close relationships between government officials and leading business actors. In such an environment, government intervention is not likely to be based on strictly economic criteria and is not, therefore, likely to be of much benefit to the economy.

For these reasons, those opposing Habibie's proposals reject the validity of comparing Indonesia with South Korea and Taiwan. While there are similarities—all ruled by authoritarian regimes at an early stage of industrialisation—the differences are more illuminating. The key difference is the nature of the authoritarian regime. Governments in Taiwan and South Korea have intervened to promote specific economic sectors over others but, importantly, those benefiting from government protection were not especially influential in political terms. By and large they became 'winners' on the basis of economic criteria.[49]

Although Habibie's criteria for government intervention are different from those put forward in Indonesia fifteen years ago, he must operate in the same political setting as the 1970s-style nationalists did. And it is therefore hard to understand how a Habibie-led round of government intervention won't meet the same fate: failure due primarily to an absence of fiscal oversight, politically motivated government–business collusion and widespread corruption. Indeed, as Chapter 6 discusses, Habibie has not been shy in the past when it comes to dealing with leading crony businessmen.

Habibie supporters like Tamara dismiss these concerns. Corruption is a problem of ethics, he told me. Since good Muslims are honest, then as long as Islamic values are upheld by the government officials implementing Habibie's plans—and Tamara believes they will be—corruption won't be a problem. Habibie's less idealistic supporters recognise the pitfalls ahead but insist these should not be an excuse for inaction. 'Can we rely on Habibie to be sufficiently insulated from political pressures?' asks Juoro. 'It's a good question. But let's remember that the technocrats aren't insulated from these pressures either. The real question, then, is who can gather enough political support to change the way the government works, to make it more insulated from privileged businessmen. The technocrats don't have any political constituency. We are trying to generate political support for Habibie so that we have more leverage to do this.'[50]

It is a sensible argument. But even those, like Juoro, who believe it concede that changing the form of interaction between the government and the business community will be a long-term process, and, moreover, one which cannot really begin until Soeharto leaves power and maybe not then either. So what will happen to the money Habibie plans to spend between now and this uncertain point in the future?

Who will pay?

No one contests the point that Habibie's projects are expensive. And as Habibie's relative influence continues to rise—as looks likely—so too will the cost of underwriting his vision.

Although Habibie accords state-owned enterprises a central role in his high-tech plans, he says he will bring in private investors—domestic and foreign—on a selective basis in order to broaden his source of funds. One of his pet ideas is to have some of the state-owned enterprises under his control raise money by listing shares on international stock exchanges.[51] But given that Habibie's existing strategic industries are not considered profitable, and that the revenues they do earn are dependent on direct government support which may or may not be forthcoming in the future, it is not likely that private interest will be widespread.

That leaves the government. The technocrats fear that Habibie's technological ambitions will have at least two adverse effects on the budget. On the income side, the danger is that tariff and non-tariff barriers erected to protect industrial 'winners' would raise costs for other Indonesian companies, especially export-oriented manufacturers. If their products become less competitive, export revenues and non-oil tax income would suffer.

On the expenditure side, government support for Habibie's projects will mean—at least for the short run—either an increase in the foreign debt or fewer budget allocations for other uses. Indonesia's government budget is not large; for fiscal 1993, total government expenditures were pegged at US$31 billion. This was to be funded by US$26 billion in domestic revenues plus US$5 billion in foreign aid and loans. What programs are to be cut to make way for new investments in high technology is an issue Habibie and his supporters have yet to address.

Habibienomics is an elitist vision. Training a corps of engineers and skilled technicians will bring immediate benefits to a relatively small number of well-educated Indonesians, but it will have little direct bearing on low-income Indonesians, a much larger community. Quite possibly, the latter group will be disadvantaged by Habibie's plans because there will be less money available to spend on programs targeted at the poor. In fact, there is compelling evidence to suggest that Habibie's approach will exacerbate the wealth gap which is so heatedly criticised by his supporters among Muslim intellectuals.

The argument used by Habibie's supporters which says a greater focus on 'technology-driven' education and human resource development will benefit all Indonesians doesn't hold much water. Training programs for workers employed in technology-intensive industries and higher government spending on engineering courses and vocational training institutes will help relatively more affluent Indonesians, not the poor.

The poor have different needs. While the incidence of poverty has declined significantly during the New Order, tens of millions of Indonesians continue to live below or just above the poverty line. Addressing the welfare of the poor and near poor, economists argue, means going beyond consumption-based measures of poverty to also include access to education, health services, clean water, etc. These are the areas in need of higher spending—not the production of airplanes or oil tankers—if the quality of life of the poor is to be increased.

By the late 1980s primary education had been made available to virtually all school-age Indonesians although, in many poor areas, the quality of that education was lacking. But beyond the primary level of education, enrolment rates begin to differ radically between the poor and the better-off. For Indonesians in the bottom 40 per cent of the income distribution, the rate of enrolment to junior high school actually declined between 1987–89.[52] And for Indonesians within the top 10 per cent of the income distribution, the rate of enrolment to senior high school is 37 times higher than for those within the bottom 10 per cent, according to the World Bank. The explanation is simple. The fees charged by senior high schools represent, on average, 'an enormous' 84 per cent of the income of poor Indonesians, the Bank says.[53]

The same disparities affect health care. Thousands of health centres built by the government provide many more poor Indonesians with access to health care compared with ten or twenty years ago. But there are large differences in the quality of health services between the poor and the better-off. For example, only 5 per cent of the poor used high-quality health-care providers—doctors and hospitals—when sick in 1990, compared with nearly half of the better-off, the Bank says.[54]

For the poor, what is most important is that economic growth be as high as possible and that jobs be created so that as many of them as possible can rise above the poverty line. Habibie's willingness to sacrifice economic growth in the short run while Indonesia invests heavily in high-tech industries would have to be considered, in World Bank parlance, strongly anti-poor.

The balance of power

Even though his standing has risen, there are limits on what Habibie can accomplish, some self-imposed, some not. As for the former, it is important to remember that there is more to Habibie than his notions of economic development. He also has high-reaching political aspirations. Like Soeharto, Habibie is a complex man and it is difficult to separate out his motivations and objectives. But there is no denying that he has a political agenda—even if it isn't clear what it is—and that, in political terms, he is a conservative. He is loyal to Soeharto and very much in favour of sticking with the political status quo. The politician Habibie understands that economic development is at the heart of Soeharto's claim to power. Policy changes, therefore, if they are to happen, must be smooth, non-disruptive and non-damaging to economic growth. As befits an avid student of Soeharto's leadership style, he believes in harmony and consensus, in victory without imposing defeat. He does not intend to rock the boat.[55]

Some of Habibie's supporters have already begun grumbling about what they see as his excessive caution and his unwillingness to become a more forceful advocate for his own views. 'Habibie talks a lot about value added and high-tech but he resists strengthening the concept. He is not prepared to fight the economists. He always tells us: don't attack Widjoyo,' says CIDES researcher Juoro. 'Habibie is willing, it seems, to work with anyone who shares his central goal of preserving the [political] status quo.' From the ICMI camp, there are some who, while publicly supportive of Habibie's economic program, are privately pessimistic that Habibie has the managerial skills or political astuteness to transform his ideas into reality. 'Habibie's [economic] ideas won't work because his ego is too big,' said Sri Bintang Pamungkas. 'He doesn't want any qualified people around him. He prefers loyal aides to brilliant ones.'[56]

To be sure, as he has become more politically influential, Habibie has taken pains to dispel the impression that his economic vision implies a loss of influence for the technocrats. 'There has never been an era of Widjoyonomics and there never will be a Habibienomics,' Habibie said a month after the new cabinet was formed in March 1993. 'What there has always been is Soeharto as head of state, and he picks ministers to help him.'[57] (An old joke about Habibie puts his relationship with the technocrats in a slightly different light. In it, a young Habibie just wants to ride up in the front seat with the technocrats. I can be the gas, Habibie says, and they can be the brake.)

Other limits are imposed from outside. While he enjoys Soeharto's favour at present, Habibie is just one of several powerful players in Indonesia. Although the 'Habibie group' was well represented in the cabinet formed in March 1993, Habibie did not get all he wanted. His supporters did not crack the key technocrat portfolios of finance minister or central bank governor, for example, nor was Habibie appointed as the coordinating minister for industry and trade, a job he coveted. 'Habibie got his due share in the new cabinet, no more,' says Sucipto Wirosardjono, a top ICMI official.

The technocrats, for obvious reasons, form one of the groups arrayed against Habibie. The technocrats appointed to run the leading economic portfolios in March 1993 had a reasonably productive first year in office. They pushed through two sets of deregulatory measures aimed at lowering tariffs and non-tariff barriers, encouraging more foreign investment and simplifying land licensing procedures. Although the first package was deemed grossly inadequate by business executives and economists, the second received generally favourable reviews.[58] The technocrats also made a start on cleaning up the balance sheets at the seven state-owned banks and, confronted by declining oil prices, they successfully resisted pressures for fiscal pump priming and drew up a relatively austere budget for the 1994/95 fiscal year.[59]

The technocrats, of course, are not alone in wishing to see Habibie's influence circumscribed. The military hierarchy resents Habibie's interfering in the procurement of military hardware in order to drum up business for his 'strategic industries'. The military also sees Habibie's rising influence with Soeharto as having come at the expense of its own influence. Lastly, Habibie's attempts to carve out a bigger role for himself within Golkar have alienated some of the ruling party's civilian and longer serving leaders.

A final and arguably most important factor working against Habibienomics is the urgent need to maintain economic growth. Indonesia cannot lightly afford a dip in growth which may be brought about by substantial investments in protected industries and new government regulations. One of the unavoidable realities facing any policymaker is that some 2.3 million Indonesians join the workforce each year. The World Bank estimates that 320 000 fewer jobs would be created annually if the growth of non-oil gross domestic product declined by one percentage point.[60] A related dynamic, as noted earlier, is the imperative of reducing poverty. Soeharto's instructions to national planning board chief Ginanjar Kartasasmita in mid-1993 to focus on poverty alleviation are likely to dent Habibie's momentum, at least for a while.

A second reality is that oil, while less important to Indonesia than a decade ago, still accounts for more than a third of total export revenues. But Indonesia's rising domestic demand for oil combined with declining production rates means that Indonesia is likely to become a net oil importer by the end of the decade. Any slowing of non-oil export growth, therefore, especially if combined with a drop in oil prices, would have a serious impact on the country's balance of payments.

Thirdly, maintaining the continued goodwill of foreign donors and the trust of the international financial community is crucial to Indonesia's near-term economic fortunes. Foreign donors have backed the technocrats' economic deregulation drive with large annual aid allotments in recent years. In 1988, for example, the level of foreign aid pouring into Indonesia was more than twice as high, as a percentage of gross national product, than the average of all nations the World Bank calls 'lower middle income countries'.[61] And while the government budget's reliance on foreign funds has declined, foreign aid still made up one-eighth of total budget revenues in fiscal 1993.

Private foreign capital is just as important to Indonesia as foreign aid. Both the state and private sectors are dependent on foreign lenders to fund ongoing operations and business expansions. Foreign investors, meanwhile, have provided needed funds and expertise to Indonesia's non-oil export sector. But competition for overseas capital is stiff. In recent years, China, India and Vietnam have all made efforts to attract foreign investors to their shores. If Indonesia is not to fall behind in the regional competition for foreign capital, the deregulation drive has to continue.

It is impossible to know, of course, how all these sources of funds would be affected by a shift to Habibienomics. But a good guess is that foreign aid donors would be deeply reluctant to underwrite heavy government investment in Indonesia's strategic industries. Likewise, foreign investors and bankers would look amiss at the imposition of new tariffs and other trade barriers which would hamper Indonesia's export drive and threaten the capacity of Indonesian exporters to service their debts.

And lastly, a shift in economic policies would not be welcomed by many domestic business groups which have prospered under the technocrats' reforms. One of Indonesia's leading businessmen, fed up with the pervasive corruption in Indonesia and worried that a shift to Habibienomics would only aggravate the situation, said in April 1993 that he had decided to put new domestic investment plans on hold. 'I am going to concentrate on doing business abroad for the time being,' he said.[62]

Notwithstanding his fondness for Habibie, Soeharto is a pragmatic enough politician to recognise these concerns. In a move that surprised many in the Indonesian elite, among them Habibie's supporters in ICMI and elsewhere, Soeharto in late March 1993 re-appointed Widjoyo Nitisastro and Ali Wardhana, the two most powerful technocrats, as his personal advisers on the economy. The move, coming less than two weeks after the unveiling of a new cabinet, was seen as being intended to mollify foreign businessmen, bankers and donors who feared that a sharp shift in Indonesia's economic policies was imminent.

The retention of the low-profile Widjoyo was the more understandable of the two. The more outspoken Wardhana, on the other hand, had become increasingly critical of the obstacles placed in the way of economic reform. I asked him why Soeharto would want to keep him on the payroll. 'I don't know. Maybe to maintain some kind of continuity with international organisations. Maybe to show there is not going to be any major shift in economic policy. Or maybe he just wants us around to be the firemen in case something goes wrong.'[63]

Wardhana, of course, is not the only one who is confused. Although there are many dynamics affecting the economic policymaking process, Soeharto is perhaps both the most important and the most difficult to understand. He is a man of many conflicting signals. Some of his recent statements and actions suggest there will, in fact, be a shift to Habibienomics. At other times he appears to endorse the technocrats' policies. Is this all a Soeharto ploy to keep contenders for power at bay? Or is he, too, confused about where Indonesia's economy should be headed?

In this uncertain climate, can anything at all be said about economic policy in the mid-1990s, other than to observe that uncertainty is not generally conducive to economic growth? Provided Soeharto can keep political pressures bottled up, then the most likely scenario—though by no means the only one—would be a policy of muddling through until the presidential succession issue is clarified. The basic thrust of the technocrats' policies will be maintained along with some modifications to accommodate Habibie. There will be new deregulation packages aimed at removing barriers to trade and investment but it is less likely that there will be real progress on the broader goals such as improving state-owned enterprises, legal reform and, most importantly, changing the nature of the government–business relationship. These are likely to come only after a process of political reform.

5

The race that counts

From top to bottom commerce marked the Chinese. They were shippers, warehousemen, and labour contractors; builders and repairmen, and suppliers of *all things* to town and country.

James Rush[1]

The current situation, with Chinese firms dominating the top ranks of the business world, is not what the founders of this country had in mind.

Kusumo Martoredjo[2]

To most Indonesians, the word 'Chinese' is synonymous with corruption.

Slamet Bratanata[3]

The wealth gap? That's the topic of the year. In the final analysis we have to admit that it may trigger upheaval and disturbances.

Air Vice Marshall Teddy Rusdy[4]

The leaders of Indonesia's 31 largest conglomerates received an unusual summons late in February 1990. The following Sunday, 4 March, they were expected at President Soeharto's Tapos cattle ranch in West Java. Most of them had not been there before and none knew why that was about to change. A glance at the invitation list, though, offered a useful hint. All but two of the 'guests' were ethnic-Chinese Indonesians.

The previous two years had brought many changes for Indonesia's Chinese-owned conglomerates. Economic reforms had made available a host of new business opportunities, and they had responded with a massive investment spree. But their feverish activity had turned public opinion against them. Resentment of the ethnic Chinese and their economic clout was nothing new; it dated back nearly to their arrival in Indonesia centuries before. What *was* new was that the resolutely low-profile Chinese tycoons had been thrust into the public spotlight like never before. By selling shares on the stock market, for example, businessmen had to disclose a degree of corporate information previously unthinkable. Their fast-growing banks became household names as they advertised furiously for new customers. Their real estate investments spread their corporate existence throughout Java's cities and countryside. The press played its part, with business newspapers and general-interest magazines falling over each other to dig up details of Indonesia's corporate elite. The biggest of the Chinese firms had been very wealthy for many years, but now their wealth was visible to everybody.

More disclosure of corporate activity, of course, had been part of the technocrats' design to create a more transparent business environment; they just hadn't realised that the exposure of Chinese wealth would be the first major consequence. The result was a wave of 'anti-conglomerate' fervour. Fuelled by some of the leading *pribumi* (indigenous Indonesian) business executives, socialist-leaning academics, populist parliamentarians, and some grassroots Muslim leaders, it became (and remains) a serious social problem.

Businesses owned and run by ethnic-Chinese families play an integral part in Indonesia's economy, responsible for perhaps as much as 70 per cent of all private economic activity. Their companies have contributed mightily to the rejuvenation of Indonesia's economy in recent years, especially in the key areas of job creation and non-oil exports. But if the ethnic Chinese are an economic asset to the nation, they are also—and always have been—a political liability. Ethnic Chinese make up less than 4 per cent of the population, far less than their economic influence would suggest. Ever since independence, coping with *pribumi* resentment of the ethnic Chinese has been a constant concern of the government. Despite— and partly because of—the fact that many of the government's past initiatives to address this problem have been enormously expensive, polarising and largely ineffective, the perceived need to counter the strength of Chinese-run businesses remains a defining characteristic of many Indonesian leaders.

This view was strengthened by the late 1980s anti-conglomerate debate which, like many aspects of the political debate in Indonesia, was broader than it appeared. 'What Indonesians feel is often different from the terminology they use,' explains economist Kwik Kian Gie. 'When they criticise conglomerates they are really calling for social justice, fair competition and a more equitable distribution of wealth.'[5] Criticism of conglomerates, to put it another way, was on one level simply a safe way to criticise leading ethnic-Chinese businessmen and the more rapacious of Soeharto's relatives, a group which is regularly accused of violating the spirit of 'fair competition'. More broadly still, it was a way of expressing resentment at the closed nature of Indonesia's political system and the advantages this system has conferred on the business elite.

Soeharto chose to respond to the conglomerate-bashing from a narrower perspective. For him, as for many members of the so-called 1945 generation, complaints about social justice and fair competition trigger an almost reflexive defence of cooperatives. The 1945 Constitution, as mentioned earlier, spells out an important role for cooperatives, and Soeharto has taken pains to stress his fealty to the cooperative movement. In reality, however, cooperatives have fallen far short of their constitutionally prescribed place in society. The roughly 34 000 active cooperatives account for less than 5 per cent of gross domestic product, and they are by far the junior partner to private and government-owned companies. Predominantly rural-based and engaged in agricultural production, cooperatives are largely viewed as inefficient, corrupt and smothered by central government bureaucracy. When cooperatives hold important meetings, for example, an official of Jakarta's Ministry of Cooperatives must attend.

Their performance aside, cooperatives retain a certain rhetorical value. In his autobiography, Soeharto wrote about Indonesians' fears that 'Chinese capital' had become an 'economic dynasty'. That is, he said, consolingly, 'only a temporary situation. In the near future the government will direct this set of circumstances so that [Chinese-owned] capital assets are truly employed in the process of development to improve the welfare of the people.'[6] By 1990, it seemed, the time had come. In his annual budget speech in January of that year, Soeharto 'appealed' to private companies to transfer up to 25 per cent of their equity to cooperatives. Banks, he suggested, should help out by lending money to them. And on 4 March, Indonesia's corporate titans arrived at Soeharto's Tapos ranch to have the message drummed in. The cameras of the state-owned television network, TVRI, were rolling.

Soeharto told the assembled businessmen their success came from the struggles of all Indonesian people and that they were obliged to contribute to all three legs of Indonesia's 'development trilogy': growth, national stability and equitable distribution of wealth. To do their bit for the third leg, Soeharto said, businessmen should sell their shares to cooperatives. 'In this way, the social gap can be minimised.' The event, with Soeharto playing teacher to the Chinese schoolchildren, was broadcast in its entirety that evening.[7]

Soeharto's ploy hit Jakarta's business community like a tidal wave. Foreign investors were spooked. Owners of shares listed on the Jakarta Stock Exchange worried that their holdings would be diluted. In the following weeks and months the conglomerate heads scrambled to demonstrate their commitment to narrowing the 'social gap'. Elaborate rules were drawn up to clarify which cooperatives were eligible for the share purchases and how they would be financed (by the selling companies themselves). The technocrats, meanwhile, who clearly had not been consulted by Soeharto, scurried around privately reassuring businessmen there would be no forced share sales. It was agreed, quietly, that conglomerates would aim to transfer 1 per cent, not 25 per cent, of their shares to cooperatives. Most Chinese leaders simply resigned themselves to the economics of the new program. 'It's like they raised the tax rate by one per cent. It's no big deal. It's just part of the cost of doing business here,' one of the Tapos invitees said.[8]

Gradually, the initial alarm over Soeharto's 'appeal' subsided. Cynics viewed the exercise as little more than a clever piece of politicking. It had shown Soeharto was cognisant of the resentment building up against the conglomerates and that he was prepared to distance himself, at least rhetorically, from the business magnates he had helped create. If the initiative did not really address the underlying problems, no matter. But for others, and especially for the Chinese business groups, the Tapos episode engendered a sense of disquiet. Even for those who consider Soeharto's political acuity second to none, it was largely inexplicable.

Flinging away his normal caution, Soeharto had in effect highlighted for the entire nation that, in his view, the Chinese business community was responsible for Indonesia's 'social gap'. In one fell swoop, Soeharto had undone a great deal of New Order effort to sweep ethnic divisions under the carpet. Paradoxically, it reinforced the impression held by many that the Chinese businessmen were collectively a stronger economic force than the government. But worst of all, the Tapos interlude resolved nothing. It addressed, at best, only a part of the Chinese–*pribumi* problem and even then not very effectively. The 'social gap' was a real issue, no doubt, but handing over equity shares to ineptly run cooperatives was hardly likely to make a difference.

Soeharto's Tapos initiative was unsettling for the economy because it made the Chinese nervous without really lowering *pribumi* concerns. And given the role ethnic Chinese play in the private sector, any measures which sap their confidence are by definition bad for the economy. But more to the point, Soeharto's plan was more an attempt to avoid the Chinese–*pribumi* issue than an effort to deal with it. This was largely due to his failure to gauge the underlying reasons for the anti-conglomerate sentiment, one of which is a feeling held by many in the Indonesian elite that Soeharto, through favouritism to his Chinese cronies, was locking the larger *pribumi* businessmen out of the corporate big leagues. It is a grievance aimed squarely at the centre of Soeharto's patrimonial style of rule.

The Chinese in history

Economic success for the Chinese in Indonesia is not a new phenomenon.
Prior to independence, the Dutch relied primarily on the Chinese to keep
the colonial enterprise ticking over, a role which served the interests of
both sides. The merchant Chinese occupied a nebulous middle ground
between the colonised and the colonisers: Chinese merchants were granted
monopolies on a wide assortment of commodities and goods; in many
areas they acted as de facto tax collectors for the Dutch; and Chinese
lending syndicates took care of most of the colony's banking needs. Over
time, their economic links with the Dutch powers enabled the Chinese to
put peasants, Dutch officials and the *priyayi*—Javanese aristocracy—in
their debt, figuratively and literally. Economic clout entitled the Chinese
to a degree of protection not available to other colonial subjects. Writing
about the Chinese in Java in the nineteenth century, historian James Rush
says, 'Where the economy was concerned, the Chinese were ubiquitous
and essential. Sooner or later everyone doing business in Java had to do
business with a Chinese—from the Dutch planter needing wagons and
tools to a Javanese villager with fruits and eggs to sell.'9

But it was not only business affairs which set the Chinese apart. In
many other ways, Rush says, Chinese 'separateness' was emphasised by
the Chinese themselves or forced on them by the Dutch. Legally, the
Chinese enjoyed a higher status than the Javanese. In civil and criminal
matters, they were subject to the legal codes for the 'Natives' but in
commercial matters they were on a level with the Europeans. Chinese
officers 'advised' Dutch judges in legal matters involving a Chinese. The
Chinese were separated by education, with most Chinese children studying
at Chinese-language schools. The Chinese were also segregated into
specially marked neighbourhoods. These Chinese quarters live on today
in many Indonesian cities. Even in everyday appearance, the Chinese were
different. The Dutch required Chinese men to wear a long braid down
their back—the mark of the Manchu—and to dress in typically Chinese
fashion.

Not surprisingly, all these factors helped open up a gulf between the
Chinese and the indigenous aristocracy, the latter being employed by the
Dutch as officials in the colonial administration. The Javanese and other
indigenous groups deeply resented the economic advantages enjoyed by
the Chinese and, as one consequence, came to look down on business as
an unworthy vocation. In the mid-1800s, however, Chinese fortunes took
a turn for the worse when Dutch reformers, repelled by colonial exploitation, began to chip away at Chinese power. In this, they were aided by
colonial officials—both Dutch and Javanese—who were themselves
uncomfortable with the degree of influence the Chinese had accumulated.

At the same time, rifts were developing within the Chinese community between what were called *totok* and *peranakan* Chinese. *Totoks* were the 'pure' Chinese, usually recent immigrants, who took naturally to the hustle and bustle of commerce. The longer established *peranakans*, in contrast, were more deeply assimilated into the Javanese culture; many had inter-married, and they tended to stand out less, at least in terms of occupation, from other groups. Many *peranakans* shared with the *priyayi* a view that the *totoks* were crass and unscrupulous. For their part, *totoks* considered *peranakans* uppity and soft. Although a century has passed, many of these attitudes linger on.

Such nuances mattered little to the Javanese. As the Chinese links with—and protection from—the Dutch withered, Javanese antipathy toward all Chinese increased. The Javanese began to look on Chinese business practices as not merely serving colonial interests but as a principal cause of poverty among the non-Chinese colonial subjects.[10] By the turn of the century, the indigenous aristocracy had become deeply hostile to the Chinese, an antipathy passed on to the very earliest leaders of the budding Indonesian nationalist movement. As Rush puts it: 'Amidst the masterless commotion of commercial competition in the [twentieth] century's first decade, sinophobia infected the embryo of the modern Indonesian national consciousness.'[11]

During the eighteenth and nineteenth centuries, many Chinese were employed as coolies on rubber, tobacco or palm-oil plantations, or in mines. In the 1920s, however, when a new wave of *totok* immigration caused the Chinese population to rise by more than fifty per cent to over 1.2 million, 'large numbers of Chinese in Indonesia began to move [off the plantations] . . . into what today are commonly regarded as their characteristic roles as small-scale traders, *warung* (small shop) operators, commodity dealers, and money lenders,' explains Jamie Mackie.[12] One consequence of this occupational shift was to widen the rift between *totoks* and *peranakans*. The great explosion of Chinese commercial activity in the 1920s and 1930s came from the *totoks*. They moved in great numbers to rural areas and opened retail stores, trading outlets and restaurants. But the *peranakans*, already comfortable in the cities, sought different kinds of jobs. 'Their greater access to education and a more settled lifestyle,' Mackie notes, 'inclined them toward salaried and professional jobs, wher-ever possible.'[13]

Indonesia's struggle for independence did little to improve the stature of the Chinese in the eyes of indigenous Indonesians. Although some ethnic Chinese took part in battles against the Dutch, many Indonesians, acutely aware of the benefits the Chinese enjoyed under colonial rule, tended to suspect the Chinese community's true commitment to Indones-ian independence and sovereignty. The view of Chinese as essentially outsiders—as spectators to rather than participants in the nationalist cause—is still widely held in Indonesia. In 1991, for example, Soeharto's half-brother Probosutedjo criticised Chinese firms for not selling enough shares to cooperatives: 'We still doubt their sense of nationalism,' he said.[14]

The first twenty years of Indonesian independence was for the Chinese a period of extreme political vulnerability. Citizenship was not automatic. In 1950, by one estimate, slightly more than one-half of the 2.1 million Chinese living in Indonesia were considered aliens.[15] Throughout the 1950s their citizenship status was vague, prone to change and the subject of sharp disagreement among the country's early political leaders. Sukarno had room for the Chinese in his Pancasila society but there were limits to how much protection he could give them without alienating other parts of his constituency. In the earliest days of the Old Order, some Chinese looked to the Indonesian Communist Party for protection, but that didn't last. In 1952 the communist leader D. N. Aidit removed the Chinese from the party's leadership, believing them to be a political liability in the campaign for mass popularity.

If anything, public perceptions of the Chinese deteriorated as the 1950s progressed. Independence had altered neither the dominating presence of the Chinese at the petty trading level, nor the resentment that this caused.[16] And to many newly independent Indonesians, the Chinese penchant for secluding themselves socially and residentially struck them as arrogant and haughty. The non-stop political ferment both under parliamentary democracy and later under Sukarno's Guided Democracy made life increasingly awkward for the Chinese, who found themselves the scapegoats for a variety of political grievances. The parallel with the Jewish experience in Europe is an apt one. Like the Jews, the Chinese in Indonesia are considered to be commercially driven, economically successful, demographically few, politically vulnerable and socially reclusive. One scholar, writing on Thailand, portrayed the Chinese minority in that country as 'pariah entrepreneurs'.[17] This unbecoming description would not be out of place in Indonesia.

Within the Chinese community, different views emerged on how to adjust to the new political environment. A debate was joined between those who favoured 'assimilation' and those for 'integration'. The assimilationists felt the Chinese would best be able to protect themselves by abandoning their ethnic identity and merging into the majority *pribumi* culture. The integrationists, on the other hand, argued that the Chinese community was just another of Indonesia's many indigenous groups, along with Javanese, Acehnese, Bugis, Dayaks and so on. Like these other sub-groups, the pro-integration Chinese felt they should be able to maintain a degree of cultural autonomy. A prominent Chinese organisation, Baperki, carried the banner of integration from 1954 until it was banned in the aftermath of the 1965 coup. Pancasila, and the religious tolerance it espoused, also helped the integrationist cause by permitting the Chinese to cling to one measure of identity. Many Chinese found in Buddhism, Confucianism and to a lesser extent Christianity a means to maintain their distinctiveness.[18]

By the end of the 1950s, anti-Chinese sentiment had reached a new peak. In 1959, Indonesia passed a law forbidding alien-owned retail stores from operating in rural areas, setting off another bout of nationalist sentiment and exacerbating the hostility aimed at the Chinese, both those who had become Indonesian citizens—who were not ostensibly targeted by the new law—and those who were still considered aliens. The law, which was coupled in West Java and South Sulawesi with a ban on rural residence for aliens, had several notable effects.[19] One was to push many Chinese toward the Indonesian Communist Party which, alone among Indonesia's political parties, attempted to defend the rights of the Chinese. Second, the communists' help for the Chinese exposed the party to ever more virulent attack from its political opponents. And lastly, the 1959 law convinced many Chinese that worse times lay ahead and they decided to leave altogether. Offered repatriation by Peking, more than 130 000 Chinese emigrated from Indonesia in 1960. In practical terms, the law was vigorously enforced in only a few areas. But the episode had a profound impact on the Chinese by illuminating just how politically weak they were.

Chinese in the New Order

An even clearer message for the Chinese was to be found in the purge of the Indonesian Communist Party which marked the beginning of the New Order. Mackie describes the period as one 'of terrifying insecurity and spasmodic violence for the Indonesian Chinese. The victors in the 1965–66 power struggle were the very people who had earlier been their most feared enemies, the military and the Muslim right-wing.'[20] Contrary to a widely-held perception, the Chinese were not the primary victims in the slaughter of the communists.[21] For this they owe Aidit's earlier decision to remove Chinese supporters from the party's leadership and the government's retail trade ban in 1959. Most of the killings in 1965–66 took place in rural areas which many Chinese had been forced to leave years before. In Jakarta, anti-Chinese violence was relatively minor. In fact, some of the leaders of the student groups which played such an important role in driving Sukarno from office were ethnic Chinese.

But it is also true that the general climate of hostility surrounding the anti-communist purge put the Chinese in an extremely difficult position. And in some areas, they suffered badly. They were all but driven out of Aceh and parts of North Sumatra and West Kalimantan. And at the very end of 1966, the East Java military commander, then Major General Soemitro, introduced draconian measures seemingly intended to eradicate all Chinese presence from the province. 'I didn't allow them to live in villages, I didn't want them to trade, I didn't even want them in business. No public use of the Chinese language, no Chinese books, no public speaking of Chinese, no Chinese shrines, nothing. We needed a comprehensive solution,' is how he later described it.[22] Soemitro's assault was more than the Chinese were prepared to take quietly. And after a series of protest demonstrations, Soemitro was obliged to take a slightly more conciliatory approach.[23]

At the national level Soeharto also became a strong advocate for Chinese assimilation rather than integration. The 1967 'Basic Policy for the Solution of the Chinese Problem' and other measures set out strict rules for Chinese behaviour. All but one Chinese-language paper were closed and Chinese were told that expressions of religious beliefs should be confined to their homes. Chinese-language schools were gradually phased out; in 1974 the last was closed. Chinese script in public places was outlawed. And Chinese were encouraged to take on Indonesian-sounding names. The last measure produced some unusual results. Liem Bian Kie, a young Chinese intellectual involved in the 1966 student movement, took the name Jusuf Wanandi because 'wana' in Indonesian and 'liem' in Chinese dialect both meant 'forest'. His brother Liem Bian Koen, also active in the student movement, happened to be in Sofia, Bulgaria when the measure was announced. So he took the name Sofyan.

Most Chinese had little choice but to comply with the measures; in the mayhem of the late 1960s they had virtually no means to defend themselves politically. When Indonesia froze diplomatic ties with China in 1967, the isolation of Indonesia's Chinese was complete. Although the Chinese have found in Soeharto's New Order a more conducive economic climate, they have largely remained political and cultural outsiders. Not a single Indonesian of Chinese origin has served in any of Soeharto's cabinets. There are no Chinese in the top ranks of the armed forces and Chinese students find it tough going gaining admission to Indonesia's better universities. It is not hard to find Chinese parents who say that it is cheaper to send their children to study at American or European universities than to pay the bribes necessary for a spot at the University of Indonesia.

Seen from this perspective, it is remarkable that the Chinese have prospered in the New Order and that, in a largely hostile cultural milieu, the biggest of the Chinese tycoons have grown so enormously wealthy.[24] Even more remarkable—and even more disturbing to many *pribumis*—is that Chinese wealth accrued under Soeharto's authoritarian rule has given the Chinese business community a (relative) degree of political influence far in excess of what it would enjoy in a more democratic setting.

How did this transformation come about?[25] The simple answer is that the Chinese are good at business. But there is more to it than that.

Culturally, the Chinese had a head start in the game of capitalism. Business and commerce have long been acceptable to the Chinese; for *pribumis*, this idea is relatively new. Traditionally, the Chinese have put a high priority on education and, in general, it remains true that the Chinese in Indonesia are better educated than their indigenous counterparts. Perhaps as a consequence of their political vulnerability, the Chinese tend to save much of their money, distrust strangers and depend to a great extent on personal relationships and family networks, all of which are conducive to the rapid growth of family-run businesses. Often, their family networks extend into broader affiliations with overseas Chinese communities throughout the region.

These alliances, in turn, give Chinese firms 'access to well-established networks of credit, market information, and domestic and overseas trading contacts, which enable the stronger among them to ride out fluctuations of business cycles,' says Mackie, a frequent writer on the Chinese in Southeast Asia. Of course, he adds, most Chinese firms 'also have to rely on political connections, bribes, and payoffs to ensure immunity from arbitrary imposts.'[26] The closing off of other activities—military service, academia, government—to the Chinese reinforced their business concentration. Lastly, it's hard to deny that the Chinese have a certain flair for entrepreneurship. They are, as one writer puts it, 'a hardy, self-reliant and, above all, a risk-taking lot'.[27] Equally, there is no denying that the Chinese have benefited from the changes Soeharto has wrought. On the one hand, the gradual depoliticisation of Indonesia reduced the Chinese community's political vulnerability while, on the other, Soeharto's attention to economic development created a climate in which the business skills of the Chinese could be put to good use.

The Chinese learned to adapt themselves strikingly well to the new state of affairs. Instead of turning to the left for protection—as they had under Sukarno—they increasingly turned to the right. Chinese businessmen built up strong and mutually beneficial bonds with new powers: the military. The term *cukong* came into use, meaning 'boss' or 'master' and denoting a relationship between a Chinese 'who knew how to raise money and an Indonesian official (often an army officer) who could provide protection and influence'.[28] The *cukong* relationship repeated itself up and down the bureaucracy, from Soeharto to the top generals to regional military commanders, provincial governors and lesser administration officials. The mutual benefits were obvious: Soeharto wanted to encourage new investment in Indonesia, the military was always short of budget resources, and the Chinese desperately needed powerful patrons. By the 1980s, Dick Robison says, 'the economic fortunes of the . . . Indonesian ruling class [were] firmly intertwined with those of the Chinese'.[29]

In exchange for generating new business activity and for supplying funds to their political patrons, the big Chinese *cukongs* received the usual litany of favours: tax breaks, state bank funding, access to import and trading licences, introductions to foreign investors and freedom from harassment. Sudjono Humardhani, one of Soeharto's top fix-it men in the early New Order period, reportedly arranged a series of joint ventures between leading *cukongs* and major Japanese investors. According to Sofyan Wanandi, the previously mentioned student activist who became a leading businessman, Humardhani was responsible for, among others, bringing together Toyota with William Soeryadjaya and Matsushita with Thajeb Gobel.[30] Both men are ethnic Chinese. Today, the Astra Group founded by Soeryadjaya is Indonesia's largest automobile producer and the Gobel Group is Indonesia's largest manufacturer of electronic appliances.

By the early 1970s resentment of the *cukongs'* privileges fuelled criticism of Soeharto's regime by students, journalists and disaffected politicians, and was a principal cause of the Malari riots in 1974. Following the mid-1970s oil boom, however, the typical *cukong* relationship became less common, although less because of a conscious decision by Soeharto than because oil wealth gave the bureaucracy—and the military—less need to seek outside sources of funding. For many Chinese-owned firms, the nationalist phase of economic policymaking is remembered for an ever greater number of bureaucratic obstacles being placed in their path although, to be sure, it was a profitable period for the most politically well-connected among them.

Paradoxically, government regulations on investment and production in the early 1980s encouraged many of the Chinese firms to diversify their businesses and create the conglomerates which became the targets of such heated criticism by the end of the decade. 'If you had a profit,' explains economist Djisman Simandjuntak, 'and you wanted to re-invest in your business, oftentimes you couldn't because there were restrictions on production capacity. So, businesses had to invest in other sectors. [The nationalists'] policies promoted extensive investment, not intensive investment.'[31]

Throughout the 1980s, the biggest Chinese groups maintained close ties to government ministries important to their businesses but for the most part the government *fasilitas* (facilities) which put them on the road to corporate success became gradually less important within their business empires. Many, though certainly not all, of the big Chinese firms have made or are making the switch from family-run enterprises to modern, professionally-run corporations. Collectively, the Chinese firms, with their ability to attract financing and investment from abroad, have played a crucial role in the Indonesian economic resurgence which began in the late 1980s.

By no means has the Chinese need to 'buy' protection disappeared. With resentment of their economic domination lying so close to the surface, the Chinese remain acutely aware of the importance of cultivating friends in powerful places. As noted above, the Chinese were reminded of their political vulnerability in the late 1980s when their business activities came under closer public scrutiny. As deregulation lifted the veil on corporate wealth in the late 1980s, it was revealed that of Indonesia's top corporations, all but a handful were owned by ethnic Chinese. One business consulting firm, Data Consult, estimated in a 1989 survey that 163 of Indonesia's top 200 business groups were controlled by Chinese interests. More recently, the Indonesian economist Sjahrir estimated that of the 162 companies listed on the Jakarta Stock Exchange in mid-1993, 'at least 80% [were] owned by ethnic Chinese'.[32]

Leading businessmen Mochtar Riady, Eka Cipta Wijaya, Prajogo Pangestu, The Nin King, Soehargo Gondokusumo, Teguh Sutantyo and Tan Siong Kie fall into the *totok* category. Most of them have received a Chinese-language education and remain more comfortable speaking Chinese than Indonesian. All of them, though to varying degrees, owe their corporate pre-eminence to mutually beneficial relationships forged with top government officials. As the Data Consult report put it: 'The road to success in the formation of conglomerates [in Indonesia] always involves the participation of those in power.'[33]

Standing above all the others is Liem Sioe Liong, a *totok* tycoon who has amassed great wealth and achieved more than a little notoriety in Soeharto's Indonesia. (Liem's Indonesianised name is Sudono Salim and his business empire is known as the Salim Group.) Some argue that Soeharto's close, trusting relationship with Liem is one important explanation for why the Chinese business community has done so well in the New Order. True or not, a sizeable portion of the *pribumi* business community takes a dark view of Liem's relationship with Soeharto. For them, Liem is both the most visible beneficiary of Soeharto's patronage and a good example of much that is wrong with Soeharto's patrimonial style of rule.

Case study: Liem Sioe Liong

Twenty-one-year-old Liem Sioe Liong left China's Fujian province in 1937 and arrived in Central Java all but penniless. As a petty trader, he sold peanuts, cloves, bicycle parts and myriad other products, much of it on credit. Liem gained profits and some important contacts in the 1940s by selling clothes, medicine, soap, food and military supplies to the nationalist forces. In the 1950s, he became an important supplier to the army's prestigious Diponegoro division headquartered in Semarang, Central Java. The division's chief supply and financial officer—and later in the decade its commander—was Lieutenant Colonel Soeharto.[34]

Soeharto evidently trusted Liem and was comfortable with his low-profile manner. Apart from forming this one crucial relationship, however, Liem's business history prior to the mid-1960s is undistinguished. His trading activities grew and allegedly extended into smuggling cloves and sugar. He started some small manufacturing operations making nails and textiles and moved his headquarters to Jakarta. A banking joint venture with an army foundation did poorly. By the mid-1960s Liem was a passably successful Chinese entrepreneur but not especially well-known. Soeharto's ascension to power, however, would soon change that.

In 1990 the sprawling Salim Group's revenues reached an estimated US$8–9 billion, with about 60 per cent of that amount coming from its Indonesian operations. Salim's domestic sales alone were equivalent to about five per cent of Indonesia's gross domestic product. The group, employing some 135 000 Indonesians, encompasses over 300 separate companies involved in a dizzying array of activities. Liem is the single biggest player in private banking, cement and several key commodities. He has major stakes in automobile manufacturing, processed foods, natural and oil-based chemicals, and property. The group is growing rapidly in wood-based industries, retailing, sugar processing, electronics and tele-communications. Overseas, the Liem empire stretches from hotels in Singapore and Hong Kong, to drugstores in the Philippines, to computers in Australia, to banking in the United States, to car-making in Holland, to telephones in Malaysia, to shoe factories and hotels in China and to other locales far and wide. The Salim Group is, by a factor of two or three, Indonesia's largest privately owned enterprise.

Liem has built his empire with a true entrepreneur's eye for business opportunities and a talent for attracting first-rate partners. He is not considered a particularly able manager in his own right. The majority of Liem's most successful businesses are run by his partners, like Mochtar Riady in banking, Ciputra in property, Eka Cipta Wijaya in palm oil, Djuhar Sutanto in cement, and Malaysian Robert Kuok in flour. But his greatest asset is his relationship with Soeharto. It is through this relation-ship that Liem accumulated the capital for his later empire-building and which enables him to keep many paces ahead of his competitors.

Liem's capital-accumulating phase began in the earliest days of the New Order. He was awarded in 1968 one of two licences to import cloves, the key ingredient in Indonesia's ubiquitous clove-scented *kretek* ciga-rettes. Two other Liem trading companies, Waringin and Waringin Kentj-ana, prospered from the trade in coffee and rubber. (In 1970 a Commission of Inquiry into Corruption appointed by the president identified Waringan as one of five companies needing 'urgent' investigation, but the matter was never pursued.) Liem came across one of his most durable cash cows in 1969 when he was granted a partial monopoly—which later became complete—on the import, milling and distribution of flour. In 1990 Liem's Bogasari Flour Mills, then the world's largest commercial buyer of wheat, posted revenues of about US$460 million. Although Bogasari imports wheat directly, its purchases are funnelled through the national logistics board Bulog. The price at which Bulog 'sells' wheat to Bogasari is heavily subsidised by the government—equivalent to about US$80 per tonne of milled flour, according to the World Bank. Bogasari mills the wheat into flour and 'sells' it back to Bulog after tacking on a margin of around 30 per cent, about five times higher than mill margins in the United States, itself a high-cost miller.[35]

Bogasari's padded returns are paid for through higher prices to consumers and downstream industries such as plywood mills, which use wheat flour as a glue, and the shrimp industry, which uses flour as a feed binder. Salim's stranglehold over wheat supplies has given the group a commanding advantage in the production and sales of noodles, pasta and other products which use wheat flour. One of Salim's products, instant noodle Sarimi, has a 75 per cent share of the domestic market. Other Salim products take up one-third of the market for milk, over half of the snack food market and more than one-fifth of baby foods.

In the mid-1970s Liem opened several cement factories. With the government setting the price of cement above world market levels, it was a lucrative business. In 1983–85, with government encouragement, Liem built an additional 4.5 million tonnes of cement-producing capacity, making his West Java cement complex Indocement the largest producer in the world. An economic downturn in the mid-1980s, however, devastated sales and put Indocement deep in the red. The government was quick to the rescue. In 1986 the government injected US$325 million into Indocement in exchange for a 35 per cent stake. It also allowed Indocement to refinance expensive foreign currency debts with rupiah loans from several state-owned banks. Three years later, Indocement wanted to raise additional capital through a share flotation on the Jakarta Stock Exchange but did not satisfy a requirement that companies going public must have at least two consecutive years of profit. A few phone calls later, the Finance Ministry issued Indocement a waiver. By 1992, Liem's cement companies accounted for more than half of Indonesia's total cement capacity.

In 1983, with the government forced to cut back on its investment commitments, Liem was persuaded to invest in a new US$875 million steel plant. Cold Rolling Mill Indonesia (CRMI) was to produce steel plates and sheets using the output of state-owned Krakatau Steel. A Liem-led consortium bought 40 per cent of CRMI directly and twenty per cent indirectly though a Luxembourg-based firm. Liem put about US$100 million into CRMI as equity and helped arrange funding from international banks. In exchange, the government gave Liem an exclusive import monopoly on a variety of steel products, the prices of which subsequently rose dramatically. Liem further covered his exposure by buying materials from Krakatau at below market prices and selling back to Krakatau at above market prices.

Despite these subsidies, by 1988 the mill had racked up debts totalling US$610 million, was operating at a loss and Liem wanted out. In 1989 Liem proposed that the government buy out the company's private share-holders for US$290 million, absolve the private shareholders of respon-sibility for the mill's past and future debt obligations and leave the private shareholders with some claim on future profits. An optimistic shopping list, considering that CRMI's 'shareholders' interests are in fact without value,' in the opinion of international banking advisers retained by the government.[36] Nonetheless, the deal went through.

Examples of the give-and-take between Liem and Soeharto extend well beyond flour, cement and steel. Liem's empire straddles the line between private enterprise and government like no other Indonesian organisation. When Soeharto decided in the late 1980s that Indonesia ought to grow and process more sugar, Liem started planting. In 1990, Liem controlled 20 000 hectares of sugar plantations and another 80 000 hectares, thanks to cheap state bank credit, were under cultivation. And when Soeharto, worried by a rice shortage in 1991, appealed to Indonesia's conglomerates to open new rice fields, Salim complied, and was also granted the licence to import the rice that Indonesia needed.

In 1989 Liem wanted to set up an in-house system of satellite-con-nected computer terminals to link his group's banking, automobile and trading operations. The only problem was that another company already had a monopoly on this product—a monopoly granted by the Telecom-munications Ministry—and its prices, in Liem's view, were too high. On 6 February 1990, Telecommunications Minister Soesilo Soedarman per-sonally wrote to Liem's son, Anthony Salim, permitting the Salim Group to lease its own channel on Indonesia's Palapa satellite, effectively allow-ing Salim to sidestep the monopoly.[37] The favour was not extended to Indonesia's other conglomerates.

Later that same year, Bank Duta, majority-owned by three social welfare foundations headed by Soeharto, announced it had lost US$420 million from speculating on foreign exchange markets. Liem promptly made good half the bank's losses, while another Chinese businessman, Prajogo Pangestu, made good the other half.

Exactly what Soeharto obtains from the relationship with Liem is hard to pinpoint. On the one hand, Liem has agreed to support development objectives favoured by Soeharto, such as in the cement, steel, sugar and rice industries. And he stands ready to help in emergencies like the Bank Duta fiasco. But there would appear to be a more personal connection as well. Most of the Salim Group's major investments—Bogasari, Indoce-ment, CRMI, among others—are owned by several businessmen known as the Liem investors. These include Liem, his old Fukian neighbour

Djuhar Sutanto, Acehnese businessmen Ibrahim Risjad and Soeharto's cousin Sudwikatmono.[38] The usual breakdown among the Liem investors is 40 per cent each for Liem and Sutanto, and 10 per cent each for Risjad and Sudwikatmono. Many speculate that Sudwikatmono acts as a front man for Soeharto. 'Charitable' foundations controlled by Soeharto have stakes in some of Liem's most profitable operations. And many Salim Group ventures have one or more of Soeharto's children as partners. Two of Soeharto's children, for example, own 32 per cent of Bank Central Asia, Liem's flagship lender and the largest private bank in Indonesia.

Liem's second son and heir apparent, Anthony, has grand designs to remake the Salim Group into a modern, professional, globally active organisation which keeps a lengthy arm's distance from Indonesia's powerholders. He plans to sell off many companies in which the group does not have management control. He intends to detach the Liem investors from the Salim Group's core activities and make the bottom line, rather than political convenience, the main criterion for entering and exiting businesses. It is an imposing task. The Salim Group is so deeply embedded in Soeharto's patrimonial network, with so many favours still owed and expected by both sides, that shifting the group's bearing may prove impossible.

Anthony, not surprisingly, tends to downplay the impact of his father's relationship with Soeharto on the Group's fortune:

> We don't deny we had good access to capital in the early days [of the New Order]. But credit shouldn't just be given to capital formation. The important thing is what happened after that. At the time, there were plenty of other people who had the same access to capital we had, but they didn't manage it properly. Capital is only one thing, but management is another thing and business vision is another thing . . . The monopolies that we were granted were like a glass of water that gets the machine going. Admittedly, the first glass of water is the most important, but relative to the size of Salim's revenues today, the [monopoly-derived] revenues are reasonably moderate.[39]

At a more general level, Anthony defends Salim's evolution as one shaped predominantly by the environment in which it existed. 'A business organisation responds not only to business opportunities but also to the [prevailing] economic, social and political situation as a whole . . . The formation of the Salim Group was by accident, not by design. [Our growth] was driven by the opportunities available to us,' he said.[40]

Few dispute that both Liem and Anthony are shrewd, tough and intrepid businessmen though the two remain more feared than admired. Although personally unassuming and soft-spoken, Liem's stature in Indonesia makes him a figure not to be crossed. Many businessmen seek partnerships with Salim not just for the business opportunities but for the protection they hope will follow. In 1990 Anthony decided that Salim and

Eka Cipta Wijaya's Sinar Mas group should split their joint holdings in palm-oil cultivation and processing. Anthony, uncomfortable with the elder Wijaya's management style—which is, curiously, not dissimilar from that of Anthony's father—wanted more control over the palm-oil operations. Wijaya, however, lobbied strenuously against a complete split of the two groups' joint assets and proposed instead that each group retain a minority stake in the companies of the other. The motivation had nothing to do with the underlying businesses, Salim and Sinar Mas executives said at the time, but with Wijaya's fear of severing links with the politically powerful Liem.

There would seem to be little likelihood that Liem will become less controversial in the 1990s than he has been in the preceding two decades. His rapid international expansion, for example, has been accompanied by criticism that he is stashing assets offshore ahead of Soeharto's departure from power. In 1990, 40 per cent of Liem's revenues and more than one-quarter of his group's assets were located outside Indonesia. 'Geography is out of date,' says Anthony, sounding every bit the modern-day manager. 'We're talking about globalisation.'[41] But many other Indonesians are talking about capital flight. Liem's investments in China are a particularly sore subject, given that many Indonesians still harbour suspicions that some Indonesian-Chinese feel more loyal to China than Indonesia. Liem fanned the flames with a November 1990 trip to China during which he told an Indonesian reporter: '*Sudah 30 tahun saya tidak pulang.* (It's been thirty years since I last went home.)'[42] In late 1993, Liem found himself mired again in a controversy about capital flight when it was revealed that the Salim Group had become the first privately owned Indonesian group to receive government permission to sell equity shares on an overseas stock market.[43]

Finally, Anthony's protestations to the contrary, it would seem that many in the Salim Group see no reason to change a business approach that has been fabulously successful. In June 1992 one Salim unit, publicly listed Indocement, acquired controlling stakes in two other Salim businesses: Bogasari Flour Mills and a package of food companies in the Indofood division. It was a typically shrewd Liem manoeuvre. The Liem investors were able to cash out of their holdings in Bogasari, using some of their own money, government funds (because the government still owned shares in Indocement) and funds raised through the public market. More importantly, by bringing the lucrative Bogasari wheat monopoly into a publicly listed company, Liem hoped to give it a degree of insulation from the economic reformers within the government. Ironically, when the news was first announced, some assumed the revocation of the wheat monopoly was imminent. That proved to be an ungrounded fear. When the Bogasari acquisition was still in the idea stage, Anthony Salim and colleagues paid a visit to Bustanil Arifin, who then headed the government's logistics board Bulog, the source of Bogasari's monopoly. 'They signed an agreement with me,' explained Arifin, 'that the [wheat import] monopoly will stay in place after the Indocement acquisition. So, for as long as I'm around, we won't be deregulating wheat imports.'[44] As it turned out, Arifin was replaced in the cabinet formed in March 1993 and three months later the government announced an 'opening' of the wheat trade. Once the fine print was scrutinised, however, it became clear that enough restrictions remained on new investments in wheat milling operations—such as Bulog retaining control over wheat imports—that Bogasari's hold over the domestic wheat market was unlikely to be threatened, at least not in the short run.

In a more general sense, Liem owes his controversial stature not to the conduct of his companies in the 1990s but to his close relationship with Soeharto from the very beginning of the New Order. It is a history that will not go away and will not be forgotten, especially by Liem's *pribumi* rivals. On the contrary, it is a matter of intense envy and dissatisfaction to many *pribumi* businessmen that Soeharto's help—Anthony's 'glasses of water'—is what lay behind Liem's initial rise to prominence. These businessmen flatly reject Anthony's contention that government favouritism played only a small part in Salim's success, and they even more ardently dispute the notion that *pribumis* and Chinese shared equal access to Soeharto's patronage in the early days of the New Order or, for that matter, share equal access today.

Balancing the scales

Coping with this resentment is one of the most important, if delicate, tasks facing the Indonesian leadership in the 1990s. Politically, the prospects for a more pluralistic system are clouded by the government's fear of an upsurge in anti-Chinese sentiment and perhaps even violence. The stakes are scarcely lower on the economic front. If, for example, the technocrats are to generate wider public support for further economic reform, they will have to convince *pribumi* business leaders that their program does not provide special advantages to the Chinese. To do that, the government will either have to distance itself from top Chinese tycoons such as Liem—an option Soeharto is unlikely to choose—or develop new government programs specifically aimed at helping *pribumi* businesses. The danger of the latter approach is that, if overdone, it could spark capital flight by the Chinese, dampen interest by foreign investors and damage overall economic growth.

The politically thorny task of managing a wealthy ethnic-Chinese minority is not Indonesia's alone. Apart from Singapore, which is three-quarters Chinese, and tiny Brunei, the other members of the Association of Southeast Asian Nations (ASEAN)—Thailand, Malaysia and the Philippines—all grapple with a 'Chinese problem'. But in Thailand and the Philippines, the Chinese minority has been largely assimilated into the majority population. In neither country has the government attempted to foster a specifically indigenous business class or to place hurdles in the path of Chinese corporate expansion.

There are no easy explanations for this. The degree to which the Chinese elite was willing to assimilate into the local population—and the degree of interest among indigenous elites in having this happen—is certainly an important factor. So too, probably, is religion. In comparing Indonesia and Thailand, Mackie points out that 'Islam seems to pose a barrier to acculturation and assimilation [for the Chinese], whereas Buddhism [in Thailand] attracted Chinese adherents very easily'.[45] Malaysia, where Islam is the official religion, has been the most explicit and aggressive of all ASEAN nations in attacking wealth imbalances between its Chinese community—which makes up 35 per cent of the population—and the indigenous Malay majority. It launched a comprehensive economic affirmative action program—known as the New Economic Policy (NEP)—two years after race riots broke out in 1969.

The NEP's two main objectives were the eradication of poverty and the redistribution of the nation's wealth through direct government intervention. Universities and government offices were to favour Malays over ethnic Chinese. Huge state-owned investment companies gathered equity stakes in foreign and Chinese-owned firms and distributed the gains to indigenous Malay businessmen. The NEP's twenty-year target was to increase the Malay share of the nation's capital to 30 per cent. By 1991, the Malay share had risen to about 25 per cent, short of the NEP target but a long way from the Malays' estimated 1970 share of three per cent.

Predictably, assessments of the NEP vary widely. Critics say its overtly racist character has exacerbated ethnic tensions and created a class of phoney capitalists who owe their wealth and status to government largesse rather than business acumen. Supporters note that the 1969 race riots have not been repeated. Malaysian Chinese, while resentful of the favourable treatment accorded indigenous Malays, have accommodated themselves to the situation and remain powerful in many fields.

According to members of his inner circle, Soeharto considers NEP-type policies an affront to the Javanese notions of unity and harmony. The principles of Pancasila, Soeharto often reminds, establish that all of Indonesia's myriad subgroups are to be treated the same and, indeed, many Indonesians would be uncomfortable with overtly discriminatory policies. But rhetoric aside, Indonesia since independence has engaged in numerous affirmative action initiatives, none of which has made much headway in denting *pribumi* resentment of the Chinese and all of which have been bureaucratically confused, poorly implemented and highly vulnerable to abuse.

From 1950 to 1957 Indonesia devoted considerable financial resources and political capital in support of what was called the Benteng program, a subsidised credit policy designed to help indigenous traders. By allocating foreign exchange credit and most import licences to indigenous Indonesians, the program attempted to cut into Chinese and Dutch domination of trade into and out of Indonesia. The program was a massive failure. Many Indonesian importers simply sold their licences to Chinese traders and many others defaulted on loans to state banks. Importers sprang up like mushrooms: from 250 in 1950 to 7000 by mid-1953. Thirty-seven per cent of all government foreign exchange credit was made available to Benteng importers in 1952; this rose to 76 per cent by 1954.[46]

The program's principal goal—to create a viable indigenous business class capable of competing with the Chinese—was never reached. Dick Robison, whose pioneering work on Indonesian capitalism was published in 1986, said that under the program 'what was being consolidated was not an indigenous merchant bourgeoisie but a group of licence brokers and political fixers'.[47]

The Indonesian economy in the 1960s was in such dire shape that there was little scope for government redistribution initiatives. But the Malari riots of 1974 refocused policymakers' attention on the problem. Rules requiring foreign investors to speed up the process of transferring equity to local investors and several subsidised lending programs geared to *pribumi* businessmen were introduced. A state-owned investment company Danareksa was set up in 1977 to buy shares in large corporations and sell inexpensive 'investment certificates' to the public. It envisioned a transfer of corporate ownership very similar to what was going on in Malaysia. But the plan required an active stock market, something which wouldn't materialise in Indonesia for another twelve years.

Oil wealth and the increasing influence of the economic nationalists paved the way for more affirmative action in the early 1980s. Several presidential decrees—Kepres 14 in 1979 and Kepres 14A and Kepres 10 in 1980—gave the 'weak economic group', a code phrase for indigenous businessmen, priority in obtaining certain government contracts.[48] For small projects, only the weak group would be allowed to bid. For medium-size projects worth up to US$80 000, 'weak group' bidders were given a five per cent cushion. For big government projects, a new team was set up to decide on project allocations. Team 10, as it would be known, was headed by Sudharmono, the powerful state secretary and, from 1983, chairman of the ruling party Golkar. In 1983, Sudharmono's protege Ginanjar Kartasasmita was named vice-chairman of Team 10.

Team 10, which had authority to oversee government purchases of goods and services worth more than US$800 000 (later lowered to about US$300 000), gave Sudharmono and other economic nationalists great leeway to build up their *pribumi* supporters and afforded Soeharto a new and valuable mechanism for patronage. Conversely, the team, which was initially encouraged by technocrat Widjoyo Nitisastro, proved to be a drastic setback to the technocrats' ambition to let the market determine winners and losers. In its operation, if not in name, Team 10 resembled very closely the government intervention in favour of indigenous businessmen that was taking place in Malaysia.

Throughout the 1980s, Team 10's control over government purchases expanded to cover virtually all ministries and state-owned companies. From 1980 until Team 10 was disbanded in 1988, Rp. 52 trillion worth of government procurements were awarded under its auspices. (Without knowing the annual breakdown of Team 10 contract awards, it is difficult to convert this figure into US dollars. Using 1984's exchange rate, however, it is equivalent to US$48 billion.) To put this figure in perspective, total approved domestic investment over the same period amounted to Rp. 36.2 trillion, of which only an estimated Rp. 15 trillion was actually invested.[49]

By the time it was closed down, Team 10 had become synonymous with fiscal abuse and wholly identified with Soeharto's patrimonial style of rule. 'What Team 10 did was [to] centralise the process [of dispensing patronage],' Jeffrey Winters says, 'drawing patronage power upward and into the centre, and elevate to the level of *formal* national policy a pattern of tight micro-management of opportunity and success throughout the archipelago that had not existed previously.' The recipients of Team 10's beneficence had specific characteristics. They were selected, Winters says, 'for their political and personal proximity to powerful officials in the [presidential] palace and at SEKNEG [the state secretariat], for their utility in securing support in geographical areas or among social groups where the Soeharto regime felt insecure, and for the personal ties of trust that bind different factions jostling for power in Jakarta and in the provinces.'[50]

Team 10's role as provider of corporate seed capital can be seen in the type of businesses in which the larger *pribumis* became active. In a 1989 interview, technocrat Mohammad Sadli explained:

> The existing group of *pribumi* entrepreneurs very much reflects the way they developed out of links to the government. If you look, you'll notice that they have no foothold in production, industry or trade. The *pribumi* businessmen are all lumped together in the services—especially engineering and construction. This is hardly surprising. They all got their start through government contracts to build infrastructure during the latter years of the oil boom.[51]

While the characterisation has become less complete since 1989, it remains true that many of the top *pribumi*-owned businesses depend heavily on government-related contracts. Two important political vehicles for *pribumi* businessmen are the Association of Young Indonesian Businessmen (Hipmi) and the Indonesian Chamber of Commerce and Industry (Kadin). Both are closely allied with the economic nationalist camp. 'We now have slightly more than 6000 members in Hipmi,' said the organisation's chairman Bambang Sugomo in a 1991 interview. 'I'd say about 80 per cent depend substantially on contract work from the government.'[52]

Of the *pribumi* businessmen close to Sudharmono and Ginanjar, the informal leader is Aburizal Bakrie, elected to the top post in Kadin in January 1994. Bakrie is unusual among his peers in that his father was a successful commodities trader as far back as the 1930s. Most are the first generation in their families to succeed at business. Other prominent, younger-generation *pribumi* businessmen include Fadel Muhammad, Iman Taufik, Jusuf and Achmad Kalla, Fahmi Idris, Siswono Yudohusudo, Suryo Sulistio, Rudy Pesik, Suryo Palo, Kamaludin Bachir, Kusumo Martoredjo, Bambang Rachmadi, Ponco Sutowo, Agus Kartasasmita, Abdul Latief, Adiwarsita Adinegoro, Hashim Djojohadikusumo, and Subagio Wiryoatmodjo.

Although acknowledging it was not perfect, *pribumi* businessmen argue that Team 10 has been the New Order's only concerted attempt to extend to them the capital-forming opportunities that they believe Soeharto has showered on favoured Chinese entrepreneurs. 'We lobbied hard for Team 10,' says *pribumi* industrialist Kusumo Martoredjo. 'While it lasted, you could see businesses growing.' Another leading *pribumi* businessman justified Team 10 like this: 'It was Team 10 under Sudharmono that made Bakrie big, it made me big, it made a lot of us big. We have to do more of this. This is how the Chinese got big in the first place.'[53] (Many *pribumi* business leaders are reluctant to speak for attribution on the sensitive *pribumi*–Chinese question.)

Apart from Team 10, the government has made other efforts to narrow the ethnic gap in the economic field. One is to encourage the winners of government contracts to replace imported materials with domestically produced goods wherever possible. Another is the foster-parent program, first mooted in 1980 and resurrected again by then Industry Minister Hartarto in 1990. The idea was to encourage Indonesia's larger firms to take on smaller, *pribumi*-run firms as suppliers, agents, distributors, subcontractors and retailers.[54] The program sputters on but is disliked by leading Chinese-owned firms, who find it vague and confused, as well as by leading *pribumi*-owned companies, who find it patronising and insulting.

The subsidised credit programs introduced after the Malari riots were another attempt to support *pribumi* businesses. However, a great deal of the money never reached its intended beneficiaries, much of it being grabbed by middlemen and stashed in high-yielding time deposits in the very banks which issued the credits. In January 1990, the subsidised credit programs were replaced by a new regulation requiring all banks to allocate twenty per cent of their total loan portfolio to small businesses, defined as those with fixed assets of less than Rp. 600 million (about US$330 000). It was, in a way, an attempt by the government to 'privatise' the task of wealth distribution.

The twenty per cent rule has suffered much the same fate as its subsidised predecessors. Banks have nominally complied but only by creating fictitious borrowers, a charge the chief executive of one leading (Chinese-owned) bank didn't bother to deny: 'Look, my idea was to target the corporate banking market. And then, boom, the central bank says I have to lend twenty per cent to very small companies. I don't have any experience in that market, I have no presence in that market. I don't have bankers who are trained to analyse those sorts of credits. What am I supposed to do?'[55]

Identifying the problem

Overall, Indonesia's varied and expensive endeavours to defuse the hostility aimed at the Chinese community have brought paltry dividends. Partly, this is due to a political reluctance to identify ethnicity as a significant national problem. But another reason is that the so-called Chinese issue is really two separate issues, and official policies have failed to distinguish adequately between the two. The first issue, which might be called the small *pribumi* problem, relates to the concerns of small- and medium-sized *pribumi* businesses. The second, the big *pribumi* problem, pertains to the top 100 or so *pribumi*-owned businesses.

Dealing with the small *pribumi* problem, of course, is scarcely different from the broad problem of economic growth. The priorities in both cases are creating new business opportunities, providing for job growth, generating additional sources of capital, and assuring an equitable distribution of economic gains. The technocrats believe that economic growth is the key to narrowing wealth discrepancies and helping small *pribumis*. But recognising that the private sector must play a leading role in generating economic growth, especially in export-oriented industries, the technocrats are opposed to any curbs on private enterprises, including those owned by Indonesian-Chinese.

The root cause of the 'social gap', the technocrats believe, is that the economic playing field is far from level. The bureaucracy smothers entrepreneurial talent, credit allocation is distorted by ad hoc and poorly implemented subsidised lending, tax collection is inefficient and inequitable, and the legal system is incapable of preventing predatory behaviour by the economically powerful. Government efforts at wealth distribution have simply made the situation worse. Moreover, the costs of these efforts are borne disproportionately by small firms. The best way to help small *pribumis*, the technocrats believe, is to remove government-imposed obstacles to growth, guarantee that the rich pay their fair share of tax, and ensure that the legal system does not discriminate against the politically powerless. Where direct government action is necessary, it should be targeted at the weakest players. Indonesia's former coordinating minister for the economy, Radius Prawiro, put it like this: 'The [*pribumi*-owned] Bakrie Group is already a giant. Forget about them. We have to concentrate on supporting small businesses. This is the real challenge. Our idea is not to hand out the fish, but to hand out fishing poles. Let [the businessmen] compete.'[56]

It is a view the larger Chinese entrepreneurs share. 'The deregulation campaign has improved economic growth and, at the end of the day, that means you have better opportunities for everybody,' said Anthony Salim, chief executive of the Salim Group. 'The focus has to be on 180 million Indonesians, not a few businessmen who already have Rp. 1 billion (US$500 000) but want to have Rp. 100 billion. There are 2.3 million new entrants to the workforce every year. They need jobs. They need a salary each month. They have to be the priority.'[57]

Soeharto, too, is fixing on the small *pribumi* problem when he offers cooperatives as the solution. Frustrated by the slow pace of trickle-down welfare, he believes that strengthening cooperatives is the most appropriate response to complaints about *pemerataan*, or equity. There are two flaws with this approach. The first is that it will not noticeably affect wealth distribution patterns and the second is that it will do little to quiet the loudest critics of economic inequality.

'If social justice and an equitable distribution of wealth are your objectives,' explained economist Kwik Kian Gie in December 1989, 'then there are certain things you need to do. What is very seriously lacking is a regulation on what is fair and unfair competition. We need some kind of anti-trust legislation, some kind of small business protection act. We also need a kind of safety net to protect people against capitalist excesses. There should be an enforced minimum wage, and a social security system for basic needs.'[58] Transferring wealth to cooperatives, the scheme of which Soeharto is so enamoured, contributes little to any of these objectives.

The Nahdlatul Ulama is Indonesia's largest Muslim organisation, with some 30 million followers, and many of its members belong to cooperatives. Even so, its outspoken leader Abdurrahman Wahid writes off Soeharto's cooperatives initiative as a political red herring. 'We need to develop a new approach to small businesses. Cooperatives are unhealthy for us and a burden on society. They are only killing the real entrepreneurs. Everyone knows the cooperatives are just tools of the government,' charges Wahid.[59] In 1991 the Indonesian Democratic Party, of which Kwik Kian Gie is a leading member, submitted to parliament an anti-monopoly bill which attempted to offer better protection for small businesses. The ruling party Golkar refused to consider it.

The case for the big *pribumi* problem is economically weak and politically strong. The debate here is concerned less with the country's macroeconomic performance and more with who shall control the commanding heights of the business community. As Aburizal Bakrie puts it: 'The issue is not only big or small, but who is the big and who is the small.'[60] And on this point, discontent among the top *pribumi* businessmen is rife. Even before the mid-1980s, everyone knew that Liem Sioe Liong had built an extensive business empire, but the deregulation drive beginning in the late 1980s confirmed *pribumi* suspicions that dozens of Chinese-owned businesses had become giants under the New Order. 'Now we have a few elite groups at the top of the pyramid and the large majority of Indonesians at the bottom,' complained businessman Fadel Muhammad in an interview in 1991.[61]

One way to gauge the extent of Chinese corporate influence is to look at what economists call the degree of concentration in specific business sectors. A high degree of concentration means that a high percentage of production of a particular commodity is controlled by relatively few firms. This is the case in Indonesia: a few big firms—state-owned, private and foreign—dominate many industries. By one estimate, two-thirds of all Indonesian manufacturing comes from industries in which the four biggest plants produced at least half of that industry's output.[62] With most of the biggest private Indonesian firms being owned by Chinese families, it is unarguable that the Chinese dominate Indonesian manufacturing, or at least that share of manufacturing controlled by the private sector. An Indonesian consulting firm estimated in 1991 that the sales of the top 200 conglomerates were equivalent to 35 per cent of gross domestic product.[63] In December 1993, Minister for Research and Technology B. J. Habibie said even this figure understates the true extent of Chinese corporate dominance: he told a parliamentary hearing that nearly a third of Indonesia's economy was controlled by the country's top ten conglomerates alone.[64]

The financial sector reforms of 1988 opened up the banking system to new, privately owned banks, many of which were affiliated to Chinese-owned conglomerates. Prior to the reforms, many Chinese businesses were obliged to look overseas for funding. According to *Tempo* magazine, Indonesia's largest circulation weekly, *pribumi*-owned business groups accounted for just twelve per cent of foreign loans made to private Indonesian companies in 1988.[65]

In economic terms, such a high degree of concentration is not necessarily a problem. But politically, it is an explosive issue. *Pribumi* businessmen share a perception that all the leading Chinese businesses owe at least part of their success to 'facilities' handed to them by the government. Some relatively moderate *pribumi* businessmen concede that one explanation for Chinese economic dominance is that *pribumis* are relative newcomers to the business world. Unlike the Chinese, they cannot draw on generations of accumulated commercial experience. 'My father taught me that business was a lower-class activity. He wanted me to work for the government,' says Kusumo Martoredjo, a leading *pribumi* figure. It is a frequently heard comment within *pribumi* circles. Transmigration minister Siswono Yudohusudo, who concurrently runs a sizeable construction company, stretches the point rather further than it needs to go. 'When the *pribumis* were fighting the Dutch, the Chinese were already in business. They had a head start. And in the 1950s and 1960s, the *pribumis* were busy forming the political base of the nation.'[66]

But many top *pribumi* industrialists take a much harder line. To them, it is an article of faith that all, not just some, of the big Chinese firms were given massive government help in getting started and that this is the main reason for their success. 'All the Chinese that were called to Tapos, they're all guilty. It's not true that just some of them have been given facilities and extra help. They all got it,' railed one leading *pribumi* businessman.[67] He and like-minded *pribumis* point to the relatively meagre contribution of the Chinese-owned conglomerates to the national export drive as evidence that government protection and favouritism has left the biggest business groups soft and inefficient.[68]

Anti-Chinese sentiment has not stopped virtually all of the top *pribumi* businessmen from forming joint ventures with ethnic-Chinese partners. Business, after all, is business. But the frustration felt by *pribumi* businessmen is real and often finds expression in sabre-rattling comments. 'The Chinese have to be made to understand that they can't keep the poor falling ever further behind. One day the poor will rise up and take their possessions,' said one. 'We understand the *pribumis* are less capable at business than the Chinese but the Chinese have to help us if they want to live in this country', said another. 'The Chinese need to be reminded that the bulk of the revenues have to stay in the country,' said a third.[69]

Antipathy toward Chinese-owned conglomerates is not limited to *pribumi* businessmen, of course. Some prominent Muslim leaders take the same view. Lukman Harun, a former leader of the Muhammadiyah, a large social and educational organisation for Muslims, says: '[Muslims] can't compete with the Chinese because they have the funds and better relations with the government. That's why the government has to protect the middle class.' Harun believes the government should revive its 1959 edict banning alien Chinese retailers from rural areas, only this time it should include Indonesian-Chinese citizens as well. 'My personal opinion is that the government shouldn't let the conglomerates operate in rural areas, and that includes their banks. Without such a rule, we will all have to surrender to the conglomerates.'[70]

Another Islamic leader, Dawam Rahardjo, holds up Chinese business success as one of the worst failings of Soeharto's administration. 'Unlike the indigenous entrepreneurs, businessmen of Chinese descent have a good sense about officials' taste. That's why they always receive privileges that indigenous people have never received,' he complained in a 1993 seminar. 'The unequal treatment of indigenous people,' he went on to say, 'has been going on since the administration of the late president Sukarno.'[71]

As a matter of national pride, *pribumi* businessmen are pained by Soeharto's favouritism toward the Chinese *cukongs*. 'It hurts us when we hear that Soeharto says *pribumi* businessmen can't be trusted,' said one *pribumi* businessman active in the oil business, 'that they don't repay loans or work hard or are able to keep a secret. That's all bullshit. Me or Bakrie and a number of others could be as big as Liem Sioe Liong or [former Astra Group chairman] William Soeryadjaya if we had been given the same facilities and breaks. Liem didn't have the money either when he started. But he was given opportunities.'[72] Big *pribumi* businessmen were insulted that they were not invited to the Tapos tryst and ordered along with the *cukongs* to give shares to cooperatives. 'No one asked *us* what we thought about the wealth gap,' complained one, plaintively.

These kinds of comments reveal that *pribumi* resentment of the Chinese is not exclusively economic. It is also political. In Soeharto's authoritarian system, neither the Chinese nor *pribumi* business executives enjoy direct political power. But the wealth of the Chinese and their importance to the economy gives them a degree of political influence denied the *pribumi* business class.

Differences within the big *pribumi* camp are reflected in their views about the technocrats' economic reform drive. Some blame the deregulation drive for the emergence of large conglomerates. This has created a fear that deregulation is paving the way for a Chinese annexation of the whole economy. Others take the more reasoned view that the rapid expansion of Chinese-owned businesses since 1987 is a by-product, rather than the object, of the deregulation campaign. 'Chinese were better prepared to take advantage of the opportunities that deregulation creates,' said one engineering consultant.[73]

Many of the top *pribumi* businessmen welcome the technocrats' efforts to liberalise the economy, particularly those who do not have the political connections to benefit from direct government help. They wish only that the technocrats had been more successful in ending the special treatment enjoyed by a few of the biggest Chinese operators. The moderates acknowledge that they, too, have done well under the New Order and are pragmatic enough to understand that they have much to lose if ethnic antagonisms lead to capital flight, falling investment and slower economic growth. They are wary of new affirmative action programs. They are equally wary of Minister for Research and Technology Habibie, whose influence has soared in recent years. On the one hand, they support his inclination for more active government intervention in the economy. They are not at all convinced, however, that his interventions will benefit them.

The hardline *pribumis*, in contrast, are adamant that the government must do more to 'create' *pribumi* businessmen of the same stature as the biggest Chinese *cukongs*. 'It's an important question,' one *pribumi* leader said. 'How many *pribumi* businessmen have been created under the New Order? The answer is, not very many.'[74] Success by the technocrats would mean failure for this group. Level playing fields, fair competition and a 'transparent' economy are not their top priorities. They do not want the government to stop handing out special 'facilities'. They want these facilities for themselves and less for the Chinese. 'You can't put us in a race with the Chinese if they are starting twenty metres ahead,' said one of the most prominent *pribumi* businessmen. 'I realise there are costs involved but these are part of the social costs that we have to pay. Something has to be done. I am very worried about a social revolution.'[75]

Soeharto's half-brother Probosutedjo, who heads the Association of Indigenous Indonesian Businessmen as well as the Supervisory Council of Kadin, the Chamber of Commerce and Industry, is counted as one of the most vocal critics of the economic clout wielded by the Chinese. In December 1993, the Supervisory Council published a five-yearly review of Kadin's activities in which it painted a bleak picture of an economy dominated by ruthless and predatory Chinese businessmen riding rough-shod over smaller *pribumi* entrepreneurs, ably assisted by corrupt government officials and gullible technocrats. The review, signed by Probosutedjo, charged that 'large business groups now control almost all businesses from the upstream to the downstream industries. The conglomerates' dominance is felt everywhere and it is real, controlling the economy both vertically and horizontally.' In a direct rebuke to the technocrats, the review claimed that 'each new deregulation package worsens economic imbalances because it allows big business to expand and grow through unfair competition.'[76]

The disappointment that many *pribumis* felt over the demise of Team 10 combined with frustration over their lack of leverage with Soeharto has prompted renewed lobbying efforts for the new *pribumi* promotion policies. In July 1991 a group of leading *pribumi* businessmen made a well-publicised visit to Malaysia and discussed the mechanics of Malaysia's New Economic Policy with senior Malaysian leaders, including Prime Minister Mahathir Mohamad. Since then, the frequency of contacts between indigenous businessmen in Malaysia and Indonesia has picked up sharply, leaving many on the Indonesian side convinced that the answer to Indonesia's Chinese–*pribumi* problem is for Indonesia to adopt its own New Economic Policy.

Pribumis are not alone in resenting Soeharto's relationship with businessmen such as Liem Sioe Liong. Some Chinese businessmen feel that more can and should be done to defuse rising *pribumi* antagonism. 'They're all so egotistical,' one complained, referring to the biggest of the Chinese businessmen. 'All they think about is their business.' Many Chinese-owned companies, he adds, share the *pribumi*'s resentment of the special favours bestowed on Soeharto's chosen few. 'I've lost business to Liem and [Bob] Hasan and Prajogo [Pangestu], just like the *pribumis* have,' said this executive, a *peranakan* Chinese.[77]

Astra International, which was until early 1993 majority owned by the Soeryadjaya family, is regarded by *pribumis* as the most progressive of all the top Chinese-owned firms. It has a number of *pribumi* executives and deals extensively with *pribumi* subcontractors and distributors. 'We need more *pribumi*-run and owned conglomerates in Indonesia,' says Astra president Teddy Rachmat. 'But there is a limit to what an individual company like Astra can do. I think most government contracts should go to *pribumis*. The Chinese should refrain from getting involved. But it is very hard to convince all Chinese companies that this is the right way to go.'[78]

Others, of course, in government, in business and elsewhere, take the view that the big *pribumis* are protesting too much. Anthony Salim, for example, believes the top *pribumi* businessmen are just looking for handouts. 'It took us 45 years to reach the standard we have today,' he said in an early 1991 interview. 'Some of these people haven't been in business for ten years yet.' Adds Anthony's right-hand man Johannes Kotjo: 'The political problem is being created by 200 people who already made their money, and most of them got special advantages from the government anyway.'[79]

Other critics of the leading *pribumi* businessmen reject the thesis that Soeharto doled out help only to Chinese companies in the early days of the New Order. 'Don't tell me Bakrie and the others didn't get a chance to grow big,' one cabinet minister said in early 1993. 'In the 1970s they all got an equal chance.'[80] Given the closed nature of Soeharto's government, it is hard to know how true this is. But it is certainly true that many of the top *pribumi* businesses benefited handsomely from Sudharmono and Ginanjar's stewardship of Team 10 in the early 1980s. Even many who are sympathetic to the big *pribumi* cause concede that much of that government help was wasted. 'Sudharmono and Ginanjar tried to accelerate the technical and engineering competence of people like Bakrie and Fadel Muhammad and other top *pribumi* businessmen,' says Umar Juoro, a researcher with the Centre for Information and Development Studies. 'But many of them were just brokers. They got government contracts and then turned around and gave them to the

Chinese or foreigners. A lot of those guys turned out to be better politicians than businessmen.'[81]

There is, obviously, a great deal of disagreement in Indonesia about what Soeharto gave and to whom, and how much difference it made to the recipient's business fortunes. But it is clear that the Chinese have prospered greatly during Soeharto's rule and that he has given considerable help to at least some of them. The resentment this has caused naturally feeds upon ancient antagonisms directed at the Chinese. But it would be a mistake to say that ethnicity per se is the crux of the problem.

Indonesia, after all, is home to hundreds of ethnic and cultural subgroups; while the Chinese community's history is unique, its members have been broadly accepted in Indonesia as equal citizens. What becomes clear in conversations with many leading *pribumi* businessmen, though, is that what they really resent is a government which has gone out of its way—at least as they see it—to grant special assistance to a group of businessmen who happen to be ethnic Chinese. A senior government economist put it this way: '*Pribumi* resentment is not, I think, specifically due to the fact that the biggest firms are Chinese-owned, it's because they see Soeharto *helping* the Chinese. It always comes back to the special facilities and who gets them: Liem Sioe Liong, Bob Hasan, Prajogo Pangestu and the others. This is what creates discontent,' he said [italics added].[82]

This view, then, points to Soeharto's patrimonial style of rule as an important contributor to Chinese–*pribumi* tension, at least as it concerns the 'big *pribumi*' problem. But even if Soeharto, for his own political purposes, finds it desirable to maintain close personal links with leading business players, why should they be Chinese and not *pribumi*? As much as the top *pribumi* business leaders hate to admit it, there is something to the theory that Soeharto is attracted to the competence and entrepreneurial skills of his top *cukongs*. Liem Sioe Liong, to give the most obvious example, may get special help from Soeharto but he does, at the end of the day, deliver the goods.

But a better explanation is a more strictly political one. No matter how large and powerful ethnic-Chinese businessmen become, they represent no political threat to Soeharto because they come from a relatively small minority.[83] But economically powerful *pribumi* businessmen, freed from reliance on government largesse, would be a different story. Unlike the Chinese, a class of strong, independent *pribumi* businessmen could well outgrow a need for Soeharto's favour and become a potent political faction. Whether Soeharto views his actions in these terms is hard to say, but the top *pribumi* businessmen certainly see it this way. The following case study provides a good illustration of why the top *pribumis* believe that their economic fortunes are being handicapped under Soeharto's rule.

Case study: Economic gains and political favours[84]

By the late 1980s the leading *pribumi* businessmen had fixed on oil, once the saviour of Indonesia, as their ticket to the big time. Their main cabinet patron, Ginanjar Kartasasmita, had assumed the portfolio of Minister of Mines and Energy in March 1988. Over the next two years the grip of state-owned oil and gas monopoly Pertamina over oil-related industries was gradually pried loose. Petrochemicals, especially, promised to be a lucrative business for Indonesia's young would-be tycoons.

In March 1990, three of 'Ginanjar's boys'—Aburizal Bakrie of the Bakrie Group, Fadel Muhammad of Bukaka Teknik Utama, and Iman Taufik of Gunanusa Utama Fabricators—set their sights on the design and construction contract for a giant export-oriented oil refinery known as Exor 4. The three businessmen formed a small consortium, named BBG after the first letters of their companies, and opened talks with two international engineering firms, Fluor of the United States and Mitsui of Japan. BBG, with Ginanjar's strong backing, intended to be the main domestic contractor in the US$1.8 billion project. Its role would be to procure and construct boilers, utilities and processing equipment costing about US$500 million. During the next few months, the three Indonesian companies travelled to Fluor's office in Irvine, California to thrash out the details of the project. Near mid-year, the consortium had received a letter of intent from Pertamina; the final contract signing was set for December 1990.

Meanwhile, a second consortium of *pribumi*-owned companies was making progress on a second petrochemical project. The CNT group, as it was known, included Kusumo Martoredjo and Agus Kartasasmita (the minister's brother) of Catur Yasa, Ponco Sutowo (son of former Pertamina chief Ibnu Sutowo) of Nugra Santana, and Wiwoho Basuki of Tripatra. It was to be the main local partner of Mitsui and Toyo Engineering of Japan on a US$1.7 billion project to construct a residual catalytic cracking plant in Cilacap, Central Java. The unit would produce naphtha and high-grade fuels like unleaded gasoline from crude oil. It was decided in the early stages of the negotiations that the CNT consortium's work would absorb about US$400 million of the total project cost.

In October of 1990, however, politics intervened. Minister Ginanjar was ordered by Soeharto to make Liem Sioe Liong and Prajogo Pangestu—two ethnic-Chinese businessmen—the principal domestic part-ners in the big-ticket projects. This was to be their payoff, it soon became clear, for bailing out Bank Duta the month before. (The bank, as noted earlier, is majority owned by charitable foundations headed by Soeharto. Between late 1988 and September 1990, it had lost US$420 million speculating on foreign exchange markets.)

An outraged Ginanjar protested to Soeharto but to no avail. The minister dragged his feet implementing the president's instructions, and tried to ensure that the *pribumi* businessmen would at least retain significant sub-contracting roles. Finally, in November Ginanjar was told by Soeharto's chief of staff Murdiono to install Liem and Prajogo in the two projects or face the consequences.[85] The deal was done.

In the event, less than a year later the two projects were indefinitely postponed, along with many others, by an interministerial team attempting to slow Indonesia's burgeoning foreign debt. Liem and Prajogo would get their money back some other way, of course, but the damage to *pribumi* morale had been done. Many Chinese businessmen were equally taken aback. 'I can't believe that Anthony [Salim] and Prajogo don't understand that taking those two contracts would inflame passions in *pribumis* who thought they had the contracts sewn up,' said one Chinese executive.[86]

The *pribumi* business lobby was devastated. In a face-to-face battle with two of Soeharto's leading crony businessmen, Ginanjar, the *pribumi*'s most powerful patron, had lost decisively. For the *pribumis* involved in the two projects, a choice opportunity to accumulate capital had been snatched from their hands, sacrificed to the greater needs of Soeharto's patrimonial balancing act. 'I am so fed up with the situation here,' exclaimed Iman Taufik. 'The only solution, I think, is to concentrate on doing more work abroad than in Indonesia.'[87]

The illusion of progress

The New Order regime's success in assimilating the Chinese minority should not be discounted. More than ninety per cent of Indonesian-Chinese are now Indonesian citizens. Draconian anti-Chinese measures like the 1959 law banning Chinese from retail trades in rural areas are unlikely to be repeated. Calls for the Chinese to return to China, frequently heard in the 1960s, are now rare. It would be fair to say that most Indonesian–Chinese now identify themselves fully with Indonesia. Intermarriages are common and younger Chinese exhibit fewer of the traits that, among their forebears, aggravated relations with the *pribumi* majority.

Several factors tend to restrain overt anti-Chinese behaviour. One is the pride Indonesians have in their multicultural society and a desire to present to the outside world an image of a tolerant, non-sectarian society. This is why, for example, many Indonesians would be uncomfortable if a formal affirmative action program were to be adopted as is the case in Malaysia. A second reason is that Indonesia's elite understands that a sharp increase in anti-Chinese sentiment would have immediate, recognisable costs for the economy. As Robison puts it: 'The Chinese are protected by their very economic indispensability. Any fundamental assault upon them will, without doubt, have a quite critical impact on the Indonesian economy as a whole.'[88] A final factor is that top Chinese and *pribumi* entrepreneurs have become tied together in an extensive array of businesses. One side cannot be hurt without hurting the other.

Yet for all that, a deep cleft remains in Indonesian society. Younger Chinese resent what they see as continuing discrimination against them. 'Despite full compliance with the regulations governing their social and cultural lives,' says Mely Tan, who has written frequently on Indonesia's Chinese minority, '[the Chinese] feel they are still not appreciated, recognised, or accepted as full-fledged fellow citizens by the ethnic Indonesian majority.'[89]

The fact that the national identity cards which all Indonesians must carry bear a special code for ethnic-Chinese citizens is but one example of the Chinese complaint. Within the business community, younger Chinese are in general better educated than their parents and bring a more modern, professional approach to running their businesses. Having only distant memories of the turbulence, insecurity and extreme vulnerability which afflicted the Chinese in the first twenty years of Indonesian independence, the younger Chinese businessmen see less need to build intricate support networks with government officials, the military and *pribumi* businessmen. Eschewing the low-profile, political-business approach of their fathers, they aspire to be 'modern' businessmen, at home in an increasingly globalised commercial environment. This, arguably, has made them better businessmen than the generation which preceded them, but it is, nevertheless, an attitude more likely to sharpen anti-Chinese sentiment within Indonesia than erase it.

At a broader social level, the relationship between the *pribumi* majority and the Chinese minority, while improved, is an uneasy one. Newspapers carry frequent complaints about Chinese 'exclusiveness'. Residential enclaves of Chinese families are ready targets for *pribumi* griping. Stories of Javanese parents refusing to attend weddings between their children and ethnic-Chinese Indonesians are common.

An increase in trade with China, particularly by Indonesian-Chinese owned firms, carries the seeds of future problems. Indonesia and China re-opened diplomatic ties in 1990 after a 23-year break. But a furore in August 1992 over the use of workers from China highlighted just how sensitive the issue remains. A unit of the Sinar Mas Group, owned by Eka Cipta Wijaya, one of Indonesia's wealthiest ethnic-Chinese businessmen, acquired machinery made in China for use in three power plants under construction in Java. A Sinar Mas subsidiary, Indah Kiat Pulp & Paper, also imported 700 workers from China to construct the plants. When the decision was made public, uproar ensued. Workers' groups, parliamentarians and government officials expressed outrage and Sinar Mas was forced to expedite the workers' return to China, even though it had received the appropriate permission from a variety of ministries.

'Don't abuse the opening up of relations with China,' Ginanjar

Kartasasmita warned business groups. 'I don't want to see this kind of thing happening again in the future.' Nationalist-leaning newspapers were even more shrill. 'Indonesians in this beloved republic were once again reminded of colonial times when they heard the shocking news of one thousand Chinese skilled workers brought to Indonesia just to build lousy electric power plants,' screeched the *Indonesian Observer* in an editorial in September 1992. 'Given the situation above, it is [a] naked fact, erosion of nationalism and patriotism in Indonesia is going on with all its strength.'[90]

The government feels it can do little to restrain these kinds of emotions which are rooted in long historical experience and are unlikely to fade as long as the *pribumi* elite keeps the anti-Chinese fires stoked. And for the 'big *pribumi*' camp, as we have seen, Indonesia's economic transformation of the past half-decade has brought to the surface long-simmering resentments for which there are no easy remedies. Rightly or wrongly, the larger *pribumi* businessmen believe Soeharto's patrimonial style of rule is the principal cause of the Chinese domination of Indonesia's private economy. Soeharto must stop giving 'facilities' to his trusted Chinese allies in the business world, say the *pribumis*. This, however, would strike at the core of his power apparatus and, as such, is unlikely. A second approach would be to adopt the Malaysian solution of direct government intervention. This, though, would be culturally disruptive and would be vehemently opposed by Soeharto, the army, the technocrats and Chinese businessmen.

'If a cleaner government is what the *pribumi* business leaders want, then that's fine,' said one top Chinese executive. 'But if the idea is to hold our companies back, to make our companies smaller as a way of closing the gap, then there will be problems.'[91] This businessman and other leading Chinese executives have one point in common with their *pribumi* counterparts. They too see Soeharto's tight links with the very biggest Chinese tycoons as a serious economic and social problem. These links, in their view, are making the broader Chinese community vulnerable to *pribumi* reprisals once Soeharto has left the scene. These Chinese businessmen are not necessarily keen advocates of democracy; they remember all too well the difficulties they had in the 1950s. But at the same time more and more of them feel that Soeharto's style of leadership is damaging their longer term interests. 'It doesn't matter how much we try to work with *pribumis* or help small businessmen,' said one Chinese executive whose firm does not have good relations with top government officials. 'If at the end of the day resentment boils over, all the Chinese will suffer.'[92] In response to this fear, wealthy Chinese businessmen are likely to hasten the process of moving some of their assets offshore. This will be done under the guise of international diversification but it will be understood that concerns about a possible upsurge in Chinese–*pribumi* tensions later in the decade will have played an important role.

Ultimately, the solution to the 'big *pribumi*' problem is the same as for the 'small *pribumi*' problem. The solution begins by recognising that the real problem is not that Indonesia has too many conglomerates, as some commentators believe, but that it has too few. And the keys to *pribumi*-owned corporate growth are continued economic growth, a less corrupt bureaucracy, a less personal government–business relationship, a fairer tax administration and a more effective legal system.

But conglomerate building takes time and therefore any lasting and non-disruptive solution to the Chinese–*pribumi* problem is likely to be long term, if at all. The business skills of *pribumis* will have to be raised through education and vocational training, and obstacles to *pribumi* business growth painstakingly removed. 'Ultimately,' says a resigned Astra president Teddy Rachmat, 'we will have to wait another two or three generations before we reach a satisfactory solution.'[93]

6
Family rules

He that plays the king shall be welcome;
his majesty shall have tribute of me.

Hamlet[1]

Old soldiers in Indonesia neither die nor fade away: they do business.
Some do it as a matter of self-preservation, others for a little more.

Indonesia Business Weekly[2]

What is wrong if among the children of the 1945 Generation and of those
who fought to uphold the New Order there are those who get the chance
to succeed in business?

Alamsyah Ratu Perwiranegara[3]

In early 1992 President Soeharto received a delegation of economic
ministers to his office in Jakarta's Istana Palace. The officials, led by
Agriculture Minister Wardoyo, had come seeking presidential approval for
a trade reform bill that had been in the making for more than six months
and was now overdue. The business community, concerned that Indonesia's highly touted economic reform program was running out of steam,
wanted action.

Wardoyo was expecting a difficult meeting. The trade bill contained,
among other items, a provision opening up imports of soybeans to private
traders. This seemingly innocuous measure held some important political
implications for Indonesia. Soybeans, as Western nations engaged in
international trade talks have found to their dismay, can sometimes travel
with heavy political baggage. This was one of those times.

Indonesia's only soybean crushing plant, Sarpindo, opened in 1988. It consumes about half the 500 000 tonnes of soybeans Indonesia imports annually, processing the beans into a feed stock—soymeal—for industries such as shrimp hatching and chicken farming. Before Sarpindo opened, soymeal was imported by the national logistics board, Bulog, or by Bulog-approved traders and then resold to end users at cost plus a small tariff. But with Sarpindo's opening, licences for soymeal imports dried up. Sarpindo became virtually the sole supplier of soymeal to the Indonesian market. The good news for Sarpindo was bad news for soymeal users.

Sarpindo had, to put it mildly, a generous deal with Bulog, which has the exclusive right to import soybeans into Indonesia. The agency provides the beans to Sarpindo and then pays it about US$12 for every tonne of beans crushed into soymeal. This is about 40 to 50 per cent higher than the price of imported soymeal, but it provides only a portion of Sarpindo's revenues. The processing of soybeans into soymeal throws off a by-product, soybean oil, a valuable vegetable oil which Sarpindo gets to keep for free. In 1991, Sarpindo's return on each tonne of crushed soybeans was US$84, with US$72 of that coming from soybean oil.

Overall, the government subsidy to Sarpindo amounts to some US$21 million a year. But the cost to Indonesia is much higher. The protection of soymeal raises prices for some of Indonesia's most-promising agro-businesses such as poultry production and shrimp farming which depend on high-protein soymeal as an important food supplement. For chicken farmers, for example, feed costs make up some two-thirds of the variable costs of production. Subsidising Sarpindo makes these operations less competitive on world markets. Soybean-based products are also an important source of protein for people, the World Bank notes. And artificially high prices discourage 'protein consumption by the poor'.[4]

Against these public costs are private benefits. Majority ownership of Sarpindo is in the hands of Hutomo Mandala Putra—more commonly known as Tommy—the youngest son of President Soeharto, and two ethnic-Chinese businessmen with close ties to the president that stretch back more than thirty years, Liem Sioe Liong and Bob Hasan.

Wardoyo argued during his meeting with Soeharto that the freeing of soymeal imports would lower costs on a range of processed agricultural goods and help boost Indonesia's non-oil exports, one of the chief goals of the economic reform program. An unconvinced Soeharto responded: *Kalau mau membunuh Sarpindo, silakan.* (If you want to kill Sarpindo, go ahead.) Those present instantly understood that what Soeharto meant, filtered through the prism of Javanese obliqueness, was that he would not countenance an abrupt end to the Sarpindo monopoly. The public good, in this case, would have to wait. As one participant later remarked: 'After Soeharto spoke, we didn't even dare bring up the wheat monopoly (another Liem Sioe Liong franchise). We knew what the answer would be.'[5]

Wardoyo and the other officials went back to the drawing board. Another six months went by. In July 1992 the trade reform bill was finally announced to the public. Its overall impact fell short of most expectations; of soybeans, there was no mention at all.[6]

Corruption: in the eye of the beholder

Corruption, Indonesians and foreigners like to say, is endemic in Indonesia: it was a prominent part of the scene prior to the arrival of the Dutch and has scarcely diminished since their departure. While true, the comment begs the question: what is corruption? And, perhaps more relevantly, does it matter? This chapter argues that the answer to the latter is: very much. Exploring the possible answers to the former is the subject of the following section.

In Indonesia, as in many developing countries, corruption carries different connotations than in more legalistically minded industrialised nations. In many cases it is socially tolerated. In others, not. At the risk of oversimplifying the issue, there are two kinds of corruption in Indonesia. They share many of the same characteristics and underlying causes but differ in scale.

In the first camp are the small bribes, payoffs, gratuities and other inducements that grease the wheels of the bureaucracy. Motorists in any of Indonesia's cities view the police as collectors of an unofficial road tax, rather than as upholders of the law. Obtaining a document quickly from the immigration department, for example, or the motor vehicles office, police department, Ministry of Manpower, Ministry of Information or any other government office, necessitates a small payment placed in many desk drawers. These unregistered payments do not add up to great sums but those who cannot, or will not, pay them can expect long and frustrating delays.

Anecdotes tell the story the best. In 1991, my car was stolen in Jakarta. To collect on the insurance, I needed a form from the police verifying that the car was, in fact, stolen. Negotiations dragged on. A police captain wouldn't part with the form for less than US$300, somewhat above the cost of the insurance premium. Not being particularly attached to the car, I balked at the price. Many months later, the captain tired of the wait. Suddenly, my car, minus a stereo and the air-conditioning unit, was 'found' in the police department's parking lot. I was free to take it.

This type of corruption is probably inevitable given the very low salaries paid to Indonesia's four million civil servants. Indeed, the very term 'civil servant' is something of a misnomer in Indonesia: in this quasi-feudal culture, it would be more accurate to say that government employees are the 'owners' of the nation and the general public their servants. These cultural attitudes are changing, but only very slowly.

Many government employees still tend to look upon their salaries as something more akin to a retainer, with extra payments from the public filling out the rest of their 'legitimate' compensation package. Most of the time, these payments are tolerated by a resigned public. In any case, there is little the public can do. The law is no help and complaints usually make the problem worse.

In 1990, the vice-president's office set up a special post office box for complaints about corruption. The box, by all accounts, does a brisk business but nothing seems to change. There is, after all, only so much difference administrative reforms can make. Pervasive, low-level bureaucratic corruption will not be eradicated without higher government salaries, better enforcement of the law, and a heightened appreciation of government accountability. All of these, of course, will take time.

Petty corruption is an unfortunate fact of life in Indonesia. More serious, however, are the much larger under-the-table payments made by companies to senior officials to win major government contracts. Or, the sums that foreign and domestic companies pay to politically well-connected private businessmen who obtain contracts on their behalf. This can involve a straight payment or free equity in a joint venture company. The strongest of Indonesia's crony businessmen obtain an assortment of benefits operating without partners, from lucrative distribution and supply deals with state-owned companies, to no-questions-asked financing from state banks, to preferential consideration on government-funded infrastructure projects, to monopolies on importing, exporting or distributing agricultural commodities like wheat, palm oil, soybeans or sugar.

The deregulation and economic reform campaign begun by the technocrats in the late 1980s has made little headway in curbing this sort of activity. If anything, it is on the rise, or at least it seems that way because of the meteoric expansion of the business empires controlled by several of Soeharto's children. In recent years, for example, hardly a single major infrastructure contract has been awarded without one Soeharto relative or other having a piece of it. Oftentimes, it seems that the tendering process is just for appearances' sake. The only suspense is over *which* crony will emerge victorious.

To Soeharto, this is not corruption. Rather, it is the petty graft of the bureaucracy which attracts his attention. 'Corruption in our country is not the result of corrupt minds but of economic pressures,' Soeharto writes. 'Eventually, when economic development has gone so far as to produce a good overall standard of living, government employees will receive adequate salaries and have no reason to practise corruption. [But] no corrupt act,' he adds, 'even under the pretext of helping people, can be justified.'[7] Curbs on the press allow this fundamental confusion between 'big corruption' and 'little corruption' to continue unchallenged. Occasionally, public frustration seeps through. 'That corruption is rampant in

Indonesia is an undeniable fact,' lamented the *Jakarta Post* in a late 1992 editorial. 'We . . . have the impression that the government seems unable to deal with the problem [and we] cannot help wondering that perhaps, if we really wanted to crack down on corruption, it would not be timely for the government to stop the rhetoric and really take firm measures to combat it.'[8]

There is more than a little resemblance between the 'big corruption' problem and the 'big *pribumi*' problem discussed in the previous chapter. In both cases, the 'problems' are rooted within Soeharto's patrimonial style of rule, itself a product of ancient cultural traditions. For Soeharto, the personal dispensing of government largesse falls well within the prerogatives of the Javanese ruler. It is, quite simply, the spoils of office. Many Indonesians agree with this, at least up to a point. That Soeharto, his family, his ministers or, for that matter, the holder of any powerful office enriches himself in the course of executing his duties is accepted by many as the natural order of things. The quote by former minister Alamsyah Ratu Perwiranegara at the beginning of this chapter exemplifies this attitude.

But there are limits. And a sizeable segment of Indonesia's elite feels that Soeharto's family and a few privileged cronies have long since passed those limits. It is important to stress that 'corruption' is not an alien concept to Indonesians. While many forms of government–business collusion that would be considered corrupt in the West are not defined that way in Indonesia, government and business leaders do not enjoy some kind of cultural carte blanche to do anything they want. On the contrary, the activities of Indonesia's top crony businessmen and their partners in government are a source of deep resentment and disillusionment for many Indonesians.

Rampant corruption, particularly of the big-ticket variety, is more than merely disillusioning, of course. It has profound implications for Indonesia's economic and political future. Corruption is profitable for the few, expensive for the many. Bureaucratic inefficiencies and large-scale corruption both add to the cost of making products in Indonesia and, more broadly, retard the growth of the economy. Soeharto's links with top crony businessmen also pose a political dilemma. As will be discussed more fully below, arranging a smooth transition of power at the top is complicated tremendously by the existence of powerful business actors—most especially Soeharto family members—who can be expected to push the president to stay in office as long as possible.

Cronyism is not a new phenomenon. The charge of high-level corruption has been levelled at the Soeharto regime since almost its first day in office. Then, as now, Soeharto has tended to respond with indifference, occasional anger and more than a trace of confusion. Strident criticism of high-level corruption in the early days of the New Order led to the formation of a so-called 'Commission of Four' in 1970 which, among its other comments, noted that corruption was so rampant that 'people no longer know what is corrupt and what is not'.[9] However, none of the cases which the commission identified as needing 'urgent action' was pursued by the government. In 1971, the reform-minded police chief Hugeng Santoso uncovered a car-smuggling racket in Jakarta in which, it appeared, Soeharto's wife was involved. Hugeng was fired for his efforts; the investigation was dropped.[10]

Throughout the New Order, the state-owned oil giant Pertamina has been linked, directly or indirectly, with a slew of corrupt activities. Indonesians were given a glimpse of the sums involved in the late 1970s thanks to a protracted legal battle between Pertamina and the heirs of Achmad Thahir, a senior Pertamina official close to its former director Ibnu Sutowo. After Thahir died in 1976 his second wife Kartika reportedly withdrew more than US$45 million from two banks in Singapore. However, she was blocked from withdrawing a further US$35 million from Sumitomo Bank's Singapore branch in 1977 and a 15-year legal tussle began. It transpired that Thahir had collected bribes from two German companies—Siemens and Kloeckner Industrie-Anlagen—who, not coincidentally, had won large construction contracts in the early 1970s for Indonesia's Krakatau Steel project. The bribes were equivalent to about twenty per cent of the value of the contracts awarded to the two firms.

Benny Murdani, who would later rise to armed forces commander, met Kartika in 1977 in Geneva and reported her as saying that the bribes were intended to be split three ways between Thahir, Ibnu Sutowo and another Pertamina executive.[11] In December 1992, the Singapore High Court finally ruled that the Sumitomo Bank deposits—by then equal to over US$80 million with accrued interest—rightfully belonged to Indonesia. 'I am convinced Thahir had struck his dishonest deals with the German contractors and to the knowledge of Mrs Kartika Thahir, they were making banking arrangements to deposit the bribes in a shroud of secrecy,' said Singapore Judge Lai Kew Chai in his ruling.[12]

The ruling came as little surprise. Even Kartika didn't deny that Thahir—whose annual salary never exceeded US$9000—had accepted illegal payments from the German contractors. Her defence rested on the contention that such payoffs are accepted practices in Indonesia, which, by all accounts, they are. More surprising was that the court case didn't generate demands for Pertamina's books to be examined more closely. Reflecting a widely held view, a leading Indonesian newspaper said in an editorial after the Thahir judgment was handed down: 'We believe there are many "Thahirs" around us even now.'[13] One Indonesian lawyer, Mulya Lubis, bravely called on the government to investigate the sources of Ibnu Sutowo's considerable wealth but it is highly unlikely the suggestion will be taken up.[14]

More broadly, Pertamina's importance to Indonesia's crony business-men extends far beyond straightforward bribery cases like the Thahir episode. As the controller of Indonesia's most valuable natural resource, Pertamina has been a crucially important source of capital formation for the cronies. Soeharto's children, in particular, have benefited from lucra-tive offtake agreements with the oil monopoly. Several have been granted allocations of crude and other petroleum-related products by Pertamina to market overseas or distribute within Indonesia, activities which could be carried out more efficiently and cheaply by the government oil company itself. It is impossible to say how much revenue these sorts of middlemen activities throw off in commissions each year. At a conservative estimate, though, the Pertamina links have netted many hundreds of millions of US dollars for Soeharto's children.

The players

Trying to establish a definition for crony businessmen in Soeharto's Indonesia is not an easy affair. Given the extensive links between gov-ernment and business leaders, a lack of transparency and a politicised legal system, almost any member of Indonesia's corporate elite could be considered a crony. As Chapter 5 discussed, almost all of the wealthiest ethnic-Chinese businessmen owe their start in business to special favours handed out by friends in the government. But for the purposes of this chapter, which focuses on crony businessmen in the 1990s, a stricter definition will be used. The entrance requirement for this group is a continuing close, personal relationship with Soeharto. Using this criterion, the top rank of Indonesia's crony businessmen can be said to form a fairly exclusive club. It consists mainly of a few ethnic-Chinese businessmen— the most important being Liem Sioe Liong, Bob Hasan and Prajogo Pangestu—and relatives of Soeharto. Of Soeharto's six children, four are active in business while two others are showing increasing interest. In the past, Soeharto's wife has been linked to a number of controversial deals but her business profile has declined since the mid-1980s.

Like Liem Sioe Liong (see Chapter 5), Bob Hasan's ties to the president extend back to the 1950s when Soeharto was commanding the army's Diponegoro division in Central Java. It is a poorly kept secret in Jakarta that Hasan (whose Chinese name is The Kian Seng) had a role in a sugar smuggling deal that eventually led to Soeharto's premature removal from the prestigious Diponegoro post. Today, Hasan's main business interests are in the forestry sector. He controls some two million hectares of forestry concession areas, mostly in Kalimantan. Through his control of the Indonesian Plywood Association, the Indonesian Sawmillers Association, the Indonesian Rattan Association and the umbrella Indones-ian Forestry Community, Hasan wields considerably more influence over the forestry sector than the Ministry of Forestry, a fact which does not endear Hasan to the ministry's top officials. Like Minister for Research and Technology Habibie, Hasan owes his relative insulation from the usual bureaucratic controls to his close links with Soeharto.

Apkindo, the Indonesian Plywood Association headed by Hasan, forms a powerful international cartel since Indonesia accounts for some three-quarters of hardwood plywood exports worldwide. Through Apkindo, Hasan sets export volumes and prices for Indonesia's plywood manufacturers.[15] Although he earns kudos for making plywood one of Indonesia's most lucrative exports, plywood manufacturers resent his heavy handed control over the industry. Rebellious operators are dealt with harshly by Apkindo.

Environmentalists, meanwhile, blame Hasan for the shoddy enforcement of Indonesia's tree felling rules and for the poor and allegedly fraudulent use of reforestation funds.[16] The World Bank estimates that Indonesia's massive tropical forest is being harvested at a rate 50 per cent higher than that considered sustainable. And because the politically powerful Apkindo cartel has been able to resist pressure to raise the royalties and other fees levied on loggers, the government has been forced to forego an estimated US$500 million a year in additional revenues.[17]

Outside the forestry sector, Hasan has a major presence in the construction industry, which brings him into frequent conflict with aspiring *pribumi* businessmen. For a while he held a monopoly on tin-plate imports and, more recently, has moved into banking, tea plantations, pulp and paper, shipping and, together with Soeharto's son Tommy, the airline business. A number of Hasan's companies have as partners ostensibly charitable foundations headed by Soeharto. And Hasan, a regular golfing partner of Soeharto, is not shy about using his links with the president to bring recalcitrant government officials into line. Cisi Raya Utama, an Indonesian business data firm, estimated that Hasan's companies posted revenues of at least US$2 billion in 1991.

Indonesia's vast forests have spawned another of Soeharto's top cronies, Prajogo Pangestu. Born Phang Djun Phen in West Kalimantan, Prajogo had by 1991 accumulated some 5.5 million hectares of forest concession areas, a tract of land slightly larger than Denmark. The land and associated wood-processing facilities are conservatively valued at some US$5–6 billion and threw off some US$1.5 billion in revenues in 1991.[18] Prajogo is the newest member of the club of leading crony businessmen. Unlike the other cronies, however, Prajogo had built up a successful business outside the Jakarta limelight *before* becoming a crony. Even by the late 1980s, Prajogo was virtually unknown in Jakarta's business circles.

His move into Soeharto's rarefied circle was prompted by two factors. One was a desire to reduce his dependence on the forestry business which was attracting increasingly critical attention from environmentalists. A second and more important reason was the need to get beyond the long shadow of forestry czar Bob Hasan. In Indonesia, the only way to combat a crony is to become one. Several of Soeharto's six children, notably middle son Bambang Trihatmodjo and eldest daughter Siti Hardijanti Rukmana, were only too glad to join forces with Prajogo and his mammoth wood-derived cash flow. Prajogo has teamed up with Rukmana, more commonly known as Mbak Tutut (Mbak being Javanese for elder sister), in a giant sugar plantation in Sulawesi and a US$1.2 billion pulp and paper plant in Sumatra. His biggest, and most controversial, venture is a US$1.6 billion petrochemical project called Chandra Asri in which Prajogo's main partner is Bambang.

Prajogo's tie-ups with the presidential offspring give him enormous clout with Soeharto. But Prajogo, like his fellow cronies, works at the relationship. He financed the publishing of Soeharto's ghost-written autobiography, for example, and has funded several projects dear to Soeharto's wife. And, not least, he stumped up US$220 million to bail out Soeharto's Bank Duta in late 1990. In return, Prajogo is allowed to operate as a quasi-governmental agent. When the forestry department resisted Prajogo's demands that the government contribute funds to one of his timber subsidiaries, Soeharto personally wrote to the Forestry Minister in March 1991 ordering him to clear up the problem.[19] State-owned Bank Bumi Daya, meanwhile, took up the role of Prajogo's personal financing vehicle. When bank president Surasa dragged his heels on Prajogo's request for an *uncollateralised* US$550 million letter of credit in 1991, Soeharto called Surasa twice and demanded the loan be granted.[20] It was.

For his troubles, Prajogo, a personally unassuming man, is deeply resented by both *pribumi* and ethnic-Chinese businessmen who speak contemptuously of him as an ill-educated arriviste. (Prajogo's formal education stopped at junior high school.) A lot of this, of course, is sour grapes, but it contributes in no small way to the dark passions which swirl about the crony clique.

Soeharto's family fills out the rest of the top caste of crony businessmen. Some family members have been able to trade on their political connections to amass tremendous fortunes in a remarkably short period of time. Individually, four of Soeharto's children are now listed among the biggest of Indonesia's corporate empires. Collectively, the family forms by far the most powerful economic dynasty in the country.

Soeharto's second son Bambang Trihatmodjo was the first of the president's six children to enter business in an organised way. In 1982, Bambang—then 29—formed the Bimantara Group with several schoolmates and Tutut's husband Indra Rukmana.[21] Seed capital came from lucrative middlemen deals set up with Pertamina. In 1984, Bambang, his older brother Sigit Haryoyudanto and Soeharto's cousin Sudwikatmono were granted a money-spinning monopoly on the import of plastics. In the late 1980s Bimantara diversified furiously into electronics, shipping, milk-processing, plywood manufacturing, telecommunications, television broadcasting, aircraft leasing, construction, real estate, sugar and palm-oil plantations and food retailing. The thread that binds these disparate activities is Bambang's ability to ride roughshod over the bureaucracy. In less than a decade of existence, Bimantara became Indonesia's largest *pribumi*-owned business group. By 1993, the group had grown to include about 100 subsidiaries with total assets of around US$1.4 billion. A Bimantara executive said in early 1994 that the group's 1993 sales were slightly more than US$400 million, although some outside analysts put the figure considerably higher.[22]

In the early 1990s Bimantara made efforts to restructure the group along more professional lines, though this campaign has not progressed much further than the public relations stage. Bambang, according to those close to him, is a loner, personally insecure and vulnerable to clever con men, of which there is no shortage. He is forever being dragged into seedy get-rich-quick schemes that undo much of what his highly paid professional managers are trying to accomplish.

Soeharto's eldest daughter Tutut moved into business about the same time as Bambang but more quietly. In 1983, she, her husband and her two younger sisters founded the Citra Lamtoro Gung Group.[23] The group made its first real splash in 1989 when details emerged of the sweetheart deal it enjoyed on a toll road running through the middle of Jakarta. Citra Lamtoro was receiving a share of the toll revenues well above its percentage of the construction costs.[24] In 1991, the group extracted from the government a licence to broadcast a supposedly 'educational' television channel. It was the first privately owned station to broadcast nationwide and funded itself through advertising, a revenue source denied the sole state-owned channel, TVRI. The station also made heavy use of TVRI's equipment and personnel while getting started, the cost for which was absorbed by the state-owned broadcaster. Tutut's new channel was also an especially public instance of Soeharto family one-upmanship as Bambang the year before had succeeded in opening up an advertising-funded TV station but one limited to broadcasting only to Jakarta and the West Java capital Bandung. In 1993, benefiting from her family's close ties with Minister for Research and Technology B. J. Habibie, Tutut secured a licence to import Malaysia's Proton car into Indonesia. The deal was reported to be part of a counter-trade arrangement under which Indonesia imported Protons in exchange for Malaysia buying airplanes manufactured by an Indonesian state-owned company headed by Habibie.

Tutut leavens her public image with a handful of social and charitable activities such as sponsoring youth organisations and disaster relief foundations. Consequently, she has enjoyed better press than her brothers but the distinction is blurring as more and more information comes to light of her rapidly expanding business empire. Her business group has a raft of profitable middleman arrangements with various government-owned firms and, often with Prajogo Pangestu, is moving heavily into agro-business ventures. Like her siblings, Tutut's main business asset is an ability to procure government licences and state-bank financing. In 1992, Citra Lamtoro Gung's group revenues were estimated at some US$400 million.

Soeharto's youngest son Tommy is the most controversial of all the Soeharto relatives. His Humpuss Group, founded in 1984 when Tommy was 22, has followed the traditional route to fortune and fame or, more precisely, notoriety. Humpuss started with exclusive distribution contracts for two important petrochemical products manufactured by Pertamina and was granted allocations of Pertamina's crude oil to sell overseas. Humpuss is also the sole concessionaire for the export of liquefied natural gas to Taiwan.[25] In 1989, Tommy and Bob Hasan bought majority control of a charter airline from a holding company controlled by the armed forces. Later, Sempati Air became the first privately-owned Indonesian airline to break the monopoly of flag carrier Garuda Indonesia on the use of jet engine aircraft and on flying international routes. Humpuss has also moved rapidly into petrochemicals, wood manufacturing, fertiliser production, toll roads, sugar and palm-oil plantations, and advertising. Revenues of the Humpuss Group plus other companies owned personally by Tommy Soeharto were estimated to be in excess of US$500 million in 1992.

Brash, aggressive and cocky, Tommy is the most public of the Soeharto children and, as such, the most dangerous to his father. According to numerous government officials, Tommy is the least squeamish of all the Soeharto children in using his name to get what he wants. He is fond of telling potential foreign investors he spends more time with his father than his siblings. The army shares the business community view that Tommy has done more than the other crony businessmen in making nepotism and corruption a serious political liability for Soeharto.

Soeharto's oldest son Sigit Haryoyudanto has numerous business interests but does not appear to take an active management role in any of them. He has minority stakes in some of Bambang's companies and holds an estimated 40 per cent of the Humpuss Group. Like his elder sister Tutut, he has a 16 per cent stake in Liem Sioe Liong's Bank Central Asia. More recently, he has taken minority positions in several petrochemical ventures and, with his brother Tommy, acquired a mid-sized bank. His personal assets were estimated at US$178 million in 1993.

Two other Soeharto relatives fall within the crony category. A half-brother, Probosutedjo, shared a lucrative clove importing monopoly with Liem Sioe Liong from the early 1970s through the mid-1980s and today has wide-ranging interests in construction, glass-making and agro-business. A cousin, Sudwikatmono, has a lock on the import and distribution of motion pictures in Indonesia, and is a minor shareholder in many of Liem's investments. The motion picture monopoly has been a recurring irritant in Indonesia's trade relations with the United States.

A business magazine's survey of the wealthiest indigenous Indonesian businessmen in 1993 confirmed what most Indonesians had long suspected: blood ties to Soeharto were the surest route to the top of the corporate ladder. Four of Soeharto's children plus Probosutedjo and Sudwikatmono filled out six of the top 13 spots on the list.[26]

The extent to which Soeharto is directly involved in business is not clear. Nominally charitable foundations which he heads hold a wide array of gainful investments but little is known of where these funds end up. Likewise, estimating the total size of the Soeharto family empire is a tricky task. Clearly, enormous funds derived from the oil industry have ended up in Soeharto family pockets. In his doctoral dissertation, American political scientist Jeffrey Winters says the US Central Intelligence Agency estimated Soeharto's personal wealth in 1989 at US$15 billion, and twice that if the entire Soeharto family was included. 'These sums,' Winters adds, 'dwarf those reportedly stolen by Southeast Asia's better-known kleptocrat Ferdinand Marcos.'[27] Other Indonesia observers, such as economist Hal Hill of the Australian National University, believe these estimates are exaggerated. 'Suggestions that [Soeharto's] cronyism rivals that of the late Marcos era . . . are far-fetched,' he says.[28]

Samizdat humour in Indonesia suggests Winters is closer to the truth. One wry joke making the rounds in the early 1990s was a play on Supersemar, shorthand for *surat perintah sebelas maret*, or the Letter of 11 March, the controversial document which transferred presidential powers from Sukarno to Soeharto in 1966. In caustic homage to the crony businessmen close to Soeharto, acronym-crazy Indonesians came up with a second rendition of Supersemar: *sudah persis seperti Marcos,* or, roughly translated, 'it's already exactly the same here as it was under Marcos'.

Case study: The telecommunications goldmine

A long, drawn-out tendering process for a contract to install sorely needed new telephones in Indonesia provides a compelling illustration of how nepotism slows down economic development.[29] The story begins in September 1988 when Indonesia invited international suppliers of telephone switching equipment to bid for a US$300 million project which was supposed to add 350 000 new telephone lines to Jakarta's badly over-stretched telecommunications grid. The winner would be expected to take on a local manufacturer in a joint venture company. Minister for Research and Technology Habibie announced at the outset that the local manufacturer would be a unit of Bambang's Bimantara Group, no matter who won the contract.

Meanwhile, Soeharto's children competed furiously to become the 'local agents' to international firms bidding for the contract. Without such an agent, an overseas bidder would stand no chance of winning. Bambang became the agent for Fujitsu of Japan. Tutut signed on as agent for American Telephone & Telegraph (AT&T) of the United States, and Tommy was retained as agent for a joint bid by NEC and Sumitomo of Japan. In November 1989, these three foreign bidders were selected to a final shortlist of five, culled from an initial eleven bidders.

The three Soeharto children stepped up the lobbying of government officials, especially Habibie and coordinating economy minister Radius Prawiro, the two officials with the most power to select a winner. Fujitsu's bid was eventually discarded which was little nuisance for Bambang as he was already designated as the project's local manufacturer. Tokyo and Washington ratcheted up the pressure on Jakarta, campaigning for NEC/Sumitomo and AT&T respectively. The result was a predictable deadlock.

In February 1990 Jakarta declared the original tender void and called on foreign finalists to resubmit bids. Five months later, government officials figured out how to avoid alienating either Tokyo or Washington or any of the Soeharto offspring. In a Solomon-like decision, Jakarta doubled the size of the contract and, in November 1990, awarded half each to NEC/Sumitomo and AT&T. (This notwithstanding the fact that the two winners had put in the highest of the five bids resubmitted in October 1990.) One final fillip remained. With the contract doubled, an opportunity arose for a second local manufacturer to enter the picture. Lembaga Elektronika Nasional, a government-run agency with some telecommunications experience, was initially intended to be the beneficiary. But in January 1991, the government awarded the job instead to Citra Telekomunikasi Indonesia, a company established just five months previously. The company is jointly owned by Tutut, with 75 per cent of the equity, and by Minister Habibie's younger brother, with 25 per cent.

The inept handling of the telephone contract was a disaster for Indonesia in many ways. It cost the country plentiful goodwill among its major foreign donors and investors; the price of the contract was unnecessarily high; several top Indonesian officials were seen to be pawns in the hands of Soeharto's children; and last and certainly not least, the country suffered serious delays in upgrading a telephone system so ramshackle that it deters foreign investment. Such are the costs of nepotism.

In defence of nepotism

Discussions of Soeharto's family and Indonesia's other crony businessmen frequently include the remark: Soeharto's Achilles' heel. 'As long as his children are not involved, the president makes very rational economic decisions,' said one long-serving cabinet minister. 'But when the kids get involved, rationality loses. Then it is the father that speaks, not the president.'[30] Soeharto, perhaps not surprisingly, is highly defensive about criticism of his children. Since he does not consider his children corrupt, he interprets such criticism as indirect attacks on him.

Government officials who have tried to raise the issue with Soeharto receive the treatment befitting a messenger of bad news. In a 1991 interview, one of Soeharto's longest-serving ministers rather defensively explained cabinet-level silence on high-level nepotism. 'Who wants to tell the president a story he doesn't want to hear?'[31] One of the few who have risked complaining directly to Soeharto about his children is former Armed Forces Commander, Benny Murdani. As military commander from 1983 to 1988, it was part of Murdani's brief to act as protector of the Soeharto family. It was a role that became increasingly uncomfortable and indeed embarrassing for the personally austere Murdani. Approaching the end of his term, he made two critical mistakes: arguing against Soeharto's choice of Sudharmono as vice-president for the 1988–93 term, and complaining about the unrestrained greed of his children. For his troubles he was shunted upstairs to the less powerful post of defence minister and, in 1993, removed from the cabinet entirely. (Other factors contributing to Murdani's rift with Soeharto are discussed in later chapters.)

Soeharto says his children have as much right as any to be in business.[32] It is a defensible point. Less defensible, of course, is *how* they do business. Those who describe Soeharto's children as the president's blind spot assume that Soeharto is not aware of the extent to which his children take advantage of their privileged status. It is an overly generous interpretation. It is more accurate to say that Soeharto believes his children deserve privileged treatment precisely because they are his children.

Soeharto's second line of defence of his children is that they are righting the *pribumi*–Chinese imbalance in the top ranks of the business community. It is a measure of how inflamed *pribumi*–Chinese tensions are that some *pribumi* businessmen agree with this assessment. 'If that's the only choice, I'd rather see the kids grow than Liem get still more facilities. That's how bad things [with the Chinese] have gotten,' said Iman Taufik, an influential *pribumi* businessman.[33] Gadjah Mada University Professor Mubyarto, appointed in 1993 as a top deputy to Minister Ginanjar Kartasasmita at the national planning board, takes a similar view: 'If not for Soeharto's children, all those businesses would go to the

Chinese, and that would be worse.'[34] Many Indonesians would agree with Taufik and Mubyarto but the majority view is that Soeharto's children are hurting the cause of the *pribumi* business community. By cynically hold-ing up his children as *pribumi* success stories, Soeharto is able to dodge demands from more legitimate businessmen to be put on a par with the top ethnic-Chinese cronies like Liem or Prajogo. 'Instead of putting many *pribumis* into the group of big businessmen, Soeharto only puts his children and relatives there,' groused *pribumi* industrialist Kusumo Martoredjo.[35]

It could be said in defence of Soeharto's children that they could be worse. When they build a toll road, for example, they do it expensively, not terribly efficiently and probably in place of someone more qualified. But the road does get built. In contrast to, say, the worst examples of African kleptocracies, government funds spent on Soeharto's family are not totally wasted. Most of the time, anyway.

Soeharto's children and other cronies have also succeeded in breaking up several inefficient government-held monopolies. Examples include toll roads, telecommunications, airlines, certain petrochemicals, oil and natu-ral gas, shipping and fertiliser production. The Indonesian consumer is probably well served by having these and other activities opened to the private sector. Whether the same can be said for having government monopolies replaced by private quasi-monopolies is harder to say. Having relatives in sensitive business areas, though, does have political rewards, notes former Coordinating Minister for Political Affairs and Security, Admiral Sudomo. 'If you are going to allow private businesses into television broadcasting, for example, it's much safer for us if it's one of the president's sons.'[36]

Arguments for the prosecution

Rationalising First Family behaviour does little to dent the broadly held view that Indonesia's crony businessmen represent an enormous drain on the economy. Financial 'leakage' is only one way to calculate this drain. The cronies cannot be blamed entirely for the parlous state of Indonesia's seven giant state-owned banks but neither can they be completely exon-erated. After a quarter century of subsidising various credit programs and making ill-advised loans to privileged borrowers, the state banks entered the 1990s saddled with mammoth uncollectible debts. Economists familiar with the state banks' financial situation estimate the seven will need at least US$2–3 billion to shore up their capital position to the point where they might be able to reach the central bank's mandated capital-adequacy level.[37]

Given their importance to the banking industry—at the end of 1991 they accounted for about 60 per cent of total outstanding loans—the troubled state banks are rightfully considered a major obstacle to the development of the Indonesian financial system. But their role as crony financiers has undermined many efforts to improve their profitability. In early 1992, to give one recent example, the technocrats began plotting to replace the top executives at the state banks with better qualified bankers. One of their main objectives was to remove Surasa, the president of Bank Bumi Daya, a man jokingly referred to in Jakarta as Prajogo Pangestu's personal banker.

In a credit reference for Prajogo's Barito Pacific Group in July 1992, Surasa admitted as much when he wrote that his bank has 'been [Barito's] main banker for many years . . . [The] Barito Pacific Group is one of our most important and valued clients'. The bank is heavily exposed to Prajogo's operations, from plywood factories to petrochemical plants to pulp and paper mills. Sensing trouble brewing for Surasa, Prajogo in late June 1992 made a payment to the bank of US$50 million. This covered interest payments three years in advance on a credit facility outstanding to one of Prajogo's timber mills. The payment was a message intended to refute technocrat claims that the bank was in poor shape and that Surasa was a poor judge of character. Soeharto got the message. In August of that year, six of the seven state bank presidents *were* removed from their posts. The only one to survive was Surasa.[38]

The cronies' impact is also felt strongly at the policy level. Indonesia's much vaunted economic reform effort has been weakened by the technocrats' inability to move as aggressively in many sectors of the economy as they have in the financial realm. Simple bureaucratic inertia has been one cause but the vested interests close to Soeharto have been important contributing factors. On a day-to-day basis, combating crony businessmen initiatives clutters up the agenda for the technocrats and leaves less time for dealing with more worthwhile business. 'These things just pop up and we have no time to cope with them. We spend all our time fighting a rearguard action,' complained one government econo- mist.[39]

In more concrete terms, the acquisitiveness of Indonesia's crony businessmen has helped cool the technocrats' enthusiasm for privatising state-owned enterprises. Without an expectation that these enterprises would be run more efficiently under private owners, or that they would be sold off under a transparent process of competitive bidding, there is little incentive to privatise. 'We're naturally reluctant to push ahead with privatisation if all the successful ones are going to be taken over by the cronies,' said leading technocrat Ali Wardhana.[40] The *Jakarta Post*, in a 1993 editorial dedicated to questionable privatisation deals, expressed the same sentiments: 'The manner in which private firms . . . have acquired state companies or state property has given the impression that the privatisation was done mostly for the benefit of particular private companies with strong political connections . . . No wonder the allegation has emerged that many of the privatisation deals simply created rent-seekers.'[41]

The Palapa satellite program is a case in point. Palapa, a network of communications satellites, was one of Indonesia's most profitable state-owned companies. Until early 1993 it fell under the jurisdiction of the Telecommunications Ministry. But in January of that year Palapa's operations were transferred to a new company, Satelit Palapa Indonesia, or Satelindo, in which a consortium led by Soeharto's second son Bambang Trihatmodjo held a 60 per cent share. The transfer, which will cost the government some US$100 million a year in lost income, was done without a tender process. In fact, it was not even clear if the government received any payment at all for relinquishing ownership.[42]

The technocrats' credibility is another casualty of crony capitalism. As described in an earlier chapter, high-level corruption in Indonesia has been used by some as an argument to reduce the technocrats' influence over economic policy. With so many monopolies and other lucrative deals still in the hands of crony businessmen, the technocrats' championing of a level playing field for everyone else falls, not surprisingly, on plenty of deaf ears. 'The problem with [the cronies] is that they are costing us legitimacy as a government,' former minister Prawiro complained.[43] In July 1992, Public Works Minister Radinal Moochtar denied to parliament that tolls would soon be raised on the main road across Jakarta. A few days later, tolls were raised and an embarrassed Moochtar had to explain why he had lied to parliament. As it turned out, he hadn't lied. Tutut Soeharto, whose company collected the bulk of the toll revenues, had gone over his head and had her father approve the toll increase.[44]

Sometimes, government officials lose more than credibility. In 1992, several senior officials lost their jobs, including Mohammad Suparno, the Garuda Indonesia president; Cacuk Sudarijanto, the president of the state telephone company; Ishadi, the director of state-owned television channel TVRI; and Ermansyah Yamin, who headed the electricity utility PLN. Official explanations aside, the business community understood that all four were paying the price for being less than fully cooperative with Soeharto's relatives.

The injurious effects of crony businessmen acting largely outside the law cannot be measured only by the cost of individual deals they enter into or the headaches they cause government officials. Together, they set an example for how to get ahead in business which reverberates all the way through the bureaucracy. Examples abound of ministers, provincial governors, regional military commanders, district chiefs and others operating miniature patronage networks based on the model used by Soeharto. Without question, the privileges and impunities enjoyed by crony businessmen are devastating to the spirit of entrepreneurialism, something the technocrats say must be inculcated more thoroughly for the economy to prosper and, longer term, for *pribumi*–Chinese tensions to abate.

In remarks unusual only for their candour, Indonesian businessman Setiawan Djody in late 1993 spelled out in the clearest terms possible how the progression of his businesses has depended on help from the First Family, particularly Sigit Haryoyudanto and Tommy Soeharto. 'If I failed to arrange meetings with [government] ministers, I had to ring up either Sigit or Tommy. In running shipping companies, I have received help from Sigit, and in the automotive business, Tommy has helped me much,' Djody said. Already a sizeable operator in shipping, mining, textiles, construction and trading, Djody made headlines in 1993 by buying the luxury Italian sportscar maker Lamborghini. 'Tommy's help is needed if I start manufacturing cars in Indonesia,' he acknowledged at the time.[45]

For those without Djody's stellar connections, life becomes much more complicated. Small businessmen complain that as soon as they reach a certain size they are vulnerable to acquisition-hungry conglomerates, with crony businessmen being the worst offenders. Soeharto's half-brother Probosutedjo, a self-styled defender of the economically disadvantaged, explained the problem like this: 'People who want to start businesses are reluctant because they realise that Indonesian conglomerates are always out to grab all kinds of businesses.'[46] With virtually no anti-trust statutes on the books, small businessmen have no recourse to the law. With such constricted rewards on offer, the risks of entrepreneurial behaviour seem more forbidding. One of the technocrats' chief aims has been to tilt the balance more in favour of entrepreneurs but the crony factor has made progress excruciatingly slow. Despite the important accomplishments of Indonesia's economic reform program, it can still be said that for Indonesia's capitalists, 'their political ties to the powerholders [remain] the most influential variable for their economic success'.[47]

This dictum also holds true for the bigger, already established businesses. Astra International, one of Indonesia's largest conglomerates, is the dominant player in the automobile industry and is active in banking, insurance, mining, food crops and plywood manufacturing. Founded by the Soeryadjaya family, Astra was long considered Indonesia's best run conglomerate and was a frequent recipient of management awards. One distinguishing characteristic of the Astra Group was that the Soeryadjayas had achieved an unusual degree of autonomy from the First Family and other cronies, a characteristic which was especially appealing to Toyota Motor of Japan, Astra's main partner in its biggest subsidiary, car-making Toyota Astra Motor.

In 1992, the Soeryadjayas' empire collapsed thanks to massive mismanagement at Bank Summa, a unit run by Astra patriarch William Soeryadjaya's son Edward. To cover the bank's losses, the Soeryadjayas were forced to seek buyers for the family's shares in Astra. For at least a year the family tried to put together a syndicate of foreign buyers led by Toyota. The plan failed because of Toyota's reluctance to commit without knowing which other new Indonesian investors would be buying into Astra. Toyota didn't want to increase its already large stake if Soeharto cronies were to become its new partners.[48] In the end, the Soeryadjayas ran out of time. The Indonesian central bank forced the family's bank into liquidation and William had no choice but to sell to an Indonesian investment consortium. The new investors, who received the full backing of Soeharto, were led by Prajogo Pangestu and Liem Sioe Liong.

The Soeryadjayas' demise was largely of their own doing, of course. But the way the 'Astra problem' was solved highlighted the leading role the top cronies play in Indonesia. When a major corporation faltered, not only did the top cronies have the inside track as 'white knights', but they were actively encouraged by Soeharto to do so.[49] (Needless to say, the Astra takeover by ethnic-Chinese businessmen only reinforced the view held by leading *pribumi* businessmen that Indonesia is not a land of equal opportunity.)

The battle over money

The heart of the battle between Soeharto's cronies and economic reformers in the government is the struggle for control over financial resources, especially the vast pools of deposits collected by Indonesia's state-owned banks. Soeharto's cronies depend heavily on these funds to pay for their projects. State bank involvement is crucial for the cronies since some of their projects are of such dubious quality that they would be shunned by private lenders. In many cases, and increasingly after the deregulation drive accelerated in the late 1980s, the cronies' projects were funded by a consortium of foreign and Indonesian state banks. The foreign banks were prepared to overlook the questionable prospects of repayment as long as a state bank was also a lender to the project, thereby giving the underlying project a de facto government guarantee. The technocrats and many other economists believed these guarantees were an important factor in the sharp run-up in Indonesia's foreign debt in the late 1980s and the subsequent pressures on the balance of payments.[50]

In late 1991 the technocrats, disturbed by the lax credit analysis of the state banks, were forced to assert more direct control over government lending. In September of that year, Minister Prawiro announced the formation of a commercial offshore loan team (Colt) consisting of ten cabinet-level officials. All projects with any connection to the government would need approval from the team before being allowed to borrow abroad. The definition of 'government connection' was deliberately made as broad as possible. Any projects with supply or distribution arrangements with state-owned firms as well as projects receiving state bank funding all fell into the net. Purely private projects were not affected.

A month later, Prawiro announced a five-year schedule which spelled out which projects would receive Colt permission for borrowing offshore. Investments worth some US$50–60 billion were indefinitely postponed. These were mainly large infrastructure projects—such as roads, power plants, ports and telephones—and a series of petrochemical complexes. The Colt initiative was a bold move by the technocrats. But although warmly welcomed by bankers and economists, the loan screening team struck right at the heart of the crony-government symbiosis. Many of the postponed projects—and all of the largest ones—had some crony involvement.

The loan team, and by implication its control over state bank resources, immediately became a test of wills between the technocrats on the one side and cabinet level nationalists such as Habibie and Ginanjar along with crony businessmen on the other. An early test involved the US$2.4 billion Chandra Asri olefins complex planned for West Java. An olefins facility cracks naphtha, an oil by-product, into ethylene and propylene, the basic building blocks for plastic compounds. Chandra Asri's shareholders included Prajogo Pangestu, Bambang Trihatmodjo and Henry Pribadi, a businessman close to Liem Sioe Liong. Chandra Asri had fallen into the Colt orbit on two counts: it had an agreement to buy naphtha from the state-owned oil giant Pertamina and it had borrowed extensively from state-owned Bank Bumi Daya. Chandra Asri did not make it on to the five-year Colt schedule of approved projects.

Chandra Asri shareholders swung into action. They argued that the plant should be exempt from Colt restrictions because construction had already started. They hired a US consulting firm to review the project and the firm concluded, unsurprisingly, that it would be cheaper for the government to allow Chandra Asri to proceed. For six months the technocrats held the line. 'We have to stick with what [the Colt] decided. If we loosen up it will be difficult to control [new borrowing],' Finance Minister Sumarlin told me in a March 1992 interview.[51] Chandra Asri was told it would have to replace its debts with the state banks before its project could go ahead. But this condition was unacceptable to Chandra Asri's Japanese bankers who wanted the government to maintain a stake in the project's future. This was precisely the sort of government exposure, of course, that the loan team had been set up to stop.

A month later Chandra Asri shareholders prevailed. On 9 April 1992 Minister Prawiro, on the instructions of Soeharto, said the Chandra Asri could resume.[52] The US$550 million letter of credit extended to Chandra Asri by Bank Bumi Daya was to be converted into a hybrid credit facility called a merchant letter of credit, which, despite the semantics, left the state bank exposed to the project. Another US$213 million in loans to Chandra Asri from Bank Bumi Daya and a second state-owned bank, Bank Dagang Negara, was simply converted into personal loans to Prajogo Pangestu.[53]

Two weeks later the government announced new rules permitting 100 per cent foreign ownership of projects with paid-up capital of more than US$50 million. Ostensibly aimed at attracting more foreign investment, the measure also opened a loophole for firms trying to evade the Colt restrictions, since these covered only domestically-owned firms. Chandra Asri's shareholders became the first to exploit the loophole. In late April Chandra Asri, now scaled down to a US$1.6 billion project, announced it would be reconfigured into a 100 per cent foreign owned company, apparently on the assumption that this would silence those who complained that politically powerful businessmen were exempt from the government's borrowing rules. In fact, the change to foreign ownership was little more than a thinly disguised bookkeeping exercise. The three Indonesian shareholders simply transferred their shares to overseas holding companies they controlled.[54]

Case study: Cloves—the slippery spice

Arguably the most egregious display of crony businessman greed in recent years is a monopoly on the sale and distribution of cloves set up by Tommy Soeharto at the very end of 1990. The disastrous monopoly had an impressive list of casualties—President Soeharto, the technocrats, the central bank, Indonesia's cigarette manufacturers and clove farmers. About the only good thing to be said of the monopoly was that it laid bare the avarice of the Soeharto flock.

Cloves are one of Indonesia's most important commodities. They are the key ingredient in the clove-scented *kretek* cigarette ubiquitous in Indonesia. Cigarettes are a big business in Indonesia, with industry sales reaching about US$3 billion a year. An estimated one-quarter of Indonesia's 180-million strong population smoke and about 90 per cent of smokers prefer *kreteks* to all-tobacco cigarettes. Cloves, which are crushed and sprinkled into a *kretek* cigarette, typically account for about 30 per cent of a *kretek*'s raw material costs.

In the late 1980s a handful of ethnic-Chinese traders decided to corner the market in cloves. Led by an Indonesian-Chinese merchant called Tjia Eng Tek, the traders were mostly from the eastern Indonesian islands of Sulawesi and Moluccas, and some of them had been involved in a lucrative nutmeg exporting cartel earlier in the 1980s. Cloves proved to be a trickier affair. Lined up against the would-be monopolists was a powerful cigarette industry lobby, the Association of Indonesian Cigarette Companies, or Gappri. Gappri was led by the four biggest *kretek* makers—

Gudang Garam, Djarum, Bentoel and Sampoerna—who accounted for some 80–90 per cent of total industry sales. All based on Java and all owned by ethnic-Chinese families, they had been in the *kretek* business for generations. Unusual for large Indonesian enterprises, the families owning the big *kretek* firms were not well diversified. A more typical Indonesian conglomerate might have decided to sacrifice one business line to preserve others. The *kretek* makers, however, were in no position to do the same.

The eastern Indonesian commodity traders began buying cloves in 1987–88 but had trouble selling the spice. The top *kretek* makers had their own stable of traders who bought directly from farmers or farmer cooperatives and they were not about to let newcomers into the business. In early 1989 the Tjia Eng Tek-led traders, realising they would need more political muscle, drafted Tommy Soeharto, then 26, into their consortium.[55] The trading consortium, now led publicly by Tommy's company Bina Reksa Perdana, portrayed itself as the defender of the small clove farmer against the rapacious *kretek* manufacturing giants. Weakening clove prices helped their cause. A state-owned company, Kerta Niaga, was supposed to maintain a floor price of about US$3.50 per kilogram but the under-capitalised firm was unable to keep prices from dropping to an average of US$2–3 a kilogram following a larger than usual harvest of cloves in 1988.

On 19 January 1990, Tommy spelled out his plan to Industry Minister Hartarto.[56] He said he wanted to replace the ineffective Kerta Niaga with a new privately-run national clove agency, headed by his company, which would be the sole buyer of cloves from farmers and cooperatives and the sole seller to *kretek* companies and other clove consumers such as food companies and makers of traditional medicines. With annual clove consumption in Indonesia of roughly 80 000 tonnes, the middleman monopoly had the potential to be enormously profitable. Tommy's basic idea was to buy cloves from farmers at about US$3.50–4.00 per kilogram and resell to the *kretek* firms at about US$6–7 a kilogram. The difference, amounting to well in excess of US$100 million a year, would stay with the clove agency.

In what became an unusually public contest, Gappri mobilised all its lobbying power. It warned that higher clove prices would cut into cigarette sales, cost jobs and mean less tax revenue for the government. From the government's perspective, these were not threats which could be easily ignored. The *kretek* industry employs 135 000 Indonesians directly and some three million more indirectly. In addition, Gappri members pay more than US$1 billion a year into the treasury in excise taxes, making cigarettes second only to oil as a source of tax revenue for the government.

Powerful though it was, Gappri couldn't compete with Tommy Soeharto. On 28 December 1990, the then Trade Minister, Arifin Siregar, gave the go-ahead for Tommy's consortium to act as the exclusive agent for the purchase and sales of cloves. (Siregar's standing in the technocrat community was one of the first casualties of the clove monopoly.) The newly minted clove agency, known by its Indonesian initials BPPC, included Tommy and the commodity traders supporting him, Kerta Niaga and some farming cooperatives.[57] At the time of its formation, BPPC had a stock of almost 90 000 tonnes of cloves, most of it sitting in warehouses owned by Tommy's trading associates.

Siregar's announcement dropped like a bombshell. Economists objected that Tommy's plan was doomed to failure. Indonesia, they pointed out, already produced more cloves than the country was consuming. And by almost doubling the price paid to clove farmers and quadrupling the price charged to *kretek* manufacturers, it was entirely predictable that consumption would decline while supply would soar. Image-wise, BPPC was a disaster, as it appeared to signal a backtracking in the economic reform campaign. '[The clove monopoly] is completely contrary to the era of deregulation,' said Sugiharto Prajogo, the late Gappri chairman.[58] The World Bank, in its 1991 annual report on Indonesia, sharply criticised the clove agency as unworkable and likely to hurt the farmers it was ostensibly designed to help. They were prophetic words.

Having obtained the government's blessing, BPPC went in search of funds. Tommy first turned to central bank Governor Adrianus Mooy for a low-interest credit line of US$600 million. (The irony of immediately turning to the government for funds after promoting itself as a private-sector replacement of state-owned Kerta Niaga was apparently lost on BPPC's founders.) Mooy refused. In February 1991, Tommy wrote to the Sultan of Brunei asking for a loan of US$650 million, suggesting that the funds be funnelled through the Indonesian central bank, thereby forcing the government to offer an implicit guarantee of repayment.[59] The Sultan resisted. Finally, Tommy appealed to his father to order Mooy to lend government funds to BPPC.[60] In April, Mooy said the central bank would lend BPPC about US$150 million out of a special subsidised lending program set up to help farmers.[61]

The technocrats were deeply upset at being forced to finance BPPC. At the time, the central bank was trying to squeeze the money supply to control inflation; pumping money into BPPC was a setback to these efforts. In October, the central bank was obliged to pump another US$200 million into BPPC, again out of subsidised credits set aside for farmers. This particular program had an annual ceiling of US$750 million and the monies funnelled into BPPC had to be taken out of other programs. 'We'll have to reduce what has been committed to other borrowers,' a frustrated Radius Prawiro said at the time.[62] 'Pouring US$350 million into BPPC is completely counterproductive to our tight money policy,' said another leading technocrat.[63]

For a while, prices paid to clove farmers moved up to about US$3 a kilogram. But at BPPC, stocks kept growing. As predicted, the supply of cloves rose dramatically in response to the promised higher prices. The cigarette companies, meanwhile, spent 1991 using up accumulated stocks and experimenting with using fewer cloves in their cigarettes. Tommy complained repeatedly that *kretek* manufacturers were continuing to buy cloves from non-BPPC approved traders. Try as he might to force cigarette producers to buy only from him, BPPC stocks grew and grew. BPPC had been rushed into existence with virtually no planning or established procedures. Its hastily set up offices in the prime clove growing regions in Sulawesi and Moluccas were incompetent and vulnerable to widespread fraud.

In February 1992, Tommy admitted BPPC had failed. The monopoly had purchased 117 000 tonnes of cloves in 1991 to add to its starting stock of 90 000 tonnes. It had been able to sell only 37 000 tonnes, leaving the agency with a large, expensive stock of 170 000 tonnes. The agency had yet to make a single payment on its debts to the central bank. And, with 1992's clove demand estimated at only 80 000 tonnes, the imbalance was only going to get worse.

Tommy's solution to the problem, as he informed parliament on 26 February 1992, was for Indonesia's tens of thousands of clove farmers to burn half their stocks. This was too much even for Indonesia's cowed legislators. One parliamentarian, Imam Chourmen, described Tommy's proposal as 'inhumane'.[64] Agriculture Minister Wardoyo, concerned that the controversy swirling about BPPC would hurt the government's Golkar party in the parliamentary elections scheduled for May 1992, hastily reassured farmers they wouldn't have to burn their clove stocks.

Tommy, however, was unrepentant. When the Speaker of Parliament Kharis Suhud directly criticised BPPC in March 1992, Tommy retorted that Suhud had no right to publicly air such comments. A month later, Tommy lashed out at Rachmat Witoelar, then Golkar's secretary-general, for suggesting that BPPC be closed. Tommy reminded him that it was President Soeharto who had made Golkar important, not the other way around. (Later, Witoelar would write to Tommy apologising for any offence caused.)[65] It was a blunt reminder that the Soeharto children see their position in Indonesia as inseparable from that of the president.

With ample justification, clove farmers felt themselves victimised by the trading monopoly. In April 1992, clove farmers in North Sulawesi told me that BPPC hadn't purchased any of their cloves since the previous December. After having been encouraged to grow more cloves, there was no place to sell. In some areas, prices had dipped below US$1.00 a kilogram.

In the same month, the government attempted to reform BPPC but succeeded only in making the problem worse. The floor price for cloves was dropped to US$2 a kilogram to discourage new plantings. The selling price to *kretek* makers stayed the same, US$6.50–7.50. But more importantly, BPPC turned over to the Federation of Primary Cooperatives the responsibility for procuring cloves outside Java. The cooperatives were prohibited from selling cloves to *kretek* manufacturers until BPPC had disposed of its 170 000 tonne stock. In effect, that meant the cooperatives gained a monopoly in *buying* cloves and BPPC retained a monopoly on *selling* cloves, as all the major *kretek* manufacturers were located in Java. Another way to describe the 'reform' was that it shifted a massive unpayable debt away from Tommy and his trading associates and on to farmer cooperatives, the same cooperatives BPPC had claimed just a year earlier would be principal beneficiaries of its monopoly.

Corruption in the 1990s

The clove monopoly typifies, albeit in an extreme form, the economic and political distortions created by widespread corruption and nepotism. Cronyism, as this chapter has discussed, acts as a brake on economic reform. It has complicated efforts to bring down inflation and the foreign debt, and reinforced impressions that the reformers wield nothing like the same clout as the leading crony businessmen. Unable to take on the cronies directly, the technocrats' only hope is that the market will eventually do the job for them.

But by 1993 economists in and out of the government were becoming increasingly pessimistic that this strategy would be effective. Without a more direct attack on the root causes of corruption, they believe, sufficient volumes of new investment will not be forthcoming. Continued private investment, both foreign and domestic, is crucial if Indonesia's transformation to an exporting industrial nation is to remain on track. Indonesian businessmen, of course, have only limited options open to them; only a few are large or sophisticated enough to invest abroad. But for Indonesia to maintain and, preferably, to expand the interest of foreign investors, it needs to keep pace with other capital-importing nations in offering an attractive investment climate. Economic reforms in China, Vietnam and India—all of which can match Indonesia's low labour and land cost advantages—are raising the stakes, although this development does not seem to be widely appreciated in Jakarta. 'Our problem is that Soeharto is not convinced that new regional competitors pose a real threat to Indonesia,' one cabinet minister complained in mid-1992.[66]

One feature of the 'investment climate' which is considered by foreign investors is what is sometimes called 'red tape', a catch-all phrase which refers to bureaucratic obstacles to investment as well as, more euphemistically, the degree of corruption in a particular country. Indonesian 'red tape' is certainly a disincentive to many overseas investors. But not for all. Those with good enough political connections of their own and those unencumbered by too many home office constraints can and do benefit from links with Indonesia's crony businessmen. Big Japanese firms in particular, say many Indonesians, find Indonesia's corporate culture quite congenial. The majority of foreign investors in Indonesia, however, and certainly a majority of *potential* foreign investors, do not fit into this category.

In July 1992 the outgoing US ambassador to Indonesia, John Monjo, made plain this concern. At a Jakarta conference on regional trade and investment, Monjo blamed red tape and corruption for dampening the interest of American investors in Indonesia. His comments set off a barrage of complaints about interference in Indonesia's internal affairs. But many were sympathetic. 'What the ambassador pointed out was nothing new,' commented legislator Yusuf Syakir. 'But the bad thing is that we only respond when such criticism is aired by a foreigner.'[67]

Less than a year later the Hong Kong-based Political and Economic Risk Consultancy surveyed bankers and business executives on the prevalence of corruption in ten Asian countries. Indonesia suffered the ignominy of being nominated the most corrupt of all. An accompanying report described a 'culture of corruption' in Indonesia which 'has been a major contributing factor to failed projects, negative policy reversals and economic stagnation'. The major culprits, the report added, are 'confined to very high levels of society, usually with the proper political credentials, where the checks and balances are difficult to enforce'.[68] Tomiyasu Nakamura, the director of general affairs at the Jakarta office of the Japan External Trade Organisation, gave a very similar assessment in a 1994 interview when he was asked about the difficulties facing foreign investors in Indonesia. 'Everything is very unclear here: taxation, procedures, restrictions. It is often necessary to do things under the table. In China there is corruption but not so much. Here it is everywhere. It's hard to calculate business costs when invisible costs come up again and again.'[69]

The same theme is increasingly being picked up by Indonesian commentators. In the absence of 'more concerted efforts to combat malfeasance, [Indonesia] will increasingly be shunned by bonafide long-term investors with good intentions,' the *Jakarta Post* editorialised in April 1993. Instead, the paper continued, Indonesia will be attractive only to 'profiteering businessmen, monopolies, oligopolies and other kinds of rent-seekers with strong political connections, who can offset the unusually high hidden costs of doing business with abnormally high profits'.[70]

These sorts of complaints have yet to make much of an impact on Soeharto. If anything, the initial burst of economic growth following the deregulation drive in 1987–90 seems to have limited, rather than expanded, the technocrats' ability to rein in the top crony businessmen. To be sure, they have made some progress. The disbanding of Bambang

Trihatmodjo's plastics monopoly is one example. But at the same time, the cronies have been able to replace lost monopolies with a privileged presence in other fields. Bambang and his siblings, for example, have become gatekeepers to the petrochemical industry: virtually no major contract goes by without their involvement. So, while their activities may be changing, the cronies' basic relationship to the government has stayed largely the same. And, as their businesses grow bigger, they in turn grow increasingly powerful. It is a trend which is of concern not only to the technocrats but also to Minister Habibie. As described earlier, the potential for government-sponsored corruption poses perhaps the most serious risk to Habibie's plans to have the government invest more in high-technology industries.

One prominent technocrat, speaking in mid-1992, had this to say about the cronies' influence: 'In the beginning, twenty-five years ago, Soeharto picked his economic officials based on expertise. That's why they were called technocrats. But lately, more personal criteria—like loyalty to Soeharto—have become more important. There's no question that Soeharto listens more to Liem and Prajogo and Hasan and his children now compared to five or even two years ago. He seems to think that these business "practitioners" are giving him better advice than the economists.'[71] Soeharto's selection of a new cabinet in March 1993 was received by many in the Indonesian elite as confirmation of the cronies' greater clout. A frequently heard view was that Soeharto had relied heavily on the advice of his children and the likes of Liem Sioe Liong and Prajogo Pangestu before making his cabinet choices.

Given Soeharto's continued support for the leading crony businessmen, the 'big corruption' problem seems destined to get worse. The appetite of Soeharto's children for business expansion seems unquenchable. Many Indonesian businessmen believe Soeharto's children intend to use their father's remaining years in office to become as economically powerful as they can. The more powerful they are, the argument goes, the more protected they will be in the post-Soeharto era. It is expected that they will focus their efforts on the transport, communications and energy sectors, all areas currently dominated by the government. The children are also likely to structure more of their investments through offshore nominee companies, in the belief that these will be more insulated from future reformers in the government.[72]

The activities of Soeharto's cronies also must be measured in political terms. Resentment of top-level corruption is no longer limited to the elite. Although the escapades of Soeharto's children are treated with care, in recent years the press has become increasingly critical of overtly corrupt behaviour. Knowledge of the Soeharto family activities is widespread in Indonesia; even on the remoter islands, the latest First Family antics are the stuff of everyday conversation.

Public dissatisfaction with crony businessmen was used to good effect by the smallest of Indonesia's three political parties, the Indonesian Democratic Party, ahead of the June 1992 parliamentary elections. Equal access to business opportunities was a prominent plank in its campaign. 'We have to provide the same opportunities to the sons of ordinary workers as are available to the sons of ministers or of the big business-men,' is how one party delegate, Laksamana Sukardi, put it.[73] Kwik Kian Gie, a party leader and economist, argued that the rampant corruption in Indonesia had weakened the fabric of Indonesian society. 'It is very difficult to make any improvement while the whole society is demoralised like this,' he complained.[74]

But while the Democratic Party scored some gains in the 1992 elec-tions, its performance fell far short of the excitement it generated during the campaign. This was to be expected, as the electoral system is heavily rigged in favour of the ruling party Golkar. In an interview prior to the 1992 elections, Golkar's secretary-general Rachmat Witoelar claimed, cynically if correctly, that the corruption issue would not damage Golkar's performance. 'A lot of our voters have already accepted the [Soeharto family businesses] as a fact of Indonesia's development process. That's the style of the Indonesian leadership and people already know it. In fact, the worse it gets the more benefit Golkar can take from trying to improve the situation. People will forget that it was Golkar in charge when the problem got bad in the first place.'[75]

Witoelar's hoped-for collective amnesia is unlikely to outlast Soeharto's passing from power. Most of the armed forces leadership, the cabinet and the business community accept that Soeharto's children have drained legitimacy from the presidential office and tainted all associated with the New Order regime. Consequently, for those already contemplating their future in a post-Soeharto Indonesia, difficult choices have to be made. As one senior government official put it in April 1993: 'For the remaining years of Soeharto's presidency, everyone has to make their choice. Either you're with Soeharto or you're not.'[76]

Crony businessmen must also be considered a serious obstacle to a smooth, predictable and non-disruptive transfer of power from Soeharto to whatever successor emerges. Many feel that Soeharto is reluctant to leave office because he would not be able to protect his children from the sidelines. Speculation has been widespread about the possibility of a deal in which the army promises to protect Soeharto's children in return for the president stepping down. Such a deal remains an unlikely prospect. First, there is the difficulty of broaching the matter with Soeharto. Second, there is the difficulty of persuading Soeharto that any deal will be honoured after he leaves power. And third, there is only so much protec-tion the army can offer without compromising its desire to see a less corrupt administration. 'A lot of younger officers ask me why Abri [the armed forces] can't just give Soeharto a guarantee that we will protect his family,' Lieutenant General (ret.) Hasnan Habib said. 'But it is not as easy as it sounds. We can protect the family physically, but we can't make them above the law.'[77]

In fact, it is unlikely that there would be a serious government effort to investigate the wealth of Soeharto's family even after the president leaves power. The consensus among the elite is that such an investigation simply wouldn't be worth the effort and, in any case, would open a can of worms that would be hard to reclose. Soeharto's children and the other crony businessmen, after all, do not exist in isolation. Officials throughout the bureaucracy have been well compensated for not standing in their way. A serious investigation of the crony businessmen would ultimately incriminate a broad swath of civil servants, an outcome that will surely temper the Indonesian elite's desire for judicial retribution.

The former Golkar secretary-general Rachmat Witoelar—he was appointed ambassador to Moscow in August 1993—argues against exaggerating the scope of the problem. As he rightly points out, 'Soeharto could solve the problem with a snap of the fingers.'[78] But being able to solve the problem is not the same thing as wanting to solve it. It is true that Soeharto, on the advice of the technocrats, has agreed to pull the plug on some of the most flagrant examples of rent-seeking behaviour in recent years. Whether he is willing to go further remains an open question. As has been discussed elsewhere, the issue of corruption presents Soeharto with a basic conflict. On the one hand, Indonesia's need to improve its competitiveness as an exporting nation requires a cleaner administration, a more accountable government and a stronger legal framework. But these demands strike at the heart of Soeharto's patrimonial style of rule. The cleaner the administration, the fewer the sources of patronage and, by extension, the fewer tools at hand to maintain his political hegemony. Soeharto's style of rule is so ingrained that any expectations of significant change would seem overly optimistic. And indeed, it is hard to find anyone in Indonesia prepared to predict that top-level corruption will abate while Soeharto remains in power.

For most of his rule, Soeharto has been able to have it both ways. A half-decade of economic liberalisation has brought higher economic growth without requiring a fundamental change in Soeharto's leadership techniques. He can afford, to give one example, to take a plastics importing monopoly away from his son Bambang because he knows there remains fertile ground for Bambang still to plough. But in the future these trade-offs will become more difficult. The hard choices between government accountability and patrimonialism cannot be finessed for much longer. How Soeharto chooses will say much about Indonesia's economic prospects through the middle of the decade and beyond.

7
Islam: Coming in from the cold?

If someone is able to separate sugar from its sweetness, he will be able to separate Islamic religion from politics.

K. H. A. Wahab Chasbullah[1]

Using religious politics is a dangerous tendency. Let the government govern and let the religious groups take care of their own affairs.

Abdurrahman Wahid[2]

Is Islam-phobia possible in a country where most of the people are Muslims?

Nasir Tamara[3]

In the middle of March 1992, a peculiar invitation arrived at the office of Abdurrahman Wahid, the leader of Indonesia's largest Muslim organisation, the Nahdlatul Ulama. Wahid, one of the most influential if controversial figures in Indonesian society, had just weeks earlier shaken up the normally quiet world of Indonesian politics by hosting a mass rally at a Jakarta stadium. The ostensible purpose of the rally—a reaffirmation of the Muslim organisation's commitment to the state ideology Pancasila—seemed harmless enough on the surface.

But with parliamentary elections just three months away, the keepers of the New Order status quo were deeply offended by Wahid's effrontery in flaunting the extent of his support among the masses. To make matters worse, over the previous fifteen months Wahid, a firm believer in keeping mosque and state separate, had consistently refused to play along with a new Soeharto-sponsored Islamic organisation (ICMI) whose main purpose seemed, to Wahid anyway, to be to drum up political support for Soeharto

162

among leading Indonesian Muslims. Now the bill for acting independent was coming due.

The invitation had been sent by Lieutenant Colonel Prabowo Subianto, an officer with far more clout than his rank would suggest. His place in the elite constellation comes less from personal prestige than from lineage: he is Soeharto's son-in-law. Wahid was invited to meet Prabowo at the latter's battalion headquarters just outside Jakarta. Once the meeting began, Prabowo, presumably with the blessing of Soeharto, warned Wahid that he had strayed beyond the boundaries of acceptable political conduct. Henceforth, Wahid was to stick with religious issues and stay out of politics. If he insisted on dabbling in politics, Prabowo said, his first move should be to endorse Soeharto for another term of office. Later, when Wahid said maybe he would opt to leave the Nahdlatul Ulama instead, the ultimatum was dropped.[4] It was too much of a risk to push aside a figure of Wahid's stature so close to elections.

Although a showdown was averted, Prabowo's message highlighted two realities of modern Indonesian politics. One, that Soeharto is not ready for any political activity, no matter how mild and innocuous, outside his direct control. Second, that despite the New Order's nearly three-decade-long campaign to neutralise civilian opposition, Islam is still considered a potent political force. In snapshot descriptions of Indonesia, one of the most commonly cited statistics is that, with almost 90 per cent of its citizens professing a belief in Islam, Indonesia is home to the largest Muslim community in the world. It is a fine example of how numbers can mislead, for Islam in Indonesia is a heterogenous faith. This explains how Indonesia could have started as a secular state and how it has managed to survive as one. Many Indonesians—probably a majority, but it is hard to say—are content to regard Islam as the nation's leading religion but are not keen to make it the central feature of the political system. For this reason, Islam in Indonesia has been by a considerable margin a more benign and moderate presence than it has been in many Middle Eastern countries.

Given the constraints on the press and absence of free elections, it is almost impossible to say which component of Indonesia's Muslim community enjoys the most popular support. But it is true to say that the community includes many for whom Islam is but the latest addition to a mixed bag of cultural traditions. For others, Islam is more a legal requirement than a matter of religious conviction. All Indonesians are required to choose from one of five officially tolerated religions—Islam, Catholicism, Protestantism, Hinduism and Buddhism. Claiming adherence to mystical beliefs, or admitting to no religion at all, is not allowed.[5] Many who in reality would fit into the latter two categories show up in official statistics as Muslims.

Many Indonesian Muslims, of course, take their religious faith very seriously. For this group particularly, Islam in Indonesia has been a study in frustration. Shunted aside under Soeharto's authoritarian and nominally secular rule, many Muslims feel they have been deprived of their rightful place in the running of the nation. This doesn't make Muslims unique in the New Order—other groups have been denied political influence as well—but the feeling of being dispossessed burns strong. However, this has not diluted their political aspirations; if anything, these appear to be growing.

By the late 1980s, a revival of Islamic consciousness was underway in Indonesia, especially among the young. Increasingly, Islam is seen as a safe alternative to the heavily circumscribed political structure. Attendance in mosques is up and sermons are filled with grievances, complaints and yearnings of an overtly political nature. Land issues, wealth inequalities, government corruption and a perceived official favouritism towards Christians (and especially Chinese Christians) are especially contentious topics. In a society which has rid itself of formal politics, everything becomes political. Nowhere is this more true than in the case of Islam.

The revival of interest in Islam has been accompanied by Muslim demands for a stronger political voice, a trend which has broad implications for Indonesia. The implications for economic policymaking have already been discussed in an earlier chapter. But these demands, naturally, are having a profound effect on the political landscape as well.

For the military, a rising Islamic awareness is a source of considerable concern. The army is fond of defining its place in Indonesia as the defender of the centre against the extreme left—communism—and the extreme right—Islamic fundamentalism. Fearful of seeing its central relevance decline, the army has worked hard to keep the communist bogeyman alive. Hence, the black hand of communism is seen behind all manner of activity not to the government's liking. But the argument has been threadbare for a long time and, with the ending of the Cold War and the collapse of communist regimes in Eastern Europe, it is approaching the point of farce. That leaves the extreme right. (Although, as will be discussed in a later chapter, by the early 1990s the military has discovered a new threat, the 'extreme centrist', meaning those pushing for democratisation and more respect for human rights.) It is accepted wisdom in army doctrine that Islam poses a potential threat to the unity of the nation. But with pressures for more political pluralism building, more political power for Muslims is inevitable. The questions are: how much more, and which Muslims?

The debate on Islam's role in society poses a real dilemma for Indonesian proponents of democratisation. A prerequisite for a peaceful, gradual process of democratisation is to convince the army that Muslims do not, in fact, threaten national unity, and that they do not nurture dreams of a theocratic state. Without alleviating the army's fears, democratisation will be doomed before it begins.

The Muslim leaders demanding more political representation resent the need to prove their nationalist credentials but they go through the motions anyway. All pledge fealty to Pancasila, the state ideology which guarantees freedom of religion and, by extension, makes the avowal of an Islamic state a criminal offence.[6] These leaders say that they do not strive for an Islamic state as such; rather, they want the government to more fully reflect Islamic views and convictions in public policy. They claim, not without some justification, that they represent a powerful pressure group for more democratic rule and that the army, not they, should be seen as the real enemy to political change.

But many Indonesians, including non-Muslims, nominal Muslims, the Chinese business community, and some important elements of the military, continue to harbour doubts about whether this Islamic consensus behind Pancasila is genuine. The usually unstated accusation is that once Islamic groups attain political power they will reveal themselves to be, in the New Order lexicon, anti-Pancasila. This prospect revives old fears of national disintegration, an explosion of Muslim–Christian enmity, and the demise of Indonesia as a secular state.

Feeding these doubts are leading figures in the 'orthodox' Muslim camp, with Wahid being the most prominent, who say that Soeharto is backing the wrong horse. They complain that the president is helping those Muslim groups most likely to bring the army's fears to fruition, and shunning those Muslims less interested in being formal stakeholders in the political structure. Soeharto's own short-term political objectives, these critics assert, are damaging the longer term prospects for democratisation in Indonesia.

The differing views of all these groups are discussed in greater detail below. But the contemporary debate cannot be evaluated without some description, however sketchy, of Islam's beginnings in Indonesia. It is understating the case considerably to say that the divisions apparent in Indonesia's Islamic community in the 1990s have taken a long time to form.

Fighting the uphill battle

Islam arrived in what is now Indonesia about seven hundred years ago, introduced by traders from India and the Middle East. Landing first in Sumatra, the Muslim influence gradually spread down through Java. The manner of Islam's arrival had a major bearing on its subsequent influence. For the most part, Islam came to the Indonesian islands peacefully, not by conquest. Generally speaking, it did not displace or destroy existing cultural traditions—mainly Hindu and Buddhist—but was syncretised with them. Moreover, the proselytising traders arriving on Indonesian shores were mostly steeped in the more accommodating *Sufi* school of Islam, rather than orthodox Arab varieties.[7]

In the nineteenth century, by one account, Islam, 'with few exceptions, was practised throughout the [Indonesian] islands as a traditional folk religion . . . Everywhere Islam had gracefully united with local beliefs.'[8] But by the end of the century, the winds of Islamic reform had reached Indonesia from the Middle East. Reform Islam provided many Indonesian Muslims with a new, stronger identity in the confusing milieu of a modernising world. The new Islam 'stood for a return to what it called the fundamental truths of the Koran, discarding both the accretions of medieval scholasticism and the compromises with local animism, thus clearing the way for a thoroughgoing modernisation of Islam'.[9] The message of Reform Islam spread quickly, especially near the end of the century when the advent of the steamship permitted large numbers of Muslims to undertake the haj pilgrimage to Mecca, one of the Five Pillars of the Islamic faith.

The arrival of Reform, or modernist, Islam widened the already apparent divisions within Indonesia's Muslim community. In his pathbreaking study, *The Religion of Java*, the American anthropologist Clifford Geertz identified three broad strains of belief among Java's Muslims: *abangan*, *santri* and *priyayi*. For the *abangan* Indonesian, religion is a mixture of traditional mystical beliefs, Hindu-Buddhism and Islam. Avowedly tolerant and syncretic, *abangan*, or nominal, Islam remains close to its Javanese roots. The *abangan* religious tradition, in the Geertz schema, is 'made up primarily of the ritual feast called the *slametan*, of an extensive and intricate complex of spirit beliefs, and of a whole set of theories and practices of curing, sorcery and magic . . . The otherness, awfulness and majesty of God, the intense moralism, the rigorous concern with doctrine, and the intolerant exclusivism which are so much a part of Islam are very foreign to the traditional outlook of the Javanese.'[10]

For *santris*, Islam occupies a much more central place in their world view. 'What concerns the *santri*,' Geertz writes, 'is Islamic doctrine, and most especially the moral and social interpretations of it. They seem especially interested, particularly the urban 'modernist' *santris*, in apologetics: the defence of Islam as a superior ethical code for modern man, as a workable social doctrine for modern society, and as a fertile source of values for modern culture. [The *santri* outlook] tends to be marked by a strong emphasis on the necessity for unreserved belief and faith in the absolute truth of Islam and by marked intolerance for Javanese beliefs and practices they take to be heterodox.'[11] *Santris* see themselves as 'purer' Muslims than *abangans* and see the *abangan* absorption of non-Islamic traditions as backward and old-fashioned.

The *priyayi* were Java's aristocratic elite. Originally clustered around the courts of the ancient Javanese kingdoms, the *priyayi* later formed the nucleus of the colonial bureaucracy. While the educated *priyayi* look down on the animistic features of *abangan* beliefs, their world views were traditionally considered to be closer to the *abangan* than to the *santri*. In colonial times, however, the main difference between the *priyayi* on the one hand and *santris* and *abangans* on the other was more clearly seen in class than in religious terms: the *priyayi* as bureaucrats and adminis- trators and the *santris* and *abangans* as petty traders, merchants and peasants. (The *priyayi* category has become less relevant since Indonesian independence as the bureaucracy has opened up to the non-aristocratic classes.)

Both the ruling *priyayi* and the Dutch saw modernist Islam as a political threat. 'This explains why *santri* Muslims were to predominate in certain economic activities such as manufacturing and trade while being under-represented in the colonial army and administration,' points out human rights activist Liem Soei Liong.[12] While less stringent, this division of labour is still apparent in modern-day Indonesia.

The arrival of reformist Islam had another effect: not only did it illuminate differences between *santri* and *abangan*, it also deepened cleavages within the *santri* community itself. A split emerged between the modernists and the more conservative *santri* preachers. The conservative end of the spectrum came to be seen as too close to the *abangan* 'infidels' and the charges against them resembled those levelled at *abangans*. 'The modernists attacked what they called the meaningless ritual of Koranic chanting and the quibbles of traditional scholasticism, and they demanded that Javanese Islam be purged of its non-Islamic "superstitions".'[13] For their part, the conservatives felt that the 'concern of modernists with reconciling Islam to a so-called modernity . . . was an implied rejection of the eternal truth embodied in the teachings of the great scholars of classical Islam'.[14] Both groups resorted to Islamic scripture to prove the rightness of their ways.

In the early part of the twentieth century these doctrinal differences took organisational shape. Two important Muslim groupings sprang up in 1912: the Muhammadiyah and the Sarekat Islam.[15] The Muhammadiyah was founded by modernist *santris*, particularly from urban areas. The Sarekat Islam, while founded by men of similar religious temperament, saw its mission more in economic and political terms—as a defence against Chinese economic domination and as a grassroots nationalist movement. The Sarekat Islam soon became more militant and factionalised along political and religious lines. It was suppressed by the Dutch and within a decade had ceased to be a powerful movement, although the ideas it represented lived on. (One wing of the Sarekat Islam eventually formed the nucleus of the Indonesian Communist Party.) The Muhammadiyah, on the other hand, survived and grew in influence.

In 1926 the more conservative *santris* responded to the Muhammadiyah by founding a mass organisation of their own: the Nahdlatul Ulama (NU), meaning the 'Revival of Religious Scholars'. The NU was unwilling to reject Javanese cultural traditions which predated Islam's arrival in Indonesia; it was established to reverse the rising importance of the modernists vis-a-vis the rural-based *ulama*, or religious teachers, in Java. By the early 1990s, the NU claimed a membership of some thirty million, based mostly in Central and East Java. The Muhammadiyah's membership is smaller, at about fifteen million, but is more dispersed across Indonesia. With their own networks of schools and training centres, the two are the strongest non-governmental social and educational organisations in Indonesia.

In the years preceding independence, the thread of nationalism, Dutch repression and the Javanese distaste of open conflict kept the intra-*santri* debate and the *santri–abangan* differences from becoming uncontrollably divisive. After the Dutch were expelled by the Japanese in the early 1940s, the Japanese military actively courted Islamic groups and assiduously exploited Muslim anti-Dutch feelings.[16] In 1943 the Japanese required all existing Muslim organisations to join an umbrella group known by its acronym Masyumi. While it lasted, the Masyumi gave Indonesian Muslims a degree of unity and national importance previously unimaginable and later a subject of wistful nostalgia.

In the constitutional debates of mid-1945, as discussed in the first chapter, the Masyumi demanded that Islam become the state religion. Sukarno's 'Pancasila speech' of 1 June 1945 attempted to finesse the issue by stipulating a 'Belief in One God' for all Indonesians. Sukarno's purpose was, as Southeast Asian scholar Anthony Johns says, that 'although Indonesia should not be an Islamic state, it should not be a secular one either. Rather, Indonesia should have a religious state philosophy based on belief in God through which the ideals of every religious denomination could be realised.'[17] In this, Sukarno was strongly supported both by proponents of a liberal and an authoritarian state who feared that the prospect of an Islamic state would sunder Indonesia even before it had achieved independence.

But many modernist *santri* Muslims cared little for Sukarno's semantics.[18] They refused to compromise on their deeply held notion of Islam as 'a holistic religion that knows no separation of the things of God from the things of man'.[19] The Jakarta Charter, which required the 'adherents of Islam to practise Islamic law', was put forward as a constitutional compromise to mollify the Masyumi but it was dropped just before Sukarno and Mohammad Hatta proclaimed independence in August 1945. For the Masyumi, and for modernist Islam more specifically, the Charter's omission was the beginning of a long and frustrating struggle to see Islam occupy a more prominent place in Indonesian society. The Masyumi's unfulfilled desire to see Islam as the basis of the Indonesian state was not a minor ideological quibble. As Bernard Lewis explains:

> When we in the Western world, nurtured in the Western tradition, use the words 'Islam' and 'Islamic', we tend to make a natural error and assume that religion means the same for Muslims as it has meant in the Western world, even in medieval times; that is to say, a section or compartment of life reserved for certain matters, and separate, or at least separable, from other compartments of life designed to hold other matters. That is not so in the Islamic world. It was never so in the past, and the attempt in modern times to make it so may perhaps be seen, in the longer perspective of history, as an unnatural aberration which in Iran has ended and in some other Islamic countries may also be nearing its end . . . At the present time, the very notion of a secular jurisdiction and authority—of a so-to-speak unsanctified part of life that lies outside the scope of religious law and those who uphold it—is seen as an impiety, indeed as the ultimate betrayal of Islam.[20]

Heated debates on Islam's role would continue until the parliamentary democracy period ended in 1959. But in the years immediately following the declaration of independence, the main task for all Indonesians was to fend off Dutch attempts to retake their colonial possession. This struggle would take place in both the diplomatic and military arenas, and Muslim groups would play an important role in each.

At its inception in 1945, the Indonesian army was comprised largely of soldiers recruited by the Japanese into the *Pembela Tanah Air* (Peta), the Motherland Defence Force. The soldiers came predominantly from lower *priyayi* and *abangan* backgrounds and shared a distrust of *santri* militancy. But the Japanese also had armed and trained *santri* Muslim units.[21] These were known as Hizbullah, the Army of Allah, and fought against the Dutch from 1945 to 1949. During the frequent cease-fires arranged by diplomats, the Hizbullah kept up a guerilla campaign against Dutch forces. In 1947 sections of the guerilla movement took on a new name, Darul Islam, or House of Islam, and established their own armed faction called the Indonesian Islamic Army.

Two years later the Darul Islam, based in West Java and headed by Sekar Madji Kartosuwiryo, refused to submit to control by the regular army and proclaimed a separate Islamic state. Kartosuwiryo justified the new Islamic State of Indonesia as righting the wrong inflicted on Muslims by Indonesia's secular nationalist leaders. 'By rejecting Islam as the sole foundation of the state, [the government] had made itself as evil an enemy as the Dutch.'[22]

The Darul Islam insurgency attracted the support of rebels in Aceh and subsequently gained new followers in South Sulawesi and other areas.

It was not fully subdued until 1962 when Kartosuwiryo was captured and executed. (Islamic-based rebellions, however, have reappeared several times since in Aceh, including in the early 1990s.) Besides tying up army units for much of the 1950s, the Darul Islam rebellion succeeded in engendering in the (largely non-*santri*) regular army a deep-seated institutional suspicion of modernist Muslim political aspirations.

The Masyumi and other Muslim political groups used the early parliamentary democracy years to build up substantial mass-based constituencies. But unity was to be short-lived. The Nahdlatul Ulama (NU), upset at the declining influence of traditional *santris*, withdrew from the Masyumi in 1952. In the 1955 elections—the only acknowledged free elections in Indonesian history—the NU and Masyumi split just over 40 per cent of the total vote. The results of the elections should have assuaged the army's fears. Though a majority of voters professed Islam as their religion, most voted for parties not principally defined as Islamic. *Abangan* Muslims turned out in great numbers to support nationalist, communist and socialist parties. It was a bitter illustration for modernist Muslims that their cause—and especially their support for an Islamic state—did not enjoy majority support.

But the army was not mollified. While the army's worst case scenario—a mandate for modernist *santri* Muslims or for the Communist Party—did not come to pass, the elections reinforced the military belief that the existing political system was not about to produce an effective government. In the latter half of the 1950s the army, chafing at its own political impotence, became increasingly contemptuous of all civilian parties and increasingly suspicious of the Masyumi's commitment to national unity.

The Masyumi survived the parliamentary democracy period but only just. The party was disbanded by Sukarno in 1960 because several of its leaders had joined a rebellion movement based in West Sumatra two years before. (The Muhammadiyah, the largest Islamic group gathered under the Masyumi umbrella, carried on as an individual organisation.) The Nahdlatul Ulama, accommodating as ever, was able to move with Sukarno's shifting winds and its influence survived intact the transition to Sukarno's increasingly authoritarian rule.

For the whole *santri* community, however, modernists as well as traditionalists, the Sukarno-protected Indonesian Communist Party posed a real threat. The Communist Party, almost exclusively an *abangan* organisation, stirred up the rural areas by agitating for land reform and crop-sharing schemes, and these activities struck directly at the legitimacy and stature of the *kiai*, the Islamic scholars and preachers who wield enormous power at the village level, as well as damaging the material interests of *santri* landlords. After the failed coup in September 1965, *santri* Muslims joined in the witch-hunt of communists with a vengeance.

Following Soeharto's rise to power, Muslim groups expected to be rewarded for helping the army eradicate its bete noire, the communists. Instead, Muslims found themselves the new bete noire. They were treated, in a famous phrase by former Masyumi leader Muhammad Natsir, like 'cats with ringworm'.[23] With the Communist Party eliminated, only Muslim groups had the numbers and organisational strength to compete for power with the army. The Masyumi ban remained in force and Soeharto's political organisers kept modernist Muslim leaders on a tight leash. Former Masyumi leaders again pushed for the acceptance of the Jakarta Charter in the late 1960s but the appeal fell on deaf ears.

In heavily manipulated elections in 1971, the Nahdlatul Ulama did as well as it had in 1955 but Parmusi, a government-created successor to Masyumi, fared much worse, obtaining only 5.3 per cent of the vote. The election could have provided another reminder to the modernist *santri* wing of Indonesian Islam that they commanded significantly less than majority support in Indonesia but the government's obvious meddling diluted the lesson. Two years later, the government forced all parties which contested the 1971 elections, except for the government party Golkar, to merge into two amalgam parties. The four (*santri*-dominated) Islamic parties formed the *Partai Persatuan Pembangunan*, or United Development Party, in which the less militant NU was the strongest component. For most of the next two decades the New Order government followed a two-pronged approach towards *santri* Muslims. Modernists championing a purer, more literal version of Islam were 'depoliticised' through repression. A more co-optive approach was taken with the conservative wing of Indonesian Islam which, led by the NU, takes a less hostile attitude toward traditional Javanese beliefs and practices and a more accommodating stance toward secular politicians. The NU's political behaviour was not as opportunistic as it seemed. The principal 'political' objective of the NU's leaders was to secure stability and protection for the NU flock, rather than to advance a particular ideology. 'Politics [for the Nahdlatul Ulama] was not the pursuit of the ideal but the art of the possible,' says Allan Samson, 'and the clear political primacy of military and secular political power made accommodation necessary.'[24]

Soeharto, like Sukarno before him, came from an *abangan* background and in the 1970s he riled Muslim groups with his tacit support for *kebatinan*, a system of Javanese mystical beliefs which, despite not being one of Indonesia's permitted religions, has many adherents in Java. In 1973, a draft marriage law provided the context for the New Order's first serious clash with Islamic groups. It was seen as an attempt to secularise marriage law and further scale back Islamic influence in government policy.[25] Muslim youth organisations demonstrated in the streets and even occupied the parliament building for a few hours. Eventually, the draft law was watered down sufficiently to appease Muslim sentiment. It would be one of Islam's few political victories in the pre-1990 New Order.

Given the constraints on the electoral system, the United Development Party performed credibly in the 1977 and 1982 elections. It continued to fight for Muslim objectives and fashioned itself, with some success, the party of the 'little people'. But since the early 1980s, the party has been in steady decline. The Nahdlatul Ulama's new chairman, Abdurrahman Wahid, was unhappy at his organisation's declining influence in the party and announced in 1984 that it was breaking away to return to its roots as a strictly social and religious organisation. (As we shall see, this was less a case of Wahid turning his back on politics and more a reflection of his view that the Development Party was a political non-starter.) The party's share of the vote plummeted to sixteen per cent in the 1987 elections from almost 28 per cent in 1982.

The government's decision later in 1984 to require all political and social organisations to adopt Pancasila as their sole ideological basis was an even bigger blow for the Development Party, as it undercut its appeal as a specifically Muslim political vehicle. The NU, true to form, easily rationalised an acceptance of Pancasila. Wahid went so far as calling Pancasila a 'noble compromise' for Muslims. Islam, he said, 'similar to the [earlier] fate of socialism and communism, has to subordinate itself to the "national ideology" of Pancasila, and to be satisfied with merely becoming a "political orientation".'[26] But for the remaining modernist components of the Development Party, enforced acceptance of Pancasila was a bitter pill. The placing of a creation of man—Pancasila—over Allah was seen by many as heretical. For the modernists, the Koran already provided a 'sole basic principle'. But Islamic groups had no choice but to endorse Pancasila, and after considerable theological acrobatics, they did so. Pressing the point still further, the government forbade the party from using Islamic symbols. It dropped the Ka'bah—symbol of the Muslim holy shrine in Mecca—and adopted the symbolically empty star as its banner.

In the 1992 elections, the Development Party ran a dispirited campaign and garnered seventeen per cent of the vote. It had lost its image as the party of change to the even smaller Indonesian Democratic Party. For all its work in complying with government edicts, the party has little to show. It has little influence in parliament and not a single cabinet representative. The nation's real political powers—the military and the bureaucracy—continue to be heavily influenced by *abangan* and non-Muslim Indonesians. One disillusioned Islamic leader described the modern-day United Development Party as 'really not a party, not united and not a development'.[27] His view of the party as an inadequate political representative of Muslim objectives was, and is, widely shared.

Outside the political sphere, isolated incidents of violence fed army–

Muslim antipathy. Dozens of Muslims were killed when soldiers opened fire on a demonstration in 1984 in the poor Jakarta dockland neighbourhood of Tanjung Priok. The spark for the demonstration was an accusation by Muslims that several soldiers had defiled a mosque by entering without removing their shoes.[28] Fuelling Muslim anger, though, were feelings of economic deprivation and political impotence. In the aftermath of the Tanjung Priok killings, Muslims retaliated by burning and bombing banks, stores and even government-owned radio and television stations. In the wake of the violence, hundreds were arrested including some whose only crime appeared to have been publicly opposing government policies.

In 1989 an army clash left an estimated one hundred villagers dead in Lampung, Sumatra. The army initially accused the villagers of being Muslim fundamentalists but later backed down when it became clear that land rights were at the heart of the matter.[29] More serious for the army is a renewed insurgency in Aceh province at the northwest tip of Sumatra. The insurgents are ostensibly fighting for an independent Islamic state but, again, economic inequality and regional autonomy issues seem to be the real crux of the matter.[30] Since 1989, more than one thousand Acehnese have died, many under mysterious circumstances.

Islamic revivalism

Paradoxically, as the government's efforts to emasculate Islam as a political force began to bear fruit in the late 1970s and early 1980s, its popularity as a source of social, ethical and spiritual advice began to rise. Some observers, many of them in uniform, felt that Islamic revolutions in Iran and elsewhere were an important factor in the revival of Indonesian interest in Islam. This camp suspected Islamic revivalism would re-open old and divisive debates on whether Indonesia should be an Islamic state. (The Indonesian military's anxiety on this point increased upon the discovery that some leaders of the current Acehnese rebellion had been trained in Colonel Qaddafi's Libya.)

But most observers argue that international trends are largely peripheral to the heightened interest in Islam in Indonesia; more convincing explanations are to be found at home. Two main dynamics appear to be at work generating higher interest in Islam: one is religious and the second is political. The former concerns the desire of many Indonesians, particularly the young, to find in their religion a stable bedrock of belief in a rapidly changing, modernising and often confusing world. They appear to be interested neither in the traditional, ritualistic dogma of conservative *ulama* or the messianic fervour of some modernists who want Indonesia to become a theocracy. Instead, they are looking for ways to make Islam more relevant to life in the modern world. Bill Liddle explains:

[Younger Muslims] are looking for a new understanding of their religion that gives them a more realistic set of guidelines, really a code of ethics, for private and family life and for dealing with the outside world. They want to know what are the rights and responsibilities of husbands and wives, how to raise their sons and daughters to be good Muslims and good Indonesians, how to relate to a modern banking system, whether and how to revitalise the concept of *zakat* (religious tax), and even how to deal with such exotica as test-tube babies, organ transplants, and homosexuality.[31]

The political dynamic adding to Islam's attractiveness has several components. The enforced acceptance of Pancasila after 1984 brought Islam fully into the fold of acceptable New Order politics. By adopting an ideology based partly on religious tolerance, Muslim groups made themselves more attractive to many Indonesian who take—or want to take—their religion seriously but who were uncomfortable with the perception of Islam as a political rival to the existing government.

More broadly, however, the New Order government's efforts to depoliticise Indonesia have driven many to look to Islam as an alternative political arena. This trend is particularly noticeable on university campuses, where political activity has been severely circumscribed since the late 1970s. 'When I was at ITB [Bandung Institute of Technology] in the early 1970s all the student political activity revolved around the student centre,' says economist Rizal Ramli. 'But ever since the government imposed restrictions on campus politics, the student centre had been dead. All the activity is now funnelled to the mosque. Young people need an outlet for their political aspirations and they will find it where they can. This is the result of the government's "security approach".'[32] Islam's growing attraction is not just reflected in higher attendance at mosques. Islamic study groups have blossomed on university campuses and more and more women students have taken to wearing the *jilbab* headscarf.[33]

It is hard to know how far this rising Islamic consciousness has spread in society. Certainly, it has made inroads into the educated elite, the class known as *priyayi*. Some, in fact, have described the changes taking place as the *santri*-fication of the *priyayi*. (Others, decrying the elitist aspect of recent Islamic revivalism, have dubbed the process the *priyayi*-fication of the *santri* community, implying that the new Islamic converts have no roots within the Indonesian masses.) Undoubtedly, the Islamic revival also has extended well into the category of nominal Muslims known as *abangan*, but modernist Muslim claims of a thoroughgoing '*santri*-fication' of *abangan* Indonesians are probably exaggerated.

No longer is Islam seen as the opiate of the uneducated and economically deprived. Professionals and the middle class increasingly are seeing it as a religion which can provide for their spiritual needs in the context of contemporary society. 'There is a new sense of pride in being a

Muslim,' says Umar Juoro of the Centre for Information and Development Studies, a think-tank close to modernist Muslim leaders. 'To be a good Muslim is very mainstream. It is now very acceptable within the elite to study the Koran and Islamic theology. Islam is no longer seen as a backward religion.'[34]

By the late 1980s the changing social composition of the Indonesian Muslim community meant it could no longer be ignored by political leaders. After two decades spent pushing modernist Muslims into the political wilderness, Soeharto suddenly became more responsive. Without relaxing the strict curbs on Muslim political activity—such as letting the United Development Party return to its Islamic roots—he began to give ground on other issues dear to Muslims and tried in many ways to burnish his own Muslim credentials. The government relaxed restrictions on the use of the *jilbab* headscarf at public schools, introduced more Islamic elements into the national school curriculum, and gave more authority to Islamic courts. On the diplomatic front, Jakarta formally recognised the state of Palestine. Soeharto and his family began increasingly to adopt a Muslim lifestyle, including a well publicised family pilgrimage to Mecca in 1991. In the same year, Soeharto helped establish Indonesia's first Islamic-style bank. The ruling party Golkar stepped up its efforts to project a more accommodating front to Islam and to highlight government efforts to build mosques and other Islamic facilities. Together with other government bodies, it sponsored and participated in a series of Islamic festivals and conferences.

Meanwhile, a shift in the top ranks of the military, the main obstacle to the political aspirations of modernist Muslims, was welcomed by many Muslims as a sign of the changing times. Former armed forces commander, Benny Murdani, a Catholic and a leading target for modernist Muslim enmity, was gradually eased out of power by Soeharto. Murdani's successor and, as of March 1993, Indonesia's vice-president, Try Sutrisno, as well as the current armed forces commander, General Feisal Tandjung, are considered 'friendly' to Islam or, at the very least, less hostile to organised Muslim activity.

The most meaningful recent development for Islam in Indonesia, and certainly the most controversial, is Soeharto's strong sponsorship of the Indonesian Association of Muslim Intellectuals (ICMI). Founded in late 1990 and headed by Minister for Research and Technology B. J. Habibie, this hybrid organisation includes among its membership critical non-governmental Muslim leaders and long-serving cabinet members. It has been set up as a sounding board for Muslim input into public policy, rather than as a mass-based political vehicle. To help formulate and broadcast Muslim views, the association launched its own newspaper, *Republika*, and its own think-tank, the Centre for Information and Development Studies. Its stated goals are to unify Indonesia's Muslims and improve their economic well-being, as well as to ensure that Islamic values are reflected in government policy. It is the first serious attempt since the Masyumi's demise to bring together Indonesia's fractious Muslim groups under one banner. The main difference, of course, is that ICMI members disavow any overt political role. Others are not so sure and therein lies the controversy.

ICMI: The battle for control

ICMI's arrival on the Indonesian scene raised more questions than it answered. The three most important are: why did it emerge? What, really, is it? And what does it want? While there are no easy answers to any of these questions, the following section tries to cover all the leading theories.

The 'why' of ICMI has several complementary explanations. At one level, it can be seen as a natural product of the process of Islamic revivalism described above. It simply provides an institutional form through which Muslims can put forward their agenda in an organised way. But it would be a mistake to view ICMI in religious terms only. A number of political objectives are also being served by the organisation. One of these is Soeharto's need to respond to what he perceives to be declining support for him within the armed forces. Much like Sukarno once looked to the communists to counteract unhappy army officers, Soeharto now looks to Muslims to play the same balancing role. Abdurrahman Wahid, who subscribes to this view, explains Soeharto's new-found warmth for Muslim groups in general and for ICMI in particular as 'a pre-emptive strike against potential opponents'.[35]

But military dissatisfaction is not Soeharto's only concern. He must also contend with strident criticism of his rule from the more vocal modernist Muslim leaders. While he would like to channel generalised Muslim discontent into a new support group for himself, he is aware that much of this discontent is aimed at him personally and must be neutralised. Soeharto hopes ICMI can play this co-opting role. Consequently, he has been careful to structure ICMI in a way that constrains the inclinations of its more radical members. By surrounding the most vocal Muslim critics with bureaucrats and more moderate Muslim figures, the president is counting on bringing the most critical ICMI members into the establishment fold with the promise of more influence in government decision-making. Whether this promise will be fulfilled and whether all of ICMI is prepared to be co-opted are of course different questions and ones which will be dealt with later in the chapter.

First, though, it is necessary to try to identify just who ICMI represents. At the risk of oversimplifying the issue, ICMI's membership can be divided into three main categories. In the first category are the government bureaucrats and 'technologists' who work under Habibie at the Agency for Research and Technology plus a collection of Golkar leaders, university professors, businessmen and cabinet ministers who were 'encouraged' to join the organisation as it began to take shape in early 1991. Members of this group are in ICMI either to reflect Soeharto's support for the organisation or to draw political—or economic—mileage out of it. Prominent among them are ministers Azwar Anas, Harmoko, and Saleh Afiff, as well as former Habibie assistants Wardiman Djojonegoro and Haryanto Dhanutirto who in March 1993 were appointed as the Minister for Education and Culture and Minister of Transportation respectively. Generally speaking, the members of the first category serve a mostly symbolic purpose; they do not take an active role in ICMI's activities.

A second group would include moderate Muslim figures and thinkers who are happy with ICMI the way it is; that is, as an intellectual forum in which concerned Muslims can discuss how Islam can be made a more positive social force in contemporary Indonesia and how the teaching of Islam can be modified to improve the economic fortunes of poor Muslims. Prominent members of this category include the Islamic scholar Nurcholish Madjid, former Minister for Population and the Environment Emil Salim, and, sometimes, former government statistician and current *Republika* columnist Sucipto Wirosardjono. Habibie straddles the first and second categories; he has no explicitly Islamic agenda of his own but he does take an active interest in ICMI's activities. Their views are discussed in more detail below.

The third category consists mostly of non-government Muslim leaders with more ambitious plans for ICMI. They would like a more active political vehicle representing modernist Muslim aspirations. More than the other two groups, they are responsible for coming up with the idea of ICMI and for getting the organisation off the ground; consequently, they consider themselves to be the 'real ICMI'. They also represent the wing which most concerns the military and which Soeharto is trying to co-opt. The leading members of this group are Amien Rais, Sri Bintang Pamungkas, Dawam Rahardjo, Amin Aziz, Watik Pratiknya, Adi Sasono, Lukman Harun, Nasir Tamara and Imaduddin Abdulrahim.

These three categories, obviously, differ in what they hope ICMI can achieve. But before moving on to their specific objectives, it may be useful to revisit briefly Geertz' *santri–abangan* schema in an attempt to locate ICMI in the broader Indonesian context. ICMI, as an organisation which defines itself in strictly Islamic terms, is appealing primarily to the *santri* community. Not all ICMI members would agree with this assessment, however; some would argue that the *santri–abangan* division has become blurred because of the revival of Islamic consciousness in the past decade.[36] While there is some merit in this argument, it probably overstates the case. It remains true that a sizeable portion of the Indonesian population can be fairly classified as nominal Muslims.

A more relevant question, perhaps, is how the *santri* community itself should be defined. It has already been discussed how the influence of reformist Islam from the Middle East widened cleavages within Indonesia's *santri* community at the turn of the century. The conservative preachers emphasised traditional Koranic rituals and dogma and resisted attempts to strip away Javanese cultural traditions from Indonesian Islam. The modernists were 'modern' in the sense that they appealed mainly to better-educated urban dwellers but doctrinally they hewed to a more 'orthodox' view of Islam and shunned the syncretic version practised by the conservative preachers. And while relying on the fundamental principles of the Koran, the modernists were interested in updating Islam to fit the needs, spiritual and otherwise, of contemporary society.

This basic division still exists in Indonesia's *santri* community but it is not the only one. It is also necessary to further refine what is meant by the term 'modernists', given that another group of Islamic scholars calls itself neo-modernist. The main differences between the two concern the importance of ideology and the proper relationships between Islamic and non-Islamic groups and between Islam and politics.[37] The neo-modernists are more concerned with the essence of Islamic teachings rather than the form. They are less concerned, to give a specific example, with whether Muslim women wear the *jilbab* headscarf than with whether they lead ethical, productive lives. In general, they are less hostile to Western and other outside influences and they believe that social and economic interests, rather than political power, should remain the priority for Islamic organisations. Finally, they are more ready to acknowledge the legitimate interests of secular groups and cooperate with them on a sustained basis. Neo-modernist views appear to enjoy considerable support from the members of the educated elite who have moved along the spectrum to *santri* Muslim status in recent years. The second category of ICMI members described above is representative of neo-modernist thought. Other leading neo-modernists are Abdurrahman Wahid and scholar Djohan Effendi, neither of whom is a member of ICMI. The third category of ICMI members are broadly representative of the modernist camp.

It should be mentioned that outside all these groups exists a fundamentalist fringe. As Allan Samson puts it, the fundamentalists 'affirm a strict, *puristic* interpretation of Islam, oppose secular thought and Western influence as well as the syncretism of traditional belief, and insist on the primacy of religion over politics'.[38] The fundamentalists, whose ultimate goal is to see Indonesia become an Islamic state, have been driven deep underground in the New Order and their views are not well represented in the public debate. The popularity of their views, however, is impossible to gauge given the lack of political freedom in Indonesia. As the 1990s opened, fundamentalist proponents were either dead, in jail, under house arrest or clever enough to keep a low profile. The organisation closest to the fundamentalist camp is the Dewan Dakwah (Preaching Council), a private organisation, founded in 1967, composed of Islamic preachers and officials. The Dewan Dakwah, as might be expected, is deeply critical of both the conservative preachers unwilling to reject non-Islamic Javanese customs and neo-modernist intellectuals such as Nurcholish and Wahid.[39]

The ICMI agenda

The third question posed above was what does ICMI want. But again, the answer depends a great deal on which ICMI is being asked.

For the ICMI neo-modernists, perhaps their most revealing characteristic is what they don't want: they adamantly oppose the use of ICMI as a political vehicle for Islamic aspirations. By and large, they accept Pancasila as a necessary and useful compromise for maintaining harmony in a multi-religious society. In their eyes, ICMI's main purpose is to increase public awareness of the social and economic needs of Indonesian Muslims; the focus is on improving Islam as a spiritual and ethical guide to modern life.

'ICMI is not a political organisation,' says Habibie, vigorously. 'Our main objective is to make a real contribution to the ever-increasing quality of life of the whole Indonesian population, especially the Islamic community.'[40] Emil Salim describes this aim in more detail:

History proves that Islam is not the religion of an underdeveloped country. So, we have to ask: why is Islam today associated with economic backwardness? The reason, I think, is that since colonial times Islam has become too dependent on *fiqih*, its legalistic traditions. This has trivialised the energy of Islamic intellectuals. It is not Islam that is wrong but the teaching of Islam. Instead of emphasising religious rules and rituals, we need to give more emphasis to science and technology in our teaching. Only in that way can Islam become the religion of progress. That's what ICMI is all about and that's why we picked Habibie to lead it.[41]

Former Minister for Religious Affairs Munawir Sjadzali puts the case more bluntly: 'The traditional understanding and teaching of Islam is responsible for the economic backwardness of Muslims.'[42] Sucipto Wirosardjono, the former vice-director of the government-run Central Bureau of Statistics, hopes ICMI will alleviate the perception that the government, and especially the army, is unshakeably suspicious of all organised Islamic activity.

There are strong feelings of deprivation among all Muslims. Our level of representation in business, in politics and elsewhere is not in the right proportion. We need to address the root cause of this perceived deprivation—a lack of skills in business and an unrealistic approach to politics—and that is what ICMI is trying to do . . . All we want to do is participate in the policy debate in Indonesia because we think we have something sensible to say. If we remain as outsiders, everything we do will be suspected, which, for me, proves how badly we need something like ICMI.[43]

Nurcholish Madjid, along with Wahid, is the most influential of the neo-modernists. The head of the non-governmental organisation Paramadina, he shares with establishment ICMI figures like Habibie and Emil Salim a desire to focus Islamic energies on the socio-economic transformation of Indonesian Muslims. But he differs with them on the need for political change. Whereas Habibie, for example, is a staunch supporter of the political status quo, Nurcholish hews to a fundamentally democratic view of society. He agrees with the modernists that authoritarian rule has contributed to the frustrations felt by Muslims, favours democratisation, and rejects the notion that a collectivist convergence is inherently superior to a system founded on individual rights. '[Political] opposition is positive, as a way to control and supervise power in a peaceful way,' he says. 'Control is peaceful. A coup d'etat is not.'[44]

But Nurcholish does not agree with the modernists that Islam should be an agent for political change. One of his most well-known comments is: 'Islam, yes; Islamic party, no.' Well aware of how Indonesian Muslims consistently have lost out when directly confronting state power, Nurcholish argues that Muslims ought to re-orient their priorities away from 'the form of the state in which they live [and to] the moral character of their political behaviour.'[45] In a famous if controversial speech delivered in 1970, Nurcholish stated that the task for Muslims was to 'make worldly things that should be worldly, and release the Islamic community from the tendency to make them divine'.[46]

Nurcholish argues that Islam in Indonesia should be understood as Indonesian Islam, by which he means that Islamic values and Indonesian values should be seen as inseparable parts of the same societal fabric.[47] He cautions against viewing any individual Islamic group as the exclusive source of the truth and encourages Muslims to be tolerant of different religious practices.

The modernists, in contrast, generally take a dimmer view of the status quo and support a more radical agenda for change. Different modernists, of course, hold to slightly different agendas, and the views expressed in the following section are not necessarily shared by all of the figures listed earlier as belonging to the modernist faction of ICMI. Generally speaking, however, the modernist camp dismisses the neo-modernist approach as elitist and overly influenced by Western liberal thought. (The two leading neo-modernists, Nurcholish and Wahid, have spent considerable time studying and travelling in the West.) It is stridently anti-military and anti-Christian. It believes Indonesia's economic development strategy is deeply flawed and that fundamental political and policy changes are needed to improve the status of Muslims.

Adi Sasono is typical of the ICMI modernists who pin the blame for Islam's political feebleness on a hostile military. 'Whenever there is a protest the government calls it Muslim fundamentalism,' Sasono said. 'It does not talk about socio-economic problems and it doesn't refer to political opposition which can emerge from any segment of society against an authoritarian regime. It is an artificial threat created to maintain the status quo.'[48] Modernist Muslims save their harshest words for former Armed Forces Commander Benny Murdani. 'The Muslims were shot at Tanjung Priok [in 1984] and I was detained,' said preacher Imaduddin Abdulrahim. 'The 'Boss' of the intelligence did all that,' he added, referring to Murdani. 'It was [Murdani] who divided the Muslims from the government.'[49]

The fear of 'Christianisation' also pervades the thinking of many ICMI modernists, despite empirical evidence to the contrary. In the 1990 census, 87 per cent of Indonesians said they were Muslims, up from 84 per cent in 1980. 'The Christian missionaries are trying to convert our people to Christianity. They build social facilities and give the people rice and medicine. We need a code of ethics for the propagation of religion. We need some sanctions against the missionaries,' said former Muhammadiyah leader and ICMI member Lukman Harun.[50] Similarly, in a March 1993 interview, the popular Islamic preacher Zainuddin MZ stated that the two most sensitive issues for the Islamic community were 'religious proselytising and the manner of building houses of worship'.[51] In both cases he was referring to the activities of Christian missionaries.

The anti-Christian rhetoric of the ICMI modernists finds many echoes at the grassroots level of the *santri* community where intolerance of Christians, and indeed of anything considered non-Islamic, is deeply rooted. Many Islamic preachers in Java's rural areas and small towns make a habit of attacking Christians as the foes of Islam and the cause of Muslim poverty. In the last two months of 1992, a spate of anti-Christian outbreaks, including church burnings in East Java and North Sumatra, illustrated the explosiveness of the issue.[52]

The ICMI modernists harshly criticise what they see as government favouritism to Christians in staffing the government bureaucracy, and they deeply resent the perceived influence of Christian-led think-tanks such as the Centre for Strategic and International Studies and Christian-run newspapers such as *Suara Pembaruan* and *Kompas*. The Centre for Information and Development Studies and the newspaper *Republika* were set up specifically as ICMI counterparts to these Christian institutions. The modernists' ire at Christians is at least partly rooted in frustration with a political system which, in their eyes anyway, entitles religious minorities to disproportionate influence. As described in earlier chapters, anti-Christian enmity has found expression in attacks on the economic technocrats, a number of whom are Christian. Some see in the technocrats' economic reform program a plan to keep Muslims poor and the Chinese rich. The same charge is levelled even at influential technocrats Widjoyo Nitisastro and Ali Wardhana, who are Muslims. 'They might be Muslims but they don't apply Islamic thinking to economic policies,' says Sri Bintang Pamungkas. 'They just use Western thinking without values, and economics without values is nothing, just a tool.'[53]

Anti-Christian sentiment has led many but not all ICMI modernists to support Habibie's economic program of higher government investment in high-technology industries and human resource development. The more committed anti-Christians, however, appear to be concerned that support for Habibie's economic policies will draw attention away from the Muslim–Christian issue. 'People like Adi Sasono and Watik Pratiknya are behind Habibie's economic vision because it gives ICMI something to talk about other than Islam and it's a way of differentiating themselves from the ICMI bureaucrats and other political powers,' says Umar Juoro of the Centre for Information and Development Studies. 'But others want to keep the debate on the simple level of Muslims versus Christians.'[54]

ICMI modernists also want to see '*santri* ethics' disseminated to the broader Muslim community. *Santris*, says *Republika* deputy publisher Nasir Tamara, are 'honest, hardworking, trusting, rational and they believe in equal rights'. On the other hand, he says, *abangan* Muslims are 'less rational, less honest, and mystics'.[55]

The issue that most clearly delineates the modernists from fellow ICMI members, however, is politics and, more specifically, the proper relationship between Islam and the political process. The modernists believe that it is impossible to improve the economic and social standing of Muslims, much less embark upon an ethical revolution, without political power. Sri Bintang Pamungkas puts the case like this:

> Nurcholish's concept of 'Islam, yes, Islamic party, no,' is denigrating to the Islamic way of life. You can't do anything without political power. What is needed is real political representation for Islamic views and values of development. If the United Development Party can't do this—and they aren't doing this—then we need a new Islamic party. Muslims have waited a long time for this. Throughout the New Order Muslims have been in a very low position. For me, ICMI is a means to political power.[56]

In this view, political power is not merely necessary for economic and social change, it is something Muslims *deserve* for the simple reason that they comprise a statistical majority of the Indonesian population. On this point, the modernists tend to skip over the ideological and doctrinal differences which divide the Muslim community; instead, they claim to speak for all Indonesian Muslims. When talking about politics, the modernists downplay the idea of a *santri–abangan* split. The *abangan* world view, they believe, is not a sustainable condition but is, rather, a sort of way station for the uninformed. *Abangans*, they believe, are Muslims in the process of becoming *santris*.

The modernists' push for political power creates an obvious conflict with Habibie, who was installed on top of ICMI to keep a lid on precisely this kind of pressure. Each side feels it can use the other. For Habibie, ICMI represents a new and valuable support base both for his economic views and for his political ambitions.[57] But he, like Soeharto and the army, is not at all interested in seeing ICMI evolve into an independent political power; his eyes are on the ruling party Golkar.

For the ICMI modernists, Habibie provides ICMI with protection in its formative years and support for him will be conditional on him fulfilling that function. Over the longer term, however, many modernists believe Habibie's involvement in ICMI will be damaging to their cause.

For the time being, the modernists need Habibie more than he needs them. 'ICMI is nothing without Habibie, at least at present,' Juoro said in early 1993.[58] The modernists rallied strongly behind Habibie's candidacy for vice-president ahead of the presidential elections in March 1993, mostly because they see him as the only power capable of competing with the military for political influence.[59]

Privately, however, the ICMI modernists are acutely sensitive to the charge that they have been co-opted by Habibie and they remain distinctly wary of his true sympathies. Imaduddin, describing how ICMI originally came to accept Habibie as its leader, said that the modernists 'looked for a figure who is clean in the government's eyes and who is not too bad in our eyes. And we came to the conclusion that we could utilise Habibie.'[60] Juoro takes the same view: 'The "real ICMI" couldn't find any government figure better than Habibie to represent their interests. They figured Habibie was the best of the worst.'[61]

The cabinet announced in March 1993 was an early test of wills between Habibie's view of ICMI and that of the modernists. Habibie's view was the clear winner. To the outsider, it appeared that ICMI did especially well in the new cabinet, given that four important cabinet posts went to its members. In addition, the number of Christians in the cabinet dropped from six to three, a source of cheer to many Muslim leaders. But there was no mistaking the disappointment the ICMI modernists felt that the ICMI members elevated to cabinet rank were all bureaucrats close to Habibie. The group that calls itself the 'real ICMI' was shut out. 'It's clear to me that on essential matters, the "real ICMI" is not very influential with Habibie,' said Juoro. '[Habibie] lobbied with Soeharto for the ICMI bureaucrats [to become ministers] but not for the "real ICMI".'[62] Imaduddin put the case more succinctly: 'There is no ICMI in the cabinet.'[63] Pamungkas remarked that the modernists' disillusionment with Habibie is a good thing for the 'real ICMI'.

> From the very beginning I told everyone not to be too sure of Habibie. What happened with the new cabinet proves that we were right [not to trust the government]. We know that for the first five years of ICMI, the government's involvement is going to be high. But we can use this time to strengthen support for our view that ICMI has to be independent of the government. Otherwise we will lose credibility with the people. Once ICMI is more developed, then it can be taken over by the real ICMI.[64]

However, Pamungkas and other modernists don't expect that disappointment with the March 1993 cabinet will weaken the modernist commitment to ICMI or to Habibie. 'Without Habibie,' Pamungkas says, 'we'll have no opportunity to develop ICMI.' Adds Juoro: 'The "real ICMI" members understand that they can't become real decision-makers in this country until Soeharto goes. But they are willing to wait.'[65]

A final question to be asked of the ICMI modernists is what would they do with political power if they had it. Given that ICMI is an ostensibly non-political organisation, it is a topic most of them prefer not to discuss publicly, although in private they are more forthcoming. At the broadest possible level, they want to see in Indonesia a government that overtly acknowledges Islam as the authoritative guide to political behaviour and one which openly and sincerely attempts to incorporate Islamic values and views into public policy. In terms of process, the ICMI modernists generally are in favour of more democratic rule in Indonesia. They argue that Islamic values are democratic in nature and that, faithfully applied, would provide individual Indonesians with more political rights than they enjoy under the current Indonesian government. 'Islam is democratic but it depends who is in charge,' as Pamungkas puts it. 'Soeharto is a Muslim but Indonesia is not democratic.'[66]

The modernists' political agenda also includes a substantial reduction in political power for the military. This view is easy to understand, given that the military's domination of the political process is held responsible for denying a fuller political role to modernist Muslims. 'It's ICMI's job to explain to the Indonesian people that Abri [the military] should be more independent of the political process,' Pamungkas said. He believes that an Islamic political party would win a majority of votes if truly free elections were held. He also warned that a refusal by the military to relinquish political control could have dire effects in the next ten years or so. He pointed to the example of Algeria where, as he put it, a secular authoritarian regime had succeeded in severely radicalising a Muslim population by holding on to power too long. 'That could happen in Indonesia, especially on Java,' he said.[67] As we shall see, Pamungkas is not the only Indonesian Muslim leader who feels the Algerian situation is relevant to Indonesia.

The anti-ICMI lobby

ICMI's importance as a political phenomenon should not be exaggerated. Its neo-modernist members, as described above, are staunchly opposed to seeing it become a political power. And although the modernist wing claims to speak on behalf of the broader Muslim community, in fact it represents only a part of that community. Non-*santri* Muslims, still a sizeable faction, do not support efforts to raise Islam's political profile. The military, distrustful right from the beginning of ICMI aims, will surely attempt to thwart any efforts by modernists to transform the organisation into a political entity. Non-Muslims, of course, and especially the powerful ethnic-Chinese business community, also can be expected to oppose a broadening of ICMI powers. But to date, all these groups have adopted a quiet, wait-and-see approach to ICMI.

The most vocal and trenchant criticism of ICMI has come from within the *santri* community in the person of Abdurrahman Wahid, the leader of the massive Nahdlatul Ulama grouping. To be sure, the neo-modernist intellectual Wahid and the traditional NU make an unusual combination. The connection has much to do with lineage. Wahid's family has strong roots in the Nahdlatul Ulama: his grandfather helped establish the organisation and his father was one of its most prominent leaders. Still, it is not clear how much organisational support Wahid enjoys for his oftentimes radical views, and it would therefore be a mistake to view Wahid and the NU as synonymous. Comments by some NU leaders suggest that they are not at all clear where Wahid is taking the organisation, and this confusion makes them uncomfortable. Some of these leaders have joined ICMI and are strong supporters of it. But despite cracks in his NU support base, Wahid remains a very influential figure. He is widely respected not only within the broad *santri* community but also by many non-*santris* and non-Muslims. Because of his stature, Wahid's views are worth spelling out.

Wahid has problems with ICMI modernists on two counts: religious and political. With regard to the former, Wahid resents the government's marginalisation of Islam, believing it deserves a broader hearing in policymaking circles. But he is concerned less with instituting a formal political presence for Islam and more with updating it as a social and ethical guide for living in the modern world. He relishes Indonesia's multicultural, multi-religious society and believes the rights of minorities should be scrupulously protected. He cites the anti-Christian rhetoric used by modernists and rural Muslim preachers as evidence of the weakness of the *santri* Muslim leadership. 'Why are we always blaming others for our problems,' he asks. 'We should be asking ourselves: why are Muslims being left behind? If Muslims take care of their community better, people won't think of switching to Christianity.'[68]

Unlike Nurcholish, who is seemingly unconcerned with the political designs of the ICMI modernists, or Sucipto, who sees in ICMI a useful mechanism for moderating the views of its more extreme members, Wahid is an ardent foe of ICMI, not so much for what it is but for what it could become. He has little confidence in the political skills of the ICMI bureaucrats or neo-modernists and frets that the modernists will succeed in doing with ICMI exactly what they say they want to do: turn it into an independent political force. That, Wahid believes, would be a blow for Islam and fatal to democracy in Indonesia. Before discussing the reasons behind this view, it would be helpful to skim Wahid's categorisation of Indonesia's *santri* community.

Wahid divides *santri* Muslims into three camps. The first he calls sectarians or exclusivists: 'They complain about discrimination against Muslims and demand that the balance be redressed. They say Muslims need special help against the Christians and Chinese because Muslims are backward and ignorant. Because they feel that Islam is threatened by modernisation, they want to formalise the role of Islam in the life of the state and society.' Wahid places in this camp the ICMI modernists, a group he refers to as militants. 'It is the militants who propose Islam as the solution to the problems of modernisation, who cater to the fears of Muslims, and who promote religious divisions . . . ICMI is full of ambitious people who want to jump up the ladder of influence. This allows the government to manipulate Islam as a political weapon . . . ICMI is controlled really by people who want to establish an Islamic state.'[69]

Wahid's second group, in which he places himself, 'believes that minorities give life to a nation and we have to protect them. Islam should be implemented as social ethics and mores but not as a political force. We have to be able to accept the existence of other cultural strengths. The first group emphasises differences between Islam and the others, when we prefer to emphasise similarities.'[70]

The third and largest group, Wahid says, is the undecided majority. They are the 'prize' for which the two first groups are competing. 'In the next few years the battle will be fought. We can't postpone for much longer. One of the two positions will gain the upper hand. As a nation, we have to decide whether we can build a society not based on religious or ethnic domination but on the rule of law and democracy.'[71]

One of Wahid's most important differences with the ICMI modernists concerns what might be called the tactics of political change. Wahid, like most modernists, is an advocate of a more democratic political system in Indonesia. Indeed, there are few mainstream figures who have been more critical than Wahid of Soeharto's authoritarian rule. He differs sharply with the modernists, however, on the role Islam should play in the democratisation process. While he shares the modernists' view that Islamic values are essentially democratic, he contends that their fixation on Muslims' need for special help is likely to create a backlash from *abangan* Muslims and non-Muslims who, comfortable with the idea of Indonesia as a secular state, may choose continued authoritarian rule over a democracy in which religious equality is not guaranteed. He is not at all convinced of the purity of the modernists' commitment to democracy. Unlike the modernists who tend to blame all of Islam's setbacks on a perfidious army, Wahid remembers keenly the Muslim role in the anti-communist purge of 1965 and the role of Islamic parties—especially the Masyumi—in weakening the fabric of parliamentary democracy in the 1950s.[72] Wahid worries that ICMI may become a new Masyumi.

In his view, the process of achieving democracy must begin with strengthening democratic attitudes at the grassroots level, attitudes which he believes have been weakened by more than thirty years of authoritarian rule. What is needed, he says, is a 'bottom-up' approach to democratisation in which issues are openly debated. If democratic rule is to emerge, he believes, political change must be gradual enough to allow time for democratic views to be widely understood and accepted. A 'top-down' approach in which certain groups are 'granted' legitimacy and influence—which Wahid thinks Soeharto is doing by currying favour with the ICMI modernists—is in his view inimical to real democracy. His reasoning is as follows:

> We have to have a socio-economic transformation as a first step in a long-term process of democratisation. That's why I am working to create an awareness of democracy within the NU . . . I am convinced the silent majority in Indonesia is pluralistic in attitude. If we can get the government to loosen its grip on society, Indonesians will take it in their hands to counteract the sectarians and maintain the unity of the nation . . . Given time and legitimacy [for the neo-modernist approach] we can make Islam a positive force in Indonesia.[73]

Wahid saves his harshest commentary for Soeharto, warning that the president is playing with fire by trying to co-opt modernist leaders. By pandering to the modernists, Wahid contends, Soeharto is giving them a head start in the process of political pluralisation even though their commitment to the national ideology Pancasila is uncertain and despite the fact that any enhanced role for them is liable to reinforce the army's bunker-like attitude to democratisation.

> For Soeharto, ICMI is a short-term marriage of convenience. He thinks he can control [ICMI modernists] if they go too far. I'm afraid the strategy will backfire . . . Moderate Muslims will win if the system is free but the problem is that Soeharto is giving help to the militants . . .We need time to develop a full religious tolerance based on freedom of faith. Instead

Soeharto is giving an opening to a certain group of Muslims, most
especially to the militants who propose Islam as the solution to all the
problems of modernisation.[74]

In an interview in March 1992, Wahid was no less forthcoming when
I asked him why he thought his views were being disregarded by Soeharto.
'Two reasons,' he said. 'Stupidity, and because Soeharto doesn't want to
see anyone he doesn't control grow strong.'[75]

Case study: Islam and banking

Modern banking, chock-full of doctrinal potholes for Islam, provides a
good illustration of the differences between Wahid and the modernist
camp. The core of the banking problem is the charging of interest which
in Islamic scripture is synonymous with usury and as such forbidden.
Traditional teaching discourages Muslims from depositing in or borrowing
from banks. For neo-modernists like Wahid, this is a perfect example of
how outdated precepts put Muslims at a disadvantage in the modern
economy.

In mid-1990 the Nahdlatul Ulama joined forces with Bank Summa to
set up a network of rural-based community credit banks. Wahid's critics
in the *santri* Muslim community were appalled, not only because the new
banks would charge interest but because Summa was owned by the
Soeryadjaya family, who as Christians and ethnic Chinese were totems in
their view of all that is wrong with the Indonesian economy. Wahid was
nonplussed.

> If Muslims' economic fortunes are going to progress, there is no other
> way forward but to cooperate with the Chinese. I deliberately chose
> Summa because we need to alleviate fears of Chinese-controlled financial
> networks if [Muslims] are going to get the funds we need to progress . . .
> I can feel resentment against Chinese rising. The militant Muslim leaders
> keep on dwelling on the ethnicity of the Chinese. In my view, there
> should not be any confrontation. If confrontational tactics are used against
> the Chinese that would be bad for the nation as a whole.[76]

At the time, the NU–Summa alliance was heartily praised by many other
Muslims. 'It's something that should have been done much earlier,' said
former Minister for Religious Affairs Sjadzali. Dorodjatun Kuntjorojakti,
dean of the school of economics at the University of Indonesia, agreed
wholeheartedly. 'The NU–Summa venture is a magnificent idea. I wish
they had done it fifteen years ago.'[77]

Curiously, Soeharto had nothing at all to say about the banking
venture. The president, according to several senior government officials,
was unhappy with both sides of the deal. He was upset that the
Soeryadjaya family was building bridges to the Islamic community and,

by extension, lessening their dependence on him. He also disapproved of Wahid independently taking the NU beyond its traditional religious activities. Given the sound economic rationale for the venture, and the courage of both sides in attempting to bridge the chasm between Muslims and ethnic Chinese, Soeharto's myopic view is hard to defend.

Eighteen months later Islam made another foray into the banking world, this time with the full backing of Soeharto. In late 1991, Soeharto gave his blessing—and considerable funds—to a new Islamic-style bank, Bank Muamalat Indonesia. In addition, to hearty applause from many in ICMI, Soeharto leaned on top government officials and leading businessmen to contribute to the bank's start-up capital. An Islamic bank works in a manner similar to a venture capital company. Depositors are regarded as investors and are allocated a return based on how profitably the bank invests their money. In practice, customers are likely to receive a return very close to what conventional banks pay on deposits, but with significantly less protection for their funds. Wahid roundly criticised the ICMI champions of Bank Muamalat Indonesia for being prepared to sacrifice the security of depositors' funds just to comply with, in his words, an outdated tenet of Islamic scripture. Describing Islamic banks as a 'moral burden for Muslims', Wahid said 'it was hard to imagine a financial vehicle more vulnerable to abuse'. He called the new bank just another victory for 'those who want to see Islam as a political alternative'.[78]

Perhaps ironically, it was the NU–Summa depositors who had first cause to worry about the security of their funds. Financial mismanagement at the Bank Summa's head office ultimately led to that bank's closure in late 1992. Summa's demise forced the NU to seek a new partner for its banking network and in April 1993 it was announced that Summa's shares in the joint venture would be bought by the company which publishes the East Java-based *Jawa Pos* newspaper. It is not clear, however, if a new injection of funds will end the NU's banking woes. In a March 1993 interview, Wahid said he had been told by former finance minister Johannes Sumarlin that Soeharto had instructed the finance ministry 'to place obstacles in the path of the NU–Summa banks'.[79]

Islam in the 1990s

Indonesia's *santri* community is in an uneasy state. Conservative preachers remain preoccupied with the 'Christian threat' and disoriented by rapid economic growth and changes in society. Neo-modernists like Wahid have been frustrated in trying to relay their message to a broader audience and are worried that they are losing ground in the public debate because of Soeharto's support for modernist initiatives like ICMI. Wahid and like-minded neo-modernists have come under increasing criticism from rural preachers for being out of touch with the real problems facing poor

Muslims. Their standing has been questioned also by modernists in ICMI who believe that the influence of neo-modernist leaders would decline in a less authoritarian political system. For their part, the ICMI modernists are irked by the perception that they are being co-opted by the promise of power and more than a little concerned that this perception is not far off the mark. ICMI itself, while holding together, is clearly showing the strains of housing so many divergent views under the same roof.

Wahid has been a lightning rod for the frustrations of ICMI modernists. He has been attacked as a heretic, an intellectual prima donna and a friend to Christians, ethnic Chinese, the military and, worst of all, to former Armed Forces Commander Benny Murdani. 'I fail to understand why Wahid thinks the way he does,' says Amien Rais, one of the leading modernists. 'Wahid is not only exaggerating differences among Muslims but he is distorting our positions and sowing disinformation . . . I believe in Islam and democracy too, a democracy that guarantees freedom of religion, press and speech.' Fellow modernist Sri Bintang Pamungkas finds Wahid's defence of minorities misplaced in a society in which, as he sees it, the majority also needs to be defended. 'Why should the minorities be in more need of protection than the majority?' he asks. And, in a comment directed at Wahid, Pamungkas adds that 'the suggestion that Muslims are opposed to Pancasila is created by those who don't want Muslims to be great.' Even some of Wahid's friends in ICMI, like Sucipto, say his bold denunciations of sectarianism 'are just hardening the views on the other side and creating a backlash . . . What good is your intellectual excellence if your communication of it hurts people and prevents appreciation of it by important people?'[80]

Wahid was relieved when the ICMI modernists were passed over by Soeharto in forming a new cabinet in March 1993. 'I was worried that the militants would be given positions of power. That would make them more extreme and possibly pull the whole Islamic movement in a more extreme direction.'[81] But Wahid's view that this setback for the ICMI modernists will mean the end of ICMI and a permanent loss of credibility for the modernists is almost certainly exaggerated, if not plainly wrong.

A more serious problem for Wahid is that his strident condemnations of ICMI, and of Soeharto's motivations in sponsoring it, have badly damaged his relationship with many moderate Muslim leaders and with the government, leaving him a largely isolated figure by early 1993. His anti-ICMI campaigning was only one of the reasons which put Wahid on a collision course with the establishment; two other events in 1991–92 helped him on his way.

The first was the formation in April 1991 of the Democracy Forum, a loose association of 45 leading Indonesian figures. Led by Wahid, it included lawyers, journalists, Muslim intellectuals, scientists, academics and a Catholic priest. The Forum, like ICMI, disavowed any specific political role. But, like ICMI, its goals were broadly political in nature.

The event that galvanised the Forum's founders into action was the closing in October 1990 of the 700 000-circulation tabloid magazine *Monitor*. The magazine had run a popularity poll a few weeks earlier in which the Prophet Muhammad finished a disappointing eleventh, behind Soeharto in the top spot, Minister Habibie in second, Iraqi President Saddam Hussein in seventh and, worst of all, its Christian editor Arswendo Atmowiloto in tenth. Many Muslims were outraged at seeing the Prophet compared with 'common' people. The poll was denounced and Muslim youths stoned the *Monitor*'s Jakarta offices, forcing Arswendo, soon dubbed Indonesia's Salman Rushdie, to seek police protection.

Information Minister Harmoko, a part owner of *Monitor*, immediately cancelled the magazine's publishing licence and the government charged Arswendo with blasphemy. Wahid was deeply upset at the mob response to the *Monitor* poll—and with Muslim leaders who fed the flames of indignation. It showed, he said, that these Muslims were intent on placing Islam ahead of democratic traditions. He complained that the government, by withdrawing the *Monitor*'s publishing licence by fiat rather than through the legal process, had simply acquiesced to the 'Muslim mob'. Six months later Arswendo was convicted of blasphemy and sentenced to five years in jail, the maximum sentence.

The Democracy Forum's chief goal, according to Wahid, was to begin a dialogue on democracy in Indonesia. The Forum aspired to 'loosen' the political system which 'has been too long already under the tight control of the state . . . Indonesians need to have more information before they decide who to vote for. They feel there should be more control over the disbursement of public funds and a more transparent judicial system.'[82]

'We are not hostile to anyone. We merely want to act as a catalyst, to promote democratic dialogue,' said Forum member Aristides Katoppo, an editor of the mass-circulation, Christian-run newspaper *Suara Pembaruan*.[83] At present, Wahid added, 'it is futile to argue with the government. There is no dialogue. They talk and we talk. It's just a series of monologues. And it's the rigidity of government policies which is what causes repression and this in turn causes sectarianism.'[84]

More broadly, the Forum was seen by its founders as a way to offer both Muslims and non-Muslims an alternative to ICMI's view of Islam and politics in Indonesia. The Forum was intended to show the government that some of the country's most respected figures, including a handful of *santri* Muslims, saw greater democracy as a more urgent need than increasing the influence of the Islamic community. Further, that these two objectives were contradictory at least in some respects.

The government, as might be expected, reacted poorly to the Forum.

It was a breach in the strict walls around political activity in Indonesia and, moreover, one beyond the control of Soeharto. Former Minister for Political Affairs and Security Sudomo dismissed the Forum as 'unneces-sary'. The government 'has to develop democracy, not the liberal kind but Pancasila democracy. I don't take the Forum seriously. They don't represent the majority of Indonesians.'[85] The government's initial urge was to ban the group but it later adopted a wait-and-see attitude. The Forum received substantial, if quiet, support from elements within the military who share Wahid's dismay with the weakness of civilian political organisations.

The second event which helped sever Wahid's links with the estab-lishment occurred in early 1992. Concerned with Soeharto's continuing support for ICMI and other modernist Muslim initiatives, Wahid had the Nahdlatul Ulama hold a mass rally in Jakarta, an almost unheard of political exercise for most of Soeharto's New Order rule.[86] The rally, referred to earlier in the chapter, had several purposes. One was to shore up Wahid's stature within the NU, as Wahid had come under pressure from leaders within the organisation who supported ICMI and from others who worried, justifiably, that Wahid's increasingly confrontational stance vis-a-vis the government was costing the NU clout in government circles.

A second purpose of the rally was to exhibit support for Wahid's inclusivist view of Islam. The focal point of the rally was Pancasila, and particularly its first principle protecting freedom of religion. By pointing out that his way of thinking was close to the government's own interpre-tation of Pancasila, Wahid put the government in a tight corner. It could not openly contradict Wahid's support for Pancasila and yet was deeply unhappy with his flouting of the political rules of the game. Soeharto was said to be displeased that Wahid had given a ringing endorsement to Pancasila and yet omitted to endorse his rule. As described in earlier chapters, Soeharto sees Pancasila and his authoritarian rule as virtually inseparable.[87]

Wahid had predicted one million Indonesians would turn up. But the government held out granting a licence for the rally on 1 March 1992 until the day before and then limited the crowd size to 200 000. Wahid later complained the police had stopped busloads of Nahdlatul Ulama supporters from travelling to Jakarta from Java's rural areas. A bitter and angry Wahid later wrote to Soeharto complaining about the bureaucratic obstacles placed in his path. He said that by trying to weaken him, the government was putting at risk its own stated hopes for Indonesia's political future. The letter concluded with these remarks:

> By preventing the NU from obtaining conclusive legitimacy for its views, the responsibility for orienting Indonesia's religious movement now moves to the government. If the government also fails, then within ten years the strength of those who don't accept the national ideology will grow, and

they will threaten the Republic of Indonesia and Pancasila . . . What's happening now in Algeria will happen again here . . . And, if the trend continues, an Islamic state will replace the state we have now.[88]

The message, which could not have been more starkly put, was poorly received by Soeharto. As mentioned earlier, Soeharto's son-in-law pressured Wahid to stop rocking the boat, while the government increased its harassment of Wahid and the Democracy Forum. Wahid was prevented from addressing crowds in East Java in April 1992 and, in the same month, a Democracy Forum meeting was shut down by the police. A furious Wahid responded by saying that life as an Indonesian in the 1990s was akin to a 'buffalo with a ring through its nose'.[89]

Wahid's involvement in the Democracy Forum, in the March 1992 rally and in anti-ICMI attacks clearly has chipped away at his political standing. In October 1992 the government announced the roster for the 1993 People's Consultative Assembly, the body which every five years chooses a president. ICMI members were represented in large numbers while Wahid, a member of the 1988–93 assembly, was dropped. Meanwhile, Wahid's championing of political reform has firmly alienated the more conservative clerics in the Nahdlatul Ulama leadership. Wahid, who is expected to stand down as NU's chairman in late 1994, is likely to become a much maligned target in the campaign to replace him. Some of his possible successors, in fact, have already begun to campaign. In April 1993, the NU deputy chairman Chalid Mawardi lashed out at Wahid for trying to make NU members 'become intellectuals and to take a confrontational stance against the establishment and for trying to transfer his values to the organisation'. Most NU followers, he said, 'have simple minds and are loyal to the government'.[90]

If Wahid's future is unclear, it is just as hard to predict the outcome of the broader debate on Islam in Indonesia. Islamic revivalism aside, there remain wide differences of opinion over Islam's proper role in society, differences which are a long way from being resolved but which have important implications for Indonesia's political future. History may show that ICMI neo-modernists like Sucipto were right in thinking that ICMI would act as a restraining influence on the modernists and that the main body of Islamic leaders was committed to the Pancasila notion of freedom of religion. If that comes to pass, the military's fear of latent Muslim demands for an Islamic state—and thus their opposition to greater political pluralism—may abate. If that doesn't happen, historians may say that Soeharto, given a choice between accommodating two contending views of Islam's political role in Indonesia, picked the view less compatible with democracy. And they might add that Soeharto made that choice because of his need to remain not only the most powerful political actor in Indonesia, but the only political actor.

8

East Timor: The little pebble that could

Foreign visitors [to East Timor] such as . . . foreign diplomats, parliamentary delegations, journalists and dignitaries and in particular Pope John Paul II [who visited] on October 12, 1989 and their positive remarks after those visits are testimony to the prevailing favourable situation in East Timor and to the continued commitment of the Indonesian government to the protection and promotion of the full political, economic and social rights of the people of East Timor.

'Facts on East Timor', Indonesian Embassy, Washington, DC[1]

It doesn't matter how cynical a pretext may be, how gratuitous the act, how cruel its execution, so long as mouths move, words are said, statements issued, then anything can be justified. A weak argument, stated confidently, becomes a strong argument. Say anything—it's only words and they have the same valency as those of the victim.

Timothy Mo[2]

The main conclusion that I draw from my tenure as governor in East Timor is that there is a large gap between what Jakarta says it wants to do in East Timor and what actually happens in East Timor.

Mario Carrascalao[3]

Early in September 1992 President Soeharto was host-chairman of the tenth summit meeting of the 108-nation Non-Aligned Movement (NAM), a grouping of developing countries which Indonesia's President Sukarno had helped assemble almost four decades before. For Indonesia, which views the NAM as a much needed voice for poor countries in the post-Cold War international arena, hosting the NAM summit was exactly

194

the kind of foreign policy initiative the country would like to do more of.

For Soeharto the NAM chairmanship was a personal triumph. It boosted his standing at home and gained him stature overseas that he had long craved; at least for some in Soeharto's inner circle, the NAM chairmanship was seen as Soeharto's entry ticket to the world stage. Later in September, Soeharto, representing the views of the developing world bloc, delivered a lengthy address to the United Nations General Assembly. He called on industrialised nations to give developing countries a greater say in the UN and other international agencies, and warned that without stability and development in the south, the rich countries of the north would suffer economically. He rejected Western pressure for more democratisation and greater respect for human rights in poor countries, saying that economic development must remain the top priority.

But halfway through Soeharto's hour-long speech, the Indonesian president was reminded that pressures for democracy, self-determination and respect for human rights cannot be willed away. In the General Assembly gallery, a two-metre banner was unfurled with the legend: 'Free East Timor'. The protesters were soon evicted but the point was made. While no doubt much of the General Assembly audience was only vaguely, if at all, familiar with the East Timor story, it is an acutely painful issue for Indonesia.[4]

Indonesia invaded the then Portuguese colony of East Timor in 1975 and subsequently incorporated it as the nation's twenty-seventh province. Many years of brutal repression followed. Although armed rebellion in the territory has been tamed, resistance to Indonesian rule remains strong. The subjugation of East Timor's independence movement has cost both sides dearly: in East Timor a terrible price has been paid in lives; in Indonesia, reputation and international credibility have been the prime casualties.

In hindsight, Indonesia's annexation of East Timor can only be described as disastrous. The job the army said it could do in weeks has yet to be completed almost two decades later. For Indonesian diplomats, East Timor has been an unending source of acute embarrassment. A series of UN resolutions has denounced the Indonesian aggression, and years of Indonesian diplomacy have not been able to undo the damage. The UN still considers Portugal the administrating power in East Timor. A number of Western nations accept Indonesia's de facto control over East Timor but dispute Indonesia's claim that a legitimate act of self-determination has taken place.

East Timor may be just a 'pebble in the shoe', in the words of Foreign Minister Ali Alatas, but it is certainly a stubborn pebble. With the exception of the 1965–66 anti-communist purge, East Timor is the worst blot on the New Order's human rights record and persistent international condemnation of the annexation has prevented Indonesia from achieving the international profile it feels it deserves. (Criticism from the developing world undermined Indonesia's repeated efforts earlier in the 1980s to become NAM chairman.)

The point was brusquely brought home to the Indonesian government following Soeharto's UN speech. US newspapers paid little attention to his prescriptions for the new world order and instead took Indonesia to task for its own failings. An editorial in *The New York Times* minced few words:

> In yesterday's United Nations speech [Soeharto] castigated 'policies of hegemony and domination' and gave unflinching support to the 'inalienable right to self-determination, independence and sovereign statehood'—for Palestinians. But there was nary a peep about East Timor . . . Indonesia is a proud and important regional power . . . yet with respect to East Timor Jakarta behaves more like a banana republic.[5]

East Timor is not the only active insurgency in Indonesia. Small, low-intensity rebellions continue in the provinces of Irian Jaya and Aceh. But East Timor is different in one significant respect. Both Aceh and Irian Jaya formed part of the territory controlled by the Dutch colonial regime. (Irian Jaya wasn't formally incorporated into the Indonesian nation until almost a quarter-century after independence; however, there was never much doubt that such an absorption would ultimately take place.) Not so with East Timor, which was colonised by the Portuguese. In fact, East Timor was all but ignored by Indonesian nationalists fighting the Dutch in the 1940s and, even as late as 1974, top officials in Jakarta insisted that Indonesia had no designs on the territory.

In the event, East Timor has become both a tragic and highly contentious story. Tragic in the sense that it is hard to envisage a peaceful, prosperous East Timor in the near future. The army has invested much prestige in its East Timor operation and it is almost inconceivable that Soeharto would pull the rug out from under its feet. And it is equally unlikely that, despite major improvements in Timor's infrastructure and health and educational facilities since 1975, Timorese resistance to Indonesian rule will evaporate.

Jakarta vigorously sticks to its claim that only a tiny percentage of Timorese rejects integration with Indonesia but time and time again that claim has been exposed as so much wishful thinking. Its hollowness was vividly illustrated in November 1991 when Indonesian soldiers opened fire on several thousand unarmed Timorese demonstrators, killing at least fifty and wounding many more. A year later Indonesia hailed the capture of Timorese resistance leader Jose Alexandre 'Xanana' Gusmao as the death knell of anti-integration sentiment in East Timor. But Indonesia has captured or killed many resistance leaders without coming any closer to putting the East Timor problem behind it. Xanana's capture is unlikely to be different.

Undisputed facts about East Timor are few and far between. It was shut off from the outside world until the late 1980s, making it almost impossible to obtain first-hand independent accounts of what was actually happening in the territory. Ever since the initial invasion, Indonesia has dismissed as outlandish propaganda any and all claims which dispute the government's contention that an overwhelming majority of Timorese favours integration.

The Indonesian press has followed this line faithfully and, consequently, East Timor is a non-issue for the vast majority of Indonesians. However, a mountain of testimony by Timorese refugees points to a story of unrestrained brutality and repression, a story strangely and starkly at odds with the common picture of the Javanese as a gentle and moderate people. There is little middle ground between these two divergent views, although it should be added that on many of the important details the official Indonesian version is transparently lacking in credibility.

The Timor case also raises sensitive questions about the army's exalted status in Indonesia. The invasion, incorporation and subsequent management of East Timor were (and continue to be) military operations. The territory has been for the military a valuable combat training ground, a smuggling entrepot and a politically useful reminder of its own importance. The armed forces, and in particular the military intelligence services, have ruled East Timor since 1976 almost as an institutional fiefdom, accountable neither to the law nor to the political apparatus in Jakarta. For many in the Indonesian elite, the botched campaign to absorb East Timor provides compelling testimony in the case for a reduction in the military's political clout.

Doubts lurk within the armed forces as well. The Timorese resistance has illustrated an important chink in the army's 'security approach' to political dissent. Through repression and propaganda, the army has tried to crush all manifestations of political opposition. It has succeeded in pushing Timorese opponents underground but it has manifestly failed to eliminate the sentiments which fuel the resistance. Two general, if uncomfortable, questions arise from the East Timor case: has the New Order's neutering of civilian political institutions in the rest of Indonesia really succeeded in eradicating opposition to its authoritarian style of rule? Is the military's 'security approach' solving political problems, or merely postponing them?

This leads to a related point. The failure to pacify Timorese unrest has engendered in the army real doubts about the strength of Indonesian national unity and kindled fears that democracy could lead to the unravelling of the Indonesian archipelago. Whether or not this fear is well founded—a point to be addressed below—it does play into the hands of army hardliners who fervently oppose greater political pluralism. Herein lies only one of the poignant ironies surrounding East Timor. Only in a more democratic, less military-controlled Indonesia would there be any possibility of more autonomy—to say nothing of independence—for the Timorese. But it is precisely this possibility which alarms the military and feeds its misgivings about political pluralism.

The many faces of colonialism

If the East Timor story since 1976 is a particularly sad one, the historical picture can hardly be said to be a great deal happier. Occupying half the island of Timor, East Timor is slightly larger than Northern Ireland, another of the world's troubled areas. The island lies along the southern rim of the Indonesian archipelago, only about 300 miles north of the Australian city Darwin. The Timorese are mostly of Melanesian stock, with curlier hair and darker skin than the Javanese but similar to the peoples of nearby Indonesian islands. Many indigenous languages are spoken, with Tetum being the most widely used.

Prior to the arrival of European colonial powers, Timor figured in the trading networks stretching from India to China primarily for its large stands of the fragrant sandalwood tree. In the early sixteenth century Dutch and Portuguese fleets came in search of the Spice Islands, islands which now make up the eastern areas of Indonesia. The victorious Dutch then claimed domain over the rest of what is now Indonesia. The main exception was East Timor. Portuguese control over the territory was tenuous, however, especially in the mountainous interior. Portuguese merchants had to compete with Dominican friars, the occasional Dutch raid, and the Timorese themselves.[6] Colonial administrators, huddled in the East Timor capital Dili, were forced to rely on traditional tribal chieftains.

Until late in the nineteenth century, East Timor remained for the Portuguese little more than a neglected trading post. Neglect, in fact, is probably the best one-word description of Portuguese colonial rule. Little investment was made in infrastructure, health facilities and education. Sandalwood remained the principal export crop, joined in the mid-nineteenth century by coffee. What Portuguese rule there was tended to be brutal and deeply exploitative. In one succinct but lasting description, Joseph Conrad, in his novel *Victory*, described Dili in the late nineteenth century as 'that highly pestilential place'.

At the dawn of the twentieth century Portugal, desperate to shore up a faltering economy at home, tried to assert greater control over its colonies. Renewed economic exploitation became the order of the day. A Portuguese Royal Commission meeting in 1889 summed up the new approach. 'The state . . . should have no scruples in *obliging* and if necessary *forcing* these rude Negroes in Africa, these ignorant Pariahs in Asia, the half savages in Oceania to work, that is, to better themselves by work, to acquire through work the happiest means of existence, to civilise themselves through work.'[7]

The implementation of this policy predictably intensified resistance in Timor. In 1910–12 a Timorese rebellion prompted the colonial power to bring in troops from Mozambique and Macau, two of its other colonies. An estimated 3000 Timorese had been killed by the time the rebellion was crushed in 1912. At about the same time, the Dutch succeeded in putting down uprisings in the western half of the island and in 1913 the two European powers formally agreed to split Timor between them.

In early 1942 thousands of Japanese troops landed in Timor to deny the Allied powers the use of the island as a forward base for the defence of Australia. For more than a year some 400 Australian and Dutch commandos, trapped on the island when the Japanese arrived, waged a guerilla campaign, tying up the invading troops and inflicting more than 1000 casualties.[8] Timorese natives who ably assisted the guerillas paid a high price after the Allied soldiers were withdrawn. An estimated 40–60 000 Timorese died at the hands of the Japanese in the Second World War; by the time they left, the Timorese economy was devastated and famine was widespread.

When the war was over the Portuguese quickly returned to reclaim their colonial possession. (West Timor, like the rest of the former Dutch East Indies, was included in the Indonesian nation which proclaimed independence in August 1945.) The wartime interregnum had made no difference to Portugal's approach to the colony. Local chiefs were forced to supply labourers to rebuild the meagre economic infrastructure, contributing to further agricultural declines. A visit to East Timor in 1947 by the Australian War Graves Commission resulted in a report of unsparing frankness: 'Forced labour under the whip goes on from dawn to dusk, and the Portuguese colonists . . . live with the same mixture of civility and brutality as they had 350 years ago.'[9]

The postwar period also saw the Catholic Church take on a more powerful role within East Timor since, in 1941, Lisbon had entrusted the education of its colonial subjects to the Church. 'Portuguese Catholic missions are considered to be of imperial usefulness; they have an eminently civilising influence,'[10] explained a 1940 Vatican–Portuguese accord. Primary and secondary school attendance in East Timor increased sharply in the three decades after the Japanese left—relative to a scandalously low base—although only a handful of Timorese reached the tertiary level. Illiteracy in 1973 was estimated at 93 per cent of the population. Ironically, however, it was Catholic seminaries which produced in the 1960s and 1970s the small educated Timorese elite that would carry the banner of nationalism. For the Indonesians who would replace Portuguese bureaucrats as Timor's overlords, the Church could hardly be considered 'imperially useful'. An imperial nuisance was more like it.

A brief season of politics

The decisive moment for Timorese nationalism came in April 1974 and occurred not in East Timor but thousands of miles away in Lisbon, the Portuguese capital. On 25 April 1974 the leftist-leaning Armed Forces Movement overthrew the dictator Marcello Caetano in Lisbon, bringing to a close almost a half-century of authoritarian rule. The new government was committed to modernising Portugal's economy and it favoured a gradual decolonisation process for Portugal's territories in Africa and Asia. The American political scientist Samuel Huntington dubbed the Portuguese coup the 'implausible beginning of a worldwide movement to democracy', noting that the following fifteen years saw approximately 30 countries in Asia, Europe and Latin America move from authoritarian rule to democracy.[11] The April surprise in Lisbon, though, would usher in a very different fate for the all but forgotten colony on Timor island.[12]

At the time, though, the news of the Lisbon coup had an exhilarating effect in East Timor. Within weeks a handful of new political parties had formed. The first was the Timorese Democratic Union (UDT). Founded by Mario Carrascalao—later to be appointed governor of East Timor by Jakarta—Francisco Lopez da Cruz and Domingos d'Oliveira, the party's statutes called for 'self-determination for the Timorese people oriented towards a federation with Portugal with an intermediate stage for the attainment of independence' and a 'rejection of the integration of Timor into any potential foreign country'.[13] Initially the most popular of the Timorese parties, it was supported both by traditional elites in the interior and senior officials in the colonial administration.

The other major party which sprang up was the Timorese Social Democratic Association, which months later was renamed Fretilin, the Revolutionary Front for an Independent East Timor. Fretilin was popular among younger Timorese and middle-level officials of the colonial government. Like the UDT, its goal was gradual independence and it stressed the need for 'literacy programs, a priority for agricultural development, the fullest participation of Timorese in the political structure, the reassertion of Timorese culture and a widespread health program'.[14]

The Association for the Integration of Timor into Indonesia soon changed its name to the more agreeable Timorese Popular Democratic Association, or Apodeti. Its goals are fairly described by its original title. Early on it received moral and financial support from Indonesia although its popularity at the outset and for the next eighteen months would fall far short of the other two parties. Two other parties, Kota and Partido Trabalhista, never attracted more than a handful of supporters.

Until mid-1974, Indonesia officially disavowed any interest in East Timor. In June 1974, in a letter to Fretilin member Jose Ramos-Horta, Indonesian Foreign Minister Adam Malik reaffirmed that 'the independence of every country is the right of every nation, with no exception for the people in Timor . . . [W]hoever will govern in Timor after independence can be assured that Indonesia will always strive to maintain good relations, friendship and cooperation for the benefit of both countries.'[15]

But others in Jakarta had a different view. Nationalists and military hardliners saw in the Portuguese coup an opportunity to bring East Timor into the Indonesian fold. This view was put forward most strongly by leaders of the powerful intelligence agency Kopkamtib as well the secretive special operations unit, Opsus. Two key players were Soeharto's close adviser and all-around fixer Major General Ali Murtopo, who headed Opsus, and his protege Brigadier General Benny Murdani, who at the time headed the military's intelligence operations.

The intelligence officers, initially pursuing a non-military strategy of annexation, pinned their hopes on Apodeti and began describing Fretilin as a communist organisation and Carrascalao's UDT as 'neo-fascist'. Jakarta's concern seems to have been two-fold. It worried that East Timor could become a 'Cuba on the doorstep' and be used as a base for incursions by unfriendly powers into Indonesia. Second, it feared that an independent East Timor within the confines of Indonesia's national territory would spark secessionist sentiments elsewhere in the archipelago, notably in Aceh and Irian Jaya. The major foreign powers accepted these fears at face value. And for its part, a preoccupied Portuguese government all but ignored the growing political ferment in East Timor for most of 1974. Lisbon vacillated between lukewarm support for Timorese nationalists and a desire not to cross the Indonesian proponents of integration.

By the end of 1974, with Murtopo firmly in charge of the Timor project, the Indonesian propaganda campaign was in full swing. Radio broadcasts beamed in from Kupang on the Indonesian side of Timor claimed that the 'pro-integration majority' of East Timorese were being persecuted by Fretilin.[16] Timorese independence was a dead letter.

By the beginning of 1975 Timor's two most popular parties banded together in the face of Indonesia's hostility and its increasingly overt support for Apodeti. 'Apodeti never had the support of more than five per cent of the population yet Indonesia's policy was that all Timorese were their enemy except Apodeti. UDT was the majority party but we were neglected,' said Carrascalao, explaining the roots of the UDT–Fretilin solidarity.[17] A formal coalition was announced in January 1975, with an unequivocal platform of 'total independence, rejection of integration, repudiation of colonialism, and recognition of decolonisation'.[18] The coalition, bolstered by support from newly arrived military officers from the reformist government in Lisbon, proposed elections for a national assembly by November 1976.

The coalition was short-lived. The left wing of Fretilin distrusted UDT's commitment to full independence while UDT conservatives were uncomfortable with Fretilin's socialist rhetoric. Indonesia was able to play on these divisions and succeeded in persuading several key UDT leaders, such as the party's president Lopez da Cruz, of the merits of integration. In May the coalition collapsed, partly due to the growing strength of Fretilin radicals whose economic initiatives were anathema to the land-owning leaders of UDT. In May 1975 UDT pulled out of the coalition.

In the following month a commission on Timorese decolonisation was held in the Portuguese territory of Macau. Fretilin chose not to attend, citing the presence of Apodeti, which it viewed as a co-opted tool of Jakarta. Consequently, Apodeti was able to portray itself as a leading Timorese party and UDT was free to step up its criticism of Fretilin without response. At this stage it seemed that many UDT leaders were convinced that Timorese independence would never be allowed by Indonesia if a left-leaning Fretilin was to be the movement's flagbearer. The Macau talks stopped short of calling for a provisional government of Timorese parties, something the Indonesians ardently opposed. But it was proposed that elections for a popular assembly be held in October 1976 and that the assembly decide Timor's political framework.

Seeing the Macau talks as a setback for integration, Indonesia notched up the propaganda campaign against Fretilin. Intellectuals working at Murtopo's think-tank, the Centre for Strategic and International Studies, began fanning the globe seeking international support for Jakarta's position. In July 1975 Soeharto publicly stated that an independent East Timor was 'not viable'.[19] At the same time, military officers in charge of the Timor project warned UDT leaders that Fretilin was planning an August coup.

On 10 August 1975 UDT launched a coup in Dili with the avowed intention of expelling all communists from Timor. UDT members occupied the police headquarters and seized its stock of weapons. Fretilin members caught in Dili were arrested. The party's rationale was that Timorese independence was better served by a routing of leftist elements of the independence movement. But the UDT leadership was itself divided. President Lopez da Cruz' increasingly frequent contacts with Indonesian officials and especially with Murtopo made some of his colleagues deeply uncomfortable. After the coup was launched, they attempted to arrest da Cruz because they were afraid he would call for direct Indonesian intervention. Da Cruz, however, escaped to Kupang with the help of the Indonesian consul in Dili.[20]

Meanwhile, blindsided by the UDT coup, the Fretilin leadership demanded of the Portuguese governor, Lemos Pires, that he disarm the putschists and regain control of Dili. Given the conflicting demands of the two main parties, the governor decided to do nothing, gave up attempts to resurrect the UDT–Fretilin coalition and confined the Portuguese troops to their barracks.

Within a week Fretilin announced an 'armed insurrection' against 'traitors of the fatherland'. Fighting broke out in outlying areas and reached Dili by 20 August. Again refusing to deploy Portuguese troops, Lemos Pires and his staff moved the seat of government to Atauro Island just off Timor's north coast. Most of the Timorese troops, including a number who had combat experience in Africa fighting *against* independence movements in other Portuguese colonies, declared themselves for Fretilin. Party members seized thousands of NATO-standard rifles from the main army barracks in Dili. Within weeks, Fretilin had taken control of Dili and pushed UDT troops all the way back to the border with West Timor. When the main UDT force under Joao Carrascalao—Mario's brother—crossed into West Timor, they learned that Lopez da Cruz had signed a document committing UDT to Timorese integration with Indonesia.[21]

In hindsight, it seems surprising that Jakarta didn't take advantage of the chaos in Dili in mid-August to invade. By that point, it was clear that the Indonesian campaign of intimidation and propaganda was a failure. Support for Apodeti had been greatly overestimated, while the reverse was true for Fretilin. By September, Fretilin controlled all of East Timor except for a few villages close to the West Timor border. The brief civil war had cost some 2–3000 Timorese lives and forced thousands more to flee into West Timor.

Indonesia threw its full support behind what it now called the anti-communist alliance of Apodeti, UDT and the two small parties Kota and Trabalhista. Indonesian commando units infiltrated East Timor to step up the pressure on Fretilin and keep alive the notion that a civil war was raging. Military activities were scaled back in October after five journalists working for Australian television stations were killed. Indonesia responded to the international outcry by asserting that the journalists had been caught in the crossfire of a UDT–Fretilin battle near the border town of Balibo. The alternative view—that the journalists had been killed by Indonesian troops—seems more credible.

Indonesia and Portugal met for talks in Rome in early November but planned follow-up talks between all Timorese parties and Portugal never took place. The rest of the world studiously averted its eyes from the now quite public tussle for power in East Timor. Australia and the United States made it clear to Jakarta that they intended to stay uninvolved, which Jakarta interpreted to mean tacit support for its integration designs.

In the face of increasingly frequent incursions by bands of UDT and

Apodeti followers led by Indonesian army soldiers, Fretilin on 24 November called on the UN to demand the withdrawal of Indonesian troops. Four days later, it declared East Timorese independence. The following day Indonesian intelligence operatives organised a counter-declaration by the UDT–Apodeti remnants near the West Timor border which called for immediate integration with Indonesia. With the signing of this document, the time for negotiation had come to a close.

Indonesia invades

Declaring its desire to allow 'the majority's' wish for integration to prevail, Indonesia prepared a major assault by sea and air on Dili. The invasion was delayed at the last moment so as not to coincide with a visit to Jakarta by US President Gerald Ford and his secretary of state, Henry Kissinger. Kissinger gave his blessing to the Indonesian plan, asking only that it be carried out 'quickly, efficiently and [without the use of] our equipment'. As writer Hamish McDonald remarks, he was to be disappointed on all three counts.[22]

At dawn on 7 December 1975 a naval bombardment of Dili was followed by the landing of seaborne Indonesian troops; simultaneously, paratroops from the elite Kostrad command dropped in and behind the city. As a military operation, the Dili invasion was seriously flawed. The paratroopers were supposed to seal off the capital but many landed directly on top of retreating Fretilin troops and high casualties were suffered. The bulk of the Fretilin forces was able to slip through the intended blockade. The taking of Dili was a violent affair, with Indonesian troops rampaging through the city streets looting shops and homes and firing at random. 'The soldiers who landed started killing everyone they could find. There were many dead bodies in the streets. All we could see were the soldiers killing, killing, killing,' said East Timor's former bishop Monsignor Martinho da Costa Lopez.[23] Over the next few days, other Indonesian units captured the airport in Baucau further to the east and gained control of the southern coast. A strict news blackout was imposed on the territory.

A series of UN resolutions condemned the invasion and demanded Indonesian troops withdraw. Indonesia ignored them. On 17 December it formed a provisional government in Dili headed by an Apodeti official and UDT's Lopez da Cruz. In May the following year the provisional government convened a People's Assembly in which 37 hand-picked delegates voted for integration with Indonesia. On 17 July 1976 Soeharto declared East Timor to be Indonesia's twenty-seventh province.

From Indonesia's perspective, developments were much less favourable on the military front. Officially, the army maintained that it was engaged only in mop-up operations. But despite continual bombardment of major towns and villages and an overwhelming superiority in troops and equipment, the invading force encountered far more resistance than it expected. To confront an estimated 30 000 Indonesian troops, Fretilin had some 2500 troops from the former Portuguese army plus 10–20 000 part-time militia and reservists. More importantly, though, as would soon become clear, Fretilin enjoyed the support of much of the Timorese population. Over the next two years, it waged an effective guerilla campaign against Indonesian troops and was able to maintain control over large swaths of Timor's interior.

Indonesia attempted to keep the war in East Timor as secret as possible. Its plan was to wipe out the resistance movement and then present an 'integrated' East Timor to the world community as a fait accompli. On the ground, the military's strategy was to cut Fretilin off from the civilian population and destroy its food resources. Many Timorese villages were obliterated in this campaign, thousands of Timorese suspected of helping Fretilin were killed, and Timor's traditional social structure was severely dislocated. Over time, tens of thousands of Timorese fled their homes to avoid the fighting and sought refuge in mountainous areas.

Beginning in 1977 Indonesia instituted an 'encirclement' strategy which sought to uproot much of the Timorese population and move it into designated hamlets. By 1979 the US Agency for International Development estimated that 300 000 Timorese, about half the population, had been transplanted into such camps.[24] Many of the settlements were located in agriculturally poor areas and their reluctant inhabitants were not allowed to stray far from the camps. Food production plummeted and famine was common. In 1979 a delegate of the International Committee of the Red Cross was quoted as saying East Timor's economic condition was 'as bad as Biafra and potentially as serious as Kampuchea'.[25]

Timorese civilians were also conscripted into military operations as part of the notorious 'fence of legs' strategy. They were forced to walk ahead of Indonesian troops advancing on Fretilin positions, obliging Fretilin soldiers to hold their fire or shoot the civilians. Catholic clergy, Timorese refugees and foreign aid workers estimate that more than 100 000 Timorese died in military actions or from starvation and illness in the period 1976–80. Some estimates run as high as 230 000, out of a pre-invasion population of some 650 000. Although Jakarta disputes the number of Timorese that have died, Mario Carrascalao described the estimate of 100 000 dead as 'credible'.[26] Indonesian casualties are not known but some estimate up to 10 000 of its troops died in this period.

The news blackout on Timor initially prevented the scale of atrocities from becoming public knowledge. But by the end of 1976 letters from East Timor and first-person accounts from Timorese who had fled abroad had given the world a picture in stark contrast to the official Indonesian version. An Australian diplomat, James Dunn, concluded from interviews

with Timorese refugees in 1976–77 that 'the military seizure of East Timor
has been a bloody operation, in which atrocities of a disturbing nature
have been committed against the civilian population. Indeed, these
accounts of Indonesia's behaviour in East Timor suggest that the plight
of these people may well constitute, relatively speaking, the most serious
case of contravention of human rights facing the world at this time.'[27]

By 1980 the military campaign in East Timor had exacted a heavy toll
on Fretilin, which had little response to continual bombing runs and
helicopter strafing. Many senior Fretilin leaders had been captured or
killed and the movement's supply networks had been seriously disturbed
by the encirclement strategy. Indonesia concluded the Timorese resistance
had been broken and eased the cordon around East Timor, permitting some
relief workers in.

But it was to prove to be a strikingly premature conclusion. Fretilin
regrouped and, much to Indonesia's bewilderment and frustration, was
able to continue disruptive raids and ambushes year after year. Working
in small bands, its troops were able to count on a sympathetic civilian
population to supply food and intelligence. In the mid-1980s Indonesia
launched several new assaults on Fretilin, which though partially effective
were unable to eradicate the armed resistance.

In sharp contrast to the army's brutal and not particularly effective
campaign, Indonesia did succeed in making significant improvements to
Timor's economic infrastructure. Scores of new schools, hospitals and
churches were built in the 1980s and hundreds of miles of new paved
roads appeared. In 1990 per capita income in East Timor was only
US$200, less than half the Indonesian average but still five times higher
than the level prevailing at the end of Portuguese rule. On the downside,
some of East Timor's most profitable economic activities have been
monopolised since the invasion by a military-controlled firm, PT Denok.
Denok's most lucrative business was its monopoly on the export of coffee,
East Timor's most valuable cash crop. But Denok aside, Indonesia's
oft-stated commitment to 'develop' East Timor has brought material
benefits for many Timorese. It is this side of the story, naturally, that
Indonesia stresses to the outside world. And for most of that world for
most of the time since the invasion, that story has provided sufficient
reason to avoid dwelling on the less palatable aspects of the Timor saga.

Reviewing the international context

New roads and bridges notwithstanding, Jakarta has a long way to go
before sweeping East Timor off the international agenda. From 1976 to
1982 the UN adopted resolutions each year demanding that Indonesian
troops be withdrawn and that the right to self-determination be given to
the people of East Timor. Since 1982 the UN, under the auspices of the

secretary-general's office, has arranged a series of talks between Indonesia and Portugal in an attempt to find an internationally acceptable solution. These talks have continued into the 1990s but have failed to bring peace to East Timor.

At the individual country level, realpolitik in the Kissinger mould has been the rule. Indonesia's neighbours and most important trading partners averted their eyes. This attitude had much to do with the international context of the mid-1970s. The United States, whose own troops were completing their painful retreat from Indochina, was easily alarmed by Jakarta's portrayal of Fretilin as a communist party. In the US view, says Indonesia specialist Ben Anderson, 'the counterweight of a ferociously anticommunist Indonesia was [considered] essential'.[28] In geo-political terms, the US desire to see a fair decolonisation process in East Timor fell far short of its desire not to disrupt friendly relations with Jakarta. A related and important concern was the American desire to maintain its access to the deep-water straits running through Indonesia so that its submarines could pass undetected between the Indian and Pacific Oceans. US military sales to Indonesia were suspended after the invasion but resumed shortly after. The US abstained from most of the UN resolutions censuring the Indonesian invasion and did what it could to water down international condemnation.[29]

The Fraser government in Australia—which replaced the Whitlam-led administration a month before the invasion—took a similar approach. Trade with Indonesia and political ties to the rest of Southeast Asia were of too much importance to be put at risk by support for what Canberra considered a lost cause. While it could not silence a considerable public outcry against the invasion, Canberra took pains to limit any damage to its relations with Jakarta. In this regard, Canberra was strongly supported by Washington.

In the years immediately following the Indonesian invasion, Portugal appeared uncertain about how to respond. The day after the invasion it cut diplomatic relations with Jakarta and it subsequently supported UN resolutions denouncing the invasion. Later in the 1970s and into the early 1980s, though, Lisbon seemed undecided as to how strongly it should push the issue. American scholar Ben Anderson maintains that Portugal was reluctant to take a hard line on the Timor issue while its application to join the European Community was still in the balance.[30] Whatever the reason behind the change of heart, Portuguese criticism sharply mounted as the 1980s progressed. Lisbon stepped up its campaigning for Timorese self-determination and more than any other country has been responsible for keeping the East Timor case alive in international forums.

Within the domestic political context of the mid-1970s, factors which might have worked against an annexation of East Timor were gradually overwhelmed by the expansionist designs of the military. The financial debacle at oil giant Pertamina in 1974–75 required Indonesia to proceed cautiously. It could ill afford to alienate overseas donors and further alarm foreign bankers. This concern no doubt helps explain Soeharto's reluctance to go along with the military's desire to invade East Timor earlier in 1975. Gradually, though, Indonesia arrived at the conclusion, rightly as it turned out, that raising the communist bogey would be the deciding factor in swaying opinion among the major powers of the West.

What effect an independent East Timor would have had on Indonesian national unity is naturally a matter of speculation. Again, there is an important difference between other insurgencies in Indonesia's past and present and East Timor. From the West Sumatran rebellion in the 1950s to the ongoing conflict in Aceh, the motivating factor was a desire to change the government in Jakarta or its policies, rather than outright secession. (An important exception is the *Organisasi Papua Merdeka*, a separatist movement in Irian Jaya.) The areas that gave rise to these rebellions were part of the former Dutch East Indies and were home also to many who did not support the rebellions. On both these counts, East Timor is different. Indonesia, by crossing colonial borders and invading East Timor in 1975, had 'set a dangerous precedent and opened the "Pandora's Box" of secession in the archipelago', according to Fretilin spokesman Jose Ramos-Horta.[31] In his view, East Timor's threat to Indonesian unity was and is a problem of Indonesia's own making.

The Indonesian army, needless to say, took a different view. Several influential members of the military leadership, especially those within the intelligence bodies, played on the fears of national disintegration to great effect. This group was led by Ali Murtopo, a man who enjoyed enormous support and trust from Soeharto. For Murtopo, it was simply and indisputably in Indonesia's national interest to prevent an independent East Timor from emerging within the archipelago. In his view, the key to maintaining national unity lay in control of the archipelago's periphery, and that meant East Timor had to be brought into the fold.

At the time, of course, no one in Indonesia could have predicted the draining military struggle which would ensue nor could they imagine the damage that would be inflicted on Indonesia's international reputation by the annexation. It is a measure of the military's dominance that its power base has been barely dented by the major miscalculations of Murtopo and his colleagues.

The resistance changes stripes

By the late 1980s Fretilin forces had dwindled to no more than several hundred armed men. Indonesia had long since dropped the inapt communist label for Fretilin and referred to them instead simply as bandits or 'security-disturbers'. But while still a nuisance for Indonesian troops, the armed resistance no longer posed the most serious threat to Indonesia's hold over the territory. That role passed to a new, unarmed opposition. Under the initiative of its leader Xanana Gusmao, Fretilin strengthened contacts with young Timorese in the cities, especially in Dili, and encouraged a policy of non-violent resistance. Meanwhile, Fretilin members abroad, with former journalist Ramos-Horta being the most prominent, energetically propounded the Timorese case in diplomatic circles.

The emergence of civil protests in Dili came as an unwelcome shock to Indonesia. Many of the youths active in the protest movement had been small children at the time of the invasion and had been educated under Indonesian rule. Resentful of Indonesia's repression of Timor's cultural and political life and unimpressed with the territory's economic development since 1976, these youths stressed their Portuguese heritage, spoke Portuguese amongst themselves, sought protection and succour from the Church and looked to Portugal to help them achieve self-determination. They considered the Indonesian garrison, which still numbered some 10–12 000 troops, as an occupying army.

This alienation was exacerbated by economic hardship. The new schools built by Indonesia educated a generation of Timorese, but school-leavers struggled to find jobs. East Timor, neglected for centuries under Portuguese colonial rule and racked by fifteen years of military strife, remains deeply poor. Despite improvements since 1976, one government report released in 1993 estimated that in three-quarters of East Timor's 61 districts, more than half the people live in poverty.[32] Investors, domestic and foreign, have steered clear of the territory, while, as noted above, the military retains control over several key businesses.[33]

Faced with a new foe advocating only passive resistance, the government decided in 1988 to 'open up' the province in a bid to improve its commercial prospects. The decision appears to have come directly from Soeharto who, against the advice of senior military commanders, acceded to the urgings of Foreign Minister Ali Alatas for a new approach to East Timor. Beginning in 1989, Timorese no longer needed special travel permits from the army to travel within East Timor. Likewise, the travel ban on journalists was lifted. And in late 1989 the hardline military commander Brigadier General Mulyadi was replaced by Brigadier General Rudolph Warouw who promised to promote a more 'persuasive' approach to the anti-integrationists. Former governor Mario Carrascalao, whose ten-year term ended in 1992, described the switch in typically blunt terms as 'the replacement of the worst military commander East Timor ever had with the best'.[34]

True to his word, Warouw removed many roadblocks limiting travel in East Timor, released batches of political prisoners and made torture a less widespread interrogation technique. The military put increasing stress on its 'territorial approach' which included participation in a variety of civil works projects.[35] Warouw also attempted to impose a modicum of discipline on the troops under his command. In February 1990, an Indonesian soldier was brought to trial for unlawful conduct in East Timor, the first such prosecution since the original invasion. 'So ended fourteen years of zero military accountability,' said Carrascalao. 'Up to that point East Timor was a completely secret war. Killing one or one hundred or one thousand Timorese had the same consequences. Nobody was responsible to the law.'[36]

Support for the opening of East Timor was not unanimous. Carrascalao, for example, worried about an influx of unskilled labour from elsewhere in Indonesia which would threaten the already too few economic opportunities for indigenous Timorese. Hardliners in the military feared a loss of control. Soeharto, however, was swayed by diplomats who contended that Indonesia had to respond to international concerns over East Timor if it was to achieve a respectable international profile. Specifically, the diplomats argued, there would have to be some progress in East Timor if Indonesia were ever to overcome objections to its bid for the chairmanship of the Non-Aligned Movement.

For a time, the diplomatic approach looked to be working. But, less noticeable at first, the reduced fear of persecution had a galvanising effect on the civil resistance movement. Anti-integration protests greeted virtually every high-profile visitor to East Timor, including Pope John Paul II in October 1989, US Ambassador to Indonesia John Monjo in January 1990 and the Jakarta-based Papal Nuncio in September 1990. Clashes between Timorese protesters and army soldiers flared periodically. As Carrascalao had predicted, large-scale migration of Indonesians from Java and other islands into East Timor stoked the fires of resentment. By 1991 East Timor's population had risen to 750 000, of which estimated 80–100 000 were migrants. Inexperienced in the ways of the business world, Timorese lost out to savvier immigrants in many fields.

Following the Monjo protest, General Murdani, one of the hardliners who opposed the opening of East Timor, lashed out in a fiery speech in Dili. 'Don't dream about having a state of Timtim [the Indonesian abbreviation for East Timor]. There is no such thing!' Murdani thundered. 'There have been bigger rebellions, there have been greater differences of opinion with the government than the small number calling themselves Fretilin, or whoever their sympathisers are here. We will crush them all! This is not in order to crush East Timorese but to safeguard the unity of Indonesian territory physically and in other ways . . . Yelling in front of an ambassador . . . won't solve the problem. And if those who yell are those who are paid by the government, then that is treachery.'[37]

At the same time, Foreign Minister Ali Alatas was continuing a dialogue with Portugal through the office of the UN secretary-general. In 1991 plans were drawn up for a Portuguese parliamentary delegation to visit Indonesia later in the year. Military hardliners were opposed to the plan but were again out-manoeuvred by Alatas. The foreign minister, a seasoned and highly regarded diplomat, fervently desired to resolve the East Timor question so that Indonesia could concentrate on other, more pressing foreign policy issues like the war in Cambodia and regional economic and security arrangements. Believing the military's contention that all was quiet in East Timor, Alatas felt confident enough to invite the Portuguese to see for themselves.

Back in East Timor the situation took a turn for the worse. The military, more worried than it let on, began a campaign of intimidation and harassment to dissuade would-be protesters from demonstrating during the Portuguese visit. An important tool in this campaign was the use of Timorese as paid intelligence agents. As documented by Timorese refugees, priests, Governor Carrascalao, foreign aid workers and human rights activists, the tactic had a highly disruptive effect on Timorese society, turned families against one another and greatly heightened the general level of distrust.[38] Night-time raids on homes of suspected protesters became common and hundreds of Timorese were incarcerated without trial.

Exactly who was behind the increased intelligence activity has never been made clear. It is generally understood that it bypassed Warouw, theoretically the senior military commander in the territory, and was orchestrated by intelligence agencies in Jakarta. Whether these covert operatives were trying simply to undermine Warouw's 'persuasive approach'—which they succeeded in doing—or whether the real goal was to scuttle the intended Portuguese visit can only be guessed at. Many military analysts believe Soeharto's son-in-law Lieutenant Colonel Prabowo Subianto, a veteran of three tours in East Timor and who enjoys close ties with former Apodeti leaders, played a key role in the intelligence operations.

In the event, the Portuguese trip was cancelled in late October just a few days before the delegation was scheduled to arrive, ostensibly because of a dispute over the accreditation of journalists. The resistance movement was bitterly disappointed, having risked a great deal to prepare a demonstration to press their case to the Portuguese visitors and through them to the outside world. On the night following the cancellation, 28 October 1991, anti-integration and pro-integration youths clashed—with some of the latter alleged to be part of the Indonesian intelligence campaign—at the Motael church in Dili, leaving one dead on each side. The mood in Dili became still more tense and desperate.

The Dili massacre

Shortly after dawn on 12 November 1991 a memorial mass was held at the Motael church for the anti-integration youth slain two weeks earlier. Following the mass, some 2500 Timorese set off in a procession to the Santa Cruz cemetery. After laying flowers in the cemetery, at least part of the Timorese contingent intended to continue on to the Turismo Hotel, where an anti-integration demonstration, originally planned for the Portuguese, would be held for the benefit of Pieter Kooijmans, a special rapporteur visiting Dili on a mission for the UN Human Rights Commission. It was a daring, even reckless, plan by the Timorese youngsters. But recklessness, perhaps, is to be expected from people living under constant pressure.

Along the route to Santa Cruz, the mourner-demonstrators unfurled the Fretilin flag and waved banners with messages such as: 'Free East Timor', 'Long Live Independence', and 'Secretary-General, We are Waiting For You'. Some carried posters of Fretilin leader Xanana Gusmao and many chanted slogans calling for Timorese independence. While boisterous, the procession was peaceful.

Somewhere along the route a scuffle broke out between demonstrators and soldiers lining the procession route. Two of the soldiers were stabbed. The circumstances of the scuffle, like virtually all other details of the day's events, are disputed. Indonesia says the attack was unprovoked. Timorese in the procession say the soldiers waded into the crowd to grab a Xanana poster and beat and kicked demonstrators in their way.

Some twenty minutes later the end of the procession had reached the cemetery but most of the group was still lingering outside the front gate. According to many foreign and Timorese witnesses, a column of soldiers then marched up the same route the procession had followed while several truckloads of troops arrived down a different street. The witnesses report that upon rounding the street corner some 50 metres from the cemetery gate, the soldiers immediately opened fire on the crowd. The barrage lasted for two to three minutes and then continued sporadically for as much as another thirty minutes. Timorese flooded into the cemetery and those that could tried to escape over the back wall. Soldiers quickly surrounded the site and began beating and bayoneting Timorese trapped inside.[39]

Hundreds of Timorese who escaped sought refuge at the home of Dili's bishop, Monsignor Carlos Ximenes Belo, and at the office of the International Committee of the Red Cross, the only two safe havens in the city. Hundreds more were arrested at the cemetery. The dead were taken to the morgue and the wounded to the military hospital. Bishop Belo, who visited the hospital on 13 November, said the faces of many of the wounded had been beaten so badly that he couldn't recognise them.[40]

The international outcry was immediate. Seven foreigners were present at the cemetery when the shooting started. A New Zealand student was killed, two Americans were beaten and an English cameraman was arrested and later released. The foreigners immediately departed Dili and recounted to international news organisations the details of the massacre. In what would prove to be a damaging contradiction to the Indonesian account, a videotape of the procession filmed by the English cameraman was smuggled out of Indonesia and widely broadcast overseas. The European Community issued a stern condemnation on 13 November and other governments weighed in with disapproval. The Dutch, Canadians and Danish within weeks would suspend aid programs to Indonesia. Although the cost in Timorese lives was high, the Timor tragedy was back in the news.

The military responded with defiance and belligerence. The blame for the massacre was placed on the Portuguese, the foreign press and the demonstrators themselves.[41] Major General Sintong Panjaitan, Warouw's immediate superior based in Bali, gave the first official military version of events at a Dili press conference on 14 November. He said 18 Timorese in addition to the New Zealand student had been killed on 12 November and 91 others were wounded. He claimed a grenade had been thrown at troops near the cemetery (which never exploded) and that someone in the crowd fired a pistol in the direction of the soldiers. An officer's command of 'Don't shoot' was misunderstood, Panjaitan said, and soldiers subsequently opened fire. All of these details are strongly and credibly disputed by witnesses to the shooting. Timorese and church officials estimated that more than one hundred Timorese had been killed and at least that number wounded.

In Jakarta, Armed Forces Commander Try Sutrisno vigorously defended the army's actions. He had said on 13 November that 'at the most' 50 Timorese had been killed the day before, but in an unrepentant presentation to the parliament on 27 November, Sutrisno stuck with the army's official death count of nineteen. He accused foreign journalists of being involved in organising the procession, and described as 'bullshit' claims that the procession was a peaceful demonstration. Prior to his presentation, Sutrisno was quoted by an Indonesian newspaper as saying the Timorese 'continued to be obstinate. In any case, the armed forces cannot be underestimated. Finally, yes, they had to be blasted. Delinquents like these agitators have to be shot and we will shoot them.'[42]

Startled by the vehemence of international criticism, however, Indonesia announced it would form a National Investigating Commission to look into what was called the 12 November incident. The team was led by Major General Djaelani—a Supreme Court judge no longer on active duty—and included six other government officials.[43] Requests to include international monitors or representatives from Indonesian non-governmental organisations were rejected, leading, not surprisingly, to complaints of bias. Before the team had travelled to East Timor, one of its members, Foreign Ministry official Hadi Wayarabi, was quoted by the national news agency *Antara* as saying he believed the massacre was 'created' by

Portugal. Sutrisno, not a member of the team, said 'after [the Investigating Commission] comes up with the results, we will wipe out and uproot the disturbance movement which has tainted the government's dignity.'[44]

The commission announced its findings on 26 December. In a humiliating rebuke to Sutrisno, the team revised the death tally upwards to 50, said 91 Timorese were injured and estimated that 90 others were unaccounted for.[45] It described the massacre as a 'tragedy which should be deeply regretted', and concluded that orders to shoot did not come from Warouw or army headquarters in Jakarta but rather that the shootings were a 'spontaneous reaction [by soldiers] to defend themselves, without command, resulting in excessive shooting at the demonstrators'. The team also noted that some of the shooting was the work of a small, unidentified group 'acting outside of any command or control, [and they] also fired shots and beat demonstrators, adding to the casualty toll'. (Although never identified, this group is believed to include the same intelligence operatives held responsible for the wave of night-time arrests and beatings in Dili in the months prior to the massacre.) The commission criticised the army for not using proper riot-control procedures and conceded that soldiers' actions 'exceeded acceptable norms'. Finally, the team said that 'in order to uphold justice, action must be taken against all who were involved in the 12 November incident in Dili and suspected of having violated the law.'

Two days later, Soeharto replaced Warouw and Panjaitan, instructed Sutrisno to search for the missing Timorese and ordered army Chief of Staff Edi Sudrajat to form a military tribunal to determine whether any officers should be court-martialled. He further called upon the economic ministries and the interior department to improve Timor's economic condition and strengthen the provincial bureaucracy. In later comments, Soeharto reiterated his regret at what happened on 12 November and expressed his condolences to the Timorese families who lost relatives.

Given that public criticism of the military is extremely rare in Indonesia, the commission's report and Soeharto's response went considerably further than many observers had expected. Views differ on the reason for this unexpected outcome. Some Indonesian diplomats pointed to the commission as a sign of political maturity and of a higher level of accountability the military would face in the future. Some sources close to Soeharto said the president was genuinely angry at the army's crude mishandling of the Timorese demonstrators. When releasing the commission's report, State Secretary Murdiono quoted Soeharto as saying: 'Make sure what happened in Dili doesn't happen again.'[46]

The alternative view is that the decision to adopt the middle ground between the army's initial and improbable view of the Dili massacre and that put forward by witnesses was prompted by international considerations rather than by a domestic change of heart about East Timor. It is certainly true that the relatively frank report into the massacre succeeded in weakening pressure within the country's major trading partners to restrict aid and investment flows to Indonesia.

The 'international explanation' is favoured by many of Indonesia's critics abroad. But it is also a view heard within Indonesia, especially from hardline military officers who felt that Soeharto was using the army as a scapegoat to dilute international criticism. An influential retired officer, General Soemitro, is typical of this line of thinking. He called the formation of the investigating commission an act 'humiliating for the Indonesian nation. The soldier's reaction was trigger-happy, I agree, but I can't blame them. What I really regret is foreigners meddling in our business. The KPN [Investigating Commission] was forced on us by foreign countries.' Banging a fist on his desk for emphasis, Soemitro declared 'there was no possibility the soldiers were in the wrong'.[47] State Secretary Murdiono, a close aide to Soeharto, admitted that international pressure played a role in establishing the commission. 'If we didn't care about international opinion, we would never have set up an investigating commission,' he said.[48]

Leaving aside the motivations behind the commission's formation, it is worth noting briefly that even if its report was more critical than expected, it still contained some serious shortcomings. By describing the 12 November killings as an isolated incident, the report ignored the long history of repression which came before and, by so doing, failed to acknowledge the real reasons which drove several thousand Timorese to demonstrate in the first place. The report also accused the unarmed demonstrators of incitement. It said the demonstrators provoked the army by 'shouting anti-Indonesian slogans, glorifying Fretilin leader Xanana, and ridiculing the security apparatus . . . [thereby creating] a disorderly, wild and unruly atmosphere'.

In addition, the team failed to locate, much less identify, the Timorese thought to have been killed on 12 November or those presumed missing. 'I have no doubt that there were more than 50 Timorese killed,' said Carrascalao. 'I told the commission where to look for bodies but they were prevented by intelligence officers from looking in the right spot.'[49] Amos Wako, a personal envoy of UN Secretary-General Boutros Boutros Ghali who visited East Timor in February 1992, also criticised the commission's findings. 'The shooting by the soldiers . . . [was] both unprovoked and unnecessary and in utter disregard to the right to life . . . [The Investigating Commission's] efforts to locate the graves were neither thorough nor effective,' he said in a later report.[50] Finally, the commission's contention that the massacre 'was clearly not an act ordered by the government . . . or the armed forces' remains a matter of serious dispute. Many Timorese, in fact, believe that far from being a 'spontaneous' incident, the 12 November massacre was deliberately planned by intelligence officers bent on undermining Warouw and his more accommodating approach to Timorese dissent.

True or not, one of the first casualties of the Dili killings was Warouw who was blamed by some of his superiors for giving independence sympathisers in East Timor the opportunity to sully Indonesia's international reputation. Warouw's replacement, Brigadier General Theo Syafei, immediately announced that the army would revert to a more hardline approach and a wave of arrests and interrogations followed. Syafei quickly imposed more discipline over military operations in East Timor, and the freelance terrorising by mysterious intelligence operatives, whom Governor Carrascalao had denounced as bandits and thugs, came to an end.[51]

The fallout: Indonesia

If the Investigating Commission's report was able to blunt calls for international sanctions against Indonesia, it was not enough to extinguish these sentiments entirely. In February 1992 Indonesia was subjected to heated criticism from the UN Commission on Human Rights. Portugal, which assumed the European Community presidency on 1 January 1992, lobbied throughout 1992 for the Community to take a harder line with Jakarta over East Timor. In August, it forced the postponement of the signing of a planned EC–ASEAN cooperation agreement because of lingering disputes over East Timor. In June 1992, the US House of Representatives voted to cut off military training funds to Indonesia.

The discrepancy in sentences meted out in trials of soldiers and East Timorese in mid-1992 stirred a new bout of criticism. Following the completion of the military tribunal's work in February, six officers were dismissed or demoted. Nine other soldiers and a policeman were court-martialled for disobeying or exceeding their orders, though their sentences were light, ranging from eight to eighteen months. Meanwhile, thirteen Timorese were tried on a variety of charges. Four were indicted for subversion; two of them having been accused of masterminding the 12 November 1991 demonstration and the other two with organising a subsequent protest in Jakarta on 19 November. The four were jailed for between nine years and life.[52]

The Dili massacre and its aftermath represented a serious blow to military prestige. The Investigating Commission's report and the subsequent military court-martials, unprecedented in their public criticism of military behaviour, left an impression of an incompetent and divided army. 'Taken together, the trial testimonies paint a picture of a sloppy, ill-prepared, ill-informed, poorly disciplined and poorly led army, with some soldiers reacting spontaneously to the stabbing of their colleagues and others apparently panicking amid sounds of shooting at the cemetery,' said the human rights group Asia Watch.[53] The discrepancy between the army's original account of the massacre and the account given by the Investigating Commission does not lend itself to easy explanations. Either the army initially lied to the public or discipline was so poor that soldiers were able to get away with not reporting the truth up the line of command. 'There are a lot of questions being asked about [the army's] competence,' remarked former Golkar parliamentarian Marzuki Darusman shortly after the commission's report was made public.[54] For at least parts of the Indonesian elite, the questions being asked included some aimed directly at the legitimacy of the army's dominant political role in Indonesia.

For his part, Soeharto, a past master at manipulating army divisions for his own purposes, emerged from the Dili massacre with his military support strengthened. What seemed at first like a dilemma for Soeharto—whether to side with Armed Forces Commander Sutrisno or appease international critics—proved instead to be an opportunity to weaken his opponents.[55] The two senior soldiers removed from active duty, Panjaitan and Warouw, were considered proteges of then Defence Minister Benny Murdani who, since his abrupt 1988 removal from the powerful armed forces commander billet, was considered the most important cabinet-level rival to Soeharto.

Panjaitan was also considered one of the main rivals to Soeharto's brother-in-law Major General Wismoyo Arismunandar for the post of army chief of staff. He was not directly implicated in the Dili shootings, but was sacked because he had overall responsibility for military operations in East Timor. Wismoyo, who at the time headed the elite Kostrad command, was spared being held to the same standard. Despite the participation of Kostrad units in the Dili massacre, Wismoyo's name never figured in the public finger-pointing which followed. The same is true of Soeharto's son-in-law Prabowo.[56] Later in 1992, Wismoyo was promoted and made deputy to the army chief of staff and in April 1993 was elevated to chief of staff.

As it turned out, the Dili massacre did little harm to the ambitions of Armed Forces Commander Try Sutrisno. His truculent hardline response in the immediate aftermath of the incident can perhaps be best explained as an attempt to burnish his credentials within the army. Although groomed by Soeharto for a top post, Sutrisno has always had an uncertain standing in the eyes of fellow officers. But in a political sense, Sutrisno's performance can only be described as relentlessly inept. At a time when Indonesia needed to defuse international criticism, he managed instead to inflame passions. 'All the efforts to patch up the international perception of East Timor were destroyed in one fell swoop by the incompetence of Try,' remarked the retired general, Hasnan Habib.[57] Many who considered Sutrisno a shoo-in for vice-president in the 1993–98 term hurriedly revised their opinions. Nonetheless, sixteen months after the massacre a rehabilitated Sutrisno was appointed vice-president by Soeharto.

The fallout: East Timor

For the Timorese the Dili massacre signalled a period of renewed repression and a blow to nationalist aspirations. Just as the massacre represented a major setback to Indonesia's diplomatic efforts to gain international recognition for its annexation of Timor, so too did the killings heighten Timorese hatred and resentment of the massive military presence in the territory, undoing much of the progress achieved by Warouw. In the weeks following the massacre, the mood in Dili alternated between shock and anger. Relatives of Timorese wounded in the shooting were afraid to visit the military hospital in case they were branded Fretilin sympathisers. Many wounded Timorese refused to seek medical help for fear of being arrested, contributing to the confusion over the precise death toll.[58] The government's investigating commission reported that many potential witnesses were too scared to testify.

A five-day trip to East Timor in the days following the Dili massacre impressed upon me a picture of a cowed and brutalised populace. Eye contact was avoided, distrust was prevalent and people tended to speak in whispers. As is common with visiting journalists, several times during my stay I was furtively slipped notes and letters asking that the Timorese 'true' story be told to the outside world, and that pleas for help be forwarded to the UN and the United States. One note, pressed in my hand by a secretary in a government office, said: 'We can't manifestate [*sic*] what we really feel 'cause we're between the guns and the wall. I think you understand: we're under pressure. Please help the Timorese people who wants his own identification. Please don't mention where you got this note because I'm always in trouble with them.'

For leading Timorese figures like Governor Carrascalao and Bishop Belo the massacre was tragic but not completely surprising. Both said they had feared the same outcome if the Portuguese visit had gone ahead. Carrascalao, one of the first to dispute the army's death toll of nineteen, played down the popular view in Jakarta that Portugal was to blame for the incident and argued instead that the underlying problem in East Timor was the behaviour of the Indonesian military.

> According to me, we [Indonesians] are to blame. The children who demonstrated are the products of an Indonesian education, not Portuguese. Thus, we have to admit that we have made mistakes. Don't blame these children. We have to correct [our own policies] . . . I want to see preventive measures, not repressive ones. For a whole generation of Timorese that has grown up since 1975, all it has known is war. That explains a lot of the anti-Indonesia sentiment . . . It's wrong to say that all Timorese are against Indonesia. They are against the situation Indonesia has created in East Timor. They are against the way the army works. The Timorese don't want much. They want some basic freedoms, like freedom of movement and justice. They don't want to be suspected

all the time. The real cause of the anti-Indonesian sentiment is that the army has forced the Timorese to become anti-Indonesian.[59]

An angry and frustrated Belo, the territory's bishop since 1983, was similarly outspoken. He described the military's repression in the months leading up to the planned Portuguese visit as 'terrible' and painted a bleak picture of suffering and brutality. 'The majority of Timorese, whether in urban or rural areas, want the right of self-determination and independence. But they are afraid to express themselves.'[60]

The year 1992 offered ample evidence for pessimists. Attempting to deny the Timorese resistance access to the outside world, the army proceeded to round up hundreds of suspected Fretilin sympathisers in Dili and penned them in secluded areas in the interior.[61] In February, the ban on foreign journalists travelling to East Timor was reimposed.[62] In September, at the end of his second term as governor, Carrascalao was replaced by the ardently anti-Fretilin, former Apodeti official, Abilio Soares, who immediately adopted a stronger pro-military line.

In a startling interview with a new Indonesian magazine in October 1992, Soares, a friend of Lieutenant Colonel Prabowo since the latter's first tour in East Timor, gave his full support to a more forceful military approach in East Timor. According to a transcript of the interview, Soares was asked about the negative psychological effects resulting from the estimated 50 casualties of the massacre in 1991. 'As far as I am concerned,' Soares replied, 'I think far more should have died . . . What happened was an incident. It wasn't something we wanted to happen. The time will come when people will be convinced that it was an incident and that it was quite understandable.'[63]

According to senior government officials in Jakarta, Soares owes his appointment as governor to strong lobbying by Prabowo, a critic of both Warouw and Carrascalao. The former governor and Soeharto's son-in-law had clashed in the late 1980s. Carrascalao was so appalled by Prabowo's brutish behaviour that he requested that the officer be removed from East Timor. Prabowo responded by accusing Carrascalao of being a Fretilin sympathiser and calling for the governor to be sacked. 'I was ready to quit,' Carrascalao says, 'but when I explained my position to Soeharto he asked me to stay on.' Although not excessively critical of Soares personally, Carrascalao contends that his appointment is certain to worsen Timorese distrust of Jakarta. 'Since the very beginning one of the main problems in East Timor is that Apodeti, a small minority party, is in power.'[64]

Like Carrascalao, the Catholic Church in East Timor is considered an adversary by parts of the military. The Church's role has changed dramatically since the colonial period when it was seen as a repressive ally of the Portuguese subjugators. But since the Indonesians arrived, many Timorese, of which more than 90 per cent are Catholics, view the Church as their only protection from the army. Unlike other Indonesian bishops, the bishop of East Timor is directly responsible to the Vatican and consequently the clergy in East Timor enjoys some independence from the Indonesian government.

Belo created a stir in 1989 when he asked the UN secretary-general to support a referendum in East Timor on the question of self-determination. He has been sharply critical of the influx of non-Timorese into Timor and of the military's dominant role in the territory. 'All the teachers are from outside, all the civil servants are from outside. Go into any government office and all the employees are from outside. For the simplest jobs in road-building, they bring in people from outside. And these people bring their children and their brothers and sisters . . . As things are here in East Timor, the military are everywhere, in social affairs, the economy, culture, tourism, social communications. So what is left for civilians?'[65]

After the Dili massacre, General Try Sutrisno darkly warned the clergy not to allow Church property to be used by independence advocates. At the time, Belo complained that his phone was bugged, his mail intercepted and his household infiltrated with military intelligence agents.[66] The harassment increased during 1992. 'It makes me feel that this is a police state. Everything I do, all my activities, every word, are followed and monitored . . . This is not the Indonesia that aspires to Pancasila.'[67] Near the end of the year, Belo complained that the army was trying to discredit him by alleging that he was passing secret government documents to Fretilin members overseas.[68]

Carrascalao says the military's antipathy to Belo is misplaced. 'Believe me, Belo is definitely not anti-integration. Like me, he is just trying to bring happiness to the Timorese. It would be a big mistake to kick him out. The solution for East Timor is to remove the army and to give the Church more influence, not less. The bishop is the person that Timorese trust the most.'[69]

While the killings in Dili in November 1991 marked a severe blow to the resistance movement, the event was a turning point of sorts for overseas sympathisers. Fretilin representatives abroad, Portuguese officials and human rights activists used the massacre to return the East Timor case to international prominence. They argued against the Indonesian description of the massacre as an 'unfortunate accident', depicting it instead, in the words of Fretilin spokesman Jose Ramos-Horta, as 'only the latest in a sixteen-year history of gross and systematic human rights violations [in East Timor] . . . It fits into an ideology of violence very much ingrained in the Indonesian military culture in which force is an instrument of policy and violence is a means to extract loyalty and obedience.'[70] The UN personal envoy, Amos Wako, came to the same conclusion: 'The 12 November 1991 incident should not be seen in isolation but rather as the result of several factors prevailing in East Timor, including poor enjoyment of human rights and fundamental freedoms, underdevelopment and lack of infrastructures, excessive presence of military and security personnel, to mention just a few.'[71]

Ramos-Horta rejected the findings of the Indonesian investigating commission as the product of a biased and partial body. In an address to the European Parliament in April 1992, the acerbic envoy asked: 'Would it make sense if the eminent Mr Pol Pot were to be invited to head a commission to investigate the genocide of the Cambodian people? How would the world react if Mrs Imelda Marcos were to be appointed head of a commission to investigate allegations of corruption in the shoe industry in the Philippines?'[72] While Ramos-Horta is dismissed by Indonesia as an unrepresentative troublemaker, his views on army behaviour are echoed in private by some Indonesian politicians who resent the military's dominant role in society. 'Sure, the Dili incident was an accident,' one cabinet minister told me in late 1991, 'but it was the kind of accident a drunk driver gets into.'[73]

The Dili massacre also led to an unprecedented volume of coverage on East Timor in the Indonesian press. Initially it hewed close to the official army line. But as the international outcry intensified, and even more so after the investigating commission reported its findings, mainstream publications increasingly carried articles critical of the army's performance. Some publications simply ignored the army's warning not to emphasise differences between its initial version and the investigating commission's report.[74] Newspapers and magazines also gave heavy coverage to the testimony of East Timorese on trial in mid-1992, a rare glimpse for Indonesian readers of the views of the Timorese resistance.

Perhaps the most powerful and articulate testimony was delivered by Fernando de Araujo, who was eventually jailed for nine years on charges of organising groups of pro-independence Timorese studying in Indonesia. De Araujo said the Indonesian treatment of East Timor was identical to that of the Dutch in Indonesia prior to 1945, and he described Timor's development gains as poor compensation for the loss of independence:

> The concept of colonialism is not limited to the domination of a white race over a black or white skinned one. Claiming that one's own people have the right to independence is also to acknowledge the right of other nations to that same independence. Freedom is not the exclusive right of large and powerful nations. Powerful countries should not concoct reasons for robbing smaller nations of their rights . . . It is proper that the world should admire the Pancasila and the [Indonesian] 1945 Constitution because the values they embody are indeed noble ones . . . [But] there is nothing in the Pancasila about slaughter, annexation or violence. The Indonesian people should be grateful that their former leaders embraced such noble ideals. The great shame is that they have been betrayed by those who hold power today in this country . . . During the Portuguese colonial era there was no intelligence personnel in the villages, no

platoons of soldiers in every small hamlet terrorising and intimidating the population, there was no tax on livestock, homes or plantations. At a day-to-day level, there was no inspection of identity cards, nor the need for travel passes for movement between districts or towns . . . The right to independence and freedom cannot be traded off for cars, asphalted roads or other material possessions. Development is like a noose set up by the Indonesian government to ensnare the [Timorese] people. Because of their rejection of Indonesia's material gifts, they were slaughtered and their corpses now join the sand and stones in forming the foundations of Indonesian development.[75]

In late 1992 the Fretilin leader Xanana Gusmao was captured in Dili and a few months later put on trial. Shortly after his capture, Xanana appeared on Indonesian television and startled his supporters by saying that he accepted East Timor's integration into Indonesia. At the time it was suspected that he may have been coerced into making these remarks or that he may have struck a deal with the military in return for a lighter sentence. By the time his trial came to a close in May 1993, however, Xanana had changed his tune. Perhaps afraid of allowing another anti-Indonesia screed to be reported in the Indonesian media, the court prevented Xanana from reading more than two pages of his defence plea. Later released by a human rights group, the full statement recanted his earlier comments, described his trial as a 'shameful farce' and condemned Indonesia's occupation of East Timor:

> [The Indonesian invasion of East Timor] has the same standing as the advance of the Iraqi troops in Kuwait, the same dimension as the advance of Russian tanks into Kabul, the same character as the Vietnamese invasion of Cambodia . . . For 17 years East Timor . . . has been the story of the great Indonesian farce . . . The Timorese, my compatriots, are out in the street under strict surveillance. This is the blatant rule of the occupier . . . Is it that because Portugal failed to develop East Timor for four hundred years, we Timorese have had to pay for the errors of one coloniser while also paying for the crimes of the other coloniser . . . What is the worth of a law which closes its eyes to the ghastly crimes of 12 November [1991]. Which moral value, which pattern of justice, do the Indonesians uphold, to declare criminals to be heroes and condemn the victims . . . Here today . . . I acknowledge military defeat on the ground. The moment has come for Jakarta to recognise its political defeat on the ground.[76]

In May 1993, Xanana was sentenced to life imprisonment and three months later he had his sentence commuted to 20 years. Allegations of his mistreatment persist.[77]

Looking to the future

Despite the Indonesian press accounts of the trials of Xanana, de Araujo and others, it would be a mistake to overstate the impact of these sorts of disclosures on Indonesian opinion. Having been told for 18 years that the vast majority of Timorese desire integration, most Indonesians accept this to be true. As far as public opinion can be gauged, there would seem to be a fair amount of resentment towards the Timorese for ungratefully soaking up development funds. More to the point, international condemnation of the Dili massacre was seen as an unfair singling out of Indonesia for criticism. The nationalist backlash reached its apex on 25 March 1992 when Soeharto, protesting the Dutch decision to suspend aid to Indonesia because of the Dili massacre, disbanded the Dutch-led Inter-Governmental Group on Indonesia, a multilateral body which annually dispenses foreign aid to Indonesia. The move was enormously popular at home and proved to be cost-free.[78] A new aid group, the Consultative Group on Indonesia, was formed with the World Bank at the helm and in July 1992 it allocated Indonesia US$4.94 billion in new grants and low-interest loans, a four per cent rise over the amount approved the year before.

But if domestic opinion can be controlled, international opinion is another matter. The increasing attention paid around the world to the right of self-determination and to human rights issues will ensure that East Timor remains a drag on Indonesia's foreign policy profile. Much to Jakarta's dismay, a resolution passed by the UN Human Rights Commission in March 1993 censured Indonesia for its poor human rights record in East Timor. Surprisingly, support for the resolution came from the United States, which for many years had voted in similar forums in support of Indonesia. The newly installed Clinton administration, however, voted for the censure resolution and its example was followed by 21 other countries.[79] 'We were clobbered,' said an angry official at the Department of Foreign Affairs in Jakarta. 'The West is being very arrogant, castigating and unfair. The resolution is not helpful to those trying to help human rights awareness here. It only helps those who distrust the West.'[80]

Whether because of international pressure or for its own reasons, Jakarta is beginning to adjust its policies for East Timor. Keen to improve the territory's economic prospects, the government has begun applying pressure on the business sector to invest there.[81] Meanwhile, the military has removed several combat battalions and has shifted its command headquarters for East Timor from Dili to Bali. It is difficult to tell, however, if troop levels in East Timor have really declined. Some, if not all, of the departing combat battalions appear to have been replaced by 'territorial troops'. The distinction matters little to the East Timorese. Whatever their stated purpose, the presence of troops in East Timor is likely to keep alive Timorese resentment at being under constant surveillance.[82]

As has been the case since the original invasion in 1975, military behaviour in East Timor remains at odds with the official line from Jakarta. The military was accused of rounding up and arresting scores of Timorese youths ahead of visits to the territory by a personal envoy of the UN secretary-general in February 1992 and by a delegation of US congressional staffers in September 1993. In early 1993, the local military command in East Timor undermined the public relations value of lowering troop levels by organising ceremonies in which thousands of youths were compelled to swear their loyalty to Indonesia by drinking the blood of chickens and goats.[83] At the end of May in the same year, military officials in East Timor blocked a visit by delegates of the International Committee of the Red Cross (ICRC) to Timorese prisoners, leading the ICRC to suspend all prisoner visits and causing more diplomatic embarrassment for Indonesia. 'You have to realise this is a very difficult, complex, serious, heavy decision we have taken,' said Pierre Pont, the chief ICRC delegate in Jakarta.[84] (In July 1993, the ICRC visits were quietly resumed.) In June 1993, Indonesia was embarrassed again when seven Timorese students who had taken part in the November 1991 demonstration in Dili sought political asylum from the embassies of Finland and Sweden in Jakarta. Denied by the embassies, the students subsequently appealed to Lisbon to grant them asylum because of continued harassment by the military. Near the end of the year, the students were granted asylum and permitted to leave Indonesia.[85]

How the military will act in the future is hard to predict. Presumably, future troop movements will be determined by whether Fretilin manages to regroup after the captures in 1992 and 1993 of Xanana and other leaders. The military's official view is that armed resistance in East Timor has been wiped out, a position which has been proved wrong many times in the past. Many non-military analysts, including Carrascalao, argue that Fretilin will be able to rebuild its networks of support and maintain a low-intensity guerilla campaign unless Jakarta makes more fundamental changes in its approach to East Timor. As noted above, Carrascalao believes the most important of these changes would be a genuine military withdrawal from the territory.

Jakarta so far has fallen a long way short of satisfying international critics. Portugal, for example, insists there can be no acceptable solution until Indonesia ceases to argue that a valid act of self-determination has already taken place in East Timor. Indonesia is vehemently sticking to its guns, literally. 'There must be some kind of consultation with the Timorese people,' said a senior Portuguese official. 'Ideally, that would happen via a referendum under UN supervision.'[86]

The rhetoric on both sides can carry a hard edge. Portugal's Foreign Minister Jose Durao Barroso conceded in a 1992 interview that Lisbon's handling of Timor's decolonisation process was 'flawed' but quickly added that this did not 'in any way change the fact that the Indonesian invasion was a criminal act. We will continue to defend the Timorese' right to self-determination. That is one of our principles and is not negotiable . . . We have nothing against the Indonesian people or culture, but we have no respect for the brutal dictatorship now in power in Jakarta . . . If not for military rule, we are absolutely sure the people of East Timor would express a different view than integration with Indonesia.'[87]

For their part, frustrated officials of Indonesia's Foreign Ministry are caught between an unrepentant and inflexible military establishment and international entities such as Portugal and human rights groups. Desperate to clean East Timor off the foreign policy slate, Minister Alatas had gone out on a limb in convincing Soeharto to overrule military objections to a visit of Portuguese parliamentarians in 1991. That plan, while well-intentioned, backfired tragically on 12 November 1991 and the Foreign Ministry's clout on the East Timor question suffered accordingly. With national prerogatives taking priority, the Ministry spent 1992 countering international criticism with a propaganda blitz of its own.

In July 1992 the Ministry published a new brochure on East Timor, which in great detail restates the standard military refrain.[88] Accusing Portugal of 'political opportunism', the brochure charges Timor's former colonial power with 'practically instigating civil war' in the territory in 1975. Describing the civil war as a 'culmination of centuries of colonial neglect and a completely bungled decolonisation process', it says Portugal has 'forfeited any right to be still considered the administrating power of East Timor' and explains Indonesia's involvement in the territory as 'helping to ensure the democratically expressed will of the majority of the people not be overruled by the armed terror and unilateral imposition of a ruthless minority'.

The report blames Fretilin aggression in the August–November 1975 civil war for the bulk of Timorese casualties both before and after the invasion, omits mention of the coup by Carrascalao's Timorese Democratic Union on 10 August 1975, and declares that non-Fretilin Timorese forces retook Dili on 7 December 1975 with the help only of 'Indonesian volunteers'. Thirty thousand Timorese are reported as having died from war, starvation and disease since 1975, a figure several times lower than most other estimates. The brochure lists the economic gains in East Timor since its annexation, questions the economic viability of an independent East Timor and concludes by lambasting Indonesia's critics for ignoring 'the good faith efforts that have been brought to bear on behalf of the people of East Timor to assure that their rights are respected, that their lives are improved'.

The dilemma facing Indonesia is that if it is going to reach an international solution to the East Timor problem, it has to deal with Portugal. And as the above comments show, there is little trust between the two sides. Referring to the July 1976 vote by the 'People's Assembly' in East Timor, Jakarta claims that Timorese have already voted for integration with Indonesia and won't be asked to vote again. The refusal to allow a new referendum provokes accusations that Jakarta is afraid of public opinion. 'Whoever is afraid of the referendum is afraid of the truth,' Xanana said in his defence plea.[89] Carrascalao adds that Jakarta is right to be worried: 'If you give the Timorese a choice between Fretilin and Indonesia now, it's hard to say who would win.'[90]

Timorese participation in the sporadic, UN-sponsored talks between Indonesia and Portugal poses another thorny problem for Jakarta. The option of including representatives from Fretilin, especially Xanana, is not one that fills Jakarta with enthusiasm.

More embarrassing still for Jakarta, at least for a time, was what to do with Carrascalao, the East Timor-born intellectual who Jakarta appointed governor in 1982 and re-appointed in 1987. Carrascalao, still on the payroll at the Foreign Ministry, has not been invited to participate in talks with the Portuguese. 'The Foreign Ministry's position is not to involve me in East Timor diplomatic efforts,' he said in early 1993. 'I was Timorese before I was Indonesian and I am still a Timorese. I can't follow the Indonesian line when I know the truth.'[91] Later in 1993, however, Jakarta solved its problem by dispatching Carrascalao to Rumania to serve as ambassador.

One bright spot for Foreign Minister Alatas was the formation of a new cabinet in March 1993. He retained his post while some leading military figures, notably Defence Minister Benny Murdani, lost theirs. Some in Jakarta believe that with the removal from power of the military men who were closely involved with the original East Timor invasion, the negotiating room for Alatas may have widened. For his part, Alatas appears determined to push ahead with diplomatic negotiations aimed at settling the East Timor issue. It remains to be seen just how much negotiating leeway he will enjoy.

In December 1992 and April 1993, Alatas and his Portuguese counterpart Barroso met for new talks but the two sides remained far apart, especially on the central issue of Timorese participation in the negotiations. 'We don't recognise Fretilin as the sole voice of Timorese,' said Barroso's assistant Rui Quartim in a June 1993 interview. 'Apodeti can be involved but so should the Church and representatives of other Timorese views.' The two sides discussed a series of confidence-building measures such as increasing diplomatic contacts and allowing more journalists from each country to visit the other, but no firm commitments were made. The Portuguese remain wary of Alatas' ability to deliver what he promises. 'The promises and gestures of Alatas mean very little because East Timor is still the playground of the Indonesian military,' Quartim said. 'The gaps between the two governments are still very wide.'[92]

Diplomatic sources in both countries, however, hold out hope that it may be possible to finesse the issue of Timorese participation in future negotiations by establishing two separate dialogues. The trilateral discussions between Indonesia, Portugal and the UN would continue as before while a second, lower-profile dialogue would be held between Timorese groups and UN officials. In such a scenario, the UN would in effect act as the Timorese delegate to the negotiations. Whether such a compromise would satisfy either Jakarta or Lisbon is unclear.

Another development which may cool the rhetoric of both governments is the beginning of a dialogue between pro-integration Timorese living in East Timor and Timorese exiles abroad. One such meeting was held outside London in December 1993 and, while no specific results were forthcoming, the fact that the former enemies agreed to meet for talks was considered a step forward.[93] In addition, growing business links between Portugal and Indonesia may increase the willingness of both sides to compromise on the Timor question. Indonesia–Portugal 'friendship associations' have been established in each country, with the Indonesian group being headed by Soeharto's daughter Siti Hardijanti Rukmana. On their own, these ostensibly non-governmental associations aren't likely to contribute much to the government-to-government dialogue taking place under UN auspices. But the involvement of Soeharto's daughter in the process could well strengthen Alatas' bargaining power vis-a-vis the Indonesian military.[94]

In the current political context in Indonesia, meaningful changes to the East Timor policy are unlikely. The foundation of this policy is the military's 'security approach' to civil affairs in which any opposition outside the regime's control is considered an intolerable threat to national unity. No doubt the stabbing of two Indonesian soldiers on 12 November 1991 contributed to the massacre which followed. But equally important, many officers admit, is that soldiers were simply horrified to see Indonesian citizens publicly demonstrating against the government. It is an example the military does not want other Indonesians to follow.

The starting point for Indonesia's policy for East Timor is that the majority of Timorese want to be Indonesians and that Timor's incorporation into Indonesia is a closed issue never to be re-opened. For Soeharto and the army, these are non-negotiable principles. With these firmly held assumptions in mind, Indonesia explains the continued resistance to integration as the product of policies poorly implemented. The solution is two-fold: to improve Timor's economic development and provide more jobs to young Timorese, and to raise the cost of public displays of opposition.

The flaw in this approach is that the problem with Indonesia's East Timor policy is not in its implementation, but in the assumptions lying behind it. The compelling evidence from Church and aid workers, human rights groups and Timorese refugees—not to mention the continued willingness of young Timorese to resist Indonesian control at great personal risk—supports the view that most Timorese do not believe a legitimate act of self-determination has taken place. The Indonesian position, by confusing the suppression of dissent with support for Indonesia, misses this point. By so doing, it forces Timorese grievances, legitimate or not, underground where they fester and feed pro-independence sentiment. Without some movement on the self-determination issue, or at the least a significant reduction of the Indonesian military presence in the territory, it is hard to see how more roads and bridges are going to create a more peaceful East Timor.

But the prospect of an independent East Timor, or even a Timor with limited regional autonomy, is simply not countenanced by the government or most of the Indonesian elite.[95] The consensus remains that an independent East Timor not only would rip the fabric of Indonesian unity but would also destabilise the whole of Southeast Asia.

Over the longer term this consensus will come under increased pressure both from within Indonesia and from outside. The worldwide trend to democratisation and a new post-Cold War concern with self-determination and human rights will not pass Indonesia by completely. The Clinton administration in the United States, for example, while unlikely to pressure Indonesia to the point of jeopardising the bilateral relationship, will be more vulnerable than previous administrations to pressure groups lobbying on behalf of territories such as East Timor. Its support for the UN Human Rights Commission resolution lodged against Indonesia in March 1993 is one reflection of the changing times. Clinton also raised concerns about East Timor with Soeharto when the two leaders met in Tokyo in July 1993 ahead of the annual meeting of the G-7 industrialised countries. And in August of the same year, the US vetoed a plan by Jordan to sell four US-made fighter aircraft to Indonesia, citing concerns with the festering situation in East Timor.[96]

In Indonesia, as pressure for more public participation in national politics gathers steam, so too may there be an opening for changes in the government's view of East Timor. To be sure, such an opening is unlikely while Soeharto remains in power and it is not necessarily any more likely once he leaves office. Much will depend on how much political influence the Indonesian military will retain in post-Soeharto administrations. If its influence should wane, the prospect of a more autonomous East Timor in some kind of loose association with Indonesia could enter the realm of possibilities.

Already in the court of Indonesian public opinion, an occasional snippet reveals a grudging appreciation of the Timorese stand against military control. Whether this view will become more popular is impossible to say but it serves as a reminder that resentment of military domination is not limited to the country's twenty-seventh province. In a cheeky editorial published a month after the Dili massacre, the *Indonesian Observer*, normally a standard-bearer of nationalist opinion, momentarily let down its guard:

> What people in Bandung, West Java feel as government high-handedness may appear the same to people in East Timor. Hence, a stop to high-handedness against people in East Timor shall also mean its abolition in other parts of Indonesia. The fact that the East Timorese thus appear to be the most effective resistance against abuse of power should not be taken against them, instead, we have to thank the Lord for saving some Indonesians from the omnipotent cult of fear.[97]

9
Social rights, individual responsibilities

I am reminded that a nation that neglects its cultural heritage will lose its identity. A nation without its identity will be weak, and in the end, a weak nation will deteriorate from within and without . . . Only a nation with its own identity can be a nation with self-confidence . . . [and] it is this self-confidence, this ability to be self-reliant and creative that are the keys to success in development.

Soeharto[1]

For the most part, [the] carnival of expression seems absent from the Indonesian language today. Our language has been ripped from the world, stripped of shape, smell, colour and form, cleansed of the grit and graffiti, the rumpus and commotion, that make up real life . . . The language that we see forms a landscape almost barren of vegetation, dotted by sparse clumps of bamboo and threatened by blight, a landscape in which only the poorest of transmigrants might find a home.

Gunawan Mohamad[2]

Honourable Parliamentarians: Welcome to Indonesia, and the government which boasts the chair of the Non-Aligned Movement and a long list of human rights violations. Welcome to Indonesia, where workers are forbidden to organise, where political and civil rights are repressed, where detainees are tortured, sometimes to their death. Welcome to a country where to speak out and to organise means jail.

Letter to a visiting delegation of Australian legislators from the Indonesian Front for the Defence of Human Rights (Infight)[3]

After a long winter of whispers and hushed tones, 1990 offered a promising new start for freedom of expression in Indonesia. The architects of the New Order's uncompromising 'security approach' to dissent, it seemed, were beginning to have second thoughts. The strict curbs they had put on the press and on all manner of cultural expression had succeeded in silencing most of their critics but their 'success' had produced as well a number of unfortunate side-effects, one being a largely vacuous, stifled and stagnant public discourse.

The government's response was to promote a kinder, gentler approach to dissent, a policy shift which came to be known as *keterbukaan*, or openness. Government support for *keterbukaan* began in earnest in December 1989 when the then army chief of staff Edi Sudrajat stunned the reading public with the following comment: 'Having enjoyed better education, our people want differences discussed more openly. As such they want more active participation in the decision-making process on national problems and in social control. Foot-stomping father-knows-best leadership style has to stop.'[4]

The following August, in his annual Independence Day address, President Soeharto returned to the theme. 'Democracy requires a great deal of consultation, discussion, exchange of ideas and dialogue,' he said. 'It is . . . wrong if our vigilance towards security is so excessive that it restricts our own movements . . . We must view differences of opinion as dynamic . . . Our common task in the years to come is . . . to develop further the people's initiative, creativity and participation in development.'[5] Days later, Coordinating Minister for Political Affairs and Security Sudomo hinted at an easing of restrictions on journalists and an end to the practice of revoking the printing licences of 'irresponsible' publications.

These comments and others like them had an invigorating effect. *Keterbukaan* was more than a carrot dangled in front of Indonesia's intellectual elite. It promised, at heart, more opportunity for individual Indonesians to have a say in the decisions that affected them the most. It was understood that there would be no sea change in the regime's policies, but there was reason to hope for a freer-flowing debate on the important issues of the day.

It didn't take long for the *keterbukaan* dream to fade. In mid-October playwright Nano Riantiarno's *Suksesi* opened to enthusiastic reviews and standing-room-only crowds. It was the last in a trilogy of plays which rolled a satirical eye over some of the most sensitive issues in contemporary Indonesia. The first two plays focused on the tight linkages between Soeharto and Indonesia's crony businessmen and the huge riches produced by these relationships. *Suksesi* combined this theme with the equally sensitive issue of presidential succession.

Suksesi tells the story of the fictional King Bukbangkalan and his four children. To determine a successor, the king feigns an illness to see how his children will react. After much posturing, his favourite daughter Diah

Roro Suksesi gains the backing of the army, throws her siblings in jail and usurps the throne. The play flits back and forth between the political jockeying for power and a series of barbed comments about the enormous wealth the king's children have accumulated. The parallels with the real Indonesia could hardly have been more obvious. At one point the king asks a court jester about the wealth of his oldest son Absalom. 'How much is Absalom's wealth anyway?' says the king. 'Have you forgotten,' the jester Bilung replies. 'It was your Highness himself who conceded many facilities for Absalom's business . . . [It] all originates from your benevolence.' The play ends with the following chorus:

> Don't show what can be obtained
> so that the people won't want it.
> The King always tries to keep his subjects
> empty in heart,
> full in stomach,
> weak in desire,
> but strong in bones.
> The King always tries to make sure
> that the people don't know
> and those who know
> don't dare,
> let alone act.
> And in consequence
> all will be orderly and stable,
> orderly and stable. . .[6]

In the end, *Suksesi*'s thinly disguised satire proved to be not quite disguised enough. On the eleventh day of its two-week run, the police ordered that the play be closed. The government, defending its action, said the play was 'uneducative', anti-Pancasila and a threat to security. Many suspect Soeharto's eldest daughter Siti Hardijanti Rukmana, on whom the character Diah Roro Suksesi was apparently based, of pressuring the police to ban the play.

Whatever the reason, the mood had changed. Over the next few months, several public readings by the popular poet W. S. Rendra were cancelled by the police, the distribution of a foreign newspaper was banned and an Indonesian magazine was closed. Another of Riantiarno's plays, *Opera Kecoa*, was deemed 'vulgar' and banned even before it opened. Indonesian-style glasnost had made an unpromising start.

Critics of the government immediately derided the whole notion of *keterbukaan* as a cynical ploy by Soeharto to flush his critics into the open. A more generous interpretation is that the government was as confused as the public as to what *keterbukaan* really meant. Apart from a series of seemingly sympathetic comments by Soeharto and top military aides, no guidelines were handed down to define the limits of *keterbukaan*. Without any new instructions from the top, perplexed lower and middle ranking military officials figured the safest policy was to carry on enforcing the repressive restrictions and policies already in place. When the hopes raised by *keterbukaan* turned to anger and cynicism, administration officials hastened to pin the blame on an impatient public. 'We want to be more forthright but we have to go slow,' said Rachmat Witoelar, then secretary-general of the ruling Golkar party. 'Artists have to inhibit themselves and remember not to hurt the feelings of the older generation.'[7]

The backtracking on *keterbukaan* disappointed many but surprised few. Even the ticketholders to the banned performances of *Suksesi* didn't complain much. What was the point? From the beginning of his rule, Soeharto has said that restrictions on free expression and free assembly are necessary to enable the government to act on behalf of the community without being hobbled by the demands of individuals or interest groups. As Soeharto has consolidated his hold on power, the capacity of individual Indonesians to confront, much less overturn, government decisions has all but disappeared.

Officially, of course, the government contends that the people are sovereign and are able to change their government at will. It insists that the press is not censored, that torture and unlawful imprisonment do not occur, that workers are free to strike, that human rights are scrupulously respected, and that prevailing forms of public communication and expression are consistent with Indonesian cultural values. Insofar as certain 'Western-style' individual liberties are constrained, these are to be seen as the 'price' for political stability and economic development.

The extent to which the New Order government has held up its side of the bargain is discussed elsewhere in this book. This chapter looks at the other side of the equation: the weakness of the individual vis-a-vis the state. It argues that many Indonesians are increasingly unhappy with the restraints placed on their freedoms and are ever more unwilling to accept these strictures as a necessary or desirable trade-off for economic development.

Suppression of individual liberties in Indonesia takes many forms, from curbs on free speech, freedom of movement and the right of assembly, to a legal system which favours the state over the individual, to a security apparatus unaccountable for its actions. Abuses go largely unchallenged because the political system is weak and ineffectual and the press and other channels of societal grievances are limited in what they can say. The fear of being labelled anti-Pancasila is enough to tame all but the boldest critics; those who do raise their hands above the parapet are harassed, intimidated and closely watched.

But, as official comments in support of *keterbukaan* in 1990 show, it is not only critics of the government who deplore this state of affairs. Many in the government, including the army, recognise that without a freer flow of ideas and opinions, the next generation of Indonesian leaders will be poorly equipped to guide the nation in an ever more complex and interdependent world. Moreover, there is a growing awareness that Indonesians' ability to think critically will be an important determinant of the nation's future economic success. The challenge ahead, then, at least as the government sees it, is to find a balance between the authoritarian impulse for total political control and the desirability of a more vibrant public debate.

Exactly how the government will meet that challenge is difficult to predict. In the second half of 1993, for example, after Soeharto had successfully arranged to have himself elected to a sixth five-year term as president, a second round of *keterbukaan* was permitted by the authorities. Soeharto reached a conciliation of sorts with several high-profile dissidents, a handful of imprisoned Islamic radicals were released from jail, and military and government leaders uttered the requisite phrases in support of more democracy, free speech and government accountability. Labour leaders, Muslim groups, human rights activists and students wasted little time in responding, and the closing months of 1993 witnessed a rash of protests and demonstrations focused on grievances ranging from a state-sponsored lottery to the military's 'security approach' to the failure of the government's umbrella labour union in protecting workers' rights.[8] At the very end of the year, in a replay of the first bout of *keterbukaan*, the government decided it had had enough. The police arrested some two dozen students on the charge of insulting the head of state, Soeharto lashed out at protesters for using what he called the 'same tactics as those used by the Indonesian Communist Party', and army officers vowed to uphold Pancasila against any ideological rivals and keep a closer rein on street-level demonstrations in the future.[9]

Whether these steps will be enough to secure a period of renewed quietude remains to be seen. They certainly won't be enough to eliminate entirely the voices calling for change. Indeed, pressures for an 'opening up' of civil society are undoubtedly growing stronger with each passing year, and the government will need to resort to ever more heavy-handed measures to keep them in check. At the same time, however, Soeharto's government is determined to ensure that any 'opening' is limited in scope and proceeds at a pace of its choosing. Thus, the most likely scenario for the future is a continuing tug-of-war both within the government—between 'stability-first' advocates and those in favour of a limited opening—and between the government and those outside the government pushing for a more thoroughgoing change in approach. What the closing of *Suksesi* in 1990 and the clampdown on students in late 1993 illustrate, however, is that at least for the time being the defenders of Indonesia's status quo still retain the upper hand.

The marketplace of ideas

As is the case for civilian politicians, Indonesia's artists, poets, play-wrights, intellectuals, novelists and journalists are more tolerated than welcomed by the New Order government. Like would-be politicians, their activities are closely monitored. The roots of this attitude lie in Indonesia's feudal past and in the traditional Javanese—and Soeharto's—notion of power. As discussed in earlier chapters, in the 'integral' view of the state the nation is akin to a family to which all societal groups belong and contribute. Family matters can be discussed, though politely, but in the end the father makes the decisions. Continued opposition to, or excessively blunt criticism of, his decisions is considered destabilising, disloyal and in extreme cases subversive and unpatriotic. 'It is considered insulting when people oppose or even question government actions,' explains legal activist Adnan Buyung Nasution. 'Opposition is interpreted as distrust of the good faith of the ruler; just as it would be inconceivable that children demand that their father account for his acts, it is inconceivable that the people demand that the ruler be accountable for his deeds.'[10]

This is, admittedly, a simplified version of the New Order's philosophical underpinnings but it is not far from the truth. There is no space outside the family. The law and the press, to give two examples, exist to serve the family's purposes, not to critique or obstruct the family's actions. Intellectuals, not surprisingly, chafe in this climate of suspicion and control and the arts have suffered. 'Soeharto has closed the door to the nation's intellectuals,' laments sociologist Taufik Abdullah.[11]

The New Order, almost insistently anti-intellectual, is all but bereft of great plays, books and films. Indonesia's greatest living author is Pramoedya Ananta Toer, whose *This Earth of Mankind* quartet offers a riveting portrait of life under Dutch rule at the turn of the century. But in Indonesia Pramoedya is considered a subversive. Citing his links to the Indonesian Communist Party, Soeharto's government jailed Pramoedya shortly after coming to power and kept him there for fourteen years. Later, seeing in his historical account of colonial rule a disguised critique of modern Indonesia, the government banned his books.[12] Several Indonesians have since been jailed for selling Pramoedya's novels.

The film industry has suffered from a surfeit of government regulations and rules which determine how films are produced, marketed and distributed, while a national censorship board keeps a close eye on the message that films bring to the viewing audience. One way to measure the cumulative effect of the New Order's intervention in the film industry is to note the sharp drop-off in Indonesian film output: only 32 films were produced in 1992, a long way short of the industry's heyday in the 1970s when more than 100 titles were forthcoming each year. The quality of Indonesian movies has suffered as well, film-makers say, and for the same reason. 'The low quality of local films is caused by the government's domination [of the industry],' complained Soemardjono, deputy chairman of the Indonesian Film Council.[13]

Academic life also has been hard hit. Students figure prominently in Indonesia's political history, with youth groups playing key roles in both the struggle against the Dutch and in the rocky transition from Sukarno to Soeharto. In the early years of the New Order student groups kept alive this tradition, campaigning against corruption, nepotism and the increasingly authoritarian nature of Soeharto's government. But beginning with the 1978 Campus Normalisation Law, student political activity has been severely circumscribed. The climate of intellectual freedom that once was taken for granted by Indonesian universities has become another casualty of the military's security approach.

University deans are expected to keep campuses free from politics, a ban which extends to campaigning ahead of five-yearly general elections. Professors critical of Indonesia's development process or political system are denied promotion; as a result, many shy away from research or lectures that would irritate the authorities. By most accounts, classroom life is boring and uninspiring and student apathy is common. The few politically engaged students run the risk of expulsion or even arrest.

In early 1990 six students at the Bandung Institute of Technology were jailed for protesting a campus visit by then Home Affairs Minister Rudini. Their crimes included waving banners critical of government policies and shouting 'down with Rudini'. In 1991, a student from the Satya Wacana Christian University in Salatiga was detained by the police and other students questioned for their role in distributing a 'Land for the People' calendar which caricatured government leaders. In May 1992, two students in Central Java were arrested for criticising the electoral process and urging a boycott of the June elections.[14]

Many older intellectuals are disturbed by what they see as political apathy among the young. The tall, imposing poet and social critic W. S. Rendra angrily lays the blame for this apathy on the government's intolerance of intellectual dissent. Defining culture as 'the opportunity to discuss the quality of life through art', Rendra argues that 'Indonesia has been "de-culturised" to the point where our ability to regenerate has been severely damaged. What should be the most productive members of society—the young—just float along in Indonesia. They have no culture of their own, no political force, no economic voice. What you're left with is robots and zombies, unable to adapt, incapable of absorbing new influences. The campuses thwart intellectual activity, not promote it. There is no room for contemplation or interaction. As a nation of thinkers, the vital signs have almost disappeared.'[15]

Adds Gunawan Mohamad, poet, essayist and editor of Indonesia's leading newsweekly *Tempo*: 'Universities are dead. Ideas are dead. The government's obsession with security is like a black hole swallowing all independent thought.'[16]

In fairness to students, it is worth making the point that 'social awareness' has not disappeared completely from campuses; it has just become harder to identify. The rules of the game have changed and student activists have had to make more effort to disguise their activities. Rather than make use of overtly political forums on campus, student leaders have found it expedient to operate under the protection afforded by mosques and Islamic study centres. Indeed, the rash of student protests in late 1993 was notable for the high participation by students from Islamic universities and training institutes.

Today's students also have a different agenda than their counterparts of two or three decades ago, another factor which helps explain why older Indonesian intellectuals feel that university activism is all but extinct. Distanced from the political process like the rest of the civilian elite, student activists in the 1980s and 1990s have shifted their focus to grassroots issues like land compensation cases and wealth inequalities. Finally, as even some professional politicians recognise, a lack of political activism on the part of students is at least partly explained by the timid example set by their elders. 'Students shy away from political activity because the risk of persecution is too high,' said Kwik Kian Gie, a leading figure in the Indonesian Democratic Party. 'They ask, if people like party politicians who have immunity from prosecution don't take risks, why should we?'[17]

Complaints about the 'de-politicisation' of university campuses are more than idle concerns about the quality of academic life. Many in the Indonesian elite feel that the government's efforts to enforce consensus by eliminating dissenting views have had a disastrous if under-appreciated effect on the nation's ability to produce capable leaders for the future. 'How can we face the twenty-first century if we are shut off from events elsewhere?' asks film-maker Eros Djarot. 'We are not equipped to play in the world of information. Our enemy is our own backwardness, the enforced backwardness of our intellectuals. If you shut the mouths of the students, the people are going to be dumb.'[18] Adds Buyung Nasution: 'I think it is Soeharto's worst crime that he has made Indonesians afraid to think, afraid to express themselves.'[19]

Mochtar Lubis is one of Indonesia's better known novelists and journalists. He edited the critical *Indonesia Raya* newspaper until it was closed by order in 1974 and since then has remained a staunch opponent of restrictions on free speech. Lubis has been imprisoned by both of

Indonesia's presidents and is today forbidden to publish a newspaper. Austere and uncompromising, Lubis rails against the complacency he sees around him:

> There is no time to waste. Indonesians must be allowed to develop their critical faculties so they can understand what's happening to themselves, to their society and in the world. Not just understand, but be able to analyze and make choices. Members of society are not allowed to be critical so how can they be creative? How can you expect people to create, to think, if there is no climate of freedom. Without fostering our intellectual strengths, which means letting people say what they think without fear, Indonesians will remain coolies in their own country. It's terrifying to think that just to say common things you have to be so careful. When you reach that stage, and that's where we are, you have to realise we've arrived at a critical situation.[20]

These comments, though focused mostly on the low level of political consciousness in Indonesia, have dark implications for Indonesia's future economic security. The ability to think clearly and critically is crucial to the competence of any workforce. Foreign businessmen with long experience in Indonesia generally seem to regard local workers as diligent and reliable. But a consistent complaint is the difficulty of finding and keeping managers and supervisors who bring to the job initiative and a willingness to make hard decisions. The weakness of the managerial class, many believe, has its roots in the New Order's obsession with 'harmony' and 'consensus' and its unwillingness to tolerate dissent. Workers who are educated by rote and learn from an early age that the 'government always knows best' are ill-prepared to run the modern business enterprises that form the centrepiece of Indonesia's economy.

The press: more responsible than free

As with the arts, the press has seen its role eclipsed under Soeharto. The New Order opened with both good and bad news for the press. In 1965–66, about a quarter of Indonesia's 160 or so newspapers were shut down because of alleged communist links and hundreds of journalists were arrested. But many of the remaining papers, tired of the ideological rigidity of the late Sukarno era,[21] welcomed a change in government and saw themselves as partners to the new government in developing Indonesia. They were ready to be, in the New Order lexicon, free but responsible, and the government allowed them considerable leeway.

But as the press became increasingly critical of the New Order's social and economic policies, the government's resistance to criticism likewise began to grow. As the government came to identify itself more clearly as a product of a hierarchical Javanese society, its tolerance of criticism from below waned. An independent press came to be seen as an unwanted and culturally misplaced Western import.[22]

The government's ambivalence ended with the Malari riots of 1974. Following the riots, twelve publications were banned, several leading journalists—including Mochtar Lubis—were arrested and others were forced out of journalism. 'The press,' notes David Hill, 'had taken advantage of the relatively cordial government–press relations over the early New Order period to highlight dissatisfaction with a government they had basically supported since its inception.' But the 1974 crackdown brought an end to the government's 'fragile partnership with the press'.[23]

Student protests in 1977–78, faithfully reported by newspapers and magazines, further soured the relationship between government and press. Another seven Jakarta dailies were banned, although this time only temporarily. But the message had been delivered: the limits of tolerable criticism had narrowed. After this point, the Indonesian press never again mustered a concerted, industry-wide challenge to the government, although individual publications would on occasion cross the boundaries. In the 1980s, a handful of papers were shut down, some permanently, some temporarily, on a variety of pretexts. The common theme, though, was that the offending publications were considered destabilising and harmful to development.

The government's main mechanism for securing a compliant press is the SIUPP—the press publication enterprise permit—issued by the Department of Information. The SIUPP, established in 1982 and strengthened in 1984 by Information Minister Harmoko, replaced the existing system of publishing licences with a broader, more potent censorship weapon that entitled the government to shut down entire publishing enterprises, as well as individual publications. Harmoko, a Soeharto loyalist in charge of the Information Ministry since 1983, has wielded the SIUPP with great effect. As he did with the *Monitor* magazine in 1990, Harmoko is able to withdraw unilaterally a publication's SIUPP without recourse to the courts.

But the SIUPP is merely the blunt edge of the sword. While undoubtedly a potent threat, it is deployed only in extreme cases. The government really wants journalists to censor themselves. 'What I want to do is to develop in the press a sense of self-control,' is how Harmoko put it in a 1993 interview.[24] The government tries to bring this about by subjecting the press to guidance, advice and veiled threats from Information Ministry officials and, more importantly, from the military. Exactly what is and what is not allowable for journalists to print is never clearly spelled out, and the confusion works in the government's favour. Adding to the confusion is that the lines of permissible behaviour are constantly shifting over time, depending on the topic and context. An article that may leave censors unruffled one year may elicit angry reprisals the next. A story that a Jakarta paper might get away with may spell trouble for a paper in Sumatra or Kalimantan. Well aware of the draconian punishment which may befall the publisher of an offending article, many journalists steer clear of troublesome areas, a tendency encouraged by the habit of big companies and government ministries to financially reward sympathetic coverage by particular journalists.

The threat of reprisals is often enough to make journalists not only censor themselves but their sources as well. As the English-language daily *Jakarta Post* put it in mid-1991, editors and journalists 'are so careful now that they do not even have enough courage to print any stories about not-so-sensitive issues, let alone anything involving anti-Pancasila ideology which would mean a pointless and stupid suicide'.[25] A clearer acknowledgment of the New Order's success in taming the press is hard to imagine.

Journalists have learned to treat certain touchy issues with extreme care, such as stories that involve racial, religious, ethnic or class tensions. Other topics dangerous for journalists include the mechanics of presidential succession, the business activities of Soeharto's family, regional insurgencies and anything that puts the military in a bad light. The government maintains that public discussion of these issues will inflame passions and exacerbate latent animosities. 'Our people can't handle "openness" yet,' said one senior cabinet official in a 1991 interview. 'Most Indonesians are still lowly educated and they are not able to filter information properly. If we allow "openness", people opposed to Pancasila, like Islamic fundamentalists, will cause trouble by distorting information.'[26] It might be added that this view is not limited to government officials; parts of the elite—especially those nervous about a political resurgence of Islam—sympathise with it as well.

When delicate news arises, editors can expect to receive telephone calls from the military 'encouraging' placid reporting or, at times, no reporting at all. Editors ignore these directives at the risk of putting their publications out of business and their journalists out of jobs—and worse. 'I see myself as the pilot of a hijacked plane and journalists as the passengers,' says *Tempo* editor Gunawan. 'If I don't pay attention to the censors my passengers will be the first victims.'[27] *Indonesia Business Weekly*, a plucky English-language magazine founded in 1992, sized up the situation in even blunter terms: 'Most Indonesians have long resigned [themselves] to the fact that the pen is often mightier than the sword but is absolutely no match for the gun.'[28]

While the government has less control over foreign journalists, it is not without leverage. In addition to controlling the distribution of foreign publications, the government on occasion has refused to grant work permits to journalists considered unwilling to play along with the 'rules of the game'. Before being distributed, foreign publications must clear a screening committee consisting of the Information Ministry, the army and the intelligence agencies. The government no longer 'blacks out' offending articles, yet publications that report extensively on Indonesia, such as the *Far Eastern Economic Review* and the *Asian Wall Street Journal,* not infrequently have their distribution delayed or prohibited outright.

The government's control over the flow of information arguably has succeeded in taming potential social unrest. It certainly has succeeded almost completely in preventing the Indonesian press from being used as a political weapon by government opponents. By denying critics ready access to mass-based communication channels, the government has been able to keep potential opponents isolated and vulnerable. But looked at from another perspective, these 'successes' are not cost-free. Perhaps the most damaging cost is that a quiescent and cowed press cannot operate as an effective two-way communications channel between the government and the people. It is a danger that Soeharto himself recognises. 'We don't restrict the press . . . [because the press] functions as a nervous system, carrying messages from one part of the body of our nation to another, so that each part plays its proper role,' Soeharto said in a speech in 1993. 'The biggest danger would be if this nervous system failed to function, causing each part of the body to work according to its separate wills and responses.'[29] Added Information Minister Harmoko: 'I have never exercised control over the press. That's not allowed by law.'[30]

It is hard to square statements such as these with reality. The discrepancy can perhaps be best explained by returning again to Soeharto's view that his power should remain unchallenged, his desire to nurture the still fragile bonds tying the Indonesian nation together and his preoccupation with economic development. As long as 'messages' carried by the press conform with these goals, then the press is free. If the 'messages' obstruct these goals, then the press is no longer acting as it should. Efforts to prevent these unwanted messages are not seen, at least by Soeharto, as restrictions on the press; they are, rather, legitimate efforts to make the press do what Soeharto wants it to do. 'Interesting events that are divisive should be reported, if at all, with the greatest possible care,' explained Soeharto to assembled journalists on National Press Day in 1993. 'But news that will help to unify this diverse nation should be disseminated immediately.'[31] Harmoko later elaborated on the president's view of the press in an interview with an Indonesian magazine: 'Publications which don't reflect the values of Pancasila and the 1945 Constitution and instead propound different views, including liberalism, radicalism and communism, are prohibited. In practice, that means their SIUPP [press licence] will be cancelled, a step which is allowed by law.'[32]

Other Indonesians, of course, have different ideas about what the press should be doing. In their view, many of the messages that Soeharto is not prepared to countenance deserve a public hearing for the benefit of both the rulers and ruled. Because the government hears only words of praise, the critics believe, it is slow to recognise its mistakes. 'The [Indonesian] government is naturally pleased to have a frightened press,' observes Gunawan of *Tempo* magazine. 'What is not realised is that from frightened people you hear no sincerity, but distortion. You will not know whether the praise uttered by a frightened man is authentic praise or merely boot-licking.'[33]

Moreover, a carefully monitored press has left Indonesians woefully underinformed about the most pressing matters of state and society. If an informed public is a necessary precondition for a well functioning democracy, an uninformed public plays directly into the hands of an authoritarian regime. And by keeping the public uninformed, an authoritarian government can continue to defend itself indefinitely by arguing that the public is not yet ready for a more participatory form of government. Over time, the government's critics add, the lack of effective channels for public communication erodes the capacity for civilised debate, another important precondition for democratic rule. 'Indonesians have lost the habit of debating issues, of accepting differences of opinion,' says lawyer Nasution. 'So, naturally, when you loosen the controls the rhetoric can quickly become polarised.'[34]

The government's control of the press also has had a major influence on the 'public language' of Indonesia. The language of journalists has become infused with 'bureaucrat-speak' and riddled with the jargon of development. Euphemisms and acronyms become the best available substitute for truth; precision of expression—and perhaps precision of thought as well—suffer. The bureaucracy enjoys a powerful influence over Indonesian journalism because it is the source of most news. One recent survey of Indonesian papers showed that almost half the information reported came from government sources. 'Journalists have adopted the language of the bureaucracy,' says media analyst Daniel Dhakidae, 'and as a result language has become alienated from the common people.'[35] The picture presented by the media to the public, he and others say, is one-sided and permeated with the New Order's ideological overtones.

Amidst this bleak portrait, some encouraging signs have emerged in recent years. Developments on the economic front and the pressures for more 'openness' have combined to widen the scope of permissible activity for journalists, both domestic and foreign. The press, in fact, has probably benefited most from the government's halting attempts at glasnost. The army's once common practice of calling editors to discourage unwanted reporting has become less frequent. More and more mainstream publications are pressing as close as they can to the limits of official tolerance, and many of the subjects once considered off limits are now being discussed in relatively more direct terms. In the mid-1980s, for example, most publications shied away from even identifying Soeharto's children in their business coverage. Now the exploits of the president's children are commonly featured in the media, although usually in the guise of straightforward business stories. Specific allegations of government favouritism and nepotism, however, still need to be treated carefully. Discussion of human rights is another subject once considered too sensitive for the military's taste but now regularly reported, if often only to reject Western criticisms.

One factor pushing the press to become more outspoken is that competition is on the rise. The economic prosperity of the late 1980s paved the way for a smorgasbord of new magazines and newspapers catering to women, bankers, computer users, gardeners, children, stockbrokers, managers and so on. In addition, other media competition is developing. The staid, state-owned television station TVRI lost its monopoly in 1990 when Soeharto's second son Bambang Trihatmodjo extracted from the Information Ministry a licence to operate a privately owned broadcasting network.[36] Bambang's older sister, Soeharto's cousin Sudwikatmono, *pribumi* industrialist Aburizal Bakrie and tycoon Liem Sioe Liong quickly followed suit and established their own television stations. The new stations are popular with the middle class and advertisers alike. While they are prohibited from broadcasting their own news programs, their entertainment and current affairs programs have attempted, with some success, to put meaningful content back into the mass media.

The development is clearly discomfiting for the Information Ministry. Had it not been Soeharto's relatives and cronies doing the asking, private TV licences would still be a distant dream. But they did ask, and Minister Harmoko had no choice but to give. For the time being, of course, the Information Ministry can be reasonably confident that Soeharto's children will not rock the boat too far. It is, after all, their boat too.

But, equally, there is little doubt that challenges to the government's control over information will rise in the future. A handful of other private Indonesian firms have announced plans to set up television stations in different cities around the country.[37] And, in both the cities and rural areas where private television has yet to reach, satellite dishes are sprouting on more and more rooftops. The dishes receive signals not only from Indonesia's privately owned broadcasters but from foreign stations as well. Faced with both technological advances in worldwide communications and the prospect of increased commercial competition among new Indonesian broadcasters, the Information Ministry is clearly fighting a losing battle. 'We cannot hold back the tide,' a weary Harmoko said in early 1993. 'There are hundreds of satellites over Indonesia's sky.'[38]

Encouraged by these developments, the print media has stepped up its efforts to weaken the government's censorship tools. In May 1991 a delegation of leading Indonesian editors made a highly publicised plea to the parliament to ease government controls over the press. The plea, which was given a sympathetic hearing by legislators, was quickly rejected by Harmoko, who said that less government control would 'lead to anarchy'.[39] Nonetheless, the delegation did succeed in putting into question the legitimacy of the SIUPP permit and the topic has returned to public prominence several times since. In late 1992 the owners of *Prioritas*, a paper shut down by fiat in 1987, petitioned the Supreme Court to review the legality of the information minister's action. While the petition was subsequently dismissed on a technicality, the fact that it was lodged at all represents a step forward for freedom of expression. By 1993, journalists were growing still braver in reporting the once taboo subjects of Indonesia's public life but few doubted that the tide could be reversed yet again. 'There is definitely more openness now but also a lot of unpredictability. The risk factor is still high,' said Aristides Katoppo, a senior editor at *Suara Pembaruan*, in August 1993.[40]

The 'unpredictability' confronting Indonesian journalists was well illustrated by press reporting of Indonesia's parliament in the early 1990s. Concerned that the press was ignoring the parliament, the government in 1991–92 took the unusual step of publicly requesting Indonesian newspapers to pay more attention to parliamentary deliberations, a suggestion many took up. But by 1993, at least some government officials were harking back wistfully to the days of media indifference. In March of that year a robust debate began inside the ruling party Golkar on the campaign to replace the party's chairman, Wahono. Given the importance of the Golkar chairmanship, many papers gave extensive coverage to the debate. It all became too much for the newly appointed Home Affairs Minister, Yogie Memed:

> Everybody talks about this candidate, that candidate, this being wrong,
> that being right. They are acting like a mob in the street. This
> phenomenon of openness is not based on Pancasila. People are talking for
> the sake of talking.[41]

The clash of wills between the media and the government no doubt will continue for many years. Technology has forced the government to retreat faster than it would have liked but the government is not about to give in completely. After all, a great deal of disagreement within the government and within society at large still exists over what 'openness' means for Indonesia. While the government seemed willing in 1993 to give the press more leeway in reporting the news of the day, it had yet to respond to complaints aired in the media with meaningful reforms in its governing approach. On many important issues, openness remained a distant, if tantalising, dream.

Unequal before the law

Government officials are fond of describing Indonesia as a *negara hukum*, a lawful nation. And in one respect they are right. Indonesia's legal code provides many safeguards for the individual against abuse and excesses at the hands of those who hold power. But in many important respects that protection is not available in practice. This is not an accident, nor due essentially to a weak and underpaid bureaucracy. The law, like the press, is for Soeharto primarily an agent of development, not the ultimate arbiter of societal rules. In the New Order, the purpose of the legal system is not so much the enforcement of laws as the enforcement of the government's will.

In contests between the rights of individuals and the rights of the state, individuals more often than not lose. Land can be appropriated, businesses closed, overseas travel denied, arrests made and jobs lost at the whim of a government official. The legal system, unresponsive, corrupt, politicised and ineffective, offers little recourse to the individual in righting perceived wrongs. Even the government's top lawyers concede that most Indonesians distrust the legal system.[42]

The government's contemptuous view of the law was laid bare in an interview in 1993 conducted by a local magazine with Admiral Sudomo, who headed the feared Kopkamtib internal security agency from 1978 to 1983.[43] Sudomo was questioned about the government's treatment of the dissident Group of Fifty, whose members had criticised Soeharto for using the armed forces as the political muscle behind the ruling party Golkar. In 1980, the dissidents were forbidden to travel overseas, obtain credit from state banks, or attend government or diplomatic functions. Many lost their jobs.

Q: *Where is the law that regulates prohibitions like that?*
Sudomo: We can just do it . . . It's true, there's no written prohibition. But that's not a problem.
Q: *Why not just write it, it's a government decision, isn't it?*
Sudomo: The government can adopt a policy like that if it wants. The policy can be written or not. That's the right of the government.
Q: *That way, they can't take legal action against the policy, can they?*
Sudomo: This is a political matter, isn't it?
Q: *So, the only way to settle this problem, they have to ask for forgiveness, like that?*
Sudomo: Yes, ask for forgiveness.

One consequence of the government's disdain for legal norms is that many Indonesians lead anxious and apprehensive lives. Their fears are rooted in their own vulnerability to the overwhelming power of the state, fears which are reflected in how Indonesians talk about the country's economic progress. Indonesians readily acknowledge that Soeharto has accomplished much in the way of economic development, for which they are grateful. But there is not much of a sense of shared accomplishment. Many Indonesians see themselves simply as the objects of government policies, rather than as partners in a national effort. Thus, while they are pleased with and proud of the nation's economic progress, they are not especially confident about the future, an insecurity founded in the knowledge that they have little control over their own destiny. Below the superficial calm of harmony and consensus, many Indonesians do not feel the government is on their side. 'The people have become spectators to development,' says Islamic activist Dawam Rahardjo.[44]

These feelings are particularly apparent in rural areas where the civilian bureaucracy remains very much the junior partner to the military. In the cities, and especially for the middle and upper classes, the military's autonomy is constrained by the power of money and the possibility of public scrutiny by the press. But for the majority of Indonesians, rural-based, isolated, poor and relatively unsophisticated, there are few checks on military behaviour. To be sure, there is more to the lives of rural Indonesians—and, for that matter, urban Indonesians—than dealing with the government and its representatives. Men, women and children of all ages go to work, attend school, meet at parties, get married, go to the movies, worship at mosques, churches and temples, play badminton, visit relatives, travel and do the many other things that people do. But when it comes to dealing with the government, individual Indonesians are at a distinct disadvantage. 'Ordinary Indonesians have no control over what happens to them,' says Buyung Nasution. 'When they see a policeman or any figure of authority, they are scared. They know that anyone who disagrees with the government is automatically considered an opponent of the state.'[45]

On a trip through Central and East Java in early 1992, many Indonesians I met spilled over with frustration and anger when describing their impotence in contesting the power of the government. The grievances varied—from inadequate compensation for appropriated land, to the business advantages given to relatives and friends of local bureaucrats, to low wages, to the costs of subsidising Soeharto family monopolies on the distribution of cloves and television licences—but the underlying theme was the same: the fear that any complaints by *orang kecil*, the little people, would be met with military intimidation or arrest. In a typical remark, one farmer in East Java resignedly told me: 'If I say anything they will just call me a communist.'

Emha Ainun Nadjib is a young and popular Muslim leader in Central Java who speaks and writes frequently on the plight of the poor and the government's intolerance for critical views. In 1991, the Central Java government banned Nadjib from speaking publicly in the province, exasperated with comments like the following:

> All Indonesians I have ever met feel that they are the subordinates
> (*bawahan*) of the government. Moreover there are very many of our
> officials in the regions or outlying areas who feel confident that they
> really are the superiors (*atasan*) of the people. And if you say that
> popular sovereignty is above the government's sovereignty, you will not
> only be considered to oppose development, but they will be sure you are
> really an evil person.[46]

The law: theory and practice

If fear and impotence are the lot of those who balk at the New Order's
economic development process, harsher measures are doled out to those
considered a political threat. Suspected communist sympathisers who
survived the purge of 1965–66 have had their legal and political rights
severely curtailed. Some half million alleged Communist Party members
were jailed between 1966 and the early 1970s, most without trial or legal
protection of any kind. For the majority, their only crime was to belong
to what had been a legally recognised political party which had fallen out
of favour with the military. From 1969–79, 10 000 Indonesians with
alleged involvement in the September 1965 coup—including author
Pramoedya Ananta Toer—were exiled to Buru Island, an inhospitable,
impoverished outpost about the size of Bali located in the eastern Indonesian province of Moluccas. The treatment of prisoners was harsh, with
beatings and torture common.

While the exact number of Communist Party members still in jail is
not known, many former members and sympathisers continue to have their
activities closely monitored. In late 1990, the government said this group
totalled just over 1.4 million people. These Indonesians, says the US State
Department's Country Reports on Human Rights Practices published in
1992, are subject to 'surveillance, required check-ins and arbitrary actions
by officials, including the removal from government employment and
threats of removal from such employment'.[47] Since 1985, 22 prisoners
have been executed for their alleged involvement in the 1965 coup.

In areas with active insurgencies legal niceties are all but ignored.
East Timor and Aceh are the worst affected. Similar to its performance
in East Timor, the military's suppression of an Acehnese rebellion in
1990–92 was replete with extrajudicial killings, unlawful detention, forced
confessions and torture, notwithstanding the fact that the Indonesian legal
code provides protection from all these abuses. Statements from suspects
or witnesses are supposed to be extracted without pressure; prisoners are
allowed to notify their family of their arrest and they or their family have
the right to challenge the legality of their detention; arrests are supposed

to be accompanied by warrants except in special circumstances; limits are imposed on pre-trial detentions; prisoners are free to appoint their own lawyers; defendants have the right to unfettered access to their lawyers at every phase of an investigation and detention; and torture is prohibited.

'In practice,' the State Department report says, 'these safeguards are often violated . . . Torture and mistreatment of criminal suspects, detainees, and prisoners are common.'[48] A similar conclusion was drawn by Pieter Kooijmans, a UN special rapporteur on torture who visited Indonesia in late 1991. 'The Special Rapporteur cannot avoid the conclusion that torture occurs in Indonesia. In areas which are deemed to be unstable [such as East Timor, Aceh and Irian Jaya], torture is said to be practised rather routinely; it is also allegedly used elsewhere, in particular on persons who are suspected of belonging to groups which threaten the State philosophy, e.g. by advocating the creation of an Islamic State. The Special Rapporteur has no reason to doubt that irregular arrests by security agencies are far from exceptional.'[49]

Both reports stress that in practice the judiciary is not independent of the military and has little power to check military abuses. In cases where torture is alleged, for example, the complainants are obliged to file a motion not with the judiciary but directly with the security forces, the same forces accused of mistreatment.

Several dozen Acehnese have been tried on subversion charges in recent years. Many were denied access to a lawyer until the day of their trial, and then had their lawyer appointed for them by the government. Many complained of torture by the military. Testifying at his own trial in March 1991, Acehnese journalist Adnan Beuransyah recounted the interrogation process:

> My hair and my nose were burned with cigarette butts. I was given electric shocks on my feet, genitals and ears until I fainted . . . I was ordered to sit on a long bench facing the interrogator. I was still blind-folded and the wires for electric shocks were still wound around my big toes. If I said anything they didn't like they'd turn on the current. This went on until about 8:00 am, meaning I was tortured for about eight continuous hours . . . On the third night I was tortured again . . . My body was bruised and bloodied and I had been beaten and kicked so much that I coughed up blood and there was blood in my urine . . . It continued like this until I signed the interrogation deposition.[50]

In 1990–91, at the height of the most recent Acehnese rebellion, many Acehnese corpses were dumped at night on the sides of roads, in rivers or in markets. The army denied responsibility but most Acehnese thought differently, believing the corpses were a warning not to support the rebellion. More than 1000 Acehnese were believed to have died in clashes with security forces or while in military detention. 'The level of killing is such,' Asia Watch reported, 'that personal vendettas and business feuds can be carried out with impunity, since once a victim is labelled "GPK" [Indonesian shorthand for "security disturber"], no questions are asked.'[51]

Major General Pramono, the top military commander in North Sumatra, explained that many Acehnese had to be detained without trial because 'if they all went to the courts, the courts would be too full.'[52] Many who did go to trial were charged under the wide-ranging Anti-Subversion Law. Dating from 1963 and carrying a maximum penalty of death, the law makes it a crime to engage in acts which 'distort, undermine or deviate from' the state ideology of Pancasila, or which arouse hostility towards the government. The law is so vaguely worded that it can cover a wide variety of activities, including political dissent. A charge of subversion, which applies not only to acts that endanger the security of the state but also to acts that 'could' do so, is tantamount to a conviction. Only two persons have ever been acquitted of subversion charges. On occasion, it seems, subversion is charged simply because the available evidence is too scanty to meet the burden of proof of more precisely defined charges.[53]

While torture and mistreatment are less common in cases not involving issues of national security, the treatment of suspected criminals is nevertheless harsh. In one notorious episode, the police and other branches of the military responded to a rise in the crime rate in 1983–85 by executing some 5000 suspected criminals in various cities throughout Indonesia, all without benefit of trial. In many cases, the bodies were dumped in public places to serve as a warning to the community. At the time, the military vigorously denied responsibility for the wave of mysterious killings, which was called *petrus* in Indonesian.

But some years later, in his autobiography, Soeharto admitted that *petrus* had been a government-sponsored operation from the start. 'There was no mystery to these events,' he wrote. 'The peace had been disturbed . . . Of course we had to take drastic action and give [the suspected criminals] treatment commensurate with their conduct . . . Those who resisted, yes, they were shot . . . Some of the bodies were just left where they had been shot. This was meant as shock therapy so that people would realise that loathsome acts would meet with strong action.'[54] To be sure, the incidence of 'loathsome acts' declined in the wake of the *petrus* killings. But although in favour of a low crime rate, many Indonesians were disturbed nonetheless by the government's blatant disrespect for the law.

The human rights debate

For many years discussion of human rights was discouraged in the press, with many government officials dismissing criticism of Indonesia's record as part of a Western plot to undermine the country's economic and political development. These concerns certainly have not disappeared. But the rising international preoccupation with human rights—accelerated by the end of the Cold War and the defeat of communism as an international threat—and the torrent of condemnation following the widely publicised killings in East Timor in November 1991 have obliged Indonesia to state its case more assertively.

So far the debate has been mired in disputes over how to define human rights. Indonesia and some other developing countries in Asia contend that the Western view is overly focused on the civil and political rights of the individual and not enough concerned with economic and community rights. The Western view of universal human rights, the argument goes, is alien to Asian cultures, which put a premium on communal harmony, and could weaken economic progress in less developed countries. The Asian view—put forward strongly by Indonesia, Malaysia, Singapore, China and Burma—states that each country has the sovereign right to tailor civil liberties to its own cultural traditions and it flatly rejects the linking of political or economic aid from abroad with human rights concerns. The underlying message of the Asian view, as Daniel Lev puts it, is that 'developing countries . . . cannot afford the luxury of attention to human rights if doing so impedes the essential process of economic growth.'[55]

Foreign Minister Ali Alatas has been the principal spokesman for the Indonesian government's view of human rights, as well as being involved in shaping agreement on the subject within the developing world. A document on East Timor published in 1992, principally authored by Alatas, spells out at some length the Indonesian government's position on human rights:

> Undue emphasis on one category of human rights over another cannot be justified . . . As in many developing countries, Indonesia's culture and its ancient and well-developed customs have traditionally put high priority on the rights and interests of the community . . . [The] implementation of human rights implies the existence of a balanced relationship between individual human rights and the obligations of individuals toward their community. Without such a balance, the rights of the community as a whole can be denied, which can lead to instability and anarchy, especially in developing countries . . . [T]he primary objective of actions in the field of human rights is not to accuse nor to assume the role of judge and jury over other countries . . . We should not try to remake the world in our own image, but we can and should try to make the world a more humane, peaceful and equitably prosperous place for all.[56]

Soeharto, in a September 1992 speech to the United Nations, made a pitch for economic rights, including the right to be free from poverty:

> [I]t is our firm conviction that the objective of human rights is the realisation of the full potential of the human being, and human potential is not confined to the political. The fundamental right to economic and social

development, for example, cannot be separated and cannot be treated separately from the other categories of human rights.[57]

By no means is the government alone in this view. In an April 1993 speech, Professor Yuwono Sudarsono of the University of Indonesia, a well-respected political analyst, defended the need for a strong state against calls for more individual freedom:

> It is imperative . . . to understand that for many governments and states in Asia, the problem is not so much limiting the power of the state in order to safeguard the civil and political liberties of individuals and communities. Rather, the most immediate, as well as long-term problem has always been the lack of state power to maintain unity and cohesion [and] the weakness of state authorities in harnessing the forces of conciliation among disparate ethnic, religious as well as provincial interests . . . No precepts of liberal democracy should stand in the way of the state performing [the] essential tasks of state action, control, indeed of regulation.[58]

Member countries of the Non-Aligned Movement, meeting in Jakarta in September 1992, attempted to shape their views into a common platform for the developing world. The Jakarta Declaration, released at the end of the summit, rejected Western pressures on human rights practices and said disputes over human rights should be settled in a 'spirit of cooperation, not confrontation'. In March 1993, Asian governments met in Bangkok to hash out a common view on human rights to take to the World Conference on Human Rights which was held three months later in Vienna. The governments accepted in principle the 'universality' of human rights but repeated the Jakarta Declaration's admonishment that countries should not impose their views of human rights on others.

These appeals notwithstanding, it seems likely that the human rights debate will become more, not less, confrontational over the near term. Most critics of Jakarta's record on human rights, both domestic and foreign, do not take issue with its official line. The point that economic well-being is an important component of human rights is an eminently sensible one, as is the reminder that cultural differences need to be taken into account. The vulnerability of Indonesia's argument, however, lies in the supposed 'balance' between individual and community rights. While the law of the land may provide for such a balance, in practice the rights of the community—as determined of course by the government—over-whelm those of the individual. The danger of allowing 'cultural' interpre-tations of human rights to obscure this imbalance was spelled out by Australian Senator Chris Schacht at a conference in 1992:

> Human rights are about the right to live without being abused, killed, tortured, or locked up. It is a very simple human right and I think even the most ill-educated peasant understands the difference between happiness

and pain . . . I have yet to come across anyone who likes to be summarily executed, or taken off and tortured, or have their kids conscripted into the army or be beaten up without recourse to the law. No matter which culture you come from, I have yet to discover anyone who thinks cultural relativism is a good idea if it allows you to do that to your own people.[59]

Although officially rejecting international criticism of its record, the Soeharto administration recognises that the increasing attention being paid to human rights around the world could prove awkward. One danger for Indonesia is that Western criticism could have economic consequences in the form of restricted access to overseas markets or a reduction in foreign aid. Another fear is that pressure from human rights activists for all Indonesians to be allowed the right to self-determination could jeopardise its hold over East Timor.[60] A third fear is that the very issue of human rights—by calling attention to the individual—could eventually erode the government's legitimacy and hasten calls for a less authoritarian political system. As Lev notes, 'The idea of human rights encourages new thinking about the distribution of power in society, state-society relationships, the obligations and limits of political authority, and the minimum conditions essential to human life and dignity.'[61]

The 'communal' view of human rights makes a useful response to all these concerns. If the rights of the community and the government's determination of what the community wants and needs are the same thing, then virtually everything the government does can be said to further the cause of human rights. The 'communal' view, of course, also conforms nicely with authoritarian rule.

For many government officials, the issue of human rights is properly seen as a nationalist cause. Sympathy for Western criticisms of Indonesia's record is considered disloyal, if not downright unpatriotic. The nationalist cause is helped by the government's control of the press, since reporting on the military's conduct in places such as Aceh and East Timor, where many of the worst human rights abuses take place, is severely limited. Consequently, many Indonesians have no input other than the army's contention that it is acting to safeguard national unity and no reason to disbelieve the government's contention that foreign criticism is prejudiced and politically motivated.[62]

At its most extreme level, the conspiratorial explanation for Western human rights criticisms is that they are intended to keep countries like Indonesia from competing economically with the world's industrialised nations. The deepest distrust is reserved for human rights monitoring organisations such as Asia Watch and Amnesty International whose access to Indonesia has long been restricted. Professor Yuwono laid out the conspiracy argument as follows:

In the myriad world of international competition for investment, trade and market share, can it be purely coincidental that the attention of governments, parliaments, the press, non-governmental organisations, as well as self-proclaimed concerned citizens of the industrialised world be focused on governments and societies in Asia that are increasingly becoming more economically competitive?[63]

Yuwono misses the mark on two counts. International criticism is not focused only on the human rights records of 'economically competitive' nations. Few, for example, would put Burma in this category and yet the military government in Rangoon has been severely criticised for its treatment of its people. Secondly, and more importantly, Professor Yuwono is wrong to imply that human rights criticisms are the exclusive domain of foreigners. What makes human rights a potent political issue in Indonesia is not so much criticism from abroad but criticism at home. '[I]f there were no local demands for change at all,' Lev points out, 'the problem would barely exist, and it would not be taken seriously.'[64]

A similar dynamic is at work around the region. What is becoming increasingly clear is that there is no such thing as an 'Asian' view of human rights, just as there is no single 'Western' view of human rights. A growing number of non-governmental organisations (NGOs) and activists in Asia, including in Indonesia, are energetically disputing the notion that the 'Asian' view of human rights put forward by the region's governments accurately reflects what Asians actually think.

The human rights conference in Bangkok in March 1993 provided a good illustration of these divergent positions. Some 240 men and women representing 110 Asian NGOs attended the conference and came up with strikingly different views to those of the government delegates to the same conference. Asia Watch executive director Sidney Jones explains:

> No one had expected so many non-governmental organisations to be there; no one could have imagined that by precisely the democratic methods that their governments find 'un-Asian', such a diverse group of people . . . would hammer out a consensus declaration that refuted or contested every major premise of the 'Asian concept' of human rights . . . Governments were forced to recognise that their definition of what is 'Asian' is not necessarily shared by their own citizens, that economic growth is not the be-all and end-all for everyone in the region, and that Asians do not want their political and civil rights traded away in the name of development.[65]

Jones noted that Asia's more (if, in some cases, only recently) democratic governments—Japan, the Philippines, South Korea and Nepal— adopted views not dissimilar to the NGOs' position while delegates from the region's less democratic nations sharply opposed the NGO stance. She singled out Indonesia for taking an especially confrontational tone:

> From the outset, Indonesia tried to set an Asia-versus-West tone, castigating the 'tendency by a group of countries to arrogate to themselves the role of judge and jury over other countries . . . backed by the power

of their biased media and single-minded NGOs'. But as one after another
of the Asian organisations spoke, it was clear that the real confrontation
was Asia versus Asia, and that the Asian governments should take note.[66]

Despite the heavy rhetoric emanating from Jakarta, Soeharto's government has taken some steps to improve its human rights record in recent
years. It joined the UN Commission on Human Rights in early 1991, a
move which helped legitimise domestic discussion of the subject. And in
early 1993 Indonesia announced plans to set up a national Human Rights
Commission at a UN-sponsored Asia–Pacific workshop it hosted.[67] It has
promised also to take a harder line against members of the security forces
accused of mistreatment and abuse.

Whether these sorts of measures will make much difference is an open
question. The protection of individual liberties is, in the end, a political
decision. And real changes to the status of individuals in Indonesia are
possible only if there is a significant change in the way the government
views its mission. Many, if not most, government leaders continue to view
strict attention to human rights as a 'luxury' which will set back Indonesia's economic development. Indeed, many feel too many concessions
have already been made to the pressure groups. Vice-President and former
Armed Forces Commander General Try Sutrisno has said on a number of
occasions that Indonesia's decision to join the UN Human Rights Commission 'proves' that Indonesia fully respects human rights, with the
implication being that no further policy changes are needed. In November
1992, Sutrisno took the case a step further in a speech to military officers
when he described Indonesian advocates of civil liberties, democratisation
and environmental protection as a 'new generation of communists' who
require close watching by the military.[68]

Less than a year later, he lashed out again at human rights advocates,
calling them the 'new traitors . . . We cannot rule out the possibility that
there are internal elements that are prepared to commit treachery against
our nation and our people.'[69] Comments like these, naturally, convince
many critics that Indonesia's efforts to improve its human rights record
are intended primarily for international consumption.

Leading the Indonesian human rights campaign are a handful of legal
activists, non-governmental organisations, artists and intellectuals. They
argue against the notion that the communal view of human rights is the
only one compatible with Indonesia's cultural traditions. As evidence, they
note that the constitution which was drawn up in 1950 just after independence was secured dwelt at length on the rights of the individual; in
force for nine years, it should be seen as reflecting Indonesian norms and
values. And as discussed in Chapter 1, the Constitutional Assembly which
met from 1956 until it was disbanded by Sukarno in 1959, made substantial progress in agreeing to human rights provisions for a new Indonesian
constitution. In its deliberations, civil liberties were not seen as an East

versus West issue, but more as a universal concept which transcended party politics. (One important exception to this rule involved the discussions about freedom of religion.) As Buyung Nasution puts it:

> No one in the Konstituante [Constitutional Assembly] argued, as many have done since, that human rights in Indonesia had a particular meaning different from that in the rest of the world, especially in Western countries . . . Despite [the] anti-Dutch, anti-Western, anti-capitalist, and anti-liberal climate [of the period], the universal validity of human rights was endorsed by all parties.[70]

In the more than 30 years since the demise of parliamentary democracy in Indonesia, discussions of individual rights have gradually faded from the public debate and, to some extent from the public consciousness. The recent revival of the human rights debate, however, appears to be reversing this trend. Says journalist Gunawan Mohamad: 'We must admit that the value of individual liberties does not have strong roots in our social history, but we must try to develop a sense of respect for human rights when it comes to cases of torture and blatant abuse of power.' History, he adds, 'is not static or entirely predetermined by social forces. Changes in the values of society are possible.'[71]

Although nervous about the trend, the government is limited in what it can do to check the spreading awareness of 'liberal' values. The shift in Indonesia's economic strategy in the late 1980s to a more outward-oriented set of policies not only tied Indonesia more closely to the international economy but also enlarged the channels through which outside influences can pervade Indonesia. Exporters and other businesses now have much more frequent contact with their counterparts abroad while modern communications technology has brought the ethics and mores of many foreign countries and cultures to the attention of a larger number of Indonesians. The result is a mixing and blurring of cultural values. 'The globalisation of the economy means that individual communities can no longer remain isolated,' says Jusuf Wanandi, who heads the Centre for Strategic and International Studies. 'Our communal approach is definitely changing as a result of the influence of international values. What we need to find now is an appropriate mixture of individualism with continued respect for the community.'[72]

For the most part, Indonesian intellectuals and government 'moderates' advocate a slow and gradual approach to changing the government's view of human rights. They are concerned, with some justification, that a nationalist backlash against Western pressures will harden attitudes and narrow the scope for negotiation. 'It is unfair for Northern countries to use human rights as a stick to discipline Third World nations,' contends Professor Yuwono. 'But in reacting to that, the danger is that we become apologists for our own internal inequalities.'[73] Echoing a commonly heard view, State Secretary Murdiono emphasised that the way in which human rights criticisms were lodged counted as much as the criticisms themselves. 'We would like to maintain good relations with all the countries in the world. But if others are too demanding, then that is another question. A lot depends on *how* they express their views. There must be mutual respect'.[74] Soeharto's decision in March 1992 to disband a Dutch-led consortium of foreign donors to Indonesia emerged from precisely this feeling. The background to that decision was a building resentment among many Indonesian officials against what they saw as patronising and condescending comments made about Indonesia by the Dutch minister for development, Jan Pronk.[75]

Other Indonesians are less concerned with matters of style and believe the government should pay more attention to human rights criticisms, no matter how they are phrased. Author and historian Pramoedya Ananta Toer, who has spent half the New Order in jail and the rest under close surveillance, puts the case in typically strong terms. 'The theft of one's rights as a human being, without any recourse to a fair and impartial trial, is equivalent to pronouncing us dead under civil law, marginalising us as pariahs or more precisely it is the same as treating us as cattle . . . It is out of date rubbish to continue to try to convince world opinion that human rights in Indonesia "are respected in accordance with the special traits of the national culture", when all this talk is just a form of political manipulation from above in order to justify the violation of citizens' basic rights carried out to preserve the rulers' power, amongst the many other things they wish to preserve.'[76] Sociologist Taufik Abdullah, who has emerged as a staunch critic of the 'cultural relativist' school of human rights, had this to say: 'The obsession of maintaining [our] national identity is constraining our democracy. It spurs conservatism in ideology and politics.'[77]

One vocal group of critical Indonesians is composed of lawyers formerly or currently at the Legal Aid Institute, an independent non-profit organisation which is active in human rights issues and often does pro-bono work for indigent Indonesians. It has, predictably, an adversarial relationship with the government, which on many occasions has prevented its lawyers from getting involved in high-profile human rights cases. The institute's current head, Adnan Buyung Nasution, two former leaders Abdul Hakim and Mulya Lubis, and H. J. Princen, who heads the Indonesian Institute for the Defence of Human Rights, have been among the most trenchant critics of the government's selective use of the law. These men hold up greater respect for the law as the key to improving Indonesia's chequered human rights record as well as a necessary prerequisite for democracy. They dispute the notion that economic development and human rights protection are incompatible and they all see international pressure as crucial in bringing about change in Indonesia. 'The government's distinction between universal human rights and indigenous human rights is dangerous and false,' says Lubis. 'And the government's argument that to focus on human rights would be bad for economic growth is an absolute lie.'[78]

In a conference in Jakarta in 1993, Lubis described the government's welcoming attitude to foreign investment and its rejection of human rights criticisms as the 'king of [the] double standard'. Conditions attached to foreign aid and investment, he said, 'may not be accepted, but [they are] a hard fact of international relationships. After all, there is no free lunch, and it is always legitimate if donor countries want to be assured that their economic assistance will not be used to finance human rights violations . . . The conclusion is therefore, if the conditionalities are for human rights improvement, then the simple answer is why not?'[79] This view, surprisingly, is even heard occasionally from government ministers. In an interview just after the Dili massacre in November 1991 and three months before Indonesia rejected future Dutch aid, State Secretary Murdiono made much the same point. 'I don't think suspending foreign aid constitutes interference in our affairs. It's their money.'[80]

Murdiono's view was superseded in subsequent months by the statements and actions of his more nationalistic counterparts. The important point, however, is that there is no single Indonesian view of human rights, not within the government nor within the broader community. The role of individuals in Indonesian society and their understanding of human rights are matters for Indonesians to decide. But by denying the diversity of views which exists in Indonesia, the government is running a real risk of diluting the force of its own views and of finding itself eclipsed by a changing society. 'Indonesia has already reached a turning point of sorts,' said former Golkar parliamentarian Marzuki Darusman in late 1991. 'The government now has to decide whether it can exist comfortably in a world sensitised to human rights concerns.'[81]

Case study: Labour rights

Of all the foreign criticisms of human rights practices in Indonesia, none has attracted more of the government's attention and concern than charges that workers are being exploited. Accompanied by threats of economic reprisals, the charges have obliged the government to give ground, albeit reluctantly, in several policy areas.

In five of the past six years, labour groups in the United States have petitioned the US Trade Representative (USTR) to revoke Indonesia's access to the tariff concessions for developing countries permitted by the Generalised System of Preferences program. Under US law, the president is required to revoke these concessions if it is determined that a trading partner is not 'taking steps to afford internationally recognised worker rights'.[82]

Labour groups have alleged that Indonesian workers do not enjoy freedom of association, the right to organise and bargain collectively and that the government has not adequately enforced minimum wage regulations. At stake are tariff reductions on some US$600 million worth of products Indonesia exports to the United States each year. To date, the USTR has declined to recommend to the president that Indonesia's tariff concessions be cut, arguing that the Indonesian government was making efforts to improve worker rights. Labour groups, however, assert that these efforts are at least partly motivated by overseas pressure and do not represent a sincere attempt to improve the plight of workers.

Indonesian labour has been a key component of the country's economic success. Plentiful and inexpensive, the workforce includes some 80 million Indonesians—with an estimated 2.3 million new workers joining the labour market each year—while wages are among the lowest in Asia. Since the mid-1980s, the government has counted on labour-intensive, export-oriented industries such as shoes, textiles, electronics, toys and agro-business to absorb labour and generate foreign exchange. All of these industries have grown rapidly and are among the brightest successes of Indonesia's industrialisation process.

But these successes have exacted a heavy toll from workers and have produced a surge in labour unrest. As Indonesian businesses have struggled to cut costs and compete in international markets, workers have paid a price in deteriorating working conditions and stagnant wages. The sole recognised union in Indonesia, the umbrella All-Indonesia Workers' Union, SPSI, is heavily controlled by the government and is poorly equipped to defend workers against employers.

Paralleling its treatment of other mass-based organisations, the New Order government has felt it necessary to weaken unions in the cause of political stability. In the 1950s and early 1960s, many labour unions were affiliated with political parties, including the Indonesian Communist Party, and wielded considerable political clout. It is an experience the Soeharto administration has been determined to avoid. The defanging of unions has eliminated their political influence but only at the cost of exposing workers to predatory employers. 'Indonesian labourers,' noted the *Indonesian Observer* in an editorial in 1991, 'have virtually been delivered to their employers' arbitrariness and greed.'[83]

The SPSI's predecessor, a federated organisation housing a collection of individual industry and sector unions, was founded in 1973 at the same time as the nine political parties then existing were forced to merge into two opposition parties. That organisation was felt to be too autonomous and, in 1985, under then Manpower Minister Sudomo, all unions were obliged to join the SPSI, which, while faithfully complying with the government's designs, remains unrecognised by the International Confederation of Free Trade Unions and is unaffiliated with most international trade union organisations. The SPSI leadership is dominated by government appointees, including members of the ruling party Golkar, while a host of military personnel holds mid-level posts.

Companies with more than 25 employees are required to allow the establishment of an SPSI unit but only some 10 000 of the 26 000 enterprises in this category have union representation. SPSI has about one million dues-paying members, about 1.4 per cent of the total workforce. One reason why there are so few unionised workers is that employees are obliged to consult with employers before setting up an SPSI unit. In many cases, employers only give their consent if they can choose the SPSI representatives. Moreover, establishing an SPSI unit is not in itself a guarantee of worker rights. Only about half of the 10 000 SPSI units, for example, have succeeded in negotiating a collective bargaining agreement with their employers. It is little exaggeration to say that the vast majority of Indonesian workers has no idea of the rights that workers are entitled to under the law.

Under the government's notion of Pancasila Industrial Relations, labour disputes are to be settled through a process of consensus between workers, employers and the government. Unfortunately for workers, the mechanics of settling disputes strongly favour the government and employers. While the right to strike is nominally guaranteed by law, until 1990 an informal ban ensured that strikes almost never occurred. Before a strike can be called legally, employees are obliged to pass through a series of arbitration tribunals and apply for permission to the Manpower Ministry. Convinced that the process is biased against them, more and more workers are taking their grievances directly to the parliament or the press, while others join illegal wildcat strikes.

Many of the most widely publicised strikes have been in the export-oriented industries which have prospered since the late 1980s. Cost-conscious foreign investors, attracted to Indonesia by its low wages, are frequently accused of underpaying workers to boost profits. In 1992 the minimum wage in Indonesia ranged from 50 US cents to US$1.50 a day, an amount which, according to the government's own calculations, was enough to cover only a fraction of a worker's 'minimum physical needs'. And yet even this amount was apparently too high for many businesses. A survey in 1989 of 1017 Jakarta firms carried out by the SPSI and the Asian–American Free Labour Institute found that 56 per cent of the companies were paying less than the minimum wage.[84]

Not surprisingly, labour agitation is on the rise. According to the government's figures, there were some 190 strikes in 1992, up from 130 the year before and 60 in 1990. The true figure is probably much higher. Almost all these strikes were considered illegal as they did not follow the official procedures for settling disputes. Mindful of international reaction, the government has been reluctant to crack down too harshly on strikers but neither has it turned a blind eye to those accused of rocking the boat. In many instances, strike leaders and union organisers have been denied wage increases or promotions and some have been fired outright or detained by the police. The military keeps a close eye on labour leaders and has taken an active role in quelling strikes, particularly in the heavily industrialised areas around Jakarta.[85]

Since 1990, two new labour organisations have emerged but neither has been recognised by the government. One leader of the Serikat Buruh Merdeka Setia Kawan (Solidarity Free Trade Union) claimed he had been abducted for four days in June 1991 and interrogated on the sources of the union's funding and its connections with political dissidents. The union said it suspected the army was behind the kidnapping, a charge the army denies.[86] In 1993, the government banned the other independent labour union from holding what would have been its first national congress on the grounds that the organisation did not represent workers.[87]

While the government has stopped short of disbanding the new labour groups, it remains deeply suspicious of their motives. Undeterred by the ample evidence illustrating SPSI's ineffectiveness, the government is quick to see a disguised political threat lurking behind every group that pledges to help workers. In an interview in 1991, the then manpower minister, Cosmas Batubara, dismissed Setia Kawan as a 'human rights organisation using the banner of labour to organise for its own political purposes'.[88] Batubara's replacement, businessman Abdul Latief, brought the same perspective to the job. He said labour organisations set up by workers would not be allowed and blamed labour unrest on groups set up as rivals to the SPSI. 'The labour condition in Indonesia is in disorder because too many non-governmental organisations are now being drawn in to interfere in labour affairs,' he claimed.[89]

For a variety of reasons, the odds are against a strong labour movement emerging in Indonesia in the short term. The government remains wary of labour's potential political power and concerned that higher wages will slow new investment. It is afraid that a stronger labour movement will damage Indonesia's competitiveness relative to other labour-rich nations in the region, especially China, where labour rights are similarly ignored. Consequently, the government is likely to stick to its stated policy of gradually improving SPSI's enforcement capabilities, tinkering with its organisational structure, and discouraging new, more vigorous labour organisations.[90] Its top priority will remain job creation, with wages and working conditions taking a back seat.

Demographics also work against labour organisers. The workforce is largely unskilled, poorly educated and growing rapidly. About 80 per cent of Indonesian workers have no more than a primary school education and about a third of the labour force is 'underemployed', meaning they work less than 35 hours per week.[91] For most workers, the risks of union activity—unemployment, denial of promotions and wage hikes, and military harassment—will remain a significant discouragement to agitating for better protection.

But at the same time Indonesia's nascent labour movement, weak though it is, is a source of real concern for the government. The recent rise in strikes and labour protests testifies to the rising frustration felt by workers. Pressure from Western labour groups is unlikely to subside and, emboldened by the measure of protection that this pressure confers, domestic labour organisers will demand the government do much more to enforce its own laws.[92] In June 1993, the new US Trade Representative Mickey Kantor warned Indonesia it had until February 1994 to improve its labour record or face a curtailment of its trading benefits with the US. Although the US is unlikely to follow through on this threat, the warning itself was enough to induce Jakarta into making some substantial concessions, including a government-mandated rise in the minimum wage and the revocation of a ministerial decree which allowed employers to summon army troops to put down strikes. Labour activists hailed these measures, but said they never would have happened without outside pressure forcing the government's hand.

As the government peers into the future, there are no easy options. Ignoring pressure from labour organisers could well have negative economic consequences brought about by international sanctions. But acquiescing to labour demands could well spell political trouble, not only in the form of a stronger labour movement but also in exposing the government's vulnerability to outside pressures. Avoiding these twin dangers will require a deft political touch, a characteristic seemingly in short supply in the late Soeharto era.

Redefining the role of the individual is one of the most complex challenges facing the New Order government. Both the government and its critics agree on the desirability of Indonesians feeling more in control over their destinies and of cultivating a more fluid, more critical and less fearful public discourse. As Soeharto and his top military leaders have themselves acknowledged, the country's continued economic success depends to some degree on Indonesians becoming more creative, showing more initiative in the workplace and sharpening their critical faculties.

But getting there is the problem. The driving dynamic of an authoritarian regime is the need for political control. And changes which enhance individual liberties—an active press, unfettered intellectuals, an independent legal system, etc.—represent a threat to that control. Establishing a blueprint for *keterbukaan*, or openness, is replete with thorny questions. Is it possible for an authoritarian government to open up gradually? Can it be sure that it can stop the process when it wants to? Is going halfway an option? Is it able to distinguish, in Gunawan Mohamad's words, between individuals who are 'weak, thus requiring liberty and [individuals] potentially dangerous to social harmony, thus requiring control'?[93]

Many in the government suspect not; their fear is that any loosening up may spiral out of (their) control. This is the main reason why efforts at *keterbukaan* have proceeded fitfully so far. A period of relative tolerance of criticism is followed by a renewed clampdown. 'There is no guarantee,' notes *Tempo* editor Gunawan, 'that any progress you make is irreversible. Freedom is something we have to define and earn every day of our lives.'[94]

After a quarter-century in power, the New Order government has become unaccustomed to dissent. A wide gap remains between its publicly stated willingness to tolerate more criticism and its reaction to critics when they emerge. What Soeharto would like is for Indonesians to become more critical but not to criticise him or his government. The military may be prepared to give more latitude to the moderate majority but doesn't know how to do so without giving freer reign to more radical critics. Soeharto and the military say they want a more robust public debate but not necessarily on many of the critical issues facing Indonesia: the role of the Chinese, wealth inequalities, the prevalence of corruption and nepotism, Muslim aspirations, and regional dissatisfaction. But it is these issues that emerge into public view every time controls are loosened. These are the issues that Indonesians talk about in private and want to talk about in public.

On a theoretical level, the whole notion of individual liberties is a tricky one for an authoritarian government. There is a limit to how much ground can be ceded in permitting more 'space' for individual action without undermining the justification for non-democratic rule. Newly confident, assertive and critical Indonesians may well decide they want a non-authoritarian government.

Heedful of this risk, the New Order government errs on the side of caution. It insists on its ideal of social harmony and thus on 'communal' rights having precedence over individual liberties. Whether this approach can remain effective in the years ahead is uncertain. Refusing to loosen official controls is not a cost-free policy. Leaving aside the long-term economic consequences of a submissive and frightened workforce, the 'enforced silence' which is supposed to ensure political stability may well be sowing the seeds of future instability.

Wildcat strikes, increasingly frequent student brawls in major cities, riots at rock concerts, rising religious sectarianism and heightened criticism of human rights practices are all manifestations of Indonesians' frustration with the limits placed on individual and organised activity. Catholic priest Y. B. Mangunwijaya is only one of many Indonesian intellectuals who worry that Indonesians are being pushed to religious fundamentalism and to adopt 'fascist' attitudes toward other societal groups because they are unable to express themselves through officially approved channels of communication.[95]

The government's 'communal' notion of society notwithstanding, there is no doubt that a rising chorus of Indonesian voices is demanding many of the individual liberties enjoyed in the West, be they the right to free speech, or the right to a fair trial, or the right to strike. Rejecting these demands as culturally inappropriate is a useful rejoinder to foreign critics but there is a limit, points out Australian political scientist David Bourchier, to 'how long one can keep telling Indonesian critics that they are un-Indonesian'.[96]

The reality is that under Soeharto's authoritarian rule it is impossible to divine the true 'Indonesian' view of human rights, individual liberties and the preferred level of personal freedoms. What is increasingly clear, though, is that the government's static view of these matters is lagging behind that of society, and that the divergence between the two is a drain on Indonesia's economic *and* political development.

10
A democratic future?

The problem of finding a collection of 'wise men' and leaving the government to them is thus an insoluble one. That is the ultimate reason for democracy.

Bertrand Russell[1]

Contrary to what American political commentators say, I do not believe that democracy necessarily leads to development. I believe that what a country needs to develop is discipline more than democracy.

Lee Kuan Yew[2]

The essence of democracy is that people freely participate in the political process. I don't know what Pancasila Democracy is, but it isn't that.

Sri Bintang Pamungkas[3]

Modern history is full of examples of autocrats, who not only alienated their peoples, but also did everything they could to make a peaceful change of rulers and policies impossible.

Ben Anderson[4]

On 5 March 1993, Indonesian Democratic Party member Sabam Sirait felt his patience snap. With the fifth day of the People's Consultative Assembly drawing to a close, Sirait could no longer deny what he already knew to be true: his party's efforts to reform Indonesia's tightly controlled political system were going to be stymied. As he rose from his chair to make a rare interruption in the carefully managed assembly, a year's worth of frustration welled up.

Only ten months earlier the future had begun to look brighter for the

264

Democratic Party, the smallest of Indonesia's three political parties. Fashioning itself as the defender of the poor, the party ran an innovative and popular campaign ahead of the parliamentary elections held in June 1992. Attracting hordes of younger Indonesians, its star performers were the party's leader Suryadi, businessman and economist Kwik Kian Gie and, especially, Guruh Sukarnoputra, the youngest son of Indonesia's founding father. In their campaign speeches, the party's politicians broached several of the New Order's political taboos by calling for a limit on presidential terms, insisting on a thorough overhaul of the electoral process, demanding the government respect the spirit of democracy as laid out in the 1945 Constitution, and implying it was prepared to nominate someone other than Soeharto for president in the 1993 People's Assembly session. Suryadi said that having more than one candidate for president 'is simply a matter of democracy. You can't force people to all choose the same candidate.'[5] Brave words, although they would soon prove to be untrue.

In the elections, the Democratic Party obtained fifteen per cent of the votes, an improvement over its 1987 performance but much less than party leaders had expected. As in 1987, allegations of vote rigging surfaced but these were denied by the government and then set aside. Despite its worse than expected results, however, the party emerged from the elections in reasonably good shape. Its promises of political change had proved to be enormously popular, especially among the young. Several million Indonesians attended its final rally in Jakarta, a turn-out well above any that the ruling party Golkar was able to attract. But with the ending of the 'festival of democracy'—as the government likes to call the five-yearly parliamentary elections—the Democratic Party was faced with the daunting task of translating its campaign message into government policy.

When the three political parties began meeting in October 1992 to prepare the agenda for the People's Assembly the following March, the Democratic Party resurrected its campaign demands for comprehensive changes to the electoral system, and an end to the abuse of power, corruption and injustice. The most radical of its nine demands was for the People's Assembly to vote on a presidential ticket, a sharp departure from the usual practice of having a single presidential candidate 'chosen' by consensus. To prove its seriousness, the party decided not to nominate a presidential candidate until its national congress convened in January 1993, even though all the other factions in the Assembly—the two other political parties, the armed forces (Abri) and regional representatives—had already nominated Soeharto. The Democratic Party's proposals ran into heavy resistance from Golkar and Abri representatives who waged a strong defence of the status quo.

In the lead-up to its congress, the Democratic Party's president Suryadi came under extreme pressure from reformers who wanted the party to nominate someone other than Soeharto for president and thereby force the People's Assembly into a vote, as well as from the government which was equally insistent that the nation's time-honoured political approach based on consensus not be disrupted. The risks for Suryadi were high. Caving in to government pressure would damage not only his credibility but also the legitimacy of the party. But crossing the government would surely invite retribution and harassment from the authorities. The stakes were raised in early January when Guruh Sukarnoputra, the party's most popular campaigner, offered himself as a presidential candidate.

As the Democratic Party's congress opened on 12 January 1993, supporters demonstrated outside calling on Suryadi to respect the party's campaign pledges. But inside the meeting hall, the government brought its full influence to bear on Suryadi. In a blunt and unambiguous speech to delegates, Lieutenant General Harsudiono Hartas, who headed the social and political affairs department at Abri headquarters, warned his audience that 'Abri will not take the risk of closing its eyes to anything that could endanger the development of the nation . . . Abri is watchful of any issues that could shake the national stability through intellectual manipulation.'[6]

According to several delegates, military officials met privately with Suryadi on several occasions to drive the point home. The officials argued that the party's refusal to nominate Soeharto was pointless since he was going to be elected president anyway, and that to break with the consensus tradition would be bad for Indonesia and bad for Suryadi. The meetings served to remind Suryadi that, at least with regard to the issue of presidential succession, the desire for consensus means in practice an insistence on unanimity.

When the congress closed on 14 January, Suryadi announced the party's unanimous support for another Soeharto presidential term. While the decision was not unexpected, it left many delegates and supporters—including Sirait—deeply disappointed and feeling betrayed by the party's leadership. The party had also decided to drop all its demands for political change except for one measure calling for electoral reform. Objecting to Golkar's monopoly on organising parliamentary elections, the Democratic Party insisted that all three political parties be allowed representatives on the commission which sets the rules for campaigning. It also urged the government to make election day a national holiday so that civil servants would not feel pressured to vote for Golkar. Although these two demands fell a long way short of the radical reforms the party had campaigned for eight months earlier, the Democratic Party at least had the distinction of being the only parliamentary faction to enter the People's Assembly with anything resembling an agenda for change, no matter how modest.

But as Sirait and his fellow reformers would learn as soon as the People's Assembly opened on 1 March 1993, the government had no intention of accommodating any of the party's demands. Attempts to place the electoral reform issue on the Assembly's agenda were brusquely swept aside by the Golkar and Abri officials chairing the working sessions. So, as Golkar chairman Wahono banged his gavel on 5 March to close the general session, Sirait marched to the podium followed by two other delegates from his party. While other delegates shouted, whistled and called for security guards to physically remove them, the three Democratic Party representatives insisted that their electoral reform proposal at least be submitted for discussion. As a tongue-in-cheek *Jakarta Post* editorial put it: 'That dreaded incident—the interruption of procedures in the nation's highest legislative body—has happened at last.'[7]

Little would become of the dreaded interruption. Sirait and the other two renegades were subjected to intense pressure from Golkar and Abri leaders to back down—advice which was also offered by Democratic Party chief Suryadi—and back down they did. On 7 March, the party withdrew its demand for electoral reform, allowing the People's Assembly to return to its prepared script. As a weary spokesman explained: 'PDI [Indonesian Democratic Party] had no choice but to submit to the will of the majority.'[8]

Suryadi's acquiesence to military wishes in January 1993 was not enough to mollify Soeharto, however. In July 1993, the Democratic Party held a national congress to elect a new chairman, a post for which Suryadi was the leading candidate. The military leaned on Democratic Party delegates from the provinces to rebuff Suryadi and choose a chairman more to its liking. Suryadi was able to resist this challenge and secured enough votes to be re-elected, but his success was to be short-lived. Citing procedural irregularities at the Democratic Party's congress, the military pressured Suryadi's rivals in the party's leadership to set up a caretaker administration in August 1993, which then proceeded to call for new elections. It was understood in Democratic Party circles and elsewhere that the pressure to unseat Suryadi came from Soeharto, who was said to be unhappy with Suryadi for his frank criticisms of government policies and officially sanctioned corruption in the campaign for parliamentary elections in 1992.[9] 'No one can afford to be independent around here for too long,' said Democratic Party delegate Laksamana Sukardi. 'If this is a trial run for the presidential succession,' he added, 'then we're in for a real mess. Intervention like this is not just bad for the Democratic Party, it's bad for democracy in Indonesia.'[10]

As it turned out, Soeharto would have been better off sticking with Suryadi. Having forced the Democratic Party to hold new internal elections, the army assumed that chastened party delegates would choose a new chairman more sympathetic to the government. But in a sign of the times—a worrying sign from Soeharto's perspective—the Democratic Party simply refused to play along. Megawati Sukarnoputri, Guruh's elder sister, allowed herself to be drafted as a candidate for chairman and reformers in the party rallied around her.

The prospect of a Sukarno scion heading one of Indonesia's three permitted political parties was greeted with dismay inside the presidential palace. Acutely sensitive to his historical legacy, Soeharto has spared little effort in distancing himself from his flamboyant predecessor. But although New Order doctrine paints Sukarno's legacy as an unvarnished failure, Indonesia's first president remains a widely popular figure, especially among the young. The Democratic Party had used the banner of 'Sukarno-ism'—which was understood to be a code word for more democracy and greater government accountability—to great effect in the 1987 parliamentary elections. The party's followers festooned rallies with banners and posters carrying Sukarno's likeness and favourite phrases. Sukarno's resurgent popularity became such a visible rebuke to Soeharto that the government prohibited Democratic Party enthusiasts from wearing their Sukarno t-shirts in the 1992 parliamentary election campaign. And now, a year and a half later, Sukarno's daughter was quickly becoming the frontrunner to succeed Suryadi as Democratic Party chairman.

The military went back to work, pressuring the party's delegates in the provinces not to support Megawati's bid for chairman. But when the party's second congress got underway in December 1993, the delegates complained instead of military harassment and reiterated their support for Megawati. Army officers and government officials tried desperately to force the party to choose its new chairman by committee—which they could control—rather than by floor vote. When that effort failed as well, the military simply ensured that the party's caretaker administration did not attend the closing session of the congress, thereby making it impossible for the party to ratify Megawati's election.[11] Much to the government's surprise, its ham-handed attempts to intervene again in the Democratic Party's internal affairs elicited howls of outrage from other politicians, the press and many influential retired officers. It soon became clear that the government's already battered credibility would come under renewed attack if it didn't relent in its opposition to Megawati's candidacy. Finally, in the last week of the year, the government agreed to endorse Megawati as Democratic Party chairman, although it fought to the end to see that the party's most vocal critics and Megawati's closest supporters were kept off the party's new executive board.[12]

All in all, 1993 was a rough year for both the Democratic Party and the government officials charged with keeping it in line. Government interference did succeed in exacerbating the party's own internal disunities and forced the party to pass through one wrenching gathering after another. But, by the end of the year, the government came off looking the worst of the two. Its futile attempts at weakening the party and diluting its reforming instincts only succeeded in highlighting the government's own weaknesses while at the same time transforming Megawati's into a credible opposition figure and establishing the Democratic Party as a legitimate rival to Golkar in the 1997 parliamentary elections. More broadly, the government's troubles with the Democratic Party illustrate one of the most serious problems facing Indonesia: as much as the government would like to pretend otherwise, pressures for political change are rising and the existing political structure is poorly equipped to accommodate them.

As earlier chapters have discussed, Soeharto came to power in a specific historical context in which a reassertion of authority and control was of paramount importance. He succeeded beyond all expectations. His achievement in imposing order on Indonesia and building up the power of the state paved the way for other accomplishments, notably in economic development and in strengthening the bonds of national unity. But almost three decades later, the challenges of the day are different. The concerns of state authority and national unity have been joined, if not superseded, by new concerns of economic competitiveness, wealth inequalities, human rights and political pluralism. The overriding political question facing Indonesia in the 1990s, then, is whether and how to adjust its political system to deal with these new concerns. Will Indonesia be well served by maintaining a dominant chief executive and keeping civil society—represented by, among others, parliament, the press and the legal system—weak and ineffectual? Should the reins of power remain in the hands of the very few? Is it reasonable to expect that Soeharto, in power for more than half of Indonesia's existence as a nation, will be able to adapt to the new realities? Does the People's Assembly really represent the 'will of the majority', as the government maintains?

Many in the Indonesian elite would answer 'no' to all these questions. And if the response to the Democratic Party's campaign platform of 1992 is any guide, these feelings extend considerably beyond the elite. A great deal of uncertainty and disagreement exists about where Indonesia's political future lies, or should lie. But there would appear to be widespread agreement within the elite and the middle class that certain aspects of the political status quo are in dire need of change. Many Indonesians in these categories accept the need for a strong executive branch, but feel that the balance has been tipped much too far in its favour. A strictly controlled political system is no longer seen as the best approach for dealing with a variety of social tensions, from Muslims agitating for Islamic values and traditions to be reflected more overtly in government policies, to the resentment of the wealth and standing of ethnic-Chinese businessmen, to the debilitating effect of pervasive corruption, to the widespread view in the Outer Islands that Java is the first island among equals. The common thread linking all these concerns is a sense of frustration that changes in the economic and social spheres have not been accompanied by any real change in the political arena.

The transformation of Indonesia's economy is probably the most important factor behind the growing pressures for change. The robust economic growth of the past half-decade has enlarged and strengthened the business community and helped reduce Indonesians' isolation from the outside world. The move from a state-directed economic policy to a greater emphasis on private sector-led growth has given the emerging middle class more self-confidence, more leverage and a desire, says Ben Anderson, 'to have a political role commensurate with its economic stake'. The middle class, Anderson continues:

> does not have any substantial interest in Suharto's pre-1975 'security state', and does not have much sympathy with the repressions that as much as anything have spawned the recent violence in Aceh, as well as the longstanding resistances in West New Guinea [Irian Jaya] and East Timor. Many of its younger members are uncomfortable with Indonesia's international image. Businessmen dislike, or are envious of, the Suharto family's greedy monopolism; lawyers dislike the government's profound contempt for law. Students and intellectuals dislike the boring nature of the press and the dreariness of university life. More important, there is less and less feeling that all this is *necessary*.[13]

The government seems incapable of effectively responding to this deepening disenchantment. It pays lip service to the concept of 'openness'—which is, among its several meanings, also a code word for democratisation—but its actions belie its words. Within the government there remains an as yet unresolved tug-of-war between those who believe that the existing political system needs reconditioning and those who think that only tinkering is required.

Which view is likely to prevail? It is a question, unfortunately, which can be answered only with hypotheses, alternative scenarios and still other questions. Given the constraints on public expression, it is difficult to gauge how strong pressures for change are, or to predict how these pressures may be reflected in policy or political changes. Much will depend on the extent to which Soeharto is able to continue setting an agenda of limited change only. But for all the uncertainty, the debate on Indonesia's political future is real, and its broad outlines are reasonably clear.

This debate is more properly thought of as two debates. One concerns what is known as the 'succession issue', which focuses on the tricky task of removing a president who is firmly ensconced in office and who shows few signs of being willing to step down. It asks whether a coalition of forces can be assembled to force Soeharto to leave power and what are the factors that work for and against such a coalition being formed. The second debate revolves around the broader issue of political change; it focuses on what changes should or should not be made to the political system created by Soeharto. The two debates are often confused and treated as one. There is a good deal of overlap between them, for the simple reason that it may not be possible to change the political system while Soeharto is in power. But they are, in essence, two separate issues and this chapter tries to treat them separately. But before turning to these debates, it is worthwhile taking a brief look at the existing political institutions and the ways in which they serve to prop up the status quo.

The political machinery

Indonesia's two main political institutions are the parliament and the People's Consultative Assembly, the 1000-member body which meets once every five years to pick a president and vice-president and to draw up the 'guidelines for state policy'. (The 500 members of the parliament form half of the People's Assembly, with Soeharto, the military, regional bodies and the political parties choosing the other half.) The constitution charges these two institutions with translating public aspirations into government policy.

The two main political players are Abri and Golkar. They are closely related to each other, although they are not identical. Abri is the most powerful component of the 'Golkar family' but government bureaucrats and civilian politicians also hold powerful positions in the party. Soeharto provides the most important link between the two, as he is both the Abri commander in chief and the paramount leader of Golkar. As described earlier, Golkar came into its own in the early 1970s when the government forced the existing nine political parties to merge into two new ones. The idea behind Golkar was that it would represent everybody. Its name, an abbreviation for *golongon karya*, or functional groups, explains its identity. It is the intended political vehicle for all societal groups, from women's clubs to farmers to labour unions to industry associations. As well as representing the entire spectrum of society, Golkar acts as the legislative representative of the army and the bureaucracy.

In practice, Golkar has done more to serve the interests of its creators than act as a tribune of its member groups. It would appear to have two central purposes as far as the government is concerned: to dispel the notion that Soeharto is an authoritarian ruler; and to absorb societal grievances in a way that does not impinge on the executive's freedom to act. Golkar is not the only parliamentary actor—the two small opposition parties and Abri are represented as well—but it can be described fairly as a proxy for the parliament as a whole. It embodies what Soeharto believes a parliament should do—implement the government's policies, not participate in the formation of those policies.

Golkar draws support from many Indonesians because it represents a government which has an enviable record of poverty alleviation and economic development. But Golkar's dominance at the polls owes at least as much to an electoral system which is overwhelmingly tilted in its favour. The party's presence extends down to the smallest village, while its two smaller rivals are prevented from operating in rural areas. The government's resources and authority are pledged to Golkar, and areas that vote against Golkar risk seeing development funding dry up. While none of the parties is allowed to campaign except for a brief period before the five-yearly elections, the restriction is less onerous for Golkar since it is synonymous with the government which, of course, is in action all the time.

The Golkar-dominated parliament—the party collected 68 per cent of the votes cast in June 1992, about the same percentage it has held since the early 1970s—has never drafted its own legislation and has never rejected a bill submitted by the executive branch. It has no say in cabinet appointments, little influence over economic policy and virtually no role at all in the making of foreign policy. It is, in short, as effective as the government wants it to be. Like a child, the parliament is displayed for visitors (and foreign legislators and donors) but otherwise is expected to be seen rather than heard. The running joke about the parliament is that its activities can be summarised by the five Ds: *datang, duduk, dengar, diam, duit,* which, roughly translated, means 'show up, sit down, listen, shut up and collect your paycheck'.

Not surprisingly, many Indonesians view the parliament as a body more concerned with appearances than content, Golkar as an ineffectual government creation and parliamentary elections as an event rather unrelated to democracy. In most cases, parliamentary legislators have little connection with the people or area they nominally represent, and the carefully controlled electoral process largely severs the link between a legislator's performance and his or her electability. In fact, elections in Indonesia, far from empowering the people, would seem to have the opposite effect: 'Legitimate' politics is confined to an arena which is unable to make much of a difference and all other political activity is deemed 'illegitimate'. This carefully controlled electoral process 'serves to distance people from politics', says Anderson. 'It is designed to make sure people do not do all the things they might otherwise do in a participatory democracy . . . The real function of elections' political mechanism . . . is actually to pacify, to mediate and to punctuate political participation.'[14]

Attempts have been made to fashion a more independent stance for Golkar, and by extension the parliament. So far, however, these attempts have floundered against Soeharto's reluctance to reinvigorate a political system he has spent so much effort to neutralise. As the government critic Marsillam Simanjuntak tartly put it, explanations for the parliament's 'systemic paralysis' need go no further than to recognise that a 'premeditated political lobotomy [was] performed on the institution [by the executive branch]'.[15]

Golkar's experience in the mid and late 1980s highlighted the political system's resistance to change. From 1983 to 1988, the civilian wing of the party grew in stature under the tutelage and support of its chairman Sudharmono, a retired military general.[16] Together with Sarwono Kusumaatmadja and former student activists Rachmat Witoelar and Akbar Tandjung, Sudharmono believed that Golkar as a reasonably independent political party would be an ideal machine for producing a new generation of Indonesian leaders. Their hope was to lessen Golkar's dependence on the executive branch and the military and to turn the party into a proper political party.

By the end of the decade, however, these plans ran into determined opposition from Soeharto and parts of the army. The army's reaction seems to have been motivated mostly by a dislike of Sudharmono. Although he came from a military background, Sudharmono was deeply distrusted by influential figures at Abri headquarters, notably Benny Murdani, who commanded the armed forces until February 1988. As a military lawyer, Sudharmono lacked combat credentials and was considered an unreliable leader. Apart from serving as Golkar chairman since 1983, Sudharmono had held the powerful state secretary role since 1973 through which he exerted considerable influence over the disbursement of government funds.

Through mechanisms like Team 10, discussed in Chapter 5, Sudharmono cultivated a handful of indigenous businessmen by widening their access to government projects and state bank funding. The army, to put it mildly, felt Sudharmono was not looking after its interests with equal vigour and tried, without success, to persuade Soeharto not to pick him as his vice-president in 1988.

Between the People's Assembly session of March 1988 and Golkar's national congress seven months later, the military took matters in its own hands. It placed military representatives in some two-thirds of Golkar's provincial chairmanships and spread rumours that Sudharmono had links with the banned Communist Party. 'We knew Sudharmono had built up contacts in Golkar,' said General (ret.) Soemitro. 'That's why we had to put military people in the Golkar provincial slots so he wouldn't be re-elected Golkar chairman.'[17] The military got what it wanted. In the Golkar congress, Sudharmono was shunted aside and replaced with another Soeharto loyalist, Wahono, also a retired general but one with no obvious political ambitions. In hindsight, it is hard to tell whether this was a victory for Abri or for Soeharto, but it was clearly a loss for Sudharmono and his civilian supporters.

Abri opposition to Sudharmono, however, did not mean it was opposed to a relatively more independent parliament. The dominant Benny

Murdani-wing of the army, resentful at its dwindling influence with
Soeharto, saw a more active and critical parliament as serving its own
interests. The army's attitude was welcomed by Golkar reformers, the two
smaller parties and promoted by the Speaker of the Parliament Kharis
Suhud. And on a series of issues between 1989–91, the parliament parted
company with the executive branch and adopted an increasingly critical
stance. It objected to higher utility prices, jumped on the 'openness'
bandwagon, supported criticisms of press censorship laws, opened a
dialogue with the political dissidents known as the 'Group of Fifty',
championed the cause of striking labourers and offered encouragement to
new labour unions, sided with farmers in several high-profile land compensation cases and even made the occasional disparaging remark about
the business empires of Soeharto's children. On many of these issues,
military representatives took leading roles, a fact which did not go
unnoticed in the presidential palace.

By the middle of 1991, Soeharto's patience with the invigorated
parliament was exhausted. In August 1991, the leaders of Golkar's three
factions—the army, bureaucracy and civilian politicians—finished assem-
bling a tentative list of party candidates for the general elections ten
months away and made plans to seek Soeharto's approval of the list. The
so-called master list contained almost eight hundred names. Only those
at the top of the list for each province would be elected, with a few more
serving only in the People's Assembly.

The party leaders were not expecting any opposition. But when
Soeharto saw the list he made some immediate changes. Several of the
most outspoken members of the existing parliament were scratched or
moved so far down the ranks as to have no chance of re-election.
Altogether, about fifteen names were dropped. While the number was
small, the message was loud. University of Indonesia political scientist
Yuwono Sudarsono called Soeharto's move a 'retrenchment of
keterbukaan (openness). The president felt things were getting out of
hand.'[18] Marzuki Darusman, one of the legislators denied re-election, put
the case more bluntly: 'After five years of heightened parliamentary
profile, [Soeharto] has completely overturned the norms [of debate] which
have developed in recent years. The message is that Soeharto doesn't want
the parliament to be a participant in the national debate. The whole episode
makes a sham of openness.'[19]

Golkar, as would be expected of a party in power, ran a conservative
campaign ahead of the elections in June 1992. Stressing the government's
record of economic achievement, the party said with some justification
that it alone had any hope of influencing the government to address social
grievances. 'With Golkar there will be continuity,' said the party's secretary-general Rachmat Witoelar, 'and continuity leads to more productivity.' But Witoelar was also quick to concede that in practice Golkar's

leverage is slight. 'Golkar doesn't consider itself to be in a position to bargain with the president. You can't bargain within the same family.'[20] Prudently, the party avoided comment on some of the more important societal grievances. 'We will not infringe on sensitive issues,' Witoelar said. 'Talking about these things will not solve the problems but only aggravate the situation.'[21]

The hopes of Golkar reformers and their Abri sympathisers would be dashed again in October 1993 when the party met to choose a new chairman. Although the military had again built up its representation in Golkar's provincial chapters, its input into selecting the party's chairman was practically nil. And the same could be said of the civilian politicians who run the party on a day-to-day basis. Instead, Soeharto, as head of the party's all-powerful board of patrons, entrusted the management of the Golkar congress to Minister of Research and Technology B. J. Habibie, blithely ignored all dissenting views from party delegates and installed his long-serving information minister, Harmoko, as party chairman. Harmoko, a politician whose principal qualification is an unshakeable loyalty to Soeharto, was the first civilian to ascend to Golkar's top job.

But nobody confused the much-touted 'civilianisation' of Golkar with democratisation.[22] Just the opposite, in fact. The day after Harmoko's election, Golkar announced a new 45-member executive board crammed with Soeharto loyalists. The president's daughter Siti Hardijanti Rukmana was named one of the party's vice-chairmen and his son Bambang Trihatmodjo became party treasurer. In addition, sons and daughters of some of Soeharto's most trusted peers were well represented on the board. 'It's nepotism on a grand scale,' said a disgusted Marzuki Darusman, the former Golkar parliamentarian who currently sits on the national Human Rights Commission. 'The executive board was chosen for the sole purpose of re-electing Soeharto again in 1998. It's simply no longer realistic to expect Golkar to ever be independent of Soeharto.'[23]

Whatever its shortcomings, Golkar is looked on by many as a crucial player in Indonesia's political future. Its ability to absorb *and* respond to public pressures will determine the extent to which the parliament plays an active role in making Indonesia more democratic. Equally important, because Golkar can command a majority of votes in the 1000-member People's Assembly, the party will play a crucial role in finding and electing a successor to Soeharto. 'I think all areas of government are already aware that if we are going to build a democracy, we have to work through, and build up, Golkar and the parliament,' acknowledged Golkar member Theo Sambuaga.[24] Whether Golkar is able to make itself more relevant to a changing, increasingly complex and demanding society remains to be seen, however. Its performance in the People's Assembly sessions of March 1993 provided little encouragement for its reformist elements. Although apparently divided on who it favoured for vice-president, it staunchly resisted the attempt to make the People's Assembly vote on the presidential ticket. And even though a poll of Assembly members showed that more than one third of Golkar representatives favoured introducing presidential term limits,[25] Golkar leaders would not permit this issue to be discussed in the Assembly's sessions.

As might be expected, the People's Assembly of 1993 was largely bereft of suspense or surprise. The re-election of Soeharto for a sixth five-year term was never in doubt, least of all by the delegates themselves. The People's Assembly, explained the body's Deputy Speaker Ismail Hasan Metareum, is 'like a wedding ceremony. Although everyone knows who the bride and bridegroom are, the ritual is necessary to formalise the union.'[26] Perhaps, though, the most revealing comment of all about the Assembly was made by the former police chief of Jakarta, General Kunarto. Appointed as a delegate, Kunarto told journalists after the Assembly closed that he had gained nothing by attending its deliberations except that his lips had swollen from having to repeatedly shout 'Setuju!' (I agree!) to decisions made beforehand.[27]

The succession dilemma

Perhaps only two things can be said with certainty about Soeharto's eventual replacement as Indonesia's president. The first is that it will happen; mortality, if nothing else, will take care of that. The second is that, when it does happen, it will create a good deal of uncertainty.

Developing a workable mechanism for the presidential succession is the most pressing political issue facing the Indonesian leadership. Nothing less than the nation's political future is at stake. Political stability has been one of the hallmarks of Soeharto's rule but that is not the same thing as saying that Indonesia is politically stable. Before that claim can be made, it must be tested by a transition of power.[28] Only then can it be said that the political system itself is stable, and not merely that one ruler, albeit a strong one, was able to keep destabilising forces at bay while he was in power.

Many Indonesians would argue that continued political stability will depend to a great extent on *how* Soeharto leaves office.[29] Indonesia has had only one presidential succession, and it happened amidst the traumatic conditions created by the coup attempt in September 1965 and the messy confrontation between Sukarno and Soeharto which followed. It was an experience that no one in Indonesia would like to repeat, including Soeharto. But can a repetition be avoided? Will Soeharto's departure from power be any smoother than his entrance?

Soeharto could die before his current mandate expires, of course. He turned 72 in June 1993, compared with an average life expectancy in

Indonesia of about 62. But he appears reasonably healthy, if mildly overweight, and barring unforeseen consequences it seems unlikely that health reasons will prevent him from serving at least until 1998. But should Soeharto die in office before 1998, the most likely result would be for the military to reassert control over the political process. Such an event, while succeeding in changing the personality at the top, would leave unanswered the important question of Indonesia's political maturity. What the nation needs, most Indonesians would agree, is to experience a peaceful, reasonably transparent succession of power in the manner prescribed by the constitution. There is a lot of work that needs to be done before that can happen.

Perhaps the most urgent requirement for a 'successful' presidential succession is planning. Without it, said the late Lieutenant General T. B. Simatupang, the situation in Indonesia could degenerate into 'a kind of anarchy with everyone manoeuvring for position'.[30] Unfortunately, there has been little planning for the succession so far, at least in public, a fact which is making the succession process much more complicated than it needs to be. Indeed, the riskiest aspect of Soeharto's eventual departure from office is its sheer unpredictability.

One reason for this unpredictability is that presidential succession is not considered a topic fit for public discussion. Most mainstream politicians and the press are fearful that any comments on this subject will be construed by Soeharto as criticism of his leadership. When, in late 1993, several academics and Islamic leaders stated publicly that it was high time for Indonesia to discuss the presidential succession process, the newly-installed Golkar chairman Harmoko cut them off at the pass, describing their opinions as 'unethical'.[31]

Soeharto is no more willing to countenance discussion of topics that serve as proxies for the succession issue, one example of which is term limits. On many occasions the president has bluntly and often angrily rejected calls for a limit on the number of terms a president can serve. In 1992, he again dismissed the idea when it was raised in the parliamentary election campaign, calling it a form of 'political castration'.[32] Soeharto appears to be equally reluctant to discuss the succession issue in private. When the topic of his replacement arises, he invariably replies that it is a matter for the People's Assembly to deal with.

This answer, of course, sheds little light on the issue because Soeharto controls the mechanism for presidential elections. He determines who occupies the top Golkar slots and, by keeping a tight leash on the electoral process, he can ensure that the party's legislative dominance remains intact. Moreover, by having veto power over the selection of Golkar and Abri delegates to the People's Assembly, he has been able to ensure that a comfortable majority remains loyal to him. Thus, by saying that the presidential succession issue is a matter for the People's Assembly,

Soeharto is in effect saying that it is really up to himself. The problem is that nobody knows what Soeharto plans to do. He said in his autobiography published in the late 1980s that he would probably step down in 1993, but then he didn't. Is he thinking of stepping down in the middle of his current term? In 1998? In 2003? Does he want to stay in office until he dies? Is he worried about what will happen to his children and their business interests once he is out of power? What will it take to convince him to step aside? The answer to all these questions is that nobody—and this possibly includes Soeharto as well—seems to know. And because they don't know, the parts of the Indonesian elite who would like to see Soeharto out of the way are being forced to consider how they can counteract Soeharto's manipulation of the People's Assembly by manipulating it themselves. From their point of view, this is the only way forward since Soeharto has made it all but impossible to reform the political system from within.

Another factor contributing to 'succession unpredictability' is the lack of credible alternatives to Soeharto. The generally accepted profile of Soeharto's successor is that he will be Javanese, Muslim and a military officer. Identifying realistic candidates is no easy task, however. Indonesia's current president is a strong believer in absolute power and he has little room in his domain for strong, independent-minded figures whose loyalty to himself is in question. And he has proven to be adept at undercutting any potential rivals. In this respect, Soeharto's style of rule bears more than a little resemblance to that of ancient Javanese monarchs. And true to Javanese court traditions, Soeharto has shown no interest in openly grooming a successor. None of the vice-presidents chosen by Soeharto has been considered presidential material. (The current vice-president, Try Sutrisno, may be an exception to this rule but this is more by default than by design.) Restrictions on the press and on political campaigning have helped ensure that political aspirants find it hard to build any mass-based support. The resulting picture is a towering president surrounded by a host of political dwarves. It is a picture, moreover, which Soeharto uses to great effect in thwarting challenges to his rule. If there is no one who can fill my shoes, he says in effect, why should I go?

Yet another factor is that whoever replaces Soeharto will by definition be a different kind of president. Indonesia's third president, regardless of political philosophy, will have nowhere near the personal influence that Soeharto enjoys, influence that extends well beyond the powers accorded him by office.[33] Soeharto came to power in the mid-1960s when political and social institutions were in disarray. His efforts to restore order, which required strengthening the presidency, were welcomed or at least accepted by a broad cross-section of society. Building on that base, Soeharto over the years has constructed an intricate network of alliances with important sections of the military and business elite, he has gained control over Golkar and by extension the parliament and the People's Assembly, and he has learned how to silence his critics, sometimes by repression, sometimes by co-optation. Soeharto's successor, necessarily a much less experienced politician, will inherit only a fraction of his impressive array of powers. That points inevitably to a power vacuum when Soeharto finally leaves office, whenever that might be. Someone or some entity will have to fill that vacuum. It might be Abri, it might be Golkar, or it might be some other group or coalition of groups. The point is that no matter how well managed the succession process is, it will be disruptive as traditional institutional relationships will be upset. This process would be less worrisome for those groups interested in filling this vacuum if they could discuss the problem among themselves prior to the succession itself. Unfortunately, there is little reason to believe that Soeharto is prepared to allow such a dialogue to develop.

The combination of these three obstacles and uncertainties serves only to illustrate how difficult it will be to arrange a 'smooth' succession process. But for the reasons listed above, the political status quo in Indonesia is unsustainable; something has to give. Soeharto could announce at any time that he plans to step down in 1998. That would make the situation considerably less unpredictable, though not completely so. Or he could announce that he is *not* planning to step down in 1998. Or he could initiate a public debate on how the succession process will work, a debate that would go far beyond the simplistic view that it is simply 'a matter for the People's Assembly to decide'. But none of these options is terribly likely.

Much more likely is that Soeharto does nothing to reduce the uncertainty of his succession and that everyone is left guessing until the last moment. In recent years especially, Soeharto has behaved as if he is very much aware that once loyalty to him begins to slip, it could evaporate quickly. He seems keenly conscious of the need to retain the means by which he can both reward his allies and punish his enemies. And by diligently placing trusted aides in Golkar and in the top ranks of the military, he has made it more likely that the People's Consultative Assembly meeting in 1998 will be beholden to his wishes. The question, then, is can Soeharto get away with it? Could he manage to get himself re-elected again in 1998 if he chooses to stand again? If he decides to step down, will he be able to hand-pick his successor? Can he, more generally, control his own destiny? It is hard to answer 'no' to any of these questions precisely because Soeharto has been in power so long and has proven himself time and time again to be a masterful political operator. Consequently, the most plausible succession scenario is the one which has Soeharto in control of the process.

But there is another scenario worth considering. This scenario has

Soeharto gradually losing control over his own succession as 1998 draws nearer. It has a coalition of elite groups dissatisfied with all or parts of Soeharto's leadership banding together for the purpose of obliging Soeharto to step down in 1998. The key is whether the anti-Soeharto groups can find common ground. Individually, they do not pose much of a threat to Soeharto, but united they would constitute a formidable pressure group for change. What might an anti-Soeharto coalition look like, and what would hold such a coalition together?

One thread binding these forces together is the belief that Soeharto is an obstacle to Indonesia's political development and that this development, therefore, can begin only when Soeharto is out of office. By and large they are not animated by hatred or even dislike of Soeharto. They give him credit for stabilising Indonesia's political life and for overseeing an extended period of economic development. They simply feel that his paternalistic style of authoritarian rule in no longer appropriate. They think there is something seriously wrong with a political system that permits one man to stay in power for 30 years. They argue that a younger, more dynamic leader is needed to cope with the nation-building challenges of the 1990s.

They disagree among themselves on what *sorts* of political changes Indonesia needs—a topic returned to below—but they agree that some change is necessary. They want a government, generally speaking, that is less arbitrary in nature and one which depends less on personal ties between the rulers and the ruled; a government which has more respect for the law and for the political process; and a government which provides for more and better communication between itself and the people it is meant to serve.

Possible members of an anti-Soeharto coalition include many parts of the Indonesian elite which once supported the president but have become disillusioned with his leadership. They include university professors and students who abhor the intellectual rigidity of campus life; artists, journalists and intellectuals who want more freedom to express their views; activists in non-governmental organisations chafing at restrictions on their activities; Muslim leaders unhappy with the New Order's deep-seated suspicion of Islamic aspirations; economists and business leaders who believe that rampant corruption is retarding the nation's development; prominent community leaders off Java irritated by the centripetal urges of Soeharto's administration;[34] and civilian politicians or would-be politicians who want to participate more fully in government decision-making, and who want, in other words, Soeharto to give someone else a chance. Finally, and most importantly, such a coalition would contain disaffected elements of the military who for their own reasons—personal, institutional and political—believe that Soeharto has been in power long enough. The military is not likely to lead an anti-Soeharto coalition much less contemplate a military coup. Either of these actions would make a mockery of the constitution and the military's beloved dual function doctrine. But it is quite possible that efforts to ensure Soeharto steps down in 1998 will receive the sympathy and tacit support of at least parts of the military establishment. Without this support, moreover, any anti-Soeharto initiative is unlikely to be successful.

Will it be possible for the constituent members of an anti-Soeharto coalition to form an open, public pressure group with clearly stated objectives? Given that the parameters of acceptable political activity in Indonesia are narrowly drawn, it will not be easy. One of the secrets of Soeharto's longevity is that he has kept his opponents divided and therefore weak, and he is not likely to change his approach this late in the day. Direct pressure, in any case, is not likely to be the most effective way to persuade Soeharto to step down. In an open confrontation, Soeharto will prevail.

Instead, he needs to be convinced that it is best for him, his legacy and the country that he leave office in a planned, smooth and reasonably predictable fashion. It would help if Soeharto could be made to feel it is his own decision. He is, after all, not a man who likes to be told what to do. But skilled diplomacy, while necessary, will not be enough. Somehow, Soeharto has to be made to understand the consequences of a refusal to relinquish power. Coordinated political action will be difficult to arrange and carry out but there may be some scope for individual groups to bring the message of change to Soeharto's notice. Bolder voices in the parliament could step up their criticism of government policies and of the government's cosy relationship with big business; students could become more politically active; non-governmental organisations could hold demonstrations on a variety of pretexts, such as the environment, labour rights and land compensation; and the press could gird itself to highlight in even more clearer terms social, religious, economic and political grievances. Indeed, by 1993 many of these groups were already beginning to take a more confrontational approach to criticising government policies. But again, the crucial piece of the puzzle is whether Abri will continue to allow these voices to be heard. If it did, it might be in a position to persuade Soeharto to step aside in exchange for restoring order. There is an obvious parallel here, of course, with Soeharto's campaign to unseat Sukarno in 1966. But the scenario listed above is not merely a historical fantasy. It is a topic of regular, if private, debate within Indonesia's elite.

The military

What can be said of Abri's attitude to Soeharto? The first thing is that it has many attitudes. It is tempting to treat the Indonesian military as a monolithic force, given the difficulties in ascertaining what its leading officers really think and who among them has the most influence. But like any large organisation, Abri contains a spectrum of differing perspectives as well as being bound by several core principles. One of these principles is that political stability is a necessary precondition for economic development. A second is that extreme vigilance is needed to counteract forces which might fray the bonds of national unity. But it would be wrong to conclude from Abri's commitment to these principles that its support for Soeharto is unwavering. A body of opinion within the Abri family believes that Soeharto's domination of the political process is not serving the causes of political stability, economic development and national unity. These officers worry that issues such as wealth inequality, the repoliticisation of Islam, anti-Chinese sentiment and corruption could become serious political problems, and that not only is Soeharto not doing enough to address them but that he may well be contributing to them. These concerns are expressed most openly by retired generals but they appear to be shared by many active duty officers as well. 'The feeling in Abri that Soeharto has to go is widespread,' said Lieutenant General (ret.) Hasnan Habib, a former ambassador to the US. 'Even younger officers like colonels and lieutenant colonels share this view.'[35]

Another way to view Abri's relationship with Soeharto is to look at how well the military as an institution has fared under Soeharto. Taking a broad look at the entire New Order period, Abri has every reason to be pleased with Soeharto. He is a military man himself, and he has done a more than credible job in rescuing Indonesia from the political and economic morass of the mid-1960s. Relative to what came before, the New Order has dealt deftly with ethnic and religious tensions, imposed at least a modicum of discipline on the bureaucracy, and fostered a sense of national unity and purpose. And last but not least, Abri has done well by Soeharto. In pre-Soeharto Indonesia, the army was factionalised and constantly in competition for power with other groups. Under Soeharto, Abri has been relatively unified as well as the most powerful political institution in the land. The doctrine of *dwifungsi*, or dual function, has grown by leaps and bounds in the New Order, allowing the military's influence to percolate into virtually every nook and cranny of society. Military officers hold key positions all through the government, from city mayors, ambassadors and provincial governors, to senior positions in central government ministries, regional bureaucracies, state-owned enterprises, the judiciary, the umbrella labour union, Golkar and in the cabinet itself.

But as the focus narrows to the recent past, Abri has less reason to be content and more reason to support an attempt to force Soeharto to step aside. If in the first fifteen years of the New Order, Abri and Soeharto were practically synonymous, their relationship has grown more distant since the early 1980s (although it was only much later that this change came to be widely appreciated). A number of explanations for Abri's declining influence with Soeharto can be put forward. One is that the military's sources of revenue were threatened by new rivals in the 1980s. Then State Secretary and Golkar chairman Sudharmono played a role in that process, as did the emergence of Soeharto's children as serious business players. The First Family supplanted the military in a handful of areas from oil trading to airlines to timber which previously had been important contributors to Abri's budget as well as to the banking accounts of privileged generals. More generally, the collapse of oil prices in the mid-1980s and the subsequent need for significant economic reform raised the stature of civilian economic 'technocrats' and closed off some avenues of off-budget financing.[36]

A second reason is that the military's partnership with Soeharto weakened as his need for political backing from the army declined. By the early 1980s, the political landscape had been all but wiped clean of credible opponents, allowing Soeharto the luxury of disregarding the military's political opinions. The military, in effect, had fallen victim to its own handiwork. This lesson was brought rudely home to Abri in 1988 when Soeharto ignored the military's strongly worded advice and picked Sudharmono to be his vice-president. If Abri needed any further reminding of its current place in the political hierarchy, Soeharto's complete dismissal of its views during the October 1993 Golkar congress provided it.[37]

A third reason, or at least a possible reason, is that Soeharto deliberately distanced himself from Abri to enhance his own legitimacy as president and to dispel the notion that he was beholden to the military for his continued hold on power.[38] (Possibly this was why he disparaged the contributions of his closest military advisers in his 1988 autobiography.) A related dynamic was that Soeharto appeared increasingly doubtful of Abri's loyalty to him. This may have been behind his (only partly successful) attempts to cultivate a new base of support within the Islamic community in the late 1980s and early 1990s. It may also be the reason why Soeharto has endeavoured in recent years to place confirmed loyalists at or near the top of all the military services. The powerful army chief of staff billet is currently held by his brother-in-law, General Wismoyo Arismunandar.[39]

Soeharto's success in sidelining critical officers, notably former armed forces commander General Benny Murdani, also succeeded in weakening the political half of the military's dual-function role. While military personnel still occupy many important positions in the political hierarchy, the military as an institution clearly has lost some of its political leverage. The reason is that influence in Soeharto's Indonesia is personality-driven; even in the early days of the New Order the military's political leverage was secured through influential figures like Ali Murtopo and Sudjono

Humardhani. But as the military has learned to its dismay, Soeharto's tolerance of influential personalities has decreased with age. He has been able to reduce Abri's political influence simply by removing or weakening its leading political thinkers. Without any effective political 'think-tank' of its own, the military has found it hard to supply new, politically savvy thinkers to establish themes and objectives for a constructive political strategy.

What remains is a military considerably more powerful in appearance than in reality. On paper Abri's position has slid somewhat, but not markedly so. It held thirteen of the 32 cabinet positions in 1983, eleven of the 38 positions in 1988 and ten of the 41 positions in 1993. But the ten military personnel in the current cabinet have considerably less clout than their cabinet-level counterparts in 1982 simply because Abri by the 1990s had become less able to formulate and disseminate its own political opinions. 'Only Soeharto has the power to get anything done in Indonesia,' lamented Habib. 'Abri is very weak, and subservient to Soeharto. We just implement what he wants us to do.' Added another retired general, Sayidiman Suryohadiproyo: 'Soeharto no longer listens to anyone, not Abri nor anyone else. This is the danger we are facing.'[40]

Abri's dilemma is that it remains closely associated in the public mind with the New Order government even though its influence has declined. The shortcomings of Soeharto's government—corruption, disrespect for the law, favouritism to ethnic-Chinese cronies, etc.—are also held to be shortcomings of the military. If Abri is to make a convincing case for a continued political role after Soeharto goes, it will need to distance itself from the more unappealing aspects of Soeharto's rule. One way to do that is to provide tacit support to the groups manoeuvring to unseat Soeharto. Gadjah Mada University sociologist Lukman Soetrisno described Abri's predicament this way: 'Abri is going to have to choose. Is it for corruption or is it for the people?'[41]

The changing relationship between Soeharto and Abri is nicely represented by the rise and fall of Benny Murdani. After joining Indonesia's war of independence at the age of sixteen, Murdani rose quickly through the ranks and by the early 1970s had become one of Soeharto's most trusted and powerful aides. A protege of General Ali Murtopo, Murdani's strong suit was intelligence operations and, like his mentor, he was, and is, a shrewd political strategist. As a Catholic, Murdani was never a likely political rival of Soeharto. But he was—and maybe still is—enormously influential within the armed forces and as a political actor in his own right. Throughout his career as an active duty officer, up to and including his stint as armed forces commander from 1983 to 1988, Murdani remained fiercely loyal to Soeharto and was openly dismissive of retired generals who criticised the president from the sidelines, notably the generals who joined the dissident Group of Fifty. Shortly before and after his own fall from grace in 1988, however, Murdani gained a new appreciation of his retired colleagues.

Murdani lost Soeharto's trust by broaching with the president the subject of his family's business activities and objecting to Sudharmono's vice-presidency. But Murdani had also begun to sympathise with the view that *dwifungsi* had gone too far and that it was time to tone down the 'security approach' to governance. In March 1988, Murdani was named defence minister, a less powerful position than Abri commander, and five years later he was dropped from the cabinet altogether. It was a classic case of Soeharto trying to weaken Abri politically by removing one of its main political thinkers. It was also a particularly visible—though not unusual—example of Soeharto being prepared to lose the services of one of his most experienced operatives in a probably futile attempt to ensure that the military's political activities remain firmly under his control.

It is far from clear whether the treatment of Murdani will quell military unease at Soeharto's domineering leadership. After he was 'kicked upstairs' in 1988, Murdani remained an influential figure through the force of his own personality and because he could count on the loyalty of many active duty officers who owed their positions to him. The push for 'openness' and the invigoration of the parliament in 1989–91 were widely attributed to Murdani's influence, as was the decision of some 40 retired military officers to throw their weight behind the Indonesian Democratic Party in 1991. In apparent recognition of Murdani's continuing sway within active duty ranks, in early 1994 Soeharto ordered the dismantling of the powerful intelligence agency known as BAIS. The agency, once Murdani's principal power base, was considered his strongest remaining link to active-duty officers.[42] Nevertheless, Murdani is likely to remain an important behind-the-scenes operator even though his links to the current military leadership are dwindling.

How might Murdani's influence be felt in the coming years? He apparently has little ambition to become a public opponent of Soeharto; in the past he has been clearly uncomfortable at being perceived as one. But although he has strived to be a loyal team player in public, he has become increasingly critical and even contemptuous of Soeharto in private. He feels, it seems, that Soeharto has turned his back on the institution which put him in power. Moreover, he has taken some steps to strengthen Abri's hand in the coming succession battle and at the same time he has begun cultivating ties with civilian politicians and intellectuals who might also be counted on to raise the pressure on Soeharto.

His most meaningful step so far has been to corner Soeharto into accepting Try Sutrisno as vice-president for the 1993–98 term. This, at least, is how Murdani's supporters describe it. Others believe that Sutrisno, a former aide to Soeharto, would have been the president's choice anyway. Which of these scenarios is closer to the mark may never be known. More to the point, perhaps, was that many in Indonesia *believed* Abri forced its wishes on Soeharto, a rare enough occurrence in any case. Many military leaders were undoubtedly worried about the prospect of Soeharto choosing Minister of Research and Technology B. J. Habibie as vice-president, or opting to retain Sudharmono for another term. Whether Soeharto was considering either option is impossible to say. He clearly had his doubts about Sutrisno, both because of the officer's political inexperience and because he is close to Murdani, whom he succeeded as Abri commander.

A few weeks before the People's Assembly of March 1993 got under way, Abri took the unusual step of nominating Sutrisno for vice-president even though Soeharto had yet to make his wishes known. The other Assembly factions quickly followed suit. Soeharto was left with the choice of either accepting the vice-presidential nominations of all five Assembly factions or publicly rejecting the stated views of the body which is constitutionally responsible for selecting the nation's top leaders. Although he opted for the former, he later made it clear to several government officials that he was unhappy with Abri.[43]

One interesting aspect of Abri's vigorous campaign in support of Sutrisno is that the new vice-president is not especially well-regarded by his peers. An amiable man with good Islamic credentials, he is seemingly bereft of a political vision and his public utterances are often cliche-filled and at times downright silly. In his favour, however, is that he is not Habibie, he is not Sudharmono, he *is* a military man, and he provides Abri with some insurance should Soeharto die or become incapacitated before 1998. As vice-president, he also has to be considered the front-runner to succeed Soeharto should the president step down in 1998. These considerations overrode concerns about Sutrisno's (so far undisplayed) political skills. Abri's 'victory' did not come cost-free, however. Two leading Abri 'politicians'—Murdani and former Home Affairs Minister Rudini—were dropped from the cabinet, while several officers close to Murdani—like Harsudiono Hartas, who headed Abri's social-political department, and Teddy Rusdy, a top aide to Sutrisno—were unexpectedly overlooked for cabinet jobs. This was, apparently, Soeharto's payback to the Abri officers presumptuous enough to restrict his latitude in choosing a vice-president.

Faced with a still strong and wary Soeharto, the Abri leaders who are anxious to see Soeharto's tenure come to an end no doubt understand that Soeharto will not be easily pushed from power. To notch up the pressure on Soeharto they will have to reach outside their small circle and enlist the support of civilian sympathisers. It will be a delicate game for all concerned.

The civilian elite

It is not hard to fathom why many members of the civilian elite are uncomfortable with the idea of Soeharto staying in power indefinitely: they have had little political influence almost since Soeharto's ascension. They may not have much more under Indonesia's next president but they would like to find out sooner rather than later. Getting there, as always, is the problem. The following list highlights some of the roadblocks that lie ahead.

The Faustian bargain

Civilian critics of Soeharto have a tricky choice. They must have some support from Abri if they are to mount an effective challenge to Soeharto but they worry they will end up with a raw deal. 'We know we have to work with Abri if we are to achieve a transition of power but we are worried that the army will take over again once Soeharto is gone,' said Arief Budiman, a sociologist at the Satya Wacana Christian University. 'Right now we have a common cause with Abri, just like we did in 1965–66. But can we carve out enough space for ourselves so that Abri won't take it all away once their objective has been reached? This is what they did in the late 1960s and I'm afraid they could do it again. If that is going to happen, what's the point of trying to push out Soeharto?' United Development Party legislator Sri Bintang Pamungkas arrived at the same conclusion: 'We will have to cooperate with Abri. The question is will we do the using or will we get used?'[44]

Another way to describe the dilemma facing civilian reformers is that they need to chip away at Soeharto's aura of invincibility until the idea of a new president taking office in 1998 seems like a feasible alternative to the broad political elite. But they can't risk overdoing it. A full scale campaign to weaken Soeharto's authority could backfire in one of two ways. It could provide an excuse for Soeharto to strike back forcefully at his critics. And, if it succeeded too well, Abri hardliners would themselves have an excuse to step in and reassert control. In either of these scenarios, democracy advocates would come out on the losing end.

Developing the Abri–civilian dialogue

Getting military officers to communicate more with their civilian counterparts is arguably the most important prerequisite for developing an effective common front on the succession issue. 'It is imperative for Abri and enlightened civilians to work together to reduce the unpredictability of Soeharto's succession,' said former legislator Marzuki Darusman.[45] But it will not be easy. Memories die hard in Abri and one of its most enduring memories is of strife, political ineffectiveness and economic stagnation in the 1950s. Abri blames this turmoil on parliamentary democracy and the civilian politicians who led it. Many contemporary military figures doubt whether civilian politicians today are any more reliable than their precursors. 'They still regard politics,' says academic Michael Leifer, 'as too important a matter to be left exclusively to civilians.'[46] As one retired four-star general put it in an interview in early 1994, 'civilians are not yet ready to do what Abri has been doing for them'.[47]

For all its talk of being 'one with the people', Abri remains socially isolated. Mixing with the civilian elite has never been high on its priority list. When Benny Murdani was Abri commander, for example, he discouraged contacts between junior officers and civilian intellectuals because the latter were 'too Westernised and a destabilising influence'.[48] His successor Try Sutrisno followed a similar line, possibly because he believes there is no such thing as a civilian–military distinction in Indonesia. 'The dichotomy [between civilians and soldiers] only exists in a liberal democracy,' he asserted in February 1993.[49]

But it does exist in Indonesia, even if Sutrisno is not prepared to admit it. Soldiers and civilians rarely mingle in Indonesia and distrust is mutual. 'The problem with Abri is that it lacks finesse, it lacks exposure to society, it lacks political skills, and it is convinced it is its right to rule Indonesia,' said one non-military cabinet minister with close ties to Golkar. 'The military has contempt for civilians and for politics in general but they relish power,' he continued. 'Murdani is a good example. He only understands force. He can't cope with complexities.'[50]

The rapid growth of the private business sector in recent years has added a new complicating factor in the civilian–military relationship. Top students increasingly are opting for high-paying jobs in business rather than seeking careers in government service or the military. This is more than a recruitment problem for the military. With underpaid officers increasingly resentful of their higher-paid peers in the business world, developing a dialogue between civilian and military leaders becomes that much harder.

For the civilian elite, there is an additional problem: how to identify which segment of Abri might be open to a dialogue. Some argue that the so-called 1945 Generation of Abri officers offers the best hope since these officers experienced the political give-and-take of the 1950s—even if they didn't like it much—and therefore are more comfortable dealing with civilians. 'The older officers have a better feel for politics, they can handle disagreement,' said newspaper editor and Democracy Forum member Aristides Katoppo. 'The younger officers all seem to feel they have to think the same way. They are afraid to debate.'[51]

Others hope for better things from the younger officers. Jusuf Wanandi, a political analyst at the Centre for Strategic and International

Studies, points out that younger officers 'are better educated and they should better understand the problems and the needs of a more open society [and] the wishes of a larger middle class . . . But at the same time they seem also to be overly worried about the unity of the nation, the continuity of development and the continued stability of political life . . . In fact, we just don't know what they will do or think once they have the opportunity to act politically.'[52] Many prominent Muslim figures blame the older military generation for denying them the political stature they feel they deserve. 'The younger officers are much more liberal and open than the older generation,' contended Nasir Tamara, a leading member of the Indonesian Association of Muslim Intellectuals. 'At least when you talk to them you are not scared.'[53]

Overcoming Abri–Muslim suspicions

As Tamara's comment indicates, the relationship between Abri and politically active Muslims is a difficult one. Modernist Muslim leaders advocate political change in Indonesia and are interested in playing a part in a 'succession coalition'. They share with some parts of Abri a desire to see Soeharto leave office, but there the commonality ends. Abri is unhappy with what it sees as Soeharto's attempts to 'repoliticise' Islam and it knows that some Muslim activists would like to see Islam 'repoliticised' to a much greater extent. Its suspicions of Islamic political aspirations is a serious obstacle to attempts to assemble a broad-based coalition to plan the succession process. The role of the Indonesian Association of Muslim Intellectuals (ICMI) is particularly troublesome. 'Before ICMI was set up, civilians and parts of the military were already working on forming some kind of coalition,' said Arief Budiman. 'But these efforts were set back when ICMI was announced. The army got scared.'[54]

Soeharto

An important obstacle to any civilian–military coalition is of course Soeharto himself. The tools of government are at his disposal and he knows how to use them. If he senses that elite groups are aligning against him, he can be expected to take steps to weaken them. He can crack down at any time on the media by revoking a few publishing licences. And it would be difficult for Abri officers to refuse a direct order to break up public protests by, say, students or workers. Should such a situation arise, the senior active duty officers—including Abri commander Feisal Tandjung and Army Chief of Staff Wismoyo Arismunandar—and Defence Minister Edi Sudrajat will have to decide whether loyalty to Soeharto and loyalty to Abri is still the same thing and, if not, which way to turn. It is hard to predict what they would do, of course, but it would be wrong to assume they would automatically support Soeharto. Not even the views of Wismoyo, married to a sister of Soeharto's wife, can be predicted with any certainty. According to several military sources, he too shares the view that Soeharto has been in power too long.

Soeharto, in addition, still enjoys plenty of support from the Indonesian elite. Grateful for the stability and economic development he has brought to Indonesia, many are prepared to overlook the less commendable aspects of his rule. Some groups, with the ethnic-Chinese business class being a good example, are nervous about their standing in a post-Soeharto Indonesia and are reasonably content to postpone the day of reckoning. And, obviously, those who have directly benefited from his patronage, such as the top crony businessmen and his family, are anxious to have Soeharto stay in power for as long as possible. 'Thank God, my father is still entrusted to be the head of state,' his son Tommy said just after the People's Assembly elected Soeharto for a sixth five-year term in March 1993.[55]

More positively, Soeharto may decide to take the wind out of the sails of a succession coalition by loosening the political controls he has imposed. In his Independence Day speech in August 1993, for example, Soeharto promised that 'in the political field, we shall continue to develop openness and promote political norms, morals and ethics'.[56] How sincere he is in this regard is impossible to predict. At the time, some prominent Indonesians felt that Soeharto had no choice but to give way before a 'democratising tide', in the hopeful words of leading Indonesian Democratic Party member Kwik Kian Gie.[57] Many others took a more sceptical view, remembering that Soeharto has promised a measure of political openness before and not delivered. The sceptics viewed Soeharto's apparent change of heart as yet another ploy to undermine opposition to his rule without permitting anything remotely resembling a meaningful change to the political rules of the game. As usual, no one quite knew what Soeharto was up to.

The economy

One of the wild cards in the succession debate is the state of the economy; this is both Soeharto's strength and vulnerability. Economic development has been the centrepiece of his administration. As long as growth can be maintained, jobs created and incomes raised, Soeharto will be in a powerful position to undermine efforts to unseat him. But development is a two-edged sword. Some serious weaknesses remain in Indonesia's economy and some difficult measures will need to be taken if it is to become more internationally competitive. Yet it is not clear if the political will exists to take these steps. Soeharto's refusal to act resolutely to reduce corruption is clearly a brake on growth as well as a drain on his own legitimacy as ruler. The apparent emergence of Minister of Research and Technology B. J. Habibie as an important political player in the early 1990s has further clouded the issue. Many feel that Habibie's plans to turn Indonesia into a technological powerhouse would derail economic growth instead. And finally, the unpredictability of Soeharto's succession is itself becoming an economic cost: foreign investors in particular say that the uncertainty surrounding Soeharto's succession is adding to the political risk of an investment in Indonesia.

Only time will tell how well the government will manage the economy in the years ahead, but the initial reactions to the cabinet appointed by Soeharto in March 1993, in which Habibie loyalists were well represented, were mixed at best. Many observers described the cabinet as weak and inexperienced; a number of first-time ministers were said to owe their appointment more to their personal loyalty to Soeharto than to any skills they could bring to their individual portfolios. United Development Party legislator and Muslim intellectual Sri Bintang Pamungkas expressed, in typically blunt terms, a not uncommon view: 'This is a lousy cabinet, an act of a tiring president. It seems like there is new blood there, but that's not really the case. They are all bureaucrats. It is not a cabinet designed to help development.' But, he added, 'this cabinet will probably provide a good opportunity for us in the parliament. A weakening economy will damage Soeharto and allow the parliament to become more critical.'[58]

These sorts of views may be little more than wishful thinking, of course. While there is little doubt that a faltering economy would weaken Soeharto, there is no way of knowing whether the economy *will* falter. Soeharto has adjusted well to economic crises in the past. And even if economic growth did slow, it is still not clear whether a 'succession coalition' could capitalise on it to pressure Soeharto to move aside. Any such coalition would contain widely differing views on what economic policy should be. All would agree that some of the worst features of Soeharto's record—such as corruption—needed to be remedied, but after that opinions would begin to diverge. Economic 'technocrats' believe Indonesia's basic policies are on target and need only minor changes. 'Technologists' in the Habibie camp argue for a significant re-orienting of public expenditures toward capital-intensive industries. Some *pribumi*, or indigenous, business leaders want a government-sponsored affirmative action program to close the gap between *pribumis* and Indonesian-Chinese. Populist academics and politicians insist that more emphasis be placed on equity than growth. Abri doesn't appear to have an economic strategy of its own but is too conservative an institution to accept dramatic change. Whether all these groups would be able to overcome their political, social and economic differences to forge a common front on the succession issue is a question waiting for an answer.

The politics of change

As noted earlier in the chapter, the political debate in Indonesia has two basic components. One is the succession issue. The other is political change: should there be any, and what sorts of changes are needed? The debate is complicated because these two components are tightly interconnected: it may not be possible to arrange a smooth succession without first changing the prevailing political approach. And it also may not be possible to make any meaningful political changes while Soeharto remains in power. Before focusing on the question of political change, it is important to note that the many differing views of Indonesia's political future constitute still another obstacle to the formation of a 'succession coalition'.

Perhaps the most appropriate place to start a discussion of Indonesia's political future is the present. Soeharto describes the nature of his government as Pancasila democracy. He believes it to be 'democratic' but not in a Western liberal sense. Instead, Pancasila democracy is meant to be a communitarian form of government in which decisions are made by consensus in a nation conceived of as a family. Open confrontation is thought to be damaging to the welfare of the community, which is much more important than the interests of individual family members. Soeharto contends that Pancasila democracy, infused by the 'family spirit', is the form of government most closely congruent with Indonesia's cultural traditions.

In reality, Indonesia is far from the ideal of Pancasila democracy. Not only is it not democratic in the Western liberal sense, it is not democratic in the Pancasila democracy sense either. The imperative of 'consensus at all costs' leaves Indonesians with little scope to disagree with official policy. The dismantling of political parties, the manipulation of the People's Assembly, the controls placed on the press, and the enforced weakness of the legal system have done much more than empower the guardians of the community. They have created a government that is far more authoritarian—as that term is commonly understood—than democratic.

So what is to be done? Virtually the entire Indonesian elite, both in and outside the government, agrees that the political system can and should be improved. Consequently, there is a great deal of talk about democratisation, though it means different things to different people. When Soeharto speaks of 'democratisation', for example, he has in mind improvements to Pancasila democracy:

> We have all testified that Pancasila as the sole basic principle continues to
> provide room to move in our political life and democracy, enriches our
> ideas, stimulates our religious life, guarantees the right to express opinions
> and evolves the execution of human rights . . . Obviously, we are not

going to look back in developing a political life. Our experience has shown the failure of liberal democracy and Guided Democracy. On the contrary, we have to look ahead to enhance the application of democracy based on Pancasila that is in line with the progress we achieve in development in general.[59]

It is the rare Indonesian who would claim to know what Soeharto means exactly by 'enhanc[ing] the application of democracy based on Pancasila'. Although there has been some movement toward *keterbukaan* (openness) in recent years, with the press for example becoming more forthright than a decade ago, there has been little movement on the political front. The elections in 1992 and the People's Assembly of 1993 were no more indicative of a political renewal than were the same events in 1982 and 1983. Voting in Indonesia remains largely unrelated to the political process, and a significant part of the Indonesian elite believes Soeharto intends to keep it that way. This is why these same Indonesians believe that real political change is possible only after Soeharto is gone. The question, says Democracy Forum member Marsillam Simanjuntak, is 'whether the president is to be relied upon . . . to solve the problem of democratisation, or [is he] a problem, a complex one at that, to be solved first'?[60]

But what, exactly, is the 'problem of democratisation' in Indonesia? Most agree that it means a process of opening up the political system and making 'society' a less subservient partner to the 'state'. But there is deep disagreement over what the stages of this process are and how quickly they should be reached. The enhancement of Pancasila democracy, as Soeharto puts it, is at the most conservative end of the spectrum of change. But what is at the other end, and what is in between?

Guillermo O'Donnell and Philippe Schmitter described two general categories of change in their studies of authoritarian states in Latin America. They called the first liberalisation and the second democratisation. To put these concepts in the Indonesian context, liberalisation is seen by advocates for political change as being somewhere in the middle of the spectrum; democratisation, on the other hand, is at the end opposite from Pancasila democracy. O'Donnell and Schmitter define liberalisation as

[t]he process of redefining and extending rights . . . By liberalization we mean the process of making effective certain rights that protect both individuals and social groups from arbitrary or illegal acts committed by the state or third parties. On the level of individuals, these guarantees include the classical elements of the liberal tradition: habeas corpus; sanctity of private home and correspondence; the right to be defended in a fair trial according to pre-established laws; freedom of movement, speech, and petition; and so forth. On the level of groups, these rights cover such things as freedom from punishment for expressions of collective dissent

from government policy, freedom from censorship of the means of communication, and freedom to associate voluntarily with other citizens.[61]

A process of democratisation incorporates and expands upon these rights and freedoms. The guiding principle of democracy, they say,

> is that of *citizenship*. This involves both the *right* to be treated by fellow human beings as equal with respect to the making of collective choices and the *obligation* of those implementing such choices to be equally accountable and accessible to all members of the polity . . . What specific form democracy will take in a given country is a contingent matter, although . . . there is likely to exist a sort of 'procedural minimum' which contemporary actors would agree upon as necessary elements of political democracy. Secret balloting, universal adult suffrage, regular elections, partisan competition, associational recognition and access, and executive accountability all seem to be elements of such a consensus in the modern world.[62]

The interesting thing about Indonesia's Pancasila democracy is that it includes many of the features of democratisation—secret balloting, universal adult suffrage, regular elections—but relatively few of the individual and group freedoms on the liberalisation agenda. It has, in other words, the form of (Western) democracy but not the content. The result is a formalistic democracy that is not easy to distinguish from authoritarian rule.

It is a result, as well, which poses something of a dilemma for Indonesian advocates of political change. Within the elite there appears to be considerable agreement that Indonesia ought to provide more of the freedoms inherent in liberalisation. Recent moves toward 'openness' are one example. But 'openness' on the political front has sputtered precisely because of disagreement over where 'openness' is headed. At the risk of oversimplifying the issue, there are two broad views on this subject. One is in favour of adopting some features of 'liberalisation' but without altering the basic structures of Pancasila democracy. The group hewing to this view would like to see a freer, more dynamic society but is not necessarily in favour of making the executive more directly accountable to the people. This is the 'enhancing Pancasila democracy' group, for want of a better term. A second, more radical view is that liberalisation ought to be the first step to 'real' democratisation, to a form of democracy that 'doesn't need an adjective in front of it', in the words of the neo-modernist Islamic leader Abdurrahman Wahid.[63]

The dilemma is that the former may not be possible and the latter probably will not be allowed. So what can we say about the prospects for political change in Indonesia? Perhaps only this: since the 'enhancing Pancasila democracy' group is by far the stronger of the two, the most likely scenario is that it will set the agenda at least for the immediate future. But it would be a mistake to suppose that political considerations alone are responsible for the weak prospects for 'real' democratisation. Economic and social considerations play a role as well.

Society

A well functioning democracy requires a shared awareness of what democracy is about. It requires an ability to publicly debate—and disagree on—important matters of state without rendering the government of the day impotent; it presumes knowledge of what it means to win and lose on the political battlefield; and it assumes a common understanding of citizens' rights *and* responsibilities. These conditions do not apply in Indonesia. It is true that Indonesia has experienced 'Western-style' democracy, in which a free press and a free political system actively engaged in public debate. But the 1950s have faded from the collective memory. More than half the Indonesian population has experienced only the regulated public discourse of Pancasila democracy. Moreover, the enduring memory of the 1950s is of public divisiveness, a memory kept alive by tireless reminders by Soeharto's government. The philosophical underpinnings of the New Order are infused with fears of national disunity—fears which emanated from the 1950s and were further strengthened by the societal breakdown in 1965–66—and these fears have been bought by the public. The result is a society, and a relatively lowly educated one at that, which is ill-equipped for and deeply nervous about political change.

Economy

The structure of Indonesia's economy offers another clue into why democratisation remains an elusive goal. At first glance, it seems surprising that the steady growth of Indonesia's economy over the past two decades has not created more of a push for a political opening. But, in fact, economic success has tended to strengthen the authoritarianism of the New Order government.[64] Usually, when people reach a certain level of wealth, they generally desire a greater say in their political destiny. In Asia, a recent example of this phenomenon is the shift beginning in 1987 from authoritarianism to democracy in South Korea. Mass protests against military rule in Thailand in mid-1992 provide another example. This same dynamic in all likelihood will be at work in Indonesia, but probably not soon.

Demands for political pluralism, if propelled by economic factors, are related to the level of economic wealth, rather than the pace of economic growth.[65] Indonesia, despite its rapid growth in recent years, remains a poor country. It will take several decades for per capita income to rise to the level attained by South Koreans in 1987. But equally important, Indonesia's business community has decidedly mixed views on democratisation. It desires a dose of economic liberalisation but it is less sure that political democratisation is in its best interests.

The economic reform program begun in the mid to late 1980s shifted Indonesia away from a government-directed, import-substituting focus to a private sector-led, export-oriented approach. In the new economy, cost competitiveness is critical. Greedy monopolies, bureaucratic corruption and nepotism, all prominent features of Soeharto's rule, push costs up and make Indonesian products more difficult to sell overseas. Secondly, the private business sector needs a reliable, predictable and effective legal system. Banks need legal protection against bad debtors, investors need legal protection against fraudulent business practices, and entrepreneurs need legal protection against unfair competition.

The business community is anxious for reforms in all these areas but its demands for more economic 'transparency' are tempered by political considerations. The most powerful segment of Indonesia's private sector is composed of ethnic-Chinese businessmen. While economically dominant, the Chinese are politically weak, or at least they would be in a more representative political system. Well aware of the streak of anti-Chinese sentiment which runs through society, ethnic-Chinese businessmen have a stake in maintaining the current political system in which they can 'buy' protection via personal alliances with government officials or through financial contributions to the institutions charged with maintaining the status quo. Liem Sioe Liong's close relationship with Soeharto and the financial support given by the Chinese business community to Golkar are two obvious examples. For the immediate future, these considerations are likely to carry more weight with the ethnic Chinese than a desire for a more rational business climate. To many of them, the risks of a political opening outweigh the benefits of having a government 'which is accountable to the requirements of the market'.[66]

For the much more numerous *pribumi* businessmen, a different set of considerations apply but they too are nervous about weakening Indonesia's 'strong state'. They regard economic liberalism with trepidation and are not at all sure about political democratisation. For ease of argument, the *pribumi* business lobby can be broken down into two parts: small and big.

Small businessmen, merchants and petty traders feel themselves vulnerable in the face of an onslaught of big business—domestic and foreign—and see a big, powerful government as their only salvation. Their political views tend to populism, nationalism and often xenophobia.[67] Their political activities, as far as they go, have 'taken the form of a constant appeal for protection and favour from big government and criticism of the government for failing to deliver'.[68] They see their interests being best served by currying favour with Golkar and other government-controlled organisations. They suspect—and not without some justification—that a more democratic polity would be prone to manipulation by big business.

Similar views are held by larger *pribumi* businessmen. They, too, feel that economic liberalism is a mixed blessing. Many believe that they can only catch up with the leading Chinese businessmen if they have government help. While they want Soeharto to stop helping the Chinese, they don't want him to stop helping businessmen such as themselves. It might be thought that these businessmen would favour democratisation as a way to secure their economic interests but that does not seem to be the case. Most seem to believe they can better secure the 'political favours' they feel they need through alliances with Golkar and the bureaucracy than through a competitive political system. 'Eighty per cent of my business is government-related,' explained one leading *pribumi* businessman, Fadel Muhammad. 'I can't join the PDI [Indonesian Democratic Party]. I have to be realistic. I have to be with Golkar.'[69]

Naturally, within all these groups there are dissenting opinions. Many medium-sized *pribumi* businessmen, for example, who don't have strong enough contacts to benefit from political favouritism are more warmly disposed to economic liberalisation and democratisation. And some Chinese businessmen are so fed up with the corruption and bureaucratic politics of Soeharto's rule that they are ready to back any reform mandate, even democratisation. However, in general it remains true that the 'business lobby' tends to conservatism.

What about the middle class? Will it emerge as a powerful force for democratisation before the end of the century? Doubtful, is the short answer. The weight of evidence rests with the pessimists who believe the middle class by and large is still taking advantage of economic opportunities recently made available, and is not yet concerned with agitating for a relaxation of political controls. 'At this stage . . . they are thinking less about politics and more about making money,' says Jusuf Wanandi.[70] A healthy percentage of the middle class shares with the army a concern that national stability is not as secure as it seems, a view militating against political activism. Democratisation, for this group, could open the door to sectarian impulses which would threaten economic prosperity. As Robison puts it: 'The bulk of the middle class are prepared to acquiesce in New Order authoritarianism because they see little prospect for an orderly democratic state.'[71] For the time being, it would seem that the broad political objective of the middle class is for a reformed authoritarianism—incorporating some of the liberalisation agenda listed above—rather than democratisation.

The battle within Abri

Just as it holds the key to the success of any 'succession coalition', so too has Abri the power to set the agenda for political reform. Its power has been weakened by Soeharto but it remains the most powerful institution in Indonesia, a role it is almost certain to keep even after Soeharto has left the scene. Generalising about Abri's political views is a hazardous business, but a few clearly defined threads can be discerned.

Like other members of the inner power circle, top military officers are content to operate in a system in which their removal by political means is all but impossible. While parts of the military establishment want Soeharto to step down, Abri as an institution is not remotely interested in dismantling the strong state structure which he—with its help—has built up, nor with bringing the masses back into the political process. Abri remains acutely concerned with achieving the Holy Grail of national unity, political stability and economic development, and feels that all of these goals require the maintenance of a strong state. And finally, Abri believes that it must continue to play an integral role in the political process.

Within these broad outlines, however, there are many differences of opinion on what political development means—or ought to mean—in the Indonesian context. Some military leaders, while sympathetic to some items on the liberalisation agenda, are practically paralysed by the fear that any process leading to real democratisation could quickly unravel and spiral out of their control. Their major concern is that ethnic, racial and regional tensions could splinter Indonesia, just like similar tensions succeeded in breaking up Yugoslavia and the Soviet Union. They are not yet convinced that adherence to the ideology of Pancasila is universal and they sense that the sectarian impulses which they see themselves keeping in check still lie uncomfortably close to the surface. For them, the secret of success lies in limiting control of the political process to as small a group as possible.

Defending the need for restrictions on political rallies prior to parliamentary elections, former Coordinating Minister for Political Affairs and Security Sudomo said 'the problem is that any assembled mass can turn into a mob'.[72] General (ret.) Soemitro, in an interview in late 1991, expressed the same fear: 'It's very dangerous for us to allow public demonstrations. We could lose control.'[73] A related if usually unspoken concern for this group is the fear that in a more democratic Indonesia the military would have to answer for the many human rights abuses it has committed in the name of national unity, most especially in trouble spots like East Timor and Aceh.

Other influential military figures, however, are open to some movement on both the liberalisation and democratisation agendas, provided Abri's *dwifungsi*, or dual function, doctrine remains in force. One example is former Home Affairs Minister Major General (ret.) Rudini who, while he was still in office, publicly advocated a shift away from the military's traditional 'security approach' and praised the virtues of democracy. 'We cannot talk about a developed and honourable Indonesia in the eyes of the world community,' he said, 'without promoting democracy and democratisation.'[74] Hasnan Habib, the former ambassador to Washington, offered the same view when considering the question of *dwifungsi*'s elimination in a 1992 speech:

> The answer is a definite 'never'. *Dwifungsi* is here to stay. [But] what will definitely change is the implementation of *dwifungsi*. That is to say, in Indonesia's future political development, Abri will gradually shift its role from emphasising the 'security cum stability' approach to the 'prosperity cum stability' approach . . . Pancasila is not supposed to be 'from, by, and for' the Armed Forces; nor is it 'from and by Abri for' the nation. It must be 'from, by, and for' the people.[75]

Habib argued that *dwifungsi* could only be considered successful if the political system became more meritocratic, a process which implies more political influence for civilians.[76] The flip side of this argument is that Abri must change its approach to wielding political power. General (ret.) Abdul Haris Nasution, the man who is credited with authoring the original dual-function doctrine in 1957—then called the 'Middle Way'—has been throughout the New Order one of the most strident critics of how *dwifungsi* has evolved. Nasution wanted the military to have political influence but not through intervention in day-to-day politics. He saw the military as a kind of political referee which could step in to settle disputes amongst political parties but one which would stay above the fray of party politics. The whole point, in his view, of giving Abri a reserved allocation of seats in the parliament was to obviate the need for Abri to engage in party politics. Needless to say, Abri's extensive involvement in, and overt support for, Golkar is a frequent target of criticism from Nasution and like-minded retired generals. 'Abri should become a watchdog only,' said Lieutenant General (ret.) Ali Sadikin, a leader of the dissident Group of Fifty. 'It should not play an active political role. The way it stands now, it would be better to change Abri's name to *Angkatan Bersenjata Golkar* (Armed Forces of Golkar).'[77]

More generally, the starting point for Abri political 'softliners' is that some sort of political opening is inevitable and that it is better to be part of the process in order to retain some control over it. Moreover, they argue that it is better for the government to give ground during a period of relative economic success—such as the present—since this would make it easier for Abri to claim a meaningful political role even in a more open political system. (Partly, it must be added, the reformers' optimism on this point is grounded in their belief that Abri remains an extremely popular institution. Rudini, for example, argued that if Abri were allowed to run as an independent political party, it would win 90 per cent of the votes.[78]) The reformers' fear is that if they fail to 'reform' Pancasila democracy, outside pressures will continue to build up until more radical and uncertain change—such as real democratisation—could become unavoidable.[79]

Whose views will prevail in the coming years is impossible to say. The views of Abri hardliners and softliners both appear to have substantial support. What can be identified with slightly more confidence are a number of obstacles that Abri reformers will have to overcome if their hope for a more 'dynamic' political process is to become a reality.

The viability of the halfway approach

The first obstacle, to repeat the point made above, is that what Abri reformers want to do may not be possible. Giving ground on the liberalisation agenda may only increase, not deflate, the pressures for democratisation. 'Once some individual and collective rights are granted,' O'Donnell and Schmitter acknowledge, 'it becomes increasingly difficult to justify withholding others . . . [A]s liberalisation advances so does the strength of demands for democratisation.'[80] Darusman makes the same point: 'Can you go halfway democratic?' he asks. 'That's the way authoritarian governments want to do it but it doesn't work.'[81]

The conservative opposition

At least for the immediate future, the most serious opposition facing Abri reformers is that coming from Abri hardliners, a group in which Soeharto should be included. For the reasons noted above, the conservative wing in Abri favours a very cautious approach to political change. Habib, for example, contended that the 'openness' campaign in Indonesia made such a fitful start in the early 1990s because Soeharto, uninterested in real change, ordered Abri to slow down the process. 'There are certainly some in Abri,' he said, referring to the softliners, 'who feel that if Abri was more independent from Soeharto then Indonesia would be more democratic.'[82] The succession issue, of course, is itself a major obstacle to political change. If the succession process gets 'messy', as one cabinet official put it, 'army hardliners will move in quickly and install themselves'.[83]

One of the key battlegrounds will be Golkar. If power is to travel from the 'state' to 'society', its likely first stop is Golkar, the New Order's grand corporatist creation. At present, Indonesia has the characteristics of a one-party state, with Golkar acting—albeit inefficiently—the part of a Leninist-type party whose main purpose is to relate the policies of an all-powerful government to a mostly powerless civil society. The reformist vision is to turn Golkar into a different kind of political organisation, one which, while continuing to be an elite-centred party acting in a 'strong state' system, will provide for a broader participatory role for the military–civilian elite in national policymaking. Abri and moderate civilian reformers argue that the transformation of Golkar along these lines offers the best hope for preserving Indonesia's 'strong state' in the post-Soeharto era.

Sarwono Kusumaatmadja, the environment minister and a former Golkar secretary-general, warns that Golkar is in danger of being left behind by emerging social forces. Business lobbies, urban professionals and middle-class organisations are all looking for a political vehicle to protect their interests, he says, and it is up to Golkar to make itself relevant to these constituencies. He argues that Golkar's mission is to make the 'gradual shift from the politics of ideology—which characterised our older political system—to the politics of interests'. He says the politics of ideology, which aimed at ensuring unanimous acceptance of Pancasila, has accomplished its purpose and must now make way for a more dynamic, if more rambunctious, political environment. Golkar's task, then, is to reshape its amorphous collection of 'functional groups' into a true political party.[84]

While Abri reformers subscribe to the basic thrust of this argument, they recognise that any tinkering with Golkar could have unintended negative consequences for Abri as an institution. Herein lies one of the many dilemmas facing Abri in the mid-1990s, as well as a fine illustration of how difficult it is to disengage the succession issue from the question of political change. As mentioned earlier, Abri is determined to retain a significant political role in Indonesia for the indefinite future. To do that, it needs to continue justifying the need for its dual function doctrine, and that in turn can best be accomplished by ensuring that Golkar remains the pre-eminent political party and, secondly, that Abri remains very much within the 'big Golkar family'. But by lending its efforts to keep Golkar strong, Abri also contributes to keeping intact Soeharto's power base and to making it harder for a 'succession coalition' to nudge Soeharto from office.

The liberal opposition

Another obstacle facing Abri reformers are the critics outside the government who demand change at a faster rate than Abri as an institution is prepared to tolerate. The more radical of these critics tend to reinforce in Abri hardliners the belief that Indonesia is not yet ready for change. Generally speaking, the civilian critics reject the notion that authoritarianism is 'in keeping' with Indonesia's cultural traditions. They argue that Abri—including its reformist members—has considerably underestimated the pressures for change and favours therefore an overly tame reform agenda. 'The outburst of emotion in 1965 came about because pressures had been bottled up for so long,' said Darusman, the former Golkar legislator ousted from parliament by Soeharto in 1992. 'We're heading that same way now.' Darusman and other civilian reformers contend that Soeharto doesn't appreciate the strength of society's desire for change partly because he has surrounded himself with sycophants and yes-men and consequently has lost touch with the people, and partly because authoritarian rulers in general, say O'Donnell and Schmitter, 'tend to interpret . . . [a] lack of perceivable opposition as evidence of "social peace" among previously conflicting classes and of "tacit consensus" for their policies'.[85]

Similar to their concerns about joining with Abri in a 'succession coalition', some civilian reformers are deeply sceptical of its stated commitment to gradual democratisation. Abri is seen by this group as being fundamentally anti-democratic and its sympathy for some political liberalisation a kind of trick intended both to put pressure on Soeharto and to let off the steam of elite dissatisfaction without altering the basic structures of power. 'This is our dilemma,' said legal activist Adnan Buyung Nasution. 'We need an army strong enough to get rid of Soeharto but an army that strong is incompatible with democracy.'[86] Arief Budiman, who shares this view, identifies two types of pseudo-democracies that are often mistakenly confused for real, or as he says structural, democracy:

> The first is what I would call *loan democracy*. This democracy exists when the state is very strong so it can afford to be criticised. A sort of democratic space then emerges in which people can express their opinions freely. However, when the state thinks the criticism has gone too far, it will simply take back the democracy that it has only lent. The people have no power to resist. There is, second, *limited democracy*. This democracy exists only when there is a conflict among the state elites . . . People can criticise one faction of the 'powers that be' and be protected by the opposite faction . . . However, when the conflict within the elite is over, this democratic space will probably disappear also.[87]

Budiman describes Pancasila democracy as a form of loan democracy and the brief campaign of *keterbukaan*, or openness, as a period of limited democracy. As for real democracy, that 'is still far away'.[88]

Democracy Forum member Simanjuntak rejects the notion that gradual, controlled change is possible inside an authoritarian regime. To believe in it, he says, is 'to doggedly defy the logic of change, or to simply mistake an unending status quo [for a] slow journey through a long, winding road to democracy'. To believe that recent 'symptoms of openness' represent the beginnings of substantive change, he continues, the gradualists are making two basic assumptions.

> First, that political powerholders have freed themselves from the ruling idea that the unity of the plural society is precarious and that the national

integrity is fragile and must be constantly protected by means of coercion. Secondly, we are accepting that there is a sort of altruism on the part of the power holder, i.e. the military, such that it is prepared to relinquish voluntarily its position through a sustained gradual release of its once strict control.

Simanjuntak adds, convincingly, that there is little evidence to suggest that either of these assumptions is correct. Openness, he concludes, such as it is, has not come about because of 'real democratisation, but more as a gradual process of [Abri] employing subtler . . . means of control and appeasement'.[89]

Other civilian reformers zero in on Abri's *dwifungsi* doctrine and say this is where real change must begin. In mid-1992, a few politicians and political scientists reopened the old question of why the 500 000-strong military, 0.3 per cent of the population, should be handed twenty per cent of the parliamentary seats. Said United Development Party delegate Sri Bintang Pamungkas at the time: 'Abri is an obstacle to democracy and Abri's domination of the political system has to be stopped. Many countries in Latin America have already realised this.'[90] (Soeharto quickly put this argument to rest by warning that Abri 'may take up arms' if it is excluded from parliamentary representation.[91]) Pamungkas, undeterred, said in 1993: 'Look at what has happened or is happening in Russia, South Korea and Thailand. There is a message there for Abri and we have to deliver it. *Dwifungsi* has to be scaled down.'[92] Lawyer Buyung Nasution saw the civilian reformers' task in essentially the same terms: 'We have to disabuse the military of the notion that they can follow the Singapore model and fend off democracy indefinitely.'[93]

Abri hardliners, needless to say, react poorly to these kinds of comments. In early 1994, the new Coordinating Minister of Political Affairs and Security, Soesilo Soedarman, darkly warned that 'intellectuals penetrated by liberal democracy' posed a serious threat to national unity. At about the same time, Armed Forces Commander General Feisal Tandjung cautioned agents of the national security agency that pro-democracy advocates were trying to 'undermine and destroy the credibility and position of the government . . . [Their] acts are designed to change the system, mechanism and structures of Pancasila Democracy.'[94]

The international arena

The final piece of the puzzle is the effect on Indonesia of events in the world outside its borders. The international arena impinges on Indonesia in two ways; by example and by direct pressure. It is possible to identify 'positive' and 'negative' aspects of each type as they relate to Indonesia's democratisation process; it is impossible to predict, however, which of these various aspects will dominate in the years ahead.

In terms of 'positive examples', the fall of communist regimes in Eastern Europe and the former Soviet Union has given the democratic governments of the West an aura of success. While there are some important differences between the totalitarian regimes of the former communist bloc and authoritarian governments like Soeharto's, the 'triumph' of Western democracies in the Cold War struggle tends to chip away at claims that strong nations need non-democratic governance. Second, information about life in the world abroad is flooding into Indonesia faster and more thoroughly than ever before, thanks to advances in communications technology and Indonesia's ever-expanding interdependence with the global marketplace. This is not to suggest that Indonesia's dominant cultural traits—marked by a deference to authority, tolerance and a premium on harmony—are under siege. Rather, it is to make the point that Indonesians, especially those living in urban areas, are vastly more aware of the outside world than they were ten or even five years ago. To be sure, much of what they see taking place elsewhere they would just as soon do without. Nevertheless, a familiarity with other societies does give Indonesians the knowledge that there are alternatives, some successful, some less so, to their current form of government.

In the 'negative example' category, many in Abri share the view of Singapore's former prime minister, Lee Kuan Yew, that Western-style democracy is 'inimical' to economic development. The 'Asian' view of liberal democracies, explained Tommy Koh, the respected former Singapore ambassador to the United Nations, is that they

> often lead to contention and political instability. And it is very difficult in a democracy to persuade the electorate to accept wise polices that may be painful in the short-term. There is often no industrial peace because management and unions are locked in a class conflict.[95]

State Secretary Murdiono, a retired major general, articulated Abri's deepest fears of liberal democracy in an interview in 1991. 'Shall we go the way of Pakistan, India and the Philippines, the so-called democracies in the region?' he asked. 'No, because multiparty democracy will not solve the real problems that we face like creating jobs or building schools. So, is it for the sake of democracy that we will ruin this country?'[96]

International pressure also works two ways. One consequence of the ending of the Cold War is that it has raised the profile of democracy advocates in the West. The foreign policies of leading Western nations are becoming increasingly concerned with the promotion of democratisation and respect for human rights around the world. The prominence, if perhaps not yet the influence, of human rights monitoring organisations is rising. Certainly some in the Indonesian civilian elite believe pressures from abroad can help further the process of democratisation in Indonesia, although they rarely make this point in public.

The more common view is that any kind of foreign pressure constitutes interference in Indonesia's affairs. Ardently nationalist, Indonesian leaders are opposed adamantly to any attempts to link economic relations with human rights or political development. International pressure clearly has forced changes in some aspects of domestic policy—notably in the area of labour rights—but it is highly improbable that the army will be swayed by foreign pressure alone to relinquish its hold on the political process. Moreover, international pressure may actually inhibit moves toward a political opening by creating a siege mentality within Abri. Obsessed with its own uniqueness, Abri is convinced that its Western critics are biased, simplistic and either unable or unwilling to understand the challenges it faces in developing a young nation or the historical experiences which gave rise to the concept of *dwifungsi*. In a typically defensive remark, Benny Murdani complained to a gathering of Abri leaders in October 1992 that the 'West and its one-sided media keeps itself busy gossiping about Abri's social-political activities'.[97]

Yuwono Sudarsono, the University of Indonesia political scientist, puts the case against, and implications of, foreign pressure in more general terms:

> Today's more competitive and intense international political, economic and security system works to the distinct disadvantage of Asian nations. In this era of global production, global marketing and global sourcing, the nations of Asia not only have to compete for market access, trade expansion and foreign investment. They are at the same time under constant pressure from powerful unions and lobbies in the parliaments of the developed world [for] a wide range of sins ranging from undemocratic government, environmental degradation, human rights violations, unfair trade practices, dumping, market restrictions, non-adherence to intellectual property rights and assorted other issues . . . As with other nations of Asia, we do not have the luxury accorded to the nations of the North in forming the bed in which the seeds of democratic forms of government and political development could flourish. Indeed, precisely because the international environment is more intense there is sometimes more need to stress deliberate and slower development of forms of political modernisation.[98]

An uncertain future

One final point needs to be made about the differences of opinion within the Indonesian elite regarding both the need for political change and the nature of that change: it is quite possible that the best case that can be made for democratisation in Indonesia is that it will happen in spite of, rather than because of, what the Indonesian elite wants.

The period leading up to Soeharto's eventual departure has the potential to be a profoundly uncertain time. A dizzying array of elite groups will be jockeying for influence and trying to reform and update existing mechanisms for protecting their interests. The military will be positioning itself to regain the political high ground, manoeuvring to get Soeharto to step aside gracefully, and trying to keep the whole process as smooth as possible. Soeharto has his own set of needs. He wants to hand power to a successor willing and able to preserve his design for Pancasila democracy, his own personal image for posterity, and the more immediate interests of his children. Chinese and *pribumi* businessmen need to make accommodations with whoever the future national leaders will be. Islamic groups will be looking to support military officers sympathetic to their cause. Civilian politicians will attempt to secure in the uncertainty of the transition period a higher profile for the parliament, a more equitable sharing of power with the military, and some safeguards against the possibility of another 30-year president. And so on down the line.

Each of these groups will have to assess its own leverage and its ability to get what it wants. Alliances will be sought and may be formed. Inevitably, there will be some 'repoliticisation' of Indonesian society, no matter how hard the military tries to keep this to a minimum. And this melange of informal politicking will undoubtedly put the cohesion of the elite under strain. The various components of the elite have different interests and will have to compete to protect them. And it is these possible cracks in the elite which present, perhaps, the most optimistic case for real political change in Indonesia.[99]

Already, in fact, elite divisions are making themselves felt. Abri's quiet support for the Indonesian Democratic Party in 1987 and 1992 and for 'openness' in the years in between, and Soeharto's wooing of support from Muslim groups are both examples of this trend. The possibility that this 'political broadening' will extend still further is certainly one plausible scenario. The fact that democratisation per se is not the objective of either Soeharto or Abri does not guarantee that democratisation will not occur. Events can have unintended consequences.

Indonesia is approaching a crucial moment in its history. There have been only a few such moments since independence was declared a half-century ago. The struggle to remove the Dutch was one such moment, of course, as was the shift from parliamentary democracy to Sukarno's Guided Democracy in 1959 and also the transition to Soeharto's New Order seven years later. In each of these last two shifts, Indonesia attempted in effect to reinvent itself. In each case, the future represented a sharp, discrete break from the past. Both were draining and even painful episodes for a young nation. Indonesians of all political ideologies would like the next transitional moment to be smoother.

Whether this will happen is largely up to Soeharto. Will he leave office before being pushed? Will he act to reduce the unpredictability of his own succession? There are few signs which would suggest a positive answer to either of these questions, unfortunately, and that augurs poorly for a smooth transition.

Soeharto has undeniably achieved a great deal during his rule. And in assessing the present challenges for Indonesia, it makes little sense to downplay his achievements. The government he has headed has forged a stronger, more prosperous nation. It has fostered a sense of nationhood, raised living standards and improved the welfare of its subjects. There have been flaws and these too should not be overlooked. But the point is that Soeharto's record contains many important accomplishments, and Indonesians, by and large, are grateful for them.

But the history of Soeharto's rule cannot yet be written. He has at least one more major task to accomplish: to remove himself from power without making Indonesia reinvent itself yet again and without putting the nation through all the turmoil and dislocation this would involve. Realising this task begins with the recognition that different times require different rulers. It begins, also, with the understanding that the economic development and societal changes that he has overseen have themselves given rise to new demands, desires and needs: a demand for more political participation, a desire for a more accountable government and a need for a more rational, more transparent and less personal system of government decision-making. Herein lies the *perjuangan*, or struggle, of the 1990s.

If Soeharto fails the succession challenge, he fails also in the broader and more important challenge of political development; the latter, simply, has fallen hostage to the former. And while Soeharto ponders his succession options, the nation waits. Indonesia's problem, however, is that it cannot afford to wait much longer. A once-a-generation transition takes planning. And planning, for all the reasons outlined in this chapter, remains at a very early stage. Unless Soeharto begins to show some willingness to permit the planning process to proceed, history books may well write of him that the worst aspect of his rule was the way in which he left it.

11
The fall of Soeharto

We are all victims of Soeharto. He made us fight each other.

Salim Said[1]

Dictators always concede when it's too late.

Sarwono Kusumaatmadja[2]

The end of an era

Shortly before midnight on 20 May 1998, Indonesia's State Secretary Saadilah Mursjid stood for a moment outside the office door of President Soeharto. Inside, the besieged president was scrambling to contain the damage to his political standing. Seemingly invincible only weeks before, Soeharto's hold on power had unravelled with astonishing speed. Eight days before, soldiers had shot dead four students at a Jakarta university, precipitating three days of the worst rioting ever seen in the Indonesian capital.

The economy, which for decades had underpinned Soeharto's authoritarian rule, lay in shambles. The military, riven by dissent within its top leadership, was growing nervous about its ability to quell further unrest. Foreigners and many members of the traumatised ethnic-Chinese community were fleeing Indonesia as fast as they could. On the streets, student demonstrators were calling for Soeharto's resignation in increasingly strident tones.

Two days earlier, Soeharto had made one last bid to retain control of his fate. Desperate to find a face-saving exit, he promised to disband the crony-laden cabinet he had assembled just two months earlier and to form a new one. Soeharto also promised to set up a special reform committee

308

and pledged to hold new elections later in the year, in which, he said, he would not run.

But his power had vanished so suddenly and so completely that these concessions fell on deaf ears. As he soon discovered, even the men and women he had protected, cultivated and showered with largesse wanted nothing to do with him. Mursjid had just learned that Ginanjar Kartasasmita and 13 other cabinet members belonging to the ruling Golkar Party refused to join the new cabinet. The rejection by Ginanjar, the senior economics minister and one of the president's most loyal servants, made the task of forming a credible cabinet virtually impossible.

Mursjid knew that Soeharto's choices were now limited to either resigning or being further humiliated by others rejecting invitations to join a new cabinet. Still, there was the matter of bringing this news to Soeharto. Before entering Soeharto's office, Mursjid, a pious, soft-spoken man, said a quick prayer to Allah asking for strength. Once inside, Soeharto asked him, 'Who is in the cabinet?'. Mursjid paused, then replied, 'It's just you and me'. After another long pause, Soeharto sighed. Finally he said, 'Well, that's it then'. The game was over.[3]

The next morning, in a brief ceremony in the presidential palace, Soeharto abruptly announced his resignation and walked out of the room. A flustered B. J. Habibie, the diminutive vice-president who had been on the job for all of 10 weeks, nervously made his first speech as Indonesia's third president. He pledged to move ahead with political reforms and pleaded for support from the public. General Wiranto, the armed forces commander, then stepped up to the microphone to say the military was determined to protect both Soeharto and Habibie.

Soeharto and his 32-year-old New Order regime had come to an end at last. Asia's longest-serving leader had reached the end of the road— unpopular, unloved and unrepentant. His departure carried some uncanny similarities to his own assumption of power from his predecessor Sukarno in 1966: a divided military, political chaos, an economy in dire straits, and a terrified community of ethnic-Chinese. And, just as Soeharto first took office pledging a complete break with the past, so did Habibie's assumption of power promise wholesale changes to Indonesia's political climate. Transparency, accountability and the rule of law were in; corruption, collusion and nepotism were out. Or so the slogans said.

Some progress has been made. Restrictive rules on the media, labour unions and political gatherings have been dropped. Political prisoners have been freed and political parties have mushroomed in the fertile soil of Indonesia's nascent democracy. New laws providing greater checks and balances on the powerful executive branch are emerging, and an electoral process now underway could produce by the end of 1999 a president with a legitimate, democratically produced mandate to rule. But the reality is that Indonesia's departure from Soeharto's authoritarianism is likely to be more gradual and halting than many pro-democracy advocates expect and yearn for. Democracy requires more than elections and political parties. It requires its own building blocks, its own software. Democracy is an attitude as much as a political system, and it will be neither quick nor easy for Indonesians to shuck off the authoritarian attitudes formed in the past four decades. There are many battles to be fought and many questions still to be answered before Indonesia will succeed in completing its democratic transition.

It is worth recalling Indonesia's one truly democratic election, which took place in 1955. How much resemblance the elections scheduled for 1999 will have to 1955 is a hotly debated issue, and one to which I return in chapter 12. For now it is enough to remember that, far from producing an effective government with majority support, the 1955 elections polarised existing differences within Indonesian society—differences which almost succeeded in breaking the country apart.

The task facing Indonesia is enormous. The challenge of shifting political gears once the firmly entrenched Soeharto had left the scene was going to be a daunting one, even in a healthy economic setting. Providing for his own succession on his own terms would have been a major contribution by Soeharto to Indonesia's much-needed political renewal, a contribution he was unwilling to make. Indonesians are left with the thankless task of overhauling Soeharto's sclerotic, outdated system of governance with scant preparation, little time and a vast array of discredited characters and institutions. Confronting this challenge in a climate of soaring poverty and declining national income raises the degree of difficulty exponentially.

As earlier chapters in this book discuss, the most fundamental questions about Indonesia's political identity were not resolved during Soeharto's tight-fisted rule—merely delayed. What political role will Islam play? How will the ethnic-Chinese and other minorities fare in a democratic Indonesia? What sorts of new relationships will be forged between Java and the outer islands? Will economic policy be inward- or outward-looking? How and on whose terms will the military learn to cede power to civilian forces? For these and many other questions, Indonesia remains a nation in waiting.

THE NEW ORDER GROWS OLD

Why did Soeharto leave power the way he did? The economic crisis that began in the middle of 1997 was the trigger, but only that. Soeharto had overcome economic shocks before, and had emerged stronger as a result. What brought Soeharto down ultimately was the weakness of the political system he created, not the economy. Right until the end, Soeharto's hold on power appeared secure. But in truth his rule had grown brittle, his legitimacy eroded. To understand how Soeharto found himself all alone on the evening of 20 May 1998 and to appreciate the scope of the political reconstruction that lies ahead, we need to go back to the early 1990s, about where chapter 10 leaves off.

The story of the hollowing-out of Soeharto's authority is complex. External factors played a role, such as the horrendous drought of 1997. But for the most part Soeharto's humiliating downfall was self-engineered. It came about after a string of poorly thought-out decisions as well as acts of omission, such as his stubborn refusal to plan his own succession. Like his predecessor, Soeharto was undone in the end by hubris, arrogance and a grossly inflated view of his own popularity.

We cannot know, even in hindsight, which of Soeharto's decisions and policies undermined his position most. Later I discuss Soeharto's response to the economic crisis that emerged in 1997 and the chaotic swirl of events leading up to his resignation. But first I will review developments in five key areas—the economy, politics, foreign policy, the Islamic community, and the military—in the final few years of Soeharto's rule. I leave it to historians to rank them in order of significance to Soeharto's demise.

The economy: troubles under the surface

According to many macroeconomic indicators, Indonesia's economy continued to perform well during the period 1993–96. Growth averaged 7.5 per cent a year, and the number of Indonesians living under the poverty line steadily declined. Inflation was kept in check, averaging just under 9 per cent annually. Foreign investors remained bullish on Indonesia's prospects: approved foreign investment averaged more than US$25 billion annually over the period. A series of reform packages lowered tariffs, removed non-tariff barriers and opened up new areas for foreign investment. A World Bank report published a month before the Asian crisis began in July 1997 giddily noted that if Indonesia could sustain an annual growth rate of 7.5 per cent until 2005, GDP per capita would more than double, to over US$2300, turning Indonesia into one of the world's 20 largest economies.[4]

But behind the macroeconomic success lay a number of worrisome trends. Protectionist measures remained widespread: half of Indonesia's non-oil exports, nearly 2000 products, still faced some kind of export restriction by 1996. Scores of new banks opened, far outpacing the capacity of regulatory authorities to monitor them. The high costs resulting from corruption and market-distorting measures began to affect the competitiveness of some key non-oil exports. The growth rate of textile exports, for example, declined from 6 per cent in 1993 to a negative 7.2 per cent in 1996. A sizeable portion of the new foreign investment went into unprofitable areas such as real estate, or into projects that depended on continued import protection. Private sector debt more than tripled from US$23 billion in 1992 to almost US$80 billion in 1997, most of it unhedged.

As more of Indonesia's workforce moved into the urban-based manu-facturing sector, labour unrest soared. In 1994 about 150 000 workers went on strike, compared with just 1000 five years earlier. Although official unemployment rates remained low, the World Bank in 1996 estimated that more than a third of the 90-million strong labour force was working less than 35 hours per week.[5] Unemployment trends were particularly alarming for the young: Indonesians between the ages of 15 and 24 accounted for just 20 per cent of the workforce in the mid-1990s, but 70 per cent of the unemployed.

In comments that would prove disturbingly prescient, Yuwono Sudarsono, then deputy governor of the National Defence Institute, described the urban poor in 1996 as

> the single most important factor of future Indonesian politics. It's the urban poor who are the most politicised, the most deprived and therefore the most volatile, and it's not difficult to incite them to violence. It happened in 1974, it happened in 1996 and you may not have to wait another twenty years for it to happen again.

Indeed, the wait would be less than two years.[6]

The government made some minor concessions to rising labour demands, such as introducing programs for accident and health insurance and mandating an annual bonus equal to one month's salary. But the government spent most of its energy trying to repress independent labour unions and their leaders. Mochtar Pakpahan, who headed the largest independent union, was arrested in 1994, convicted of inciting riots in Medan and sentenced to four years in jail. A year later, the Supreme Court set Pakpahan free, saying there was no evidence tying him to the riots. In 1996 the Supreme Court, apparently on Soeharto's orders, decided to hear the case again. In a verdict that surprised no-one, the court found Pakpahan guilty and sent him back to jail.

The rise and fall of the technocrats

As noted in chapter 4, Soeharto turned to his economic technocrats to wrest Indonesia from an economic slump in the mid-1980s. But by the mid-1990s they had become largely marginalised, although their reduced influence was not immediately apparent. Their success in restoring eco-nomic growth proved to be their undoing, as Soeharto felt increasingly free to disregard their policy prescriptions. Instead, in the colourful phrase of former cabinet minister Sarwono Kusumaatmadja, Soeharto sought advice from 'tinkerers, technicians, and other crazy characters'.[7]

The technocrats' declining clout was apparent even before 1993 (as discussed in chapter 4). But it accelerated after 1993 for a number of reasons. One was the rising political influence of Research and Technology Minister B. J. Habibie, who placed several figures close to him in Soeharto's 1993–98 cabinet. Some became major embarrassments, confirming for many Indonesians that Habibie is a poor judge of character. One of his loyalists, Wardiman Djojonegoro, was considered a disastrous minister of education. Another, Haryanto Danutirto, became embroiled in a major corruption scandal at the ministry of transportation.

Among Habibie's early endeavours in the 1993–98 term was the highly controversial purchase of 39 ships from the former East German navy. What began as a US$12.7 million deal to buy the ageing ships became, in typical Habibie fashion, a gigantic US$1.1 billion public works package which included upgrading 15 shipyards, constructing a new deepwater port in Sumatra and acquiring a pair of oil tankers. The underlying purpose of the deal appeared to be attracting some much-needed business for PT PAL, the state-owned shipbuilding facility in Surabaya under Habibie's control.[8] Habibie brought the plan directly to Soeharto for his approval, making an end run around the technocrats and the navy, both of which adamantly opposed the purchase. Although the plan was later watered down, Habibie let it be known that he would not be shy in using his clout with Soeharto. Habibie's controversial aircraft manufacturing plant, IPTN, also benefited from Soeharto's largesse. In 1994 Soeharto authorised a US$190 million 'loan' to IPTN from a fund set up to finance reforestation efforts.[9]

Habibie was not the only challenge the technocrats faced in making economic policy. Competition heated up between conglomerates owned by indigenous (or *pribumi*) businessmen and their ethnic-Chinese counterparts, drawing in their respective supporters in the cabinet and elsewhere in the government. The prizes included shares of privatised contracts, no-questions-asked loans from state-owned banks, and government-issued contracts for major infrastructure projects.

An estimated three-quarters of the foreign investors who set up joint ventures in Indonesia by the mid-1990s had chosen an ethnic-Chinese-owned firm as a local partner.[10] This flood of foreign capital solidified the dominant economic position of the ethnic-Chinese in key industries, and exacerbated the resentment felt by many non-Chinese. Passions were further inflamed in 1994 when an ethnic-Chinese businessman named Eddy Tansil was caught stealing hundreds of millions of dollars from the state-owned bank, Bapindo.[11]

Nepotism and the New Order

But the biggest challenge to economic policy coherence came not from Habibie or the dominance of the ethnic-Chinese, but from the children and cronies of President Soeharto. Along with the reforming communist states of China and Vietnam, Indonesia was routinely rated throughout the 1990s as one of the most corrupt nations in Asia.[12] All six of Soeharto's children stepped up their rapacious assets grab in the mid-1990s, led by eldest daughter Siti Hardijanti 'Tutut' Rukmana, middle son Bambang Trihatmodjo and youngest son Hutomo 'Tommy' Mandala Putra. The children, joined by business cronies such as Mohamad 'Bob' Hasan, competed furiously for Soeharto's favour. Scarcely a single infrastructure project was awarded without the participation of one Soeharto relative or another. In a typical case, one of the children, acting as local agent, would receive, for free, a 10–15 per cent equity stake in contracts to build water-treatment facilities, toll roads, power stations, petrochemical plants and the like. By the middle of the decade the children had stakes in many hundreds of companies.[13]

In 1996 several of the children joined an unusually public and unseemly scramble to get a piece of a promising gold mine in Kalimantan. Tutut Rukmana, eldest son Sigit Haryoyudanto and Bob Hasan all insinuated themselves into the Busang gold mine deal before it was revealed to be a giant hoax in 1997.[14] Also in 1996, Tommy Soeharto received tax breaks and state bank loans to build a national car, despite having no experience in the automobile industry. The move undercut the country's leading automobile manufacturer, Astra, infuriated foreign investors, and generated a series of complaints to the World Trade Organisation.[15]

Soeharto's grandson, Ari, became the first second-generation Soeharto to get in on the game. In 1995 he acquired a monopoly on collecting a provincial tax of Rp. 200 on each bottle of beer sold in Bali. In good monopoly fashion, he tacked on a Rp. 400 per bottle fee on top of the tax. Only when the distributors of domestic beer halted deliveries of beer to Bali, raising howls of protest from tourism officials, was the monopoly quietly rescinded.[16]

The expanding privatisation program offered new opportunities to the children, especially in telecommunications, power generation and other infrastructure-related fields. In many cases, privatisation of state companies was little more than a transfer of assets to Indonesia's political elite, with only a modest increase in competition. In 1996 the World Bank, which spectacularly misunderstood the ravaging effect of corruption on Indonesia's economy, heaped praise on Indonesia's attempts to bring new private players into the telecommunications sector. Sales of new licences, it said, were carried out with 'full transparency and strict adherence to clearly defined rules'.[17]

Analysts with a better feel for developments on the ground quickly disagreed. The Hong Kong-based Political and Economic Risk Consultancy, which regularly surveys business leaders across the region, said that as far as [Indonesia's] telecommunications industry is concerned, the presidential family is into almost everything where there is good money to be made, and state-run Telkom takes the cream off just about everything else. The first family or their business partners are associated either directly or indirectly with every cellular telephone operator in the country.[18]

In addition to raising costs, eroding Soeharto's political legitimacy and generating massive popular resentment, the children's business activities greatly undermined bureaucratic discipline. Many ministers, governors and lesser officials simply replicated on a smaller scale what Soeharto was doing on a national scale. 'Soeharto encourages ministers' families to get into business. It's like a mafia boss who protects himself by making everyone around him corrupt as well', said Laksamana Sukardi, a top aide to Megawati Sukarnoputri.[19]

Ministers and other government officials who rebuffed the advances of the First Family often found themselves out of a job. After the partial privatisation of telecommunications provider Indosat in 1995, several finance ministry officials were shunted off to lesser jobs. Their mistake, as it turned out, was not allocating enough of the attractively priced shares to First Family members. In the same year, the president of the state-owned Merpati Airlines was sacked by Habibie ally and transportation minister Haryanto Danutirto. Ridwan Fatarudin's 'crime' was refusing to lease aircraft at well above market rates from a leasing firm owned by Tommy Soeharto.[20]

How was it possible for the disease of corruption to spread so rapidly throughout Indonesian society? The lack of a free press or other means of accountability certainly helped fashion Indonesia into what Australian political scientist Dick Robison called 'a Stalinist system sitting atop Dodge City'.[21] Ultimately the responsibility lies with Soeharto, helped in no small measure by the greed of his offspring. Despite overseeing major improvements in Indonesia's economic development over the course of his rule, Soeharto's notion of governance did not change much from when he assumed power. Lacking a vision of a modern state, Soeharto continued to wield power much like a village chief, doling out favours to friends, family and hangers-on. Although he went along with Indonesia's opening to the outside world and a reduction in protectionist barriers, he never understood the political consequences these moves implied. The requirements of globalisation ultimately impaired his ability to keep his patronage machine up and running. As sociologist Ariel Heryanto put it: 'The deepening of Indonesia's incorporation into the world economy means that the state can no longer be the ever-reliable benevolent patron to favourite cronies'.[22] The national car controversy, which pitted Tommy Soeharto against American, Japanese and European automobile manufacturers, offered a vivid illustration of the problem.

The abuse of foreign capital

But Soeharto was not the only actor in the drama: foreign investors played their roles, currying favour with Soeharto's cronies and pouring billions of dollars into projects with First Family connections. Contrary to the common assumption that economic integration with the West would lead to further economic and political liberalisation, Indonesia's absorption of massive foreign investment merely reinforced an entrenched political elite. 'This assumption needs some questioning', Robison dryly noted: 'Foreign investors in Southeast Asia have shown a remarkable degree of accommodation to state-led economic systems and to systems where political power determines access and success in the markets'.[23]

International donors also played a major part. Each year, the World Bank organised donors' conferences that committed billions of dollars to Indonesia. It was common knowledge, even to Bank staff, that much of this money was siphoned off into corrupt deals. Yet the Bank never made more than a token protest, confirming to Soeharto that he could do what he pleased with the national purse. In July 1997 an American academic, Jeffrey Winters, estimated that up to a third of World Bank funds were being lost to corruption, a charge immediately and vigorously disputed by the Bank's resident representative in Jakarta, Dennis de Tray.[24] A year later, leaked World Bank documents showed that even as de Tray was denying the charge, the Bank was finishing an internal study which confirmed the substance of the allegation and demonstrated that the Bank knew in great detail how its money was being stolen:[25]

> In aggregate, we estimate that at least 20–30 per cent of GOI [Government of Indonesia] development budget funds are diverted through informal payments to GOI staff and politicians, and there is no basis to claim a smaller 'leakage' for Bank projects as our controls have little practical effect on the methods generally used.
>
> Most GOI agencies have sophisticated informal systems for diversion of 10–20 per cent of the development budget under their management and for utilizing the proceeds diverted to supplement both their inadequate operations funds and their compensation.

The report then described in precise detail the myriad ways in which Indonesian agencies skimmed money off the pool of development funds, and concluded with a ranking of the ministries by 'estimated magnitude of development budget diversion'. The ministries of home affairs, transmigration, cooperatives and forestry were deemed the most corrupt, each losing a quarter or more of the funds made available to them.

World Bank officials say they often raised the corruption issue with senior government officials, including Soeharto, and always received the same answer: 'Prove it'.[26] Whether the Bank was unable ever to provide solid evidence on a single case of corruption or, the more likely alternative, was unwilling to offend the leader of a country it considered one of its prime success stories, the result was the same. The World Bank consistently pursued a 'Don't ask, don't tell' policy.

Bank officials also defended themselves by arguing that 'a little leakage' was an acceptable price to pay. 'Let's say we knew someone was skimming 10 per cent off of a US$100 million project', one Bank official told me: 'We could cancel the project and rebid it, but that would delay the project by at least another year. From a return-on-investment point of view, it made economic sense to stick with the original project'.[27] It was, of course, precisely this focus on economics that led the World Bank to miss the significance of corruption to Indonesia's political stability. Corruption had become so widespread that it could not be viewed merely as an economic phenomenon. It also undermined social cohesion and political legitimacy, effects the Bank pretended not to see.[28]

Finally, the technocrats deserve some of the blame as well. One of the technocrats' major achievements of the early 1990s was opening up the banking sector. This in turn opened up new flows of capital to the Indonesian corporate sector, including the firms owned by Soeharto's cronies and relatives. The technocrats erred in two ways: by not putting into place proper controls, and not enforcing the controls they did put in place.

Like Soeharto, the technocrats seemed a little unsure of what they had unleashed by liberalising the financial sector in the late 1980s. Prior to 1990 most loan capital from abroad came from official sources or through a relatively small number of major international banks. The two leading technocrats, Wijoyo Nitisastro and Ali Wardhana, had close relationships with leading foreign bankers and could influence which private projects received foreign funding.

As the number of private banks mushroomed and the importance of the state sector gradually declined, Indonesian corporate borrowers tapped into a much wider supply of foreign capital providers, bypassing the technocrats in the finance ministry and central bank in the process. In hindsight, it is clear that the technocrats were slow to appreciate how quickly their own policies reduced their influence in directing capital flows. And they failed abysmally in constructing a new regulatory framework for the booming financial sector they had brought into being. Wijoyo and Wardhana knew better than anyone the ways in which Soeharto's children exploited their position. By not installing adequate safeguards against fraudulent and imprudent lending, the technocrats exposed the banking system to dangers that would come back to haunt Indonesia in the late 1990s.[29]

To their credit, the technocrats did try to enact some safeguards, but the cronies regularly outfoxed them. As described in chapter 6, in 1991 the technocrats set up an offshore loan monitoring team to rein in offshore borrowing by private companies. Well-connected businessmen quickly undermined the team by exploiting loopholes in the team's rules, with Soeharto's blessing. The technocrats also enacted legal lending limits that stipulated how much a bank could lend to companies owned by the same shareholder. Again, banks routinely ignored the rules, and the technocrats were helpless to do anything about it. On several occasions, middle-ranking central bank officials who tried to enforce the lending limits were fired for their efforts.

It is important to stress the important role the technocrats played in two areas. On the one hand, the technocrats were the principal interlocutors between Soeharto and international aid institutions, whose funds accounted for 12–15 per cent of Indonesia's budget revenues in the mid-1990s. In effect, they lent their reputation to Soeharto in dealing with the World Bank, the International Monetary Fund and bilateral donors. On the other hand, the key technocrat ministries—the finance and trade ministries, the central bank, and the national planning office—were also responsible for authorising or implementing contracts, loans and presidential instructions which benefited the cronies and Soeharto's children. In private, many of the technocrats complained bitterly about being forced to steer lucrative business opportunities towards the president's children. And yet, for the duration of Soeharto's rule, not a single technocrat resigned in protest or made his complaints public. The technocrats defended their decision to stick with Soeharto by arguing that they needed to stay 'inside the establishment' to limit the damage the First Family could do. This argument carries little weight with many Indonesians, who accuse the technocrats of moral cowardice or of being corrupt themselves. 'The technocrats are very naïve, not to say stupid', said the Muslim leader Amien Rais: 'They believe national development only means the growth of the economy. They don't want to look at the social and political realities. Where are their human values'?[30]

An interview in late 1998 by the business magazine *Kontan* with Ma'rie Muhammad, the 1993–98 finance minister, nicely illustrates the technocrats' well-meaning but ineffectual approach to combating corruption.[31]

Kontan: Why didn't you say anything [about corruption] while you were Finance Minister?

Muhammad: I brought these issues to Soeharto's attention many times, to no avail.

Kontan: During your term in office, there were tax holidays given to the president's cronies and relatives, weren't there?

Muhammad: There were presidential decrees pertaining to certain companies. They came as a surprise even to me.

Kontan: Come on, isn't the function of the department of finance to manage the national treasury?

Muhammad: Officially, yes. But these were decisions taken over my head, unofficially.

Kontan: They may have been presidential decrees, but are you saying that you weren't aware of them?

Muhammad: If I said anything to Soeharto, he would say 'I'm in charge'.

Kontan: When you were minister, didn't you notice that all your colleagues had huge properties and houses all around the world?

Muhammad: So what? What did you expect me to do?

Politics: the tightening hand

During Soeharto's last full term in office, he steadily concentrated power in his own hands. Eschewing any attempts to justify or explain policies to the citizenry, Soeharto increasingly resorted to manipulation and repression to keep dissident voices at bay.

As described in chapter 10, Soeharto was re-elected to a sixth term as president by the typically quiescent People's Consultative Assembly (MPR) in March 1993. He quickly turned his attention to cleaning up loose ends. He first went to work assuring Golkar's continued subservience to him by designating a trusted lieutenant, Information Minister Harmoko, as the party's new chairman.[32] He then set his sights on neutering the political effectiveness of the armed forces (a topic to be discussed later). His next order of business was putting the Indonesian Democratic Party (PDI), which had been an irritant to Soeharto in both the 1987 and 1992 parliamentary elections, back in its place. He successfully dislodged Suryadi from the leadership of the party, only to see his predecessor's daughter, Megawati Sukarnoputri, take over the helm at the end of the year.

Soeharto's heavy-handed response to Suryadi's mild calls for reform set the stage for the rest of the New Order. It not only reflected Soeharto's vanishing tolerance for dissident voices but revealed that Soeharto had become his own worst enemy. His inability to stomach criticism from even moderate, mainstream figures galvanised the opposition and lay the groundwork for his own demise.

The end of openness

In 1994 Soeharto put the final nail in the coffin of *keterbukaan*, a policy of increased openness introduced in the late 1980s. In June of that year he ordered shut three publications—*Tempo, Editor* and *Detik*—out of pique with their critical reporting on Habibie's controversial decision to buy the naval fleet of the former East Germany.[33] The closing of *Tempo*, the most respected publication in Indonesia, came as a shock to

Indonesia's burgeoning middle class. It confirmed for many that Soeharto's earlier promises of a freer public discourse were merely empty rhetoric and that there was little reason to expect that Soeharto would countenance moves to open up the political system.

Tempo's closing also had the effect of radicalising what had previously been moderate, inside-the-establishment critics of the Soeharto regime. Goenawan Mohamad, *Tempo*'s highly regarded editor, was a prime example. The soft-spoken Mohamad was stunned by *Tempo*'s closing. Like many Indonesian intellectuals, he chided himself for having clung to the vain hope that change could be wrought from within. 'To me', Goenawan wrote in an essay, 'anyone involved in the political conflict of the past 35 years was a participant, however unwittingly, in a conspiracy of repression'. In an interview, Goenawan returned to the theme: 'We didn't work hard enough to get around the government's efforts to silence us. We were silent too long about so many things, about East Timor, about the treatment of [novelist] Pramoedya [Ananta Toer], about the rebellion in Aceh and Irian Jaya, about how Soeharto came to power'.[34]

Goenawan founded the Center for the Free Flow of Information, a research organisation that also helped distribute underground publications. He later went on to head an election-monitoring team, KIPP, that was strongly opposed by the government.[35] The then armed forces commander Feisal Tandjung led the charge against KIPP and Goenawan. 'The 1945 Constitution makes no mention of independent monitoring committees. It is obviously unconstitutional', Feisal said.[36]

Tempo journalists migrated to other publications, some toning down their coverage, some turning more radical. Dozens of Indonesian journalists joined a new, independent association of journalists, the Alliance of Independent Journalists (AJI), which opened its own magazine, *Forum Wartawan*. In response, Information Minister Harmoko decreed that all AJI members no longer belonged to the sole, government-sanctioned journalist association and therefore could not be employed by accredited publications. To drive the point home, in early 1995 the government arrested three AJI members and sent them to jail under a colonial-era 'hate-sowing' law.[37] Editors at leading publications began to receive a flurry of calls from the military and the information ministry warning them to lay off sensitive stories, including articles critical of Harmoko and those supportive of Megawati Sukarnoputri. Meanwhile, the government issued new publishing licences to friends of Soeharto such as Bob Hasan, who could be relied on to respect the government's diktats on press censorship.

The net effect of Soeharto's efforts to quash the press was simply to push critical reporting underground. Many Indonesians turned to *Samizdat* newsletters or the Internet for information on their own country, much to the annoyance of the government. The military, frustrated at its inability to shut out unwanted news found on the Internet, set up its own bulletin board in late 1995 to counter 'negative and bad' information. 'There is a lot of junk information on the Internet, especially misinformation on our country', complained Air First Marshall Sri Diharto, the man charged with leading the military's Internet counterattack.[38]

Soeharto's iron-fist approach to the media was mirrored in his response to political critics. In 1995 Soeharto was outraged that disgruntled Indonesians, including parliamentarian and Islamic activist Sri Bintang Pamungkas, demonstrated against him while the president was on a trip to Germany. Pamungkas allegedly called Soeharto 'a dictator'. On returning to Jakarta, Soeharto launched into a rare public diatribe against his critics, calling them 'mad, crazy and irrational. How can they sell out their own people in another country? They should be sternly dealt with'.[39] And they were. Soeharto orchestrated Sri Bintang's ouster first from the United Development Party, and then from the board of the Indonesian Association of Muslim Intellectuals (ICMI). In 1996, having lost his parliamentary immunity, Sri Bintang was arrested on the charge of 'insulting the president' and later sentenced to 34 months in jail.

In April 1996 Soeharto's wife of 48 years, known universally as Ibu Tien, died of a heart attack. Tien's death deprived Soeharto of his closest confidante as well as the chief arbiter of disputes between his fractious children. Many Indonesians cited Tien's absence to explain the increasingly public quarrels that would soon break out within the family on business deals such as the Busang gold mine and the national car. Two months after his wife's death, Soeharto was rushed to Germany for treatment for 'undisclosed health problems', which later turned out to be kidney stones. The treatment was successful, but the public relations exercise surrounding it was a disaster.[40] Indonesians were given no warning of Soeharto's health problems, and after Soeharto had departed ministers and Soeharto's children quarrelled in public over what information to release. For the business community, Soeharto's health problems brought to the fore the unresolved succession issue and provided a reason to dump Indonesian stocks.

Shutting down the opposition

After his return, Soeharto set his sights on Megawati and the Indonesian Democratic Party, or PDI. Since taking over the PDI in late 1993, Megawati had introduced more democratic procedures in the PDI, allowing delegates with genuine grassroots support to rise through the ranks. Her calls for more government accountability and political pluralism won Megawati a wide following among the young, and the enmity of Soeharto. Looking forward to the 1997 parliamentary elections, which would involve 20 million new voters, one-fifth of the electorate, the PDI was posed to substantially increase its share of the vote.

Apparently fearing that the PDI would nominate Megawati to run against Soeharto in the 1998 presidential elections, the government ordered the PDI to hold a special congress in June 1996. Held in the Sumatran city of Medan, Megawati and all her supporters on the party's executive board were excluded from the congress. Under heavy military protection, dissidents in the party complied with government instructions and voted to bring back Suryadi as party chief. The government immediately recognised Suryadi as the legitimate head of the party—despite the fact that three years earlier he had been deemed unacceptably independent-minded—and told Megawati to make her peace with him. She refused. As one of her aides, Laksamana Sukardi, put it: 'It's like being robbed and then being told by the police to share your possessions with the thief'.[41] The government's overt manipulation of the PDI instantly added to Megawati's popularity. Disaffected groups of all kinds rallied to her cause. Her loyalists camped out at the PDI headquarters on a quiet, leafy street in central Jakarta, holding 'free-speech' forums and demanding Megawati's reinstatement. Hundreds gathered daily, many wearing motor-cycle helmets in anticipation of a military assault.

The government at first tried to quash press coverage of Megawati and waited for the furore to die down. When that did not work, military-backed thugs burst into PDI headquarters in late July and evicted Megawati's supporters by force. This, in turn, prompted two days of riots that left five dead, 149 injured, and caused considerable damage to buildings and other property. Twenty-three others were listed as missing.

In the aftermath, deciding there was little to be gained from further demonising Megawati, the government pinned the blame for the riots on a small group of activists called the People's Democratic Party, known as the PRD. Led by a wispy, 27-year-old dropout from Gajah Mada University in Yogyakarta, the PRD counted about 200 students and other activists as members. The group had formed alliances with various labour groups and had helped organise a number of strikes across Java in the preceding two years. Historians noted the similarity between the PRD and the People's Democratic Front, a leftist organisation that flourished briefly in the late 1940s. It, too, had worked with workers' and peasants' organisations to put pressure on the government of the day.[42] Military leaders labeled the PRD activists as communists and traitors, and launched an all-out publicity assault against them. Soeharto was quoted as saying the PRD 'follows the (outlawed) Communist Party' and wants to 'overthrow the government'.[43]

Some 124 Megawati loyalists were arrested at the start of the July riots, with 115 later convicted to short prison terms for disobeying police orders. Nine were charged with subversion, which carries a maximum penalty of death. All the charges were eventually dropped. None of the roughly 200 alleged Suryadi supporters who raided the PDI headquarters were arrested.

Megawati responded to her ouster in a relatively restrained manner, disappointing many of her supporters who were keen to take on the government more directly. She brought her case to the courts, where it languished for the remainder of Soeharto's rule. Suryadi, meanwhile, was instantly labeled a traitor by many of the PDI faithful who had once supported him. He required, and received, police protection when he campaigned around the country before the 1997 parliamentary elections. Students, activists and Megawati supporters responded to her ouster by becoming more radical. Having learned from an older generation of political opponents that playing within the system was a dead end, younger activists decided to fight from the outside. By 1996 some 60 per cent of Indonesians had been alive fewer years than Soeharto had been president. As each year passed, warnings about the turmoil of the pre-Soeharto days fell on increasingly deaf ears. The threat of being labeled a communist or being sent to jail on a political charge became a badge of honour among the new breed of activists rather than the social stigma the government believed them to be. Defiance replaced fear in confronting the military.[44] To many middle-class Indonesians, Soeharto's vendetta against Megawati seemed incomprehensible. Although popular, she stood little chance of posing a credible challenge to Soeharto, given his control of the political process. By drumming her out of a position to which she was popularly elected, Soeharto reminded Indonesians that he would brook no challenge to his rule, however minor, and that the military stood ready to crack down on political challenges when they arose. In the process, Soeharto exacerbated the unease many Indonesians felt about the inevitable presidential succession.[45] As the Australian academic Harold Crouch put it, 'if a relatively small issue like the leadership of the PDI can set off serious rioting in the center of the capital, what might happen if military and other factions cannot agree on the national leadership after Soeharto?'.[46] Indonesians would find out less than two years later.

New alliances respond

A number of other less well-publicised developments in 1996 deserve mention. Non-governmental organisations, independent labour unions and dissident activist groups such as the People's Democratic Party (PRD) succeeded, despite continuous harassment by the government, in linking elite dissatisfaction with grassroots rumblings. In particular, they were able to turn labour discontent into political protest. In addition to clamouring for higher wages and more freedom to organise, workers began demanding the repeal of laws banning political parties and the end of the military's participation in politics. While the independent labour union, SBSI, and the independent journalists' association, AJI, both faced constant persecution from the government, their steadfast existence nevertheless weakened Soeharto's corporatist state.[47]

The same could be said for the creation of the Partai Uni Demokrasi Indonesia (PUDI), set up by Sri Bintang Pamungkas in May 1996 while appealing his conviction for 'insulting the president'.[48] PUDI overtly claimed to be an opposition party, breaking one of the main New Order taboos, and pledged to succeed the Soeharto government through constitutional means. Groups such as the PRD and PUDI posed no direct threat to Soeharto's rule. But, as Ariel Heryanto points out, their emergence made 'a substantial contribution to a mental breakthrough for most Indonesians after three decades of depoliticisation and a general sense of powerlessness'.[49] There were other signs that the elite consensus underpinning Soeharto's rule was beginning to fray, including a series of attempts at judicial independence, a rarity in the New Order. Individual judges initially refused to uphold the directive to close *Tempo*, threw out the trumped-up case against labour leader Mochtar Pakpahan, and procrastinated in endorsing Soeharto's wish to expel Megawati from the Indonesian Democratic Party. In the end, Soeharto got his way on all these cases, but the resistance from the judiciary provided one more sign of public dissatisfaction with Soeharto's iron-fisted rule, even from within the elite.[50]

As Indonesia approached the parliamentary elections in May 1997, the government issued strict new campaign regulations, largely aimed at preventing a repetition of the large rallies the PDI had convened in 1992. Government and military leaders, still apparently nervous about Golkar's electoral prospects, publicly reminded civil servants and military personnel they were to vote for Golkar. Soeharto took the added precaution of putting four of his six children on the Golkar delegate list.

In drawing up its list of delegates for the coming elections, the PDI wing controlled by Suryadi left out Megawati and all her supporters. Megawati, meanwhile, was forbidden from submitting her own delegate list.[51] After a short campaign marked by frequent clashes and acts of violence, Golkar emerged with a commanding 74 per cent of the votes. When the economic crisis arrived a few months later, Soeharto was secure in power but increasingly aloof from both the elite and the people at large. Since the death of his wife, his circle of advisers and confidantes had shrunk, leaving him dependent for advice on such figures as his eldest daughter Tutut who, like the rest of her siblings, had a skewed notion of what Indonesians really thought. Political feedback mechanisms had all but broken down. On issues ranging from rumblings by labour unions, forest fires in Kalimantan and the resentment caused by his children, Soeharto's responses were slow, misguided and often counterproductive.

'You can't even hold a conversation with Soeharto anymore', complained former cabinet minister Sarwono Kusumaatmadja: 'He just gives lectures on everything under the sun. He knows everything'.[52]

Foreign policy: testing the waters

Making a break from the inward-looking focus of his earlier terms, Soeharto sought a larger role on the world stage in the 1990s. Indonesian troops participated in UN peace-keeping efforts in Bosnia and Cambodia, and Indonesia served a term on the United Nations Security Council. The foreign ministry helped negotiate settlements of conflicts in Cambodia and the Philippines, and hosted talks attempting to resolve competing claims in the South China Sea.

Assuming the chairmanship of the Non-Aligned Movement from 1992 to 1995 was a foreign policy highlight for Soeharto. Although the group's *raison d'être* had vanished with the end of the Cold War, leadership of the 113-nation body nevertheless brought Soeharto considerable international stature.[53]

Hosting the 1994 heads-of-state meeting of the Asia–Pacific Economic Cooperation (APEC) forum was another highlight. Held in Bogor, about an hour's drive from Jakarta, the leaders agreed to create a tariff-free trading regime in the region by 2020 for developing countries and 2010 for developed countries. Other heads of state heaped praise on Soeharto for adroitly getting all APEC states to agree to the plan and for resisting protectionist lobbies at home. Within Indonesia, the Bogor Declaration received a more lukewarm response. Indonesians were impressed that Soeharto agreed to hold a press conference for journalists attending the summit, his first and only press conference in 32 years in power. But, unlike the foreign heads of state, Indonesians knew Soeharto's willingness to abide by international trade agreements extended only to the point that they began to encroach uncomfortably on his capacity to personally intervene in the economy.

Soeharto's higher international profile was a mixed blessing, however. The troubled province of East Timor continued to blacken Indonesia's profile abroad. Following the Santa Cruz massacre in 1991, a dialogue of sorts was established between pro-integration and pro-independence Timorese. Although useful as a mechanism to bring together rival camps, the dialogue had little impact on Jakarta's negotiations with Portugal and the United Nations. Neither Soeharto nor the military was prepared to deal directly with the main Timorese resistance figures or to broach the subject of a referendum on Timorese independence. In East Timor, reports of military-backed thugs, known as ninjas, terrorising the civilian population continued to leak out. In 1996 East Timor Bishop Carlos Ximenes Belo and the Timorese resistance spokesman Jose Ramos-Horta received the Nobel Peace Prize. Jakarta was outraged. Foreign Minister Ali Alatas called Horta a 'political adventurist' who 'represents no-one but himself'.[54] Jakarta boycotted the prize ceremony in Stockholm and pressured its ASEAN neighbours to do the same. Indonesia also demanded that Malaysia, Thailand and the Philippines break up or prohibit meetings and seminars on East Timor, and they all complied. On other fronts, too, Indonesia came under renewed pressure from abroad, especially from the United States. Complaints about Indonesia's restrictive labour laws led the USA to threaten a revocation of Indonesia's access to tariff reductions under the Generalised System of Preferences. In response to continued human rights violations in East Timor, the USA vetoed a sale of F-5 jets to Jakarta. And the USA was virtually alone among Indonesia's trading partners in publicly criticising Soeharto's treatment of Megawati and the restrictions placed on the 1997 parliamentary elections.[55] Even so, it would be a mistake to exaggerate the impact of criticism from Washington. US trade to and investment in Indonesia helped Soeharto much more than the occasional barb from Washington hurt him.

In any case, with the Asian economies roaring along and the Asian values argument in full swing, Soeharto brushed off most of the criticism aimed his way. The ASEAN policy of non-interference also helped shield him from outside pressure. The embrace of Soeharto's authoritarianism by former Singaporean Prime Minister Lee Kwan Yew, the principal Asian-values cheerleader, disguised the fundamental differences between variations of authoritarianism. Indeed, the authoritarian regimes in Indonesia and Singapore had about as much in common as Indonesia had with, say, American democracy. Singapore, for all its repression of domestic political activity, is a nation managed under the rule of law; in Soeharto's Indonesia, the law played second fiddle to the ruling elite.

In hindsight, the Asian-values bandwagon and ASEAN's craven attitude towards Soeharto clearly did Indonesia no favours. It merely helped deafen Soeharto to those voices warning of the escalating political tensions at home. On the economic front, the Asian critique of Western-style welfare systems began to unravel once the economic crisis hit. With jobs disappearing and poverty rates soaring, arguments against unemployment insurance and other elements of a social safety net found few supporters among the newly poor. Jusuf Wanandi of the Center for Strategic and International Studies in Jakarta is typical of Indonesians angry at the proponents of the Asian-values argument for providing cover for Soeharto's authoritarian politics. Speaking at a conference in Singapore in late 1998, Wanandi said 'this values debate has really given a false impression to all of us. That we are all so special. This is really BS, I tell you'.[56]

Islam: seeking a higher profile

Taking on a political prominence not seen since the 1950s, Islam moved to the fore of Indonesian politics in the 1990s. Indonesia has been undergoing an Islamic revival since the 1980s (as discussed in chapter 7). Many Indonesians describe the process as santrification, a reference to the growing number of Indonesians who could be described as *santri*, or pious, Muslims.[57] *Santris* are often contrasted with *abangan* Indonesians, nominal Muslims usually of Javanese ethnicity. While *abangan* Muslims may follow Islamic customs and practices in their private lives, they do not support an overtly Islamic presence in government. Generally speaking, they are unlikely to support political parties with a specifically Islamic agenda. Historically, *santris* have tended to support Islamic parties, although here too significant differences persist: some *santri*-supported parties demanded a stronger role for Islam within the government; some did not.[58]

One of the great unanswered questions about Indonesian politics is the effect of decades of santrification on Indonesians' political preferences. Few dispute that Islam as a religious and moral force became more prominent throughout the New Order, particularly in the last two decades. But there is plenty of disagreement about what this social trend means for Indonesian politics. Many Muslims (as described below and in chapter 12) are convinced that santrification has paved the way for Islam's political dominance. But other analysts disagree, arguing that many Indonesians who have embraced Islam as an ethical and spiritual guide still support a government that does not discriminate between religions.[59]

These divisions are apparent between and within two categories of the *santri* community, the traditionalists and the modernists. Traditionalist Muslims are generally found in the rural, less affluent parts of the country, especially Java. Conservative in their social views, they hold to a syncretic view of Islam, which incorporates some of the cultural traditions predating Islam's arrival in the Indonesian archipelago. They are relatively tolerant of different professions of the Islamic faith; politically, as Robert Hefner writes, 'they are imbued with populist or progressive nationalist sentiments'.[60] The 30-million strong Nahdlatul Ulama (NU), led by Abdurrahman Wahid, is the main traditionalist Islamic organisation.

Modernist Muslims follow a more literal interpretation of the Koran. They have a broader national base than the traditionalists, and are generally more urban, wealthy and formally educated. The more militant wing of the modernist community has objected since independence to the secular approach followed by the country's leadership, including the military. The mainstream Muhammadiyah, led by Amien Rais from 1995 to mid-1998, is the largest modernist grouping.

The rise of modernist Muslims

In the last years of his rule, Soeharto reached out to the modernists by endorsing the formation of the Indonesian Association of Muslim Intellectuals (ICMI), a collection of mostly modernist intellectuals and civil service bureaucrats close to Soeharto. Headed until recently by Soeharto's former vice-president and the current president, B. J. Habibie, ICMI has been vigorously criticised by some traditionalist leaders, especially Wahid.

Wahid's particular criticisms of ICMI are discussed in detail in chapter 7. Here, I want briefly to test Wahid's predictions against developments of the past half-decade. Wahid argued that Soeharto's patronage of ICMI would unfairly provide modernist Muslims with political influence disproportionate to their actual support in society. (The political strength of modernist Muslims is discussed in chapter 12.) A number of ICMI leaders, together with researchers in its affiliated think-tank, the Center for Information and Development Studies, did follow Habibie into positions of power after Soeharto resigned. Many ICMI stalwarts, convinced that Soeharto was grooming Habibie to be president, clung to Habibie in the hope that he would sweep them into the halls of power.[61] They were right, although it is unclear how long-lived the victory will be.

But Habibie did not become a true convert to the modernist Muslim cause, at least not in the political sense. In 1994–98 Habibie did his best to make ICMI the co-opted tool Soeharto meant it to be. He kept the ICMI-affiliated newspaper *Republika* on a tight leash, and did not hesitate to expel ICMI members who Soeharto considered disloyal. Amien Rais and Sri Bintang Pamungkas are two such examples.

Wahid also charged that the political clout Soeharto gave the modernists would slow the pace of democratic reform. He thought the military, wary of the threat posed by the modernists to Indonesia's secular traditions, would grow more resistant to political liberalisation. He also felt the modernists were more interested in 'Islamising' Indonesia than making it a true democracy. As it turned out, the military played a largely reactive role when the pressure began to build against Soeharto in 1998. And some modernist leaders did, in fact, show less than wholesale support for the democratic opposition. The criticism of Megawati after her ouster in July 1996 by ICMI secretary-general Adi Sasono and other ICMI militants is but one example.[62]

These examples notwithstanding, many modernist figures did play key roles in the movement to push Soeharto from power, a necessary first step in making Indonesia more democratic. Amien Rais, for example, was a key leader of the pro-reform movement. And he was not alone: many modernists showed a deep commitment to democratic reform and actively participated in the resistance to Soeharto's rule. As Hefner puts it: 'Nowhere in the Muslim world have Muslim intellectuals engaged the ideas of democracy, civil society, pluralism, and the rule of law with a vigor and confidence equal to that of Indonesian Muslims'.[63]

Wahid claimed that Soeharto's cultivation of modernist Muslims would polarise the Islamic community and give strength to its radical fringe. On this count the evidence supports Wahid, but not completely. Two of the more important developments of the past five years were the evolution of Amien Rais from a religious to a national leader, and the rising political influence of militant, right-wing Islam. The first came as a surprise to Wahid; the second did not.

Rais, a 55-year-old political science professor at Gajah Mada University in Yogyakarta, was born in Solo, Central Java, into a modernist Muslim family. He spent more than five years studying in the USA in the late 1970s and early 1980s. He received a master's degree in political science from Notre Dame in 1974 and his PhD from the University of Chicago seven years later. He spent a year in Egypt doing doctoral research on the Islamic Brotherhood, a militant Muslim group pushing for an Islamic state. When he returned to Indonesia in 1982, he quickly developed a reputation for harbouring anti-Christian sentiments. 'I was traumatised at first by the sight of big, beautiful churches being built in the midst of Muslim poverty, at the centre of the Muslim communities', Rais admitted: 'It's true I made some strong statements against the Christians'.[64] Among these were his frequent complaints that Christians held too many jobs in the cabinet and within the military leadership.

In the early 1990s Rais joined the ICMI, heading its Council of Experts and with a regular column in the ICMI newspaper, *Republika*. In 1995 he was elected chairman of the Muhammadiyah, Indonesia's largest grouping of modernist Muslims. His experiences in ICMI and Muhammadiyah changed his views of politics, Rais concedes: 'I felt my responsibilities become greater, no longer restricted just to the Muslim community. My views have become more reasonable, tolerant and I hope wiser'.[65]

As the 1990s wore on, Rais increasingly voiced support for the protection of minority rights and Indonesia's pluralistic traditions. 'We must treat minorities in a fair and respectful way', Amien said in an interview: 'This is the position of Islam'.[66] He rejected the accusation that he secretly favoured an Islamic state in Indonesia and that he was sympathetic to the aims of Egypt's Islamic Brotherhood. He was quick to point out that, from his research on the Brotherhood, he concluded the Brotherhood's idea of an Islamic state did not solve the basic questions of political legitimacy.[67] He also became increasingly convinced that the fundamental problem facing Indonesia's Muslims was not the Christian community but Soeharto and his authoritarian regime.

Rais was among the first mainstream leaders to publicly identify the lack of planning for a presidential succession as a major threat to Indonesia's political stability. He also often criticised First Family corruption.

By early 1997 Rais had clearly gotten under Soeharto's skin. In February Soeharto complained to ICMI chairman Habibie that Rais was making 'subversive' statements and was 'more dangerous' than his rival, Nahdlatul Ulama leader Abdurrahman Wahid.[68] Later in 1997, not long after Soeharto had him expelled from ICMI, Rais called for a referendum on Soeharto's handling of the economic crisis.

Still, many Christians, ethnic-Chinese and nominal Muslims continued to harbour suspicions about Rais's true aims. Wahid remains one of the skeptics. 'Amien still needs to give more explanation of why in the past he was so close to the fundamentalists', Wahid said in an interview in 1998. 'But it would be a good thing if his changes are real', he conceded.[69] Rais realised he still needed to do some work to overhaul his image. 'Indonesia changed and I changed', Rais told journalist Margaret Scott in mid-1998: 'I don't want to try to erase my past. But through my actions, I am slowly gaining the trust of Chinese businessmen and Christians'.[70]

The influence of Islamic radicals

While Rais moved to the centre, the radical fringe began to flex its own muscles. Militant modernist groups such as Dewan Dakwah Islamiyah Indonesia, the Indonesian Islamic Preaching Council, and KISDI, the Indonesian Committee for Solidarity with the Islamic World, became much more influential than in earlier decades of New Order rule. Dewan Dakwah has its roots in the Masyumi, a modernist organisation committed to making Indonesia an Islamic state and which Sukarno banned in the early 1960s. KISDI, founded in 1986 in support of the *intifada* in Palestine, has a younger, more activist membership. In the early 1990s it mobilised small numbers of Indonesians to fight with Muslim guerillas in Bosnia. For most of the New Order, militant Islamic groups were treated as a threat to national unity and were repressed by the military. Not surprisingly, they were bitterly opposed to Soeharto. But beginning in the early 1990s they had a change of heart, becoming, in Bill Liddle's words, 'more royalist than the king, defending Soeharto, his ministers, and his policies against all comers'.[71]

The militant Islamic groups were lured into Soeharto's camp by the president's efforts to accommodate modernist wishes. Soeharto installed officers considered sympathetic to Muslims in top jobs in the military. Equally important was Soeharto's estrangement from General Benny Murdani, a Christian whom many modernist Muslims considered anti-Islamic. The militants applauded the formation of ICMI, the opening of an Islamic bank, Soeharto's pilgrimage to Mecca in 1991, and a more Islamic school curriculum. 'From 1966 to 1990, Soeharto was the enemy because he marginalised Muslims', said Ahmad Soemargono, the KISDI chairman: 'After 1990, Soeharto became more conducive to Muslim wishes so we supported him'.[72]

In terms of policy, the militants follow a strict interpretation of Islamic law, at least by the standards of Indonesian Islam. Their foreign policy views are fiercely anti-Western and anti-semitic. At home, they are sharply critical of ethnic-Chinese and Christians, who both have far more economic and political clout than the militants believe they deserve. They demand that 90 per cent of the members of the cabinet, Golkar, the military, the bureaucracy and other leading institutions be Muslims to reflect the percentage of Muslims in society.

Their fervent support for Soeharto put them in a distinct minority of defenders of Soeharto's family. 'The Soeharto family businesses are not considered conglomerates. They are very small and have many shareholders', said Fadli Zon, who heads KISDI's foreign affairs department: 'I don't know if they are involved in corruption. It's the people around Soeharto's children who are the ones taking advantage, not the children'. In any event, Zon added, 'in other developing countries, the family of the president is always involved in business. It's a natural thing'.[73]

Ethnic conflicts ignite

Finally, Wahid predicted that Soeharto's swing to the modernists would exacerbate ethnic and religious conflict. Undoubtedly, intra-ethnic and religious relations have worsened in the past five years. Militant Muslims pin the blame for this on ethnic-Chinese and Christians, arguing that it is their fault for depriving Muslims of the political dominance they feel they deserve. Many others agree with Wahid's assessment.

To be sure, resentment of the ethnic-Chinese has always been strong in Indonesia, even dating back to the colonial period. And because many Chinese are Christians, ethnic and religious tensions often overlap. Rhetoric by Islamic preachers took a sharper anti-Christian and anti-Chinese tone as the 1990s progressed. For most of the New Order, physical violence against the Chinese was relatively rare. But anti-Chinese riots erupting in Medan in 1994 and in scattered locations across the country in 1995 put an end to that.[74]

Religious and ethnic intolerance became more prevalent in 1996. Anti-Chinese and anti-Christian riots broke out in October in the East Java city of Situbondo after the trial of a man accused of blaspheming the Prophet Muhammad. Rioters burned some 20 churches and five died. 'It will happen again as long as we are not ready to change our orientation in leading the Islamic community', Wahid said at the time.[75] And it did. In December, in the West Java city of Tasikmalaya, two Muslim teachers were beaten by the police after disciplining the son of the local police chief. In response, Muslims burned down another 10 churches and a handful of Christian schools, Chinese shops and Chinese residences, killing four in the process. Christian sources said more than 500 churches were burned to the ground between 1992 and 1997.[76]

The riots in Situbondo, a Nahdlatul Ulama stronghold, came as a shock to NU leaders. Many in NU, including Wahid, believed the riots were instigated by outside forces to weaken Wahid's political standing and put traditionalist Muslims in a bad light. Wahid publicly identified ICMI–linked militants as responsible for the provocation, a charge ICMI leaders denied.[77]

Wahid mends fences with Soeharto

Unsurprisingly, given his constant criticism of Soeharto and of the modernist Muslims close to Habibie, Wahid faced a tough battle to retain his NU chairmanship when his term expired in December 1994. Wahid prevailed against the government's campaign to unseat him, but became further convinced that ICMI militants and their supporters in the military were out to get him. Wahid singled out the Abri commander Feisal Tandjung and Army chief of staff Hartono for 'leading the efforts to stop me being elected as head of the NU in 1994'.[78]

In 1995 Wahid stepped up his support for Megawati and her bid to strengthen the Indonesian Democratic Party. When Megawati was ousted from the party in July 1996, Wahid grew still more alarmed about the rising strength of modernist Muslims, who he felt had a hand in Megawati's removal. In response, Wahid threw his support behind Golkar in the 1997 parliamentary elections—even to the point of accompanying Soeharto's eldest daughter Tutut, by now a senior Golkar official, on the campaign trail. It was a decision that disappointed and confused many of Wahid's supporters.

Wahid explains his decision in *realpolitik* terms. 'Everybody knew I was close to Megawati. And I knew that if Megawati felt intimidated by the government, she would withdraw from the 1997 elections, which would have the effect of pushing voters to the PPP [United Development Party] and Golkar. If that happened, then Metareum and Hartono would say the NU doesn't really support me', he said, referring to PPP secretary general Ismail Hasan Metareum and General (ret.) Hartono, a senior Golkar official close to Tutut: 'So I thought I better try to split the votes between Golkar and the PPP. That's why I supported Tutut'.[79]

The argument does not make a lot of sense. Throwing his weight into a fraudulent, highly manipulated election on the ruling party's behalf helped neither Megawati, himself nor the democratic reform movement. In any event, Golkar hardly needed Wahid's help in winning parliamentary elections, which it had won handily every five years since Soeharto came to power. If any party needed help, it was the PPP. A more plausible explanation for Wahid's behaviour is that he was motivated primarily by the desire not to see the modernist-dominated PPP benefit from Megawati's absence in the elections. Many Indonesians sympathetic to Wahid felt the NU leader had put the NU's institutional interests ahead of the democratic agenda, and his credentials as a democratic reformer suffered as a result. Marsillam Simanjuntak, a long-time Soeharto critic and Wahid ally, complained that 'Wahid is a good democrat but a bad reformer'.[80]

The armed forces: stalemate at the top

The Indonesian armed forces, Abri, went through a profound change in Soeharto's last full term. The reasons are complex but can be boiled down into three general categories, two of them a function of Soeharto's politicking and the third a function of Abri's own personnel requirements.

The greening of Abri

As discussed in earlier chapters, Soeharto's handling of military promotions in the early and mid-1990s was motivated by two objectives: the removal of former armed forces commander Benny Murdani and those close to him; and the elevation of officers more agreeable to modernist Muslims. Murdani, a Catholic, had run afoul of Soeharto in the 1980s for resisting demands by Soeharto's children for military procurement projects. According to Murdani, Soeharto's eldest daughter Tutut and youngest son Tommy had both arranged to act as agents for foreign companies bidding to sell minesweepers to the Indonesian navy: 'I told my staff that the president's children should be treated like any other businessmen, and not be given favourable treatment. I told Soeharto I had done this. He just smiled and I interpreted this as his approval'. Later, Murdani said, a former aide to Soeharto was made chief of the navy and 'gave the children everything they wanted, which made me and soldiers under me look bad. At the time, I thought it was a trivial thing. Why should the president care about something like this?'.[81] Like many other government officials, Murdani would learn to his regret that the First Family's business success was far from a trivial matter to Soeharto.

Murdani's ties to Soeharto soured further in the run-up to the People's Consultative Assembly (MPR) in March 1993. Soeharto accused Murdani of forcing his hand into choosing the then armed forces commander Try Sutrisno as vice-president for the 1993–98 term, an accusation Murdani does not reject:

> At the end of 1988, I chaired a meeting of the *dewan sospol* [council for social and political affairs] at armed forces headquarters. We talked about

the 1993 MPR and agreed that we would try to make Try vice-president or president. We didn't want [former Vice-President] Sudharmono or Habibie. That's why Abri was ready to announce Try's candidacy in early 1993.[82]

Soeharto, he added, did not take the news well.

In the aftermath of the 1993 MPR, Soeharto set about killing two birds with one stone. He dropped Murdani from the 1993–98 cabinet and sidelined officers considered loyal to him. 'The Presidential Palace was unsure how deeply "contaminated" the officer corps was by Murdani's influence when it embarked on the purge', wrote Takashi Shiraishi, an expert on the Indonesian military: 'Some analysts suggested that when Murdani left the government in 1993, perhaps as many as 50 per cent of officers with the rank of colonel or above had direct links to Murdani. Christian generals and intelligence officers became major targets in the purge because Murdani himself was a Christian and had spent much of his career in military intelligence agencies'.[83]

Soeharto used the shake-up to install officers considered 'more Islamic' in the top reaches of the military. In practice, this benefited a number of officers from Sumatra and Sulawesi who were close to the modernist Muslim community. Habibie, himself a native of Sulawesi, clearly had a major influence on Soeharto's decisions on military promotions. Within the military, the purge of Murdani loyalists was overseen by former armed forces commander Feisal Tandjung and former army commander Hartono. Soeharto's son-in-law, Prabowo Subianto, also played a key role in the process.

Competition within the ranks

A third factor determining the rapid rotation of officers in the mid-1990s was the flood of officers reaching the end of their careers. On average, 269 officers graduated each year from the Indonesian military academy between 1965 and 1969; they were due to retire between 1985 and 1990. But class sizes jumped sharply in the early 1970s. In 1970–74 the average graduating class totalled 405 officers, who in turn were scheduled for retirement between 1990 and 1995.[84]

As the number of top billets in the military remained roughly constant, the jump in class sizes in the early 1970s created problems for the military hierarchy in the mid-1990s. 'The larger the class size, the greater the competition between officers, and consequently the worse the career success of the class as a whole', noted Doug Kammen, a student of the Indonesian military.[85] The military leadership under Feisal Tandjung, wrote Takashi Shiraishi,

> responded to the logjam in several ways. It sought non-military
> assignments for officers on active duty, and early retirement for officers

deemed expendable. And it accelerated the transfer and rotation of officers, thus giving as many as possible a chance in the much-coveted command positions. Frequent, large-scale personnel changes [became] a striking feature of military life. Major reshuffles took place in 1993, twice in 1994, three times in 1995, twice in 1996, and again in 1997, each involving more than 100, and sometimes more than 300, senior officers.[86]

One effect of the constant rotation of officers was Abri's loss of what political influence it had left. With soldiers passing through commands at such a rapid rate, no officer had time to build a power base outside Jakarta. By the mid-1990s, Soeharto had effectively neutered the military as a political force just as he had neutered all other political actors earlier in his rule. As military officers were later to say in their own defence, Abri became a tool of Soeharto—nothing more, nothing less.

A divided military

The weakening of Abri as a political actor was not cost-free. By disrupting the military's intelligence network in order to weed out General Murdani's influence, Soeharto also weakened one of his main tools to neutralise opponents. The take-over of the intelligence apparatus by Prabowo Sub-ianto, Soeharto's son-in-law, and officers close to Prabowo, made Abri subservient again to Soeharto, but at a much less effective operational capacity. A series of heavy-handed and clumsy interventions by intelli-gence units—among others, the ousting of Megawati from the Indonesian Democratic Party, the harassment of labour leader Mochtar Pakpahan, and the scapegoating of activist groups such as the People's Democratic Party—succeeded only in drastically weakening support for both Soeharto and the military. Prabowo's push to double the size of the Special Forces command from 3000 to 6000 troops reinforced the public perception that the military's main function had become the suppression of domestic political activity. 'Prabowo was unable to distinguish between enemies of the state and domestic critics of Soeharto', said retired general Hasnan Habib. A disgusted Benny Murdani charged Prabowo with 'trying to make the Special Forces into the Iraqi secret service'.[87]

The rapid reshuffling of the military leadership in the mid-1990s also created a divide within Abri along religious lines. The so-called red-and-white faction represented the military's nationalist, secular wing. Its leader in the period leading up to Soeharto's resignation was the current armed forces commander, General Wiranto, together with his deputy for social and political affairs, Lieutenant General Susilo Bambang Yudhoyono. A green faction composed of officers close to modernist Muslims was led by Soeharto's son-in-law, Lieutenant General Prabowo Subianto, until May 1998.

By ensuring that both Wiranto and Prabowo had important allies in key military commands, Soeharto made it still more difficult for the

military to reach any sort of consensus independent of his wishes. Even
during the last weeks of Soeharto's rule, the military remained divided
on how to respond to street-level demonstrations and unable to muster a
single voice with which to communicate with Soeharto.[88]

Radical Muslim groups, however, welcomed the split in Abri. Much
as their view of Soeharto changed in the early 1990s, so too did the radical
Muslims switch from seeing Abri as a force of repression to that of a
political ally. The military's efforts to reach out to radical Muslims were
led by Prabowo. A highly ambitious officer, Prabowo graduated from the
military academy in 1974 and served with the army special forces,
Kopassus, until 1986, before taking on a seven-year stint with the army
strategic reserve, or Kostrad. Prabowo had a reputation as a brilliant but
brutal officer; he has been accused of a variety of human rights violations
throughout his career. Within the military hierarchy, he was widely
resented for his rapid rise through the ranks and his willingness to use
his personal relationship with Soeharto to get around the chain of command. For many Indonesians outside the military, Prabowo was simply a
dangerous man. Former cabinet minister Sarwono Kusumaatmadja called
Prabowo 'a nut case, a toy soldier'. When asked his views of Prabowo,
the Muhammadiyah leader Amien Rais replied 'a mercenary intellectual'
and 'a criminal'. A Western defence analyst called Prabowo 'the most
charismatic, enigmatic, unusual and weird guy I've ever known in my
life. He's also laudable and detestable . . . Pick an adjective and it fits'.[89]

Early in his career, Prabowo was a protégé of General Murdani. At
some point in the mid-1980s the two men had a falling out. Since then,
Prabowo has been consumed by an obsessive hatred of Murdani, according
to officers close to Prabowo. Military sources say Prabowo worked
assiduously to undermine Murdani's relationship with Soeharto.[90] Exactly
what triggered Prabowo's intense dislike for Murdani is not clear. Murdani
suspects it was his decision in the mid-1980s to recall Prabowo from a
tour in East Timor:

> When I was armed forces commander, I sent Prabowo to East Timor to set
> up long range patrols. He became obsessed with catching [East Timor
> resistance leader] Xanana [Gusmao]. He had gone out of control. I heard
> reports that Prabowo was beating patrol leaders when they came back
> empty-handed. I had no choice but to bring him back to Java.[91]

Some Indonesians close to Prabowo say a simple case of envy is the
explanation for Prabowo's obsession with Murdani. Prabowo aspired to
assume the powerful soldier–statesman role that Murdani had, and the
only way to get it was to knock Murdani out of the picture. Whatever his
motivations, Prabowo's ambitions pushed him into an alliance with radical
Muslim groups and led to his (and their) involvement in a seemingly
endless series of dirty-tricks campaigns. Many Indonesians believe these

included the effort to unseat Abdurrahman Wahid as Nahdlatul Ulama leader in 1994 and the ouster of Megawati from the Democratic Party in 1996. 'I see them as friends', Prabowo said of the radical Muslim groups: 'They shouldn't be treated as outcasts. When they were chased like dogs by Benny Murdani, no human rights groups defended them. They have an inferiority complex'.[92]

In early 1998, Prabowo was given a third star and promoted to commander of the army strategic reserve, the same post Soeharto held in 1965. His chief allies included Major General Syafrie Syamsuddin, who assumed command of the Jakarta military district in September 1997; Major General Muchdi Purwopranyoto, who succeeded Prabowo as commander of army special forces in March 1998; and Major General Kivlan Zein, Kostrad's chief of staff.[93]

To many Indonesian analysts, it seemed clear that Prabowo was manipulating his radical Muslim supporters for his own political purposes. But his Muslim apologists did not see it that way. They saw Prabowo and his chief allies as heroes. In an interview in early 1998, KISDI's Fadli Zon said: 'Muslims are very happy with Abri now. Prabowo, Syafrie and Muchdi are all sincere and close to the people. We don't know yet about Wiranto. He never shows his sincerity to the people'.[94] As discussed in chapter 12, Prabowo's flirtation with radical Muslim groups would continue to have a major impact on the political scene, even after Prabowo was dismissed from active service.

FROM PROSPERITY TO CRISIS

July–December 1997

All of these factors fed into Soeharto's response to the economic crisis, which emerged in 1997. On 2 July 1997 Thailand floated its currency, the baht, after its foreign exchange reserves came under attack by currency speculators. The Thai finance ministry had counted on a depreciating baht and rising interest rates to boost Thailand's export revenues and to make foreign investors more keen to hold the baht. It was a vain hope. In August, Thailand turned to the IMF for help, signing a US$17 billion rescue package with the Fund.

The Thai crisis marked the end of the Asian miracle, although few could have predicted how quickly the Thai crisis would be replicated elsewhere in the region. For a decade or more, foreign investors had thrown money into non-Japanese Asia with abandon. But the Thai crisis jolted the foreign investment community into taking a much-delayed and hard look at the numbers. When investors realised how much they did not know—such as the true foreign exchange reserves of Thailand and, later, South Korea—they dumped Asian currencies and assets as fast as they could.

Foreign capital departs

Indonesia, which suffered the most severely from the 'Asian flu', initially earned high marks from investors and economic analysts. Rather than depleting its foreign reserves, on 14 August 1997 Indonesia freed the rupiah from its 'dirty peg' with the dollar and allowed it to float freely. As discussed in chapter 3, Soeharto had a record of responding well to economic crises. Many pundits said at the time they expected Indonesia to weather the storm better than its neighbours. But investors were about to learn an uncomfortable truth: history does not always repeat itself.

Many investors took comfort in the thought that a crisis would strengthen the hand of the economic technocrats in the cabinet, as it often had in the past. The technocrats did emerge stronger, but only for a while. What most investors did not know was that the economic ministers responded to the Thai crisis by proposing a wide-ranging reform package intended to shore up investor confidence in Indonesia before it disappeared.[95] But Soeharto, convinced Thailand's case had no relevance for Indonesia, baulked at the proposal. In hindsight, it seems unlikely that the reform package would have bought a respite for Indonesia; among other structural weaknesses, the country's enormous private-sector debt was a time bomb waiting to explode. But Soeharto's inability to see this allowed ownership of the reform process to be taken out of Indonesian hands.

In September, Indonesia made tepid moves to attract new foreign investment and rein in spending by postponing a number of big-ticket infrastructure projects, some with First Family involvement.[96] The currency markets barely noticed. Indonesian firms, panicked at the continuing depreciation of the rupiah and saddled with US$80 billion in foreign-currency debts, were buying dollars furiously, putting ever more downward pressure on the Indonesian currency. At the same time, the worst drought in half a century promised to cut deeply into the coming rice harvest.[97] On 31 October, the government raised the white flag; Jakarta sought and received a US$43 billion bailout package from the IMF.

The IMF arrives

Just a few days before, the US stock market had plunged 554 points, or 7 per cent, its 12th-worst day on record, forcing a suspension in trading.[98] The scare on Wall Street brought the Asian crisis to US shores. The USA had not participated in the IMF's US$17 billion package for Thailand in August 1997, greatly disappointing one of its staunchest allies in the region. But by the end of October fears of a contagion effect were widespread, and the USA decided to commit US$3 billion to the 'second line of defence' within the IMF package for Indonesia.

Following its standard crisis-management menu, the IMF demanded a fiscal tightening, including the winding down of food and fuel subsidies. It ordered the closure of 16 privately owned banks and encouraged central bank officials to raise interest rates in what became an unsuccessful attempt to make the rupiah more attractive to offshore investors.[99]

The first IMF package failed dismally to show the world that Soeharto was serious about reform. As the Indonesian scholar Jack Bresnan pointed out, the agreement was attacked for doing too much *and* doing too little. The closure of the 16 banks accomplished little more than a run on the rest of Indonesia's banks. Without any form of deposit insurance or any idea whether more banks had been ordered closed by the IMF, Indonesian depositors did the prudent thing and withdrew their savings. Billions of rupiah were taken out of circulation, further restricting the banks' ability to lend. The IMF was also criticised for insisting on a fiscal tightening when the government was not running a budget deficit; cutting government spending merely exacerbated deflationary pressures on the private sector.[100]

At the same time, critics assailed the IMF for not doing more to attack the roots of Soeharto's patronage network. For example, the IMF shied away from putting an immediate stop to public subsidies for Tommy Soeharto's national car project. This argument gained favour when Soeharto's middle son, Bambang Trihatmodjo, who owned one of the 16 closed banks, reopened it under a new name only a week later. Bambang charged the IMF with trying to bring his father down and hinted the technocrats had gone around Soeharto's back in signing the IMF package. 'I see this as an attempt to sully our family name in order to indirectly topple my father, so that father won't be chosen as president again', he complained to reporters on 4 November.[101] In any event, the weakened technocrats were powerless to stop Soeharto's children and cronies from undermining the IMF accord.

As would be the case throughout the crisis, Soeharto and his greedy children proved the principal stumbling block to economic reform. By refusing to hold his children in check, Soeharto convinced investors he was unwilling to take the necessary steps to reverse the dwindling confidence in Indonesia's economy. The IMF, however, did its part in making the process messier than it needed to be, responding to Indonesia's request for help with a powerful mix of arrogance and ignorance. Despite having little institutional knowledge of the political and economic complexities of Indonesia, the IMF dismissed the advice of the World Bank and the Asian Development Bank, both of which had a much larger presence on the ground. Confident that it and it alone had the answers to Indonesia's problems, the IMF marched into Indonesia like a bull in a china shop. Former cabinet minister Sarwono Kusumaatmadja likened Indonesia to 'an ill, confused patient treated by an arrogant and ignorant doctor'.[102]

Indonesia's economy continued to decline in the last months of 1997. December found South Korea within days of going bankrupt, pushing the Asian crisis into a particularly virulent phase. On 9 December, Indonesia's crisis escalated sharply when Soeharto, citing undisclosed health problems, cancelled a trip to Kuala Lumpur to attend a summit meeting of ASEAN heads of state. As in mid-1996, Soeharto's worsening health and the subsequent fears of an unpredictable and messy succession panicked the financial markets. The economic crisis in Indonesia began to evolve into a political crisis, although it would be some time before either Soeharto or his international donors recognised it.

January–February 1998

On 6 January 1998 Soeharto unveiled a budget for the coming fiscal year, containing a number of assumptions considered wildly optimistic by the markets. Panic turned into a rout. Convinced that Soeharto neither understood the magnitude of the problem Indonesia faced nor was capable of overcoming it, both domestic and foreign investors abandoned rupiah-denominated assets.[103] The rupiah lost half its value in five days. Shoppers fought pitched battles in supermarkets as Indonesians began to hoard food.

Misjudging Soeharto's intentions

Senior IMF officials, now deeply worried that Indonesia's troubles would cascade around the region and possibly to emerging markets elsewhere, rushed to Jakarta to stem the damage. Led by Stanley Fischer, the IMF's deputy managing director, the Fund drew up a new 50-point reform package for Indonesia. Humbled by its sobering experience in October and November, the IMF worked closely with the World Bank and Indonesia's economic technocrats in drafting the new accord. But when it came time to hammer out the final details, the IMF officials found themselves dealing directly with Soeharto. In the end little negotiation was required, as Soeharto agreed without much resistance to the package. Soeharto apparently felt that simply signing a comprehensive, IMF-orchestrated package would be enough to restore confidence in the faltering Indonesian economy.

Reflecting a more realistic view of the looming food shortages in Indonesia, the 15 January package eased the conditions on fiscal austerity that had been part of the earlier plan. The package also included many of the measures the technocrats had been advocating for many years, such as the end of government support for Tommy Soeharto's national car project and Habibie's expensive aircraft-manufacturing plant. It proposed a gradual phasing out of public subsidies on fuel, cooking oil and sugar. It promised the end of a slew of monopolies held by Soeharto's relatives and business cronies. In short, it cut deeply into the finely etched patronage network Soeharto had built up over three decades. But within weeks it became clear that he had little intention of implementing it faithfully.

The euphoria surrounding the announcement of the second IMF package dissipated almost immediately. 'The package certainly hasn't done what we expected it to do', said Dennis de Tray, the World Bank's chief representative in Indonesia: 'I really don't have a good explanation'.[104] Indonesians did. They understood much better than the IMF or foreign investors that the chances of Soeharto complying with the package were practically nil. Soeharto, aware that the demands for reform were increasingly incompatible with his own political maneuvrability, did not disappoint the skeptics. Within weeks, the beneficiaries of Soeharto's largesse began to fight back. Long-time crony Bob Hasan tried various back-door techniques to preserve his stranglehold over the forestry sector. Tommy Soeharto demanded that the government continue special tax breaks to his national car project.[105] Eldest daughter Tutut struggled once again to resuscitate a previously cancelled power project in which she held a minority share. On 22 January, the rupiah hit its low-water mark of 17 000 to the US dollar, compared with 2400 just six months earlier.

As confidence continued to evaporate, a flurry of finger-pointing ensued. Some critics blamed the technocrats for pushing for too much in the 15 January package. An American businessman in Jakarta accused the technocrats of 'grossly overplaying their hand' and trying to weaken Soeharto politically.[106] Douglas Ramage, Jakarta representative for the US-based Asia Foundation, took a similar line: 'The technocrats failed Soeharto and they failed the country. They didn't recognise that this crisis was different from crises in the past'.[107] The accusations are misplaced. By the time the final negotiations for the 15 January package started, the technocrats were reduced to playing a bit part. Even by then, Soeharto had lost confidence in them. In fact, the dean of the technocrats, Wijoyo Nitisastro, was so angry at the way the IMF and World Bank had handled the negotiations that he refused to speak with World Bank officials for months. 'Wijoyo was enraged at us', said a senior World Bank official: 'He said: we've been working with Soeharto for thirty years and now you are destroying everything'.[108]

Others pin the blame on the IMF, for a variety of reasons. Some, like Harvard economist Jeffrey Sachs, say the IMF misdiagnosed the causes of Indonesia's crisis. Sachs is particularly critical of the IMF's decision to slash public spending in the face of private-sector deflation and of its insistence on closing banks as its first order of business. He likens the decision to pouring oil on a fire.[109] Others, such as economist Martin

Feldstein, say the IMF had no business pursuing structural reforms in a country suffering from a financial crisis.[110] The IMF would have done better, he and others say, by trying to boost the currency and helping relieve the crushing burden of private-sector debt. Still others, like Malaysian Prime Minister Mahathir Mohamad, say volatile capital flows caused the crisis, and blame the IMF for pressuring countries to liberalise their banking sectors too quickly.[111]

Each of these arguments has merit. Sachs, for example, is certainly right in criticising the IMF for insisting on immediate bank closures in Indonesia after the 31 October package was signed. There is little doubt that forced rises in interest rates helped push the stricken economies deeper into recession. And those finding fault with 'hot money' make a valid point: the enormous volume and volatility of international capital flows have made smaller economies pay a deadly price for opening their markets too quickly. It is unarguably the case that the herd-like behaviour of foreign banks—in throwing loans at emerging market firms and then pulling them out as fast as they could—played a major role in turning a liquidity crunch into a full-blown financial crisis.[112]

But much of the criticism misses the point. First, the IMF, just like private investors, was operating on poor data. Efforts by the Thai and South Korean central banks to disguise the true level of their foreign exchange reserves succeeded. Once the truth came out, there was little the IMF or any institution could have done to stem the panicked outflows of private foreign capital. In Indonesia's case, neither the IMF nor government officials knew the scope of the private debt overhang. The central bank governor, Soedradjad Djiwandono, admitted in late 1997 that he had no idea how serious the debt problem had become.

Second, Feldstein and others in the USA ideologically opposed to the IMF misread the Indonesian situation entirely when arguing that the IMF should have stayed away from structural reforms. Their mistake, not uncommon among economists, was to insist that Indonesia's crisis was fundamentally an economic crisis. Economic reasons—in particular the massive, unhedged private-sector debt—triggered the crisis but do not explain its severity or Indonesia's inability to respond effectively to it. Indonesia suffered from the Asian flu more than any other country, not because its economic situation was more dire or because the IMF prescribed the wrong medicine but because its political system was fatally flawed.[113] The bond between the political leadership and the citizenry had been severely weakened, corroded by rampant corruption and abuse of power. Foreign investors were not alone in losing confidence in Soeharto's ability to overcome the crisis: Indonesians too had lost the faith, and these perceptions inside and outside the country reinforced each other. Economic growth had become Soeharto's only claim to political legitimacy and when growth evaporated, so too did Soeharto's mandate to govern. Indeed, one could well argue that decades of World Bank winking at Soeharto's corruption contributed far more to the messy end of the New Order regime than anything contained in the IMF menu of reforms.[114]

To be sure, the IMF's initial approach to the Indonesian crisis had its share of mistakes, as discussed above. But, as the crisis evolved, the Fund recognised that the solution to Indonesia's private-sector crisis also lay in the private sector. The scale of the problem far exceeded what official flows of capital could cover. International institutions and bilateral donors could provide seed money to a solution, but the key to putting Indonesia's economy back on track was in restarting private capital flows to Indonesia, including direct investment, equity capital and loans. Shortcuts and gimmicks were not going to work.

The Fund's goal as 1998 began was to convince the providers of foreign capital that Soeharto was capable of making difficult choices in reorienting the Indonesian economy onto a more competitive path. This meant unwinding the symbiotic relationship between government and business and reducing graft and corruption. The IMF tried this approach by pushing for a host of structural reforms in the 15 January package. The fact that the package failed wasn't necessarily the IMF's fault. 'We can't say the IMF failed because Soeharto never implemented the reforms', noted the Indonesian economist Djisman Simanjuntak.[115]

The announcement of a new IMF package brought with it a flurry of foreign officials to Jakarta. Japanese Prime Minister Ryutaro Hashimoto and German Chancellor Helmut Kohl both placed telephone calls to Soeharto. Singaporean Prime Minister Goh Chok Tong dropped in for a quick visit. US President Bill Clinton sent Deputy Treasury Secretary Lawrence Summers to Jakarta in January and a special envoy, former Vice-President Walter Mondale, in March.[116] He also called Soeharto at least four times between January and March. The message of all these visits was virtually the same: stick to the IMF program and rebuild investor confidence. By all accounts, the message fell on deaf ears.

Politics to the fore

The confusion surrounding the 15 January package was an important factor in the precipitous fall of the rupiah, but it was not the only one. A number of other political developments played a role. First, Soeharto let it be known in mid-January that he wanted his Research and Development Minister B. J. Habibie to be his vice-president for his next term in office, which was due to begin with a meeting of the People's Consultative Assembly in March. The high-spending Habibie had long been an enemy of the technocrats and his political ascendancy further soured the mood among foreign investors.[117] Habibie's Muslim supporters were elated at the news, confident that Soeharto was grooming the

German-trained engineer to be his successor, a prospect that further
dimmed the hopes of foreign investors.[118] The news of Habibie's rise also
raised fears of a military split, as the military establishment had long
resented Habibie's meddling in their procurement projects. But military
support was secured by two of Habibie's staunchest allies, Armed Forces
Commander Feisal Tandjung and soon-to-be Kostrad Commander Prabowo
Subianto. (Army Commander Hartono, previously close to Habibie, split
with Habibie around this time, due to his own ambitions to become
vice-president.) For Prabowo, who also had ambitions for higher political
office, Habibie was a perfect choice. Habibie's dependency on Muslim
support would strengthen the hand of the so-called green faction in the
military, of which Prabowo was a leading member. A Habibie vice-
presidency also kept the job from a military figure from the red-and-white
faction who would be in a position to thwart Prabowo's political rise.

Second, Soeharto made it clear that he had lost faith in the technocrats,
whom he blamed for being unable to stem the crisis. Desperate to shore
up the declining rupiah, which he rightly sensed was a proxy vote on his
own leadership, Soeharto began openly to flirt with the idea of imposing
a currency board. His children ferried in an American expert on currency
boards, Steven Hanke, to meet Soeharto secretly. Hanke held out the
tantalising prospect of a quick fix to the faltering rupiah.

With a currency board in place, the central bank stands ready to
exchange all local currency with a reserve currency, such as the US dollar.
It effectively replaces a central bank and forfeits control over monetary
policy. In fact, many analysts concluded that undermining the central bank
was the real goal of Soeharto's children, still upset about bank closures
from the previous October. 'The whole purpose of [the currency board]
is not to stabilise the currency, it's to try to destroy the central bank',
said David Cole, an American economist with many years' experience in
Indonesia: 'There is no economic motive whatsoever'.[119]

By installing a currency board and fixing the rupiah at 5000 or 6000
to the dollar, Hanke told Soeharto, 'the currency could return to stability,
inflation would decline while interest rates would dramatically collapse'.[120] Leaving aside the problem of Indonesia not having nearly
enough foreign-exchange reserves to make a currency board credible,
Hanke and Soeharto also misunderstood the nature of Indonesia's problem.
Investors had not lost faith in the macroeconomic policies of Indonesia
or of its central bank; rather, they had lost faith in Soeharto, a problem
a currency board was not going to solve. The flirtation with the currency
board further soured foreign investors and threatened to unravel the Fund's
US$43 billion rescue package.[121] Among other concerns, contributors to
the package worried that a currency board would do little more than
deplete Indonesia's dwindling reserves while allowing Soeharto's children

and cronies to cash in their rupiah-denominated assets using an artificially low exchange rate.

Undermining his lost confidence in the technocrats, in February Soeharto fired the central bank governor, Soedradjad Djiwandono, who became one of the few cabinet ministers to be dismissed during the New Order. Explanations for Soedradjad's dismissal vary: some say Soeharto was trying to shift the blame for the crisis onto the technocrats, others that Soeharto fired Soedradjad because the central bank governor was opposed to the currency board plan. Still others say Soedradjad was fired because he had authorised billions of dollars in central bank loans to bail out leading Indonesian banks, most of which were owned by ethnic-Chinese business-men. And still others say Soedradjad was done in by Soeharto's children, who were enraged at the closing of the 16 banks the previous October.

The truth is probably a mixture of the four, although only Soeharto knows for sure. What we do know is that Prabowo and his fiercely anti-Chinese, radical Muslim supporters were out to get Soedradjad. Many radical Muslims suspected Soedradjad, a Christian, was improperly using public money to help out his ethnic-Chinese friends. Prabowo appears to have shared this view, notwithstanding the fact that Soedradjad is married to Prabowo's sister, Bianti. Prabowo was also irate because one of the 16 closed banks was partly owned by his brother, Hashim Djojohadikusumo. Friends of Soedradjad say Prabowo threatened to kill the central bank governor shortly after the 16 banks were closed. The issue caused a major rift in the Djojohadikusumo family, one of the most prominent in Indo-nesia, with Soedradjad's wife Bianti telling friends that she thought Prabowo had 'gone crazy'.[122]

The ethnic blame game

A third factor destabilising Indonesia in early 1998 was a spate of attacks on ethnic-Chinese, mostly in small towns of Central and East Java. Chinese shops and homes were looted and burned in a foretaste of occurrences in Indonesia's main cities a few months hence. The circum-stances of the attacks were murky. Long-standing resentment of the Chinese minority clearly underpinned the violence. But there is evidence that at least some of the riots were provoked.[123] The identity of the provocateurs is unknown, although many Indonesians were quick to suspect Prabowo and his special forces unit of playing a role. In any event, the violence directed at ethnic-Chinese had the effect of disrupting food supplies, as the Chinese controlled much of the wholesale food distribution network. Many Chinese refused to stock goods for fear of being accused of hoarding.

In Jakarta, an attack of a different sort was aimed at the ethnic-Chinese elite. Rhetoric at the top of the political leadership began to take on an overtly anti-Chinese tone, with hints that the Chinese were responsible for Indonesia's dire economic straits. Soeharto's daughter Tutut sought to pin the failure of her 'I Love Rupiah' campaign onto Chinese-owned businesses.[124] Senior military figures such as Feisal Tandjung and Prabowo Subianto made a number of anti-Chinese remarks. Soeharto himself began using expressions such as 'we Muslims', which many people saw as a snub to the ethnic-Chinese.[125] The rhetoric marked an abrupt change for Soeharto, who had long insisted on keeping divisive ethnic and religious issues out of Indonesia's public discourse. To many, it appeared Soeharto had decided to sacrifice this principle, not to mention the Chinese, as he came under increasing political threat. 'Soeharto thinks only of his and his family interests,' said the Muslim leader Amien Rais, the first prominent leader to defend the ethnic-Chinese: 'He is willing to make every other group a scapegoat. We must not victimise people. We should blame the government for this crisis, not the Chinese'.[126] Military analyst Salim Said was even more critical: 'Soeharto is like Stalin. First he eliminated the left, and then moved on to the rest of the political spectrum. Then he divided the Muslims and finally he turned on the minorities. In such a broken down geography, anything can happen'.[127]

In February, Sofyan Wanandi, a leading Chinese businessman, was picked up for questioning in relation to an alleged plot to disrupt the upcoming People's Consultative Assembly. The People's Democratic Party (PRD), the small group which had shouldered the blame for the Jakarta riots in July 1996, was again fingered as chief culprit by the military. No evidence was ever produced to support the charge. According to Wanandi, 'the police investigating me admitted they had no evidence but were just acting on instructions from higher up'.[128]

The order to frame Wanandi appears to have come from Soeharto, with Prabowo again playing a role. Earlier in 1998 Wanandi had publicly expressed his preference for the current vice-president, Gen. (ret.) Try Sutrisno, to remain as vice-president for the 1998–2003 term. Soeharto was outraged, sensing a repeat of 1993, when military officers led by Benny Murdani forced his hand in choosing Try as vice-president for the 1993–98 term. Soeharto and Prabowo both suspected Murdani was intent on playing the same game. After leaving the armed forces, Murdani occasionally used an office in the Center for Strategic and International Studies, a think-tank he helped start. CSIS is headed by Sofyan's brother Jusuf, and is financially supported by Sofyan. Both the Wanandi brothers are close to Murdani. According to Sofyan:

> When I went to the police station, the intelligence officers only spent fifteen minutes asking me about the PRD. Then they wanted to know all about how and why I supported Try and why I don't like Habibie. They accused me, [Finance Minister] Ma'rie [Muhammad], and Soedradjad of masterminding the economic crisis and of encouraging capital flight. Then

they told me the investigation would be stopped if I agreed to stop talking about Try.[129]

From the behaviour of the investigating officers, it seems clear that the purpose of the trumped charges against Sofyan Wanandi was to draw a link between the ethnic-Chinese, Benny Murdani and Try Sutrisno, and in the process undermine Sutrisno's prospects of remaining as vice-president.[130]

After the police questioned Sofyan, radical Muslim groups protested outside the offices of CSIS in central Jakarta. The protesters carried placards saying 'CSIS—Parasite' and 'Sofjan Wanandi—*pengkhianat* [traitor]'. According to Jusuf Wanandi, a check of the licence plates on the buses that brought the Muslim groups to CSIS showed they belonged to the Jakarta military garrison, then headed by Major General Syafrie Syamsuddin, a close ally of Prabowo.

Prabowo, as described above, suffers from a severe case of paranoia when it comes to Murdani, a condition that also afflicts much of the radical Muslim community. And by early 1998 his anti-Chinese instincts had come to the fore. Shortly before the Sofyan Wanandi incident, Prabowo attended a fast-breaking ceremony with thousands of Muslim preachers, including representatives of the most radical groups. According to people present, Prabowo told the preachers that a handful of wealthy Chinese businessmen, including Sofyan Wanandi, were unhappy about how close Soeharto had become to the Muslim community and that they were trying to replace Soeharto with Try Sutrisno. He implored the Muslims to join him in fighting 'traitors of the nation', a reference everyone understood to mean the ethnic-Chinese.[131] Privately, Prabowo told several close associates he had recorded a conversation in which Sofyan Wanandi tried to bribe him to turn against Soeharto, a charge Wanandi vehemently denies. Although the tape has never seen the light of day, Prabowo's radical Muslim supporters firmly believe in its existence.[132] A Chinese businessman who saw Prabowo in early 1998 was shocked by what he heard: 'Prabowo told me the Chinese are responsible for the economic crisis. He said he intends to drive all the Chinese out of the country even if that sets back the economy twenty or thirty years. He thinks the Christians are trying to topple Soeharto'.[133]

Like Prabowo, his radical Muslim supporters became convinced by early 1998 that Indonesia's crisis was due to a nebulous conspiracy involving greedy Chinese and anti-Muslim Westerners with the ultimate purpose of bringing down Soeharto. They stepped up their criticism of the pro-democracy activists and of their supporters in the mainstream Muslim community. The KISDI leader Ahmad Soemargono called Amien Rais and pleaded with him to support Soeharto.[134] A March 1998 interview with the KISDI activist Fadli Zon provided a blueprint of sorts on the radical Muslim world view:[135]

- *On the ethnic-Chinese and capital flight.* 'If the Chinese don't bring back their money to Indonesia, we should kick them out of the country. The government is able to stop them from doing business here. How can we consider them Indonesian if they take all the money they took from Indonesians and put it in Singapore? Those Chinese who want to leave, just go. They can stay here if they show a sense of nationalism by bringing back their money from overseas. But for most Chinese, it is too late for them to show their nationalism.'
- *On the need for political change.* 'There is no need to change leaders. In Thailand and South Korea, the economy didn't improve after a political change. So this is not the solution for Indonesia.'
- *On the IMF.* 'The IMF provisions are impossible. They make everything cheap for foreigners. Soeharto only signed the agreement because it was a crisis situation, but most Indonesians don't agree with the IMF package. The IMF does not want to help us. It would be better for us to close the country like Myanmar.'
- *On the West.* 'The West is trying to make our crisis worse and take advantage of us. Mondale demanded that Indonesia give the U.S. military bases in East Timor and Irian Jaya in exchange for financial assistance. It's just like after Iraq was provoked into attacking Kuwait, now the U.S. has military bases all over the Middle East. Of course, Soeharto rejected it. Because Indonesia is the fourth largest country in the world, and 90 per cent Muslim, the U.S. is afraid this large country with all these Muslims will take off economically.'
- *On the US Democratic Party.* 'The Democrats are bad for Indonesia. It's full of radical Jews and Catholics. The Republicans are Protestant, more conservative and they don't meddle so much. [Treasury Secretary Robert] Rubin, [Federal Reserve Chairman Alan] Greenspan and [Secretary of State Madeleine] Albright are all Jews. They want to keep Indonesia down. Rubin tried to talk the rupiah lower. A month after Albright became secretary of state, she wrote to Soeharto asking him to open diplomatic relations with Israel.'
- *On Prabowo.* 'It's very unfair to say Prabowo is anti-Chinese. Actually, he restrains the Muslims in not going after the Chinese.'

The voice of protest grows louder

Elsewhere in the political arena, events were picking up speed. Amien Rais, the Muhammadiyah leader, was the first mainstream political figure publicly to challenge Soeharto's leadership. In January he said he was prepared to run for president: 'Our crisis can be overcome if Soeharto disappears. He is the problem. He is trying to solve our economic problems with political manipulation and it won't work'.[136] In January he had tried to join forces with Nahdlatul Ulama leader Abdurrahman Wahid and Megawati Sukarnoputri to step up the pressure on Soeharto. Wahid declined the offer. Shortly thereafter, Wahid suffered a stroke and was absent from the political scene until a few weeks before Soeharto resigned.

Students and younger political activists began clamouring for change as well, although they were more vulnerable to repression. A number of activists, some associated with the People's Democratic Party, disappeared in the early months of 1998 in a manner reminiscent of the 'mysterious killings' described in chapter 9. Pius Lustrilanang, an activist who was abducted and later released, claimed he had been tortured at what appeared to be a military installation.[137] Again, suspicion fell on Prabowo and his special forces unit. In all, 25 activists went missing between mid-1997 and early 1998. Nine resurfaced after months of detention and one was found dead; 14 are still listed as missing and are presumed dead.[138] (After Soeharto resigned, a military honour council was convened to hear evidence on the abductions. The council discharged Prabowo from the armed forces and shifted two other officers, including the special forces chief, Major General Muchdi, from active duty for their role in the abductions. Details of their role, or of the fate of the missing activists, were not forthcoming.)

Meanwhile, the economy continued to spiral downward. The central bank escalated money supply growth to finance lending to the insolvent banking sector, setting the stage for sharply higher inflation later in the year. Outstanding liquidity credits from the central bank reached Rp. 127 trillion by April 1998, up from just Rp. 17 trillion in September 1997.[139] Unemployment was soaring higher as debt-strapped companies shut down production lines or closed up shop completely. Even healthy companies suffered as banks no longer provided working capital. Exports slowed because firms could not open letters of credit to import raw materials. Most foreign banks, especially those from Japan, refused outright to discuss writing down or renegotiating Indonesian debt.[140] Food prices rose steadily, encouraging fears of malnutrition and a sharp rise in the incidence of poverty.

The government began to implement some of the provisions of the IMF's 15 January package, but progress was uneven. In late February Soeharto invoked a clause in the constitution in criticising the IMF package for weakening the government's control over the economy. Picking up on Soeharto's mood, would-be cabinet ministers honed their nationalist rhetoric. Businessman Aburizal Bakrie, who headed the Indonesian Chamber of Commerce and Industry, urged parliament to use the economic crisis to redistribute corporate assets to *pribumi*, or indigenous, businessmen.[141] Soeharto's children and friends began taking potshots at the IMF. 'We do need the IMF, yes, but not if we are continually being repressed with this and that condition', complained

Soeharto's daughter Titiek, who is married to General Prabowo. Her elder sister Tutut agreed that Indonesia needed foreign funds but only 'those which would not tie us. If the funds sacrifice and degrade our nation's dignity, we do not want them'.[142] For its part, the IMF, hoping to dissuade Soeharto from further consideration of a currency board, decided to delay further disbursement of its aid money.

Meanwhile, the government-friendly media stepped up criticism of Amien Rais and the pro-reform movement. The *Indonesian Observer*, an English-language daily owned by a business partner of Soeharto's son Bambang, editorialised that:

> Amien Rais is making a big mistake if he thought that a 'power to the people movement' would get underway in Indonesia, similar to that headed by Corazon Aquino several years ago in the Philippines . . . In the Philippines, the political process of democracy has lived on. This has made it possible for the masses to hit the streets and demand the downfall of President Marcos. This will never happen in Indonesia, where the government is the embodiment of the will of the political parties.[143]

March–April 1998

The People's Consultative Assembly, or MPR, convened on the first day of March to endorse Soeharto for another five-year term as president. The mood was sombre. An economic success story just nine months earlier, the wheels had come off for Indonesia. 'It's a perfectly co-ordinated catastrophe,' said Sarwono Kusumaatmadja: 'Corruption, a succession dilemma, forest fires, air crashes, drought, Wahid's stroke—we got it all'.[144]

Tens of thousands of soldiers were deployed in Jakarta to keep students and protesters from disrupting the assembly. Inside the assembly, Soeharto's eldest daughter Tutut and her close ally Hartono, the former army commander, choreographed the meetings from their perches as senior officials in the ruling Golkar Party. The sessions soon took on a surreal air. The 1000 carefully screened members of the MPR and Soeharto went about their business with scarcely an acknowledgement of the crisis raging outside. In his opening speech to the assembly, Soeharto referred only briefly to the crisis and offered no new thoughts on how to combat it. Soeharto and Habibie were unanimously sworn in as president and vice-president for the 1998–2003 term. The only event of interest was the MPR's decision to grant Soeharto's wish for a new decree giving the president sweeping authority to take extra-constitutional measures if faced with an emergency. Many suspected Soeharto had insisted on the measure to give himself more leeway to handpick his own successor or to override the military chain of command in dealing with political protests.[145]

A controversial cabinet

A week after the MPR meeting Soeharto announced a new cabinet, which accomplished the unusual feat of offending nearly everyone. The composition of the cabinet appeared to be mostly the work of Tutut, reflecting how much Soeharto had come to depend on her for advice. Fadli Zon, the KISDI activist and close friend of Tutut, said Tutut showed him the cabinet list in her house just prior to the MPR and it was identical to the cabinet Soeharto announced two weeks later.[146] Tutut herself was in the cabinet, as were a number of officials close to her. Perhaps the most controversial selection was Bob Hasan as trade minister. Hasan, an ethnic-Chinese with very close ties to Soeharto, controlled the monopoly on plywood exports targeted by the IMF two months earlier. One of the chief beneficiaries of Soeharto's crony capitalism, Hasan's promotion to trade minister was seen as a direct rebuff to the IMF. Some speculated that Soeharto meant to appease the ethnic-Chinese by making Hasan the first ethnic-Chinese ever to serve in a Soeharto cabinet. If so, it was a cruel joke: Hasan was as reviled among the ethnic-Chinese as he was by other Indonesians. Hasan got off to a poor start by defending the very monopolies the IMF was trying to abolish in his first statement as trade minister. 'Monopolies are OK . . . as long as [they] are in line with the constitution', he said.[147]

Habibie and his modernist Muslim supporters made out poorly in the cabinet, a reflection of both the intense animosity between Habibie and Soeharto's children and Soeharto's poor regard for Habibie's political skills. Prabowo, said a general close to him, 'went berserk' when he heard the cabinet line-up.[148] He felt the dearth of modernist Muslims in the cabinet would undercut his support among radical Muslim groups. Even the radical Muslims, otherwise diehard Soeharto loyalists, were dismayed. Fadli Zon called the cabinet 'the last and biggest mistake Soeharto made. Even though there was only one Christian in the cabinet, we were still very unhappy. What can you expect from Bob Hasan? He's just a big thief. If he had picked a better cabinet, Soeharto might still be president'.[149]

Shortly before the MPR session, Soeharto put Prabowo in charge of the 27 000-troop army strategic reserve, which together with the special forces is the best-trained and best-equipped military unit. He also made Subagyo, an ally of Prabowo, commander of the army. In the cabinet announced in March, however, Soeharto made Wiranto his defence minister but left him as armed forces commander. Thus, the military remained factionally divided between Soeharto loyalists, led by Prabowo, and those referred to as professional soldiers. But as much as Soeharto sought to keep the military politically impotent, he was clearly concerned about

Prabowo as well. As Sarwono put it: 'Soeharto doesn't trust Prabowo, but he needs him there to keep the military off-balance'.[150]

Much of the international community greeted the announcement of the new cabinet with dismay. Far from picking a cabinet to soothe investor concerns, Soeharto appeared to go out of his way to do the opposite. A more nuanced explanation of Soeharto's behaviour is that he really had no idea what the market wanted or why he was under so much pressure. But he knew the pressure was rising and decided to surround himself with figures whose loyalty was unquestioned. Soeharto and his economic team had more than three decades' experience negotiating with international financial institutions and bilateral donors. He could play that game masterfully. He knew when to concede and when to call a bluff. When pushed into a corner he could, and did, play the sovereignty card.[151] He knew from long experience that the major industrialised nations, the IMF and the World Bank had little appetite to push him where he did not want to go.

But the enemy he faced in 1997–98 was unknown to him. The market had no sovereignty and its decisions were unaffected by diplomatic niceties. Foreign investors were not nearly so easy to stigmatise as, say, the IMF. Diffuse and anonymous, they were immune to Soeharto's bluffs and threats. Soeharto had come up against a 'conspiracy of far more potent subversives: capitalism, markets and globalisation', remarked journalist Nick Kristof: 'These forces set off the Asian financial crisis, and Soeharto's armaments were suddenly useless. His sophisticated military equipment can detect a guerilla in the jungle of East Timor at night, but it was unable to discern bad loans or prop up a tumbling currency'.[152]

Unlike the Soeharto who deftly handled economic crises in years past, the Soeharto of 1998 had been in power so long that he had seemingly lost any capacity for distinguishing between his family's interests and the interests of the nation. He had gone along with the globalisation trend, confident that he could continue to successfully reconcile the demands for economic growth and family enrichment. But by March 1998 it had become painfully clear, even to Soeharto, that his juggling act was satisfying no-one.

In April Indonesia signed a third agreement with the IMF in an attempt to open the aid spigot. Another month had been wasted as Indonesia's new economic team came to grips with the crisis. The agreement called for faster action on bank restructuring, a new bankruptcy law and a new court to handle bankruptcy cases. It also laid out a schedule for privatising state-owned enterprises. After the poor implementation of the previous two packages, the IMF insisted on closer monitoring mechanisms in the 8 April 1998 agreement.

Growing civil unrest

Students protested regularly just before the MPR meeting and again immediately after its conclusion. Protests were generally largest and most frequent in Yogyakarta, home to the prestigious Gajah Mada University, although students were active across the country. Over 25 000 students staged a demonstration at Gajah Mada on 11 March, the day Soeharto took the oath of office beginning his seventh term. Among the biggest of the student groups were the leftist-leaning People's Struggle Committee for Change (KPRP); the Indonesian Islamic Student Movement (PMII), which was linked to the Nahdlatul Ulama; and the Indonesian Muslim Students Committee (KAMMI), which was the largest Muslim grouping. In addition, various student senates emerged which acted as coalitions of student groups.[153]

For a time, student groups and the military coexisted peacefully, with most of the protests confined to university campuses. But, thanks to modern forms of communication, different student organisations were able to keep abreast of events elsewhere in the archipelago and to coordinate actions against the government. The New Order's control of the traditional mass media proved to be little defence against the Internet and mobile phones that wired the student movement together. In April 1998, KPRP, among the most radical of the student groups, led the charge to get students off the campuses and into direct confrontation with the military. At the same time, Soeharto began calling on the military to take more repressive action against the students, putting the army leadership in a tight spot. The military's stark choice, said the Islamic leader Amien Rais, was to defend the people's interests or Soeharto. It could no longer do both.[154]

By this time, Rais had become the principal leader of the opposition movement. His position as head of the Muhammadiyah afforded him some protection, similar to that of Abdurrahman Wahid and Megawati, but, unlike Wahid and Megawati, Rais was prepared to use his stature to lead a full-scale assault on Soeharto. 'The economic disease has spread too far', he said at the end of April: 'It's too late for Soeharto to recover. The bottom line is that the people have lost all confidence in him'. Among mainstream leaders, Rais was one of the first to see the potential for a mass uprising against Soeharto. 'We must not be afraid of the term "people's power"', he said: 'That, after all, is how we gained independence and again how we toppled Sukarno in 1966'.[155]

Abroad, no governments were prepared to voice such sentiments and neigbouring governments continued to express support for Soeharto. Australia, panicked at the thought of vast migration southward out of Indonesia, sharply criticised the IMF for demanding too much of Soeharto. Many private-sector analysts also missed the fundamental changes occurring in Indonesia. On 21 April the non-governmental Asia Foundation held a briefing on Indonesia in Washington; five representatives with years of experience in Indonesia criticised the foreign media for giving too much attention to the student protests and 'caricaturing' Indonesia. The Foundation's chief representative in Jakarta defended the new cabinet, saying it contained a good number of competent people. He said Soeharto 'was very much in control, on top of his political form' and insisted there was no 'people's power' movement to speak about.[156] In early May, a *Washington Post* report from Jakarta stated: 'Soeharto appears firmly in control . . . Indonesia is still far from seeing the kind of widespread "People's Power" movement that toppled other authoritarian regimes in the Philippines or South Korea'.[157]

Soeharto's children, unsurprisingly, also paid no heed to what was happening on the streets of Jakarta and other major cities. They continued to demand special privileges right until the very end of Soeharto's rule. In April, Soeharto's son Bambang and daughter Titiek duelled over who would collect the middleman fee on the privatisation of a state-owned cement factory. Youngest son Tommy maneuvred to keep his clove monopoly alive for a few more months and wangled himself a new monopoly distributing goods provided by foreign donors.[158] Like their father, the children remained oblivious to the galvanising role the issue of corruption was having on the political opposition.

THE LAST DAYS OF SOEHARTO

Soeharto's last month in office began with yet another ill-fated decision. On 4 May the government announced a reduction of subsidies on fuel, resulting in an immediate price rise for gasoline of 70 per cent and smaller but still substantial hikes in bus fares. Under the IMF program, Indonesia was given until the end of October to reduce the subsidies.[159] Indonesian officials said Soeharto personally decided to slash the subsidies all at once, confident of being immune from public protest. He could not have been more wrong.

The riots

The reaction was sharp and immediate. Large-scale riots broke out in the North Sumatran city of Medan. Looting and burning, much of it targeting ethnic-Chinese areas, went on for three days and received full coverage from the main television stations in Jakarta.[160] At about the same time, student activists took their protests off university campuses and onto the streets of the main cities in Java. The London-based War Risks Rating Committee, an arm of the international insurance industry, placed Indonesia on a list of countries at high risk of war and labour strife.[161] On

9 May, Soeharto left on an extended trip to Cairo to attend an economic summit of developing countries, still confident that the situation at home was well under control. As he departed, he warned protesters they would be quashed by the army: 'The security forces will take action against whoever disturbs and ruins national stability'.[162]

Three days later 6000 students staged a protest at and around Trisakti University in central Jakarta, located not far from the parliament building. Late in the afternoon, as the students were moving back into the campus, men wearing the uniforms of the police mobile brigade unit took positions on an overpass looking down on the campus. Shots rang out. Stunned, the students ran for cover inside university buildings. The shooting continued. When the firing stopped, six students had been shot, four fatally.

The identity of the shooters is not known. The police chief insisted his men had been issued only rubber bullets. Forensic analysis showed the students had been shot with Steyr rifles, which are issued to only a handful of special police units. The soldiers who did the shooting appeared well trained and were clearly aiming to kill. The dead students had all been shot in the head or the chest. Weeks later, a report surfaced claiming that uniforms had been stolen from a mobile brigade unit a few weeks prior to the incident, adding to the suspicion that renegade soldiers wearing police uniforms had done the killing.[163] Many Indonesians speculated that special forces units loyal to Prabowo were somehow involved, and that the police were merely scapegoats. A few weeks later, two police officers were charged with 'not controlling their troops' in connection with the Trisakti killings. But many analysts say the manner of the shootings suggests the involvement of more highly skilled units, such as the special forces. 'This was not an unfortunate action', said Marzuki Darusman, deputy chairman of the Indonesian Human Rights Commission: 'The high degree of skill that went into Trisakti and the sophisticated weaponry indicates only certain units which have that'.[164]

The following day, 13 May, funerals for the slain students were followed by angry, embittered processions of students. To many older Indonesians the scene bore an uncanny resemblance to the funeral of Arief Rachman Hakim, a medical student shot in February 1966 during an anti-Sukarno protest. Just as Hakim's funeral served to unify the student-led opposition to Sukarno, the funerals of the four Trisakti students fed the growing movement to push Soeharto from power. The students' courageous stand against Soeharto further weakened the elite's dwindling support for the president as well as winning widespread sympathy from the population at large.

As the funeral processions wound down, the mood turned ugly in Jakarta. Rioting and looting broke out on a scale never before seen in the capital, and continued for three days. Bands of hoodlums were seen directing the violence, which was primarily directed at the ethnic-Chinese. Hundreds of shops and houses were burned to the ground, including the home of Liem Sioe Liong, Indonesia's wealthiest tycoon. Scores of ethnic-Chinese women were raped in what appeared to be a systematic attempt to terrorise the Chinese. Dozens of women were stripped naked and assaulted. Several shopping malls were burned down, killing hundreds of looters.[165] Panicked Jakartans fled if they could, hid if they could not. An estimated 150 000 foreigners and ethnic-Chinese evacuated Jakarta, flying to Singapore, Perth, or wherever the next available flight was heading.[166] An IMF team in Jakarta to discuss the economic reform program bolted for the airport at dawn on the second day of rioting. By the time the rioting had subsided, over 1000 Indonesians were dead. Thousands of shops and house were destroyed. And Indonesia's capital city was traumatised.

The aftermath

Many unanswered questions remain about the riots of 13–15 May. Were they a spontaneous outpouring of resentment and rage? Did parts of the military instigate the riots and, if so, which parts? There is no doubt that tension in the city reached a fever pitch after the Trisakti killings, and resentment against the ethnic-Chinese was widespread. But the manner in which the riots progressed strongly suggests they were not spontaneous. Numerous eyewitness reports describe an organised pattern of destruction. Bands of men with short-cropped hair were seen directing looters into shops, malls and banks. Testimony from rape victims suggests a targeting of ethnic-Chinese women. Some victims said they heard their rapists discussing where else they had been and where they intended to attack next.[167] 'It's very hard to believe the riots were spontaneous', said Habibie advisor Dewi Fortuna Anwar: 'It was all done with military precision'.[168]

Underworld figures and other assorted hoodlums, known as *preman*, clearly took advantage of the mayhem of 13–15 May and contributed to it. Less clear is what, if anything, connected the *preman* to the military.[169] James Riady, the ethnic-Chinese deputy chairman of the Lippo Group, was in a helicopter above the residential complex at Karawaci, west of Jakarta, on the first day of the riots. He saw security personnel leave the complex and, shortly thereafter, hundreds of rioters arriving in trucks which appeared to be military vehicles. The mall at Karawaci was destroyed.

The military's behaviour during the riots was also suspect. Few troops were seen on the streets on the first day of rioting. Syafrie Syamsuddin, a Prabowo ally and commander of the Jakarta military garrison, was ordered by Armed Forces Commander Wiranto to deploy his troops in Jakarta on 13 May, according to military sources. Syafrie either refused or deployed his troops in areas where there were no rioters.[170] On 14 May, Wiranto ordered troops from Central and East Java to come to Jakarta but they did not arrive until late in the day. Strange things were also happening with the city's communications networks. The communications system in the vice-president's office was jammed throughout 13 May, noted Habibie advisor Anwar, something only the military would be able to do. An unconfirmed report surfaced a few weeks later claiming that Syafrie's office was in radio contact with the paramilitary gangs terrorising the city during the riots.[171]

Why the military would instigate riots is also not clear. One theory is that military elements loyal to Prabowo and close to his radical Muslim supporters saw an opportunity to strike at the ethnic-Chinese in what sociologist Ariel Heryanto called an 'act of state-sponsored terrorism', which aims 'to spread greater fear among the large population against whom similar violence could happen at any time'. Journalist Taufik Darusman argued that 'what happened in May comes close to an ethnic cleansing on a smaller Bosnia scale—but in a shorter period of time and in no less barbaric manner'.[172]

Another theory is that Prabowo and the generals close to him helped foment the riots in a bid for power. According to this theory, Prabowo hoped the riots would discredit Wiranto and convince Soeharto to appoint Prabowo as armed forces commander or chief of a new security agency. Earlier in the month, Soeharto had reportedly considered reconstituting the disbanded internal security agency, Kopkamtib, and putting Prabowo or Army Commander Subagyo in charge of it. He would have been able to do this thanks to the new powers given to him in March at the MPR session. The Kopkamtib chief would have wide-ranging powers and be outside Wiranto's chain of command. On the afternoon of 14 May, several senior generals and influential civilians held a meeting at armed forces headquarters. The purpose of the meeting is disputed, but several members of a government-appointed team which investigated the riots believe the meeting discussed the restoration of Kopkamtib and the granting of emergency powers to Prabowo.[173] In its formal report, the fact-finding team said there were links between the abduction of pro-democracy activists earlier in the year, the killings at Trisakti University on 12 May and the riots that began the next day. 'The range of incidents climaxing on May 13 to May 15 gives the perception that the situation was engineered to create an emergency which required extra-constitutional force to control', the report said.[174]

A more benign theory is that the military initially stood aside as the riots began in order to let some steam blow off, never thinking they would become as violent as they did. According to military analyst Salim Said, the military was spread thin from 'putting out brush fires non-stop since the beginning of the year. They had troops to guard strategic installations but not enough to guard the whole city'. Said says the military leadership was also hampered by soldiers going AWOL, and others refusing to protect ethnic-Chinese areas.[175] Whatever the truth of the military's motives, its behaviour during 13–15 May did lasting damage to its reputation.

Soeharto, still in Cairo, seemed taken aback by the news from Jakarta. He said he would not use force to keep himself in power 'if I am no longer trusted by the people'. Using Javanese expressions, he said he was prepared to become a *pandito*, or sage, and that he would 'follow a course of *tut wuri handayani* [leading from behind]'. Soeharto's comments raised a flutter of excitement back in Jakarta, but not for long. First, Soeharto's comments revealed he still did not appreciate that he was the core of the problem, and that Indonesians did not want him to lead from any direction. Second, no-one quite knew what he meant by 'the people': he could well have been referring to the 1000 hand-picked people in the People's Consultative Assembly, which had endorsed his presidency just 10 weeks before. Third, Soeharto's hint that he might step aside did not have a very convincing ring to it. The Javanese expression *lengser keprabon, madeg pandito* refers to the practice of stepping down as king and becoming a priest, or sage. As the Irish scholar Ben Anderson had noted some months before, 'no king ever voluntarily does *lengser keprabon* in the Javanese chronicles. Kings [are] forced to do *lengser keprabon*, yes, often'.[176]

Soeharto cut short his visit to Cairo and returned to Jakarta on Friday, 15 May. He cancelled the fuel-price rises announced at the beginning of the month and ordered the military to crack down on trouble-makers. Hartono, the hard-line home affairs minister and former army commander, reflexively termed the student protesters communists. 'I have warned you all that behind this was the Communist Party's remnants', Hartono exclaimed after his meeting with Soeharto.[177]

Soeharto's support dwindles

As the weekend opened, the action started to accelerate. Military officers, parliamentarians, cabinet members and a host of non-government actors went into a frenzy of scheming, plotting and palace intrigue. Over the next week, acts of betrayal and venality became commonplace, as did scenes of great courage. 'Nothing moved for 32 years, and then in three days everything happened', noted Dewi Fortuna Anwar.[178]

On Monday, 18 May, Soeharto's last week in office began on a suitably surreal note. Harmoko, speaker of the parliament and of the People's Consultative Assembly, held a press conference early in the afternoon and stunned the assembled journalists by calling on Soeharto to resign. The leaders of parliament, Harmoko said, 'hope the president will act wisely and with wisdom, and step down for the sake of unity and integrity of the nation'.[179] He gave Soeharto until Friday to comply, or impeachment hearings would begin. Adding to the absurdity of the scene, Harmoko was joined in his declaration by Lieutenant General Syarwan Hamid, who headed the 75-member military faction in parliament. When Harmoko called on Soeharto to resign, Hamid enthusiastically punched the air with his fist. This was the same Hamid, former armed forces chief of staff for social-political affairs, who helped orchestrate the ouster of Megawati from the Indonesian Democratic Party two years earlier.[180]

The resignation demand could hardly have come from a more unlikely source. With the possible exception of Habibie, no minister had served Soeharto for longer or more loyally—many would say obsequiously—than Harmoko. But even Harmoko had his breaking point, those close to him say. He became disenchanted with Soeharto the previous year after being unceremoniously dumped as information minister right after leading Golkar, which he also chaired, to a resounding victory in the 1997 parliamentary elections. Earlier in 1998 he was disappointed again at being passed over for vice-president. And now he faced a revolt in the Golkar ranks. The Kosgoro veterans group, a small but influential component of the ruling party, called for Soeharto's resignation and threatened to pull out of Golkar. Student protesters patrolling the parliamentary grounds raised the temperature even higher. So Harmoko, sensing his long-time mentor's days were at last numbered, jumped on the reform bandwagon.

However strange the source, Harmoko's demand electrified the pro-democracy movement. News that Armed Forces Commander Wiranto was to make a television address to the nation that evening set off speculation that the military had blessed Harmoko's overture. But the excitement was short-lived. Instead of seconding Harmoko's call, Wiranto dismissed the impeachment threat as simply an 'opinion' of Harmoko. According to the constitution, Wiranto said, 'such an opinion does not have legal power'.[181] Most of the military leadership, including Wiranto, understood by this point that Soeharto needed to go. But Wiranto, a Javanese general deeply loyal to Soeharto, was dead set against seeing Soeharto run out of town by the mob. And he had little interest in seeing Habibie take over the presidency, the likely result of an immediate Soeharto resignation. For Wiranto and much of the pro-reform opposition, a preferable option was to hold new elections, after which both Soeharto and Habibie could be replaced.[182]

Orchestrating Soeharto's ouster

Meanwhile, two key players outside the power structure were ratcheting up the pressure on Soeharto. The Muhammadiyah leader Amien Rais was working closely with student groups as well as his own followers in Muhammadiyah to maintain a virtually non-stop series of street protests clamouring for Soeharto's resignation. He pledged to bring a million protesters onto the streets of Jakarta to mark National Awakening Day on 20 May.

Another influential Muslim leader, Nurcholish Madjid, who headed the non-governmental Paramadina Institute, was at the same time laying the groundwork for a resignation process acceptable to Soeharto. On the previous Thursday, 14 May, Nurcholish was invited to present a paper on political reform at armed forces headquarters.[183] The main points of his paper were that Soeharto should apologise in public for the economic crisis and admit that he had made mistakes; give up power after new elections in January 2000; create a social safety net; and 'relinquish gains accumulated from wrong policies', a reference to corruption-linked First Family wealth.

According to Nurcholish, the 20 generals who attended the meeting had mixed feelings about the plan. On the one hand, they were happy to see an outline of a possible resolution to the crisis. On the other, none of the generals had any appetite for bringing such a message to Soeharto. The generals also thought an election date of January 2000 too soon.

On Saturday, 16 May, Nurcholish and another Muslim leader, Emha Ainun Nadjib, held a press conference to publicise details of Nurcholish's paper. The press gave the ideas favourable coverage, although, contrary to the military view, the consensus was that new elections in January 2000 represented too long a delay. The next day, Soeharto's cabinet secretary Saadilah Mursjid saw the press reports of Nurcholish's ideas and invited Nurcholish and businessman Fahmi Idris to discuss the plan with him on Monday, 18 May.

Prior to the meeting, Nurcholish, Fahmi and Amien Rais went on television to implore students to keep their demonstrations orderly and to avoid further rioting. When the meeting started, Mursjid, Nurcholish and Fahmi discussed at length the best way to present the reform plan to Soeharto. While they were talking, the army strategic reserve commander, Lieutenant General Prabowo, walked into Mursjid's office to offer his own thoughts. 'Prabowo said I was crazy to demand that the First Family return their wealth because they didn't have any', reported Nurcholish: 'Prabowo also told me I should suggest to Soeharto that he make Habibie president. I said the problem with that is that the military doesn't support Habibie'.

Prabowo replied: 'Don't worry about that. I will protect Habibie'. Prabowo then suggested that Nurcholish ask Habibie to make Prabowo the armed forces commander so that Prabowo would have more power to protect Habibie. 'Why don't you just ask Soeharto yourself?', retorted Fahmi Idris. 'Because Soeharto doesn't like me', Prabowo replied, and then left Mursjid's office.

After the meeting Mursjid conveyed the gist of Nurcholish's ideas to Soeharto, who requested a meeting with Nurcholish at the presidential palace on the evening of Monday, 18 May. 'I said to Soeharto that the people's understanding of reform is that you resign', Nurcholish said. Soeharto replied: 'I don't have a problem with that. I already hinted at that in Cairo'. According to Nurcholish, Soeharto claimed Harmoko misled him earlier in the year. 'I asked Harmoko before the MPR session whether the people still wanted me to be president', Soeharto told Nurcholish: 'And Harmoko said he had checked all the way down to the district level and reported to me that all the people still wanted me to be president'.[184]

At the conclusion of their meeting Soeharto told Nurcholish he would resign 'as soon as possible' but gave no date. He said he would make an announcement to this effect the next day but first he wanted to meet with leaders of the Muslim community. Nine Muslim leaders were chosen. Soeharto rejected Nurcholish's suggestion that Amien Rais be included, insisting that Abdurrahman Wahid, the ailing leader of the traditionalist Muslim organisation Nahdlatul Ulama and long-time thorn in Soeharto's side, be included. It remains something of a mystery why Soeharto was so insistent that Wahid be present, given the effort his government had made in recent years to minimise Wahid's influence.

One final attempt

The meeting with the Muslim leaders took place on Tuesday morning, 19 May. Soeharto opened the meeting by saying he planned to announce a new reform committee and a new cabinet, which he proposed to call a reform cabinet. Several of the Muslim leaders present, including Nurcholish, stressed to Soeharto that his resignation must be the centrepiece of any reform program. 'You have to end your presidency gracefully and honourably', Nurcholish told Soeharto: 'Not in the Latin American way. Not a repeat of our 1965–66 experience'. Nurcholish, who had conferred with Amien Rais just before the meeting, also insisted that the nine Muslim leaders at the meeting not be included on the reform committee or the reform cabinet: 'I said if he did then people would suspect us and accuse us of being co-opted. I said to Soeharto, help us to protect ourselves so we can help you'.

The meeting, which was supposed to last 30 minutes, stretched to two hours. Soeharto was 'very relaxed' in the meeting, Nurcholish reports, although not so relaxed that he accepted the suggestion to hand back his family's ill-gotten gains. He also refused to name a date for new elections. Soeharto said several times he was bored or fed up with being president (in Indonesian: *saya bosan jadi presiden*). Soeharto also took a dig at Habibie. In resisting pleas for an immediate resignation, he noted that this would mean Habibie's assumption of the presidency. 'There is a question of whether he is capable', Soeharto said.[185] Soeharto's contemptuous dismissal of Habibie confirmed for many that he had never had any intention of grooming Habibie for the presidency. Rather, he had picked Habibie as vice-president to make himself look better by comparison. In effect, Soeharto was arguing: stick with me or you'll end up with Habibie as president. Actually, had it not been for the economic crisis, the argument would have been fairly convincing. As it was, it came across as mere desperation.

After the meeting, Soeharto addressed the nation. He announced his plans to reshuffle the cabinet and establish a reform committee that would make preparations for new elections to be held 'as soon as possible'. He disavowed any interest in being renominated: 'There is no need to worry I will remain president. I will feel honoured to return to being an ordinary citizen . . . provided I am able to give services to the nation'.

Soeharto's concessions made barely a dent on the protesting students and reformist leaders such as Amien Rais. Many suspected Soeharto of trotting out yet another gambit to defuse the popular protests, without any real intention of stepping down. Reporting on the student protests a few days earlier, Australian journalist David Jenkins noted Soeharto's long history of unfulfilled promises to leave power. One such example was his comment to the People's Consultative Assembly in 1977 that 'this may be the last opportunity for me to address you from this rostrum'.[186] Another Australian journalist likened Soeharto's ploy on 19 May to 'a technically perfect, ten-point dive into an empty swimming pool'.[187] Soeharto's attempts to fall back on constitutional niceties to remain in control of the reform process won little sympathy from supporters of Megawati, who recalled that Soeharto had offered no such graceful exit to Megawati's father, Sukarno.

Rais and other pro-reform leaders criticised the nine Muslim leaders for thwarting their attempts to make Soeharto resign immediately. They were especially critical of Wahid's public appeal on the afternoon of 19 May for the students to stop protesting, get off the streets and give Soeharto a chance to implement his promises. At the meeting with Soeharto, Wahid said little except that he was surprised Nurcholish had come 'to hammer' Soeharto, a remark some of the other Muslim leaders present interpreted as meaning Wahid was opposed to efforts to force Soeharto to resign. Rais described Wahid's performance at the 19 May meeting with Soeharto as 'sycophantic'.[188] Some secular supporters of Wahid were bitterly disappointed. 'Wahid had no faith in the students, who were the most effective agents of change', said Marsillam Simanjuntak, who worked with Wahid in the Democracy Forum: 'He abandoned his chance to play a key role in history'.[189]

According to Wahid, Soeharto told him privately that Wahid had been right all along in his suspicions about modernist Muslims posing a threat to Indonesia's political stability. Wahid took this to mean that Soeharto realised he had made a mistake in giving modernist Muslims, and especially the ICMI, his political support earlier in the decade.[190]

After Soeharto's comments to the media, the political scheming, if anything, accelerated. Habibie, deeply hurt by Soeharto's comments, was strongly advised by his supporters to confront Soeharto directly, which he did. 'Soeharto's dismissive remarks about Habibie were the turning point for Habibie', said Dewi Fortuna Anwar, a top aide to the then vice-president.[191] Habibie claimed he had been the most loyal minister to Soeharto, and that he was capable of handling the presidency. Habibie also told Soeharto his best chance for a dignified retirement was ceding power to the vice-president: if an impeachment process moved forward, there could be no guarantees.[192]

For his part, Amien Rais moved ahead with plans to hold a major demonstration in Jakarta the following day, 20 May. But as the evening of 19 May wore on, he came under increasing pressure to call off the rally. In the early hours of 20 May he received a message from Kivlan Zein, the chief of staff of the army strategic reserve and a close ally of Prabowo. According to Rais, the message was the military would use strong measures to prevent the planned rally from happening. The military was not afraid of 'another Tienanmen' and threatened a 'sea of blood' if the rally went ahead.[193] Before dawn on 20 May, Rais went on the radio to call off the rally. 'It would have been unconscionable of me to sacrifice hundreds of young lives to a killing machine', Rais said later.[194]

The final hours

On Wednesday, 20 May, an eerie silence descended on a tense Jakarta. The military put on a massive show of force, with tanks and armoured personnel carriers cruising the streets and protecting strategic locations, including the presidential palace. Barricades blocked off major arteries. Students, disappointed that the National Awakening Day rally had been called off, continued camping out on the grounds of the national parliament, where they had been since Monday. Marines, considered the military units most sympathetic to the students, patrolled the parliament grounds and did not attempt to dislodge the students. Rifles slung over their backs, the maroon-bereted marines made idle conversation with the students. Their hands-off approach reminded many observers of the military's support for anti-Sukarno demonstrators in 1965–66.

Intentionally or not, the military's tolerance of student protesters occupying the national parliament clearly heightened the pressure on Soeharto.[195] The military leadership remained divided: Prabowo and his allies clearly preferred a more hard-line approach to the protesters; but Wiranto and the staff at armed forces headquarters recognised that Soeharto's days were numbered and that the military as an institution was also on trial. They pursued a more accommodative approach to the students.

Wiranto spent Wednesday shuttling back and forth between armed forces headquarters, Soeharto's home, and several meetings with constitutional experts. At a meeting with constitutional lawyers on Wednesday evening, Wiranto wanted to know the various options. He rejected the suggestion that a triumvirate of ministers or a military leader take over from Soeharto, arguing that this would be perceived as a coup. His objective remained an honourable exit for Soeharto and a peaceful resolution to the crisis. In the end, they decided the only solution was to support a transfer of power to Habibie.[196] It is unclear, however, whether the military decided to communicate its position to Soeharto. The *Jakarta Post* quoted informed sources as saying Wiranto went to Soeharto's house on Wednesday evening and, speaking on behalf of the military leadership, 'asked the president to resign'. Wiranto's assistant for social and political affairs, Susilo Bambang Yudhoyono, put a subtler spin on the same line: 'We communicated to Soeharto that he should realise that the people want change, that the situation is critical, and to consider the possibility of handing over power'.[197]

Some believe the military's version of events exaggerates its role after the fact in order to appear on the side of the reform movement. Military analyst Salim Said claims: 'Wiranto just reported to Soeharto what was going on without encouraging Soeharto to do one thing or another. Until the last minute, Soeharto was in control of the army'. Hasnan Habib, a retired general and former ambassador to the United States, took the same view. 'Wiranto was Soeharto's favourite aide-de-camp. There is no way a Javanese soldier like Wiranto told Soeharto to resign', he said, adding that 'lots of my colleagues think Wiranto was too passive'.[198]

While Wiranto huddled with lawyers, Soeharto and his allies scrambled to find people to sit on the reform committee and the new cabinet. Soeharto's speech-writer, the Muslim activist Yusril Mahendra, together with cabinet secretary Saadilah Mursjid, assembled a list of 45 prospective members for the reform committee on 20 May at Soeharto's house. Mahendra agreed to serve as secretary of the committee. Given the chaos in Jakarta at the time, some prospective members simply could not be reached. Many of those contacted refused to join. As Wednesday dragged on, Soeharto repeatedly sent emissaries to Nurcholish urging him to join the reform committee, including Mursjid and the minister of religion, Quraish Shihab. But Nurcholish refused.

Meanwhile, existing cabinet members finally acknowledged their fate and began plotting a future without Soeharto. They were led by the coordinating minister for the economy, Ginanjar Kartasasmita, a nationalist figure close to the *pribumi* business lobby and a long-time protégé of Soeharto. Ginanjar, along with Habibie, was mentioned by name in

Soeharto's autobiography as a promising young official.[199] The politically ambitious Ginanjar had struggled for months over how and when to break with Soeharto, according to businessmen close to him.

Before the People's Consultative Assembly in March, Ginanjar had abandoned one of his friends and supporters, Arifin Panigoro, when Panigoro was accused by Habibie of plotting against Soeharto.[200] But in April the two men made up, and Panigoro began urging Ginanjar to distance himself from Soeharto. Still, Ginanjar hesitated. He sensed Soeharto could not last much longer but did not know how the end would come. Would it be a gradual, constitutional process conducted by the People's Consultative Assembly? Or would Soeharto be forced out by public pressure? If the former, Ginanjar thought he would be better off keeping his cabinet post as well as his influential post with the Assembly; if the latter, he might be better situated for the post-Soeharto era by resigning from the cabinet. Throughout March and April the cautious Ginanjar doubted the emergence of a credible people's power movement, and resisted entreaties to resign.[201]

But by the middle of May even Ginanjar recognised Soeharto had lost control of his destiny. On 20 May he met with 13 fellow cabinet members who were also members of the Golkar faction in parliament. The group included Akbar Tandjung, who two months later would become Golkar chairman. Ginanjar's group drafted a letter to Soeharto saying there was no need to form a new cabinet because it was up to Soeharto 'to solve the political problems first'. Thus, the group added, they would refuse to join a new cabinet. Oddly, instead of delivering the letter personally to Soeharto, they sent the letter by courier to Soeharto's office, where it remained unopened until the next day. But Akbar Tandjung gave the Muslim activist Yusril Mahendra a copy of the letter that afternoon, and he in turn gave the letter to cabinet secretary Mursjid.

At about the same time, Soeharto's daughter Tutut learned of the Ginanjar plan and told her father, who dismissed the story as an unfounded rumour. Soeharto ordered Habibie to contact Ginanjar about the new cabinet, but Habibie and Ginanjar appeared to have agreed only that Ginanjar would support Habibie taking over the presidency. On Wednesday evening, in a meeting with Habibie, Soeharto broached the possibility of resigning but said he wanted to pick Habibie's cabinet for him, an offer Habibie rejected.[202] At the parliament Harmoko sent word to Soeharto that impeachment proceedings would commence if Soeharto did not resign by Friday, 22 May. Mursjid, as described earlier, finally delivered Ginanjar's letter to Soeharto at about 11 p.m. on 20 May. Soeharto was out of options. The pressure had continued to rise on the streets. Even moderate leaders such as Nurcholish Madjid refused to serve on his reform committee, and the core of his existing cabinet had abandoned him. Soeharto decided, finally, to resign.

In a brief, strained ceremony at 9 a.m. the next day, 21 May, Soeharto asked forgiveness for his mistakes, announced his immediate resignation and introduced the nation to President Habibie. Wiranto took the microphone to offer military support for Habibie and to inform the public that 'the armed forces will continue to protect the safety and the honor of former presidents . . . including Father Soeharto and his family'.[203] In an equally brief presentation, a tired-looking Habibie said 'I want to affirm my commitment to the people's aspirations' and 'extend my deepest gratitude to . . . Soeharto for all his services and dedication to the nation and country'.[204]

Soeharto shuffled off without a word to Habibie or Wiranto.[205] He seemed as surprised as everyone else at how quickly the end had come. He retired to his modest house in central Jakarta to ponder where it had all gone wrong. The New Order was over.

12
Starting over

The first president (Sukarno) was crazy about women. The second president (Soeharto) was crazy about fortune. The third president (Habibie) was truly crazy.

Abdurrahman Wahid[1]

It's a fight between those who want to re-establish democracy and those who want to suppress the people and take away their sovereignty.

Mochtar Buchori[2]

This is the beginning of the destruction of religion, because it's being used for political purposes.

Ali Sadikin[3]

A new day dawns

President B. J. Habibie's honeymoon lasted about as long as his acceptance speech. He had barely returned home from the presidential palace when he was confronted with a possible split in the military. A glance out the window revealed that two sets of troops had moved in to protect his house: the presidential guards, who reported to Armed Forces Commander Wiranto, and who were supposed to be there; and units of the army strategic reserve, or Kostrad, who were not. On the afternoon of 21 May, Habibie received a visit from an agitated Lieutenant General

367

Prabowo, the commander of Kostrad, who was eager to consolidate his own position in the military.

Prabowo, slow to recognise he was no longer the president's son-in-law, had once again jumped the chain of command to register his demands. Worried about losing ground to Wiranto, Prabowo insisted that Habibie put him in charge of the army and promote the current army commander and close Prabowo ally, Subagyo, to armed forces commander. He reminded Habibie of his loyal support and defence of Habibie, first for the vice-presidency and then for the presidency. According to Habibie's aide Dewi Fortuna Anwar, Prabowo then 'showed Habibie evidence of his support, including pamphlets supporting Habibie and of the demonstrations he had covertly organised to counter pro-democracy activists at the DPR'. Prabowo 'still considered himself a kingmaker', Anwar said, adding: 'Habibie did not appreciate his advice'.[4]

Habibie, who was immediately escorted back to the presidential palace for his own safety, acted quickly to neutralise the threat. 'The next morning . . . I called in Wiranto and instructed him to replace Prabowo and to bring the Kostrad troops back to the barracks', Habibie said. Habibie wanted 'to consolidate the military', Anwar explains, 'which meant he had no choice but to replace Prabowo'.[5]

That is one version of events. Another is that Habibie and Wiranto struck a deal before Soeharto resigned. In this version, Wiranto pledged to support Habibie as president and, in return, Habibie gave Wiranto free rein to sideline his rivals in the armed forces.[6] Both versions agree on Prabowo's attempt on 21 May to gain control of the military; they differ on whether it was Habibie or Wiranto who made the decision to cashier Prabowo. A defence analyst in Jakarta, who subscribes to the second version, says Wiranto visited army headquarters on 21 May and was refused entry by guards ordered not to admit anyone without Prabowo's permission. 'That was the last straw for Wiranto', the analyst says.[7] Regardless of who made the decision, Prabowo was relieved of his command on 21 May and transferred to Bandung to head a military college.

Meanwhile, pro-democracy student protesters were still camped out at the parliament. Although unaware of Prabowo's machinations, they had their own problems to deal with. The mood at the parliament had moved rather quickly from jubilation at the news of Soeharto's resignation to disappointment at Habibie's assumption of power. Many of the more moderate students began leaving the parliamentary grounds during the afternoon, hoping to avoid a split within the student movement.[8] But late on 21 May the remaining students found themselves in conflict again, not with the military but with Muslim groups loyal to both Habibie and Prabowo.

Fadli Zon, the Muslim activist with the Indonesian Committee for Solidarity with the Islamic World, or KISDI, claimed that 43 Muslim groups met at KISDI's office in central Jakarta and proceeded to the parliament to confront the pro-reform students and to support Habibie. A Habibie ally in the Indonesian Association of Muslim Intellectuals (ICMI), Jimly Asshiddiqie, also helped organise the pro-Habibie demonstrations by militant Muslims. 'We can't have instability', Fadli said: 'We want constitutional reform'.[9] The clashes between the two groups continued through the evening of 22 May, when the marines arrived to escort the students off the parliamentary grounds.

Back at the presidential palace Habibie, fearing for his safety, spent the night at the state guesthouse instead of his home. Wiranto deployed units of the air force special forces and marines to guard the compound, apparently distrusting the loyalty of troops under Major General Syafrie Syamsuddin, the Jakarta military garrison commander and Prabowo ally. On the morning of 22 May, Habibie announced a new cabinet in which Wiranto served as both minister of defence and armed forces commander. Later that day, in a state of disbelief, Prabowo tried to force another meeting with Habibie. Prabowo could hardly believe that Habibie's first act as president would be to side with Wiranto against him. Prabowo arrived for the meeting in battle fatigues and accompanied by several truckloads of Kostrad troops. Lieutenant General (ret.) Sintong Panjaitan, who had gone to work for Habibie after his retirement from the military, denied Prabowo entry to Habibie's office in a tense confrontation.[10]

Although Prabowo had undoubtedly contributed to the unrest in Jakarta and elsewhere, paving the way for Habibie to take over the presidency, Habibie was shrewd enough to prevent Prabowo from doing the same to him. Fearing retaliation from Kostrad and special forces troops, Habibie also spent the next evening at the state guesthouse and preparations were made to airlift him to safety if the need arose.

But by this point Prabowo was left with few options. Although he was considered close to army chief Subagyo, it appears Subagyo remained loyal to Wiranto during these crucial hours. Subagyo relieved Prabowo's close ally Muchdi Purwopranyoto of his command of the special forces some time on 22 May. Prabowo was thus left with a small number of troops still loyal to him, too few to challenge the troops under Wiranto's command. On the same day Prabowo, who is married to Soeharto's second-youngest daughter, had visited Soeharto at his home in a last-ditch attempt to salvage his career. The visit did not go well. Soeharto rebuked Prabowo for causing so much trouble, while Soeharto's eldest daughter Tutut bitterly assailed him for failing to defend Soeharto and for plotting with Soeharto's enemies to bring down the ex-president. 'I was flabbergasted', Prabowo said later: 'I was the loyal son and I was the one who was banished'.[11]

On Saturday 23 May, Prabowo met with Wiranto and agreed to accept the offered post at the military college in Bandung without further trouble.

But Wiranto's troubles with the military chain of command were not over. The evening before, he had assigned his assistant for operations, Major General Johny Lumintang, to take over the Kostrad command from Prabowo, which set off a firestorm of protest. Lumintang, though a highly regarded officer, was a Christian. The prospect of a Christian officer taking over the powerful strategic reserve command was anathema to the militant Muslim groups. Having supported Habibie for so long, the last thing they expected was plum military jobs handed over to Christians. A number of ICMI leaders are believed to have complained strenuously to Habibie, as did Feisal Tandjung, the new coordinating minister for politics and security. Prabowo and his allies in senior military positions also voiced their objections. Wiranto decided he could not afford to risk a military split and backed down. Seventeen hours after being appointed Kostrad chief, Lumintang was replaced by a Muslim, Major General Djamari Chaniago, who had served as an infantry division commander at Kostrad under Wiranto.[12]

Publicly, the military denied that the sudden switch was based on religion, although failing to come up with a convincing alternative explanation. Wiranto's assistant for social and political affairs, Lieutenant General Susilo Bambang Yudhoyono, said the decision to replace Lumintang 'was based on a comprehensive calculation at the time. It was not outside military logic'. Religion, he added, 'did not influence Wiranto's decision'.[13]

Few believed the military denial. 'The Muslims close to Prabowo panicked at the thought of Lumintang taking over Kostrad', said military analyst Salim Said: 'They thought that meant the return of Benny Murdani and his influence. They used all their channels to get Habibie to overrule the decision. I think later they realised they overreacted'. A Western defence analyst spoke about the Lumintang case with Brigadier General Zen Maulani, a senior adviser to Habibie who later in the year would be appointed to head Bakin, the state intelligence coordinating board. A pious Muslim with a dim view of Benny Murdani, Maulani told the analyst that Lumintang and the other Christian officers needed 'to be reacquainted with the importance of Islam in Indonesia'. For his part, Fadli Zon of KISDI made no apology for protesting Lumintang's appointment. 'It was Wiranto who decided to replace Lumintang because he realised the decision to put Lumintang in Kostrad was too drastic', Fadli said. Why was it too drastic? 'Because Lumintang is a Christian', Fadli replied.[14]

The Lumintang case profoundly disappointed many military figures, who took pride in the military's emphasis on merit over religion or ethnicity. 'There is no discrimination within Abri', insisted Yudhoyono. 'And we have to maintain this corporate culture', he added, banging his fist on the table for emphasis. Benny Murdani, the former armed forces commander, was one of many retired officers disappointed with Wiranto's decision to switch Lumintang: 'The Lumintang case is very strange to me. In my day, you asked a man's religion only to know how to bury him. This sort of screening weakens the military'.[15]

Within 72 hours of taking office, Habibie had confronted what would remain two of the most serious challenges to his presidency: a disgruntled, confused military unsure of its role in society; and demands for preferential treatment by segments of the modernist Muslim community.

It did not take long to convince Habibie that he was sailing in uncharted waters. An authoritarian reign longer than the lifetimes of most Indonesians had come to an abrupt end, and a new political roadmap had yet to be sketched. Strong forces for reinventing Indonesia in a more democratic, open fashion faced strong forces interested in preserving much of Soeharto's political framework. Writing in 1994 I titled the last chapter of the first edition of this book, 'A democratic future?'. The question mark still belongs. While it is too soon to draw a clear picture of Indonesia's immediate future, one can describe, as I attempt to do in this chapter, the major actors and societal forces. To each I ask: what sort of Indonesia do you want?

BACHARUDDIN JUSUF HABIBIE: MAN ON A MISSION

When B. J. Habibie assumed power, a loud groan emanated from the pro-democracy movement. After labouring so long to evict President Soeharto from power, the emergence of Soeharto's long-time protégé as president made for a bittersweet victory. Sensing his popular support as less than overwhelming, the 62-year-old, German-educated Habibie immediately began refashioning his image. Describing himself as a transitional president, Habibie said it would be his legacy to bring Indonesia into a more democratic future. Claiming that his many years in Germany taught him the virtues of democracy, Habibie promised a slew of new laws to upend Indonesia's authoritarian political system. He freed dozens of political prisoners, pledged to remove controls on the media, and annulled the ban on new political parties.[16] Most importantly, he called for new parliamentary elections in mid-1999 and the selection of a new president by the end of 1999.

Aware of his shaky support within the armed forces, he gave armed forces chief Wiranto free rein to consolidate control of the military. As discussed above, Wiranto removed Prabowo from a troop command within hours of Soeharto's resignation. He then made a clean sweep of Prabowo's allies. Major General Muchdi Purwopranyoto was removed from his command of the special forces the day after Soeharto resigned and was replaced a few days later by Major General Syahrir. A Wiranto ally, Major General Djaja Suparman, replaced the head of the Jakarta military command, Major General Syafrie Syamsuddin, on 25 June. A handful of other key Prabowo allies, including army strategic reserve chief of staff Major General Kivlan Zein, were also sidelined in Habibie's first month in office. Major General Zacky Makarim, who headed the military's main intelligence unit, was replaced by a retired military officer and close Habibie aide, Zen Maulani, in September.[17]

Just another illegitimate leader?

While the threat of a military split receded, other challenges to Habibie's rule grew more strident. The imploding economy (discussed more fully below) left Habibie unable to buy off his critics and with only limited means to satisfy his supporters. His attempts at liberalising the political system won Habibie only a modicum of breathing space. Habibie's core problem was that he lacked legitimacy as president. No amount of pleasing rhetoric could overcome this fundamental weakness. Behind the forces that drove Soeharto from power was a belief that Soeharto and his political machinery lacked legitimacy. The strict controls on the media, sharp limits on political activity and fraudulent elections once every five years produced a governing elite that had no right to claim (although it often did) to represent the Indonesian body politic. By calling for new parliamentary elections and a new People's Consultative Assembly meeting in 1999, Habibie implicitly conceded that the earlier elections that had kept Soeharto in power lacked legitimacy. But it was those same flawed electoral devices that had elevated Habibie to the vice-presidency. If the elections had not conferred legitimacy on Soeharto, neither did they confer any on Habibie.

For most of the political opposition forces, Habibie was merely a more talkative version of Soeharto. Habibie often referred to Soeharto as 'my professor', or SGS, for Super Genius Soeharto. He once described Soeharto as 'the hero of all other heroes'.[18] Prior to Soeharto's resignation, Habibie had never publicly articulated any political vision other than endorsements of Soeharto's authoritarian rule. Despite attempts by his aides to portray otherwise, Habibie played no role whatsoever in pushing Soeharto from power. On the contrary, he immediately quashed an initiative in early May 1998 of the Association of Muslim Intellectuals, which he headed, which tepidly supported the convening of a new People's Consultative Assembly. In reality, he remained steadfastly loyal to Soeharto until 19 May, the day Soeharto finally revealed his low opinion of Habibie's political talents. In short, Habibie owed his rise to the presidency to nothing other than being the last beneficiary of Soeharto's manipulation of the political system.

Needless to say, Habibie came to power with few natural constituencies, although this didn't appear to faze him. 'Maybe I am the most stupid guy in Indonesia . . . I am a stupid, naïve and whatever guy,' Habibie mused in an interview. 'It's all right with me. The fact is that I'm the president'.[19] Habibie did have some support, however, particularly from the nationalist wing of the modernist Muslim community, civil servants who had prospered under Soeharto, and non-Javanese businessmen and politicians happy to see the Javanese monopoly on power broken. The cabinet he appointed on 22 May reflected his bases of support. He kept 21 members from Soeharto's last cabinet and appointed 15 new members.[20] Many of the new appointees were drawn from Habibie's Muslim supporters in the Indonesian Association of Muslim Intellectuals. But he proved fairly adept at using the office of the presidency to accumulate support. In addition, his authority to hire and fire military leaders allowed Habibie to keep armed forces chief Wiranto in check.

Ironically, one of Habibie's strongest new constituencies was the international aid community, including the International Monetary Fund. As described in chapter 11, in January 1998 the IMF had targeted Habibie's aircraft manufacturing plant as one of the wasteful public-sector projects needing to be eliminated. Once settled into the president's chair, Habibie quickly moved to patch up relations with the Fund. He appointed Ginanjar Kartasasmita as his senior economics minister and rehired the two elderly technocrats, Wijoyo Nitisastro and Ali Wardhana, as his economic advisers. All three men had good relations with the international financial community. After Habibie took power, the IMF and the World Bank resumed disbursement of the US$43-billion rescue package as well as raising US$14 billion more to cover Indonesia's projected budget shortfall for 1998 and 1999. The two institutions and numerous countries contributed to humanitarian assistance programs for Indonesia. To his domestic audience, Habibie claimed credit for the renewed flows of assistance. To many reform-minded Indonesians, it appeared the IMF and the World Bank were propping up Habibie, just as they used to prop up Soeharto. But the Fund and the Bank had little choice: to help Indonesia meant helping Habibie.

Building a political foothold

In his first six months in power, Habibie had to navigate through two political meetings to preserve his hold on power: the first was a congress of the ruling Golkar Party in July; the second was a special session of the People's Consultative Assembly in November. By July, Habibie had already dropped the pretence of serving as a transitional president and had let it be known he was interested in staying in power after 1999. But he faced an early challenge from Golkar, Soeharto's formidable patronage machine. Habibie and his ICMI supporters settled on State Secretary Akbar Tandjung as the new Golkar chairman. He was challenged by Edi Sudrajat, the former armed forces chief, who was supported by Try

Sutrisno, another general who had been vice-president in 1993–98. With a majority of the Golkar provincial chairmen coming from the military, many analysts expected Sudrajat to prevail in a vote. But Habibie's supporters effectively painted Sudrajat as a puppet of Soeharto and tarred Sutrisno's Muslim credentials on account of his role in the Tanjung Priok killings in 1984. Meanwhile, Habibie reportedly issued an ultimatum to Wiranto: support Tandjung for Golkar chairman or I will replace you as armed forces chief. In the end Wiranto conceded, and pressured a number of Golkar provincial chairmen to vote for Tandjung. The final vote was 16 to 11 in favour of Tandjung. The threats, bribes and backroom intrigue that coloured the proceedings reminded many of how little Indonesian politics had changed from the Soeharto era.

In the run-up to the provisional People's Consultative Assembly in November, known as the MPRS, Habibie faced another set of challenges from pro-reform groups. When the school year began in September 1998, student groups revived regular protests against Habibie's rule. The students complained that the 1000 members of the MPRS had been mostly hand-picked by Soeharto and thus had no more legitimacy than Habibie. The more radical student groups demanded Habibie be removed from the presidency at the MPRS and replaced with a presidium of national leaders. The students received behind-the-scenes support from a group of retired generals and nationalist figures known as the *Barisan Nasional*, or National Front. The plan to remove Habibie at the MPRS never got off the ground, principally because the potential members of a ruling presidium—Megawati Sukarnoputri and the Islamic leaders Amien Rais and Abdurrahman Wahid—had no interest in joining. All three planned to contest the parliamentary elections scheduled for mid-1999 and had no desire to see the democratic process short-circuited.

Even before the four-day MPRS opened on 10 November, the meeting was already mired in controversy. The military had armed over 100 000 civilians with sharpened bamboo staves to 'protect' the meeting. The civilian militia was apparently conceived by Generals Feisal Tandjung and Kivlan Zein, the latter having become an adviser to Wiranto after being dislodged as chief of staff of the army strategic reserve.[21] Supported by militant Muslim groups, the militia's objective was clearly to protect Habibie from the student groups demanding his ouster. Among its other flaws, the militia represented a dangerous blurring of the line between religion and politics. Militia members patrolled the streets of Jakarta, clashing repeatedly with student demonstrators. At one point, Wiranto promised to disband the militia in the face of widespread criticism, not only from the students but from many mainstream figures. But the vigilantes were not withdrawn until several had been killed in violent clashes with student protesters and irate citizens offended at their heavy-handed tactics.

By the time the MPRS finally opened, the students' main demands were boiled down to two: an independent investigation of Soeharto family wealth, and an end to the military's role in politics. Student protesters congregated around the assembly hall to keep the pressure on the delegates inside. On the first point, the MPRS reluctantly gave ground. It passed a decree calling for an investigation of corrupt activities, mentioning Soeharto by name. The MPRS was less willing to compromise on the second point. The army faction in the MPRS conceded the military would phase out its dual-function role over time, but refused to set any dates.[22]

On Tuesday 10 November, leading opposition figures Rais, Wahid, Megawati and the Sultan of Yogyakarta met at Wahid's home to discuss the students' demands. The so-called Ciganjur group, named after the neighbourhood where Wahid lives, issued an eight-point statement urging Habibie to move up the date of elections, declaring Habibie's government a transitional regime, and demanding an end to the military's role in politics within six years. But, much to the disappointment of the students, they refused to endorse student demands for Habibie to step down or for an immediate end to the military's involvement in politics. The 10 November meeting marked a parting of the ways between the increasingly frustrated student movement and the mainstream opposition. 'The radicalisation will deepen and spread, and the loyal "opposition" will be increasingly frightened', insisted Ma'ruf, a leader of the banned People's Democratic Party: 'Amien Rais now talks like the military'.[23]

On 13 November, the last day of the MPRS, Jakarta experienced a repeat of the mayhem in May. Soldiers opened fire with live ammunition on more than 50 000 protesting students thronging the assembly building. By the time the shooting stopped on Black Friday, as it was soon dubbed, at least 15 students lay dead and hundreds more were injured.[24] The violence, unsurprisingly, further radicalised the student movement. The students added the ouster of armed forces chief Wiranto to their list of demands, and broke completely with the main political parties, who were willing to tolerate a phased reduction of the military's political role.[25] From his home in central Jakarta, Soeharto added the final surreal twist to the proceedings. The violence occurred because 'the students' aspirations were not heard and appreciated', Soeharto said, apparently without irony: 'If [the government] had respected them, the problem could have been overcome'.[26] On one level, Habibie emerged from the MPRS relatively unscathed. He was forced to investigate Soeharto's wealth, which he did not want to do, but he left the meeting with a constitutional mandate to continue as president.

The MPRS called for new parliamentary elections but did not specify a date. From a broader perspective, Habibie's political standing suffered. The lack of input by pro-democracy forces into the MPRS deliberations and the violence inflicted on the students by the military merely reinforced the impression of an elite trying desperately to hold onto power. For many students, what happened at the MPRS convinced them that the political opening promised by Habibie was just a trick. Following the MPRS, Habibie ordered the leading members of the National Front detained for questioning. A few weeks later, the attorney-general announced that several of them would be charged with the crime of treason for demanding that Habibie step down.[27] Once again, the pro-reform community concluded Habibie had learned nothing from Soeharto's ouster, and was determined to treat dissident voices just as his mentor had.

Investigating Soeharto's corruption

In his first 10 months in office, Habibie confronted two crucial issues that would leave a lasting imprint on his presidency. The first was the issue of corruption, the second the fate of the ethnic-Chinese. The corruption issue can itself be divided into two separate challenges: how to handle Soeharto family wealth, and how to deal with corruption allegations about sitting cabinet ministers and other government officials.

From the day Soeharto resigned, both Habibie and Wiranto made it clear they did not favour a sweeping investigation of Soeharto, despite protesters' demands. Publicly, both men said they wished Soeharto a dignified retirement as a reward for his contributions to Indonesia's economic development. In fact, Habibie knew that any credible investigation of Soeharto family corruption would undoubtedly result in an indictment of the New Order itself and its major beneficiaries, including himself. Like many ministers who served Soeharto, Habibie made sure his family was well provided-for. Numerous reports detailed Habibie family wealth, especially on the island of Batam.[28]

In an early indication of his sentiments, in June 1998 Habibie abruptly sacked the attorney-general, Sujono Atmonogro, who had a reputation as a reasonably independent-minded official. He was replaced by an active-duty military officer, Andi Ghalib, a switch many Indonesians assumed was meant to protect Soeharto. Umar Juoro, a researcher with the Center for Information and Development Studies, says the expulsion of Sujono was also meant to protect Habibie. 'Sujono was actually close to the Soeharto family, and Habibie and Ginanjar were afraid he would investigate them (rather than Soeharto)', Juoro said: 'Ghalib, on the other hand, is loyal to Habibie'.[29]

As the months progressed, it became more difficult to ignore the corruption issue. A newly liberated press reported day after day the details of how Soeharto's family and friends had stolen from the national purse. Freed from the fear of prosecution and worse, government officials went public with information on scores of contracts and loans corruptly acquired by Soeharto's inner circle. Major state-owned enterprises like oil giant Pertamina and the national flag-carrier Garuda cancelled a slew of middleman deals that had enriched Soeharto's children.[30] Foreign companies rushed to disentangle themselves from First Family companies, adding still more information on the extraordinary reach of Soeharto's children.

Although hundreds of other examples could be given, the case of Astra International provides one illustration of the economic damage wrought by corruption. After Soeharto awarded the 'national car franchise' to his youngest son Tommy in 1996, he said other automobile companies that met specified local content requirements would also qualify for the tax breaks and other benefits given to Tommy. Astra, as the country's largest automobile manufacturer and generally considered the country's best-run firm, had no choice but to increase the domestic production content of its vehicles. To do so, Astra went on a borrowing spree, pushing its foreign debt from US$900 million in February 1996 to US$2 billion in August 1997. The crisis hit Astra with a double whammy: automobile sales plummeted, from 15 900 units a month just before the crisis hit to 2200 units at the end of 1998, causing Astra to shut down entire production lines for months on end. And its forced accumulation of debt rendered it insolvent as the rupiah depreciated to a fraction of the level at which the debt was originally contracted. Astra was not the only one damaged by Tommy's foray into the automobile business. The attorney-general's office said in December 1998 the national car project cost the government US$1.6 billion in lost taxes and soured bank loans.[31]

While eager to shield Soeharto from public accountability, Habibie said his children would not be granted the same protection. But this ploy was doomed from the start. It was impossible to hold Soeharto's children accountable without exposing Soeharto's role in directing illicit wealth to them.[32] In September, Soeharto appeared on a television station owned by his daughter Tutut to deny he had even 'one cent' in a foreign bank account, and challenged his critics to prove him wrong. Two months later Soeharto 'returned' to the government seven foundations he controlled with assets of US$530 million. Soeharto repeatedly denied he had amassed great wealth and refused to apologise for the rampant corruption of his administration.[33]

Soeharto's relatives, true to form, managed to pour oil on the flames. Soeharto's step-brother Probosutedjo once again trotted out the view that Soeharto's children were merely innocent bystanders duped by greedy underlings. 'These Soeharto children have only been used by bad people', he said: 'What can his children do, they are not even so good in business'. In November, Tommy Soeharto lashed out at critics of his father, vowing 'we'll prove that father isn't guilty'. Tommy's comments had the predictable result of stoking the students' fury to an even higher pitch. Many Indonesians were deeply affronted that Soeharto's children continued to actively pursue their business interests, oblivious to the controversy about them. 'The children still walk around like they're all-powerful', said Umar Juoro: 'No wonder students are angry'.[34] At the Provisional People's Consultative Assembly meeting in November, Habibie tried valiantly to keep his options open on dealing with Soeharto. But, as described above, the assembly delegates issued a resolution specifically requiring Habibie to launch an investigation of Soeharto. As even Habibie's supporters noted, without the inclusion of the specific reference to Soeharto, Habibie was unlikely to act on the resolution.

But the story does not end there. In mid-November 1998 Habibie approached noted human rights lawyer Adnan Buyung Nasution to lead an independent commission investigating New Order corruption. Before joining, Nasution demanded that the commission be granted sufficient powers to compel testimony, funds to hire attorneys and investigators, and the authority to instruct the attorney-general's office to prosecute. But Habibie refused. He insisted on placing figures loyal to him on the commission and refused to grant the commission subpoena power. While these discussions were taking place, Soeharto's lawyer went public with a thinly veiled threat. If the investigation of Soeharto proceeded, said the former president's legal advisor Yohannes Yacob, the case 'will also drag down government officials, ex-officials and all the cronies. The legal process will be very long and tiring'. In the end, Nasution refused to join the commission. Instead, Habibie endorsed a team led by Attorney-General Ghalib; its findings would be referred to Habibie for follow-up action.[35]

Two things about Soeharto's corruption are certain: one, it will continue to play a major role in the political discourse for some time to come; two, Indonesia will not reach a satisfactory resolution of the issue until Habibie is gone from power. The issue is about more than money, something Habibie understands as well as his critics. Estimates of Soeharto family wealth vary widely, from a few billion dollars up to US$40 billion. The exact amount of wealth hived off by the Soeharto clan is not known and probably never will be. Soeharto family assets are tied up in many hundreds of companies and foundations, both in Indonesia and abroad. It will take years of accounting sleuthing to track down.[36] Even if the assets are properly identified, it is far from certain how much money Indonesia will actually recover. If the Philippines' experience with tracking down the wealth of its former strongman Ferdinand Marcos is any guide, the answer is probably: not much. But in a political sense the pursuit of Soeharto's wealth is a process Indonesia cannot avoid. The wealth of Soeharto and his children symbolises for many Indonesians the fundamental flaw of the New Order: its lack of accountability and transparency. The demands for a genuine investigation of Soeharto are inseparable from the demand for a new political order.

Of course, current government officials were also tarred with the corruption brush. One of the most prominent examples of this group was Ginanjar Kartasasmita, Habibie's senior economics minister. Several newspaper and magazine articles delved into Ginanjar's connections to the American mining firm, Freeport McMoRan, which operates a massive copper and gold mine in Irian Jaya. The articles alleged that Ginanjar and businessmen close to him had fraudulently benefited from distribution and construction contracts awarded by Freeport, as well as from a sale of Freeport shares in the early 1990s. An American academic, Jeffrey Winters, repeated the allegations at a press conference in Jakarta in October 1998. Ginanjar heatedly denied the allegations, and Winters was temporarily banned from the country.[37] But the charges weakened Ginanjar's political standing nonetheless, and made him less of a threat to Habibie. Allegations of corrupt behaviour of a number of other cabinet ministers lurk just below the surface, adding both to the uneasiness of top government officials and to a reluctance to endorse a sweeping investigation of Soeharto-era corruption. 'Habibie is trying to clean the floor with a dirty mop', said former cabinet minister Sarwono Kusumaatmadja. 'The harder he tries, the dirtier it gets'.[38]

The failure to settle the accounts of the past hobbled Indonesia's efforts to move forward economically. The much-touted privatisation campaign provided a good example. Compromised officials in leading government ministries, as well as numerous vested interests sprinkled throughout the government, did all they could to slow down reforms of state-owned enterprises. An early casualty was the East Java-based cement company, Semen Gresik. Shortly after Habibie took power, the ministry handling state-enterprise reform reached a provisional deal to sell 35 per cent of Gresik's shares to the Mexican cement company, Cemex, along with an option to sell another 30 per cent over the next five years. In return, Cemex agreed to assume US$260 million in debts Gresik had incurred to build a new plant, and to export at least 4 million tonnes of cement after three years. Cemex also agreed not to lay off any workers for at least two years. 'It was a great deal for the government', said one official who worked on the deal: 'It took a chunk of debt off our books, put a new plant to use, began generating foreign exchange and retained all the old jobs'.[39]

But after the deal's announcement vested interests swung into action. Gresik's top managers stirred up protests in West Sumatra, where one of the firm's plants is located. Meanwhile, former members of Gresik management and other West Sumatran officials who had taken up government jobs in Jakarta also worked to undermine the deal, which would have cut off their access to funds generated by Gresik. In the end, the Habibie administration, on the advice of senior technocrat Wijoyo Nitisastro, backed down and settled for a smaller sale of Gresik shares. 'I didn't used to think this way but after the experience with Gresik I realised that we need a clean break with the past', said the official involved with the deal: 'There are too many old ghosts hanging around holding us back'.[40]

Habibie and the ethnic-Chinese

The other major issue confronting Habibie in his first months in office involved the ethnic-Chinese community. The Chinese entered the post-Soeharto era deeply traumatised. Both poor and rich Chinese were stunned by the violence directed at them in the first half of 1998, culminating in the riots and rapes of 13–15 May. They were, to put it mildly, unsure of their role in society with Soeharto gone and the military discredited. Chinese businessmen considered Habibie anti-Chinese long before he rose to the vice-presidency in March. Habibie did little to assuage their fears in his first few months as president. In several interviews with foreign publications, Habibie revealed a remarkable lack of sympathy for the plight of the ethnic-Chinese. 'If the Chinese community does not come back because they don't trust their own country and society, I cannot force, nobody can force them', Habibie said in one interview: 'But do you think we will then die? Their place will be taken over by others.'[41]

Habibie's insistence that he held no animosity towards them failed to comfort the ethnic-Chinese community. And it was not merely the Chinese who worried about the rise of ethnic conflict. Abdurrahman Wahid, the influential leader of the Nahdlatul Ulama, accused several cabinet ministers by name of being anti-Chinese, including Adi Sasono, A. M. Saefuddin, Fahmi Idris, Tutty Alawiyah and Muslimin Nasution. 'Habibie has paid lip service to Chinese concerns, but appointed anti-Chinese ministers to his cabinet', Wahid said.[42]

Perhaps most troubling for the Chinese was Habibie's handling of the investigation into the rapes of Chinese women in May. He appointed a fact-finding team to look into the May riots containing both government officials and civilian leaders.[43] Human rights groups originally claimed that 168 women were raped during the rioting. The fact-finding team later said it could confirm 52 rape cases, but it did not dispute claims that the true number was higher. According to human rights groups, many Chinese rape victims fled the country or were too afraid of testifying in public. Meanwhile, Indonesian groups working with the victims as well as medical personnel treating the victims came under constant harassment. Romo Sandyawan, a Jesuit priest who headed the Volunteer's Team for Humanity, said he and his staff received numerous threatening phone calls and warnings 'to stop making trouble'. The identity of those making the threats was unknown, but Romo Sandyawan and other human rights workers were convinced they were linked to the military, if not actually in the military. Karlina Leksono, who worked with Sandyawan, said military officers visited the hospitals where rape victims were being treated and threatened the doctors: 'The doctors and the victims were very scared. We had to move one of the victims out of the hospital and into a safe house'.[44]

Like the human rights groups, the ethnic-Chinese community did not believe for a moment that the rapes were committed spontaneously by looters and rioters. They were convinced the rapes were instigated by factions of the military—once again the suspicion fell on Soeharto's son-in-law Prabowo—as a deliberate attempt to drive the Chinese out of the country. While the truth may never be known, the Habibie administration and the military did go to extraordinary lengths to ensure the truth would remain buried for as long as possible.

The impression of a governmental cover-up solidified when senior members of Habibie's cabinet, including armed forces chief Wiranto and Women's Affairs Minister Tutty Alawiyah, denied on several occasions there had been any rapes at all.[45] When the government's fact-finding commission released its report in November, human rights groups demanded the government use the report as a starting point for prosecuting those who had instigated and participated in the riots and rapes. But 10 months after the May riots the Habibie administration remained steadfastly unenthusiastic about getting to the bottom of the May 1998 riots. Wiranto dismissed the fact-finding team's report, saying it was only 'an analysis', not an investigation.

Habibie's shifting winds

It is not only the Chinese who harbour serious misgivings about Habibie's true intentions. Many Indonesian politicians and community leaders struggle to discern what Habibie really thinks about anything. A non-stop talker, Habibie drowns his listeners with verbiage but seems bereft of a political vision or even a consistent message. One moment he preaches pluralism and protection of minority rights, the next moment he is disparaging the Chinese. One day he endorses neo-classical economists and promises a level playing field in the economy; the next day he sings the praises of affirmative-action programs. Habibie's views 'are the same as the last person he spoke with', explained Marzuki Darusman of the Human Rights Commission. Others are considerably less charitable. Jusuf Wanandi of the Center for Strategic and International Studies dismissed Habibie as 'a clown, a joker, an entertainer'. Former armed forces commander Benny Murdani looked puzzled when asked for an impression of Habibie. Like many Javanese, he is uncomfortable with Habibie's hyperactive style. 'He is not really dignified, is he?', Murdani asked.[46]

Habibie aggravates his supporters by regularly speaking off-the-cuff. One of his much-derided suggestions was for Indonesians to overcome the country's food shortage by fasting one day a week. In August 1998

Habibie raised eyebrows by awarding Indonesia's highest honours to some of his close associates, as well as his wife. In late 1998 he alarmed many relatively well-off Indonesians by suggesting a prohibition on Indonesian students going to school abroad, notwithstanding the fact that he had educated his own sons overseas. Indonesia's neighbours have also been taken aback by Habibie's penchant for articulating whatever is on his mind. In February 1999, for example, Habibie infuriated Singaporeans by calling them 'racists'.[47]

On more substantive matters as well, Habibie's actions belie the democratic image he tries hard to cultivate. Government critics have been harassed by the tax department and threatened by the attorney-general's office.[48] Members of the left-leaning People's Democratic Party have languished in jail while other political prisoners have been released. Promises to respect workers' right to freedom of association were undercut by continued military suppression of labour protests.[49] Moves to free the media from Soeharto-era controls have been followed by other efforts to keep the media in check.

It is equally difficult to fathom what Habibie has in mind for his political future. It did not take long for Habibie to forget his plans to be a transitional president and to declare himself interested in another term. Sounding eerily like Soeharto, Habibie said it would be 'arrogant' of him to turn down the people's wishes for him to remain president, if that's what they wanted. He dawdled for as long as he could on setting a date for parliamentary elections in 1999 and for the People's Consultative Assembly meeting to pick a new president later in 1999. Umar Juoro, who works for Habibie as an adviser posted to the still vacant vice-president's office, said Habibie wanted to delay the elections 'so he could make his first term in office as long as possible'. In December 1998 Habibie finally announced that parliamentary elections would be held in June 1999.[50]

Habibie appeared to be counting on support from a range of parties, principally those appealing to modernist Muslims. But his hopes for remaining in power past 1999 hinged mainly on Golkar. As discussed above, he successfully positioned his ally Akbar Tandjung as the new Golkar chairman in July 1998, but it remains unclear just how strong an ally Tandjung would be. Many analysts felt Tandjung had presidential ambitions of his own. Habibie's spokeswoman Dewi Fortuna Anwar conceded Habibie's control of Golkar was shaky when she noted in October 1998 that 'Habibie's main competitor for president [in the future comes] from within Golkar itself', a comment that did not sit well with Tandjung.[51] Habibie himself is an unlikely politician. He is a mediocre public speaker whose ramblings often leave listeners confused, if not downright alarmed. A Western banker who has met Habibie on a number of occasions said: 'Habibie has the worst political instincts of anyone I've ever met'.[52]

Reshaping Golkar

Even if Habibie retains the support of Golkar, it remains to be seen how effective a political force Golkar will be. Golkar began the post-Soeharto era with a major public relations challenge. Along with the military, Golkar is the institution most closely identified with Soeharto and his authoritarian politics. Although Habibie dismissed a number of renowned Soeharto cronies from the Golkar faction in the parliament and the People's Consultative Assembly, the party is still seen by many as inseparable from the New Order.

From its beginning (described in chapter 2), Golkar was an artificially assembled amalgam of different interest groups, with the bureaucracy and the military as its two core components. Its intended function was to legitimise Soeharto's rule rather than to represent the interests of its followers. Cracks in the system appeared as soon as Soeharto left the scene. In the rural areas, hundreds of village chiefs were accused of corrupt behaviour and hounded from office. As the chiefs were the bottom rung of Golkar's vote-buying machine, their removal from positions of authority weakened the party.[53] A number of retired officers withdrew their support in the wake of Edi Sudrajat's defeat as Golkar chairman and founded the National Front. In January 1999 Sudrajat joined several other former ministers, generals and Golkar officials in launching their own party, called the Justice and Unity Party. The PKP, as the party is known, intends to be a 'neo-Golkar', says Sarwono Kusumaatmadja, who has close links to the PKP leaders: 'People want a vehicle that can bring people together. Golkar is stuck in the past. Today, patronage has a bad name. You can't buy votes like before'.[54]

With what was left of Golkar, several groups jockeyed for control. One centred on Cooperatives Minister Adi Sasono, who was also Golkar chairman for the important province of Central Java. A Muslim activist, secretary-general of the Indonesian Association of Muslim Intellectuals (ICMI), and a strong supporter of Habibie, Sasono appeared intent on turning Golkar into a political vehicle for modernist Muslims. Another group revolved around Akbar Tandjung, who is also a modernist Muslim but does not share Sasono's zeal for turning Golkar into an overtly Islamic party. 'There are no religious differences between the two', says Umar Juoro, who is close to Sasono: 'But Adi wants the government to help Muslims whereas Akbar is just a power seeker. He doesn't really want to accomplish anything'.[55]

Tandjung's view of Golkar seems similar to those of former Golkar leaders such as Sudharmono and Sarwono Kusumaatmadja—that is, as a secular, broad-based party similar to the Liberal Democratic Party in Japan. Sasono and Tandjung shared the view that Golkar urgently needed to transform itself from the party of the elite to the party of the people, a strategy reflected in Golkar's new-found support for *Ekonomi Rakyat*, or People's Economy. The difference is that Sasono's vision has a pro-Muslim, anti-Chinese flavour to it. In January 1999 Sasono concluded he was losing the battle for Golkar's leadership. He was said to be unhappy both about Habibie's close relationship with Armed Forces Commander Wiranto as well as the rising stature within Golkar of Marzuki Darusman, who headed the party's faction in the People's Consultative Assembly and who was close to secular, pro-democracy figures. Sasono announced he would remain a Golkar member but that he considered himself 'inactive' as a party leader.

According to Mohammad Jumhur Hidayat, secretary-general of the CIDES think-tank and a close Sasono ally, Sasono intended to lend his support to, but not join, a new party to be named the People's Sovereignty Party. Like Habibie, Sasono seemed reluctant to tie his flag to any one party. Also like Habibie, he seemed to feel his policies would earn him support across the political spectrum. He strove for a pan-Islam appeal that would draw support from a range of modernist Muslim parties. 'It would reduce Adi's popularity if he joined one party. He should be the umbrella of the nation. That way he could get support from many parties to be president', Hidayat said.[56]

Sasono's dwindling support for Golkar left Tandjung in a stronger position and eased military fears that Islamic activists would capture the party. But the party continued to face a long, uphill climb in refashioning its image. Darusman argued the party needed to apologise for its past, slavish service to Soeharto before it would be taken seriously by Indonesian voters. He made such an apology in November 1998 but, tellingly, others in the party immediately denied he was speaking for the party. The strength of the conservative wing of the party was also seen in the Provisional People's Consultative Assembly, when conservatives tried, ultimately without success, to keep Soeharto's name off the decree calling for an investigation into corruption. In January 1999, however, Darusman's argument finally won over the party leadership, and Tandjung joined in with an apology for Golkar's past 'faults and mistakes'.[57]

Despite its past record, Golkar does carry some significant advantages into the coming elections. Unlike the scores of new parties, Golkar has a nationwide infrastructure of party branches already in place. Golkar can no longer tap Soeharto's foundations for unlimited funds and is likely to get less financial support from the ethnic-Chinese business community than it did in the past. But, thanks to its continuing close relationship with the government and ministers such as Sasono, it is better off financially than all the new parties.

Darusman believes Golkar 'is finished in Java' because of its past association with Soeharto but that it can continue to retain the support of poorer Indonesians, especially on the outer islands. 'Golkar's future constituency is farmers, especially off-Java', he said: 'People are confused. They will vote for what they know, and that's Golkar. And the most confused, unsophisticated voters are farmers'. Leading *pribumi* businessman Aburizal Bakrie, a Golkar member and Habibie supporter, also expects Golkar to do well nationally. He predicted Golkar would win less than 10 per cent of the vote on Java but 'up to 60 per cent' of the vote off-Java. 'Golkar's association with Soeharto is only a liability on Java', he said: 'But the people outside Java will support Golkar because it's the only party there. Nationwide, Golkar will win at least 30 per cent of the vote'.[58]

ISLAM TO THE FORE

One of the most striking characteristics of the post-Soeharto era in Indonesia was the emergence of Islam as a pivotal political player. In the eyes of much of the modernist Muslim community, Islam had been denied its rightful political prominence since Indonesia's birth. With the political opening created by Soeharto's abrupt resignation, many modernists felt their time had come.

On one level, the modernists are certainly right. The transition from a secular authoritarian regime to a democratic government in a country that is almost 90 per cent Muslim will undoubtedly lead to greater prominence for Islamic issues and concerns, but exactly how much prominence is hard to say. To repeat a point discussed in several earlier chapters, there is not a single, homogeneous Muslim community in Indonesia. The community of devout, or *santri*, Muslims is itself divided into traditionalists and modernists, and each of these encompasses a broad range of political outlooks. There is also a large community of nominal, or *abangan*, Muslims, which prefers to keep religion and politics largely separate.

Since the lifting of the ban on new political parties, more than 140 new parties were established, with at least two dozen of them tied to Islamic groups. But this in itself says little about how much more 'Islamic' the politics of Indonesia are likely to become. The National Awakening Party, linked to the traditionalist Nahdlatul Ulama grouping headed by Abdurrahman Wahid, is comfortable with a continued political role for the military and stresses Islam as an ethical and moral force. But other, smaller parties with mainly traditionalist Muslim supporters define themselves in more strictly Islamic terms.[59]

The conservative modernist Crescent and Star Party fashions itself as a reincarnation of the Masyumi, an umbrella modernist organisation banned by Sukarno in the early 1960s. Although it stops short of calling for an Islamic state, it insists that Islam be both religiously and politically predominant in Indonesia. But other modernist-dominated parties, such as the National Mandate Party led by Amien Rais, see themselves as inclusive, pluralistic parties trying to appeal also to non-modernists and even non-Muslims. The modernist ICMI, formerly headed by Habibie, reflects the heterogeneity of opinion within the modernist community. Habibie, his senior aide Jimly Asshiddiqie, ICMI's secretary-general Adi Sasono and other senior ICMI figures are linked to Golkar. Leading ICMI thinkers such as Amien Rais, Dawan Rahardjo and Umar Juoro are connected to the National Mandate Party. And cabinet ministers such as Hamzah Haz and A. M. Saefuddin are with the United Development Party, as well as being members of ICMI.

Unsurprisingly in a society that has gone so long without free elections, none of the Muslim groups know how much support they will garner when elections are held. Many of them believe they are representative of a majority of Indonesians and at most only one of them can be right. And in a political climate manipulated and constrained for decades, the level of mistrust and paranoia is high. This is particularly true of the conservative modernist segment of the community. The same Muslims who feel they have been unfairly marginalised throughout Indonesia's history are convinced there are all manner of plots and conspiracies afoot to keep them marginalised. The conspirators are rarely identified, but the suspicion generally falls on Christians, Chinese and the military. 'We helped push-start the New Order bus thirty years ago', said the Muslim leader Cholil Bisri: 'But when it started, the driver and other passengers, far from offering us a place, spat on us. Muslims don't want to be left behind again'. The Muslim activist Mohammad Jumhur Hidayat put it more simply: 'This is our era'.[60]

Conservative modernists are also the most anxious to achieve Muslim unity. They tend to view both traditionalist and *abangan* Muslims as modernists in waiting, and are the most prone to thinking that all Indonesian Muslims have the same basic political aspirations. The fact that Indonesia's Muslims are not a unified political force is blamed not on the underlying heterogeneity of the Muslim community, or on the fact that modernist Muslims have been politically divided since the early part of the century, but rather on sinister forces keeping Muslims apart. Their frustration is reflected in several ways. One is in their frequent calls for Muslims to put aside their differences and to be more vigilant against attempts to divide them. 'Do not let differences among Muslims be exploited by enemies of Islam', implored the Muslim student leader Mannarul Hidayat, speaking to a pro-government rally in Jakarta. Otherwise, 'Muslims will become weak, disunited, powerless and become oppressed again by the tyranny of a minority'.[61]

Turning to violence

Modernist frustration can also be seen in a sharp rise in religious violence. One gruesome example occurred in Jakarta on 22 November 1998. Hundreds of Muslims, told that stones had been thrown at a nearby mosque, went on a Christian-killing rampage. While police stood by watching, Muslim youths burst into churches, ripping up pews and setting the churches ablaze. In full view of the domestic and international press, marauding Muslim youths hunted down a handful of Christians from the eastern island of Ambon who were accused of throwing rocks at a mosque the night before. The Ambonese were paraded through the streets, beaten to a pulp and eventually killed. By the end of the day, at least ten Christians had been killed and more than a dozen churches destroyed.[62]

A few days later, hundreds of Christians in West Timor retaliated. Dozens of Muslim-owned houses and mosques were burned. Muslim migrants from Sulawesi were chased into the sea. Rampaging Christian youths set up road blockades and made passing Muslims motorists lay flowers as a sign of mourning. Threatening to mount a secessionist movement, the students demanded Habibie condemn the previous week's violence against Christians and prosecute the killers of the Ambonese Christians.[63]

Muslim and Christian leaders quickly denounced the violence.[64] But, despite the soothing words, the orgy of religious violence had dealt another body-blow to Indonesian confidence. As usual, there were claims that the violence in Jakarta and West Timor had been instigated by unknown forces trying to derail the political reform process. There were unsubstantiated reports that unidentified men with short-cropped hair similar to soldiers were seen throwing stones at the mosque in Jakarta, precipitating the violence there, and setting fire to Muslim homes in West Timor.[65] Even if the violence was precipitated, it did not take much to provoke a vicious response. For the Chinese, the Christians and other religious and ethnic minorities, fears rose anew about their future in a nation led by a Muslim majority.[66]

An even worse outbreak of religious violence opened the new year. On 19 January 1999 a petty dispute between a Christian minibus driver and a Muslim passenger on the island of Ambon erupted into vicious communal clashes which flared on and off for months. As many as 200 were killed and tens of thousands left homeless. The religious violence in Ambon, which prided itself on the relatively good relations between its Muslim and Christian inhabitants, came as a shock to national political leaders. Christians, who blamed the military for siding with Muslims, contemplated mounting a secessionist movement. Muslims, who blamed the military for siding with Christians, called for a holy war to avenge Muslim deaths. Speaking at a rally in Jakarta, the militant Muslim labour activist Eggy Sudjana called on Muslims around the country to launch 'a *jihad* since more and more Muslims are being shot down'.[67]

Political analysts blamed Soeharto's policies for inflaming religious tensions in Ambon, especially his decision in 1997 to appoint a Muslim governor there and for encouraging an influx of Muslim migrants from other parts of the country into the province. Others blamed young thugs reputedly close to the Soeharto family for instigating the violence.[68] In any case, the speed with which the violence spread from hamlet to hamlet reflected deep-rooted and profound resentments between Muslims and Christians. Military and political leaders in Jakarta seemed unsure how to react and, not for the first time, were obliged to question their cherished belief in Indonesians' religious tolerance. Sidney Jones, the executive director of Human Rights Watch, argued that 'more than any other communal incident that has taken place around Indonesia, the civil war in Ambon has ripped apart the notion of Indonesia as a society tolerant of all faiths'. Another political analyst noted that 'people used to say Bosnia was a good example of religious tolerance, and look what happened there'.[69]

Mainstream Muslim leaders such as Abdurrahman Wahid and Amien Rais were acutely aware that the 'Bosnian scenario' was not as far-fetched as many Indonesians had once thought. Both men were deeply saddened by the use of religion to settle old political scores. Both sought to broaden their political base beyond their core Muslim constituencies, with varying results. Like the broader Muslim community they represented, the Islamic political parties took widely differing approaches to their pursuit of power. A review of the main Islamic parties reveals how wide those differences can be.

The National Awakening Party

The National Awakening Party, or PKB, is the main party linked to the traditionalist Islamic grouping, the Nahdlatul Ulama (NU). Matori Abdul Jalil, a former secretary-general of the United Development Party, heads the PKB, but its main draw is the NU's charismatic and widely popular chairman, Abdurrahman Wahid. The NU encompasses a broad network of Islamic schools in East and Central Java, and it is considered a more hierarchical, disciplined organisation than its modernist counterpart, the Muhammadiyah. The NU is said to have a following of 30–35 million Indonesians, although there is no member list. (The same goes for the Muhammadiyah, which claims 28–30 million followers.) While there are other parties for traditionalist Muslims to choose from, Wahid is confident most NU members will vote for the PKB. 'The PKB has the blessing of the Nahdlatul Ulama. I am convinced it will be the biggest party', Wahid said.[70]

Ascertaining what the PKB stands for is no easy task. There is no coherent policy platform, and PKB leaders do not appear bothered by the absence of one. The PKB leadership seems confident that the great bulk of NU followers will vote for the PKB because it is the party of the NU, regardless of what it stands for. Wahid's own view for the PKB is to represent the interests of the traditionalist Muslim community. As described in earlier chapters, Wahid believes political parties should be inclusive, and he is open to non-Muslims joining the PKB. The PKB also reflects the NU's cautious, accommodating relationship with the political establishment. Like Wahid, the PKB is likely to support a moderate, gradual reform process. It is comfortable with a continuing if gradually scaled-back political role for the military. Like Megawati's Indonesian Democracy Struggle Party, the PKB sees the army as a still necessary bulwark against the political ambitions of modernist Muslims. Most of all, the PKB is anxious to stem the political strength of modernist Muslims. The rivalry between the NU and the Muhammadiyah on an institutional level, and between Wahid and modernists leaders on a personal level, is deep, long-lasting and bitter. The rivalry has had, and will continue to have, a profound impact on the development of Indonesian politics.

Despite Wahid's immense popularity, the PKB's dependence on him carries a number of risks. First, Wahid's health is poor: the Muslim leader suffered a serious stroke in early 1998 and a year later remained wheel-chair-bound and almost blind. Another setback to his health could weaken support for the PKB. Second, Wahid's close alliance with Megawati may prove problematic for the more conservative NU preachers, who may not be enthusiastic about aligning the NU with a party led by a woman. Wahid had strongly supported Megawati before she was ousted from the Democratic Party in 1996 and reaffirmed his support shortly after Habibie took power, even as the PKB was being set up. Some observers believe Wahid was initially lukewarm about the PKB, seeing it as a rival power centre to him within the NU. These observers saw Wahid's support for Megawati as a way for the NU chairman to keep his political options open.[71] By the end of 1998, however, Wahid had become convinced that the PKB would not dilute his power within the NU and pledged to spend the first half of 1999 campaigning exclusively for the PKB. As 1999 opened, Wahid grew increasingly concerned about resistance within the NU community to his support for Megawati: 'I personally will support her, but most NU ulamas [religious teachers] still believe that a woman cannot become a leader'. By March 1999 Wahid determined it would be too risky to continue supporting Megawati as a presidential candidate. Although the PKB and Megawati's party planned to campaign together in parts of Java, Wahid said the PKB would not support Megawati as its presidential candidate. Instead, the party intended to nominate Wahid or the Sultan of Yogyakarta, Hamengkubuwono X.[72]

Finally, Wahid's political maneuvring in 1998 alienated parts of the pro-reform community and even caused many of his friends to question his motivations. As described in chapter 11, Wahid was slow to join the opposition to Soeharto in late 1997 and early 1998. Historically, the NU has always pursued an accommodative approach to the political establishment—since Indonesia's independence and even before.[73] The exception was in the early 1990s, when Wahid became increasingly critical of Soeharto, a stance that almost led to his losing the NU chairmanship in 1994. By 1996 Wahid was already looking for ways to repair his damaged relationship with Soeharto, and this accounted for his surprisingly muted role in late 1997. He disappointed many of his followers by refusing to join forces with Megawati and the Muhammadiyah leader Amien Rais in an attempt to ratchet up the pressure on Soeharto in early 1998.[74] And in Soeharto's meeting with nine Muslim leaders on 19 May 1998, Wahid was virtually alone in not pushing Soeharto to resign. Many felt Wahid was putting the NU's institutional interests ahead of the democratic reform movement, a similar charge that Wahid had long levied at modernist Muslims.

Wahid has never held a high opinion of Habibie, and Habibie's selection of a modernist Muslim-dominated cabinet did little to change his opinion. Habibie's flirtation with politically ambitious modernist Muslims, the frequent attacks on the ethnic-Chinese, and a deeply dispirited armed forces left Wahid feeling deeply pessimistic. 'I'm afraid there will be a social revolution that will destroy all our institutions, including the Nahdlatul Ulama and the military', Wahid said: 'Abri could become like the military in Burma and North Korea. Or we could have chaos like the Congo. I spend my days between hope and despair'.[75]

Wahid responded by moving closer to the military. He supported Armed Forces Commander Wiranto's plan to set up a civilian militia, even though many of his supporters opposed it. He also tempered his criticism of Wiranto following the shootings of unarmed students at the Provisional People's Consultative Assembly in November 1998. Although he was appalled by the deaths of the students, he worried that the removal of Wiranto would open the door to a new military chief more sympathetic to modernist Muslims.[76] At the end of 1998, Wahid irritated reformers again by meeting Soeharto several times. Wahid was convinced that Soeharto still held sway over parts of the military and was responsible for instigating a series of violent actions, including the killings of Muslim clerics in East Java and the burning of churches in Jakarta.[77] He argued that the violence would continue unless Soeharto was brought into the national dialogue on political reform. The suggestion infuriated much of the opposition, and almost all the student groups, who wanted Soeharto isolated from the political arena and investigated for corruption.

Wahid's current support base within the NU is strong, and he remains personally popular among non-Muslims and nominal Muslims. 'To Christians and other minorities Wahid is infallible, a kind of Muslim Pope', said a prominent journalist: 'He can do no wrong'.[78] However, Wahid is the target of stinging criticism from more militant segments of the Muslim community for refusing to endorse a more prominent political role for Islam.[79] In addition, Wahid's cautious approach to political reform could make it more difficult for the PKB to broaden its reach beyond the core NU membership.

The United Development Party

Unlike the PKB, the United Development Party, or PPP, welcomed the possibility of comprehensive change. One of two legal opposition parties in the New Order—the Indonesian Democratic Party being the other—the PPP had been relegated to the margins of politics since the early 1980s. The party did reasonably well in the 1982 parliamentary elections but lost support shortly thereafter when the NU withdrew from the party, a decision that left the PPP dominated by modernist Muslims. Invigorated by Habibie's assumption of power, the PPP quickly went to work revamping its image to place the party in the vanguard of the reform movement. In July 1998 party leaders attempted to entice Amien Rais to join the party and make him PPP chairman later in the year. Rais hesitated but eventually said no. A keen student of Indonesian history, he believed the leader of a religious party would never gain majority support. 'PPP wanted to change its past image by recruiting me', Rais said: 'But I sensed strong resistance from the Nahdlatul Ulama wing of the party. More importantly, I believed the PPP, as an Islamic party, could only give me a captive market, and from that I don't gain anything'.[80]

At the PPP's national congress held in November, Investment Minister Hamzah Haz defeated Food Minister A. M. Saefuddin to become the party's new chairman. Haz won crucial support from traditionalist Muslim groups off-Java, revealing a blurring of the lines between traditionalist and modernist Muslims as well as cracks in Wahid's hold over the traditionalist Muslim community. At the Provisional People's Consultative Assembly meeting in November 1998, PPP delegates threatened to walk out of the Assembly if a resolution calling for a corruption investigation did not mention Soeharto by name. Reflecting the modernist Muslim community's deeply ingrained suspicion of the military, the PPP also campaigned strenuously for a sharp and immediate reduction in the army's role in politics.[81] In early 1999, the party vigorously supported legislation banning civil servants from active participation in party politics, a sharp change for the 4-million strong bureaucracy that voted almost en bloc for Golkar in past elections. The PPP also took steps to burnish its Islamic image. It reclaimed the Ka'bah, symbol of the Muslim holy shrine in Mecca, as the party's symbol, after being forced to drop it in 1985 when it was required to adopt Pancasila as its sole ideological basis.[82]

Many observers believe the PPP will do reasonably well in the elections. Unlike the new parties created since Soeharto's resignation, it has a national network of branches and experience in campaigning. The PPP faces a number of formidable opponents, however, among them Megawati's Indonesian Democracy Struggle Party. The food minister, Saefuddin, ignited a controversy in October after questioning Megawati's fitness to run for president. After seeing a picture of Megawati inside a Hindu temple on Bali, Saefuddin said Indonesians could not vote for Megawati because she was not a Muslim. Tens of thousands of Balinese staged immediate protests and demanded Saefuddin's resignation.[83] Muslim groups rallied to Saefuddin's defence, and Habibie studiously ignored the issue. A more serious obstacle for the PPP is the fierce competition for the Muslim vote. The PPP's natural constituency is the modernist Muslim community, which has a range of parties to pick from.

The National Mandate Party

One of these parties is Amien Rais' National Mandate Party, or PAN. As described above, Rais turned down the offer to take over the leadership of the PPP because he felt a party with a strictly religious orientation could not garner majority support. 'If I stick completely with a Muslim constituency, I will never make a difference', Rais said in an interview in August 1998: 'I will never be able to push the country in a democratic direction'.[84] In the year prior to Soeharto's resignation, Rais saw his popularity soar, both within the modernist Muslim community and among many nominal Muslims and non-Muslims, thanks to his public and courageous stand against corruption and for greater political accountability. After Soeharto resigned, Rais set out to create a political vehicle to take advantage of this broad-based support.

The result was PAN, launched in August 1998 as a pluralistic, non-sectarian reform party. It immediately attracted the support of leading intellectuals, including journalists Goenawan Mohamad and Albert Hasibuan and economist Emil Salim. It also won the support of leading lights in the Indonesian Association of Muslim Intellectuals (ICMI), such as Dawam Rahardjo and Umar Juoro. Unlike ICMI leaders such as Adi Sasono and Dewi Fortuna Anwar, Rahardjo and Juoro did not see the need to continue lending their political support to Habibie. For them, Habibie had served his purpose by providing protection to modernist Muslim intellectuals in the last years of Soeharto's rule. But they were never particularly enamoured of Habibie's leadership style, and once Soeharto had left the scene they gravitated to Rais' camp.

PAN was the first party to produce a platform.[85] It called for the abolition of appointed military seats in the parliament, although it favoured keeping some reserved seats for the military in the People's Consultative Assembly. With equal controversy, the party said it was open to the idea of moving towards a federal system of government to appease regional resentment of Jakarta's dominance of economic resources.[86]

For Rais personally, PAN represented an enormous gamble. He was obliged to relinquish his chairmanship of the Muhammadiyah, which wanted to keep its social and religious activities at a distance from the political arena. But Rais' bigger hurdle was escaping from his own past. His earlier involvement in the Indonesian Association of Muslim Intellectuals made many pro-reform Indonesians wonder whether Rais had truly broken his ties with Habibie. 'My acceptance of Habibie at present is because we have no alternative', Rais explained: 'But politically speaking, Habibie is just a continuation of the Soeharto regime. My position is clear: Habibie is a transitional figure. His one job is to write new rules of the game for Indonesian politics'. Habibie going back on his initial promise to serve only as a transitional figure disappointed Rais: 'Unfortunately, he was surrounded by vested interests, including some of my old friends, and now he wants to continue as president'.[87]

Rais also had a reputation in some quarters for being anti-Chinese and anti-Christian. Although he made considerable headway in reversing this image, many Indonesians continued to suspect Rais' true commitment to religious tolerance and the state ideology Pancasila. 'Actually, the resistance to PAN has been lighter than I expected', Rais said: 'But I realise this is a risky venture. On the one hand, Muslim leaders are suspicious because they think I am too accommodating to religious minorities. The second risk is that the [religious] minorities still aren't particularly comfortable with a Muslim leader. And I suppose a third risk is that I give up because I am unable to reconcile the various groups in PAN who are worried about the first two risks'.[88]

Rais made numerous overtures to the ethnic-Chinese in a bid to convince skeptics that he had genuinely changed his stripes. He pledged to include ethnic-Chinese figures in his cabinet if elected, and to make Confucianism an official, state-approved religion. He condemned in the strongest terms the continuing violence against the ethnic-Chinese and, like Wahid, blamed Soeharto and his supporters for instigating social unrest. He denied accusations that he secretly favoured turning Indonesia into an Islamic state and, uncharacteristically for a modernist Muslim leader, spoke approvingly about Pancasila: 'To me, Pancasila is more than enough to be our state ideology and as a Muslim I don't see any contradiction whatsoever between the five principles and Islamic teaching'.[89]

Responding to his overtures, many Christian leaders and top ethnic-Chinese businessmen came out in support of Rais. But he continues to face entrenched opposition from Abdurrahman Wahid, the leader of the traditionalist Muslims. Wahid, in turn, has a strong influence on Megawati's political outlook, and has not been shy in conveying to her his suspicions of Rais. Consequently, although the political views of Rais, Wahid and Megawati are remarkably similar, the strained personal relationship between Wahid and Rais dimmed the prospects of their three parties forming a coalition.[90] In the beginning of 1999, Rais and Wahid met in a series of highly publicised meetings that succeeded in lowering the temperature of their rivalry. It remained unlikely, however, that the two men would be able to work together easily as political allies.[91]

Many opinion polls near the end of 1998 showed Rais and Megawati as the two most popular politicians in Indonesia, but some observers wondered how successful Rais would be in translating his personal popularity into political support.[92] PAN had to start from scratch to build a national network of branches, and it had to do so on a very tight budget. There were also doubts about whether urban intellectuals' enthusiasm for PAN would translate into significant grassroots support. 'When the intellectuals in PAN get together we all agree we would make a good university but we're not so sure we'll make a good political party', admitted Juoro. Like the United Development Party, PAN's biggest constituency is the modernist Muslim community, especially members of the Muhammadiyah. A confident Rais expects '90 per cent of modernist Muslims will vote for PAN. And, if we work hard, we can get 25–30 per cent of the total vote in the elections'.[93] PAN's dependence on the modernist vote, however, is precisely what concerns many of the younger, more secularly minded activists who joined the party at its inception. As PAN moves into the campaign season and beyond, it may well come to be seen as more of a Muslim party than a broad-based, pluralistic party, and that in turn may cause some of its less pious supporters to switch their allegiance to other parties.

The Crescent and Star Party

The last of the large modernist parties is the Crescent and Star Party, or PBB, which appeals to the conservative wing of the modernist community. Other parties are competing for the same constituency, such as the Justice Party and the New Masyumi Party, but the PBB received the most attention, at least in the first 10 months of Habibie's presidency.[94] Although the PBB was slow to produce a party platform, it is the party that most closely models itself on the old Masyumi party. Headed by a former Soeharto speechwriter, Yusril Izha Mahendra, the party draws support from militant Muslim groups that have long sought a larger role for Islam in Indonesian politics. Cooperatives Minister Adi Sasono is close to a number of PBB leaders, and shares the PBB view that modernist Muslims have been unfairly denied their political dominance. 'In China, we don't see any Indonesians running the government and the economy', he said: 'Why should we have our majority repressed? It's the same in the Philippines. You don't see any Muslim generals or ministers there. Why should we have so many Christian ministers and generals in Indonesia?'.[95]

Ahmad Soemargono, who chairs the Indonesian Committee for Solidarity with the Islamic World, or KISDI, and is also a top PBB official, denied any ambition to turn Indonesia into an Islamic state. But he argued that 'people of every religion want their beliefs applied in government on a day-to-day basis. We need new regulations so that Islamic values will be applied. For example, the sale of alcohol should be banned in Muslim areas'.[96] Soemargono also says the PBB will campaign to put the 'Jakarta Charter' back in the 1945 constitution. The Charter, drawn up in mid-1945, obliges the adherents of Islam to implement Islamic law (*shariah*). It was dropped from the constitution just before independence was proclaimed in August 1945, to the lasting chagrin of conservative modernists. Modernists later tried to resuscitate the Charter in the constitutional debates of the late 1950s and shortly after Soeharto came to power in the mid-1960s, but were rebuffed again both times.

Soemargono insists that the PBB is committed to protecting the pluralistic nature of Indonesian society. As an example, he says the PBB does not intend to oblige all Indonesian women to wear the *jilbab*, or headscarf. Like other PBB leaders, however, Soemargono's commitment to democracy is unclear. Although a number of conservative Muslim student groups support the PBB, the party's leadership is deeply suspicious of much of the student movement, which they regard as leftist and secular. The party is also strongly opposed to Megawati, whom it considers insufficiently Muslim to be leader of Indonesia.[97] 'We don't want liberal democracy', Soemargono said, in an unconscious imitation of Soeharto: 'We want democracy with responsibility'.[98]

Reflecting the views of the militant groups that support it, the PBB is likely to develop a strongly anti-Western bias in its foreign policy. The KISDI activist Fadli Zon, who also heads the PBB's foreign relations department, said Indonesian Muslims are convinced the 'United States is against all Muslim leaders, even in democracies'. Soemargono worries that the 'U.S. will try to bully Habibie, just like it bullied Soeharto'. PBB supporters launched demonstrations outside the US embassy in Jakarta on several occasions in 1998.[99] The PBB leader Mahendra believes a coalition of sinister outside forces was responsible for toppling Soeharto from power: 'There were many actors involved, including the CIA, Mossad,

George Soros, and Lee Kwan Yew. We will need 30 years to learn the whole truth'.[100]

PBB leaders are also strongly anti-Chinese. PBB officials accused the Chinese of making up the allegations that ethnic-Chinese women were raped in the May 1998 violence as a way to tarnish the name of Islam and to weaken Habibie politically. 'There were no rapes', Zon insists: 'It's all just propaganda to damage Muslims'. The PBB leader Mahendra agreed: 'People hate the Chinese. The Chinese try to hide this fact by making up stories of rape, which cannot be proven'.[101]

Like other parts of the modernist Muslim community, the conservatives supporting the PBB saw Habibie's assumption of power as a historic opportunity to achieve political dominance. They strongly support Habibie, much as they supported Soeharto in the last years of his rule. KISDI and other Islamic activist groups defended Habibie in battles with pro-democracy students at the national parliament on the day Soeharto resigned. They have attacked the homes of businessmen Arifin Panigoro and Sofyan Wanandi, whom they accuse of supporting anti-Habibie students. In an interview in November 1998, Soemargono warned Indonesians that to be against Habibie was to be against Islam.[102] And during the Provisional People's Consultative Assembly in November 1998, militant Muslim groups participated in a civilian militia set up to protect the assembly building from protesting students. Carrying sharpened bamboo spears, the Muslim militia carried banners saying: 'If You're Against Habibie, You're Against Islam', and 'If You're Against Islam, You're a Communist'.[103] In the outcry following the military's use of deadly forces against pro-democracy students, killing at least 14, the militant Muslims were quick to defend the military.[104]

But although the militant Muslims supporting PBB were strongly in Habibie's corner, they were not fully convinced of his support for them. Soemargono said Muslim activists were disappointed that Habibie was slow to release some right-wing Islamic preachers in jail and because he failed to protest loudly when US planes bombed suspected terrorist sites in Sudan and Afghanistan.[105] By the end of the year, the militants began to wonder whether Habibie was using them. Indications that Habibie was trying to distance himself from militant modernist aims, including strong denunciations of calls for Indonesia to become an Islamic state, set off warning bells in militant corners. Even so, Habibie remained the best bet for the militants among the likely presidential candidates, and their support for him is likely to continue. As Soemargono put it: 'Habibie will always be preferable to Abri'.[106]

More worrying for the militant Muslims is the sidelining of officers considered sympathetic to Islam from top military positions. 'I'm worried about Abri', Soemargono said: 'Prabowo, Syafrie, Muchdi, and Kivlan Zein are already out. That means Abri no longer represents all

Indonesians'. Zon said that with the Muslim generals shunted aside, 'Abri is demoralised. It has no more dignity'.[107] Evidence of Prabowo's violations of human rights is especially problematic for the militant Muslims. Considered a hero by many of the militants, Prabowo's humiliating discharge from the army was a bitter pill to swallow. 'Habibie got disinformation', said a disgusted Fadli Zon: 'That's why he was scared of Prabowo [on the day he assumed power]. Habibie knows nothing about the military. He is a very naïve president. He doesn't know anything except how to build a plane'.[108] At the same time, the militants recognised that a continued defence of Prabowo was not likely to be helpful to their cause in the run-up to the parliamentary elections. Militant leaders attempted to explain Prabowo's controversial conduct as a product of his questionable commitment to Islam. Prabowo 'is a very nice man', Soemargono said: 'But I doubted his commitment to Muslims because his father is a socialist and his mother is Christian'.[109]

Similar acrobatics were required in the case of Soeharto. After serving as Soeharto's staunchest supporters for much of the 1990s, the militant Muslim groups suddenly found their one-time hero the object of contempt and disgust by most of the political spectrum. Some of the militants tried to defend Soeharto as the unlucky victim of perfidious plotting by secular-minded student groups and Islam-phobic generals. Others, such as Fadli Zon, took the more pragmatic approach of disavowing their earlier support. 'We were happy to see Soeharto step down', Zon said in an interview in September 1998, in direct contrast to sentiments he had expressed only a few months earlier: 'Our smiles to Soeharto were only cosmetic. In fact, Soeharto was too powerful, since he was backed by Abri'.[110]

Many other Muslim leaders had nothing but scorn for the militant's behaviour. 'It's because they suffer from a vast inferiority complex', the National Mandate Party leader Amien Rais said of the militants: 'They felt so inferior to Abri, which is why they were so pleased to have some officers court their support. This is the only way to explain how they could be so misled'. Rais argued that the militants' fervent support for Soeharto would damage their political prospects: 'The PBB leaders are all stooges of Soeharto. They worshipped Soeharto right until the last minute. I don't think many Muhammadiyah members will vote for them'.[111] The Nahdlatul Ulama leader Abdurrahman Wahid was equally critical of the PBB leaders. 'They come from the legalistic side of Islam,' he said: 'They want Islam to be formalised in the life of the nation. I am not satisfied at their appearance'.[112]

Among many secular leaders and nominal Muslims, the PBB generates more fear than scorn. The fear is that the militants' commitment to democracy, such as it is, is secondary to their desire to see Islam become the foundation of the Indonesian state. Their distrust of militant modernist ambitions stretches back to the early part of the century, when modernist leaders such as Muhammad Natsir insisted the nascent nationalist movement be inextricably tied to Islam. It was not enough for Muslims to struggle for independence, Natsir argued. They must also struggle, in the words of historian Merle Ricklefs, 'for a state which would serve Islam and in which Islamic law and Muslim leaders would be dominant'.[113] As described in earlier chapters, the same sorts of divisions arose in the 1950s during the parliamentary democracy period. Many Indonesians, including many Muslim leaders, believe the modernist insistence on making Islam the basis of the state played a major role in undermining Indonesia's early experiment with democracy. And they worry that the same may happen again.

The PBB constituency appears to be largely urban-based. However, there is no doubt that the rhetoric of many rural mosques grew more anti-Chinese and more anti-Christian as the 1990s progressed, and this may suggest more support for the PBB than many urban analysts predict. Moreover, as the economic crisis deepens, the search for scapegoats is likely to accelerate. And the PBB is unique in its willingness among leading parties to identify scapegoats for Indonesia's troubles. As for the PBB's own leaders, they are wary of making predictions. Says party leader Mahendra: 'I don't know how many people will vote for PBB. We offer our program to the people and we will see'.[114]

MILITARY IN RETREAT

Like Golkar, Soeharto's ruling party, the Indonesian military entered the post-Soeharto period under a dark cloud. The military was ultimately responsible for keeping Soeharto in power for so long. When he fell, the military found itself on the receiving end of widespread invective and hatred. The only people who were surprised at the response, it seemed, were military personnel. Since independence, the military has perceived itself as one with the people, the neutral arbiter of societal relations. To the extent that 'errors' were committed under Soeharto's term, military officers tended to blame these on Soeharto himself or the political system he created. The military, officers said, was merely a tool of Soeharto. Many Indonesians, of course, had a very different perception. They viewed soldiers as bullies and bandits, unaccountable to the law. When the shackles on free expression were removed after Soeharto's ouster, Indonesians were not bashful about letting Abri know how they felt.[115]

Moral defeat in Aceh

In a number of provinces outside Java, where resentment at Jakarta's dominance is deep and long-standing, the depth of hatred towards Abri came as a shock to military leaders. The northern Sumatran province of Aceh, where the military had battled separatist insurgents for the past decade, was one such example. In August 1998, Armed Forces Commander Wiranto apologised to the people of Aceh for the military's past violations of human rights and pledged to reduce the number of combat troops deployed in the province.

For Wiranto, the apology was a laudable, if all too rare, example of the military owning up to its own faults. But as an attempt at closing the book on the military's performance in Aceh, the apology failed miserably. Wiranto immediately came under attack from more conservative members of the military hierarchy, aghast at the idea of the military asking for forgiveness. They viewed their mission in Aceh as defending the integrity of the Indonesian state, a mission bound to have casualties on both sides. 'People want an apology for Aceh, but they will keep demanding more', complained the former armed forces commander Benny Murdani: 'Wiranto never served in Aceh. Does he really know what happened? Libyan-trained terrorists were shooting at us. Our reaction was justified at the time. Why should we pretend we are angels now?'.[116]

The apology also failed to mollify the Acehnese, who demanded a full accounting of the many who were tortured or killed. As troops began to leave Aceh they were stoned by irate Acehnese, a move that convinced Wiranto to revoke the withdrawal order. The pelting of departing troops was hardly the gratitude the military expected for its apology, and it reminded reformists within the military that they faced an uphill battle in the court of public opinion. 'In Aceh, we have to apologise for excesses and deviations from procedures but not for the mission itself', said General Susilo Bambang Yudhoyono, assistant to the armed forces commander for socio-political affairs and a leading military reformist: 'Our mission was given by the state to fight an insurgency movement. Society needs to distinguish the military's legal operations with deviations from those operations'.[117]

As 1998 wore on, the situation in Aceh deteriorated. Acehnese led journalists to sites of suspected mass graves, and many came forward with gruesome tales of being kidnapped and tortured by soldiers. Human rights groups put the total number of Acehnese civilians killed by the military at over 2000. The military claimed only 760 had been killed, including 111 soldiers.[118] In late December 1998, Acehnese rebels dragged seven off-duty soldiers off a bus and killed them, an act the military blamed on followers of Ahmad Kandang, a previously little-known member of the Aceh Merdeka separatist movement. In response, soldiers invaded a detention centre holding suspects in the attack and began beating the detainees, killing four of them. The military commander in Aceh promised a swift court martial for the soldiers involved, but the damage had been done.[119] Military–civilian relations are likely to remain tense for some time to come.

Anarchy reigns

Although Aceh emerged as a particularly troubling case, the military's reputation went on a sharp downward slope across the country. In post-Soeharto Indonesia, the military commanded neither respect nor fear, resulting in an explosion of looting and petty vandalism, often right before the military's eyes. Trucks driving across Java were routinely stopped and their cargo stolen. In rural Java, villagers looted food warehouses and stole rice left on the side of the road to dry. In the cities, gangs of youths stalked passengers on public transportation and robbed people riding in taxis.[120] On numerous occasions, police attempting to arrest vandals were themselves attacked, leading the police to look the other way.

Communal violence also arose with worrying frequency. As described above, religious clashes broke out in Jakarta, West Timor and Ambon. In early 1999 indigenous Dayaks in West Kalimantan went on a rampage against devout Muslim migrants from the island of Madura, located off the east coast of Java. In less than two weeks several hundred Madurese were killed, many with incredible brutality, and tens of thousands were forced to flee their homes.[121]

One of the more mysterious breakdowns in law and order occurred in the later months of 1998 in East Java. Practitioners of black magic, or those suspected of being so, were hunted down and killed by bands of vigilantes. The killings soon spread to include Muslim clerics, mostly from the traditionalist Muslim organisation, Nahdlatul Ulama. Most of the victims were brutally hacked to death. In some cases the victims were decapitated and their heads paraded through villages on sticks. By the time the killing wave ceased, about 200 Indonesians had been murdered.[122] Both the military and the government took a curiously detached view of the killings. When a visiting diplomat raised the issue with Habibie in late October 1998, the president replied: 'I've got 200 million people to take care of, I can't worry about 200 people in East Java'.[123] Few arrests were made, and many reports circulated of military personnel refusing to intercede to defend victims being chased by a mob.

Theories to explain the killings mushroomed almost as fast as the number of victims. Some blamed the killings on Soeharto, who was believed to retain control of his own private army. This camp believed Soeharto wanted to disturb the peace to slow the pace of democratic reform, convince Indonesians they needed a strong military, and distract attention from demands that he be investigated for corruption. Some thought Prabowo or the military itself was behind the killings, for much the same reasons. Others blamed the killings on surviving sympathisers of the banned Indonesian Communist Party set on avenging the deaths of their loved ones three decades earlier.[124] Still others attributed the surge in violence to the societal stresses caused by the deepening economic crisis.

By the beginning of 1999, military commanders had issued shoot-on-sight orders to deal with looters and violent protesters in many areas.[125] Although human rights campaigners worried the military would use the worsening lawlessness as an excuse to retake power, many Indonesians began to grow increasingly nostalgic for the relative orderliness of the New Order. Aburizal Bakrie, a leading *pribumi* businessman, and other business executives argued that the non-stop social unrest was scaring off new investment. In a January 1999 meeting with Habibie, he criticised the president for not taking strong enough measures to quell the violence. 'What do you want me to do', a frustrated Habibie asked: 'do you want me to be like Benny Murdani and just start shooting people?'. To which an equally frustrated Bakrie replied: 'Yes! That's exactly what you need to do'.[126]

Confusion in the ranks

The combination of public expressions of hatred for the military and the growing lawlessness of society left many Abri officers bitter. For some it confirmed suspicions that Indonesia was not yet ready to be ruled by civilians. The military, however, did little to further its cause. Its treatment of protesters was often heavy-handed, a reflection of its lack of riot-control training and equipment and of an ingrained military disbelief in the concept of peaceful protest. In the New Order, protest was akin to dissidence, if not subversion, and was to be treated as such. For those on the receiving end of military brutality, the army's behaviour merely reinforced the view that democracy was incompatible with the military's retaining a role in politics. Repeated denials by military leaders that ethnic-Chinese women had been raped in the May 1998 riots infuriated the Chinese community and human rights workers. The military's laggardly response to the killing of Muslim clerics in East Java incensed Muslim leaders, especially the NU chairman, Abdurrahman Wahid. Abri's decision to use a civilian militia to help guard the Provisional People's Consultative Assembly in November proved to be a disastrous experiment. Wiranto's later decision to form a full-time, 40 000-strong militia only compounded the problem.[127] The shooting of unarmed protesters at the Assembly on 13 November 1998 radicalised much of the student protest movement. Marzuki Darusman, who heads the National Commission on Human Rights, said Abri's shooting of the students was akin to shooting itself, and therewith its hopes for sustaining a political role over the medium term.[128]

On other issues as well, the military displayed an extraordinary propensity to shoot itself in the foot. In July 1998, following Habibie's pledge to grant greater autonomy to East Timor, the military announced a troop withdrawal from the troubled province. Weeks later, it was revealed that the military had surreptitiously shipped in new military personnel to replace the departing platoons, an act of trickery that damaged the military's credibility both at home and abroad.[129] In addition, the military's clear reluctance to support public demands for a comprehensive investigation of New Order corruption elicited a rising chorus of protest, as well as a flurry of charges that the military itself was guilty of corrupt business dealings.[130]

While the military's external public relations campaign was foundering, efforts to impose more discipline internally were having only mixed success. In the immediate aftermath of Soeharto's fall from power, Wiranto removed or sidelined a number of so-called 'green' officers who were considered close to the militant Muslim groups. Chief among these was Soeharto's controversial son-in-law, Prabowo Subianto. But Wiranto's own position was also suspect. As described above, he was forced to rescind his first choice to replace Prabowo at the Army Strategic Reserve because of complaints from Muslim generals. In July he was obliged to support Habibie's choice for Golkar chairman over a military rival. Wiranto was also convinced to delay moving loyalists into top military positions for fear of a backlash from green officers. According to one source, Wiranto feared a military split or even a civil war if he were to remove too many green officers too quickly.[131]

Wiranto's dilemma, and a principal reason why pro-democracy groups became disenchanted with him, was well illustrated by the treatment of Prabowo. In August, a military honour council convened to hear evidence of Prabowo's involvement in the abduction and torture of pro-democracy activists earlier in the year. A few days before the conclusion of the hearing, the council's presiding officer, Army Commander Subagyo, said there was enough evidence to warrant a court martial of Prabowo. But a few days later Wiranto announced Prabowo's discharge from active duty, making no mention of a court martial. The widely reviled Prabowo would be allowed to receive full pension benefits. The decision caused an immediate outcry among many civilian leaders. 'I tell Abri leaders that if they think dismissing Prabowo is enough, they're wrong', said the Muslim politician Amien Rais: 'It's a cover-up. The Indonesian people have worked hard for Abri. It's our tax dollars that pays them. We are entitled to the full story'.[132]

As for Prabowo, he promptly left the country and settled in Jordan 'to pursue business interests'. He reportedly travelled on an official passport issued by armed forces headquarters. A Jordanian official later claimed Prabowo had requested Jordanian citizenship, although Prabowo denied this. Meanwhile, Prabowo's relatives launched a short-lived campaign to restore his reputation. His younger brother, businessman Hashim Djojohadikusumo, was 'very proud' of his brother, while Prabowo's father, economist Sumitro Djojohadiksumo, complained that his son had been the victim of 'black propaganda'.[133] Even his sister, Bianti, who six months earlier had described her brother as 'homicidal', privately complained to friends that Prabowo was now being framed.[134]

Wiranto did not publicly explain his reasons for letting Prabowo off the hook. The most likely explanation, according to military sources, was what he feared Prabowo would say in a court martial. Prabowo had told his associates the decision to abduct pro-democracy activists was ordered by his superiors, including Soeharto, Wiranto and the then armed forces commander Feisal Tandjung. Wiranto's concern was that a Prabowo court martial would not only indict Soeharto, whom Wiranto had pledged to protect, but would land Abri in still more disrepute in the eyes of Indonesians. On the one hand, Wiranto recognised the value of having the military make some effort to atone for its past misdeeds and to acknowledge a willingness to change with the times. On the other, Wiranto was averse to any moves that would further discredit the military. In the case of Prabowo, Wiranto seemed to consider the second objective the more compelling of the two, at least through the end of 1998. As Benny Murdani put it in September 1998: 'We do not know if Abri can handle more bad PR at this point'.[135]

Another factor weighing on Wiranto was the fear of a Muslim backlash. Although a number of high-flying Muslim officers had been shunted aside after Soeharto's fall, their civilian supporters continued to watch Wiranto's maneuvring with a critical eye. Prabowo's many fans within the militant Muslim community interpreted calls for a court martial as an attack on Islam. If it went forward, they threatened to demand investigations of past military repressions of Muslims. 'It's OK if Prabowo goes to jail but only if the military investigates other cases like Tanjung Priok and Lampung', said Fadli Zon of KISDI and the Crescent and Star Party: 'We want Prabowo to go to court so he can defend himself. If you open one case you have to open them all. If not, we will fight you'.[136] The common theme among militant Muslims was that the military should not prosecute Prabowo unless it hauled the retired Christian general Benny Murdani into court as well.

While it might have seemed rational from a military point of view to avert a Prabowo court martial, civilian leaders and student groups were outraged. In the face of mounting public pressure, the military eventually charged 11 junior special forces officers for the abductions of the pro-democracy activists. As their court proceedings opened in December 1998, uniformed special forces soldiers filled the courtroom to show their support for their detained comrades. To most Indonesians, the military's attempt to scapegoat the junior officers while letting Prabowo off the hook was nothing short of ludicrous. The respected chairman of the Indonesian National Human Rights Commission termed the trial 'a miscarriage of justice' and demanded that it be stopped.[137]

As the trial continued, Wiranto announced a major reshuffling of top military leaders. Apparently feeling more secure in his control over the military, Wiranto sidelined several more leading Muslim generals and replaced them mainly with officers considered loyal to him.[138] Among the losers in the reshuffle were the commanders of East Java and Aceh, two provinces that had been particularly hard-hit by violence since Soeharto's fall. He also felt confident enough to promote a Christian general, Johny Lumintang, to deputy army commander. As described above, Lumintang had been appointed commander of the Army Strategic Reserve on 22 May 1998, but the decision was quickly revoked under intense pressure from Muslim circles.

Militant Muslim groups were unhappy to see more Muslim generals pushed further away from the centre of power, but there was little they could do. Their wholehearted support for the disgraced Prabowo left them with little leverage. And many student groups were displeased with the reshuffle as well. Noting the retention or promotion of officers considered Soeharto loyalists, they concluded that the reshuffle made the military even less likely to allow a genuine investigation of Soeharto's wealth. They also lost hope that the military would permit a real inquiry into the killings at Trisakti University on 12 May 1998 and during the ensuing three days of riots that engulfed Jakarta.

The future of Dwifungsi

Over the medium term, the dominant issue for the top military brass will be to preserve what they can of the cherished dual-function doctrine, or *dwifungsi*. There is general agreement in the military leadership that the military's involvement in politics during the New Order expanded far in excess of the originators' vision of the dual-function doctrine. In the words of Benny Murdani, '*dwifungsi* is a nice thing but you can have too much of a nice thing. It was misused. And now we have a mess'.[139]

In a meeting of several hundred top military officers in August 1998, more than 70 per cent agreed that *dwifungsi* needed to be redefined. But the devil, as always, is in the details. One of the military's first attempts to appease public opinion was to concede that *dwifungsi* was not a permanent feature of Indonesian politics, although it was sparing with details of a timetable. At the Provisional People's Consultative Assembly in November, it agreed reluctantly to a vague commitment to wind down *dwifungsi* within five years.[140]

The military also abolished the post of armed forces assistant for socio-political affairs, the most senior billet overseeing the military's political role, although this was mostly a cosmetic change. Susilo Bambang Yudhoyono, who held the post, was given a new title (armed forces assistant for territorial affairs) but his job description remained largely the same.[141] In addition, the military said it would no longer support Golkar. Instead, it would strive to play more of a background part, concentrating on setting and enforcing commonly agreed rules of the game, somewhat along the lines of the Turkish model. In another important concession, the military leadership said in November 1998 that officers seconded to civilian jobs would have to retire from active duty first. Finally, the military attempted to sell a skeptical public on the notion that it had been a servant to Soeharto, rather than his partner. 'In the first 15 years of the New Order, Abri and Soeharto were indistinguishable in terms of policy and strategy', said Yudhoyono: 'But in the last 15 years, we have to make a distinction between the two. Actually, all power was held by Soeharto'.[142]

The task of redefining *dwifungsi* poses two main challenges to the military leadership: one in the realm of military politics, the other involving national politics. *Dwifungsi* provides the military with an important source of jobs. At the beginning of 1998, about half the provincial governors and about 40 per cent of district chiefs came from a military background; altogether, some 12 300 military personnel were seconded to non-military posts. The military is prepared to see a number of high-profile jobs switch to civilian hands. Yudhoyono, for example, said in October 1998 that he authorised civilians to replace military figures as governors of two provinces—Nusa Tenggara Barat and Nusa Tenggara Timor—and as chiefs of six districts (*kabupaten*) in Java.[143]

At the same time, the military is not anxious to see military figures pushed out of their non-military jobs *en masse*. There are no jobs for them within the military, no budget to create any, and only very poor prospects of finding civilian positions in Indonesia's crisis-stricken economy. For example, if military personnel were to be removed entirely from local legislatures, an estimated 2800 jobs would be lost. Military leaders were justifiably concerned that a wholesale dismissal of military personnel holding civilian jobs would create a small army of armed, bitter, unemployed young men. As military analyst Douglas Kammen noted: 'At the very moment that Abri needs more posts to which to second its excess number of commissioned officers, it finds itself confronted by not one but two obstacles: an economy in tatters and calls for the military to retreat from the position it so cherishes'.[144]

As for national politics, the military's principal concern is the ability of civilian leaders to hold the country together. Since independence, the military has held a generally low opinion of civilian politicians. At present, it is reluctant to make this point publicly, given its own role in creating and perpetuating Soeharto's authoritarian rule. But privately many officers continue to view civilian rule as a recipe for national disintegration. 'Don't you understand what would happen if we just simply go back to the barracks', asked one senior officer: 'Don't you think there will be huge problems for different groups in society to communicate with each other, to practice democratic values?'.[145]

In the short run, the debate over *dwifungsi* is likely to remain centred on the number of seats allocated to the military in the national parliament. In the current parliament the military holds 75 seats. In a compromise hammered out by the national parliament in January 1999, the military agreed to reduce its seats to 38 in the parliament to be elected in June 1999, and to reduce its share of seats in local legislatures from 20 per cent to 10 per cent. The decision angered many student leaders and other pro-reform activists. They had campaigned for the military to lose all of its seats from both the parliament and the People's Consultative Assembly, or MPR. If the military was allowed to keep seats in the parliament, they believed, the path to democracy would be blocked and the military would eventually rebuild its political dominance. They were highly skeptical of the military's capacity to play a neutral role in the parliament. 'The president is the commander in chief of the armed forces', noted one student leader: 'If he tells the military in parliament to vote a certain way, how are they going to refuse?'[146]

Although a valid point, it is one that is not embraced by the leaders of most political parties. Senior Muslim figures, both modernist and traditionalist, generally support a gradual reduction of the military's political clout. 'Longer term, Abri has to go back to the barracks', said Amien Rais: 'But for the time being we cannot do it. I believe in incremental change. I support Abri keeping seats in the MPR, but not the parliament. It would be better if they did not vote'. Fadli Zon of the Crescent and Star Party concurred: 'The PBB supports Abri seats in the MPR only, but it's negotiable'.[147] The NU leader Abdurrahman Wahid and the nationalist politician Megawati Sukarnoputri, on the other hand, were content to see the military retain seats in both the parliament and the MPR. Although Rais, Zon and others were unhappy with the decision to allow the military 38 seats in the parliament, they were wary of pushing the issue too far. In a dilemma common to post-authoritarian political transitions, Indonesia's democratic reformists were still struggling to find a balance between pushing the military out of politics altogether and avoiding the risk of a military backlash that could derail the democratisation process before it even started. Nevertheless, the agreement to permit the military 38 seats is not likely to last long. The soon-to-be directly elected parliament is almost certain to revisit the issue.

As far as the military is concerned, the immediate worries about national stability take precedence over the broader, philosophical debate about the military's role in politics.[148] And although military reformists would be content to have the military only represented in the MPR at some future date, they are not willing to concede that much for the time being. 'We want to be in the parliament at least for the next term because we are not sure yet about how things will work out with civilian leaders', said one reform-minded officer: 'If things work out, we can negotiate about Abri's seats in the parliament in the next term, but not this one'. Longer-term, he continued, Abri was prepared to cede its political role entirely: 'If society is mature, and national unity is assured, and the commitment to democracy is there, then everything can be like it is in democratic countries in the West. There will no longer be any need for Abri to defend the country from enemies within, and we can be purely a professional military'.[149]

But it is far from clear whether the reformist view will prevail inside Abri, or whether the conditions for Abri's withdrawal from politics will be met. The reformists face entrenched opposition not only from the more radical civilian leaders but from much of the military establishment. Many older, retired generals who still wield considerable influence are staunch believers in *dwifungsi*, and blame the younger generation of military leaders for implementing it so poorly as to generate widespread calls for its elimination. The reformists also must overcome an institutional reluctance to atone for past misdeeds. One of the prerequisites for restoring Abri's reputation, concedes Yudhoyono, 'is to resolve past problems such as the Trisakti killings and the abduction of [pro-democracy] activists. We must identify and punish wrongdoers'.[150]

Needless to say, the military's unwillingness to clear up these issues is doing little to help the reformist cause within Abri. The same is true of Wiranto's hesitation in prosecuting Prabowo. Although not normally categorised as a reformist officer, even Benny Murdani appreciates that Wiranto's cautious handling of Prabowo is not doing the military's image any good: 'I still support Abri having seats in the parliament but I'm not sure how we will justify it. If the military honour council could have dealt with Prabowo properly, it would have been easier. I don't understand why there isn't a court-martial'.[151]

Ironically, one of the best arguments in favour of a continued political role for the military is the increasing lack of public safety across the country. Indonesians are understandably alarmed at the violence and chaos following Soeharto's resignation, and they recognise that the military, at least in the short term, is the only institution capable of restoring order. Yet the bulk of the military leadership has no desire to return to the authoritarian ways of the past, or to see the military take power. The problems besetting Indonesia's economy and society are highly complex and even the military brass recognises it does not have the answers. It is worthwhile keeping in mind, however, that the military sees as its paramount mission the protection of Indonesian stability and integrity. If these come under severe threat, the military may well conclude that it has no alternative but to set aside the democratic process.[152]

ECONOMIC WATERLOO

B. J. Habibie came to power in May 1998 as Indonesia was suffering what the World Bank called the worst economic collapse suffered by any large country since World War II. Habibie saw the deepening economic malaise as posing a clear threat not only to Indonesia's experiment with democratic reform but to his own political prospects. He immediately turned his attention to patching up relations with the international financial institutions, which were at that point virtually the only source of foreign capital available to Jakarta. He retained Ginanjar Kartasasmita, the coordinating economics minister in Soeharto's last cabinet and an aspiring presidential candidate in his own right, as his top economics minister. Putting aside for the time being his active promotion for state-supported industries, Habibie did what Soeharto had done in every economic crisis before the present one: he turned to the technocrats for help. He hired his long-time nemeses, technocrats Wijoyo Nitisastro and Ali Wardhana, as consultants. Wijoyo and Wardhana would play key behind-the-scenes roles in dealing with the IMF and the World Bank, with which they had built personal connections for over 30 years.

By the time Habibie reopened discussions with the IMF, the Fund had long since abandoned its efforts to impose fiscal discipline and had agreed to allow Jakarta to run a budget deficit of 8.5 per cent of GDP in the 1998/99 fiscal year. Together with the World Bank, the IMF organised several donors' conferences for Indonesia, which raised an additional US$14 billion in aid.[153] The Fund also resumed regular monthly aid disbursements of about US$1 billion that had been pledged in the original US$43-billion IMF rescue package signed in October 1997.

Within a few months the influx of money appeared to be making a dent on the unrelenting gloom surrounding the economy. By October 1998 the rupiah had strengthened to around 8000 to the dollar, a level more in line with the degree of inflation-adjusted depreciation that hit other regional currencies.[154] Inflation also dropped dramatically. Although the cost-of-living index rose by almost 80 per cent in 1998, the rate of inflation dropped sharply by the end of the year. Some rural areas benefited from a rise in agricultural prices and the removal of export barriers. And several of Indonesia's key non-oil exports began to show new signs of life at the end of the year; the government optimistically predicted that exports would grow 3 per cent in the fiscal year beginning in April 1999.

No-one, however, predicted in early 1999 that Indonesia's economic crisis would soon end. On the contrary, many analysts expected the crisis to worsen before bottoming out. As had been the case since the crisis began, Indonesia's economic prospects were inextricably tied to the political process; until the political situation started to settle and investors had some idea of who would be in charge of economic policy, the best the economy could do was muddle along.

The crisis bites deep

Indonesia's economy contracted by 13.6 per cent in 1998 and was expected to shrink a further 2–4 per cent in 1999. The unemployment rate rose steadily following the onset of the crisis. According to the government's conservative estimate, the number of unemployed jumped to almost 20 million in the 18 months to December 1998, representing about a quarter of the workforce. Bomer Pasaribu, director of Jakarta-based Centre for Labour and Development Studies, predicted the unemployed rolls would swell to 30 million in 1999.[155] Poverty rates also climbed, but by how much was a source of considerable controversy. The Indonesian Central Bureau of Statistics estimated that the incidence of poverty had soared to 40 per cent of the population, or 80 million people, by the end of 1998, compared with just 11 per cent at the start of the crisis. In December 1998, Social Affairs Minister Yustika Baharsyah put the number of impoverished at 100 million.[156] World Bank economists dismissed these numbers as alarmist. They pointed out that many rural areas, where most of Indonesia's poor live, had fared relatively well in the crisis compared with urban areas. In early 1999 the Bank estimated that the rate of poverty had risen only slightly, to perhaps as high as 15 per cent of the population.[157]

The difference in these views is not as wide as it may appear. The poverty line, after all, is an artificial construct.[158] Whether the group classified as impoverished had risen dramatically, or whether the group considered 'near-poor' had ballooned in size, the result was the same: a large number of Indonesians had seen their quality of life eroded to a considerable degree. Many middle-class Indonesians abruptly encountered the problems familiar to the poor. Millions of mothers, for example, suddenly found themselves unable to afford baby milk or formula. In another measure of declining purchasing power, the number of Indonesians who made the Haj pilgrimage to Saudi Arabia dropped by 70 per cent in 1998 compared with 1997. At a national level, Indonesia's per-capita income dropped to about US$400 in 1998, compared with a little over US$1000 in early 1997, a stunning 60 per cent in the space of one year.

The sharp fall in purchasing power combined with a disruption to the food distribution network led to a disturbing rise in malnutrition. Steven

Woodhouse, who heads the Jakarta office of the United Nations Children's Fund, noted that malnutrition posed a particular risk for infants and young children. Twenty-three million Indonesians are under the age of 5, and the number of deaths attributed to malnutrition began to climb as 1998 wore on. 'Even mild and moderate malnutrition can affect the development of intellectual capacity', he said: 'The critical time is in the first 6 to 18 months of life. That means one year of malnutrition will affect an entire generation of workers'.[159]

Information on health statistics is incomplete, but anecdotal evidence pointed to a sharp deterioration across the board. A survey by the UN Children's Fund of six hospitals in East Java discovered a 60 per cent rise in maternal mortality in 1998 over 1997. Hospitals in many areas of the country reported falls in child weight and rises in diarrhoea, both resulting from the increasing unaffordability of safe water. Data collected by the Helen Keller Foundation in Central Java revealed that milk and egg consumption had fallen by 50 per cent in 1998, while reported cases of anaemia in children had risen by 40–60 per cent. An estimated 12 million preschool-aged children were said to be suffering from vitamin deficiencies.[160]

The crisis also had a drastic effect on the health-care delivery system. The poor could no longer afford health care, and virtually all clinics and hospitals encountered severe shortages of medicine and health supplies. The sharp rise in female unemployment and the growing cost of contraceptives undermined Indonesia's previously successful family planning program and set the stage for a higher birth rate in coming years. The educational system was similarly affected. Teacher salaries dwindled to almost nothing, and schoolbooks became a luxury few could afford. Many poor families could no longer afford to send their children to school at all, another trend that promised to have a negative, long-term effect on the productivity of Indonesian workers. Yuwono Sudarsono, the new education minister, said in February 1999 that as many as 5 million students had dropped out of school since the onset of the financial crisis. According to another ministry official, an audit of the public school system revealed that half the nation's 70 000 elementary schools were so run-down they needed to be closed.[161] More girls were dropping out of school than boys, and many areas reported a steep rise in the number of prostitutes. School-aged girls, along with pregnant women and children under the age of 2, were deemed the groups most vulnerable to the crisis.

International financial institutions and bilateral donors initiated large-scale humanitarian programs in the middle of 1998, with many of the largest being managed or coordinated by the World Bank. The programs aimed at shoring up, or in some cases creating, a social safety net for those worst affected by the crisis. They included public works projects to absorb idle labour, subsidies on food and clean water for the very poor, and scholarships for students unable to afford school fees. Although well-intentioned, many of the programs failed to reach their intended recipients. Corruption was a familiar problem. Some of the deliveries of subsidised rice were re-exported or sold on the black market by Indonesian officials.[162] Some funds delivered to local and provincial governments were instead deposited in banks for weeks or even months so that local officials could profit from high interest rates. And some of the humanitarian aid was believed to be siphoned off by central government officials to help Golkar ahead of the parliamentary elections.

Many foreign donors argued that most of the aid should be funneled through large non-governmental organisations such as the Nahdlatul Ulama and the Muhammadiyah, both of which had national networks. Many smaller donors did work through these two organisations and other Indonesian NGOs, but the World Bank, which controlled the bulk of the aid, worked mostly through the Indonesian government. 'The World Bank wants to work with NGOs, but it is forced to work with the government which wants to avoid the NGOs', said Ann Thomson, a former Indonesia director for CARE International.[163] Many aid workers believed the Habibie administration was loath to work with the NU and the Muhammadiyah because they were headed by men seen as political rivals to Habibie.

Meltdown of the banking system

The worst-hit sector of the modern economy was the banking system, where the crisis began. Deteriorating balance sheets left almost all of Indonesia's banks technically insolvent, even the state-owned institutions. An audit of the banking system showed that only some 60 banks out of a total of more than 200 could claim a capital-adequacy ratio greater than 4 per cent.[164] An estimated two-thirds of all outstanding loans were thought to be non-performing. Even higher rates of delinquency were recorded at the state-owned banks, the principal lenders to Soeharto's children and close cronies. Lending dropped precipitously, as banks understandably had a tough time locating creditworthy borrowers. Bankers' hesitation to lend, however, merely exacerbated the crisis, starving even viable businesses from obtaining working capital and letters of credit. Banks desperate to rebuild their capital base were slow to lower interest rates, even after the rate of inflation eased near the end of the year. Export–import banks from a number of countries, including Japan and the USA, offered to guarantee trade credits to Indonesian exporters via Indonesian banks. But Indonesian banks were so reluctant to lend that most of the guaranteed credits went unused.[165] The government announced it would merge four of the seven state-owned banks into one institution, although the potential efficiency gains from the move were hotly debated.[166]

In January 1999, Habibie announced a massive bank recapitalisation plan that was expected to cost at least US$30 billion. Most of the money was to come from new bonds issued by the government, with the remainder coming from sales of assets seized from problem banks. To be eligible to participate in the plan, bank owners were required to commit new equity to their banks. Although restoring some semblance of health to the financial system was undoubtedly a necessary step to economic recovery, the recapitalisation plan was immediately criticised as unrealistic. Critics of the government objected to public monies being used, as they saw it, to bail out corrupt banks. And bankers claimed there was no way for them to meet their expected contribution. The controversy deepened in February when the central bank announced that Lippo Bank, an Indonesian-Chinese-owned institution, would receive 88 per cent of the US$500 million expended in the first tranche of the recapitalisation program. Subsequent delays in the plan, apparently at the urging of politically well-connected owners of insolvent banks, added to the furore.[167]

Related to the banks' woes was the seemingly intractable problem of foreign debt. The private sector held an estimated US$80 billion in foreign-currency debt at the beginning of the crisis. The enormous depreciation of the rupiah raised the debt burden on many Indonesian firms by a factor of three or four when denominated in rupiah. One indication of the damage wreaked on Indonesia's corporate health can be seen in the calamitous drop of the Jakarta Stock Exchange. In dollar terms, the Jakarta Stock Exchange index lost 90 per cent of its value between September 1997 and September 1998, although it recovered somewhat in the fourth quarter of the year.[168]

Unlike in South Korea and Thailand, the foreign currency debt in Indonesia was mostly held by non-bank corporations. This made the search for a solution all the more complicated, as a banking sector recapitalisation would solve only part of the problem. The Habibie government's first attempt to address the debt issue, known as the Frankfurt Agreement, provided for an eight-year rollover of principal including a three-year grace period. Indonesia agreed to guarantee foreign exchange to debtor companies but only at prevailing exchange rates. Few debtors took advantage of the agreement, however, as it made no provision for a write-down of debt. 'The Frankfurt Agreement is meant for companies with a liquidity problem', one Indonesian banker said: 'But it doesn't do much for insolvent companies, which is what most of ours are'.[169]

The Jakarta Initiative, a second attempt, provided a set of principles for debt-restructuring deals as well as an offer to facilitate negotiations between creditors and debtors. It fared scarcely better than the Frankfurt Agreement. Indonesian debtors argued there could be no lasting solution to Indonesia's debt crisis without creditor banks agreeing to write down a portion of their loans. They said a simple restructuring of the debt would not suffice, given the huge gap between their cash flow and what they owed. But many creditors remained unwilling to consider write-offs until they had more information on Indonesian debtors' capacity to repay. Many suspected the shareholders of indebted Indonesian companies of having considerable assets offshore. Japanese banks were especially reluctant to write down any of their Indonesian loans because of their already fragile balance sheets.[170] Creditors were also disappointed with what they saw as the government's foot-dragging on setting up a functional bankruptcy court. An early decision by the court rejecting a bankruptcy application further soured the mood among foreign bankers.[171]

A business community in tatters

The near dissolution of the banking sector had a profound impact on the rest of the business community. Lending rates remained punitively high and many companies found they could no longer roll over even working capital credits. A number of sectors were particularly hard-hit. Textile and shoe exports dropped precipitously, with the latter falling by almost 30 per cent in 1998. Car sales plummeted almost 80 per cent to around 30 000 units. Misguided government policies hindered the export of several agricultural products. One example widely criticised by economists was a 60 per cent tariff the government imposed on palm oil exports in July 1998, ostensibly in a bid to assure a continued domestic supply of the commodity. Economists argued that Indonesia would have been better off switching to alternative sources of cooking oil, such as coconut oil, while benefiting from the rise in the world prices of palm oil. The palm-oil export tax cost Indonesia perhaps as much as US$1 billion of lost revenue at a time when it was desperately short of hard currency reserves.[172]

Foreign direct investment slowed markedly in the last months of Soeharto's rule and scarcely picked up after Habibie took over. Investment commitments by both foreign and domestic investors plunged by more than 50 per cent in 1998. Foreign investors recognised that Habibie's assumption of power marked the beginning of a process, not an end. With Indonesia's political future uncertain, it took a brave investor to make a long-term commitment in the country. Most foreign investors had not bothered to understand Indonesian politics during Soeharto's tenure. They clung to a few simple truths: Soeharto was in charge; the technocrats controlled economic policies; the armed forces were all-powerful; and all decisions of note were made in Jakarta. But when Soeharto left the scene, foreign investors' uncomplicated map of Indonesian politics was rendered useless and they grew cautious. Some foreign investors did come to

Indonesia in the second half of 1998 looking to take advantage of the fall in asset values. But most were put off by the uncertainty of the political process and concern about Indonesia's continued commitment to open markets and free trade. Others were frustrated by the insistence of Indonesian shareholders on valuing their assets at prices well above market value.

Foreign investors took their cues from the ethnic-Chinese business community, which made them even more cautious. Many investors had ethnic-Chinese partners or employees. The palpable fear that infused the ethnic-Chinese community and the departure of tens of thousands of ethnic-Chinese to foreign lands sobered foreign investors. The foreign investment community also had to come to grips with the changing nature of Jakarta's relations with outlying provinces. After Soeharto fell, provincial and local governments immediately began asserting their authority. Anxious to claim a larger share of the profits earned by foreign-invested companies in their area, they demanded that foreign companies open their books and reveal how much they had remitted to Jakarta. A few firms suspected of polluting the environment faced a continuous series of protests and demands for redress, but the government and the military no longer came to their aid. The Indorayon pulp plant in North Sumatra was closed for months when villagers, who said toxic emissions from the plant had polluted the local water supply and caused respiratory ailments, barricaded the plant and refused to allow supplies to be delivered.[173]

A number of high-profile foreign companies also found themselves on the wrong end of the anti-corruption drive sweeping the nation. Many firms with connections to Soeharto relatives quickly tried to distance themselves from their erstwhile partners.[174] The US mining giant Freeport McMoRan was accused of bribing government officials in exchange for an extension of its mining contract. It was also accused of helping the Indonesian military repress an insurgency movement active near its mining site in Irian Jaya. In a similar vein, the US oil company Mobil was accused of helping the military put down an insurgency near its production site in Aceh.[175]

The ethnic distribution of wealth

Redistribution of wealth is likely to be the most contentious topic in the debate on Indonesia's long-term economic health. As described in earlier chapters, the ethnic-Chinese play a significant role in Indonesia's economy, although measuring their degree of control is no easy matter.[176] Regardless of what share of the national wealth they used to control, two factors have altered the picture dramatically. One is the economic crisis itself. Ethnic-Chinese families owned the majority of the most heavily indebted firms hurt by the crisis. Many lost their holdings entirely, while others have watched their wealth dwindle to a fraction of its former size. Second, the political transformation underway in Indonesia will almost surely result in a less favourable climate for ethnic-Chinese businesses.

It was a measure of the strength of Soeharto's authoritarian control that the ethnic-Chinese community, representing less than 4 per cent of the population, amassed as much economic clout as it had during the New Order. The Chinese possessed entrepreneurial talent, access to overseas financial networks and a strong commitment to education. But another essential ingredient of their success in New Order Indonesia was a tightly controlled political system that nullified the demographic weight of the *pribumi*, or indigenous, majority. With the fall of Soeharto, that ingredient is now missing.

Consequently, erosion of the ethnic-Chinese economic clout is likely. How that will be accomplished, and at what cost to Indonesia's near-term economic prospects, is much more difficult to predict. Many ethnic-Chinese businessmen readily concede that a rebalancing of Indonesia's ethnic distribution of wealth is inevitable and indeed welcome. For obvious reasons, they are aware of the dangers they face as a consequence of the widespread resentment their business success has created.[177] Their goal is to participate as equals in a long-overdue national dialogue on how to reduce social resentment of the ethnic-Chinese community. Their fear, however, is that they will be victimised in a national witch hunt aimed at eliminating their economic presence once and for all. All but the most radical redistributionists agree that such a course of action would prolong the current crisis for many years to come. 'There is no doubt there is a lot of resentment against the Chinese', concedes the NU chairman Abdurrahman Wahid: 'But we have to deal carefully with the problem. We will need one or two generations to resolve it. We cannot do it overnight like Adi Sasono says'.[178]

The fear of the future has a number of disturbing implications. Chinese-owned firms have sharply reduced their investments in new and existing operations, a trend that has exacerbated the growing unemployment problem. Uncertain of their future political standing in Indonesia, they have been reluctant to repatriate offshore capital and many have dragged their feet in negotiating with offshore creditors. As a result, the flow of private capital into Indonesia has slowed to a trickle and a resolution to the massive foreign-debt problem remains distant. On a more human level, the trauma inflicted on the ethnic-Chinese community led to an exodus of precisely those skills Indonesia will need most in years ahead. Indonesian and foreign companies have seen many of their Chinese employees pack up and leave, creating vacancies in accounting, finance, operations and middle management.

A number of officials who came to power with Habibie have attempted to move ahead with various plans for redistributing wealth. Together with their civilian supporters, they see the current weakened position of the ethnic-Chinese as a once-in-a-generation opportunity to redress the wealth equation. Only the most radical publicly admit their goal is to reduce the economic clout of the Chinese, but that will be the result, direct or indirect, of the programs they advocate. Much of the jockeying centred on a newly created entity, the Indonesian Bank Restructuring Agency. Ibra, as the agency is known, was charged with collecting the roughly US$14 billion in credits the central bank lent out earlier in 1998 to keep the banking system afloat. In the process, Ibra took over or closed a number of formerly high-flying banks that could not pay back their central bank credits. It emerged that some of the banks had violated a series of banking regulations, especially laws limiting how much a bank could lend to companies owned by the same shareholders. Bank Dagang Nasional Indonesia, owned by the Nursalim family, was said to be the worst offender. 'It was ridiculous what the Nursalim family was doing', said a senior banker in Jakarta: 'BDNI did nothing but fund the Nursalim companies. The central bank credits went into BDNI and right out the back door to the family firms'.[179]

The shareholders of the indebted banks were obliged to meet their commitments to the government by transferring to Ibra their equity stakes in dozens of firms. In return, the shareholders of the indebted banks were given immunity from future prosecution for misusing the central bank credits. The Salim Group, for example, paid back the roughly US$4 billion it had received from the central bank by surrendering to Ibra an equivalent value of equity it held in scores of companies. To its credit, Ibra took pains to dispel the impression that its main objective was to confiscate Chinese-held assets. For example, it allowed the Salim Group to retain management control of many of the companies partially turned over to Ibra and offered the group the opportunity to buy back its shares in the future.

Ibra's collection efforts had two immediate effects. First, they represented a major shift of corporate ownership from the private to the public sector, reversing a trend that had gained steam during the previous decade. Second, they converted Ibra into arguably the country's most powerful economic institution.[180] In the space of several months, Ibra evolved from an office of several dozen bureaucrats to an agency controlling a sizeable chunk of Indonesia's corporate jewels. Unsurprisingly, there was no shortage of people looking to separate Ibra from its newly acquired assets. Large, *pribumi*-owned businesses urged the government to use the Ibra-held assets to build up or create a class of *pribumi* tycoons, pointing approvingly to Malaysia's New Economic Policy (NEP). Underlying the position of the *pribumi* big-business lobby was a fear that IMF-imposed reforms would create too open a market too soon. Many felt themselves unable to compete effectively with either foreign investors or the Indonesian-Chinese, and they wanted the government to retain considerable capacity to intervene in the economy. Ibra offered a particularly attractive target.

'There is a lot of envy and hatred in Indonesia', said Aburizal Bakrie, a leading *pribumi* businessman: 'Most Indonesians are afraid to say we have a problem because they are afraid of being called racists. But this is not a racist issue; it's an economic one. The bottom line is that we have to redistribute assets'.[181] Bakrie urged Habibie to initiate a wide-ranging affirmative action program along the lines of Malaysia's NEP and to instruct Ibra to sell its assets to *pribumi*-owned banks. 'This is the best opportunity to redistribute wealth because the government, via the central bank, already owns lots of Chinese companies', added businessman Suryo Sulistio, who also supports an NEP-type approach: 'The government needs to convince the people it is no longer helping the Chinese'.[182]

Malaysia's Prime Minister Mahathir Mohamad jumped into the debate on the side of businessmen such as Bakrie and Sulistio. He said Indonesia's refusal to pursue NEP-type policies was 'why the Indonesians attack the Chinese'. But while there were plenty of other *pribumi* businessmen in Indonesia who supported Bakrie's views, there was also plenty of skepticism that they could be put into practice. 'I support an NEP-type program in theory, but I don't think it will happen for a long time', said businessman Kusumo Martoredjo: 'For one thing, there aren't enough competent *pribumi* businessmen to take over from the Chinese'.[183]

Minister for Cooperatives Adi Sasono had his own plans for Ibra. He wanted to use the Ibra assets to finance a larger economic role for cooperatives. Deswandhy Agusman, a senior official of the cooperatives ministry, said the ministry expected to receive 20 per cent of the assets collected by Ibra, although the ministry later disavowed the statement in the face of widespread criticism.[184] Like-minded ministers developed their own plans. Forestry Minister Muslimin Nasution, a former senior official at the cooperatives ministry, pledged to limit the size of the forestry concession areas held by any one firm and to force current concession holders to relinquish at least 20 per cent of their firms to cooperatives.[185] Sasono attempted to give cooperatives a monopoly on the distribution of cooking oil, a business formerly dominated by ethnic-Chinese traders, although he was later forced to water down the plan. He later succeeded in establishing a subsidised credit facility for cooperatives and small businesses.

In late September 1998 the Habibie government put a stop to Ibra negotiating asset swaps with the shareholders of indebted banks. Some ministers worried that Ibra was not driving a hard enough bargain with the banks. Others wanted the shareholders to come up with cash instead of assets. Initially, the government decided that the recipients of central bank credits would be given one year to repay their debts. After both the banks and the IMF protested vigorously, the timetable was extended to four years.[186] Meanwhile, the ethnic-Chinese saw the debate as additional evidence that anti-Chinese ministers were driving policy.

Within months of Habibie taking power, Sasono had become enemy number one within the ethnic-Chinese business community. They saw Sasono as anti-Chinese and anti-capitalist and fretted about his apparently close relationship with Habibie. A string of media profiles emerged with such headlines as: 'Is Adi Sasono the Most Dangerous Man in Indonesia?'.[187] Many non-Chinese businessmen and economists were also alarmed by Sasono's plans, which they condemned as racist and harmful to Indonesia's economic health. Many economists warned that Sasono's subsidised credit program was a recipe for more corruption. Sri Mulyani Indrawati, a prominent economist at the University of Indonesia, derided Sasono's economic agenda as 'nonsense'.[188] How far Sasono is able to push his program of building up cooperatives will depend on how much support he can muster in the political arena.

Sasono is popular in the more militant part of the Muslim community thanks to his background in Muslim non-governmental organisations as well as his leadership of the Indonesian Association of Muslim Intellectuals. He appears to enjoy considerable support from Habibie, and his ministry has enjoyed a much higher level of funding since Habibie came to power. He is an able politician who tirelessly travels around the nation spreading his populist message and championing the cause of small-scale farmers and businessmen. How successful this approach will be at the polls is hard to say, but it is likely to be considerable.

Sasono's overt appeal to the poor and disenfranchised has long been absent from Indonesian politics. The Indonesian Communist Party, wiped out in the mid-1960s, was the last party to make its political appeal strictly on class grounds. An earlier example, and no doubt a more comforting one to Sasono, was the Yogyakartan prince, Pangeran Surjodiningrat, who built up Indonesia's largest political organisation in the 1930s, a decade before independence. Like Sasono, Surjodiningrat alienated the bureaucracy and the elite by cultivating the support of the peasantry. And, like Sasono, he organised the peasantry by developing and expanding cooperatives.[189] In the months after Habibie assumed power, Sasono pushed Golkar to adopt a more populist line in a bid to change its elitist image. And in November 1998 the party dedicated itself to a 'People's Economy' program that promised to steer government credit to small and medium-sized businesses.

Sasono denies accusations that he is anti-Chinese: 'The issue is not about Chinese or non-Chinese. The issue is against the concentration of the productive assets in the hands of the few. We must fight against poverty, not minorities'.[190] Although many Indonesians think of him as a radical, he sees himself as a moderate holding the radical fringe at bay:

'I'm worried that if people like me fail, the radicals will take over'. He also disavows any interest in emulating Malaysia's experience with an ethnic-based affirmative action program. At the same time, he has little sympathy for the complaints emanating from the ethnic-Chinese business community: 'Those who had privileges before in a non-democratic system are naturally unhappy when they lose them'.[191]

While Sasono is careful to frame his ambitions in strictly economic terms, his militant Muslim supporters want to keep the ethnic issue front and centre. They view the Chinese economic success as purely a product of illicit collaboration with Soeharto and the military, and see little reason why they should be allowed to continue in business. 'The Chinese were given special advantages because the government was dirty', says Ahmad Soemargono of the Crescent and Star Party: 'Without corruption, Chinese business wouldn't exist. I agree with what Adi Sasono is doing with cooperatives. We have to prepare Indonesians to take over from the Chinese'. The government, he added, 'should nationalise the Chinese companies and redistribute their assets to *pribumis*'.[192] These sorts of views attract some support from the top ranks of *pribumi* businessmen, but not much. One leading *pribumi* businessman shares the militants' dim view of the ethnic Chinese, saying that 'the humbling of the Chinese shows that this crisis has some merit'. But in the next breath the businessman, himself a Muslim, heaped scorn on the militant Muslims: 'The last thing I'd want is for them to take power. We would end up like Iran'.[193]

POLITICAL RENEWAL

As 1999 began, the outcome of Indonesia's experiment with political liberalisation was far from certain. A democratic Indonesia committed to open markets and regional stability was the hope of many Indonesians and many of Indonesia's friends abroad. But there were no guarantees that Indonesia would turn out this way. No-one could say whether regional tensions would spiral out of control, turning Indonesia into an Asian version of strife-torn Yugoslavia. No-one could say whether the military would agree to a lower political profile, or whether continuing civil unrest would lead to a return of authoritarianism. And no-one could say whether Islam would or would not become the dominant force in Indonesian politics.

Few, however, would dispute that all these outcomes were possible. The conditions underlying Indonesia's attempt to secure a new political system could hardly have been more adverse. Political institutions had been severely weakened under three decades of Soeharto's rule. Soeharto himself had made no provisions for his own succession, and he hounded into submission those who tried to do it for him. Eighteen months of deteriorating economic conditions had stretched the social fabric almost to breaking point. And distrust prevailed at every level: between political rivals, between the political opposition and the government, between religions and ethnic minorities, and between provinces.

Many analysts viewed the threat of national disintegration as perhaps the most serious obstacle to consolidating democratic rule. The military viewed as its primary mission the protection of Indonesia's national unity. Indeed, it had long defended its powerful political role as necessary to prevent the country from coming apart at the seams. Many in the pro-democracy movement feared that the prospect of secessionist movements arising across the archipelago would convince the military to retake power from civilian leaders and stop the democracy movement in its tracks.

Trouble in the provinces

It did not take long to put this fear to the test. Almost immediately after Habibie assumed power, separatist sentiment picked up steam in the three traditional trouble spots: Aceh, Irian Jaya, and East Timor. In Aceh, as described earlier, a nationalist movement gathered strength shortly after Soeharto resigned, and the military pledged to reduce its presence in the province. As news filtered out about the torture and killings of civilians during the past decade, anger at Jakarta grew. In the easternmost, resource-rich province of Irian Jaya, secessionist rebels pushed their campaign for independence. As in Aceh, a repressive military approach and a freer press combined to harden separatist views.[194]

East Timor presented the most troubling case of all. Soon after Habibie took power, Indonesia presented its plan for granting greater autonomy to East Timor. Vague on most details, the plan was explicit on two points: Indonesia would not countenance a referendum to be held in East Timor, and it would not discuss autonomy as a prelude to independence. Jakarta pinned its hopes on Timorese support for independence waning after a period of greater provincial autonomy. It was not, however, willing to put its hopes to the test. Foreign Minister Ali Alatas remained adamantly opposed to a referendum. And despite numerous appeals from foreign governments, Habibie refused to release the jailed leader of the Timorese opposition, Jose Xanana Gusmao.

From his cell in Jakarta's Cipinang prison, Xanana was willing to take a moderate approach in negotiating with the government. He was prepared to accept a limited period of autonomy, but insisted that a referendum on remaining part of Indonesia would have to take place at some point. 'Jakarta is now trying not to lose face, and it doesn't serve our purposes to make them do so', Xanana said in a September 1998 interview inside Cipinang prison:

> The Timorese are agreed that full independence is the goal. We will not settle for anything less. But we can agree to a transitional period to prepare the political landscape in East Timor, to establish political parties, develop local government offices, and so on. But the maximum we are willing to wait would be three years.[195]

Many East Timorese, however, were not willing to wait. They wanted the Indonesian military withdrawn immediately and a referendum on independence to be held as soon as possible. Pro-independence activists in East Timor saw the political turmoil in the Indonesian capital as a golden opportunity to finally achieve their goal, and they viewed all of Jakarta's offers short of independence as another in a long line of tricks and false promises. Clashes between independence rebels and the military grew more frequent, and temperatures rose on both sides. As 1998 wore on, Xanana's moderate approach appeared to be losing the day, and some analysts felt the movement's leader was losing credibility with his more impatient supporters back in East Timor. In the capital city of Dili, petty crime, vandalism and small skirmishes became commonplace. On several occasions migrants who had moved to East Timor from elsewhere in Indonesia had their homes and shops attacked, leading to a steady exodus of non-native East Timorese.[196] Human rights groups blamed bands of vigilantes funded and armed by the Indonesian military for stirring up much of the trouble. Many feared the run-up to the parliamentary elections scheduled for June 1999 could degenerate into widespread violence, as the military and military-backed thugs attempted to force Timorese to participate in the parliamentary elections.

In January 1999 Australia changed its policy toward East Timor. Although it continued to recognise East Timor as part of Indonesia, Canberra urged Jakarta to permit a genuine 'act of self-determination' in East Timor. Australia had been one of the few Western countries to support Jakarta's position on East Timor since its annexation in 1976, and its 11th-hour turnaround infuriated the government in Jakarta, especially Foreign Minister Alatas. Within weeks of the Australian announcement, Habibie succumbed to the inevitable. On 27 January he said he was prepared to grant independence to East Timor if the Timorese rejected the earlier offer of greater autonomy. He pledged to have the issue settled one way or another by the beginning of 2000. One of Habibie's aides said Indonesia would support East Timor's application to join ASEAN if it chose the independence route.[197]

While the news was welcomed, it was not long before a new set of worries emerged, including a great deal of speculation about Habibie's motivation in putting independence on the table. Some of his aides said the president wanted a resolution to the seemingly intractable East Timor problem to be a historic legacy of his brief presidency. Others argued that Habibie hoped to gain considerable goodwill from the international community. Still others believed Habibie and Alatas were motivated primarily by frustration and pique.[198] The predominantly Catholic East Timor had been a black mark on Indonesia's record for more than two decades and a constant irritant for Alatas in his 11 years as foreign minister. Both men were said to be annoyed at the East Timorese refusal to be grateful for the offer of enhanced autonomy, and Habibie in particular was put out by the refusal of East Timor's widely respected Bishop Carlos Ximenes Belo to meet him.

Whatever its motivations, Jakarta's new position immediately came under attack. Many analysts, in and outside East Timor, warned that East Timor was not ready for an immediate move to independence. It remained something of a mystery why Jakarta rejected the offer by East Timorese leaders for a transitional period of three to five years before putting the independence question to a vote. Alatas seemed intent on keeping East Timorese participation in the negotiations to a minimum, preferring to deal with Portugal and the United Nations as the lessor of two evils. He also adamantly ruled out a referendum in East Timor. He argued that it was a decision of Indonesia's People's Consultative Assembly (MPR) to incorporate East Timor into Indonesia in the first place and it was up to the MPR to decide whether it should be set free.[199] Instead of a referendum, some measure of sampling Timorese opinion was to be devised. The Timorese were left with a take it or leave it proposition: accept Indonesia's offer of limited autonomy or take immediate independence and risk civil war.[200]

Many Timorese who worked in the local bureaucracy or who supported integration with Indonesia were the unhappiest of all. They stood to lose their jobs, their social standing and perhaps their lives. Across the province, clashes erupted between pro-independence and pro-integration camps, the latter armed by the Indonesian military. Many pro-independence Timorese thought the military's efforts to arm pro-integration civilians was intended to foment civil war in Timor and thus to show the world that Jakarta was right all along in its contention that East Timor was not viable as an independent state.[201] Independence advocates found themselves in a dilemma: they wanted more time to educate the Timorese about the consequences of independence, but they were loath to admit to Jakarta, and to the outside world, that they were in any way dependent on Indonesia. Responding to the Timorese who wanted to keep East Timor inside Indonesia, Jose Ramos-Horta, a co-winner of the Nobel Peace Prize, said he found it 'mind-boggling to think we would fear Indonesia's withdrawal if its only [legacies] are war, abuse, humiliation, rape, corruption and mismanagement'. The outspoken independence advocate also made it clear that suspicions of Indonesia's motivations had in no way been eased following Jakarta's change of heart. 'I do not trust them', Horta said, referring to Habibie, his ministers and the army leadership: 'I have known them for 23 years. These people thrive on lies, on deception, which is a culture deeply ingrained in the Indonesian military hierarchy and political elite'.[202]

Another line of criticism questioned East Timor's ability to sustain itself economically. East Timor has few natural resources, although there may be considerable quantities of oil in the waters south of the province. Xanana took pains to assure the Australian firms who had been exploring in those waters that their interests would be protected: 'We will honor commitments made by the previous regime. And if we make changes to the [Timor Gap] treaty, they will not be detrimental to existing parties'.[203] Coffee, tourism and sandalwood are other potential revenue sources. Optimists have noted that there are 35 sovereign nations in the world today with fewer than 500 000 people, most of them with higher incomes than Indonesia. East Timor too, they said, could manage on its own.[204]

But few denied that an independent East Timor would face a daunting challenge in meeting the expectations of its people. Education levels in the provinces are low, even by Indonesian standards. Some 90 per cent of high school teachers were sent in from elsewhere in Indonesia and many were likely to leave if East Timor became independent. The younger generation of East Timorese have known nothing but violence, an upbringing that left them poorly prepared to settle disputes with other East Timorese peacefully.[205] Nevertheless, independence leaders tried to put the best face possible on the province's economic viability, and argued that Indonesia was hardly in a position to lecture East Timor on sound economic management. 'Is Indonesia in a position to lecture anyone on economic feasibility?', asked the acerbic Ramos Horta: 'I don't think I would trust Habibie running our economy. I'd rather have Imelda Marcos running a shoe store in Dili'.[206]

In Jakarta there was little public opposition to Habibie's change of heart on East Timor. Until very recently, most Indonesians knew little of what was going in East Timor and accepted the government's line that the majority of East Timorese were happy being part of Indonesia. Muslim groups often complained that Western support for the predominantly Catholic province amounted to another form of Western Islamophobia. But attitudes began to change after Soeharto left power and the press was at last free to report the East Timor story.[207] The Timorese tales of military atrocities seemed less far-fetched to ordinary Indonesians once similar stories had emerged elsewhere in the archipelago. On a more personal level, a number of influential politicians who had been tossed into Cipinang jail by Soeharto came to appreciate East Timor's plight after long talks with Xanana, a cellblock neighbour. Among them were the Islamic politician Sri Bintang Pamungkas and the labour leader Mochtar Pakpahan, both of whom were released from jail shortly after Habibie came to power.

The leaders of the opposition parties were divided on the issue, however. Amien Rais strongly supported the need for a referendum to accurately gauge Timorese opinion. Abdurrahman Wahid hoped East Timor would remain part of Indonesia, but said the decision was up to the Timorese. Megawati was the coolest to the idea of Timorese independence. In a curious role reversal, Kwik Kian Gie, one of Megawati's top advisers, mimicked the government's earlier position by asserting that only a small minority of Timorese opposed integration with Indonesia.[208] In public, the military establishment supported the new policy. In private, many officers saw the offer of independence as a betrayal of their long struggle against pro-independence forces, while others worried that the offer of independence to East Timor would generate similar demands from other provinces. In February 1999 military fears on this score were validated when independence activists in Irian Jaya demanded the same deal that had been offered to East Timor.[209]

The division of views in Jakarta highlighted another flaw of Habibie's new approach to East Timor. Given the transitional nature of Habibie's administration and the objections of leading opposition leaders such as Megawati, it was unclear whether Jakarta could uphold its side of any deal offered to the Timorese. As in so many other areas, Habibie's lack of legitimacy severely limited his latitude in pushing major new initiatives. Many in East Timor distrusted Habibie, seeing him as a clone of Soeharto. For some, it was preferable to wait and deal with whoever assumed the presidency in late 1999, even if this were to be the skeptical Megawati.

Although East Timor received the most attention, provincial discontent was on the rise across the archipelago. Local officials in numerous provinces voiced complaints about the ruling elite in Jakarta. In North Sumatra, Aceh, Riau, East Kalimantan, North Sulawesi and the Moluccas, provincial officials and local notables wondered aloud whether they would not be better off outside Indonesia.[210] These views were particularly noticeable in provinces that had weathered the economic crisis reasonably well. Much of the discontent concerned Jakarta's highly centralised control of the country's economic resources. Some 80 per cent of taxes collected in the districts and provinces is sent to Jakarta, an irksome requirement to resource-rich provinces.[211]

Jakarta's response

Jakarta's answer to the problem was to promote economic and political decentralisation. A bill discussed in early 1999 promised to give provinces more control over their resources. A second bill promised to devolve more political power onto local governments. To avoid strengthening separatist sentiment at the province level, the bill planned to bolster the power of district-level governments in the hope that districts, of which there are more than 300, would be less inclined than provinces to go their own way. Jakarta was optimistic in early 1999 that a genuine decentralisation of economic decision-making would appease provincial elites and help keep national borders intact. This optimism even extended to Aceh and Irian Jaya, although not to East Timor.[212]

Even so, a number of important caveats remained, with timing being the most important. Jakarta needed to move quickly to convince skeptical provincial officials that it was serious about decentralising control over economic resources and devolving more power to the provinces. Skepticism about Jakarta's motives ran high, and the early drafts of the bills mentioned above did little to improve confidence. In the bill on political decentralisation, for example, provinces and local legislatures would be given more authority on a range of issues. But provincial governors still needed Jakarta's approval. As written, the bill merely 'decentralises administrative tasks, not power, away from Jakarta's hands', editorialised the *Jakarta Post*: 'There is no doubt who the real boss is; loyalty is to Jakarta first and to people in the region last'.[213]

Jakarta had little time to waste. Every ethnic and religious clash and every violent encounter with military forces exacerbated provincial unease with the status quo and hardened separatist sentiment. Aceh provided a good example. In the third quarter of 1998, demonstrators in Aceh were principally concerned with getting combat troops out of the province and winding back the military's dual-function role. By early 1999, after a series of bloody clashes between separatist rebels and army units, student and Muslim demonstrators began campaigning for a referendum on independence.[214] The longer Jakarta dawdled on genuine decentralisation efforts, the more likely that this trend would be emulated in other provinces.

Other threats to democracy

Provincial unhappiness was only one of a series of obstacles blocking the path to a democratic future. The economy was another. Just as the uncertain political situation was holding up prospects for an economic recovery, so too was the economic crisis complicating the process of political reform. The urban middle class provided the main impetus for the societal push for more political accountability and an end to Soeharto's rule. But these were also the people most severely hurt by the economic crisis. And it was unclear how their worsened economic condition would affect their commitment to political change. The poor did not play a major role in the movement against Soeharto, although they too supported efforts to secure greater social justice and more restraints on military behaviour. But the primary concern of the poor was economic survival, and it did not go unnoticed that Soeharto's departure coincided with a sharp run-up in prices of basic commodities and a breakdown of law and order. Although they may not have understood the reasons why, some poor Indonesians blamed pro-democracy leaders for their economic problems and the growing lawlessness in society.[215]

On the other hand, the crisis also had a moderating effect on political discourse. Indonesia's desperate need for foreign capital kept in check those parts of the political spectrum that were ideologically opposed to globalisation and eager to see a bigger state role in the economy. With the country heavily dependent on continued international assistance, most political leaders saw fit to tone down their criticism of the IMF and the World Bank. At the same time, the IMF and other donors used their leverage to lobby Habibie to back off from politically disruptive policies, such as attempts to weaken the standing of the ethnic-Chinese. For example, the IMF threatened to withhold aid if Habibie used the Indonesian Bank Restructuring Agency as a wealth redistribution tool.[216]

Religious and ethnic tension posed another threat to the political reform process. As described above, the first 10 months of Habibie's presidency were marked by an almost continuous string of violent incidents against the ethnic-Chinese and between Muslims and Christians. It was, of course, the fear of just this type of sectarian violence that underpinned Soeharto's justification of authoritarian rule, and many saw the violence as the factor most likely to spark a return to the authoritarian ways of the past. Political scientist Soedjati Djiwandono argued that religious and ethnic conflicts posed a greater threat to the national fabric than separatist sentiments on the outer islands: 'I, for one, am more concerned with national unity than with disintegration, if the former should mean the unity of the Indonesian people, and the latter the falling apart of the unitary state'.[217]

As noted early in this chapter, another issue poisoning the political debate was Habibie's lack of legitimacy. Many politically active Indonesians had little faith that Habibie and his government would be impartial in administering the elections. 'The problem is that we can't expect Habibie to be fair in setting the rules of the game', complained Amien Rais: 'After all, he learned politics from Soeharto'.[218] One example of the distrust was the bitter debates on whether civil servants should continue to hold senior positions in political parties. Most of the parties wanted to ban the practice in order to promote a politically neutral bureaucracy. But Golkar vigorously resisted the move, once again calling Habibie's impartiality into question. Only in late January 1999 did Golkar finally agree to laws freeing the 4-million-strong bureaucracy from its previous obligation to support the party. Even so, many reformists suspected Golkar would still benefit disproportionately from bureaucratic largesse at the expense of newer political parties.

Many in the pro-democracy community also distrusted the Indonesian elite, who had benefited most from Soeharto's rule. In some cases, this distrust was aimed at Soeharto personally, who many felt continued to manoeuvre behind the scenes in an attempt to disrupt the democratic process.[219] In other cases, it was directed at the elite more generally, including the military leadership. And many democracy campaigners were convinced that Soeharto and the military had played a role in instigating some of the worst episodes of violence in Habibie's first 10 months in power.

Although the elite no longer voiced support for Soeharto, many shared the former president's view that Indonesia was 'not ready' for democracy. Many saw democracy as a threat not only to Indonesia's ethnic and religious pluralism but to their own economic and political standing. They feared both radical students on the left and militant Muslims on the right, and almost all favoured retaining a strong army to keep both on the margins. 'Members of the political elite fear more than losing the perks and prerogatives of power', noted political scientist Jeffrey Winters: 'There is a real possibility they could be tried and jailed for the crimes of corruption and brutality they perpetrated together with Soeharto during three decades of authoritarian rule'.[220]

Elite-level concern was apparent in numerous provisions to the proposed laws for political parties and new electoral bodies.[221] For example, one provision required all political parties to acknowledge Pancasila as the national ideology of Indonesia. Another required that politicians be 'loyal to Pancasila' and not be members of the Communist Party or other banned organisations. A joke going around Jakarta was that the elite would vote overwhelmingly for the SQ Party (the Status Quo Party). Although relatively few in number, the elite retained enormous influence due to their financial resources. Students and other activist groups took for granted that the elite would use these resources to prop up Golkar and the other instruments of Soeharto's political machine. Indeed, several ethnic-Chinese businessmen complained in early 1999 of Habibie administration officials demanding they contribute funds to Golkar's campaign war chest, just as Soeharto had done in earlier elections.[222]

With some oversimplifying, all of these obstacles can be boiled down to one: a disturbing shortage of social trust. Societies use the political process to articulate demands and to negotiate compromises between conflicting views. Soeharto's elite-centred, authoritarian rule brought this sort of politics to a standstill. In what is arguably Soeharto's most damaging legacy to the Indonesian people, he allowed resentments and sectarian antagonisms to fester out of sight while at the same time disemboweling the political institutions needed to mediate them. Democracy requires more than campaigns, elections and political parties. It also requires a societal understanding of democratic principles and behaviour— what might be called democracy software. It requires the ability to bargain and compromise, and a belief that political institutions can implement elections impartially. It requires a willingness to lose, which in turn requires the belief that there will be another chance to compete.

Virtually all these attributes are in woefully short supply in today's Indonesia. There is precious little respect for the government, the military and other official institutions. Soeharto's winner-take-all approach to politics taught Indonesians that the winner really does take all.[223] This is one reason why campaigning for the upcoming parliamentary elections is likely to be so intense: few are convinced that the winners will treat the losers any better than Soeharto did.

Indonesia's crisis of alienation and distrust is most visible in the student movement. Unlike in 1965–66, the current crop of student leaders has assiduously avoided the urge to work with the military or older civilian leaders. The consensus view, supported by considerable historical evidence, is that the risk of forming an alliance with the military is unacceptably high. Students fear that once a common aim has been reached the military will reassume a dominant political position and marginalise its former allies. Consequently, the main student groups jealously guarded their autonomy leading up to Soeharto's fall, and were reluctant to change course after Habibie came to power. Indeed, Habibie's coming to power convinced them that the elite's commitment to reform was only skin-deep and that they were better off staying independent. By staying true to their self-image as a 'moral force', the students have been effective in keeping Habibie's feet to fire. The threat of massive student protests forced Habibie's hand in a number of ways, such as the inclusion of Soeharto's name in the anti-corruption decree passed in November 1998.

But the students' posture has also kept them largely aloof from the formal political process, which has weakened their influence. There is a great deal of mistrust of the motives of all the main party leaders, although some are distrusted more than others. Amien Rais' forceful critiques of Habibie made him the preferred choice of many students over Abdurrah-man Wahid and Megawati Sukarnoputri. Even so, the students were disappointed that Rais, together with Wahid and Megawati, refused to join with the students in the attempt to oust Habibie from the presidency during the Provisional People's Consultative Assembly in November 1998. The students had hoped to replace Habibie with a committee of national leaders, notwithstanding the fact that the prospective candidates for the committee were also leaders of rival political parties. Asked who should take over the presidency in light of the lack of credible alternatives, one student said: 'Better to leave it empty!'. When it was pointed out that no country had ever functioned without some kind of leader, the student replied: 'Make Indonesia the first!'[224]

The students see 'politics as inherently dirty', said Robin Madrid, who has followed the development of the student movement for many years:

'To them, it meant the elite struggle over the profits of development: which child or crony of Soeharto would get the toll road, which the clove monopoly'.[225] On the whole, the student movement is convinced the elections planned for June 1999 will not be fair, and some of the more radical groups have promised to boycott the elections.

The students have been sharply criticised by many mainstream politicians for being naïve, idealistic and even 'narcissistic', in the words of Indonesia's ambassador to the USA, Dorodjatun Kuntjoro-jakti.[226] Older civilian politicians have been frustrated by the failed efforts to bring students into the political fold, or even to support a particular party. 'Understandably, the students see power as a negative force', said one leading civilian politician: 'It has always been used negatively against them. But power can also be used to accomplish positive things. By staying outside the formal political system, the students are hurting, not helping, the democratic process'.[227] A rueful Amien Rais said that winning the support of the students 'may be the most difficult political task of all'.[228]

The Indonesian Democracy Struggle Party

Given the fractured nature of Indonesian politics, many parties have focused on religious loyalties or on the personalities of their leaders. This is at least partly true of Megawati's branch of the Indonesian Democratic Party, or PDI. After being evicted from the party's leadership in mid-1996, Megawati launched a series of unsuccessful legal actions to reclaim control of the party. After Habibie assumed power, she again sought to regain control of the party and its nationwide network of branches. But the judiciary under Habibie proved to be as impervious to political realities as it had been under Soeharto. The government continued to recognise as the official Indonesian Democratic Party the widely unpopular faction of the party handed control after Megawati's ouster. Megawati's party was obliged to choose a new name, and settled on Partai Demokrasi Indonesia-Perjuangan (Indonesia Democracy Struggle Party), or PDI-P.

In October 1998 the PDI-P held a national congress on the island of Bali, which attracted more than 100 000 supporters. Highlighted by a rousing closing-day speech by Megawati, the congress illustrated the party's impressive grassroots strength. Like Abdurrahman Wahid, Megawati promotes a pluralistic, secular nationalism, and strongly supports the political and religious tolerance embedded in the state ideology Pancasila. And, like Wahid, Megawati is enormously popular among many *abangan* Muslims and non-Muslims. Many observers expect Megawati's party to finish first or second in the parliamentary elections and be a leading contender to replace Habibie as president later in 1999. Given the close relationship between Megawati and Wahid, their two parties would make natural allies in a possible coalition government.

But Megawati draws mixed reviews from other parts of the political spectrum. As noted above, many *santri* Muslims consider her insufficiently Islamic and her candidacy a setback to Muslim political aspirations. Some Muslim leaders have argued she is unfit to be president because she is a woman.[229] Ahmad Soemargono, one of the leaders of the Crescent and Star Party, says his party 'will do whatever necessary' to ensure Megawati does not win'.[230]

Businessmen are leery of the party's views on economic policy. The Democratic Party draws many of its supporters from the old Indonesian Nationalist Party (PNI), which was founded by Megawati's father, Sukarno, Indonesia's first president. The PNI, like Sukarno, distrusted capitalism and favoured support for state-owned enterprises and cooperatives. Megawati has distanced herself from the inward-looking economic policies of her father—much to the chagrin of some of her siblings—and has taken on a number of highly regarded economic advisers. The PDI-P's treasurer, Laksamana Sukardi, a former managing director of Lippo Bank, made several trips abroad to assure potential foreign investors that Megawati is committed to free-market policies.[231] Nonetheless, suspicions persist that Megawati may swerve toward a more populist, nationalist economic agenda if elected. 'Many in our party still cling to the old Sukarno maxim: capitalism leads to colonialism which leads to imperialism', concedes Mochtar Buchori, who chairs the party's executive board and is an ally of Laksamana: 'The "nationalists" in the party don't know what they want. They're just allergic to the word capitalism because they don't acknowledge that global capitalism has changed. If Megawati comes to power, it will be our job to set up an environment for her to think in rational terms vis-à-vis economic policy'.[232]

Economics aside, many Indonesian intellectuals complain that Megawati lacks a broad vision for Indonesia's future.[233] She speaks in public rarely and often limits her speeches to vague generalities. Some critics say Megawati resembles former Philippines President Cory Aquino, in that her popularity derives principally from loyalty to a deceased male relative. Those of more macabre bent liken her to Evita Peron. A feisty critic while still a member of parliament, Megawati seemed sure of herself when criticising Soeharto. But since being tossed into the political wilderness in mid-1996, Megawati has grown more subdued and less sure of her bearings. At times she appears downright frightened by the zeal of her young supporters.

Many reformists launch some of the same criticisms at Megawati that they do at Wahid: among others, that she was overly cautious in the last months of Soeharto's rule and is too close to the military. Unlike Amien Rais, Megawati played at best a peripheral role in the movement that toppled Soeharto; like Wahid, she seemed content to sit on the sidelines and wait for developments to unfold. 'I don't like Megawati', said Arry, a freshman at the University of Indonesia: 'She rose up when the reform movement was already completed. She did not do anything'.[234] A number of senior retired generals have taken leadership positions in the PDI-P, and Megawati has angered many of her supporters by continuing to support a substantial political role for the military. Like Wahid, Megawati remains wary of the political aspirations of modernist Muslims, and believes a strong military is necessary to preserve Indonesia's secular approach to government. Many attributed Megawati's initial opposition to East Timorese independence to her close ties to military figures.

Despite these concerns by intellectuals and students, Megawati's party is certain to do well provided the elections are reasonably fair. Buchori says the PDI-P will win a quarter of the votes 'in the most pessimistic scenario and perhaps up to 35–40 per cent of the total'. He expects the PDI-P and Wahid's National Awakening Party to form a coalition in the People's Consultative Assembly convened to choose a new president. But even between parties as close as Megawati's and Wahid's, coalition building is not likely to be easy. 'The art of forming coalitions has been forgotten', Buchori says: 'How to treat partners fairly, how to compromise, all these things have been lost after so many years of monolithic politics. Even Megawati is very stubborn, but she will have to learn'.[235]

Predictions from the past

Many Indonesians harbour deep misgivings about the coming elections. No-one disputes that elections are necessary to put in place a legitimate government, but many wonder whether elections can produce a stable, effective government. Older Indonesians, in particular, remember first-hand the excitement of 1955, the only free and fair elections in Indonesian history, and the disappointment that followed. Less than four years after the elections Sukarno ended Indonesia's nine-year-long tumultuous experiment with democratic government and instituted his own brand of authoritarian rule.

With little else to go on, many Indonesians are digging through their history books to see what went wrong in 1955 and what lessons can be learned.[236] Four main parties captured 80 per cent of the vote in 1955: the Indonesia Nationalist Party, or PNI (22.3 per cent); Masyumi (20.9 per cent); Nahdlatul Ulama (18.4 per cent); and the Indonesian Communist Party, or PKI (16.4 per cent).[237] None of the other two dozen or so parties contesting the elections received more than 3 per cent of the vote. Before drawing parallels with the contemporary political scene, a few caveats are in order. Four decades of social development have surely altered the political currents that dominated the 1950s, although by how

much is harder to say. And prior to the 1955 elections few predicted that
the four main winners would do so much better than the other contestants.
Those parties that appear popular in early 1999 may also fall far short of
expectations in the elections scheduled for mid-1999. As noted above,
some rivals of Amien Rais believe that his party, Partai Amanat Rakyat
(PAN), will suffer the same fate as the Indonesian Socialist Party. The
PSI, as the party was known, was enormously popular among urban
intellectuals in the mid-1950s. But in the 1955 elections it won a mere
2.0 per cent of the vote. Jumhur Hidayat, secretary-general of the CIDES
research institute and a supporter of Adi Sasono, expects PAN to encounter
the same disappointment. 'PAN is an urban, elite phenomenon', he says:
'It doesn't have any grassroots support'.[238]

Of the four largest parties in the 1955 elections, only the NU remains
intact. It will do well in its heartland of East Java, where it won 34 per
cent of the vote in 1955, but it faces competition from half a dozen other
parties competing for the traditionalist Muslim constituency. Many former
NU strongholds in Central Java and on the outer islands are likely to
support the United Development Party and other Muslim parties. Many
supporters of Sukarno's party, the PNI, which was involuntarily merged
with the Indonesian Democratic Party in 1973, had links to the bureaucracy and tended to support Golkar in New Order elections. Some are
expected to stick with Golkar in the 1999 elections, while others will
gravitate to the PDI-P, the party of Sukarno's daughter. Sukarno banned
the Masyumi, the party of modernist Muslims, in 1960 on account of its
leaders' support of a military rebellion in Sumatra. In 1999 the modernist
Muslim vote is likely to be spread over a number of parties, including
the National Mandate Party, the United Development Party and the Crescent and Star Party.[239]

The Indonesian Communist Party has no obvious successor in 1999.
Much of the party's base was eliminated in the bloodbath of 1965–66,
and surviving sympathisers were driven deep underground in Soeharto's
New Order. It is not clear which party, if any, they might support in the
current political line-up. Leftist student groups, for example, are among
the most alienated and radical, and some of them plan to boycott the
elections entirely. Some analysts believe there is no grassroots base for a
leftist party. They argue that the gradual *santrification* of Indonesian
society, by which they mean the process of nominal Muslims becoming
more devout, has whittled away what once was the *abangan* base of the
Communist Party. Nevertheless, it is odd that the left edge of the political
spectrum remains largely unrepresented by political parties, and new
parties may well emerge to fill this space.

In the official New Order history books, the experiment with constitutional democracy in the 1950s is portrayed as an unvarnished failure.
Supporters of Soeharto's authoritarian rule blamed 'Western-style

democracy' for many of the decade's ills, including a deteriorating economy, sectarian tensions and sporadic separatist movements. Although
much of this critique is one-sided and biased, the 1950s were in fact
marked by continuous political uncertainty and ferment, a state of affairs
that the 1955 elections did little to resolve. Many in the elite fear that
the 1999 elections will similarly fail to heal Indonesia's political wounds.
Worse, they worry that democracy and party politics will again aggravate
religious and ethnic tensions, encourage secessionist sentiment and
damage the economy.[240]

One of the key lessons of the 1955 elections, and one of the critical
factors for the success of the 1999 elections, concerns the behaviour of
the election's winners and losers. The 1955 elections were seen as a
victory by Java over the Outer Islands, and a victory by traditionalist
Muslims over modernist Muslims.[241] Exchange-rate policies in the late
1950s, for example, benefited import-dependent Java and hurt many
export-dependent Outer Islands. Modernist Muslim ambitions were
thwarted repeatedly by Sukarno and in the constitutional assembly that
met in 1956–59. The frustration felt by the losers of the 1955 elections
provided the impetus for a series of regional rebellions that emerged in
1957–58. The rebellions, in turn, played a key role in the decision by
Sukarno and the military leadership to end the constitutional democracy
in July 1959 and replace it with Sukarno's increasingly authoritarian
regime, which he called 'guided democracy'. It is too early to predict the
reaction of the political losers in the 1999 elections. If the Outer Islands
do not get the economic and political autonomy they are demanding, they
could well react in a manner reminiscent of 1957–58. Likewise, modernist
Muslims may end up with less clout than they feel they deserve. The
modernist vote is likely to be split among a number of parties, and many
modernist Muslims may cast their votes for reasons that have little to do
with their religion. The result is likely to be heightened tension between
devout and secular Muslims. It remains to be seen whether the political
framework under construction in Indonesia can accommodate and amelio-
rate this tension, or be fatally weakened by it.

Summing up

Indonesia's path to democratic reform is almost certain to be long and
strewn with obstacles. The institutions necessary for democratic rule are
non-existent or have been hollowed out by decades of authoritarianism.
Ethnic, religious and regional tensions have burst forth after a long period
of repression. The military, the long-time guarantor of national peace and
stability, is in disrepute and faces an unsure future. Social trust, an
admittedly hard-to-define notion, is in short supply. This trust is essential
to the compromises inherent in any sustainable democratic polity and the

avoidance of further communal violence. Important parts of the economy lie in tatters, and a key economic resource—the Indonesian-Chinese—remains traumatised by the violence of the final days of Soeharto's rule. Powerful forces from the *ancien regime* are determined to retard the pace of reform, and they have the money and the means to pose a very real threat.

Above all, Indonesia is short of time. Indonesia is attempting nothing less than a revolutionary shift in its political orientation. It is doing so against a backdrop of economic collapse and in an exceedingly short time frame. To some extent, Indonesia is engaged in a race against itself. It must install and then consolidate a democratic process while fending off a range of threats. These include a demagogic populism that reduces Indonesia's access to the global trading system; a military take-over in the name of restoring law and order; a flowering of separatist sentiment that is breaking the country apart; and an Islamist surge that shatters Indonesia's multi-religious mosaic.

But even in the face of these very real fears there are grounds for hope. Virtually every point of Indonesia's political compass acknowledges the necessity of free and fair elections in producing a legitimate government. This is true of the opposition forces, which have long clamoured for a more representative system. But it is also true of the military, the economic technocrats, senior civil servants, the ethnic-Chinese business community and other actors that have long supported either Soeharto's brand of authoritarianism or the fiction that Soeharto's government was in its own way representative. Even President Habibie recognises the need for quick elections, implicitly acknowledging his government's own lack of legitimacy. Indonesia is blessed with a range of competent, moderate politicians leading many of the major parties. Abdurrahman Wahid, Amien Rais, Megawati Sukarnoputri and Sultan Hamengkubuwono of Yogyakarta are by definition untested politicians, but they share a commitment to democratic reform and a desire to preserve Indonesia's tradition of ethnic and religious pluralism. Their views enjoy widespread support from a population yearning for a political system that is more fair, just and representative than what came before. The impressive legal reforms accomplished by early 1999 should ensure a more level playing field for future political contests and limit the scope of corruption and vote-buying.

The military angered some opposition leaders by insisting on continued representation in the parliament and the People's Consultative Assembly. It is noteworthy nonetheless that the decision to give the military seats in the parliamentary bodies was a result of compromise and bargaining rather than fiat. Moreover, reformists in the military are prepared to see the military's direct political role scaled down further. There is also widespread agreement that Jakarta's dominant economic and political role must be reduced if the nation is to keep its present boundaries. Discussions on regional autonomy, in both political and economic terms, were well advanced by early 1999. If Jakarta maintains its commitment to a genuine decentralisation of power, there are solid grounds for optimism that East Timor's insistence on independence will not be repeated in other parts of the archipelago. Perhaps most importantly, Indonesians at every level of society yearn for a different and more just form of government. The fear of returning to a new form of Soeharto's corrupt authoritarianism is reason enough for many Indonesians to tolerate considerable uncertainty and doubt during Indonesia's democratic transition. As Amien Rais put it in early 1999: 'The status quo forces can slow us down for weeks, maybe months, but they can't stop the political reform movement. It is too strong now'.[242]

In sum, all that one can confidently say of Indonesia's short-term prospects is that they are uncertain. A contest is underway between powerful forces for change and powerful forces supportive of the status quo, and the outcome is still in doubt. Indonesia's economy will recover, but the timing of its recovery will depend on the success and the speed of political reform. Indonesia's political system, as this book has endeavoured to explain, remains in dire need of an overhaul from top to bottom, a fact apparent for many years. The good news is that Soeharto's departure from office has enabled the overhaul to begin.

Bibliography

International publications and news organisations

Agence France Presse
American Reporter
Asian Wall Street Journal
Australian Associated Press
Australian Broadcasting Corporation
Australian Financial Review
Bristish Broadcasting Corporation
Bulletin of Indonesian Economic Studies
Dow Jones Newswires
Far Eastern Economic Review
Financial Times
Indonesia
Inside Indonesia
International Herald Tribune
Melbourne Age
Reuter
Singapore Straits Times
South China Morning Post
Sydney Morning Herald
The Australian
The Independent Monthly
The New York Times
Time
Washington Post

Indonesian publications and news organisations

Antara
Bisnis Indonesia
Detik
Editor
Eksekutif

Forum Keadilan
Horison
Indonesia Business Weekly
Indonesian Business Watch
Indonesian Observer

Indonesian Political Watch	*Media Indonesia*
Info Business	*Prisma*
Jakarta Jakarta	*Prospek*
Jakarta Post	*Republika*
Jawa Pos	*Suara Pembaruan*
Jayakarta	*Tempo*
Kompas	*Van Zorge Report*
Matra	*Warta Ekonomi*

Publications of non-governmental organisations, research institutes, advocacy groups and think-tanks

Amnesty International
Human Rights Watch/Asia
Asian–American Free Labor Institute
Centre for Information and Development Studies
Centre for Strategic and International Studies
Committee to Protect Jounalists
Index on Censorship
Infight
Indonesian Institute for the Defence of Human Rights
Lawyers Committee for Human Rights
Legal Aid Institute
TAPOL
US–Indonesian Society
Walhi

Books and journals

Adnan, Zifirdaus. 'Islamic Religion: Yes, Islamic (Political) Ideology: No! Islam and the State in Indonesia', in *State and Civil Society in Indonesia*, ed. Arief Budiman, Centre of Southeast Asian Studies, Clayton, 1990

Amsden, Alice. 'The State & Taiwan's Economic Development', in *Bringing the State Back In*, eds Peter Evans, Dietrich Rueschemeyer and Theda Skocpol, Cambridge University Press, Cambridge, 1985

——*Asia's Next Giant: Late Industrialization in Korea*, Oxford University Press, New York, 1990

Anderson, Benedict. 'Last Days of Indonesia's Suharto?', *Southeast Asia Chronicle*, No. 63, 1978

——ed. *Language and Power: Exploring Political Cultures in Indonesia*, Cornell University Press, Ithaca, 1990

——*The Spectre of Comparisons: Nationalim, Southeast Asia and the World*, Verso, London, 1998

Anderson, Benedict and Ruth McVey. *A Preliminary Analysis of the October 1, 1965 Coup in Indonesia*, Cornell Modern Indonesia Project, Ithaca, 1971

Anwar, Dewi Fortuna. *Indonesia in ASEAN: Foreign Policy and Regionalism*, Institute of Southeast Asian Studies, Singapore, 1994

Arndt, H. W. 'Survey of Recent Developments', *Bulletin of Indonesian Economic Studies*, July 1974

Benda, Harry. 'Democracy in Indonesia', *Journal of Asian Studies*, May 1964

Booth, Anne, ed. *The Oil Boom and After: Indonesian Economic Policy and Performance in the Soeharto Era*, Oxford University Press, Singapore, 1992

Bresnan, John. *Managing Indonesia: The Modern Political Economy*, Columbia University Press, New York, 1993

——'The United States, the IMF and the Indonesian Financial Crisis', in *The Politics of Post-Suharto Indonesia*, eds Adam Schwarz and Jonathan Paris, Council on Foreign Relations, New York, 1999

Broinowski, Alison, ed. *Asean into the 1990s*, Macmillan Press, London, 1990

Budiman, Arief, ed. *State and Civil Society in Indonesia*, Centre of Southeast Asian Studies, Clayton, 1990

——'Indonesian Politics in the 1990s', in *Indonesia Assessment, 1992: Political Perspectives on the 1990s*, eds Harold Crouch and Hal Hill, Research School of Pacific Studies, Canberra, 1992

Chomsky, Noam. *Towards a New Cold War: Essays on the Current Crisis and How We Got There*, Pantheon Books, New York, 1982

Chomsky, Noam and Edward S. Herman. *The Washington Connection and Third World Fascism. The Political Economy of Human Rights: volume I*, Hale & Iremonger, Sydney, 1980

Cole, David C. and Betty F. Slade. *Building a Modern Financial System: The Indonesian Experience*, Cambridge University Press, Cambridge, 1996

——'Why Has Indonesia's Financial Crisis Been So Bad?', *Bulletin of Indonesian Economic Studies*, August 1998

Cribb, Robert, ed. *The Indonesian Killings, 1965–1966: Studies from Java and Bali*, Centre of Southeast Asian Studies, Clayton, 1990

Crouch, Harold. *The Army and Politics in Indonesia*, Cornell University Press, Ithaca, 1978 (revised edition, 1988)

——'Patrimonialism and Military Rule in Indonesia', *World Politics*, Vol. 31, No. 4, 1979

——'Military–Civilian Relations in Indonesia in the Late Soeharto Era', *The Pacific Review*, Vol. 1, No. 4, 1988

——'Indonesia: The Rise or Fall of Suharto's Generals', *Third World Quarterly*, Vol. 10, No. 1, 1988

——'The Politics of Islam in the Asean Countries', in *Asean into the 1990s*, ed. Alison Broinowski, Macmillan Press, London, 1990

Crouch, Harold and Hal Hill, eds. *Indonesia Assessment, 1992: Political Perspectives on the 1990s*, Research School of Pacific Studies, Canberra, 1992

Crouch, Harold and James W. Morley. 'The Dynamics of Political Change', in *Driven by Growth: Political Change in the Asia–Pacific Region*, ed. James W. Morley, M. E. Sharpe, Armonk, 1993

Dahl, Robert. *Polyarchy: Participation and Opposition*, Yale University Press, New Haven, 1971

Deyo, Frederic, ed. *The Political Economy of the New Asian Industrialism*, Cornell University Press, Ithaca, 1987

Doig, C. D. *A History of the 2nd Independent Company and 2/2 Commando Squadron,* Trafalgar, Victoria, 1986

Dunn, James. *Timor, A People Betrayed*, Jacaranda Press, Milton, Queensland, 1983

'East Timor: Building for the Future. Issues and Perspectives', Department of Foreign Affairs, Republic of Indonesia, July 1992

Emmerson, Donald. 'The Bureaucracy in Political Context: Weakness in Strength', in *Political Power and Communications in Indonesia*, eds Karl Jackson and Lucian Pye, University of California Press, Berkeley, 1978

——'Exit, Aftermath, Outlook: The Crisis of 1997–98', in *Indonesia Beyond Suharto: Polity, Economy, Society, Transition*, ed. Donald Emmerson, M.E. Sharpe, Armonk, NY, 1999

Evans, Peter, Dietrich Rueschemeyer and Theda Skocpol, eds. *Bringing the State Back In*, Cambridge University Press, Cambridge, 1985

Esposito, John, ed. *Islam in Asia: Religion, Politics & Society*, Oxford University Press, New York, 1987

Far Eastern Economic Review, *Asia Yearbook*, various issues

Fealy, Greg. 'The 1994 NU Congress and Aftermath: Abdurrahman Wahid, Suksesi, and the Battle for Control of NU', in *Nahdlatul Ulama, Traditional Islam and Modernity in Indonesia*, eds Greg Barton and Greg Fealy, Monash University, Melbourne, 1996

Feith, Herbert. *The Decline of Constitutional Democracy in Indonesia*, Cornell University Press, Ithaca, 1962

——'East Timor: The Opening Up, the Crackdown and the Possibility of a Durable Settlement', in *Indonesia Assessment, 1992: Political Perspectives on the 1990s*, eds Harold Crouch and Hal Hill, Research School of Pacific Studies, Canberra, 1992

Feith, Herbert. *The Indonesian Elections of 1955*, Modern Indonesia Project, Cornell University, 1957

Feldstein, Martin. 'Refocusing the IMF', *Foreign Affairs*, March/April, 1998

Fischer, Louis. *The Story of Indonesia*, Harper, New York, 1959

Forrester, Geoffrey. 'Introduction', in *The Fall of Suharto*, eds Geoff Forrester and R.J. May, Crawford House Publishing, Bathurst, Australia, 1998

Geertz, Clifford. *The Religion of Java*, University of Chicago Press, Chicago, 1960

——*Peddlers and Princes: Social Development and Economic Change in Two Indonesian Towns*, University of Chicago Press, Chicago, 1963

——'Afterword: The Politics of Meaning', in *Culture and Politics in Indonesia*, ed. Claire Holt, Cornell University Press, Ithaca, 1972

Gelb and Associates, *Oil Windfalls: Blessing or Curse?*, Oxford University Press, New York, 1988

Gillis, Malcolm. 'Micro and Macroeconomics of Tax Reform: Indonesia', *Journal of Development Economics*, 19, 1985

Glassburner, Bruce. 'In the Wake of General Ibnu: Crisis in the Indonesian Oil Industry', *Asian Survey*, No. 12, December 1976

Habib, Hasnan. 'The Role of the Armed Forces in Indonesia's Future Political Development', in *Indonesia Assessment, 1992: Political Perspectives on the 1990s*, eds Harold Crouch and Hal Hill, Research School of Pacific Studies, Canberra, 1992

Habir, Ahmad. 'State Enterprises: Reform and Policy Issues', in *Indonesia Assessment*

1990, eds Hal Hill and Terry Hull, Research School of Pacific Studies, Canberra, 1990

Hanna, Willard and Des Alwi. *Turbulent Times Past in Ternate and Tidore*, Yayasan Warisan dan Budaya Banda Naira, Banda Naira, 1990

Haseman, John. 'Indonesia and ABRI: Challenges for the Future', *Southeast Asian Affairs*, 1997, Singapore, 1997

Hefner, Robert. 'Islam, Class, and Civil Society: ICMI and the Struggle for the Indonesian Middle Class', *Indonesia*, No. 56, October 1993

——'Islamization and Democratization in Indonesia', in *Islam in an Era of Nation States*, eds Robert Hefner and Patricia Horvatich, University of Hawaii Press, Honolulu, 1997

——'Print Islam: Mass Media and Ideological Rivalries Among Indonesian Muslims', *Indonesia*, No. 64, October 1997

——'Islam and Nation in the Post-Suharto Era', in *The Politics of Post-Suharto Indonesia*, eds Adam Schwarz and Jonathan Paris, Council on Foreign Relations, New York, 1999

Heij, Gitte. *Tax Administration and Compliance in Indonesia*, Asia Research Centre on Social, Political and Economic Change, Murdoch, Western Australia, 1993

Heryanto, Ariel. 'Indonesia: Towards the Final Countdown?', *Southeast Asian Affairs*, 1997, Institute for Southeast Asian Studies, Singapore, 1997, p. 109

Hewison, Kevin, Richard Robison and Garry Rodan, eds. *Southeast Asia in the 1990s: Authoritarianism, Democracy and Capitalism*, Allen & Unwin, Sydney, 1993

Higgott, Richard, Richard Leaver and John Ravenhill, eds *Economic Relations in the Pacific in the 1990s: Conflict or Cooperation?*, Allen & Unwin, Sydney, 1993

Hill, David. 'The Press in New Order Indonesia', Asia Paper 4, University of Western Australia Press, 1994

Hill, Hal, ed. *Unity and Diversity: Regional Economic Development in Indonesia since 1970*, Oxford University Press, Singapore, 1989

——'Manufacturing Industry', in *The Oil Boom and After: Indonesian Economic Policy and Performance in the Soeharto Era*, ed. Anne Booth, Oxford University Press, Singapore, 1992

——'Survey of Recent Developments', *Bulletin of Indonesian Economic Studies*, Australian National University, Canberra, Vol. 28, No. 2, August 1992

——ed. *Indonesia's New Order: The Dynamics of Socio-Economic Transformation*, Allen & Unwin, Sydney, 1993

——*The Indonesian Economy Since 1966: Southeast Asia's Emerging Giant*, Cambridge University Press, Cambridge, 1996

Hill, Hal and Terry Hull, eds. *Indonesia Assessment 1990*, Research School of Pacific Studies, Canberra, 1990

Hitchcock, David. 'Asian Values and the United States: How Much Conflict?', Center for Strategic and International Studies, Washington, DC, 1994

Holt, Claire, ed. *Culture and Politics in Indonesia*, Cornell University Press, Ithaca, 1972

Hull, Terence and Valerie Hull. 'Population and Health Policies', in *The Oil Boom and After: Indonesian Economic Policy and Performance in the Soeharto Era*, ed. Anne Booth, Oxford University Press, Singapore, 1992

Human Rights Watch, *Academic Freedom in Indonesia: Dismantling Soeharto–Era Barriers*, New York, 1998

Huntington, Samuel. *Political Order in Changing Societies*, Yale University Press, New Haven, 1968

—— 'Will More Countries Become Democratic?' *Political Science Quarterly*, Vol. 99, No. 2, Summer 1984

—— *The Third Wave: Democratisation in the Late Twentieth Century*, University of Oklahoma Press, Norman, 1991

Indonesia Source Book, National Development Information Office, Jakarta, 1992

Jackson, Karl and Lucian Pye, eds. *Political Power and Communications in Indonesia*, University of California Press, Berkeley, 1978

Jenkins, David. *Soeharto and his Generals: Indonesian Military Politics 1975–1983*, Cornell Modern Indonesia Project, Monograph Series no. 64, Ithaca, 1984

Johns, Anthony. 'Indonesia: Islam and Cultural Pluralism', in *Islam in Asia: Religion, Politics & Society*, ed. John Esposito, Oxford University Press, New York, 1987

Johnson, Chalmers. 'Political Institutions and Economic Performance: the Government-led Business Relationship in Japan, South Korea and Taiwan', in *The Political Economy of the New Asian Industrialism*, ed. Frederic Deyo, Cornell University Press, Ithaca, 1987

Jolliffe, Jill. *East Timor: Nationalism and Colonialism*, University of Queensland Press, Brisbane, 1978

Jones, Howard. *The Possible Dream*, Harcourt Brace Jovanovich, New York, 1971

Kahin, George. *Nationalism and Revolution in Indonesia*, Cornell University Press, Ithaca, 1952

Kell, Tim. *The Roots of the Acehnese Rebellion, 1989–1992*, Cornell University Press, Ithaca, 1995

Kunio, Yoshihara. *The Rise of Ersatz Capitalism in Southeast Asia*, Oxford University Press, Singapore, 1988

Legge, J. D. *Sukarno: A Political Biography*, Penguin Press, London, 1972

Leifer, Michael. 'Uncertainty in Indonesia', *World Policy Journal*, Winter 1990–91

Lev, Daniel. *The Transition to Guided Democracy: Indonesian Politics, 1957–1959*, Cornell Modern Indonesia Project, Ithaca, 1966

Lewis, Bernard. *The Political Language of Islam*, University of Chicago Press, Chicago, 1988

Liddle, R. William. 'Participation and the Political Parties', in *Political Power and Communications in Indonesia*, eds Karl Jackson and Lucian Pye, University of California Press, Berkeley, 1978

—— 'Soeharto's Indonesia: Personal Rule and Political Institutions', *Pacific Affairs*, Vol. 58, No. 1, Spring 1985

—— 'The Relative Autonomy of the Third World Politician: Soeharto and Indonesian Economic Development in Comparative Perspective', *International Studies Quarterly*, Vol. 35, No. 4, December 1991

——'Indonesia's Democratic Past and Future', *Comparative Politics*, Vol. 24, No. 4, July 1992

——'Indonesia's Threefold Crisis', *Journal of Democracy*, Vol. 3, No. 4, October 1992

—— 'The Politics of Development Policy', *World Development*, Vol. 20, No. 6, 1992

——'*Media Dakwah* Scripturalism: One Form of Islamic Political Thought and Action in New Order Indonesia', in *Intellectual Development in Indonesian Islam*, eds Mark Woodward and James Rush, Center for Southeast Asian Studies, Arizona State University, Tempe, 1993

——'Improvising Political Cultural Change: Three Indonesian Cases', in *Indonesian Political Culture: Asking the Right Questions*, ed. James Schiller, Ohio University Center for Southeast Asian Studies, Athens

——'Indonesia's Unexpected Failure of Leadership', in *The Politics of Post-Suharto Indonesia*, eds Adam Schwarz and Jonathan Paris, Council on Foreign Relations, New York, 1999

Liem, Suei Liong. 'Indonesian Muslims and the state: accommodation or revolt?', *Third World Quarterly*, Vol. 10, No. 2, April 1988

Lubis, Mochtar. *Indonesia: Land under the Rainbow*, Oxford University Press, Singapore, 1990

Lubis, Todung Mulya. *In Search of Human Rights: Legal-Political Dilemmas of Indonesia's New Order, 1966–1990*, PT Gramedia Pustaka Utama dan SPES Foundation, Jakarta, 1993

MacIntyre, Andrew. *Business and Politics in Indonesia*, Allen & Unwin, Sydney, 1991

——'Indonesia, Thailand and the Northeast Asia Connection', in *Economic Relations in the Pacific in the 1990s: Conflict or Cooperation?*, eds Richard Higgott, Richard Leaver and John Ravenhill, Allen & Unwin, Sydney, 1993

——'The Politics of Finance in Indonesia: Command, Confusion and Competition', in *Government, Finance, and Development*, eds Stephan Haggard, Chung Lee and Sylvia Maxfield, Cornell University Press, Ithaca, 1993

Mackie, J. A. C. 'Report of the Commission of Four on Corruption', *Bulletin of Indonesian Economic Studies*, No. 2, November 1970

——*Konfrontasi:* The Indonesia–Malaysia Dispute, 1963–1966, Oxford University Press, London, 1974

—— ed. *The Chinese in Indonesia*, Thomas Nelson, Melbourne, 1976

——'Economic Growth in the Asean Region: The Political Underpinnings', in *Achieving Industrialization in East Asia*, ed. Helen Hughes, Cambridge University Press, Cambridge, 1988

——'Towkays and Tycoons: The Chinese in Indonesian Economic Life in the 1920s and 1980s', in *The Role of the Indonesian Chinese in Shaping Modern Indonesian Life*, Cornell Southeast Asia Program, Ithaca, 1991

——'Changing Patterns of Chinese Big Business in Southeast Asia', in *Southeast Asian Capitalists*, ed. Ruth McVey, Cornell Southeast Asia Program, Ithaca, 1992

——'Overseas Chinese Entrepreneurship', *Asian Pacific Economic Literature*, May 1992

——'Indonesia: Economic Growth and Depoliticization', in *Driven by Growth:*

Political Change in the Asia–Pacific Region, ed. James W. Morley, M. E. Sharpe, Armonk, 1993

Mackie, Jamie and Andrew MacIntyre. 'Politics', in *Indonesia's New Order: The Dynamics of Socio-Economic Transformation*, ed. Hal Hill, Allen & Unwin, Sydney, 1993

Manning, Chris and Joan Hardjono, eds. *Indonesia Assessment 1993. Labour: Sharing in the Benefits of Growth?*, Research School of Pacific Studies, Canberra, 1993

McDonald, Hamish. *Suharto's Indonesia*, Fontana Books, Blackburn, 1980

McKendrick, David. 'Acquiring Technological Capabilities: Aircraft and Commercial Banking in Indonesia', PhD dissertation, University of California, Berkeley, 1989

——'Obstacles to "Catch Up": The Case of the Indonesian Aircraft Industry', *Bulletin of Indonesian Economic Studies*, Vol. 28, No. 1, April 1992

McVey, Ruth. 'Faith as the Outsider: Islam in Indonesian Politics', in *Islam in the Political Process*, ed. James Piscatori, Cambridge University Press, Cambridge, 1983

——ed. *Southeast Asian Capitalists*, Cornell Southeast Asia Program, Ithaca, 1992

Madjid, Nurcholish et al. *Pembaharuan Pemikiran Islam*, Islamic Research Centre, Jakarta, 1970

Madjid, Nurcholish. *Islam: Doktrin dan Perabadan*, Yayasan Wakaf Paramadina, Jakarta, 1992

Makarim, Nono Anwar. 'The Indonesian Press: An Editor's Perspective', in *Political Power and Communications in Indonesia*, eds Karl Jackson and Lucian Pye, University of California Press, Berkeley, 1978

Mietzner, Marcus. 'Between *Pesantren* and Palace: Nahdlatul Ulama and Its Role in the Transition', in *The Fall of Soeharto*, eds Geoff Forrester and R.J. May, Crawford House Publishing, Bathurst, Australia, 1998

Mo, Timothy. *The Redundancy of Courage*, Chatto & Windus, London, 1991

Mohamad, Goenawan. *Sidelines: Thought Pieces from TEMPO Magazine*, trans. Jennifer Lindsay, Hyland House Publishing Pty Limited, Melbourne,1994

Mondale, Walter F. 'Asia is still our future', *Brookings Review*, 22 June 1998

Moore, Barrington, Jr. *Social Origins of Dictatorship and Democracy: Lord and Peasant in the Making of the Modern World*, Beacon Press, Boston, 1967

Morley, James W. ed. *Driven by Growth: Political Change in the Asia–Pacific Region*, M. E. Sharpe, Armonk, 1993

Nasution, Adnan Buyung. *The Aspiration for Constitutional Government in Indonesia: A Socio-legal Study of the Indonesian Konstituante 1956–1959*, Pustaka Sinar Harapan, Jakarta, 1992

Notosusanto, Nugroho and Ismail Saleh. *The Coup Attempt of the 'September 30th Movement' in Indonesia*, Penbimbing Masa, Jakarta, 1968

O'Donnell, Guillermo and Philippe C. Schmitter. *Transitions from Authoritarian Rule: Tentative Conclusions about Uncertain Democracies*, The Johns Hopkins University Press, Baltimore, 1986

O'Donnell, Guillermo, Philippe C. Schmitter and Laurence Whitehead. *Transitions from Authoritarian Rule: Comparative Perspectives*, The Johns Hopkins University Press, Baltimore, 1986

Paauw, Douglas. *Financing Economic Development: The Indonesian Case*, The Free Press, Illinois, 1960

Pranowo, Bambang. 'Which Islam and Which Pancasila? Islam and the State in Indonesia: A Comment', in *State and Civil Society in Indonesia*, ed. Arief Budiman, Centre of Southeast Asian Studies, Clayton, 1990

Radelet, Steven and Jeffrey Sachs. 'The Onset of the East Asian Financial Crisis', Harvard Institute for International Development, 30 March 1998

Rakmat, Jalaluddin. 'Islam di Indonesia: Masalah Definisi', in *Islam di Indonesia: Suatu Ikhtiar Mengaca Diri*, ed. Amien Rais, Rajawali, Jakarta, 1986

Ramli, Rizal and Jonathan Pincus. 'Indonesia: From Showcase to Basketcase', *Cambridge Journal of Economics*, Vol. 22, No. 6, November 1998, pp. 723–34

Ramos-Horta, Jose. *East Timor Debacle: Indonesian Intervention, Repression, and Western Compliance*, Red Sea Press, Trenton, 1986

Rasyid, Ryaas. 'Indonesia: Preparing for Post-Soeharto Rule and Its Impact of Democratization', *Southeast Asian Affairs, 1995*, Institute of Southeast Asian Studies, Singapore, 1995

Reeve, David. *Golkar of Indonesia: An Alternative to the Party System*, Oxford University Press, Singapore, 1985

Reeve, David. 'The Corporatist State: the Case of Golkar', in *State and Civil Society in Indonesia*, ed. Arief Budiman, Centre of Southeast Asian Studies, Clayton, 1990

Repetto, Robert et al. *Wasting Assets: Natural Resources in the National Income Accounts*, World Resources Institute, Washington, 1989

Riantiarno, N. *Time Bomb & Cockroach Opera*, ed. John H. McGlynn, The Lontar Foundation, Jakarta, 1992

Ricklefs, M.C. *A History of Modern Indonesia since c. 1300*, Stanford University Press, Stanford, California, 2nd edition, 1993

Riggs, Fred. *Thailand: The Modernization of a Bureaucratic Polity*, East–West Center Press, Honolulu, 1966

Robison, Richard. *Indonesia: The Rise of Capital*, Allen & Unwin, Sydney, 1986
——'After the Gold Rush: the Politics of Economic Restructuring in Indonesia in the 1980s', in *Southeast Asia in the 1980s: the Politics of Economic Crisis*, eds Richard Robison, Kevin Hewison and Richard Higgott, Allen & Unwin, Sydney, 1987
——'Authoritarian States, Capital-Owning Classes, and the Politics of Newly Industrializing Countries: The Case of Indonesia', *World Politics*, Vol. XLI, No. 1, October 1988
——'Structures of Power and the Industrialisation Process in Southeast Asia', *Journal of Contemporary Asia*, Vol. 19, No. 4, 1989
——*Power and Economy in Suharto's Indonesia*, Journal of Contemporary Publishers, Manila, 1990
——'Indonesia: An Autonomous Domain of Social Power?', *The Pacific Review*, Vol. 5, No. 4, 1992
——'Indonesia: Tensions in State and Regime', in *Southeast Asia in the 1990s: Authoritarianism, Democracy and Capitalism*, eds Kevin Hewison, Richard Robison and Garry Rodan, Allen & Unwin, Sydney, 1993

Robison, Richard and Vedi Hadiz. 'Economic Liberalisation or the Reorganisation of Dirigisme? Indonesian Economic Policy in the 1990s', *Canadian Journal of Development Studies*, Special issue, December 1993

Roeder, O. G. *The Smiling General*, Gunung Agung, Jakarta, 1969

Roy, Olivier. *The Failure of Political Islam*, trans. Carol Volk, Harvard University Press, Cambridge, MA, 1994

Rush, James. 'Placing the Chinese in Java on the Eve of the Twentieth Century', in *The Role of the Indonesian Chinese in Shaping Modern Indonesian Life*, Cornell Southeast Asia Program, Ithaca, 1991

Rustow, Dankwart. 'Transitions to Democracy: Toward a Dynamic Model' *Comparative Politics*, No. 2, 1970

Ryter, Loren. 'Permuda Pancasila: The Last Loyalist Free Men of Suharto's Order?', *Indonesia 66*, October 1998

Sachs, Jeffrey and Wing Thye Woo. 'The Asian Financial Crisis: What Happened, and What Is To Be Done', *The Asia Competitiveness Report 1999*, World Economic Forum, Geneva, 1999

Said, Salim. 'The Political Role of the Indonesian Military: Past, Present and Future', *Southeast Asian Journal of Social Science*, Vol. 15, No. 1, 1987

——*Genesis of Power: General Sudirman and the Indonesian Military in Politics, 1945–1949*, Pustaka Sinar Harapan, Jakarta, 1992

——'Suharto's Armed Forces: Building a Power Base in New Order Indonesia, 1966–1998', *Asian Survey*, Vol. XXXVIII, No. 6, June 1998

Samego, Indria et al, eds. *Bila Abri Berbisnis*, (When the Armed Forces Goes Into Business), Mizan Press, Bandung, 1998

Samson, Allan. 'Conceptions of Politics, Power, and Ideology in Contemporary Indonesian Islam', in *Political Power and Communications in Indonesia*, eds Karl Jackson and Lucian Pye, University of California Press, Berkeley, 1978

Schacht, Chris. 'Opening Address', in *Indonesia Assessment 1992: Political Perspectives on the 1990s*, eds Harold Crouch and Hal Hill, Research School of Pacific Studies, Canberra, 1992

Schwarz, Adam. 'Indonesia's Economic Boom: How Banks Paved the Way', in *Finance and the International Economy (4): The AMEX Bank Review Prize Essays*, eds Richard O'Brien and Sarah Hewin, Oxford University Press, New York, 1991

——'In Indonesia, Freedom Hope is Dim', *Nieman Reports*, Vol. XLIX, No. 4, Winter 1995

——'In Indonesia After Suharto', *Foreign Affairs*, July/August 1997

——'Introduction', in *The Politics of Post-Suharto Indonesia*, eds Adam Schwarz and Jonathan Paris, Council on Foreign Relations, New York, 1999

Schwarz, Adam and Michael Vatikiotis. 'Indonesia: Price of Security', in *Japan in Asia*, ed. Nigel Holloway, Review Publishing Company Ltd, Hong Kong, November 1991

Shin, Yoon Hwan. 'Demystifying the Capitalist State: Political Patronage, Bureaucratic Interests, and Capitalists-in-Formation in Soeharto's Indonesia', PhD dissertation, Yale University, May 1989

Shin, Yoon Hwan. 'The Role of Elites in Creating Capitalist Hegemony in Post-Oil Boom Indonesia', in *The Role of the Indonesian Chinese in Shaping Modern Indonesian Life*, Cornell Southeast Asia Program, Ithaca, 1991

Shiraishi, Takashi. 'The Indonesian Military in Politics', in *The Politics of*

Post-Suharto Indonesia, eds Adam Schwarz and Jonathan Paris, Council on Foreign Relations, New York, 1999

Simatupang, T. B. *Indonesia: Leadership and National Security Perceptions*, Institute of Southeast Asian Studies, Singapore, 1987

Sjahrir. 'The Indonesian economy: the case of macro success and micro challenge', in *Indonesia Assessment 1993. Labour: Sharing in the Benefits of Growth?*, eds Chris Manning and Joan Hardjono, Research School of Pacific Studies, Canberra, 1993

Soeharto. *My Thoughts, Words and Deeds: An Autobiography*, Citra Lamtoro Gung Persada, Jakarta, 1991

Soesastro, Hadi. 'East Timor: Questions of Economic Viability', in *Unity and Diversity: Regional Economic Development in Indonesia Since 1970*, ed. Hal Hill, Oxford University Press, Singapore, 1989

——'The Political Economy of Deregulation in Indonesia', *Asian Survey*, Vol. 29, No. 9, September 1989

Steinberg, David Joel, ed. *In Search of Southeast Asia: A Modern History*, University of Hawaii Press, Honolulu, 1985

Sukarno. *Sukarno: An Autobiography as told to Cindy Adams*, Bobbs-Merrill Co., Indianapolis, 1965

Sundhaussen, Ulf. 'The Military: Structure, Procedures, and Effects on Indonesian Society', in *Political Power and Communications in Indonesia*, eds Karl Jackson and Lucian Pye, University of California Press, Berkeley, 1978

Suryadinata, Leo. *Pribumi Indonesians, the Chinese Minority and China*, Heinemann Asia, Singapore, 1978

—— *Military Ascendancy and Political Culture*, Centre for International Studies, Ohio University, Athens, 1989

Tan, Mely. 'The Social and Cultural Dimensions of the Role of Ethnic Chinese in Indonesian Society', in *The Role of the Indonesian Chinese in Shaping Modern Indonesian Life*, Cornell Southeast Asia Program, Ithaca, 1991

Tanter, Richard. 'The Totalitarian Ambition: Intelligence and Security Agencies in Indonesia', in *State and Civil Society in Indonesia*, ed. Arief Budiman, Centre of Southeast Asian Studies, Clayton, 1990

Taylor, John. *Indonesia's Forgotten War: The Hidden History of East Timor*, Zed Books, London, 1991

US Agency for International Development. 'East Timor—Indonesia—Displaced Persons', Situation Report No. 1, 9 October 1979

Vatikiotis, Michael. *Indonesian Politics Under Suharto*, Routledge, London, 1993

Wade, Robert. *Governing the Market: Economic Theory and the Role of Government in East Asian Industrialization*, Princeton University Press, Princeton, 1990

——'East Asia's Economic Success: Conflicting Perspectives, Partial Insights, Shaky Evidence', *World Politics*, 44, January 1992

Wanandi, Jusuf. 'Political Development and National Stability', in *Indonesia Assessment, 1992: Political Perspectives on the 1990s*, eds Harold Crouch and Hal Hill, Research School of Pacific Studies, Canberra, 1992

Wertheim, W. F. 'Suharto and the Untung Coup: The Missing Link', *Journal of Contemporary Asia*, 1970 (Winter)

Winters, Jeffrey A. 'Structural Power and Investor Mobility: Capital Control and

State Policy in Indonesia, 1965–1990', PhD dissertation, Yale University, December 1991

World Bank. 'Indonesia: Developing Private Enterprises', 9 May 1991

——*World Bank Development Report, 1990*, Oxford University Press, Oxford, July 1991

——'Indonesia: Growth, Infrastructure and Human Resources', 26 May 1992

——'Indonesia. Agricultural Transformation: Challenges and Opportunities', Volume I, 18 June 1992

——'Indonesia: Public Expenditures, Prices and the Poor', draft report, 8 December 1992

——'Indonesia: Sustaining Development', 25 May 1993

——'Indonesia: Dimensions of Growth', 1 May 1996

——'Regional Development in Indonesia', 27 February 1997

——'Indonesia: Sustaining High Growth with Equity', 30 May 1997

Wu, Yuan-li. 'Chinese Entrepreneurs in Southeast Asia', *American Economic Review*, Vol. 73, No. 2, 1983

Zakaria, Fareed. 'The Rise of Illiberal Democracy', *Foreign Affairs*, November/ December 1997

Notes

Introduction

1 Interview Goenawan Mohamad, 23 July 1996.
2 Soeharto, like many Javanese, has only one name. In this book, his name is written using the older spelling system. In 1972, the Indonesian and Malaysian governments established a common system of spelling, under which the main changes were that the old *dj* becomes *j*; *j* becomes *y*; *tj* becomes *c*; and *oe* becomes *u*. In most instances, this book uses the modern spelling system for the names of people and places. Some exceptions are made for names, like Soeharto, which are commonly spelled in the Indonesian press using the old system. A further confusion arises in references to individuals with a first and a family name. In the Indonesian press, some individuals are always referred to by their first name, others by their surname. I have endeavoured to follow the system of references employed by the Indonesian media.

Chapter 1   Growing pains

1 Quoted in Louis Fischer, *The Story of Indonesia*, Harper, New York, 1959, p. 154.
2 Leon Wieseltier, 'Total Quality Meaning', *The New Republic*, 19 and 26 July 1993, p. 18.
3 The account of Soeharto's meeting with Sukarno in early 1966 comes from Soeharto, *My Thoughts, Words and Deeds: An Autobiography*, Citra Lamtoro Gung Persada, Jakarta, 1991, pp. 138–44. The book was published originally in Indonesian as Soeharto, *Pikiran, Ucapan dan Tindakan Saya: Otobiografi*, Citra Lamtoro Gung Persada, Jakarta, 1988. References in this book are to the English-language version. In Soeharto's autobiography, some personal

448

names have been shortened or nicknames have been used. When quoting from the autobiography, I have inserted the full name where this occurs.

4 Accounts of the Dutch colonial period are drawn primarily from David Joel Steinberg, ed., *In Search of Southeast Asia: A Modern History*, University of Hawaii Press, Honolulu, 1985. See also Willard Hanna and Des Alwi, *Turbulent Times Past in Ternate and Tidore*, Yayasan Warisan dan Budaya Banda Naira, Banda Naira, 1990; Mochtar Lubis, *Indonesia: Land Under the Rainbow*, Oxford University Press, Singapore, 1990; and Mochtar Lubis, 'Woman Warrior', *Far Eastern Economic Review*, 9 March 1989, p. 67. Information on the colonial-era economy is drawn from Richard Robison, *Indonesia: The Rise of Capital*, Allen & Unwin, Sydney, 1986, pp. 3–35.

5 Steinberg, ed., *In Search of Southeast Asia*, pp. 185–6.

6 ibid., p. 296.

7 Two good works on Sukarno are Sukarno, *Sukarno: An Autobiography as told to Cindy Adams*, Bobbs-Merrill Co., Indianapolis, 1965; and J. D. Legge, *Sukarno: A Political Biography*, Penguin Press, London, 1972.

8 Steinberg, ed., *In Search of Southeast Asia*, p. 377.

9 Slamet Bratanata, 'Indonesia since the Dutch', unpublished manuscript.

10 Steinberg, ed., *In Search of Southeast Asia*, pp. 377–8.

11 Quoted in Adnan Buyung Nasution, *The Aspiration for Constitutional Government in Indonesia: A Socio-legal Study of the Indonesian Konstituante 1956–1959*, Pustaka Sinar Harapan, Jakarta, 1992, p. 29.

12 This section draws primarily from Nasution, *The Aspiration for Constitutional Government*. See also Marsillam Simanjuntak, 'Unsur Hegelian Dalam Pandangan Negara Integralistic', unpublished masters thesis, University of Indonesia, 1989; David Bourchier, 'Totalitarianism? Recent controversy about the basis of the Indonesian state', a paper written for the conference: Indonesian Culture: Asking the right questions, Adelaide, 28 Sept.–4 Oct. 1991; David Reeve, 'The Corporatist State: the Case of Golkar', in *State and Civil Society in Indonesia*, ed. Arief Budiman, Centre of Southeast Asian Studies, Clayton, 1990, pp. 151–76; and Richard Robison, 'Indonesia: Tensions in State and Regime', in *Southeast Asia in the 1990s: Authoritarianism, Democracy and Capitalism*, eds Kevin Hewison, Richard Robison, and Garry Rodan, Allen & Unwin, Sydney, 1993.

13 *Indonesian Observer*, 5 December 1990, p. 3. In its Observatory column, authored by Abdullah, the *Observer* ran a three-part series in late 1990 on Indonesia's constitution. Abdullah is a pseudonym used by several writers. Slamet Bratanata is believed to have written the three-part series on the constitution.

14 Quoted in the *Indonesian Observer*, 5 December 1990, p. 3.

15 Nasution, *The Aspiration for Constitutional Government*, p. 422.

16 The point is taken from Allan Samson, 'Conceptions of Politics, Power, and Ideology in Contemporary Indonesian Islam', in *Political Power and Communications in Indonesia*, eds Karl Jackson and Lucian Pye, University of California Press, Berkeley, 1978, p. 219.

17 The quote is from Daniel Lev, *The Transition to Guided Democracy: Indonesian Politics, 1957–1959*, Cornell Modern Indonesia Project, Ithaca, 1966, p. 123.

18 Nasution, *The Aspiration for Constitutional Government*, pp. 88, 412.

19 ibid., esp. pp. 122–30.

20 *Indonesia Source Book*, National Development Information Office, Jakarta, 1992, p. 13.

21 R. William Liddle, 'Indonesia's Democratic Past and Future', *Comparative Politics*, Vol. 24, No. 4, July 1992, p. 449.

22 Nasution, *The Aspiration for Constitutional Government*, p. 421, n. 246.

23 Quoted in Nasution, *The Aspiration for Constitutional Government*, p. 106.

24 Interestingly, support for constitutional safeguards against an all-powerful presidency was forthcoming from Supomo and some other proponents of the integralist state. 'We may suppose,' says Nasution, 'that by this time Supomo had already learned from experience during the existence of the Indonesian state that abuse of power and violations of human rights can also be committed by Indonesians.' See Nasution, *The Aspiration for Constitutional Government*, p. 423, n. 248.

25 Benedict Anderson, 'Elections and Democratisation in Southeast Asia: Thailand, the Philippines and Indonesia', a lecture broadcast on the *Indian Pacific* program of the Australia Broadcasting Corporation, August 1992. The lecture was published in *ABC Radio 24 Hours*, September 1992. The quotation is on p. 58.

26 Nasution, *The Aspiration for Constitutional Government*, p. 407.

27 See Ruth McVey, 'The Case of the Disappearing Decade', paper delivered to the Conference on Indonesian Democracy, 1950s and 1990s, Monash University, 17–20 December 1992, p. 6.

28 Jamie Mackie, 'Inevitable or avoidable? Interpretations of the collapse of parliamentary democracy, 1956–59', paper delivered to the Conference on Indonesian Democracy, 1950s and 1990s, Monash University, 17–20 December 1992.

29 For a summary of the *Konstituante*'s debates on Sukarno's proposal, see Nasution, *The Aspiration for Constitutional Government*, pp. 366–74.

30 For a good account of military thinking in the immediate post-independence period, see Salim Said, *Genesis of Power: General Sudirman and the Indonesian Military in Politics, 1945–1949*, Pustaka Sinar Harapan, Jakarta, 1992; and Salim Said, 'The Political Role of the Indonesian Military: Past, Present and Future', *Southeast Asian Journal of Social Science*, Vol. 15, No. 1, 1987.

31 Article 2 (1) of the 1945 Constitution reads: 'The Majelis Permusyawaratan Rakyat [People's Consultative Assembly] shall consist of members of the Dewan Perwakilan Rakyat [House of Representatives] augmented by delegates from the regional territories and *the groups* in accordance with regulations prescribed by statute' [italics added]. See also Nasution, *The Aspiration for Constitutional Government*, pp. 294–7, 309–10.

32 *Pos Indonesia*, 13 November 1958. Quoted in Ulf Sundhaussen, 'The Military: Structure, Procedures, and Effects on Indonesian Society', in *Political Power and Communications*, eds Jackson and Pye, p. 47.

33 Said, *Genesis of Power*, p. 24.

34 Two fine books on the parliamentary democracy period are Herbert Feith, *The Decline of Constitutional Democracy in Indonesia*, Cornell University

Press, Ithaca, 1962; and Nasution, *The Aspiration for Constitutional Government*. Several papers on the same topic were delivered at the Conference on Indonesian Democracy, 1950s and 1990s, Monash University, 17–20 December 1992. See Jamie Mackie, 'Inevitable or avoidable? Interpretations of the collapse of parliamentary democracy, 1956–59'; Ruth McVey, 'The Case of the Disappearing Decade'; Herb Feith, 'Indonesia's constitutional democracy of the 1950s: How serious was its malfunctioning?'; and Daniel Lev, 'On the Fall of the Parliamentary System'.

35 Sukarno, *Sukarno: An Autobiography*, p. 279.

36 A good account of the campaign is in J. A. C. Mackie, *Konfrontasi: The Indonesia–Malaysia Dispute, 1963–1966*, Oxford University Press, London, 1974.

37 See Ahmad Habir, 'State Enterprises: Reform and Policy Issues', in *Indonesia Assessment 1990*, eds Hal Hill and Terry Hull, Research School of Pacific Studies, Canberra, 1990, pp. 90–107.

38 See Hal Hill, 'The Economy', in *Indonesia's New Order: The Dynamics of Socio-Economic Transformation*, ed. Hal Hill, Allen & Unwin, Sydney, 1993.

39 See Gunawan Mohamad, 'The "Manikebu" Affair: Literature and Politics in the 1960s', *Prisma*, No. 46, 1989, pp. 70–88.

40 The point is elaborated in Robison, 'Indonesia: Tensions in State'.

41 A thorough account of the coup and its aftermath is in Harold Crouch, *The Army and Politics in Indonesia*, Cornell University Press, Ithaca, 1978 (revised edition, 1988). See also Hamish McDonald, *Suharto's Indonesia*, Fontana Books, Blackburn, 1980.

42 It is generally thought that Soeharto was the most senior general not targeted for abduction by the coup plotters. Some have speculated that Soeharto may have been in league with the rebel officers, although the evidence for this assertion is slim. This theory is detailed in W. F. Wertheim, 'Suharto and the Untung Coup: The Missing Link', *Journal of Contemporary Asia*, 1970 (Winter). Doubts about whether Soeharto had prior knowledge of the coup have been fed by the treatment of Colonel A. Latief, one of the key figures in the attempted coup. Latief, who served under Soeharto in Central Java and in the Irian Jaya campaign, visited Soeharto the night of the coup and allegedly informed Soeharto of the impending coup, an allegation Soeharto denies. However, Latief was not permitted to appear as a witness in trials of other plotters until 1972, giving rise to the impression that the government feared what he might say in a public forum. Latief is still in jail for his role in the coup.

43 The official army version of the coup is Nugroho Notosusanto and Ismail Saleh, *The Coup Attempt of the 'September 30th Movement' in Indonesia*, Penbimbing Masa, Jakarta, 1968.

44 Benedict Anderson and Ruth McVey, *A Preliminary Analysis of the October 1, 1965 Coup in Indonesia*, Cornell Modern Indonesia Project, Ithaca, 1971.

45 See, for example, 'Soeharto warns that PKI lurks', *Jakarta Post*, 18 December 1993.

46 Communist Party membership estimates come from Kopkamtib, Indonesia's powerful internal security agency. Quoted in Robert Cribb, 'Problems in the historiography of the killings in Indonesia', in *The Indonesian Killings,*

1965–1966: Studies from Java and Bali, ed. Robert Cribb, Centre of Southeast Asian Studies, Clayton, 1990, p. 41.

47 Central Intelligence Agency, Directorate of Intelligence, 'Intelligence Report: Indonesia—1965, the coup that backfired', Central Intelligence Agency, Washington DC, 1968, p. 71. Quoted in Cribb, 'Problems in the historiography', p. 5, n. 8. For a chilling first-person account of the killings in East Java, see Pipit Rochijat, 'Am I PKI [Indonesian Communist Party] or Non-PKI?', *Indonesia*, No. 40 (October 1985), pp. 37–56.

48 Cribb, 'Problems in the historiography', p. 3, 21.

49 McDonald, *Suharto's Indonesia*, p. 53.

50 J. A. C. Mackie, 'Anti-Chinese Outbreaks in Indonesia, 1959–68', in *The Chinese in Indonesia*, ed. J. A. C. Mackie, Thomas Nelson, Melbourne, 1976, pp. 126–9.

51 Nasution, *The Aspiration for Constitutional Government*, p. 428.

52 'Vengeance with a smile', *Time*, 15 July 1966, p. 26.

53 Soeharto, *My Thoughts*, p. 144.

Chapter 2 Soeharto takes charge

1 Soeharto, *My Thoughts, Words and Deeds: An Autobiography*, Citra Lamtoro Gung Persada, Jakarta, 1991, pp. 193–4.

2 Interview with Rachmat Witoelar, secretary-general of the ruling party Golkar, 1 April 1992.

3 The comment by the former head of Indonesia's state-owned oil company Pertamina is quoted in Jeffrey A. Winters, 'Structural Power and Investor Mobility: Capital Control and State Policy in Indonesia, 1965–1990', PhD dissertation, Yale University, December 1991, p. 159, n. 301.

4 Harold Crouch, *The Army and Politics in Indonesia*, Cornell University Press, Ithaca, 1978, p. 180.

5 ibid., pp. 190–1.

6 ibid., see chap. 7.

7 Soeharto, *My Thoughts*, p. 148.

8 Information on Soeharto's childhood is drawn largely from his 1988 autobiography. See also Hamish McDonald, *Suharto's Indonesia*, Fontana Books, Blackburn, 1980, chap. 1; and O. G. Roeder, *The Smiling General*, Gunung Agung, Jakarta, 1969.

9 Soeharto, *My Thoughts*, pp. 6, 196.

10 Crouch, *The Army and Politics*, p. 40; and McDonald, *Suharto's Indonesia*, p. 29. Soeharto once told a US diplomat that he was removed from his Diponegoro command in the late 1950s for moving too aggressively against communists. See Howard Jones, *The Possible Dream*, Harcourt Brace Jovanovich, New York, 1971, p. 438.

11 Ruth McVey, 'The Case of the Disappearing Decade', paper delivered to the Conference on Indonesian Democracy, 1950s and 1990s, Monash University, 17–20 December 1992, pp. 5, 8. The seminal theoretical work connecting political and social order with economic development is Samuel Huntington, *Political Order in Changing Societies*, Yale University Press, New Haven, 1968.

12 McVey, 'Disappearing Decade', p. 5.
13 Interview with General (ret.) Soemitro, 24 May 1989.
14 David Reeve, 'The Corporatist State: the case of Golkar', in *State and Civil Society in Indonesia*, ed. Arief Budiman, Centre of Southeast Studies, Clayton, 1990, p. 164. Good histories of Golkar are in Leo Suryadinata, *Military Ascendancy and Political Culture*, Centre for International Studies, Ohio University, Athens, 1989; and David Reeve, *Golkar of Indonesia: An Alternative to the Party System*, Oxford University Press, Singapore, 1985.
15 For details of Golkar campaign tactics ahead of the 1971 elections, see R. William Liddle, 'Participation and the Political Parties', in *Political Power and Communications*, eds Karl Jackson and Lucian Pye, University of California Press, Berkeley, 1978, pp. 182–3.
16 Quoted in David Jenkins, *Suharto and his Generals: Indonesian Military Politics 1975–1983*, Cornell Modern Indonesia Project, Monograph Series no. 64, Ithaca, 1984, p. 37.
17 Soeharto, *My Thoughts*, pp. 221, 226.
18 Slamet Bratanata, 'Fortunes of Democracy', unpublished essay, p. 4.
19 Crouch, *The Army and Politics*, ch. 12.
20 ibid., p. 315.
21 John Bresnan, *Managing Indonesia: The Modern Political Economy*, Columbia University Press, New York, 1993, pp. 137–8.
22 Jamie Mackie and Andrew MacIntyre, 'Politics', in *Indonesia's New Order: The Dynamics of Socio-Economic Transformation*, ed. Hal Hill, Allen & Unwin, Sydney, 1993.
23 Soeharto, *My Thoughts*, p. 298.
24 Interview with Arief Budiman, 7 April 1991.
25 Jenkins, *Suharto and his Generals*, pp. 13–4.
26 Interview with General (ret.) Soemitro, 24 May 1989.
27 For a fuller description of the 'security approach', see Richard Tanter, 'The Totalitarian Ambition: Intelligence and Security Agencies in Indonesia', in *State and Civil Society*, ed. Arief Budiman, pp. 215–88. A personal example: One Friday in early 1991, I met with Brigadier General Nurhadi Purwosaputro, the head of the armed forces information office. We were talking about the problems in Aceh, where an Islamic-based insurgency was fighting government troops, but we got around to discussing Islam in Indonesia more generally. I asked him if he was concerned with Muslim preachers fomenting dissent in the mosques. Not at all, he replied, we keep a close eye on what they are saying. Just then, an aide dropped a report on his desk. It was a summary of what was said at midday prayers at Jakarta's main Istiqal Mosque less than an hour before.
28 The relevant provision in the 1945 Constitution reads: 'All decisions of the [People's Consultative Assembly] shall be determined by majority vote.'
29 Harold Crouch, 'Patrimonialism and Military Rule in Indonesia', *World Politics*, Vol. 31, No. 4, 1979, pp. 571–87.
30 R. William Liddle, 'Soeharto's Indonesia: Personal Rule and Political Institutions', *Pacific Affairs*, Vol. 58, No. 1, Spring 1985, pp. 69–90. See also R. William Liddle, 'The Relative Autonomy of the Third World Politician: Soeharto

and Indonesian Economic Development in Comparative Perspective', *International Studies Quarterly*, Vol. 35, No. 4, December 1991, pp. 403–27.

31 David Bourchier, 'Pada masa liberal timbul semacam anarki: the 1950s in New Order ideology and politics', paper delivered to the Conference on Indonesian Democracy, 1950s and 1990s, Monash University, 17–20 December 1992, p. 1.

32 See John McBeth, 'Irrelevant No More', *Far Eastern Economic Review*, 11 November 1993; and 'RI seeking Security Council seat', *Jakarta Post*, 5 January 1994.

33 Dewi Fortuna Anwar, 'RI grips high profile foreign policy', *Jakarta Post*, 4 January 1994.

34 Confidential interview, 11 September 1991.

35 Although Pertamina's financial disintegration was well under way by early 1975, Sutowo was not fired until early 1976. Soeharto apparently believed that the Pertamina debacle was at least partly the fault of foreigners. Explaining the non-action against Sutowo, Soeharto says in his autobiography (p. 261): 'I had to be fair [because] Pertamina also had many enemies abroad, people who were envious of us.' Several sources, in fact, claim that Sutowo's ultimate ouster had nothing to do with Pertamina's problems. They say the real reason was that Sutowo embarrassed Soeharto at an ASEAN meeting in Bali in early 1976. Sutowo, off playing golf with Ferdinand Marcos, was late for a meeting with Soeharto (as was Marcos). The following day, Sutowo was fired. For more details, see Winters, 'Structural Power', pp. 114–15, n. 214.

36 Soeharto, *My Thoughts*, pp. 378–9.

37 Benedict Anderson, 'The Idea of Power in Javanese Culture', in *Language and Power: Exploring Political Cultures in Indonesia*, ed. Benedict Anderson, Cornell University Press, Ithaca, 1990, pp. 17–77. (The essay was originally published in *Culture and Politics in Indonesia*, ed. Claire Holt, Cornell University Press, Ithaca, 1972.)

38 ibid., p. 23.

39 This point is drawn from Jenkins, *Suharto and his Generals*, p. 36, n. 10.

40 Soeharto, *My Thoughts*, pp. 481–2.

41 Karl Jackson, 'The Political Implications of Structure and Culture in Indonesia', in *Political Power and Communications*, eds Jackson and Pye, p. 41.

Chapter 3 The emerging tiger

1 Interview with former finance minister, Johannes Sumarlin, 14 September 1989.

2 Interview with Mubyarto, a professor at the Gadjah Mada University in Yogyakarta, 25 March 1992.

3 Adam Smith, *An Enquiry into the Nature and Causes of the Wealth of Nations*, ed. E. Cannan, Random House, New York, 1937.

4 For more details, see Steven Jones, 'Suharto's Kin Linked With Plastics Monopoly', *Asian Wall Street Journal*, 25 November 1986.

5 Confidential interview, 6 March 1992.

6 R. William Liddle, 'The Relative Autonomy of the Third World Politician: Soeharto and Indonesian Economic Development in Comparative Perspective', *International Studies Quarterly*, Vol. 35, No. 4, December 1991, p. 419.

7 Quoted in Jeffrey A. Winters, 'Structural Power and Investor Mobility: Capital Control and State Policy in Indonesia, 1965–1990', PhD dissertation, Yale University, December 1991, pp. 112–13. For a description of the 'low politics' style of the technocrats, see Hadi Soesastro, 'The Political Economy of Deregulation in Indonesia', *Asian Survey*, Vol. 29, No. 9, September 1989.

8 H. W. Arndt, 'Survey of Recent Developments', *Bulletin of Indonesian Economic Studies*, July 1974, p. 31.

9 For accounts of Sutowo's rise and fall, see Richard Robison, *Indonesia: The Rise of Capital*, Allen & Unwin, Sydney, 1986, esp. chap. 5; and Hamish McDonald, *Suharto's Indonesia*, Fontana Books, Blackburn, 1980, pp. 143–65. Information on Indonesia's 'oil windfall' is taken from Hal Hill, 'The Economy', in *Indonesia's New Order: The Dynamics of Socio-Economic Transformation*, ed. Hal Hill, Allen & Unwin, Sydney, 1993; Anne Booth, ed., *The Oil Boom and After: Indonesian Economic Policy and Performance in the Soeharto Era*, Oxford University Press, Singapore, 1992; and World Bank, 'Indonesia. Agricultural Transformation: Challenges and Opportunities', Volume I, 18 June 1992, pp. 1–4.

10 Bruce Glassburner, 'In the Wake of General Ibnu: Crisis in the Indonesian Oil Industry', *Asian Survey*, No. 12, December 1976.

11 Radius Prawiro, 'Back to the Wisdom of the Market Economy', speech to Indonesian Institute for Management Development, 15 December 1989, p. 12. One of the negative aspects of the oil boom was that it brought a virtual end to tax reform efforts. Malcolm Gillis, a Duke University economist who helped Indonesia reform its tax system in the mid-1980s describes the earlier state of affairs like this: 'Perhaps the only redeeming feature of the tax regime in force in the early eighties was that enforcement of the income tax on oil companies was reasonably effective. Otherwise, the system was unproductive of revenue, ineffective in redistributing income, highly vulnerable to manipulation in compliance and administration, and was replete with incentives for inefficiency and waste.' See Malcolm Gillis, 'Micro and Macroeconomics of Tax Reform: Indonesia', *Journal of Development Economics*, 19, 1985, p. 224.

12 For a fuller account, see Guy Sacerdoti, 'Overdraft of Inefficiency', *Far Eastern Economic Review*, 29 May 1981, pp. 44–9.

13 For Indonesia, the oil price collapse meant that oil exports in 1986 amounted to only US$5.2 billion, 65 per cent less than 1982's receipts.

14 Prawiro, 'Back to the Wisdom', p. 12.

15 ibid., p. 13.

16 Ali Wardhana, 'Structural Adjustment in Indonesia: Export and the "High-Cost" Economy', speech to the 24th Conference of South-East Asian Central Bank Governors, Bangkok, 25 January 1989. See also Soesastro, 'The Political Economy', pp. 854–5.

17 For a fuller history of Indonesia's financial sector liberalisation, see Adam Schwarz, 'Indonesia's Economic Boom: How Banks Paved the Way', in

Finance and the International Economy (4): The AMEX Bank Review Prize Essays, eds Richard O'Brien and Sarah Hewin, Oxford University Press, New York, 1991, pp. 188–207.

18 Information for the following section on the New Order's economic record is drawn primarily from Hill, 'The Economy'; Booth ed., *The Oil Boom and After*; Robison, *The Rise of Capital*; annual World Bank reports on the Indonesian economy, various years, esp. 'Indonesia: Developing Private Enterprises', 9 May 1991; 'Indonesia: Growth, Infrastructure and Human Resources', 26 May 1992; 'Indonesia: Sustaining Development', 25 May 1993; World Bank, 'Agricultural Transformation'; and Far Eastern Economic Review, *Asia Yearbook*, various issues.

19 Among oil-exporting countries, Indonesia's performance stands out starkly. Consultants Gelb and Associates compared Indonesia with five other members of the Organisation of Petroleum Exporting Countries over the period 1974–84. In most economic categories, and especially in agriculture, Indonesia came out on top. It also did relatively well in avoiding a crippling dependency on oil. '[O]nly Indonesia and possibly Ecuador managed to strengthen and diversify the non-hydrocarbon traded sector during the windfall decade', the consultants noted. See Gelb and Associates, *Oil Windfalls: Blessing or Curse?*, Oxford University Press, New York, 1988.

20 Andrew MacIntyre, 'The Politics of Finance in Indonesia: Command, Confusion and Competition', in *Government, Finance, and Development*, eds Stephan Haggard, Chung Lee and Sylvia Maxfield, Cornell University Press, Ithaca, 1993.

21 Hill, 'The Economy'.

22 World Bank, *World Bank Development Report, 1990*, Oxford University Press, Oxford, July 1991; and Terence Hull and Valerie Hull, 'Population and Health Policies', in *The Oil Boom and After*, ed. Booth, pp. 423–33.

23 World Bank, *Development Report, 1990*, p. 45.

24 Hill, 'The Economy'.

25 Robert Repetto et al., *Wasting Assets: Natural Resources in the National Income Accounts*, World Resources Institute, Washington, 1989, p. 6. Indonesia loses some 10 000 sq km of forest cover annually, an area roughly the size of Lebanon. Most of the losses are due to shifting cultivators, logging and forest fires.

26 Hill, 'The Economy'.

27 J. A. C. Mackie, 'Economic Growth in the Asean Region: The Political Underpinnings', in *Achieving Industrialization in East Asia*, ed. Helen Hughes, Cambridge University Press, Cambridge, 1988, p. 316.

28 Liddle, 'Relative Autonomy', p. 412. For a good discussion of Indonesia's 'patrimonialism', see Harold Crouch, 'Patrimonialism and Military Rule in Indonesia', *World Politics*, Vol. 31, No. 4., 1979, pp. 571–87.

29 These figures are calculated from the government's statistical data. Many economists believe the government's actual role in the economy is considerably higher than even these figures suggest.

30 Hill, 'The Economy'.

31 Between 1988 and 1992, seven state-owned firms were wholly or partially sold to private investors, six were liquidated and seven were merged into

other state-owned firms. During the same period, 15 new state-owned companies were established. See 'Assessing state firms', *Jakarta Post*, 29 December 1993. A more optimistic account of Indonesia's privatisation prospects is in 'Total Exposure', *Indonesia Business Weekly*, 29 October 1993, pp. 4–9.

32 Interview with Sjahrir, 10 February 1994.

33 For an excellent province-by-province analysis of Indonesia's economy, see Hal Hill, ed., *Unity and Diversity: Regional Economic Development in Indonesia since 1970*, Oxford University Press, Singapore, 1989. A thought-provoking piece on the same subject is Anne Booth, 'Can Indonesia Survive as a Unitary State?', Indonesia Circle Annual Lecture, School of Oriental and African Studies, University of London, 19 March 1992.

34 Booth, 'Unitary State'.

35 Interview with Taufik Abdullah, 24 October 1990.

36 Interview with Rachmat Witoelar, 20 December 1990.

37 Booth, 'Unitary State'. Interview with Dorodjatun Kuntjorojakti, 6 June 1990. See also 'Governors—who do they truly represent?', *Jakarta Post*, 4 January 1994; and Amir Santoso, 'Local administrations deserve greater autonomy', *Jakarta Post*, 4 January 1994.

38 World Bank, 'Indonesia: Public Expenditures, Prices and the Poor', draft report, 8 December 1992.

39 Booth ed., *The Oil Boom and After*, p. 348.

40 'Saya Bukan Karbitan', *Matra*, March 1991; and interview with Barnabas Suebu, 29 May 1991.

41 Interview with Taufik Abdullah, 24 October 1990. I am also grateful to Iwan Jaya Aziz for his views on this issue.

42 Booth, 'Unitary State'.

43 ibid.

44 Gitte Heij, *Tax Administration and Compliance in Indonesia*, Asia Research Centre on Social, Political and Economic Change, Murdoch, Western Australia, 1993, p. 20.

45 Hill, 'The Economy'. See also 'Indonesia needs to adopt modern business laws', *Jakarta Post*, 9 December 1993.

46 Information for the following section is drawn from several dozen interviews from July 1991–November 1993 with executives of the Rajawali Group, its financial advisers Jardine Fleming Nusantara and its outside accountants; with executives at Business Advisory Group; with representatives of Indonesian, American, French, British and Japanese creditors of Bentoel; with Bentoel's legal advisers; with lawyers for the creditors; with executives of the Humpuss Group; with research analysts at Jakarta-based merchant banks; with executives at Bentoel's major competitors Gudang Garam, Djarum and Sampoerna; and with senior government officials. Most of the interviewees spoke on background basis and insisted on not being identified by name. A good history of Bentoel is 'Pertikaian Keluarga Melanda Bentoel', *Warta Ekonomi*, 2 September 1991, pp. 22–34. Some material in this section previously appeared in articles by the author, including 'Out of the Ashes', *Far Eastern Economic Review*, 7 November 1991; and 'Behind the Smoke', *Far Eastern Economic Review*, 21 November 1991.

47 The auditors, KPMG Hanadi Sudjendro & Rekan, submitted their findings to the Rajawali Group on 7 February 1992. The report was entitled: 'Bentoel Group of Companies: Report on the Financial Position as at 31 October, 1991'.
48 Confidential interview, 3 March 1993.

Chapter 4 The politics of making policy

1 World Bank, 'Indonesia: Sustaining Development', 25 May 1993, pp. 87–8.
2 Quoted in 'Perjalanan Industrialisasi', *Editor*, 17 April 1993, p. 32.
3 Interview with Ali Wardhana, 1 April 1993.
4 The account of Soeharto's initial meeting with Habibie is found in Soeharto, *My Thoughts, Words and Deeds: An Autobiography*, Citra Lamtoro Gung Persada, Jakarta, 1991, p. 64.
5 Sumarlin, Habibie and Soeharto letters supplied confidentially by a senior government official.
6 See Adam Schwarz, 'Growing Pains', *Far Eastern Economic Review*, 2 April 1992; and 'No Cure in Sight', *Indonesia Business Weekly*, 14 January 1994. A more optimistic reading of the situation is in Dean Yates, 'Indonesia apparently winning bank bad debt battle', *Reuter*, 15 January 1994.
7 Interview with senior government official, 2 July 1993. See also 'Specter of Bad Debt', *Indonesia Business Weekly*, 25 June 1993, pp. 8–12.
8 Interview with Johannes Sumarlin, 14 September 1989; and interview with Adrianus Mooy, 14 August 1991.
9 Interview with Nasir Tamara, 12 March 1993.
10 Interview with Johannes Sumarlin, 20 March 1991.
11 Confidential interview, 18 October 1990.
12 Interview with Ali Wardhana, 1 April 1993.
13 Interview with Iwan Jaya Aziz, 27 February 1992.
14 Interview with Nasir Tamara, 12 March 1993.
15 Rizal Ramli, 'Hutang Luar Negeri: Kontraksi dan Beban Ekonomi Nasional', working paper, Centre for Policy and Implementation Studies, Jakarta, 4 March 1993.
16 World Bank, 'Indonesia: Sustaining Development', p. 11.
17 The Gini Ratio is a commonly used measure of wealth distribution; on this scale, zero equals perfect equality, one perfect inequality. A ratio of 0.3 indicates low wealth inequalities by international standards, while a ratio in excess of 0.5 suggests higher discrepancies. Economists calculate that Indonesia's Gini Ratio was 0.35 in 1965 and 0.32 in 1990. See Hal Hill, 'The Economy', in *Indonesia's New Order: The Dynamics of Socio-Economic Transformation*, ed. Hal Hill, Allen & Unwin, Sydney, 1993.
18 Interview with Rizal Ramli, 18 March 1993. See also Rizal Ramli, 'Deregulasi: Suatu Evaluasi Kritis', working paper, Centre for Policy and Implementation Studies, 27 February 1993.
19 Interview with Adrianus Mooy, 14 August 1991.
20 Hill, 'The Economy'.
21 Interview with Sri Bintang Pamungkas, 22 July 1992.
22 'Negara Kita Bisa Disebut Negara Islam', *Detik*, 1–7 April 1993, p. 21.

23 Article 33 of the 1945 Constitution reads as follows: (1) The economy shall be organised as a common endeavour based upon the principle of the family system. (2) Branches of production which are important for the State and which affect the life of most people shall be controlled by the State. (3) Land and water and the natural riches contained therein shall be controlled by the State and shall be utilised for the people.

24 Jamie Mackie, 'Indonesia: Economic Growth and Depoliticization', in *Driven by Growth: Political Change in the Asia–Pacific Region*, ed. James Morley, M. E. Sharpe, Armonk, 1993, p. 92.

25 Interview with Mubyarto, 25 March 1992. In April 1993, Mubyarto was retained as an adviser by Ginanjar Kartasasmita, who heads the national planning board.

26 Soeharto, *My Thoughts*, pp. 301–4, 323–5, 448–53.

27 The two surveys are described in R. William Liddle, 'Improvising Political Cultural Change: Three Indonesian Cases', in *Indonesian Political Culture: Asking the Right Questions*, ed. James Schiller, Ohio University Center for Southeast Asian Studies, Athens, forthcoming.

28 'Negara Kita Bisa Disebut Negara Islam', *Detik*, 1–7 April 1993, p. 21.

29 Along with Professor Mubyarto, Sri Edy Swasono was retained in April 1993 as an adviser to Ginanjar Kartasasmita.

30 Interview with Sri Bintang Pamungkas, 30 March 1993. See also 'Sri Bintang Pamungkas: Status Quo Ada Batasnya', *Forum Keadilan*, 1 April 1993, pp. 14–16.

31 Interview with Nasir Tamara, 12 March 1993.

32 Interview with Umar Juoro, 29 March 1993.

33 A letter from the World Bank's Jakarta office to Radius Prawiro dated 24 September 1991 recommended the postponement of several large oil-related projects due to Indonesia's worsening current account deficit. On 12 October 1991, the projects were postponed.

34 B. J. Habibie, 'Kertas Posisi Seri Dialog Pembangunan: Pembangunan Ekonomi Berdasarkan Nilai Tambah Dengan Orientasi Pengembangan Teknologi Dan Industri', paper delivered at a conference organised by the Centre for Information and Development Studies, 25 January 1993.

35 On the background to the formation of the 'strategic industries' group, see Adam Schwarz, 'Arms and the plan', *Far Eastern Economic Review*, 23 November 1989, p. 73. A more recent account is Mark Clifford, 'Promises, Promises', *Far Eastern Economic Review*, 29 July 1993, p. 58–61. For a lengthier description of Habibie's views, see David McKendrick, 'Acquiring Technological Capabilities: Aircraft and Commercial Banking in Indonesia', PhD dissertation, University of California, Berkeley, 1989.

36 Indonesia's 1993 purchase of ships belonging to the former East German navy is one example of an offset deal which generated work for one of Habibie's 'strategic industries'. See Adam Schwarz and Mark Clifford, 'Naval Manoeuvres', *Far Eastern Economic Review*, 13 May 1993.

37 World Bank, 'Indonesia: Sustaining Development', p. 142.

38 David McKendrick, 'Obstacles to "Catch-Up": The Case of the Indonesian Aircraft Industry', *Bulletin of Indonesian Economic Studies*, Australian National University, Canberra, April 1992, pp. 59, 51 and 63.

39 Interview with Nasir Tamara, 12 March 1993.
40 'Jejak-Langkah dari Malang sampai Senayan', *Tempo*, 10 October 1992, p. 24.
41 Soeharto, *My Thoughts*, pp. 389–90.
42 ibid., pp. 391–2.
43 Interview with Umar Juoro, 29 March 1993.
44 Interview with Nasir Tamara, 12 March 1993.
45 Interview with Ali Wardhana, 1 April 1993.
46 'Komparatif Menjadi Kompetitif', *Editor*, 17 April 1993, p. 27.
47 World Bank, 'Indonesia: Sustaining Development', pp. 87 and xiii. See also Clifford, 'Promises, Promises'.
48 Interview with Ginanjar Kartasasmita in 'Daya Tahan Ekonomi dan Kekuatan Dalam Negeri', *Prisma*, 6, 1985, pp. 42–7.
49 For writings on the 'statist' view of Northeast Asian development see Alice Amsden, *Asia's Next Giant: Late Industrialization in Korea*, Oxford University Press, New York, 1990; Chalmers Johnson, 'Political Institutions and Economic Performance: the Government-led Business Relationship in Japan, South Korea and Taiwan', in *The Political Economy of the New Asian Industrialism*, ed. Frederic Deyo, Cornell University Press, Ithaca, 1987; and Robert Wade, *Governing the Market: Economic Theory and the Role of Government in East Asian Industrialization*, Princeton University Press, Princeton, 1990. For analyses which compare Indonesia's development with the East Asian model, see Andrew MacIntyre, 'Indonesia, Thailand and the Northeast Asia Connection', in *Economic Relations in the Pacific in the 1990s: Conflict or Cooperation?*, eds Richard Higgott, Richard Leaver and John Ravenhill, Allen & Unwin, Sydney, 1993; Richard Robison, 'Structures of Power and the Industrialisation Process in Southeast Asia', *Journal of Contemporary Asia*, Vol. 19, No. 4, 1989; and Yoshihara Kunio, *The Rise of Ersatz Capitalism in Southeast Asia*, Oxford University Press, Singapore, 1988, esp. chap. 6.
50 Interview with Umar Juoro, 29 March 1993.
51 See 'Total Exposure', *Indonesia Business Weekly*, 29 October 1993, pp. 4–9. It appears that Habibie's long-term plan for making his aircraft manufacturer IPTN economically sustainable includes the establishment of assembly plants overseas. Iran and the United States have been mentioned as two possibilities. See 'Habibie Eyes N. American Market', *Indonesia Business Weekly*, 28 January 1994.
52 World Bank, 'Indonesia: Sustaining Development', p. 107.
53 World Bank, 'Indonesia: Public Expenditures, Prices and the Poor', draft report, 8 December 1992.
54 ibid.
55 See 'Current political system not perfect but the best: Habibie', *Jakarta Post*, 19 January 1994.
56 Interview with Umar Juoro, 29 March 1993; interview with Sri Bintang Pamungkas, 30 March 1993.
57 'BJ Habibie: Widjojonomics dan Habibienomics Itu tidak Ada', *Kompas*, 24 April 1993.

58 See Mari Pangestu, 'Pakto '93: Kepenatan Deregulasi?', *Tempo*, 6 November 1993, p. 93.
59 See Richard Borsuk, 'Indonesia's Budget Relies Heavily on Private Sector', *Asian Wall Street Journal*, 7–8 January 1994.
60 World Bank, 'Indonesia: Sustaining Development', p. 43.
61 Hill, 'The Economy'.
62 Confidential interview, 2 April 1993.
63 Interview with Ali Wardhana, 1 April 1993.

Chapter 5   The race that counts

1 James Rush, 'Placing the Chinese in Java on the Eve of the Twentieth Century', in *The Role of the Indonesian Chinese in Shaping Modern Indonesian Life*, Cornell Southeast Asia Program, Ithaca, 1991, p. 17.
2 Interview with Kusumo Martoredjo, 28 August 1991.
3 Interview with Slamet Bratanata, 18 May 1989.
4 Presentation by Air Vice Marshall Teddy Rusdy to Jakarta-based foreign journalists, 14 January 1991.
5 Interview with Kwik Kian Gie, 13 December 1989.
6 Soeharto, *My Thoughts, Words and Deeds: An Autobiography*, Citra Lamtoro Gung Persada, Jakarta, 1991, pp. 328–9.
7 An account of the Tapos meeting is in Michael Vatikiotis and Adam Schwarz, 'Sharing the goodies', *Far Eastern Economic Review*, 29 March 1990, pp. 21–2.
8 Confidential interview, 16 July 1990.
9 Rush, 'Placing the Chinese', p. 17.
10 ibid., p. 23.
11 James Rush, speech delivered to a Cornell University symposium on the Indonesian-Chinese, 13–15 July 1990.
12 J. A. C. Mackie, 'Towkays and Tycoons: The Chinese in Indonesian Economic Life in the 1920s and 1980s', in *The Role of the Indonesian Chinese in Shaping Modern Indonesian Life*, Cornell Southeast Asia Program, Ithaca, 1991, p. 84.
13 ibid., p. 89.
14 'Non-indigenous businessmen criticized', *Jakarta Post*, 20 June 1991.
15 Leo Suryadinata, *Pribumi Indonesians, the Chinese Minority and China*, Heinemann Asia, Singapore, 1978, pp. 114–15.
16 For a fine portrait of Indonesian life at the village level, see Clifford Geertz, *Peddlers and Princes: Social Development and Economic Change in Two Indonesian Towns*, University of Chicago Press, Chicago, 1963.
17 Fred Riggs, *Thailand: The Modernization of a Bureaucratic Polity*, East–West Center Press, Honolulu, 1966.
18 Leo Suryadinata, 'The Long Slow March to Integration of the Chinese in Indonesia', *Far Eastern Economic Review*, 22 March 1984, pp. 40–1.
19 J. A. C. Mackie, 'Anti-Chinese Outbreaks in Indonesia', in *The Chinese in Indonesia*, ed. J. A. C. Mackie, Thomas Nelson, Melbourne, 1976, p. 82.
20 Mackie, 'Towkays and Tycoons', p. 90.
21 Mackie, 'Anti-Chinese Outbreaks in Indonesia', esp. pp. 79, 111.

22 Interview with General Soemitro, 25 March 1991.

23 Mackie, 'Anti-Chinese Outbreaks', pp. 120–2.

24 On a less positive note, some 300 000 ethnic Chinese in Indonesia remained stateless in the early 1990s. See US Department of State, 'Country Reports on Human Rights Practices for 1991', February 1992.

25 The following section draws on Richard Robison, *Indonesia: The Rise of Capital*, Allen & Unwin, Sydney, 1986; J. A. C. Mackie, 'Overseas Chinese Entrepreneurship', *Asian Pacific Economic Literature*, May 1992, pp. 41–64; J. A. C. Mackie, 'Changing Patterns of Chinese Big Business in Southeast Asia', in *Southeast Asian Capitalists*, ed. Ruth McVey, Cornell Southeast Asia Program, Ithaca, 1992, pp. 161–90; Ruth McVey, 'The Materialisation of the Southeast Asian Entrepreneur', in *Southeast Asian Capitalists*, ed. Ruth McVey, pp. 7–34; and Yoon Hwan Shin, 'The Role of Elites in Creating Capitalist Hegemony in Post-Oil Boom Indonesia', in *The Role of the Indonesian Chinese in Shaping Modern Indonesian Life*, Cornell Southeast Asia Program, Ithaca, 1991, pp. 128–43.

26 Mackie, 'Changing Patterns', p. 165.

27 Wu Yuan-li, 'Chinese Entrepreneurs in Southeast Asia', *American Economic Review*, Vol. 73, No. 2, 1983, pp. 112–17.

28 Mackie, 'Changing Patterns', p. 179.

29 Robison, *The Rise of Capital*, p. 317.

30 'Sofjan Wanandi', *Jakarta Jakarta*, 5 February 1993, p. 32.

31 Interview with Djisman Simandjuntak, 12 December 1989.

32 Sjahrir, 'The Indonesian economy: the case of macro success and micro challenge', in *Indonesia Assessment 1993. Labour: Sharing in the Benefits of Growth?*, eds Chris Manning and Joan Hardjono, Research School of Pacific Studies, Canberra, 1993, p. 24, n. 3.

33 Quoted in Adam Schwarz, 'Call for Constraints', in *Far Eastern Economic Review*, 28 December 1989, p. 55.

34 Material in this section is drawn from a profile of Liem Sioe Liong's Salim Group in Adam Schwarz, 'Empire of the Son', *Far Eastern Economic Review*, 14 March 1991, pp. 46–9, 52–3; and Jonathan Friedland, 'And Now the World', *Far Eastern Economic Review*, 14 March 1991, pp. 49–50. Two good histories of Liem's business background are Robison, *The Rise of Capital*, pp. 296–315; and Yoon Hwan Shin, 'Demystifying the Capitalist State: Political Patronage, Bureaucratic Interests, and Capitalists-in-Formation in Soeharto's Indonesia', PhD dissertation, Yale University, May 1989, pp. 321–86.

35 World Bank, 'Indonesia. Agricultural Transformation: Challenges and Opportunities', vol. I, 18 June 1992, pp. 99–102.

36 'Cold Rolling Mill Indonesia Utama', a memorandum prepared by 'The Advisory Group' for Minister of Finance Johannes Sumarlin and Junior Minister of Industry Tungky Ariwibowo, 23 May 1989, p. 12. The document was supplied to me by a government official.

37 Soedarman's letter was supplied by a senior government official in March, 1990.

38 The economic clout these four men wield is well illustrated by the tax office's annual list of the country's top taxpayers. For the 1992 tax year,

the Liem investors occupied four out of the top seven slots. See 'Govt unveils largest taxpayers', *Jakarta Post*, 1 February 1994.

39 Interview with Anthony Salim, 13 February 1991.

40 ibid.

41 ibid.

42 'Pulang Kampung Setelah 30 Tahun', *Tempo*, 24 November 1990, p. 35.

43 See Richard Borsuk, 'Salim Studies Listing Company Offshore to Raise Up to $1 Billion', *Asian Wall Street Journal*, 15 December 1993.

44 Interview with Bustanil Arifin, 16 July 1992.

45 Mackie, 'Changing Patterns', p. 166.

46 Robison, *The Rise of Capital*, p. 45.

47 ibid.

48 Material on *pribumi* promotion policies in the 1980s is drawn from Robison, *The Rise of Capital*, pp. 323–30; Shin, 'The Role of Elites'; and Jeffrey A. Winters, 'Structural Power and Investor Mobility: Capital Control and State Policy in Indonesia, 1965–1990', PhD dissertation, Yale University, December 1991, pp. 151–72.

49 Team 10 procurements and domestic investment figures are taken from Winters, 'Structural Power', pp. 164–5.

50 Winters, 'Structural Power', p. 172, n. 330; and p. 167.

51 Quoted in Winters, 'Structural Power', p. 222.

52 Interview with Bambang Sugomo, 16 October 1991.

53 Confidential interview, 3 September 1991.

54 A fuller description of the foster-parent program is in Adam Schwarz, 'Piece of the Action', *Far Eastern Economic Review*, 2 May 1991, pp. 39–41.

55 Confidential interview, 12 September 1991.

56 Interview with Radius Prawiro, 15 October 1991.

57 Interview with Anthony Salim, 13 February 1991.

58 Interview with Kwik Kian Gie, 13 December 1989.

59 Interview with Abdurrahman Wahid, 30 May 1990.

60 Interview with Aburizal Bakrie, 12 September 1991.

61 Interview with Fadel Muhammad, 13 February 1991.

62 Hal Hill, 'Ownership in Indonesia', in *Indonesia Assessment 1990*, eds Hal Hill and Terry Hull, Research School of Pacific Studies, Canberra, 1990, p. 61.

63 PT Data Consult, *Anatomy of Indonesian Conglomerates*, June 1991.

64 'Indigenous Indonesians warn of Chinese dominance', *Reuter*, 11 December 1993. Habibie offered no empirical data to support this claim.

65 'Menuju Kesejajaran Pri dan Nonpri', *Tempo*, 20 July 1991, p. 83.

66 Interview with Kusumo Martoredjo, 5 February 1991; and interview with Siswono Yudohusodo, 16 September 1991.

67 Confidential interview, 9 August 1991.

68 See, for example, the comments of Dawam Rahardjo in 'Perlu Penyesuaian Seperempat Abad', *Prospek*, 3 April 1993, pp. 27–8.

69 Confidential interviews, 11 December 1990; 19 June 1991; and 28 August 1991. Fears of capital flight escalated in mid-1991 when a survey by an American consulting firm revealed that 41 per cent of all Asian Currency Unit deposits in Singapore—or approximately US$26 billion—originated from Indonesia. ACUs are popular foreign currency dollar deposits which

enjoy tax-free status in Singapore. The offshore deposits, headline writers repeatedly emphasised, were greater than Indonesia's 1991 budget revenues. See, for example, 'Dana RI "parkir" di LN US$76 milyar', *Bisnis Indonesia*, 3 August 1991.
70 Interview with Lukman Harun, 5 June 1990.
71 'Big changes vital to cure imbalance in economy', *Jakarta Post*, 23 December 1993.
72 Confidential interview, 19 June 1991.
73 Confidential interview, 11 December 1990.
74 Confidential interview, 5 February 1991.
75 Confidential interview, 9 August 1991.
76 'Conglomerates blasted for lack of ethics', *Jakarta Post,* 27 December 1993; and 'Indonesia's conglomerates attacked for social ills', *Reuter*, 27 December 1993.
77 Confidential interview, 12 September 1991.
78 Interview with Teddy Rachmat, 21 February 1991.
79 Interview with Anthony Salim, 13 February 1991; and interview with Johannes Kotjo, 15 August 1991.
80 Confidential interview, 31 March 1993.
81 Interview with Umar Juoro, 29 March 1993.
82 Confidential interview, 13 May 1991.
83 The point is elaborated more fully in Adam Schwarz, 'Plastic Properties', *Far Eastern Economic Review*, 2 May 1991, pp. 40–1.
84 Some of the information in the following section first appeared in Schwarz, 'Plastic Properties'.
85 Confidential interview, leading business executive, 12 December 1990.
86 Confidential interview, leading business executive, 16 January 1991.
87 Interview with Iman Taufik, 15 January 1991.
88 Robison, *The Rise of Capital*, p. 318. See also Mackie, 'Anti-Chinese Outbreaks', p. 133.
89 Mely Tan, 'The Social and Cultural Dimensions of the Role of Ethnic Chinese in Indonesian Society', in *The Role of the Indonesian Chinese in Shaping Modern Indonesian Life*, Cornell Southeast Asia Program, Ithaca, 1991, p. 124.
90 'Something's Wrong', *Indonesian Observer*, 14 September 1992. The Lippo Group, one of Indonesia's fastest-growing conglomerates, has been another frequent target of nationalist criticism. Lippo, headed by an ethnic-Chinese businessman, Mochtar Riady, has been assailed in the press for making investments in mainland China. See ' "Saya Bukan Bangsa Cina . . ." ', *Tempo*, 23 October 1993, pp. 90–2.
91 Confidential interview, 2 April 1993.
92 Confidential interview, 22 February 1991.
93 Interview with Teddy Rachmat, 21 February 1991.

Chapter 6   Family rules

1 William Shakespeare, *Hamlet*, Act II, Scene two.
2 Savitri Setiawan and Alex Mirza Hukom, 'The Enterprising Military', *Indonesia Business Weekly*, 6 July 1992, p. 5.

3 The quote by Alamsyah, a former Coordinating Minister for People's Welfare, was cited in *Jakarta Post*, 1 May 1992.

4 World Bank, 'Indonesia. Agricultural Transformation: Challenges and Opportunities', 18 June 1992, Vol. 1, p. 95. In June 1993, prohibitively high import tariffs on soymeal were lowered to a more reasonable 5 per cent. Only two weeks later, however, the government issued a new decree requiring soymeal consumers to purchase at least 40 per cent of their supplies from Sarpindo, at a price set by the latter. See Sjahrir, 'The Indonesian economy: the case of macro success and micro challenge', in *Indonesia Assessment 1993. Labour: Sharing in the Benefits of Growth?*, eds Chris Manning and Joan Hardjono, Research School of Pacific Studies, Canberra, 1993, p. 23.

5 Confidential interview, 11 July 1992.

6 Information for this section was drawn from author's interviews with government officials, economists and commodity traders from March–July 1992; and from the World Bank, 'Agricultural Transformation'. The debate over Sarpindo's monopoly is discussed in Adam Schwarz, 'Biting the Bullet', *Far Eastern Economic Review*, 23 July 1992, pp. 34–5.

7 Soeharto, *My Thoughts, Words and Deeds: An Autobiography*, Citra Lamtoro Gung Persada, Jakarta, 1991, p. 213.

8 'The Thahir Phenomenon', *Jakarta Post*, 5 December 1992.

9 J. A. C. Mackie, 'Report of the Commission of Four on Corruption', *Bulletin of Indonesian Economic Studies*, No. 2, November 1970.

10 Harold Crouch, *The Army and Politics in Indonesia*, Cornell University Press, Ithaca, 1988, p. 292.

11 Sutowo's proclivity for helping himself to extra-budgetary revenues was well known, even in the mid-1970s. In 1958, Sutowo, then a colonel serving on the general staff in Jakarta, was removed from his post by then Minister for Defence and Security, General Nasution, allegedly for various corrupt activities.

12 Quoted in Raphael Pura, 'Pertamina Wins Its Legal Battle Over Deposits', *Asian Wall Street Journal*, 4–5 December 1992. The case is currently under appeal.

13 'The Thahir Phenomenon', *Jakarta Post*, 5 December 1992.

14 In late 1993, an Indonesian business magazine published a survey of the wealthiest indigenous Indonesians. Ibnu Sutowo came in number one on the list, with estimated assets of US$138 million. See 'Suharto children among wealthiest Indonesians', *Reuter*, 9 November 1993.

15 The mechanics of the Apkindo cartel are described in Adam Schwarz, 'Timber Troubles', *Far Eastern Economic Review*, 6 April 1989.

16 Adam Schwarz, 'Trade for Trees', *Far Eastern Economic Review*, 4 June 1992.

17 World Bank, 'Indonesia: Sustaining Development', 25 May 1993, pp. 17, 130. The calculation of foregone revenues assumes the government could theoretically collect 85 per cent of the 'economic rent' produced by the forestry sector, the same percentage which is currently collected from the oil industry. At present, the government collects less than 30 per cent of the forestry 'rent'.

18 For a fuller profile of Prajogo's business empire, see Adam Schwarz and Jonathan Friedland, 'Green Fingers', *Far Eastern Economic Review*, 12 March 1992, pp. 42–4. An account of the listing of Prajogo's wood-manufacturing operations on the Jakarta Stock Exchange is in Adam Schwarz, 'Elusive Evaluation', *Far Eastern Economic Review*, 12 August 1993, p. 82.

19 Prajogo wrote to Soeharto on 8 March 1991 asking that a state-owned forestry company, Inhutani II, contribute US$45 million in equity capital to Enim Musi Lestari, a company owned by Prajogo's Barito Pacific Group. The following day, in a letter to Minister of Forestry Hasjrul Harahap, Soeharto ordered that Prajogo's request be filled. Both documents supplied by a senior government official.

20 Confidential interview with senior government official, 6 March 1992.

21 Good accounts of Bimantara's corporate beginnings can be found in Paul Handley, 'Coming to the Defence of the Family Business', *Far Eastern Economic Review*, 22 May 1986; Steven Jones, 'Suharto's Kin Linked With Plastics Monopoly', *Asian Wall Street Journal*, 25 November 1986; and Raphael Pura, 'Suharto's Family Tied to Indonesian Oil Trade', *Asian Wall Street Journal*, 26 November 1986. More recent accounts of the group's progress are Raphael Pura, 'Indonesia's Bimantara Tries to Revamp Image', *Asian Wall Street Journal*, 17 September 1990; and Adam Schwarz, 'From Oil to Aircraft', *Far Eastern Economic Review*, 30 April 1992.

22 See Richard Borsuk, 'Indonesia's Bimantara Says Assets Increase 75% and Profit Doubles', *Asian Wall Street Journal*, 13 January 1994.

23 Material on Tutut's business interests is drawn from Adam Schwarz, 'Corporate Catalyst', *Far Eastern Economic Review*, 30 April 1992, pp. 56–7.

24 For more details, see Richard Borsuk, 'Jakarta Draws Criticism for Road Project', *Asian Wall Street Journal*, 16 January 1990.

25 For a profile of the Humpuss Group, see Adam Schwarz and Jonathan Friedland, 'No Mere Middleman', *Far Eastern Economic Review*, 23 August 1990. A more recent account of Humpuss activities is in Adam Schwarz, 'Monopoly under Fire', *Far Eastern Economic Review*, 30 April 1992.

26 The survey, which did not include ethnic Chinese businessmen, was published by *Info Business* magazine on 9 November 1993.

27 Jeffrey A. Winters, 'Structural Power and Investor Mobility: Capital Control and State Policy in Indonesia, 1965–1990', PhD dissertation, Yale University, December 1991, p. 76, n. 94.

28 Hal Hill, 'Survey of Recent Developments', *Bulletin of Indonesian Economic Studies*, Australian National University, Canberra, Vol. 28, No. 2, August 1992.

29 Some material in this section appeared in Adam Schwarz, 'Indonesia on Hold', *Far Eastern Economic Review*, 24 January 1991.

30 Confidential interview, 6 March 1992.

31 Confidential interview, 15 October 1991.

32 Soeharto's views on his children's business activities are discussed more fully in Adam Schwarz, 'All is Relative', *Far Eastern Economic Review*, 30 April 1992, pp. 54–6.

33 Interview with Iman Taufik, 15 January 1991. This same argument has been used by Soeharto's children themselves. Bambang Trihatmodjo in particular

has argued that the privatisation of state-owned enterprises should be aimed at helping *pribumi* businessmen. For a discussion of this point, see Richard Robison and Vedi Hadiz, 'Economic Liberalisation or the Reorganisation of Dirigisme? Indonesian Economic Policy in the 1990s', *Canadian Journal of Development Studies*, Special issue, December 1993, pp. 13–32.

34 Interview with Mubyarto, 25 March 1992.

35 Interview with Kusumo Martoredjo, 5 February 1991.

36 Interview with Minister Sudomo, 8 May 1992.

37 See Adam Schwarz, 'Growing Pains', *Far Eastern Economic Review*, 2 April 1992, pp. 43–4; 'State banks violate legal lending limits: Soedradjad', *Jakarta Post*, 10 December 1993; and '$430m lost to L/C issue collusion', *Jakarta Post*, 1 February 1994.

38 The credit reference for Barito Pacific written by Bank Bumi Daya president Surasa was supplied by a government official. A note accompanying Barito's US$50 million prepayment on 29 June 1992, and Surasa's 4 July 1992 letter confirming receipt of this payment, were supplied by a senior executive of an Indonesian timber firm. Fourteen months after this transaction took place, the technocrats finally were able to convince Soeharto to approve Surasa's dismissal. In September 1993, the finance minister announced Surasa had retired. See 'Tugasnya Telah Selesai', *Tempo*, 25 September 1993, p. 91.

39 Confidential interview, 6 March 1992.

40 Interview with Ali Wardhana, 1 April 1993.

41 'Questionable privatization', *Jakarta Post*, 14 April 1993.

42 Richard Borsuk, 'Jakarta's Methods Cloud Satellite Plan', *Asian Wall Street Journal*, 15 April 1993.

43 Interview with coordinating economy minister Radius Prawiro, 15 October 1991.

44 Confidential interview, leading Indonesian businessman, 24 July 1992.

45 'Setiawan Djody', *Indonesia Business Weekly*, 7 January 1994, p. 4; and 'Wah Djody, Wah', *Tempo*, 13 November 1993, p. 92.

46 'Probosutedjo', *Indonesian Business Weekly*, 21 January 1994.

47 Yoon Hwan Shin, 'Demystifying the Capitalist State: Political Patronage, Bureaucratic Interests, and Capitalists-in-Formation in Soeharto's Indonesia', PhD dissertation, Yale University, May 1989, p. 402.

48 See, for example, 'Sumitro defends policy on Astra', *Jakarta Post*, 18 December 1992. The story quotes Astra's chairman Sumitro Djojohadikusumo as saying: 'Toyota . . . felt uncomfortable about the new would-be investors in Astra'. See also Richard Borsuk, 'Professor Placed in Eye of Astra Storm', *Asian Wall Street Journal*, 18–19 December 1992.

49 Completing the cronies' absorption of the former Soeryadjaya empire, Soeharto's eldest daughter Tutut announced plans in early 1994 to take over Bank Summa. See Richard Borsuk, 'Takeover Plan Could End Saga Of Bank Summa', *Asian Wall Street Journal*, 26 January 1994.

50 See 'Hati-Hati Kolusi', *Tempo*, 18 December 1993, p. 91.

51 Interview with Finance Minister Johannes Sumarlin, 6 March 1992.

52 On 7 March 1992, Prajogo wrote to Soeharto asking for his help to unfreeze the funds committed to Chandra Asri by Bank Bumi Daya and other state-owned banks. Prajogo wrote that the petrochemical project was

'extremely vital and strategic for national development'. The following day, Soeharto sent a message to Finance Minister Sumarlin and Bank Indonesia Governor Mooy instructing them to release the state bank funds promised to Chandra Asri. Both documents supplied by a senior government official.

53 In a sharply worded letter dated 19 April 1992, Bank Indonesia Governor Adrianus Mooy instructed that 'BBD is not authorised to have any further direct or indirect contacts with PT Chandra Asri in either the rupiah or any other currency.' Document supplied by a senior government official.

54 Material on Chandra Asri is drawn from Adam Schwarz, 'Personal Chemistry', *Far Eastern Economic Review*, 12 March 1992, pp. 45–6; and Carl Goldstein, 'Flexible as Plastic', *Far Eastern Economic Review*, 7 January 1993, pp. 50–3. Bambang and Prajogo are not alone in trying to evade the Colt restrictions. Soeharto's youngest son Tommy has used the loophole made available by the April 1992 ruling on foreign investment to resuscitate several petrochemical projects in which he is a shareholder.

55 The member firms of the consortium are detailed in Adam Schwarz, 'Spice of strife', *Far Eastern Economic Review*, 19 July 1990, pp. 56–7.

56 Tommy's letter to Industry Minister Hartarto supplied by a government official.

57 The formation of BPPC is discussed in Adam Schwarz, 'No Smoke Without Ire', *Far Eastern Economic Review*, 17 January 1991.

58 Cited in Schwarz, 'Spice of strife'. See also Elizabeth Pisani, 'New Clove Monopoly May Spell Doom For Indonesian Deregulation', *Reuter*, 5 January 1991.

59 Tommy's letter to Sultan of Brunei, Haji Hassanal Bolkiah, was dated 9 February 1991. Copies were sent to President Soeharto and Finance Minister Johannes Sumarlin. The letter was supplied to me by a senior government official.

60 Confidential interview with a senior government official, 13 May 1991.

61 State funding for the clove monopoly is discussed in Adam Schwarz, 'Tying the Clove Hitch', *Far Eastern Economic Review*, 25 April 1991, pp. 56–7.

62 Interview with Radius Prawiro, 15 October 1991.

63 Confidential interview, 16 March 1992.

64 Cited in Adam Schwarz, 'Burning Issue', *Far Eastern Economic Review*, 12 March 1992, p. 40.

65 Confidential interview, senior Golkar official, 8 July 1992.

66 Cited in Schwarz, 'Biting the Bullet'.

67 ibid. Australia also has had its problems with Indonesia over the corruption issue. A 1986 article in an Australian newspaper commenting on the Soeharto family's business involvements caused a rift in bilateral relations with Australia that has yet to fully heal. The article was written by David Jenkins, 'After Marcos, now for the Soeharto billions', *Sydney Morning Herald*, 10 April 1986.

68 See 'Corruption: Alive and Well', *Indonesia Business Weekly*, 30 April 1993. In a similar survey carried out in late 1993, the Political and Economic Risk Consultancy again found that Indonesia was considered the most corrupt of the ten Asian nations considered. See Political and Economic Risk Consultancy, '*Comparative Country Risk Report*, 1994', pp. 30–2.

69 'Indonesia Lost a Big Chance', *Indonesia Business Weekly*, 21 January 1994.
70 'Licensed to corrupt', *Jakarta Post*, 27 April 1993.
71 Confidential interview, 11 July 1992.
72 See Richard Borsuk, 'Salim Studies Listing Company Offshore to Raise Up to $1 Billion', *Asian Wall Street Journal*, 15 December 1993; and Raphael Pura, Stephen Duthie and Richard Borsuk, 'Plywood Tycoon May Purchase Malaysian Firm', *Asian Wall Street Journal*, 3 February 1994.
73 Interview with Laksamana Sukardi, 23 March 1992.
74 Interview with Kwik Kian Gie, 2 April 1992.
75 Interview with Rachmat Witoelar, 1 April 1992.
76 Confidential interview, 1 April 1993.
77 Interview with Lieutenant General (ret.) Hasnan Habib, 2 April 1993.
78 Interview with Rachmat Witoelar, 1 April 1992.

Chapter 7   Islam: Coming in from the cold?

1 Quoted in Allan Samson, 'Conceptions of Politics, Power, and Ideology in Contemporary Indonesian Islam', in *Political Power and Communication in Indonesia*, eds Karl Jackson and Lucian Pye, University of California Press, Berkeley, 1978, p. 213.
2 Interview with Abdurrahman Wahid, 9 July 1992.
3 Nasir Tamara, 'Islam under the New Order: A Political History', *Prisma*, No. 49, June 1990, p. 20.
4 The details of the meeting between Wahid and Lieutenant Colonel Prabowo were related to me by Wahid in an interview on 9 July 1992.
5 Some four hundred 'misleading religious cults' are specifically banned by law. The exact breakdown of Indonesians according to faith is as follows: Muslims, 87 per cent; Protestants, 6 per cent; Roman Catholics, 4 per cent; Hindus, 2 per cent; and Buddhists, 1 per cent.
6 The belief in one, supreme God is the first of the five Pancasila principles. The other four are: justice and civility among peoples; the unity of Indonesia; democracy through deliberation and consensus among representatives; and social justice for all.
7 See Anwar Nasir, 'House and Household', *Far Eastern Economic Review*, 2 July 1987, pp. 38–43. A fuller account of Islam's role in Indonesia is in Anthony Johns, 'Indonesia: Islam and Cultural Pluralism', in *Islam in Asia: Religion, Politics & Society*, ed. John Esposito, Oxford University Press, New York, 1987, pp. 202–29.
8 David Joel Steinberg, ed., *In Search of Southeast Asia: A Modern History*, University of Hawaii Press, Honolulu, 1985, p. 288.
9 ibid.
10 Clifford Geertz, *The Religion of Java*, University of Chicago Press, Chicago, 1960, pp. 5, 160.
11 ibid., p. 127.
12 Liem Soei Liong, 'Indonesian Muslims and the state: accommodation or revolt?', *Third World Quarterly*, Vol. 10, No. 2, April 1988, p. 871.
13 Steinberg, ed., *In Search of Southeast Asia*, p. 291.
14 Samson, 'Conceptions', p. 199.

15 This section draws on Steinberg, ed., *In Search of Southeast Asia*, pp. 291–8.

16 Johns, 'Islam and Cultural Pluralism', p. 208.

17 ibid., p. 210.

18 Not all modernist *santris* supported the Masyumi cause. Mohammad Hatta, one of Indonesia's founding fathers, was a devout Muslim but also a staunch supporter of Pancasila and its message of religious tolerance. See Zifirdaus Adnan, 'Islamic Religion: Yes, Islamic (Political) Ideology: No! Islam and the State in Indonesia', in *State and Civil Society in Indonesia*, ed. Arief Budiman, Centre of Southeast Asian Studies, Clayton, 1990, p. 446.

19 R. William Liddle, 'Improvising Political Cultural Change: Three Indonesian Cases', in *Indonesian Political Culture: Asking the Right Questions*, ed. James Schiller, Ohio University Center for Southeast Asian Studies, Athens, forthcoming.

20 Bernard Lewis, *The Political Language of Islam*, University of Chicago Press, Chicago, 1988, pp. 2–3.

21 This section draws on Liem, 'Indonesian Muslims and the state', pp. 872–6.

22 Johns, 'Islam and Cultural Pluralism', p. 211.

23 Quoted in Ruth McVey, 'Faith as the Outsider: Islam in Indonesian Politics', in *Islam in the Political Process*, ed. James Piscatori, Cambridge University Press, Cambridge, 1983, p. 199.

24 Samson, 'Conceptions', p. 224. For a longer discussion of the government's two-pronged approach, see Harold Crouch, 'The Politics of Islam in the Asean Countries', in *Asean into the 1990s*, ed. Alison Broinowski, Macmillan Press, London, 1990. On the NU's conception of politics, I am grateful to Greg Barton and Greg Fealy for their insightful comments.

25 See Liem, 'Indonesian Muslims and the state', p. 884.

26 Abdurrahman Wahid, 'Islam, Politics and Democracy in Indonesia in the 1950s and 1990s', paper delivered to the Conference on Indonesian Democracy, 1950s and 1990s, Monash University, 17–20 December 1992.

27 Jalaluddin Rakmat, 'Islam di Indonesia: Masalah Definisi', in *Islam di Indonesia: Suatu Ikhtiar Mengaca Diri*, ed. Amien Rais, Rajawali, Jakarta, 1986, p. 38.

28 For a full account of the incident, see Amnesty International, 'Indonesia: Arrests of Muslim Activists Relating to the Tanjung Priok Incident of 12 September 1984', London, July 1985. Some later accounts of the incident put the death toll at several hundred.

29 See Michael Vatikiotis, 'Islam's hidden warriors', *Far Eastern Economic Review*, 23 February 1989.

30 Adam Schwarz, 'Deadly Suspicion', *Far Eastern Economic Review*, 25 July 1991, pp. 18–20. For a thorough account of alleged human rights allegations in Aceh, see Asia Watch, 'Indonesia: Continuing Human Rights Violations in Aceh', New York, 19 June 1991.

31 Liddle, 'Three Indonesian Cases'.

32 Interview with Rizal Ramli, 18 March 1993.

33 For a discussion of university-based Islamic study groups, and their various views on Islam, see 'Pembaruan', *Tempo*, 3 April 1993, pp. 13–21.

34 Interview with Umar Juoro, 29 March 1993.

35 Interview with Abdurrahman Wahid, 9 July 1992.

36 For a critique of the *santri–abangan* paradigm, see Adnan, 'Islamic Religion: Yes, Islamic (Political) Ideology: No!' pp. 441–78.
37 This point is taken from Samson, 'Conceptions', p. 199. A good description of neo-modernist thought within the Indonesian Muslim community is in Greg Barton, 'The Impact of Islamic Neo-Modernism on Indonesian Islamic Thought: The Emergence of a New Pluralism', paper presented to the Conference on Indonesian Democracy, 1950s and 1990s, Monash University, 17–20 December 1992.
38 Samson, 'Conceptions', pp. 199–200.
39 The views of Dewan Dakwah followers are described in R. William Liddle, '*Media Dakwah* Scripturalism: One Form of Islamic Political Thought and Action in New Order Indonesia', in *Intellectual Development in Indonesian Islam*, eds Mark Woodward and James Rush, Center for Southeast Asian Studies, Arizona State University, Tempe, 1993, pp. 71–107. Liddle found strident anti-Semitism to be characteristic of the Dewan Dakwah mentality.
40 Interview with B. J. Habibie, 13 February 1992.
41 Interview with Emil Salim, 18 February 1992.
42 Interview with Munawir Sjadzali, 2 June 1990.
43 Interviews with Sucipto Wirosardjono, 18 February 1991, 21 July 1992 and 1 April 1993.
44 'Tidak Usah Munafik!', *Matra*, December 1992, p. 23.
45 Liddle, 'Three Indonesian Cases'.
46 Nurcholish Madjid, 'Keharusan Pembaharuan Pemikiran Islam Dan Masalah Integrasi Ummat'. The speech was published subsequently in Nurcholish Madjid, Abdul Qadir Djaelani, Ismail Hasan Metareum, and Saefuddin Anshari, *Pembaharuan Pemikiran Islam*, Islamic Research Centre, Jakarta, 1970, pp. 1–12. For a fuller description of the speech and its implications, see Liddle, 'Three Indonesian Cases'. Nurcholish's views are spelled out at length in a collection of his essays, *Islam: Doktrin dan Perabadan*, Yayasan Wakaf Paramadina, Jakarta, 1992.
47 Interview with Nurcholish Madjid, 31 July 1992. See also 'Tidak Usah Munafik!', *Matra*, December 1992, pp. 13–23.
48 Quoted in Nasir, 'House and Household'.
49 'Negara Kita Bisa Disebut Negara Islam', *Detik*, 1–7 April 1993, p. 20.
50 Interview with Lukman Harun, 5 June 1990.
51 'KH Zainuddin MZ', *Jakarta Jakarta*, 20–26 March 1993, p. 66; see also 'Government moves to limit activities of missionaries', *Jakarta Post*, 11 October 1993.
52 See Margot Cohen, 'Religious Feuds Rattle New Order', *Asian Wall Street Journal*, 14 December 1992.
53 Interview with Sri Bintang Pamungkas, 22 July 1992.
54 Interview with Umar Juoro, 29 March 1993.
55 Interview with Nasir Tamara, 12 March 1993.
56 Interview with Sri Bintang Pamungkas, 30 March 1993.
57 See 'Habibie takes credit for govt, Moslem relations', *Jakarta Post*, 1 February 1994.
58 Interview with Umar Juoro, 29 March 1993.
59 An ICMI modernist, Dawam Rahardjo, in an interview published just before

Soeharto made his choice for vice-president, gave Habibie a ringing endorsement for the job. See 'Dawam Rahardjo: Pak Try Sulit Diterima Presiden!', *Detik*, 10 March 1993.

60 'Negara Kita Bisa Disebut Negara Islam', *Detik*, 1–7 April 1993, p. 20.

61 Interview with Umar Juoro, 29 March 1993.

62 ibid.

63 'Negara Kita Bisa Disebut Negara Islam', *Detik*, 1–7 April 1993, p. 21.

64 Interviews with Sri Bintang Pamungkas, 22 July 1992 and 30 March 1993. The concerns of Pamungkas and others that ICMI will be dominated by members working for the government, and specifically Minister Habibie, are described at length in 'Payung ICMI Dengan Makna Ganda', *Editor*, 16 February 1991, pp. 12–20.

65 Interview with Sri Bintang Pamungkas, 30 March 1993; interview with Umar Juoro, 29 March 1993.

66 Interview with Sri Bintang Pamungkas, 30 March 1993.

67 ibid.

68 Interview with Abdurrahman Wahid, 26 March 1993. Some material in this section appeared in Adam Schwarz, 'Charismatic Enigma', *Far Eastern Economic Review*, 12 November 1992, pp. 34–6.

69 Interviews with Abdurrahman Wahid, 12 April 1991, 25 February 1992, 29 April 1992 and 9 July 1992. Some material in this section appeared in Adam Schwarz, 'Islam and Democracy', *Far Eastern Economic Review*, 19 March 1992, p. 32.

70 Interview with Abdurrahman Wahid, 25 February 1992.

71 Interview with Abdurrahman Wahid, 29 April 1992.

72 For a discussion of the latter, see Djohan Effendi, 'The Contribution of the Islamic Parties to the Decline of Democracy in the 1950s', paper delivered to the Conference on Indonesian Democracy, 1950s and 1990s, Monash University, 17–20 December 1992. Referring to the late 1950s, Djohan writes: 'At a critical time in our recent history the Islamic parties in Indonesia did much to reduce and weaken their potential as an instrument for democracy, and therefore to their image as 'clean' players in the process of democratisation in Indonesian political life, and their role as a channel for realising the sovereignty of the people.'

73 Interviews with Abdurrahman Wahid, 12 April 1991, 9 July 1992 and 26 March 1993.

74 Interviews with Abdurrahman Wahid, 29 April 1992 and 9 July 1992.

75 Interview with Abdurrahman Wahid, 5 March 1992.

76 Interviews with Abdurrahman Wahid, 30 May 1990 and 12 April 1991. For more detail on the NU–Summa joint venture, see Adam Schwarz, 'The Prophet Motive', *Far Eastern Economic Review*, 12 July 1990, pp. 60–1.

77 Interview with Munawir Sjadzali, 2 June 1990; interview with Dorodjatun Kuntjorojakti, 6 June 1990.

78 Interviews with Abdurrahman Wahid, 12 November 1991 and 29 August 1991. For more information on Bank Muamalat Indonesia, see Adam Schwarz, 'Profit and the Prophet', *Far Eastern Economic Review*, 21 May 1992, pp. 45–6.

79 Interview with Abdurrahman Wahid, 26 March 1993.

80 Interview with Amien Rais, 27 February 1992; interview with Sri Bintang Pamungkas, 22 July 1992; interview with Sucipto Wirosardjono, 21 July 1992.

81 Interview with Abdurrahman Wahid, 26 March 1993.

82 Interview with Abdurrahman Wahid, 12 April 1991. For an account of the Democracy Forum's formation, see Adam Schwarz, 'A Worrying Word', *Far Eastern Economic Review*, 25 April 1991, p. 23.

83 Quoted in Elizabeth Pisani, 'Indonesians take democracy into their own hands', *Reuter*, 5 April 1991.

84 Interview with Abdurrahman Wahid, 12 April 1991.

85 Interviews with Minister Sudomo, 5 April 1991 and 8 May 1992.

86 The rally, and the government's reaction to it, is described in Schwarz, 'Islam and Democracy'.

87 For a recent account of *santri* Muslim thinking on Pancasila, see Douglas Ramage, 'Pancasila Discourse in Soeharto's Late New Order', paper delivered to the Conference on Indonesian Democracy, 1950s and 1990s, Monash University, 17–20 December 1992. See also Bambang Pranowo, 'Which Islam and Which Pancasila? Islam and the State in Indonesia: A Comment', in *State and Civil Society*, ed. Arief Budiman, pp. 479–502.

88 A copy of the letter was supplied to me by an associate of Wahid.

89 'Gus Dur dan Suksesi', *Forum Keadilan*, 14 May 1992, p. 75.

90 'Chalid says NU chair has lost touch with fold', *Jakarta Post*, 20 April 1993.

Chapter 8   East Timor: The little pebble that could

1 The report, distributed by the embassy's information division, was published in February 1991.

2 Timothy Mo, *The Redundancy of Courage*, Chatto & Windus, London, 1991. Mo's novel is loosely based on events in East Timor.

3 Interview with Mario Carrascalao, the East Timor governor from 1982–92, 26 March 1993.

4 For an account of Soeharto's speech, see 'Ketua Dari Selatan', *Tempo*, 3 October 1992, pp. 32–3; and 'Langkah Pinheiro', *Tempo*, 3 October 1992, p. 36.

5 'The cemetery called East Timor', *The New York Times*, 25 September 1992.

6 Two of the best accounts of Timor's history are in John Taylor, *Indonesia's Forgotten War: The Hidden History of East Timor*, Zed Books, London, 1991; and James Dunn, *Timor, A People Betrayed*, Jacaranda Press, Milton, Queensland, 1983.

7 Cited in Taylor, *Indonesia's Forgotten War*, p. 10.

8 For a highly readable first-person account of the guerilla campaign, see C. D. Doig, *A History of the 2nd Independent Company and 2/2 Commando Squadron*, Trafalgar, Victoria, 1986. I am grateful to Lieutenant (ret.) Harry Morgan for the reference.

9 Francis Glen, 'Slavery in Timor', *Observer* (Australia), 29 October 1960.

10 Cited in Taylor, *Indonesia's Forgotten War*, p. 13.

11 Samuel Huntington, *The Third Wave: Democratisation in the Late Twentieth*

Century, University of Oklahoma Press, Norman, 1991. For the record, the first two waves, Huntington says, began in 1828 and 1943.

12 Taylor, who is deeply critical of Portugal for not supporting Timorese nationalists in 1974–75, has this to say: 'It was ironic that a movement which had overthrown a right-wing dictatorship in its home country should end up succumbing so early to the requests of an even more brutal and authoritarian military regime. Yet perhaps it was a fitting end to its 450 years of colonial rule. For all leaders of Portugal, there had always been one rule for its corporate elite and another for its incorporated and disenfranchised colonies.' See Taylor, *Indonesia's Forgotten War*, p. 54.

13 In addition to the sources cited in note 6, a good account of the formation of Timorese parties is in Jill Jolliffe, *East Timor: Nationalism and Colonialism*, University of Queensland Press, Brisbane, 1978.

14 Taylor, *Indonesia's Forgotten War*, p. 27.

15 Statement of Jose Ramos-Horta to the Human Rights Sub-Committee of the European Parliament, Brussels, 23 April 1992, p. 3.

16 Hamish McDonald, *Suharto's Indonesia*, Fontana Books, Blackburn, 1980, p. 199.

17 Interview with Mario Carrascalao, 26 March 1993.

18 Coalition Document, translated into English and published by the campaign for an Independent East Timor, Sydney, Australia, March 1978.

19 Taylor, *Indonesia's Forgotten War*, p. 46.

20 ibid., p. 52.

21 McDonald, *Suharto's Indonesia*, p. 209.

22 ibid., p. 211.

23 Cited in Taylor, *Indonesia's Forgotten War*, p. 68.

24 US Agency for International Development, 'East Timor—Indonesia—Displaced Persons', Situation Report No. 1, 9 October 1979.

25 McDonald, *Suharto's Indonesia*, p. 214.

26 Interview with Mario Carrascalao, 26 March 1993.

27 James Dunn, 'The East Timor Situation. Report on Talks with Timorese Refugees in Portugal', Legislative Research Service, Australian Parliament, Canberra, 1977.

28 Benedict Anderson, 'East Timor and Indonesia: Some Implications', paper delivered to the Social Science Research Council Workshop on East Timor, Washington, DC, 25–26 April 1991.

29 See the introduction by Noam Chomsky in Jose Ramos-Horta, *East Timor Debacle: Indonesian Intervention, Repression, and Western Compliance*, Red Sea Press, Trenton, 1986. For a penetrating critique of Washington's very different responses to atrocities carried out by anti-communist stalwarts like Soeharto in Indonesia and atrocities committed by left-wing regimes in, for example, Cambodia and Vietnam, see Noam Chomsky and Edward Herman, *The Washington Connection and Third World Fascism*, Hale & Iremonger, Sydney, 1980, pp. 129–218; and Noam Chomsky, *Towards a New Cold War: Essays on the Current Crisis and How We Got There*, Pantheon Books, New York, 1982, pp. 337–70.

30 I am grateful to Herb Feith for bringing this point to my attention.

31 Ramos-Horta, Statement to the Human Rights Sub-Committee of the European Parliament, Brussels, 23 April 1992, p. 3.

32 The report was issued by the national planning board in April 1993. See 'Report says poverty reigns in 33.7% of Indonesia's sub-districts', *Jakarta Post*, 29 April 1993.

33 A 1990 report prepared by Professors Mubyarto and Lukman Soetrisno of the Gadjah Mada University in Yogyakarta—'A Social-Anthropological Study of East Timor'—remarked that Timorese feel their land is being 'used as a milking cow by powerful economic groups from Java'. (The Indonesian military blocked domestic publication of the report.) For a thorough profile of East Timor's economic structure, see Hadi Soesastro, 'East Timor: Questions of Economic Viability', in *Unity and Diversity: Regional Economic Development in Indonesia since 1970*, ed. Hal Hill, Oxford University Press, Singapore, 1989, pp. 207–29.

34 Interview with Mario Carrascalao, 26 March 1993.

35 For a review of this period, see Herb Feith, 'East Timor: The Opening Up, the Crackdown and the Possibility of a Durable Settlement', in *Indonesia Assessment, 1992: Political Perspectives on the 1990s*, eds Harold Crouch and Hal Hill, Research School of Pacific Studies, Canberra, 1992.

36 Interview with Mario Carrascalao, 26 March 1993.

37 The speech was secretly taped and passed on to human rights groups abroad. Large extracts of the speech appear in 'Don't dream, or else. . .', *Inside Indonesia*, No. 23, June 1990, pp. 14–15.

38 See, for example, 'East Timor: Amnesty International Statement to the United Nations Special Committee on Decolonisation', August 1991.

39 This account is drawn primarily from personal interviews conducted in East Timor, 13–17 November 1991. See Adam Schwarz, 'Over the Edge', *Far Eastern Economic Review*, 28 November 1991, pp. 15–18; Asia Watch, 'East Timor: The November 12 Massacre and its Aftermath', New York, 12 December 1991; and Amnesty International, 'East Timor: The Santa Cruz Massacre', London, 14 November 1991.

40 Interview with Mgr Carlos Ximenes Belo, 14 November 1991.

41 See Adam Schwarz, 'No Apologies', *Far Eastern Economic Review*, 12 December 1991.

42 See *Jayakarta*, 14 November 1991; and Adam Schwarz, 'Reaction and Inquiry', *Far Eastern Economic Review*, 5 December 1991.

43 In August 1993, Djaelani was elevated to Vice-Chief Justice of the Supreme Court.

44 See *Antara*, 22 November 1991; and Amnesty International, 'Indonesia/East Timor. Santa Cruz: The Government Response', London, 6 February 1992.

45 Excerpts from the Investigating Commission's report cited in the following section are drawn from Adam Schwarz, 'Burden of Blame', *Far Eastern Economic Review*, 9 January 1992.

46 Schwarz, 'Burden of Blame'.

47 Interview with General Soemitro, 16 December 1991.

48 Interview with State Secretary Murdiono, 20 December 1991.

49 Interview Mario Carrascalao, 26 March 1993.

50 Confidential report by Amos Wako to Secretary-General Boutros Boutros Ghali, February 1992.

51 Interview with Mario Carrascalao, 14 November 1991.

52 See 'Report on the Trial of the East Timorese Students in Jakarta', published by the Indonesian Front for the Defence of Human Rights (Infight), undated; and Asia Watch, 'East Timor: The Courts-Martial', New York, 23 June 1992.

53 Asia Watch, 'East Timor: The Courts-Martial', 23 June 1992, p. 5.

54 Interview with Marzuki Darusman, 27 December 1991.

55 Adam Schwarz, 'Suharto's Dilemma', *Far Eastern Economic Review*, 26 December 1991.

56 One prominent businessman close to Prabowo told me that Prabowo blamed Benny Murdani for orchestrating the Dili massacre as a way to embarrass Soeharto ahead of an upcoming world tour. The evidence offered for this theory was that the Immigration Department, which was alleged to be under Murdani's orders, allowed the foreign journalists present in Dili on 12 November 1991 to easily leave Indonesia on the same day after which they 'maliciously' attacked the Indonesian government. Confidential interview, 20 July 1992.

57 Interview with Hasnan Habib, 2 April 1993.

58 In the days after the massacre I spoke with several Timorese hiding in houses near the Santa Cruz cemetery with serious injuries. One boy about twelve with gunshot wounds in the arm and thigh and an older man with a broken leg said they had crawled through the neighbourhood north of the cemetery to escape. Both felt they would be killed if they went to the hospital. Many families in the same neighbourhood said at least one family member had not returned from the demonstration.

59 Carrascalao's comments are taken from 'Saya Tidak Akan Diam', *Editor*, 14 December 1991, pp. 16–17, and from interviews with the author, 14 November 1991 and 26 March 1993.

60 Interview with Mgr Carlos Ximenes Belo, 14 November 1991.

61 Amnesty International, 'Indonesia/East Timor: Arbitrary Detention/Fear of Torture and Ill-Treatment', London, 23 November 1992.

62 Jonathan Thatcher, 'Indonesia Bars Journalists From East Timor', *Reuter*, 26 February 1992. Asked about the possibility of such a ban two months earlier, Australian Foreign Minister Gareth Evans said that 'would be a most unhappy development. What is needed in East Timor are more confidence-building measures, not less'. The Australian government made no official comment when the ban was reimposed. Evans made his comments at a Jakarta press conference, 21 December 1991.

63 See Tom Hyland, 'Even More Should Have Died in Dili: Governor', *Sydney Morning Herald*, 4 November 1992. The interview was first published in the 29 October 1991 edition of *Forum Keadilan*. See also 'Yang Bimbang Jadi Tenang', *Tempo*, 5 December 1992, p. 24.

64 Interview with Mario Carrascalao, 26 March 1993.

65 See 'We want to be free', *Inside Indonesia*, September 1992, pp. 10–12.

66 Interview with Mgr Carlos Ximenes Belo, 14 November 1991. See also Pascal Mallet, 'Roman Catholic Bishop shelters 257 Timorese after Dili shooting', *Agence France Presse*, 14 November 1991.

67 'We want to be free', *Inside Indonesia*, p. 12.
68 Interview with Jose Ramos-Horta, 21 December 1992.
69 Interview with Mario Carrascalao, 26 March 1993.
70 Jose Ramos-Horta, statement to the Human Rights Sub-committee of the European Parliament, Brussels, 23 April 1992, p. 2.
71 Confidential report by Amos Wako to Secretary-General Boutros Boutros Ghali, February 1992.
72 Jose Ramos-Horta, statement to Human Rights Sub-Committee of the European Parliament, Brussels, 23 April 1992, p. 2.
73 Confidential interview, 16 December 1991.
74 The weekly *Jakarta, Jakarta*, combined its coverage of the commission's report with testimony from Timorese witnesses to the Dili massacre, including accusations that many Timorese injured in the Santa Cruz cemetery had been tortured after being brought to the military hospital outside Dili. Subsequently, the magazine's owners were pressured into dismissing three senior editors.
75 Defence plea of Fernando de Araujo presented to the public prosecutor's team in the Central Jakarta court, 11 May 1992. See also Amnesty International, 'Indonesia/East Timor: Fernando de Araujo, Prisoner of Conscience', London, May 1992.
76 'Defence Plea of Xanana Gusmao', Dili district court, 17 May 1993. Xanana's statement was translated from Portuguese and distributed by TAPOL, a London-based human rights group.
77 See Amnesty International, 'East Timor: State of Fear', London, 13 July 1993; Wilson da Silva, 'Jailed Timorese rebel leader offers to serve longer term', *Reuter*, 9 January 1994; and 'Xanana visitation ban for "disgracing the nation" ', *Jakarta Post*, 13 January 1994.
78 Adam Schwarz, 'Tilting at Windmills', *Far Eastern Economic Review*, 9 April 1992, pp. 10–11.
79 On 25 November 1991, then Senator and current Vice-President Al Gore joined 51 other US senators in writing to President George Bush denouncing the Dili massacre and imploring the administration to do more to bring about 'true self-determination' for the East Timorese. For Indonesia's response to the United States' shifting position on East Timor under the Clinton administration, see 'Dari Dili sampai Roma', *Tempo*, 17 April 1993; and 'Setelah Portugal Melobi Clinton', *Tempo*, 8 May 1993.
80 Confidential interview with a senior Foreign Ministry official, 27 March 1993.
81 Confidential interview with a prominent Indonesian businessman, 29 March 1993.
82 This point is elaborated on in Asia Watch, 'Remembering History in East Timor: The Trial of Xanana Gusmao and a Follow-up to the Dili Massacre', New York, April 1993. A description of the military's plans for troop withdrawal is in Margot Cohen, 'Velvet Fist', *Far Eastern Economic Review*, 29 April 1993, pp. 24–5.
83 See Lindsay Murdoch, 'The trials of Timor', *Melbourne Age*, 19 February 1993.

84 'Red Cross suspends visits to East Timor political prisoners', *Agence France Presse*, 30 May 1993.
85 Simon Sinaga, 'Indonesia agrees to let Timorese students leave', *Reuter*, 29 December 1993.
86 Interview with Rui Quartim, director of political affairs at the Portuguese Foreign Ministry, 4 June 1993.
87 Interview with Jose Durao Barroso, 12 June 1992.
88 'East Timor: Building for the Future. Issues and Perspectives', Department of Foreign Affairs, Republic of Indonesia, July 1992.
89 'Defence Plea of Xanana Gusmao', Dili district court, 17 May 1993.
90 Interview with Mario Carrascalao, 26 March 1993.
91 ibid.
92 Interview with Rui Quartim, 4 June 1993.
93 'Meeting with E. Timorese in exile warmly welcomed', *Jakarta Post*, 24 December 1993.
94 'RI-Portugal forum set up with strong political backing', *Jakarta Post*, 10 January 1994; and 'Persahabatan Tutut untuk Tim-Tim', *Tempo*, 15 January 1994, pp. 29–30.
95 For a rare dissenting view, see Arief Budiman, 'Timtim: Berpikir Dingin dan Mencari Alternatif', *Editor*, 30 November 1991, pp. 26–7. In the article, Budiman makes the obvious point about guerilla warfare, although one rarely uttered in Indonesia: 'It would better for us to be brave enough to honestly look at what is going on [in East Timor]. A guerilla war can only continue if it has the support of the people.'
96 Susumu Awanohara, 'The Right To Arm', *Far Eastern Economic Review*, 23 September 1993, p. 13. For the Indonesian reaction to these measures, see 'Indonesian general slams "unfair" arms treatment', *Reuter*, 21 September 1993.
97 'Those East Timorese', *Indonesian Observer*, 17 December 1991.

Chapter 9   Social rights, individual responsibilities

1 Soeharto, *My Thoughts, Words and Deeds: An Autobiography*, Citra Lamtoro Gung Persada, Jakarta, 1991, pp. 334–5.
2 From a speech by Gunawan Mohamad in acceptance of the A. Teeuw Award in Leiden, the Netherlands, May 1992. Reprinted in 'RI language, culture grow up together', *Jakarta Post*, 5 June 1992.
3 'An Open Letter to the Australian Parliamentary Delegation on its Indonesian Study Tour', Indonesian Front for the Defence of Human Rights, 20 October 1992.
4 *Kompas*, 4 December 1989.
5 See Jonathan Thatcher, 'Suharto says Indonesia needs to be more open', *Reuter*, 16 August 1990; and *In the Censor's Shadow: Journalism in Suharto's Indonesia*, Committee to Protect Journalists, New York, August 1991.
6 For a fuller description of *Suksesi*, see Andrea Webster, 'Play politics: policing theatre in Indonesia', *Index on Censorship*, No. 7, 1991. Andrea Webster is a pen name of Julia Suryakusuma.

7 Interview with Rachmat Witoelar, 20 December 1990.

8 'Priok, Sampang, Apa lagi?', *Tempo*, 16 October 1993, pp. 29–40; Jeremy Wagstaff, 'Indonesia's lottery debate raises wider concerns', *Reuter*, 26 November 1993; and 'Students Pushing the Limits', *Indonesia Business Weekly*, 24 December 1993.

9 'Soeharto warns that PKI lurks', *Jakarta Post*, 18 December 1993; 'Demonstran dan Hukumannya', *Tempo*, 15 January 1994, pp. 21–7; and 'Defend Pancasila, ABRI told', *Jakarta Post*, 24 January 1994.

10 Adnan Buyung Nasution, *The Aspiration for Constitutional Government in Indonesia: A Socio-legal Study of the Indonesian Konstituante 1956–1959*, Pustaka Sinar Harapan, Jakarta, 1992, p. 423.

11 Interview with Taufik Abdullah, 24 October 1990.

12 See Margot Cohen, 'Pramoedya Still Awaits His Country's Awakening', *Asian Wall Street Journal*, 1–2 October 1993.

13 'Industry morass threatens RI's annual film festival', *Jakarta Post*, 19 February 1993.

14 For a description of the students' trial, see Margot Cohen, 'A Telling Trial', *Far Eastern Economic Review*, 2 September 1993; and Asia Watch, 'Indonesia: Government Efforts to Silence Students', 4 October 1993.

15 Interview with W. S. Rendra, 24 December 1990. Some material in this section appeared in Adam Schwarz, 'Opening Gambits', *Far Eastern Economic Review*, 24 January 1991, pp. 30–1.

16 Interview with Gunawan Mohamad, 21 December 1990.

17 Interview with Kwik Kian Gie, 10 January 1993.

18 Interview with Eros Djarot, 15 December 1990.

19 Interview with Adnan Buyung Nasution, 27 March 1993.

20 Interview with Mochtar Lubis, 20 December 1990.

21 A number of Indonesia's most prominent intellectuals and writers, including Pramoedya Ananta Toer, joined the Communist Party-linked People's Cultural Institute, or Lekra, in the early 1960s. Lekra became a powerful organ in pressuring Indonesian writers and artists to support the communists' political struggle. For an account of Pramoedya's role, see Margaret Scott, 'Waging War With Words', *Far Eastern Economic Review*, 9 August 1990, pp. 26–30. For a first-hand account of efforts by Indonesian intellectuals to resist Lekra's influence, see Gunawan Mohamad, 'The "Manikebu" Affair: Literature and Politics in the 1960s', *Prisma*, No. 46, 1989, pp. 70–88.

22 See Nono Anwar Makarim, 'The Indonesian Press: An Editor's Perspective', in *Political Power and Communications in Indonesia*, eds Karl Jackson and Lucian Pye, University of California Press, Berkeley, 1978.

23 David Hill, 'The Press in 'New Order' Indonesia: Entering the 1990s', Working Paper No. 1, Asia Research Centre, Murdoch University, October 1991, p. 4.

24 'Silakan Kritik Siapa Saja', *Forum Keadilan*, 15 April 1993.

25 'Not so impressive show', *Jakarta Post*, 27 June 1991.

26 Confidential interview, 28 January 1991.

27 From comments by Gunawan Mohamad to the Jakarta Foreign Correspondents Club, 4 September 1991.

28 'Final Word on Press', *Indonesia Business Weekly*, 10 December 1993.

29 Santi Soekanto, 'Be more circumspect, press told', *Jakarta Post*, 10 February 1993.
30 'Silakan Kritik Siapa Saja', *Forum Keadilan*, 15 April 1993.
31 Soekanto, 'Be more circumspect, press told'.
32 'Silakan Kritik Siapa Saja', *Forum Keadilan*, 15 April 1993.
33 *Tempo*, 22 June 1991.
34 Interview with Adnan Buyung Nasution, 27 March 1993.
35 Daniel Dhakidae, 'Language, Journalism, and Politics in Modern Indonesia', paper delivered to the Conference on Indonesian Democracy, 1950s and 1990s, Monash University, 17–20 December 1992.
36 Adam Schwarz, 'Commercial Break', *Far Eastern Economic Review*, 21 June 1990.
37 'Making Airwaves', *Indonesia Business Weekly*, 27 August 1993, pp. 3–9.
38 'Govt will revamp National Film Censorship Board', *Jakarta Post*, 28 April 1993.
39 Adam Schwarz, 'Licence Lament', *Far Eastern Economic Review*, 27 June 1991, p. 18.
40 Interview with Aristides Katoppo, 18 August 1993.
41 'Yogie against open debate on Golkar chairmanship', *Jakarta Post*, 26 April 1993.
42 See, for example, comments by the head of the Supreme Court Purwoto Gandasubrata as quoted in 'Chief Justice dismayed at disrespect of law', *Jakarta Post*, 6 February 1993.
43 'Sudomo: "Lho, yang Difitnah Itu Pak Harto" ', *Forum Keadilan*, 8 July 1993, pp. 90–1. I am grateful to Bill Liddle for the reference.
44 'Perlu Penyesuaian Seperempat Abad', *Prospek*, 3 April 1993, p. 27. Rahardjo's point was tragically driven home in September 1993 when army soldiers opened fire on peasants protesting the construction of a dam on Madura island, killing four of them. See 'Priok, Sampang, Apa lagi?', *Tempo*, 16 October 1993, pp. 29–40.
45 Interview with Adnan Buyung Nasution, 27 March 1993.
46 'Mereka Menyangka Saya Kiai', *Matra*, February 1992, p. 18. Cited in R. William Liddle, 'Improvising Political Cultural Change: Three Indonesian Cases', in *Indonesian Political Culture: Asking the Right Questions*, ed. James Schiller, Ohio University Center for Southeast Asian Studies, Athens, forthcoming.
47 US Department of State, 'Country Reports on Human Rights Practices for 1992', January 1993. See also Hamish McDonald, *Suharto's Indonesia*, Fontana Books, Blackburn, 1980, esp. pp. 216–31.
48 US Department of State, 'Country Reports'.
49 UN Economic and Social Council, 'Report of the Special Rapporteur, Mr. P. Kooijmans, pursuant to the Commission on Human Rights resolution 1991/38', 8 January 1992, pp. 17–8. A description of documents, purportedly drawn up by armed forces officers based in East Timor, which set out procedures for extracting forced confessions from captured rebels, is in Richard Tanter, 'The Totalitarian Ambition: Intelligence and Security Agencies in Indonesia', in *State and Civil Society in Indonesia*, ed. Arief Budiman, Centre of Southeast Asian Studies, Clayton, 1990, pp. 215–88.

50 See Amnesty International, 'Indonesia/East Timor: The Suppression of Dissent', London, July 1992; and Asia Watch, 'Indonesia: Continuing Human Rights Violations in Aceh', 19 June 1991.

51 Asia Watch, op. cit., p. 3. See also Elizabeth Pisani, 'Curfews and killings may perpetuate Indonesian rebellion', *Reuter,* 30 April 1991; and Amnesty International, 'Indonesia. "Shock Therapy": Restoring Order in Aceh, 1989–1993', London, 28 July 1993.

52 Interview with Major General Pramono, 1 July 1991. See Adam Schwarz, 'Deadly Suspicion', *Far Eastern Economic Review*, 25 July 1991, pp. 18–20.

53 See 'Remembering History in East Timor: The Trial of Xanana Gusmao and a Follow-up to the Dili Massacre', Asia Watch, New York, April 1993, p. 12. A full discussion of the anti-subversion law is in 'Broken Laws, Broken Bodies: Torture and the Right to Redress in Indonesia', Lawyers Committee for Human Rights, New York, February 1993.

54 Soeharto, *My Thoughts*, p. 336.

55 Daniel Lev, paper delivered to the International Seminar on Human Rights, Jakarta, 11 May 1993.

56 Department of Foreign Affairs, 'East Timor: Building for the Future', Jakarta, July 1992. See also 'Live and Let Live', *Far Eastern Economic Review*, 11 July 1991, pp. 12–13, which carries extracts of an interview with Foreign Minister Ali Alatas.

57 Soeharto, speech to the United Nations General Assembly, 24 September 1992.

58 Yuwono Sudarsono, paper delivered to the 'United States–Asia Parliamentary Development Conference', Jakarta, 6–7 April 1992.

59 Chris Schacht, 'Opening Address', in *Indonesia Assessment 1992: Political Perspectives on the 1990s*, eds Harold Crouch and Hal Hill, Research School of Pacific Studies, Canberra, 1992, pp. 9–10.

60 See, for example, 'Hak Asasi di Timtim Masih Diartikan Hak Memberontak', *Kompas*, 2 March 1992. The title means: 'Human rights in East Timor still means the right to struggle'.

61 Daniel Lev, paper delivered to the International Seminar on Human Rights, Jakarta, 11 May 1993.

62 See Jeremy Wagstaff, 'Indonesia attacks overseas activists, journalists', *Reuter*, 20 January 1994.

63 Yuwono Sudarsono, paper delivered to the 'United States–Asia Parliamentary Development Conference', Jakarta, 6–7 April 1992. See also 'Scholar sees rights issue as economic tool of West', *Jakarta Post*, 27 January 1994.

64 Daniel Lev, paper delivered to the International Seminar on Human Rights, Jakarta, 11 May 1993.

65 Sidney Jones, 'Asians Deserve Their Rights, Like Everyone Else', *International Herald Tribune*, 21 April 1993.

66 ibid.

67 Almost a year later, 25 Indonesians were appointed to Indonesia's first Human Rights Commission. While some respected non-governmental figures were named to the commission, none of Indonesia's leading human rights activists were included. See 'A Few Good Men (and Women)', *Indonesia Business Weekly*, 17 December 1993.

68 'Pangab: Komunis Generasi IV Manfaatkan Isu Hak Asasi Manusia dan Demokratisasi', *Kompas*, 17 November 1992. See also 'Ancaman Disintegrasi Sudah Mulai Muncul', *Republika*, 22 February 1993.
69 'VP's Statement Stirs Political Cauldron', *Indonesia Business Weekly*, 10 September 1993, pp. 10–11.
70 Nasution, *The Aspiration for Constitutional Government*, pp. 160–1.
71 From a presentation by Gunawan Mohamad to the Centre for Human Rights Studies, Jakarta, 25 July 1992.
72 Interview with Jusuf Wanandi, 15 July 1992.
73 Interview with Yuwono Sudarsono, 29 July 1992. See also, Yuwono Sudarsono, 'The future of the Non-Aligned Movement', a research paper prepared for the Department of Foreign Affairs, July 1992.
74 Interview with State Secretary Murdiono, 20 December 1991.
75 See Adam Schwarz, 'Tilting at Windmills', *Far Eastern Economic Review*, 9 April 1992.
76 From an open letter circulated in Jakarta by Pramoedya Ananta Toer on 7 December 1992, three days ahead of Human Rights Day. The letter, not published in Indonesia, was printed in *The New York Times* on 10 December 1992.
77 From a presentation by Taufik Abdullah to a seminar hosted by the Indonesian Association of Political Scientists, Jakarta, 25 January 1994.
78 Interviews with Mulya Lubis, 1 September 1992 and 5 March 1992.
79 T. Mulya Lubis, paper delivered to the International Seminar on Human Rights, Jakarta, 11 May 1993.
80 Interview with State Secretary Murdiono, 20 December 1991.
81 Interview with Marzuki Darusman, 10 December 1991.
82 For a summary of charges brought by US labour groups against Indonesia, see Asia Watch, 'Indonesia: Charges and rebuttals over labour rights practices', New York, 23 January 1993.
83 'Some Tripartite', *Indonesian Observer*, 27 August 1991.
84 See Adam Schwarz, 'Pressures of Work', *Far Eastern Economic Review*, 20 June 1991, pp. 14–16. The Asian–American Free Labour Institute has published several reports critical of the treatment of Indonesian workers by the American sport shoe manufacturers Nike and Reebok. For a summary of those complaints, see Jeffrey Ballinger, 'The new free-trade heel: Nike's profits jump on the backs of Asian workers', *Harper's*, August 1992, pp. 46–7; and Peter Goodman, 'Plain and Simple: Reebok, Nike, and Levi Strauss on the prowl for cheap labour in Indonesia', *The Progressive*, June 1993.
85 Although physical violence against labour activists is not common in Indonesia, it is not unheard of. In May 1993, a young activist, Marsinah, was raped, tortured and killed after leading a strike for better working conditions at the watch factory where she worked in Surabaya, East Java. Labour organisers accused the government of trying to cover up the case and alleged that a local military commander had taken part in the killing. See Goenawan Mohamad, 'In Rural Java, Death Comes to a Fighter and a Dreamer', *International Herald Tribune*, 13 January 1994; and 'Indonesian officer implicated in activist murder', *Reuter*, 5 November 1993.

86 Elizabeth Pisani, 'Indonesian labour leader disappears, believed arrested', *Reuter*, 4 June 1991.

87 Margot Cohen, 'Union of Problems', *Far Eastern Economic Review*, 26 August 1993, pp. 23–4.

88 Interview with Cosmas Batubara, 12 April 1991.

89 'Govt insists on single trade union movement', *Jakarta Post*, 3 September 1993.

90 For example, in September 1993, the government reconverted the SPSI into a federated union housing other, smaller and industry-specific unions, a structure similar to that used by SPSI's predecessor organisation from 1973–85.

91 A lengthy profile of the Indonesian labour force can be found in 'Buruh Kita', *Tempo*, 8 June 1991, pp. 21–30; and 'Labour trends in Indonesia', published by the American Embassy in Jakarta, 1989, pp. 1–42.

92 For example, in January 1994 one of Indonesia's two independent unions filed a formal complaint with the International Labour Organisation, alleging government harassment of its members. See Jeremy Wagstaff, 'Indonesian trade union challenges government', *Reuter*, 25 January 1994.

93 'Goenawan, Kayam address new human rights group', *Jakarta Post*, 27 July 1992.

94 From comments by Gunawan Mohamad to the Jakarta Foreign Correspondents Club, 4 September 1991.

95 Quoted in 'All layers of Indonesian society are haunted with common fears', *Jakarta Post*, 6 January 1993.

96 David Bourchier, 'Pada masa liberal timbul semacam anarki: the 1950s in the New Order ideology and politics', paper delivered to the Conference on Indonesian Democracy, 1950s and 1990s, Monash University, 17–20 December 1992, p. 12. Ariel Heryanto, a lecturer at the Satya Wacana Christian University, makes a similar point in 'Why should student activists be branded "un-Indonesian"?', *Jakarta Post*, 12 January 1994.

Chapter 10 A democratic future?

1 Bertrand Russell, *A History of Western Philosophy*, Simon & Schuster, New York, 1945, p. 107.

2 Lee Kuan Yew, speech to the Philippine Business Conference, 18 November 1992. Lee is the senior minister of Singapore.

3 Interview with Sri Bintang Pamungkas, a member of the United Development Party, 30 March 1993.

4 Ben Anderson, 'Last Days of Indonesia's Suharto?', *Southeast Asia Chronicle*, No. 63, 1978, p. 16.

5 Suryadi, comments to the Jakarta Foreign Correspondents Club, 19 February 1992.

6 Pandaya, 'PDI leadership meeting marred by unruly protest', *Jakarta Post*, 12 January 1993.

7 'The Awakening', *Jakarta Post*, 8 March 1993.

8 'PDI drops demand for electoral reforms', *Jakarta Post*, 8 March 1993.

9 Confidential interviews, three Indonesian Democratic Party delegates, August 1993.

10 Interview with Laksamana Sukardi, 29 August 1993.

11 John McBeth, 'Orders Awaited', *Far Eastern Economic Review*, 16 December 1993; and Pandaya and Lewa Pardomuan, 'PDI caretakers leave congress, seek govt aid', *Jakarta Post,* 8 December 1993.

12 Interview with Kwik Kian Gie, 2 January 1994. See also Winfred Hutabarat, 'ABRI Solves PDI Problem', *Indonesia Business Weekly*, 31 December 1993.

13 Benedict Anderson, 'East Timor and Indonesia: Some Implications', paper delivered to the Social Science Research Council Workshop on East Timor, Washington, DC, 25–26 April 1991.

14 Benedict Anderson, 'Elections and Democratisation in Southeast Asia: Thailand, the Philippines and Indonesia', a lecture broadcast on the *Indian Pacific* program of the Australia Broadcasting Corporation, August 1992. The lecture was published in *ABC Radio 24 Hours*, September 1992.

15 Marsillam Simanjuntak, 'Democratization in the 90s: Coming to Terms with Gradualism?' paper delivered at the Conference on Indonesian Democracy, 1950s and 1990s, Monash University, 17–20 December 1992.

16 See Michael Vatikiotis, 'Debate and Deference', *Far Eastern Economic Review*, 10 November 1988.

17 Interview with General (ret.) Soemitro, 24 May 1989.

18 Interview with Yuwono Sudarsono, 12 September 1991.

19 Interview with Marzuki Darusman, 13 September 1991. See also Adam Schwarz, 'President's Pleasure', *Far Eastern Economic Review*, 26 September 1991.

20 Interviews with Rachmat Witoelar, 16 May 1991 and 1 April 1992.

21 Rachmat Witoelar, comments to the Jakarta Foreign Correspondents Club, 21 May 1992.

22 See John McBeth, 'Party Patron', *Far Eastern Economic Review*, 4 November 1993; and Adam Schwarz, 'Suharto's Ever-Tightening Hand', *Asian Wall Street Journal*, 27 October 1993.

23 Interview with Marzuki Darusman, 2 January 1994. See also Winfred Hutabarat, 'Drama with Predictable Ending', *Indonesia Business Weekly*, 29 October 1993.

24 Interview with Theo Sambuaga, 6 July 1989.

25 See 'Pendapat Wakil Rakyat', *Tempo*, 6 March 1993, pp. 13–22.

26 Pandaya, 'Pessimists say nothing will come of general session', *Jakarta Post*, 1 March 1993.

27 'Kunarto's remark infuriates legislators', *Jakarta Post*, 13 April 1993.

28 See Samuel Huntington, *Political Order in Changing Societies*, Yale University Press, New Haven, 1968; Samuel Huntington, 'Will More Countries Become Democratic?' *Political Science Quarterly*, Vol. 99, No. 2, Summer 1984, pp. 193–218; and Michael Leifer, 'Uncertainty in Indonesia', *World Policy Journal*, Winter 1990–91, pp. 137–57.

29 See Harold Crouch, 'Indonesia: The Rise or Fall of Suharto's Generals', *Third World Quarterly*, Vol. 10, No. 1, 1988, pp. 160–75.

30 Michael Vatikiotis, 'Echoes From the Grave', *Far Eastern Economic Review*, 18 January 1990, p. 26.

31 See 'Mauquf Enam Kriteria Amien', *Tempo*, 25 December 1993; 'RI must set up smooth process of succession', *Jakarta Post*, 22 December 1993; and 'Indonesia urged to shun talk of Suharto successor', *Reuter*, 29 December 1993.

32 See 'To the End of Time', *Indonesia Business Weekly*, 9 November 1992.

33 The point is drawn from Richard Robison, 'Indonesia: Tensions in State and Regime', in *Southeast Asia in the 1990s: Authoritarianism, Democracy & Capitalism*, eds Kevin Hewison, Richard Robison and Garry Rodan, Allen & Unwin, Sydney, 1993.

34 The political implications of centre-region tensions are discussed in R. William Liddle, 'Indonesia's Democratic Past and Future', *Comparative Politics*, Vol. 24, No. 4, July 1992.

35 Interview with Hasnan Habib, 2 April 1993. For an account of intra-military dissension prior to 1983, see David Jenkins, *Suharto and his Generals: Indonesian Military Politics 1975–1983*, Cornell Modern Indonesia Project, Ithaca, 1984.

36 Richard Robison, 'After the Gold Rush: the Politics of Economic Restructuring in Indonesia in the 1980s', in *Southeast Asia in the 1980s: The Politics of Economic Crisis*, eds Richard Robison, Kevin Hewison and Richard Higgott, Allen & Unwin, Sydney, 1987.

37 Days after the Golkar congress closed, Major General Sembiring Meliala, an active duty officer representing Abri in the parliament, lashed out at Soeharto for engineering the election of Information Minister Harmoko as party chairman and putting Minister for Research and Technology Habibie in charge of selecting the party's new executive board. Referring to Harmoko and Habibie, Sembiring said that 'without President Soeharto's mandate they are nothing. When the president is no longer in power they will vanish.' He added that the military remains committed to playing the lead role in finding a successor to Soeharto. 'The people want [a president] from the military. Anyone without military support cannot make it.' Subsequently, a military spokesman hastened to explain that Sembiring's comment reflected his personal view only. See '1000 Orang DPR/MPR jangan Dianggap Togog', *Detik*, 27 October–2 November, 1993; Simon Sinaga, 'Indonesia's army insists it will pick next president', *Reuter*, 27 October 1993; and 'General's voice not ABRI's view', *Jakarta Post*, 1 November 1993.

38 See Harold Crouch, 'Soeharto's Balancing Act', *The Independent Monthly*, June 1993, p. 19.

39 For a recent account of military changes, see 'Current Data on the Indonesian Military Elite, January 1, 1993–April 3, 1993', *Indonesia* 55, April 1993, pp. 177–98. Another round of house-cleaning of senior military officers occurred in January 1994. See 'ABRI Shakeup More Than Skin Deep', *Indonesia Business Weekly*, 28 January 1994.

40 Interviews with Hasnan Habib, 25 January 1991 and 2 April 1992; interview with Sayidiman Suryohadiproyo, 5 August 1991.

41 Interview with Lukman Soetrisno, 27 March 1992.

42 See 'Menyorot Mata dan Telinga', *Tempo*, 22 January 1994, pp. 21–7.

43 Confidential interviews with government officials and business executives, March 1993.

44 Interview with Arief Budiman, 14 March 1993; interview with Sri Bintang Pamungkas, 30 March 1993.
45 Interview with Marzuki Darusman, 10 March 1993.
46 Leifer, 'Uncertainty in Indonesia', p. 151.
47 Confidential interview, 10 February 1994.
48 Interview with Hasnan Habib, 19 December 1991. See also Margot Cohen, 'Marching to a Crossroads', *Far Eastern Economic Review*, 3 September 1992. In addition to discouraging contacts with civilian intellectuals, Murdani also tried to prevent younger officers from mixing too freely with their counterparts in Western militaries. Each year, the four US military academies offer scholarships to cadets from friendly nations, an opportunity taken advantage of by all ASEAN nations except Indonesia. While Abri does allow middle-level officers to participate in combat training exercises in the US, Murdani was not prepared to expose Indonesian cadets to foreign influences at an early stage in their careers.
49 'Try remains low-key about his candidacy', *Jakarta Post*, 2 February 1993. See also 'Masalah Hak Asasi Manusia Harus Tetap Mengacu Kepada Pancasila', *Suara Pembaruan*, 6 December 1992.
50 Confidential interviews, 16 December 1991 and 8 July 1992.
51 Interview with Aristides Katoppo, 6 March 1993.
52 Jusuf Wanandi, 'Political Development and National Stability', in *Indonesia Assessment, 1992: Political Perspectives on the 1990s*, eds Harold Crouch and Hal Hill, Research School of Pacific Studies, Canberra, 1992, p. 100; and interview with Jusuf Wanandi, 8 March 1993.
53 Interview with Nasir Tamara, 12 March 1993.
54 Interview with Arief Budiman, 14 March 1993.
55 'Soeharto re-elected again', *Jakarta Post*, 11 March 1993.
56 Soeharto, 'Speech to the House of Representatives', 16 August 1993.
57 Interview with Kwik Kian Gie, 29 August 1993.
58 Interview with Sri Bintang Pamungkas, 30 March 1993.
59 Soeharto, 'Accountability Address', delivered at the General Session of the People's Consultative Assembly, 1 March 1993.
60 Marsillam Simanjuntak, 'Democratization in the 90s'.
61 Guillermo O'Donnell and Philippe Schmitter, *Transitions from Authoritarian Rule: Tentative Conclusions about Uncertain Democracies*, The Johns Hopkins University Press, Baltimore, 1986, p. 7. See also Robert Dahl, *Polyarchy: Participation and Opposition*, Yale University Press, New Haven, 1971; and Dankwart Rustow, 'Transitions to Democracy: Toward a Dynamic Model' *Comparative Politics*, No. 2, 1970.
62 O'Donnell and Schmitter, 'Transitions from Authoritarian Rule', pp. 7–8.
63 Interview with Abdurrahman Wahid, 9 July 1992.
64 See Jamie Mackie, 'Indonesia: Economic Growth and Depoliticization', in *Driven by Growth: Political Change in the Asia–Pacific Region*, ed. James Morley, M. E. Sharpe, Armonk, 1993.
65 The point is discussed more fully in Harold Crouch and James Morley, 'The Dynamics of Political Change', in *Driven by Growth*, ed. Morley, pp. 277–310. The authors note that higher wealth does not always lead to

demands for political pluralism. One prominent exception in Asia is the case of Singapore.

66 Robison, 'Tensions in State'.
67 Richard Robison, 'Indonesia: An Autonomous Domain of Social Power?', *The Pacific Review*, Vol. 5, No. 4, 1992, p. 344.
68 ibid., p. 345.
69 Interview with Fadel Muhammad, 3 September 1991. For a fuller discussion of the *pribumi* view of how democratisation might affect business growth, see Robison, 'Tensions in State'.
70 Wanandi, 'Political Development', pp. 104–5.
71 Robison, 'An Autonomous Domain', p. 342.
72 Interview with Admiral Sudomo, 8 May 1992.
73 Interview with General Soemitro, 16 December 1991.
74 'RI has to boost democratization to stay honourable', *Jakarta Post*, 24 December 1991.
75 Hasnan Habib, 'The Role of the Armed Forces in Indonesia's Future Political Development', in *Indonesia Assessment, 1992*, p. 94.
76 Interview with Hasnan Habib, 2 April 1993.
77 'Dulu Dibenci, Kini Dipuji', *Forum Keadilan*, 24 June 1993.
78 See the interview with Rudini in 'Saya Bisa Panas Dingin', *Matra*, March 1993, pp. 10–20.
79 The point is discussed in more detail in Mackie, 'Economic Growth and Depoliticization'.
80 O'Donnell and Schmitter, *Transitions from Authoritarian Rule*, p. 10.
81 Interview with Marzuki Darusman, 10 March 1993.
82 Interview with Hasnan Habib, 2 April 1993.
83 Confidential interview, 31 March 1993. See also R. William Liddle, 'The Complex Politics of Succession in Indonesia', *Asian Wall Street Journal*, 15 September 1992.
84 'Jangan Mengandalkan Aliansa Lama', *Eksekutif*, August 1992, pp. 45–6. See also R. William Liddle, 'Can All Good Things Go Together? Democracy, Growth, and Unity in Post-Soeharto Indonesia', paper delivered to the Conference on Indonesian Democracy, 1950s and 1990s, Monash University, 17–20 December 1992.
85 O'Donnell and Schmitter, *Transitions from Authoritarian Rule*, p. 48.
86 Interview with Adnan Buyung Nasution, 27 March 1993.
87 Arief Budiman, 'Indonesian Politics in the 1990s', in *Indonesia Assessment, 1992*, eds Crouch and Hill, p. 132.
88 ibid., p. 132; and interview with Arief Budiman, 14 March 1993.
89 Marsillam Simanjuntak, 'Democratization in the 90's'.
90 Interview with Sri Bintang Pamungkas, 22 July 1992.
91 'Dual Function to ensure Abri acts constitutionally' *Jakarta Post*, 23 July 1992.
92 Interview with Sri Bintang Pamungkas, 30 March 1993.
93 Interview with Adnan Buyung Nasution, 27 March 1993.
94 See 'Public told to watch out for liberal-minded intellectuals', *Jakarta Post*, 14 January 1994; and 'Feisal warns of attempts at subversion', *Jakarta Post*, 24 December 1993.

95 Tommy Thong-Bee Koh, 'This Way or That, Get On With Good Government', *International Herald Tribune*, 6 May 1993. Koh does not himself agree with the 'Asian' view of democracy as he has defined it. There are, he noted, 'democratic governments that have succeeded in promoting economic development and others that have failed'.
96 Interview with Murdiono, 28 January 1991.
97 'Moerdani lashes out at West for interfering in RI affairs', *Jakarta Post*, 20 October 1992.
98 Yuwono Sudarsono, paper delivered to the 'United States–Asia Parliamentary Development Conference', Jakarta, 6–7 April 1992.
99 Harold Crouch, 'Democratic Prospects in Indonesia', paper delivered to the Conference on Indonesian Democracy, 1950s and 1990s, Monash University, 17–20 December 1992. See also O'Donnell and Schmitter, *Transitions from Authoritarian Rule*, esp. p. 19; and Harold Crouch, 'Military–Civilian Relations in Indonesia in the Late Soeharto Era', *The Pacific Review*, Vol. 1, No. 4, 1988.

Chapter 11   The fall of Soeharto

1 Interview, Salim Said, 27 August 1998.
2 Interview, Sarwono Kusumaatmadja, 10 March 1998.
3 The account of Mursjid's meeting with Soeharto on the evening of 20 May 1998 is based on a series of interviews in June through September 1998 with, among others, Amien Rais, Nurcholish Madjid, Umar Juoro, Dewi Fortuna Anwar and Yusril Izha Mahendra.
4 World Bank, 'Indonesia: Sustaining High Growth with Equity', 30 May 1997.
5 World Bank, 'Indonesia: Dimensions of Growth', 1 May 1996.
6 Quoted in Adam Schwarz, 'Indonesia after Suharto', *Foreign Affairs*, July/August 1997.
7 Interview with Sarwono Kusumaatmadja, 10 March 1998.
8 Adam Schwarz and Mark Clifford, 'Naval Manoevres', *Far Eastern Economic Review*, 13 May 1993.
9 Raphael Pura, 'Suharto Lawyers Ask Court to Reject Suit over Decree', *Asian Wall Street Journal*, 1 November 1994.
10 The estimate comes from an undated study undertaken by the Prasetya Mulya Graduate School of Management in Jakarta.
11 Adam Schwarz, 'Bank Scandal Throws Indonesia off Balance', *Asian Wall Street Journal*, 13 April 1994. See also Ryaas Rasyid, 'Indonesia: Preparing for Post-Soeharto Rule and its Impact on Democratization', *Southeast Asian Affairs, 1995*, Institute of Southeast Asian Studies, Singapore, 1995. In 1996 Tansil escaped from Cipinang prison in Jakarta. Some believe he fled the country, others that he was killed. In 1998 it was alleged Tansil had moved to China and opened a brewery under an assumed name. See Greg Earl, 'Fugitive Indonesian Swindler Found Running China Brewery', *Australian Financial Review*, 30 December 1998.
12 See the annual surveys on corruption in Asia conducted by the Hong Kong-based Political and Economic Risk Consultancy.

13 For a partial listing of Soeharto family assets, see George Aditjondro, 'The Swiss Business Links of the Suharto & Habibie Oligarchy of Indonesia', report prepared for the Berne Declaration, 22 July 1998.

14 John McBeth, 'The Battle for Busang', *Far Eastern Economic Review*, 19 December 1996.

15 See Michael Shari with Edith Hill Updike, 'Dad, Can I Have the Keys to Indonesia's Auto Industry', *Business Week*, 18 November 1996; Jay Solomon, 'EU Calls National Car Plan by Jakarta "Discriminatory"', *Asian Wall Street Journal*, 24 April 1996; and Eduardo Lachica, 'U.S. Criticizes Indonesia for National Car Program', *Asian Wall Street Journal*, 8 May 1996.

16 Richard Borsuk, 'Storm Brews in Bali over Beer Levy', *Asian Wall Street Journal*, 26 January 1996. In 1997 Ari was back for another try, this time on school shoes. See Richard Borsuk, 'Suharto Halts Grandson's Plan for a School Shoe Monopoly', *Asian Wall Street Journal*, 29 August 1997.

17 World Bank, 'Dimensions of Growth', p. 55.

18 'Telecommunications Dynamics', in *Asian Intelligence*, published by the Political and Economic Risk Consultancy, 2 October 1996.

19 Interview, Laksamana Sukardi, 22 July 1996.

20 'Indonesia Sacks Airline Director', *Reuter*, 24 October 1995.

21 Quoted in Margaret Scott, 'Indonesia Reborn?', *New York Review of Books*, 13 August 1998.

22 Ariel Heryanto, 'Indonesia: Towards the Final Countdown?', *Southeast Asian Affairs, 1997*, Institute for Southeast Asian Studies, Singapore, 1997, p. 109.

23 Richard Robison, 'Economic and Political Liberalisation in Southeast Asia: Inexorable Force or Red Herring?', paper delivered to the Southern California Workshop on Political and Economic Liberalization at the University of Southern California, 21 March 1995.

24 See Jeffrey Winters, 'World Bank Must Face the Corruption Music', *Jakarta Post*, 23 September 1998; and Keith Loveard, 'The Dark Side of Prosperity: A World Bank Critic Alleges Waste and Graft', *Asiaweek*, 11 August 1997.

25 The leaked World Bank memorandum was titled: 'Summary of RSI Staff Views Regarding the Problem of "Leakage" from World Bank Project Budgets'. It was distributed on the Internet beginning late August 1998. Bank officials privately confirmed the document was genuine. See also Glenn Simpson, 'World Bank Memo Depicts Diverted Funds in Jakarta', *Wall Street Journal*, 19 August 1998.

26 Confidential interview with World Bank official, 4 September 1998.

27 Confidential interview with World Bank official, 15 July 1998.

28 See David Sanger, 'World Bank Beats Breast for Failures in Indonesia', *New York Times*, 11 February 1999.

29 See Rizal Ramli & Jonathan Pincus, 'Indonesia: From Showcase to Basketcase', *Cambridge Journal of Economics*, vol. 22, no. 6, November 1998, pp. 723–34. A good review of Indonesia's financial sector reform is in David C. Cole & Betty F. Slade, *Building a Modern Financial System: The Indonesian Experience*, Cambridge University Press, Cambridge, 1996.

30 Interview, Amien Rais, 25 February 1998

31 'Ma'rie Muhammad: The Bigger they Are, the Bigger they Fall', *Kontan*,

14 September 1998. An English translation of the interview was carried in *Castle's Insight Indonesia*, vol. 1, no. 3, 12 October 1998.

32 Adam Schwarz, 'Suharto's Ever-Tightening Hand', *Asian Wall Street Journal*, 27 October 1993.

33 After assuming the presidency in 1998, Habibie denied that he had pushed for the closing of the publications. If so, he made no mention of his opposition at the time they were closed.

34 Goenawan Mohamad, 'Indonesia's Prize Scars', *Far Eastern Economic Review*, 28 September 1995; and Adam Schwarz, 'In Indonesia, Freedom Hope is Dim', *Nieman Reports*, vol. XLIX, no. 4, Winter 1995. For a good review of the Indonesian media, see David Hill, 'The Press in New Order Indonesia', Asia Paper 4, University of Western Australia Press, 1994. For a profile of Goenawan, see Louise Williams, 'How Being Banned Set Free the Man in Sandals', *Sydney Morning Herald*, 7 June 1997.

35 The Muslim scholar Nurcholish Madjid was one of the members of KIPP who was pressured to distance himself from the election monitoring project. Nurcholish says he was warned by Soeharto's son-in-law, Lieutenant General Prabowo Subianto, to resign from KIPP. Interview, Nurcholish Madjid, 31 August 1998.

36 'Jakarta Military Slams Polls-Watchdog', *Reuter*, 10 March 1996. In late 1998, with Feisal Tandjung as his senior minister for political and security affairs, President Habibie agreed that independent teams should be allowed to monitor the parliamentary elections scheduled for June 1999. Feisal, apparently having reread the 1945 Constitution, did not object. See 'Independent Election Committee Promised', *Jakarta Post*, 9 December 1998.

37 'Indonesia: Journalists' Sentences Increased as Media Restrictions Continue', report by Amnesty International, December 1995. Journalists involved in *Forum Wartawan* say the arrest of the three AJI journalists was prompted by stories alleging that Harmoko demanded ownership shares in several dozen publications for himself and his relatives in exchange for issuing publishing permits. See Margot Cohen, 'My Word', *Far Eastern Economic Review*, 14 September 1995.

38 'Indonesian Soldiers Join Internet to Fight "Bad" Information', *Bangkok Post*, 20 October 1995.

39 'Rare Presidential Fit of Anger', *Indonesia Business Weekly*, 24 April 1995.

40 Richard Borsuk, 'Suharto's Trip Heightens Uncertainty', *Asian Wall Street Journal*, 8 July 1996.

41 Interview, Laksamana Sukardi, 22 July 1996.

42 See M. C. Ricklefs, *A History of Modern Indonesia Since c. 1300*, Stanford University Press, Stanford, CA, 2nd edn, 1993. The People's Democratic Front was wiped out after lending its support to the bloody uprising in Madiun, East Java, in September 1948.

43 Richard Borsuk, 'Crackdown Sparks Question: What Is Suharto Up to Now?', *Asian Wall Street Journal*, 16 August 1996. For more details of the government's response to the July 1996 riots, see 'Indonesia. Arrests, Torture and Intimidation: The Government's Response to its Critics', report by Amnesty International, 27 November 1996.

44 A good overview of the student movement in the mid-1990s is Edward

Aspinall, 'Intra-Elite Conflict and Civilian Dissent in Indonesia: The Case of Students', paper delivered at the Asian Studies Association of Australia Biennial Conference, Perth, 13–16 July 1994.

45 Adam Schwarz, 'Suharto Can't Turn Back the Clock', *Asian Wall Street Journal*, 16 August 1996.

46 Harold Crouch, 'Suharto's Splendid Isolation', *Asian Wall Street Journal*, 2 August 1996.

47 Heryanto, 'Towards the Final Countdown?'.

48 See Stanley et al., eds, *Saya Musuh Politik Soeharto* [I am a Political Enemy of Soeharto], Pijar Indonesia, Jakarta, 1996.

49 Heryanto, 'Towards the Final Countdown?', p. 118.

50 ibid. See also Richard Borsuk, 'Indonesia Court Rejects Closing of Magazine', *Asian Wall Street Journal*, 4 May 1995. Another case of judicial independence was the support of several judges for the election monitoring team, KIPP, set up in 1996.

51 Jim Della-Giacoma, 'Indonesia's Megawati Left off Election Roll', *Reuter*, 16 September 1996.

52 Interview, Sarwono Kusumaatmadja, 10 March 1998.

53 A good survey of Indonesia's foreign policy is in Dewi Fortuna Anwar, *Indonesia in ASEAN: Foreign Policy and Regionalism*, Institute of Southeast Asian Studies, Singapore, 1994.

54 Nicola Malbeck, 'Indonesia Minister Raps "Adventurist" Nobel Winner', *Reuter*, 11 October 1996.

55 See Nigel Holloway & John McBeth, 'Storm Clouds', *Far Eastern Economic Review*, 20 February 1997.

56 'Asiaweek Roundtable: Crisis-Time Lessons', *Asiaweek*, 6 November 1998. For a lengthy account of the 'Asian Values' debate, see David Hitchcock, 'Asian Values and the United States: How Much Conflict?', Center for Strategic and International Studies, Washington, DC, 1994.

57 Literally, *santri* means student, but it is more commonly translated as pious or devout.

58 This section is drawn from Adam Schwarz, 'Introduction: The Politics of Post-Suharto Indonesia', in *The Politics of Post-Suharto Indonesia*, eds Adam Schwarz & Jonathan Paris, Council on Foreign Relations, New York, 1999.

59 See Robert Hefner, 'Islamization and Democratization in Indonesia', in *Islam in an Era of Nation States*, eds Robert Hefner & Patricia Horvatich, University of Hawaii Press, Honolulu, 1997. For a comparative analysis of same dynamic, see Olivier Roy, *The Failure of Political Islam*, trans. Carol Volk, Harvard University Press, Cambridge, MA, 1994.

60 Robert Hefner, 'Islam and Nation in the Post-Suharto Era', in *The Politics of Post-Suharto Indonesia*, eds Schwarz & Paris.

61 See Robert Hefner, 'Islam, Class, and Civil Society: ICMI and the Struggle for the Indonesian Middle Class', *Indonesia*, no. 56, October 1993.

62 Shortly after the July 1996 riots, ICMI Secretary General Adi Sasono assailed Megawati for risking 'scorched-earth politics'. Soeharto, he said, 'is still the effective power and he determines the pace of change'. Some Muslims close to Wahid believe a handful of more militant ICMI members

cooperated with the government in plotting Megawati's overthrow. They say ICMI hard-liners considered Megawati too *abangan* and too much a threat to Habibie, charges that would recur in late 1998. See Hefner, 'Islam and Nation'.

63 ibid. See also Scott, 'Indonesia Reborn?'.

64 Interview, Amien Rais, 30 April 1998.

65 ibid.

66 Interview, Amien Rais, 25 February 1998.

67 See Scott, 'Indonesia Reborn?', for a fuller discussion of Rais' thinking.

68 An account of the meeting between Soeharto and Habibie is in John McBeth, 'Line in the Sand', *Far Eastern Economic Review*, 27 March 1997.

69 Interview, Abdurrahman Wahid, 27 August 1998.

70 Scott, 'Indonesia Reborn?'.

71 William Liddle, 'Indonesia's Unexpected Failure of Leadership', in *The Politics of Post-Suharto Indonesia*, eds Schwarz & Paris. See also Robert Hefner, 'Print Islam: Mass Media and Ideological Rivalries among Indonesian Muslims', *Indonesia*, no. 64, October 1997.

72 Interview, Ahmad Soemargono, 26 August 1998.

73 Interview, Fadli Zon, 12 March 1998.

74 See John McBeth, 'Social Dynamite', *Far Eastern Economic Review*, 15 February 1996.

75 Quoted in Schwarz, 'Indonesia after Suharto'.

76 'Nearly 500 Churches Damaged in Indonesia in Past Five Years', *Agence France Press*, 19 November 1998. A good account of the religious and ethnic violence occurring in 1996 is in John McBeth & Margot Cohen, 'Tinderbox', *Far Eastern Economic Review*, 9 January 1997.

77 See Hefner, 'Islam and Nation'.

78 Interview, Abdurrahman Wahid, 27 August 1998. See also Ryaas Rasyid, 'Indonesia: Preparing for Post-Soeharto Rule and its Impact of Democratization'; and Greg Fealy, 'The 1994 NU Congress and Aftermath: Abdurrahman Wahid, Suksesi, and the Battle for Control of NU', in *Nahdlatul Ulama, Traditional Islam and Modernity in Indonesia*, eds Greg Barton & Greg Fealy, Monash University, Melbourne, 1996.

79 Interview, Abdurrahman Wahid, 27 August 1998.

80 Interview, Marsillam Simanjuntak, 1 September 1998.

81 Interview, Benny Murdani, 3 September 1998.

82 ibid. See also Salim Said, 'Suharto's Armed Forces: Building a Power Base in New Order Indonesia, 1966–1998', *Asian Survey*, vol. 38, no. 6, June 1998.

83 Takashi Shiraishi, 'The Indonesian Military in Politics', in *The Politics of Post-Suharto Indonesia*, eds Schwarz & Paris. See also John Haseman, 'Indonesia and ABRI: Challenges for the Future', *Southeast Asian Affairs, 1997*, Institute of Southeast Asian Studies, Singapore, 1997.

84 See Douglas Kammen, 'Military Politics and Kekaryaan in Post-Soeharto Indonesia', paper delivered at the conference 'Indonesia after Suharto', University of Auckland, 9–10 September 1998.

85 ibid.

86 Shiraishi, 'The Indonesian Military'. See also John McBeth, 'New Wave, Old Ties', *Far Eastern Economic Review*, 14 August 1997.

87 Interview, Hasnan Habib, 31 August 1998; interview, Benny Murdani, 19 July 1996.

88 See Schwarz, 'Introduction' and Shiraishi, 'The Indonesian Military'.

89 Interview, Sarwono Kusumaatmadja, 10 March 1998; and interviews, Amien Rais, 30 April 1998 and 30 August 1998. The defence analyst was quoted in Cindy Shiner, 'Suharto's Once Powerful Son-in-Law under Fire', *Washington Post*, 12 August 1998.

90 Interview, Salim Said, 27 August 1998.

91 Interview, Benny Murdani, 3 September 1998.

92 Quoted in Scott, 'Indonesia Reborn?'.

93 See Shiraishi, 'The Indonesian Military', for more details. A minority view disputes Syafrie's close connection with Prabowo. Says Salim Said, a military analyst, 'Syafrie is from the same [military academy] class as Prabowo but he is his own man. Syafrie says he didn't know what Prabowo was doing'. Interview, Salim Said, 27 August 1998.

94 Interview, Fadli Zon, 12 March 1998.

95 Interview, Emil Salim, 27 October 1998. See also John McBeth, 'Action Faction: Indonesia's Economic Crisis Team Pushes Reform', *Far Eastern Economic Review*, 4 September 1997.

96 Richard Borsuk & I Made Sentana, 'Indonesia Ends Most Limits on Ownership by Foreigners', *AP-Dow Jones News Service*, 5 September 1997; and Richard Borsuk, 'Indonesia Keeps Economy Even by Postponing Large Projects', *Asian Wall Street Journal*, 17 September 1997.

97 John McBeth, 'El Nino Gets Blamed, but Indonesia Inertia is Equally Responsible for the Fires', *Far Eastern Economic Review*, 9 October 1997; and Margot Cohen, 'Unlucky Country', *Far Eastern Economic Review*, 25 December 1997.

98 For a lengthy treatment of the IMF's programs for Indonesia, see John Bresnan, 'The United States, the IMF and the Indonesian Financial Crisis', in *The Politics of Post-Suharto Indonesia*, eds Schwarz & Paris.

99 This section is drawn from Schwarz, 'Introduction'. For an excellent overview of the background to Indonesia's financial crisis, see Kevin Evans, 'The Economy: From Transition to Transformation', paper delivered at the Indonesia Update Conference, Australia National University, 25 September 1998. See also Anwar Nasution, 'Note on the Meltdown of the Indonesian Economy: Causes, Impacts and Responses', paper delivered at the conference 'Indonesia after Suharto', University of Auckland, 9–10 September 1998.

100 See Bresnan, 'The United States'. See also Jeffrey Sachs, 'IMF is a Power unto Itself', *Financial Times*, 11 December 1997. For an analysis of Indonesia's crisis in a regional context, see *Asian Contagion: The Causes and Consequences of a Financial Crisis*, ed. Karl Jackson, Westview Press, Boulder, 1999.

101 Raphael Pura & Richard Borsuk, 'Suharto's Son Criticises Minister, May Shake IMF Plan's Credibility', *Asian Wall Street Journal*, 5 November 1997.

102 Interview, Sarwono Kusumaatmadja, 10 March 1998.

103 See Philip Bowring, 'Trouble in Indonesia, and No Outside Solution in Sight', *International Herald Tribune*, 8 January 1998; and Keith Richburg, 'Suharto Appears Blind to Havoc in his Country', *Washington Post*, 9 January, 1998.

104 Paul Blustein, 'Indonesian Currency Still Falling', *Washington Post*, 17 January 1998.

105 The government was left with the choice of allowing privileges to continue to the national car project, thereby violating the IMF agreement almost before the ink was dry, or cutting off the privileges and having Tommy Soeharto default on his loans to the state banks that had been forced to lend to the project. With Soeharto still in power, the state banks would not have been permitted to seize Tommy Soeharto's assets to cover their loans.

106 Confidential interview, 13 February 1998.

107 Comments by Douglas E. Ramage, at the conference 'Indonesia: Political and Economic Challenges', organised by the Asia Foundation, Washington, 21 April 1998.

108 Confidential interview, World Bank official, 4 September 1998. The same official criticised Wijoyo for being so focused on treating Soeharto gently that he lost sight of the urgency of the problem: 'Wijoyo was so obsessed with playing Javanese politics with Soeharto he forgot about the big picture. He sort of reminded me of Colonel Nicholson, the character played by Alec Guinness in *The Bridge on the River Kwai*.'

109 Interview, Jeffrey Sachs, 31 January 1998. See also 'IMF Prescribes "Wrong Medicine"': Q&A with Jeffrey Sachs', *International Herald Tribune*, 15 January 1998.

110 Martin Feldstein, 'Refocusing the IMF', *Foreign Affairs*, March/April 1998. For other critiques of the IMF, see George Shultz, William Simon & Walter Wriston, 'Who Needs the IMF?', *Wall Street Journal*, 3 February 1998; and Henry Kissinger, 'The IMF's Remedies are Doing More Harm than Good', *Los Angeles Times*, 5 October 1998. For a rebuttal of these views from the IMF, see Michel Camdessus, 'The IMF and Its Critics', *Washington Post*, 10 November 1998; Stanley Fischer, 'In My View: Make IMF Aid Pay Off', *South China Morning Post*, 17 August 1998; and Hubert Neiss, 'In Defense of the IMF's Emergency Role in East Asia', *International Herald Tribune*, 9 October 1998.

111 Mahathir would have been pleased to learn that a painting by a Malaysian artist would be awarded first prize at the 1998 ASEAN Art Awards later in the year. Low Leong Kiang titled his work: 'Mr Foreign Speculator, Stop Damaging Our Country!'. See Samantha Marshall, 'Angst in Art: Award Paintings Reflect Ravages of Asean's Crisis', *Wall Street Journal*, 25 November 1998.

112 See Steven Radelet & Jeffrey Sachs, 'The Onset of the East Asian Financial Crisis', Harvard Institute for International Development, 30 March 1998; David Sanger, 'World Bank Report Lays Blame in Global Financial Crisis', *New York Times*, 3 December 1998; and Jeffrey Sachs & Wing Thye Woo, 'The Asian Financial Crisis: What Happened, and What Is to Be Done', *Asia Competitiveness Report 1999*, World Economic Forum, Geneva, 1999.

113 See Adam Schwarz, 'For Indonesians, the President Looks Like the Problem', *International Herald Tribune*, 13 January 1998; Jamie Mackie, 'Indonesia's Problem is Now Political', *Asian Wall Street Journal*, 9 January 1998; Andrew MacIntyre, 'We May Rue the Day the U.S. and the IMF Saved Suharto', *Los Angeles Times*, 18 January 1998; and David Cole & Betty

Slade, 'Why Has Indonesia's Financial Crisis Been so Bad?', *Bulletin of Indonesian Economic Studies*, August 1998.

114 Indonesian critics of the World Bank met with the Bank's president, James Wolfensohn, in early February 1998 to stress exactly this point. See 'Don't Just Praise: World Bank Head Wolfensohn is Attacked by Vocal Critics', *Jawa Pos*, 5 February 1998.

115 Interview, Djisman Simanjuntak, 27 October 1998.

116 Mondale's views on the Indonesian crisis can be found in Walter F. Mondale, 'Asia Is Still Our Future', *Brookings Review*, 22 June 1998.

117 See Hamish McDonald, 'Heir Apparent: As "Dr Strangelove" Rises, the Rupiah Falls Even Further', *Sydney Morning Herald*, 22 January 1998; and Keith Richburg, 'Indonesian Oracle, or Oddball? B.J. Habibie Divides a Nation', *Washington Post*, 19 February 1998.

118 In fact, as later events were to show, Soeharto had no intention of handing over power to Habibie. See Liddle, 'Indonesia's Unexpected Failure'.

119 Raphael Pura, Darren McDermott & Jay Solomon, 'President's Family Welcomes Plan as Economic Advisers Voice Fears', *Asian Wall Street Journal*, 10 February 1998. See also 'Voice of Suharto's Guru: A Q&A with Steve Hanke', *International Herald Tribune*, 20 March 1998.

120 Pura et al., 'President's Family Welcomes'.

121 For a critical account of US and IMF hostility to the idea of a currency board in Indonesia, see James Tyson, '"Dollar Diplomacy" Rises Again as U.S. Foreign-Policy Tool', *Christian Science Monitor*, 10 February 1999.

122 Confidential interviews, March 1998.

123 Jenny Grant, 'Rioters Paid to Initiate Anti-Chinese Violence, Police Say', *South China Morning Post*, 18 February 1998.

124 Andreas Harsono, 'Anti-Chinese Riots Ruin Indonesian Nation-Building', *American Reporter*, 21 February 1998.

125 David Jenkins, 'The New Dis-Order Government', *Sydney Morning Herald*, 21 February 1998.

126 Interviews, Amien Rais, 25 February 1998 and 30 April 1998. See also Adam Schwarz, 'Hunting for Scapegoats in Indonesia', *Asian Wall Street Journal*, 3 February 1998; John McBeth with Salil Tripathi, 'Playing with Ire', *Far Eastern Economic Review*, 5 March 1998; and Thomas Fuller, 'Anatomy of a Price Riot: Misunderstanding Sparked Indonesian Violence', *International Herald Tribune*, 20 March 1998.

127 Interview, Salim Said, 27 August 1998.

128 Interview, Sofyan Wanandi, 2 March 1998. After Soeharto had resigned, some of the police investigators went to see Wanandi to apologise for hauling him into the police station in February.

129 Interview, Sofyan Wanandi, 2 March 1998. See also Yang Razali Kassim, 'Difficult Time for Wanandi', *Business Times*, 11 February 1998.

130 Jenkins, 'The New Dis-Order Government'.

131 Confidential interviews, March 1998. See also Margot Cohen, '"Us" and "Them"', *Far Eastern Economic Review*, 12 February 1998; and Andreas Harsono, 'Amid Economy in Crisis, Embattled Suharto Plays Islamic Card', *American Reporter*, 15 April 1998.

132 Interview, Fadli Zon, 12 March 1998.

133 Confidential interview, March 1998. See also Scott, 'Indonesia Reborn?' for more on Prabowo's views of the ethnic-Chinese.
134 Interview, Amien Rais, 30 April 1998.
135 Interview, Fadli Zon, 12 March 1998. KISDI's views can also be found at www.kisdi.com
136 Interview, Amien Rais, 25 February 1998.
137 See testimony by Pius Lustrilanang, at a Hearing of the Committee on International Relations, United States House of Representatives, 7 May 1998. KISDI's Fadli Zon defended Prabowo's involvement in the abductions, saying the general 'was fighting a terrorist threat. It was only later that the media started describing the terrorists as democracy activists'. Interview, Fadli Zon, 9 September 1998.
138 David Jenkins, 'Scared into Silence', *Sydney Morning Herald*, 2 May 1998. See also 'Disappearances in Indonesia: The Military Must Answer', report by Human Rights Watch, 28 April 1998.
139 World Bank, 'Indonesia in Crisis: A Macroeconomic Update', Washington, DC, 16 July 1998, p. 1.9.
140 Henny Sender, 'A Tale of Why Indonesia Never Got a Debt Deal', *Wall Street Journal*, 4 November 1998; and 'Indonesia: Japanese Banks Turn Down Debt Petition', *South China Morning Post*, 21 March 1998.
141 'Call to Let Pribumis Take Control', *Singapore Straits Times*, 11 February 1998.
142 Harsono, 'Amid Crisis'.
143 'Focus on Amien Rais', *The Indonesian Observer*, 25 February 1998.
144 Interview, Sarwono Kusumaatmadja, 10 March 1998.
145 Richard Borsuk, 'Indonesian Assembly Is Likely to Expand Powers of President', *Asian Wall Street Journal*, 27–28 February 1998.
146 Interview, Fadli Zon, 12 March 1998. For a profile of Tutut, see Margot Cohen, 'Daughter-in-Waiting', *Far Eastern Economic Review*, 9 April 1998.
147 Jenny Grant, 'Trade Minister Snubs IMF Bid over Reforms', *South China Morning Post*, 17 March 1998. For profiles of Hasan, see 'Indonesia's Uncle Bob', *Economist*, 29 March 1997; and John McBeth & Jay Solomon, 'First Friend', *Far Eastern Economic Review*, 20 February 1997.
148 Confidential interview, 12 March 1998.
149 Interview, Fadli Zon, 3 September 1998.
150 Interview, Sarwono Kusumaatmadja, 10 March 1998. See also John McBeth, 'Chains of Command: Army Insiders See Curbs on Suharto Son-in-Law', *Far Eastern Economic Review*, 25 December 1997.
151 Adam Schwarz, 'A Nation Sinks under a Leader's Weight', *Washington Post*, 22 March 1998; and Adam Schwarz, Testimony at a Hearing on Indonesia, Foreign Relations Committee, United States Senate, 24 March 1998.
152 Nicholas Kristof, 'Capitalism: Suharto's Stealthy Foe', *New York Times*, 20 May 1998. See also Terry McCarthy, 'Thanks, But I'll Do it My Way', *Time*, 23 March 1998.
153 This section draws from Robin Madrid, 'Forces for Moderation: Islamic Students in the Indonesian Student Movement', *Bulletin of Concerned Asian Scholars*, forthcoming. See also *Academic Freedom in Indonesia: Dismantling Soeharto-Era Barriers*, Human Rights Watch, New York, 1998.

154 Interview, Amien Rais, 30 April 1998. See also Raphael Pura, 'Students Find their Voice as Indonesia Crisis Deepens', *Wall Street Journal*, 28 April 1998.

155 Interview, Amien Rais, 30 April 1998. See also 'A Sense of Disgust: Time is Ripe for People's Power, Says Suharto Opponent', *Far Eastern Economic Review*, 14 May 1998.

156 Comments by Douglas E. Ramage, at the conference 'Indonesia: Political and Economic Challenges', organised by the Asia Foundation, Washington, 21 April 1998.

157 Keith Richburg, 'Six Dead as Riots Rock Indonesia for 3rd Day', *Washington Post*, 7 May 1998. Other reports pushing the same line, and reliant on 'informed Western diplomats' as principal sources, include Brian Williams, 'Military Seen as Key to Indonesia's Future', *Reuter*, 11 May 1998; and Sander Thoenes, 'Indonesians Who Don't Throw Stones: Suharto May Survive Crisis', *Christian Science Monitor*, 11 May 1998. One of the few Western journalists to recognise the potential impact of the student movement and its burgeoning links with labour and farmer associations was Margot Cohen; see her 'To the Barricades', *Far Eastern Economic Review*, 14 May 1998.

158 Kate Linebaugh, 'Indonesia's Clove Monopoly Still Holds Reins Despite Deal', *Dow Jones Newswires*, 27 April 1998; and 'Yet Another Suharto Family Monopoly Created', *Dow Jones Newswires*, 6 April 1998.

159 Bresnan, 'The United States'.

160 Mark Landler, 'Riots Bare Ethnic Hatreds in Indonesia', *The New York Times*, 9 May 1998.

161 Jay Solomon & I Made Sentana, 'Flight of Ethnic Chinese Adds to Disruption in Indonesia', *Wall Street Journal*, 11 May 1998. The only other Southeast Asian nation on the list was Cambodia.

162 Christopher Torchia, 'Suharto Warns of Crackdown', *Associated Press*, 9 May 1998. See also Mark Landler, 'Suharto Seems Unconcerned as Indonesia Nears Breakdown', *New York Times*, 10 May 1998.

163 Susan Berfield & Dewi Loveard, 'Ten Days that Shook Indonesia', *Asiaweek*, 24 July 1998.

164 Keith Richburg, 'Indonesia's Unintentional Martyrs: Slayings of Four Students Transformed a Nation', *Washington Post*, 8 June 1998.

165 See Berfield & Loveard, 'Ten Days'; and Andrew Higgins & Nick Cumming Bruce, 'Burnt Corpses Haunt Suharto', *The Guardian*, 17 May 1998. The award for the most insensitive headline on riot articles goes to: 'Hundreds of Pillagers Roasted in Action', *Kompas*, 16 May 1998.

166 'Paper: 150,000 Fled Indonesia Riots', *Associated Press*, 9 June 1998. The report cited immigration chief Pranowo as saying that 70 837 Indonesians and 81 526 foreigners left Indonesia between 14 and 20 May.

167 For accounts of attacks on ethnic-Chinese women, see 'The Rapes in the Series of Riots: The Climax of an Uncivilized Act of the Nation Life', Report from the Volunteers Team for Humanity, 13 July 1998; 'Update on Rapes of Ethnic Chinese Women in Jakarta', Human Rights Watch, 2 August 1998; and Margot Cohen, 'Turning Point', *Far Eastern Economic Review*, 30 July 1998.

168 Interview, Dewi Fortuna Anwar, 28 August 1998.

169 See Loren Ryter, 'Pemuda Pancasila: The Last Loyalist Free Men of Suharto's Order?', *Indonesia* 66, October 1998.
170 Confidential interviews. See also Berfield & Loveard, 'Ten Days'.
171 Berfield & Loveard, 'Ten Days'.
172 Ariel Heryanto, 'Flaws of Riot Media Coverage', *Jakarta Post*, 15 July 1998; Taufik Darusman, 'The Guilty Must Be Punished', *Indonesian Observer*, 20 June 1998.
173 See Susan Sim, 'May 14 Meeting "pivotal" to Suharto's Downfall', *Singapore Straits Times*, 5 November 1998.
174 See Don Greenlees, 'Report on Riots Puts Heat on Jakarta Generals', *The Australian*, 4 November 1998.
175 Interview, Salim Said, 27 August 1998.
176 See David Jenkins, 'Don't Count on Resignation', Sydney Morning Herald, 15 May 1998.
177 'Indon News—Riots Blamed on Communists', *Dow Jones Newswires*, 18 May 1998.
178 Quoted in Peter Waldman, Raphael Pura & Marcus W. Brauchli, 'Suharto's Final Days as President Were Marked by Shifting Loyalties', *Wall Street Journal*, 22 May 1998.
179 See Keith Richburg, 'Seven Days in May that Toppled a Titan: Back-Room Intrigue Led to Suharto's Fall', *Washington Post*, 24 May 1998. Harmoko's house in the Central Java city of Solo was burnt to the ground the previous weekend, an event some analysts say contributed to Harmoko's change of heart on Soeharto.
180 See David Jenkins, 'The Last Domino: How Soeharto Fell', *Sydney Morning Herald*, 23 May 1998.
181 Waldman et al., 'Suharto's Final Days'.
182 See Richburg, 'Seven Days'. Richburg discusses the theory that Harmoko and Habibie were working together to push for Soeharto's immediate resignation, and that they may have been helped by General Prabowo.
183 Material from this section is drawn from an interview with Nurcholish Madjid, 31 August 1991.
184 Fadli Zon of KISDI, who a few months earlier had strongly supported Soeharto's decision to stay in office, had changed his tune by the middle of May: 'Soeharto would have stepped down in March 1998 but he was surrounded by jerks like Harmoko who gave him disinformation'. Interview, Fadli Zon, 3 September 1998.
185 Waldman et al., 'Suharto's Final Days'.
186 David Jenkins, 'Don't Count on Resignation', *Sydney Morning Herald*, 15 May 1998.
187 Peter Hatcher, 'Soeharto's "Perfect Dive Into Empty Pool"', *Australian Financial Review*, 20 May 1998.
188 Interview, Amien Rais, 30 August 1998.
189 Interview, Marsillam Simanjuntak, 1 September 1998.
190 Interview, Abdurrahman Wahid, 27 August 1998. Wahid noted that five of the nine Muslim leaders at the 19 May meeting came from Nahdlatul Ulama backgrounds and only two were from the Muhammadiyah, a decision reflecting Soeharto's increasingly suspicious view of modernist ambitions.

191 Interview, Dewi Fortuna Anwar, 28 August 1998. See also Greg Torode, 'Strongman's Grip on Nation Failed in Hours before Dawn', *South China Morning Post*, 22 May 1998.

192 See Raphael Pura, 'Habibie to Face Scrutiny over Some Worrisome Ties', *Wall Street Journal*, 22 May 1998; and Richburg, 'Seven Days'.

193 Interview, Amien Rais, 30 August 1998. According to Rais, Soeharto had ordered that Rais be arrested two weeks earlier. When the attorney-general refused to do it, Soeharto told Prabowo to arrest Rais, and Prabowo in turn delegated the task to Kivlan Zein. In the end, Zein was convinced by several influential Muslims not to do it.

194 Interview, Amien Rais, 30 August 1998. According to Soeharto's speechwriter, Yusril Izha Mahendra, it was Soeharto who instructed the military to shoot demonstrators if they reached the national monument in Jakarta during the planned 20 May rally. Mahendra says Generals Prabowo and Syafrie met with Soeharto on the evening of 19 May, and a decision was made to have soldiers use live bullets instead of rubber bullets on 20 May. Interview, Yusril Izha Mahendra, 4 September 1998.

195 The ease with which the military was able to remove the students from the parliament after Soeharto resigned tended to support the proposition that the military's tolerant approach to the students earlier in the week was carefully thought out.

196 See Waldman et al., 'Suharto's Final Days'. According to Nurcholish, Soeharto asked Wiranto to replace him but Wiranto refused. Interview, Nurcholish Madjid, 31 August 1998.

197 'Indonesian Military Nudged Suharto From Office—Report', *Dow Jones Newswires*, 22 May 1998; interview, Susilo Bambang Yudhoyono, 4 September 1998. For another account suggesting an activist military role, see Jonathan Head, 'Indonesia '98: A Year of Living Dangerously', BBC Report, 30 December 1998.

198 Interview, Salim Said, 27 August 1998; interview, Hasnan Habib, 31 August 1998.

199 Soeharto, *My Thoughts, Words and Deeds: An Autobiography*, Citra Lamtoro Gung Persada, Jakarta, 1991.

200 See John McBeth, 'A Warning Shot: Probe of Businessman Is Likely to Deter Dissent', *Far Eastern Economic Review*, 2 April 1998.

201 Information on Ginanjar's thinking in March–May 1998 comes from interviews with several businessmen close to Ginanjar, including an interview with Arifin Panigoro, 9 September 1998. Analysis of Ginanjar's motives was also provided in an interview with Marsillam Simanjuntak, 1 September 1998.

202 Interview, Dewi Fortuna Anwar, 28 August 1998. See also Geoffrey Barker, 'Soeharto Sought to Name Habibie Cabinet', *Australian Financial Review*, 26 September 1998. It appears Soeharto was particularly keen to have Habibie keep Wiranto as armed forces commander; military sources say by this point Soeharto had grown intensely distrustful of Prabowo and wanted Wiranto as armed forces chief to keep him in place.

203 *Kompas*, 22 May 1998, p. 5.

204 'President Habibie's Maiden Speech in Full', broadcast by the BBC, 22 May 1998.

205 According to Dewi Fortuna Anwar, Soeharto refused to speak with Habibie in the last few days of his presidency, save for a brief meeting around 8 p.m. on 20 May. Interview, Dewi Fortuna Anwar, 28 August 1998. Habibie recollects the swearing-in ceremony this way: Soeharto 'looked at me. He shook hands—not a single word, just a smile. That's all'. Quoted in Seth Mydans, 'Indonesia's New Leader, Self-Styled Reformer, Hopes to Stay Awhile', *New York Times*, 3 June 1998.

Chapter 12   Starting over

1 Quoted in 'Indonesia Can't Have Woman President: Top Muslim Leader', *Agence France Presse*, 24 March 1999.

2 Quoted in Anthony Spaeth, 'Indonesia's Great Experiment', *Time*, 22 February 1999.

3 Quoted in Terry McCarthy, 'Armed and Dangerous', *Time*, 30 November 1998.

4 Interview, Dewi Fortuna Anwar, 28 August 1998. See also Geoffrey Barker, 'Soeharto Sought to Name Habibie Cabinet: Aide', *Australian Financial Review*, 26 September 1998.

5 Habibie's comments are quoted in Michael Sheridan, 'The Day Civil War Simmered in Indonesia', *Sunday Times*, 8 November 1998; interview, Dewi Fortuna Anwar, 28 August 1998.

6 See the analysis in Geoffrey Forrester 'Introduction' in Geoff Forrester and R.J. May, eds, *The Fall of Suharto*, Crawford House Publishing, Bathurst, Australia, 1998.

7 Confidential interview, 3 September 1998.

8 KAMMI, the biggest of the student groups, organised a rally at the Al Azhar Mosque in Jakarta on 22 May, drawing over 30 000 people. But the event failed to prevent clashes at the parliament. See Robin Madrid, 'Forces for Moderation: Islamic Students in the Indonesian Student Movement', *Bulletin of Concerned Asian Scholar* forthcoming.

9 Interview, Fadli Zon, 3 September 1998.

10 See the analysis by John McBeth, 'Army Maverick Prabowo Falls from Grace', *Far Eastern Economic Review*, 4 June 1998; and Takashi Shiraishi, 'The Indonesian Military in Politics', in *The Politics of Post-Suharto Indonesia*, eds Adam Schwarz & Jonathan Paris, Council on Foreign Relations, New York, 1999.

11 Quoted in Margaret Scott, 'Indonesia Reborn?', *New York Review of Books*, 13 August 1998. See also Andreas Harsono, 'In Reversal of Fortune, Indonesian Strongman Becomes its "Sick Man"', *American Reporter*, 26 August 1998; and McBeth, 'Army Maverick'. On Prabowo's denial of the purported coup attempt, see 'Prabowo: Don't Believe Gossip', *Kompas*, 29 May 1998; and 'Prabowo Responds', *Indonesia Political Watch*, 22 February 1999. Prabowo claimed that the troops surrounding Habibie's home on 21 May 1998 were Kopassus troops not under his command.

12 See Shiraishi, 'The Indonesian Military'.

13 Interview, Susilo Bambang Yudhoyono, 4 September 1998.

14 Interview, Salim Said, 27 August 1998; confidential interview, Jakarta, 2 September 1998; interview, Fadli Zon, 3 September 1998. Shortly after taking the helm at Bakin, Maulani fired a dozen military intelligence operatives, most of them Christians. See 'A Step Down . . . ', *Far Eastern Economic Review*, 1 April 1999.

15 Interview, Susilo Bambang Yudhoyono, 4 September 1998; interview, Benny Murdani, 3 September 1998.

16 During Habibie's first 10 months in office, the information ministry granted 742 new press licences. See Margot Cohen, 'Fastest Gun in the East', *Far Eastern Economic Review*, 25 March 1999.

17 See Shiraishi, 'The Indonesian Military'.

18 Santi Soekanto, 'Who are the true reformists?', *Jakarta Post*, 20 February 1999.

19 Habibie's quote was broadcast in an interview with CNBC, 5 January 1999. For an analysis of Habibie's attempts to turn his political weakness into a strength, see Donald Emmerson, 'Exit, Aftermath, Outlook: The Crisis of 1997–98', in *Indonesia Beyond Suharto: Polity, Economy, Society, Transition*, ed. Donald Emmerson, M. E. Sharpe, Armonk, NY, 1999.

20 See Gerry van Klinken, 'Habibie's Cabinet: Islamic Yes, Military Yes, Reformist Perhaps', *Inside Indonesia*, online edn, 22 May 1998; and Greg Earl, 'Muslims, Technologists Fill Emperor's Court', *Australian Financial Review*, 22 May 1998.

21 'Cleaning-Up Operations', *Indonesia Political Watch*, 25 January 1999.

22 Prior to the MPRS meeting, some Abri faction members attempted to introduce an MPR decree requiring the parliament to continue allocating seats to the military, apparently to pre-empt any subsequent attempt by the parliament to deny seats to the military. As the higher constitutional body, an MPR decree takes precedence over legislation passed by parliament. See 'Indonesian Lawmakers Want Army in Parliament', *Reuter*, 2 November 1998.

23 Quoted in 'Indonesia: The Radicalisation Will Spread', *Green Left Weekly*, 25 November 1998. For an account critical of Ciganjur group for failing to support the students' demands, see Arief Budiman, 'New Order, Old School', *Inside Indonesia*, April–June 1999.

24 Louise Williams, 'Shooting to Kill on the Streets of Jakarta', *Sydney Morning Herald*, 21 November 1998; Jose Manuel Tesoro, 'Bloodshed in Jakarta Has Put Reform in Peril', *Asiaweek*, 27 November 1998; and 'ABRI under Siege: A Struggle between History and Destiny', *Indonesia Political Watch*, 30 November 1998.

25 Greg Earl, 'Abri's Chickens Coming Home to Roost', *Australian Financial Review*, 14 November 1998. Despite the criticism of his handling of the MPRS, many Indonesians continued to regard Wiranto as a viable presidential or vice-presidential candidate. See 'General Wiranto: The Presidential Dark Horse', *Van Zorge Report*, 23 March 1999. In March 1999, Golkar selected Wiranto as one of its five possible candidates for president.

26 See 'Suharto Criticises Habibie Govt over Inability to Prevent Clashes', *Agence France Presse*, 14 November 1998.

27 A description of the National Front is in John McBeth, 'Secular Soldiers: Old Generals Face Off against Habibie's Islamic Allies', *Far Eastern Economic Review*, 29 October 1998; and 'Interview with Dr Subroto, Vice Chairman of Barisan Nasional', *Van Zorge Report*, 27 November 1998. See also David Jenkins, 'Habibie Flogging a Lame Horse', *Sydney Morning Herald*, 17 November 1998.

28 See George Aditjondro, 'The Swiss Business Links of the Suharto and Habibie Oligarchy of Indonesia', report prepared for the Berne Declaration, 22 July 1998; and Shannon Luke Smith, 'Habibie's Business Empire', *Australian Financial Review*, 1 June 1998.

29 Interview, Umar Juoro, 2 September 1998.

30 '149 Major Pertamina Contracts Linked to Suharto', *Dow Jones Newswires*, 10 June 1998; and Louise Williams, 'Soeharto's Poor Little Rich Kids', *Sydney Morning Herald*, 24 October 1998.

31 Dan Murphy, 'Debt-Mired Astra Int'l Fights to Stay Afloat', *Far Eastern Economic Review*, 9 December 1998; and Ian Chalmers, 'Tommy's Toys Trashed', *Inside Indonesia*, October–December 1998.

32 See Richard Borsuk, 'Suharto Regime Bungled Many Chances to Amass Wealth', *Asian Wall Street Journal*, 30 December 1998.

33 Jay Solomon, 'Suharto's Secretive Foundations Shrouded in Mystery', *Wall Street Journal*, 26 November 1998. See also 'I've Already Said my Apologies: Soeharto', *Jakarta Post*, 12 February 1999.

34 'Half Brother Comes to the Defence of Former President Suharto, Family', *Agence France Presse*, 18 December 1998; 'Tommy Soeharto's Remarks Give Students New Spirit', *Jakarta Post*, 27 November 1998; interview, Umar Juoro, 27 October 1998.

35 A thorough account of the ill-fated corruption commission is in 'In Pursuit of Soeharto', *Van Zorge Report*, 12 December 1999; see also 'Ten Leading Indons Back Out of Suharto Probe Body', *Agence France Presse*, 3 December 1998; and 'Suharto Appears to Threaten Govt Will Fall if he Goes on Trial', *Agence France Presse*, 29 November 1998. Two months later, a transcript of a leaked phone call between Habibie and Ghalib reinforced impressions of Habibie's insincerity in investigating the wealth of his former mentor. See Jenny Grant, 'Phone Tap Points to Suharto Cover-Up', *South China Morning Post*, 19 February 1999.

36 Jeffrey Winters, 'Some Comments on Suharto's Wealth and Trying to Track it', unpublished.

37 See 'Ginanjar Defends Himself; Says Ready for Investigation', *Kompas*, 16 October 1998; and 'Ginanjar to US academic: Put up or Shut up over Graft Claim', *Agence France Presse*, 14 October 1998.

38 Interview, Sarwono Kusumaatmadja, 3 September 1998.

39 Confidential interview, 1 September 1998.

40 Confidential interview, 1 September 1998. See also Salil Tripathi & John McBeth, 'Habibie Govt Disappoints as Vested Interests Frustrate Privatization', *Far Eastern Economic Review*, 22 October 1998; Jose Manuel Tesoro,

'Anatomy of a Deal', *Asiaweek*, 22 January 1999; and 'Indonesia's Rising Populism', *Van Zorge Report*, 24 August 1998.

41 See Keith Richburg, 'Habibie Pushes for Visit to U.S.', *Washington Post*, 19 July 1998. For other accounts of the ethnic-Chinese, see Jusuf Wanandi, 'The Road Ahead', *Far Eastern Economic Review*, 30 July 1998; Michael Shari, 'Indonesia: The Plight of the Ethnic Chinese', *Business Week*, 3 August 1998; and Keith Richburg, 'Ethnic Chinese: Indonesia's Scapegoats', *Washington Post*, 23 December 1998.

42 Nisid Hajari, 'Odd Man in: Is Habibie for Real?', *Time*, 3 August 1998.

43 Two comprehensive accounts of the rapes are 'The Rapes in the Series of Riots', Volunteers Team for Humanity, Jakarta, 13 July 1998; and 'Indonesia: The Damaging Debate on Rapes of Ethnic Chinese Women', Human Rights Watch, New York, 8 September 1998.

44 Interview, Romo Sandyawan, 31 July 1998; interview, Karlina Leksono, 1 September 1998. For an account of the fact-finding team's conclusions, see 'Jakarta Admits Rape Cases in May Riots but Denies they Were Organized', *Agence France Presse*, 21 December 1998.

45 'Wiranto's Denial of Gang Rapes Infuriates Probe Team Leader', *Agence France Presse*, 7 October 1998.

46 Interview, Marzuki Darusman, 29 August 1998; interview, Benny Murdani, 3 September 1998. Wanandi quoted in Hajari, 'Odd Man in'.

47 See 'Advisor Defends Decision to Honor Habibie's Family', *Jakarta Post*, 21 August 1998; 'Habibie Wants to Ban Study Overseas', *Straits Times*, 10 December 1998; and Michael Richardson, 'Singapore Quickly Denies an Assertion of "Racism"', *International Herald Tribune*, 12 February 1999.

48 See Jenny Grant, 'Phone Tap Points to Suharto Cover-Up', *South China Morning Post*, 19 February 1999; and 'Arifin Panigoro: "I Will Sue"', *Indonesia Political Watch*, 30 November 1998.

49 Interview, Mochtar Pakpahan, 8 August 1998. See also Jeffrey Ballinger, 'Old Policies of Repression Linger in Indonesia', *Los Angeles Times*, 7 August 1998.

50 Interview, Umar Juoro, 27 October 1998. As late as March 1999, many still doubted that the June 1999 elections would take place as scheduled. Many Indonesians remember how Soeharto repeatedly delayed the elections initially scheduled for 1968 to allow enough time for his political handlers to manufacture an overwhelming victory for Golkar. The elections did not happen until 1971. It then took another two years to convene the People's Consultative Assembly to select a president.

51 'Statement on Opposition to Habibie Sparks Speculation', *Jakarta Post*, 12 October 1998.

52 Confidential interview, 4 September 1998. For an account of Habibie's political strategy, see John McBeth, 'Habibie: Little Big Man in the Hot Seat', *Far Eastern Economic Review*, 3 December 1998.

53 Margot Cohen, 'Tackling a Bitter Legacy: Reformasi Advocates in Provinces Focus on Corrupt Officials', *Far Eastern Economic Review*, 2 July 1998.

54 Interview, Sarwono Kusumaatmadja, 3 September 1998; and Susan Sim, 'New Party "will not clone Golkar"', *Straits Times*, 15 December 1998. See

also 'Even if Golkar Genuinely Did Well, People Would Not Believe them', *Van Zorge Report*, 23 March 1999.

55 Interview, Umar Juoro, 27 October 1998.

56 Interview, Mohammad Jumhur Hidayat, 12 February 1999. See also Derwin Pereira, 'Adi Sasono: Can he Be Indonesia's Next President?', *Singapore Business Times*, 21 January 1999.

57 See 'Golkar Apologizes for Past Mistakes', *Agence France Presse*, 3 November 1998; 'Indonesia's Ruling Party Denies Apologizing for Past Mistakes', *Agence France Presse*, 3 November 1998; and 'Golkar Party Makes Official Apology for Past Mistakes', *Agence France Presse*, 17 January 1999.

58 Interview, Marzuki Darusman, 3 September 1998; interview, Aburizal Bakrie, 30 January 1999. See also 'Money Politics Will Happen', *Van Zorge Report*, 23 March 1999; and 'Re-Inventing Golkar', *Van Zorge Report*, 23 March 1999.

59 See 'Restive Indonesia Faction Plans Rival Political Party', *Dow Jones Newswires*, 11 August 1998. Yusuf Hasyim, Abdurrahman Wahid's father-in-law, set up a rival party for traditionalist Muslims called Nahdlatul Ummah. The party's goal was to prevent Indonesia from becoming 'another Turkey' ruled by secular elites.

60 Quoted in Gerry van Klinken, 'Indonesian Politics Become More Islamic', *Melbourne Age*, 18 June 1998; and Jose Manuel Tesoro, 'Islam's Struggle for Power in Indonesia', *Asiaweek*, 29 January 1999.

61 Quoted in 'Moslems Rally to Support Government Election Plan', *Agence France Presse*, 5 November 1998.

62 Jenny Grant, 'The death of Tahan—Rough Justice in Jakarta', *Sydney Morning Herald*, 28 November 1998; and Don Greenlees, 'A Society's Fault Lines Exposed', *The Australian*, 5 December 1998.

63 See 'Background Briefing on Indonesia: Urgent Action Needed to Halt Communal Violence', Human Rights Watch, New York, 9 December 1998.

64 Andreas Harsono, 'Indonesian Leaders Ask Restraint after Mosques Are Burned', *American Reporter*, 1 December 1998.

65 '"Third Party" Behind Bloody Kupang Riots', *Jakarta Post*, 21 December 1998.

66 'RI Ranks among World's Worst for Religious Disharmony', *Jakarta Post*, 24 December 1998; and 'Indonesian Churches Ask Govt for Protection', *Dow Jones Newswires*, 17 January 1999.

67 Jay Solomon, 'Indonesian Religious Violence Heats Up as Islamic Leaders Call for Holy War', *Asian Wall Street Journal*, 3 March 1999. See also Richard Lloyd Parry, 'Slain for Being Young and Christian', *The Independent*, 3 March 1999; John McBeth & Margot Cohen, 'Flames of Passion', *Far Eastern Economic Review*, 4 February 1999; and Jeremy Wagstaff, 'Calls to Join "Holy War" Entice Indonesia's Youth', *Asian Wall Street Journal*, 1 April 1999.

68 Louise Williams, 'Ambon an Isolated Island of Bitterness', *Sydney Morning Herald*, 6 March 1999; 'Muslim Leader Fingers "Mastermind" of Ambon Rioting', *BBC Summary of World Broadcasts*, 23 January 1999; John McBeth & Dini Djalal, 'Ambon Violence May Have Had its Origins in Jakarta', *Far Eastern Economic Review*, 25 March 1999; and 'Kontras Reports Ambon

Riots Engineered', *Indonesian Observer*, 19 February 1999. For a description of the alleged role of the Pemuda Pancasila, a conservative paramilitary outfit with close ties to the Soeharto family, see Derwin Pereira, 'Underworld Politics in Indonesia: The Role of "Pancasila thugs"', *Straits Times*, 7 March 1999; and 'Yorrys: The Rule of Law is Not Being Upheld in Indonesia', *Indonesia Political Watch*, 25 January 1999.

69 See 'Indonesia: The Violence in Ambon', Human Rights Watch, March 1999; confidential interview, 8 March 1999.

70 Interview, Abdurrahman Wahid, 27 August 1998.

71 See Marcus Mietzner, 'Between *Pesantren* and Palace: Nahdlatul Ulama and its Role in the Transition', in Forrester & May, *The Fall of Soeharto*.

72 Jay Solomon, 'Indonesian Islamic Leader Won't Support Megawati Presidency', *Dow Jones Newswires*, 16 March 1999; and 'The Elaborate Courtship of Gus Dur and Megawati', *Van Zorge Report*, 9 April 1999. See also John Colmey, 'How a Javanese Sultan Became a Hero of Democracy', *Time*, 17 February 1999; and Tim Dodd, 'Sultan Getting Serious about Reins of Republic', *Australian Financial Review*, 19 March 1999.

73 See William Liddle, 'Indonesia's Unexpected Failure of Leadership', in *The Politics of Post-Suharto Indonesia*, eds Adam Schwarz & Jonathan Paris, Council on Foreign Relations, New York, 1999.

74 Mietzner, 'Between *Pesantren* and Palace'. Reflecting the NU's cautious approach, the student group associated with the NU, the Indonesian Islamic Student Movement (PMII), was hesitant in joining other student organisations in protesting against Soeharto. See Robin Madrid, 'Forces for Moderation: Islamic Students in the Indonesian Student Movement', *Bulletin of Concerned Asian Scholars*, forthcoming.

75 Interview, Abdurrahman Wahid, 27 August 1998. See also 'Gus Dur: Three Million May Die if Social Revolution Erupts', *Straits Times*, 12 February 1998. Habibie's initial cabinet contained only one NU member.

76 Confidential interview, 10 January 1999.

77 A few months before, Wahid had accused modernist Muslims in the Indonesian Association of Muslim Intellectuals of being behind the killing spree in East Java. Yorrys Raweyai, one of the leaders of Pemuda Pancasila, was present at the meetings between Wahid and Soeharto, adding to the speculation that paramilitary thugs close to Soeharto were involved in instigating communal violence.

78 Confidential interview, 12 February 1999.

79 Margot Cohen, 'Friction among the Faithful', *Far Eastern Economic Review*, 11 March 1999; and Jay Solomon, 'Wahid's Ambitions Point to Rifts in Indonesia', *Asian Wall Street Journal*, 25 March 1999.

80 Interview, Amien Rais, 30 August 1998.

81 'PPP Takes MPR to Brink of Vote', *Jakarta Post*, 13 November 1998.

82 'PPP Plans to Return to Former Identity as an Islamic Party', *Jakarta Post*, 24 November 1998.

83 'Megawati Views Saefuddin Blunder as an "ordeal"', *Jakarta Post*, 29 October 1998.

84 Interview, Amien Rais, 30 August 1998.

85 PAN's platform and other information can be found at: www.amanat.org

86 For an account of Rais' views on economic policy, see 'Hints of Post-Election Policy-Making: Amien Rais' Economic Views', *Van Zorge Report*, 9 March 1999.

87 Interview, Amien Rais, 30 August 1998.

88 Ibid.

89 Quoted from Rais' comments at the Foreign Correspondents Club of Hong Kong, 15 February 1999.

90 Just as Rais has had a difficult time convincing Wahid that his views have moderated over time, so too has he found it a tough task overcoming suspicions abroad. In the first half of 1998, the prevailing opinion in the US government was a deep-seated suspicion of Rais' motives. A number of influential Western media outlets took the same line. A *Los Angeles Times* article in November 1998 described Rais' views as leaning 'toward a more fundamentalist interpretation of Islam'. See David Lamb, 'Novice is Popular Choice in Indonesia', *Los Angeles Times*, 12 November 1998.

91 See 'Gus Dur Meets Amien Rais', *Jakarta Post*, 8 January 1999. It should be noted that the second tier of leaders in the parties headed by Wahid and Rais are much more willing to work with each other. It remains to be seen whether their spirit of cooperation trickles up to their respective party leaders.

92 'Polls Point to Indonesian Leadership Crisis', *Agence France Presse*, 16 December 1998.

93 Interviews, Umar Juoro, 27 October 1998; and Amien Rais, 30 August 1998.

94 Although lacking a well-known name at the helm, the Justice Party was given a credible chance to do well at the polls. It had branches in 25 of the 27 provinces, and its strongly pro-Islamic message proved popular across the country. The party is socially conservative and wants a greater role for Islamic scholars in government. The party appeared to have strong connections with Muslim groups overseas, particularly in Egypt and Pakistan. Like the PBB, the Justice Party is close to Dewan Dakwah and KISDI. See Margot Cohen, 'On the High Road: Idealistic New Muslim Party Draws Indonesian Youths', *Far Eastern Economic Review*; and Sander Thoenes, 'The Leaders of the Justice Party Put their Money where their Mouth Is', *Christian Science Monitor*, 3 March 1999.

95 Interview, Adi Sasono, 3 March 1998.

96 Interview, Ahmad Soemargono, 26 August 1998.

97 See 'Kalau Status Quo Ini Menguntungkan Islam, Mengapa Tidak' (If the status quo is good to Islam, why not?), *Tempo Interaktif*, 23 November 1998. A number of the more militant Muslim groups also object to Megawati as a presidential candidate because she is a woman. For example, one of the slogans used by the Justice Party is: 'Whoever accepts a woman as leader will not be successful'.

98 Interview, Ahmad Soemargono, 26 August 1998.

99 Interviews with Fadli Zon, 3 September 1998; and Ahmad Soemargono, 26 August 1998. In the interview with Soemargono, the KISDI chairman denied that he was involved in planning demonstrations outside the US Embassy in Jakarta. As we were speaking, a group of Muslim activists were demonstrating at the embassy. Halfway through the interview, Soemargono

received a call from a mobile telephone from one of the leaders of the demonstration asking Soemargono whether he should burn an American flag.

100 Interview, Yusril Izha Mahendra, 4 September 1998. It appears Soeharto shares the view that his ouster was orchestrated by outside forces. See the comments attributed to him in 'Foreign Power Made me Quit, Says Suharto', *Straits Times*, 28 January 1999, and 'It was a Zionist Conspiracy', *Castle Political Watch*, 26 April 1999.

101 Interviews, Fadli Zon, 3 September 1998; and Yusril Izha Mahendra, 4 September 1998.

102 'Kalau Status Quo Ini Menguntungkan Islam, Mengapa Tidak' (If the status quo is good to Islam, why not?), *Tempo Interaktif*, 23 November 1998. See also 'Indonesian Student Protesters Tear Down US Flag at Consulate', *Dow Jones Newswires*, 4 June 1998; and Robert Hefner, 'Islam and Nation in the Post-Suharto Era', in *The Politics of Post-Suharto Indonesia*.

103 Ron Moreau, 'Flames of Faith', *Newsweek*, 25 January 1999.

104 In the aftermath of the 13 November killings, the *Jakarta Post* published statements of regret from 14 political or research organisations. Only the Indonesian Muslim Forum defended the military, insisting that 'all acts of anarchy to topple the legitimate government must be condemned'. See 'Calls Mount for Habibie and Wiranto to Step Down', *Jakarta Post*, 16 November 1998.

105 Interview, Ahmad Soemargono, 26 August 1998.

106 Interview, Ahmad Soemargono, 26 August 1998. In March 1999 Habibie fired his speechwriter, Yusril Izha Mahendra, the militant Muslim leader. The decision reinforced the view that Habibie intended to distance himself from the militant Muslim community.

107 Interview, Ahmad Soemargono, 26 August 1998; interview, Fadli Zon, 3 September 1998.

108 Interview, Fadli Zon, 3 September 1998.

109 Interview, Ahmad Soemargono, 26 August 1998; and 'Kalau Status Quo Ini Menguntungkan Islam, Mengapa Tidak' (If the status quo is good to Islam, why not?), *Tempo Interaktif*, 23 November 1998.

110 Interview, Fadli Zon, 3 September 1998.

111 Interview, Amien Rais, 30 August 1998.

112 Interview, Abdurrahman Wahid, 27 August 1998.

113 M. C. Ricklefs, *A History of Modern Indonesia since c. 1300*, Stanford University Press, Stanford, CA, 2nd edn, 1993, p. 190.

114 Interview, Yusril Izha Mahendra, 4 September 1998.

115 'Majority of Public Wants Double Function Abandoned', *Kompas*, 4 October 1998.

116 Interview, Benny Murdani, 3 September 1998.

117 Interview, Susilo Bambang Yudhoyono, 4 September 1998. For a lengthy account of the military's campaign against Acehnese separatists, see Tim Kell, *The Roots of the Acehnese Rebellion, 1989–1992*, Cornell University Press, NY, 1995.

118 John McBeth, 'An Army in Retreat', *Far Eastern Economic Review*, 19 November 1998; David Liebhold, 'Spreading Fire', *Time*, 18 January 1999. See also Cindy Shiner, 'Indonesian General Apologizes', *Washington*

Post, 8 August 1998; and Ridwan Max Sijabat, 'Abri "Cannot Follow Up Aceh Rights Abuses"', *Jakarta Post*, 21 January 1999.

119 Louise Williams, 'Indonesian Soldiers Beat Rebels to Death', *Sydney Morning Herald*, 12 January 1999. For an interesting account alleging the military deliberately exaggerated the influence of the rebel leader Ahmad Kandang, see 'The Mysterious Ahmad Kandang', *Indonesia Political Watch*, vol. 1, 25 January 1999.

120 Jose Manuel Tesoro, 'Indonesia's Descent to Chaos', *Asiaweek*, 25 September 1998; and Terry McCarthy, 'Descent into Madness', *Time*, 7 December 1998. The law-and-order problem also spilled into international waters near Indonesia. See 'Economic Crisis Fuelling Upsurge in Indon Sea Piracy: Report', *Agence France Presse*, 3 February 1999.

121 Jose Manuel Tesoro, 'And the Killing Goes on', *Asiaweek*, 2 April 1999; Richard Lloyd Parry, 'Renewed Ethnic Cleansing Flares up Against Migrants to Borneo', *The Independent*, 21 March 1999; and Vaudine England, 'Indonesia Pays High Price for Insensitivity', *South China Morning Post*, 23 March 1999.

122 Nicholas Kristof, 'Fears of Sorcerers Spur Killings in Java', *New York Times*, 20 October 1998.

123 Confidential interview, 24 October 1998.

124 For a run-down of the various theories, see Greg Sheridan, 'Jakarta's Transition Must Engage Us, Too', *The Australian*, 6 November 1998.

125 Jeremy Wagstaff, 'Social Fabric Comes Loose in Rural Indonesia', *Asian Wall Street Journal*, 23 February 1999; and 'Jakartans Armed but Fearful amid Terrifying Crime Wave', *Jakarta Post*, 31 January 1999.

126 Interview, Aburizal Bakrie, 30 January 1999.

127 Andreas Harsono, 'Indonesian Military under Fire on Plan to Set up Militia', *American Reporter*, 16 December 1998.

128 Susan Sim & Derwin Pereira, 'Students Get Closer to Parliament', *Straits Times*, 13 November 1998.

129 Don Greenlees, 'Leak Shows no E Timor Troop Cuts', *The Australian*, 30 October 1998.

130 See 'Questioning the Business of Indonesian Military', *Jakarta Post*, 17 January 1999. A lengthy treatment of the military's business dealings throughout the New Order is in Indria Samego et al., eds, *Bila Abri Berbisnis* (When the armed forces goes into business), Mizan Press, Bandung, 1998.

131 Confidential interview, 27 August 1998.

132 Interview, Amien Rais, 30 August 1998. See also Cindy Shiner, 'Once Powerful Son-in-Law of Suharto under Fire', *Washington Post*, 12 August 1998; and 'Prabowo on Trial', *Van Zorge Report*, 24 August 1998.

133 'Suharto Son-in-Law Denies Taking up Jordanian Citizenship', *Agence France Presse*, 23 December 1998; 'Kostrad Meeting was "not secret"', *Jakarta Post*, 5 November 1998; and 'Soemitro Pleads for Fair Treatment of Son Prabowo', *Jakarta Post*, 27 November 1998.

134 Confidential interview, 2 September 1998.

135 Interview, Benny Murdani, 3 September 1998.

136 Interview, Fadli Zon, 3 September 1998. See also Jesse Wong 'Indonesian General Target for Islamists', *Asian Wall Street Journal*, 27 January 1999.

In the article, the militant Muslim leader Ahmad Soemargono describes Lt-Gen. Luhut Panjaitan as 'one of those Christian extremists'. In a separate interview, Soemargono accused Benny Murdani of instigating religious violence in a bid to weaken Habibie. See 'Ahmad Soemargono: Secularism Is in Fact a Jewish Concept', *Indonesia Political Watch*, 25 January 1999.

137 'Marzuki Lashes out at Court Martial', *Jakarta Post*, 28 December 1998.

138 Good accounts of the military reshuffle are in 'Wiranto's Army: Marching into Unknown Territory', *Van Zorge Report*, 10 February 1999; and Derwin Pereira, 'Musical Chairs in Indonesia', *Straits Times*, 17 January 1999.

139 Interview, Benny Murdani, 3 September 1998.

140 'MPR Wants Gradual Phasing out of ABRI from Parliament', *Agence France Presse*, 12 November 1998.

141 John Haseman, 'Credibility Gap', *Jane's Defence Weekly*, 18 November 1998.

142 Interview, Susilo Bambang Yudhoyono, 4 September 1998. See also 'Indonesian Military Blames Policies of Old Regime for its Past Deeds', *Agence France Presse*, 21 August 1998; and 'Habibie Aide Sees Turkish Model for Indonesian Military', *Agence France Presse*, 24 November 1998.

143 Interview, Susilo Bambang Yudhoyono, 27 October 1998. According to Yudhoyono, the number of military personnel seconded to non-military posts had been reduced from 14 600 in 1995 and 13 200 in 1997. See also Susilo Bambang Yudhoyono, 'The Roles of the Indonesian Armed Forces in the Process of Democratisation', paper delivered at the conference 'The Relations between the European Union and Indonesia in the Context of the Asian Crisis', The Hague, Netherlands, 26–27 October 1998.

144 Douglas Kammen, 'Military Politics and Kekaryaan in Post-Soeharto Indonesia', paper delivered at the conference 'Indonesia after Suharto', University of Auckland, 9–10 September 1998. Another worrying factor for the military leadership was the extent to which the economic crisis had reduced the revenues from military-owned businesses that supplement the military's budgetary allotments.

145 Confidential interview, September 1998.

146 Confidential interview, August 1998.

147 Interviews, Amien Rais, 30 August 1998; and Fadli Zon, 3 September 1998.

148 Two excellent analyses of the military are in Harold Crouch, 'Wiranto and Habibie: Military-Civilian Relations since May 1998', paper delivered at the conference 'Democracy in Indonesia? The Crisis and Beyond', Melbourne, 11–12 December 1998; and John Haseman, 'Indonesia's Armed Forces: Difficult Challenges, New Future', *Southeast Asian Affairs*, forthcoming.

149 Confidential interview, September 1998.

150 Interview, Susilo Bambang Yudhoyono, 4 September 1998. For examples of the military refusing to address past problems, see 'Military Police Probe of Black Friday Shooting Draws a Blank', *Agence France Presse*, 15 February 1999; and Cindy Shiner, 'Families Seek Missing Indonesian Activists', *Washington Post*, 16 September 1998.

151 Interview, Benny Murdani, 3 September 1998.

152 For Wiranto's rejection of this alternative, see 'Army Chief Wiranto Rules

Out Military Junta in Country', *BBC Summary of World Broadcasts*, 16 February 1999.

153 Jay Solomon, 'Indonesia Secures Extra $6 billion; Creditors Agree to Reschedule Debts', *Asian Wall Street Journal*, 17 July 1998.

154 Not everyone took solace in the rupiah's strengthening from 12 000 to the dollar to 8000 in the fourth quarter of 1998. Some economists ascribed the rise principally to the government's daily conversion of US dollar-denominated loans into rupiah. They warned that the rupiah was likely to weaken again once the supply of foreign-currency aid was exhausted.

155 Praginanto, 'Gloomy Forecast for Indonesia Causes Worry', *Nikkei Weekly*, 23 January 1999.

156 'Indonesia's Poor Jumps to Close to Half its 202 Million People', *Agence France Presse*, 13 December 1998.

157 Jeremy Wagstaff, 'Survey Finds Indonesia Crisis is Less Severe than Estimated', *Asian Wall Street Journal*, 25 January 1999. The Bank also argued that Indonesian estimates of unemployment and school dropout rates were grossly exaggerated.

158 The definition of poverty used in Indonesia is relatively strict. Only those unable to earn enough to consume at least 2200 calories a day are considered impoverished. Other, internationally accepted definitions of poverty show a much higher incidence of poverty in Indonesia. A good review of the poverty debate is in Anne Booth, 'The Causes and Consequences of Indonesia's Economic Crisis', paper delivered at the conference 'The Relations between the European Union and Indonesia in the Context of the Asian Crisis', The Hague, Netherlands, 26–27 October 1998.

159 Interview, Steven Woodhouse, 30 August 1998. See also Jenny Grant, 'Malnutrition Stunts Growth of Generation', *South China Morning Post*, 24 September 1998.

160 Information provided by Steven Woodhouse at the conference 'Indonesia: The Social Costs of the Financial Crisis and International Aid', Asia Society, Washington, DC, 22 January 1999. See also Andreas Harsono, 'Indonesia's Economic Crisis Wrecks the Dreams of its Poor', *American Reporter*, 11 January 1999; and 'Indon Warned of Danger of Mentally-Deficient Generation', *Straits Times*, 27 March 1999.

161 Derwin Pereira, 'Over 5m School Dropouts Yearly', *Straits Times*, 23 February 1999; Margot Cohen, 'Lessons in Hardship', *Far Eastern Economic Review*, 24 September 1998; and 'Indonesian Government to Close, Cut 20 000 Elementary Schools', *Agence France Presse*, 16 December 1998.

162 Grainne McCarthy, 'Indonesia Aid Spending Slowed by Corruption Fears', *Dow Jones Newswires*, 29 October 1998; and 'Official Admits Diverting Half of Jakarta's Rice: Report', *Agence France Presse*, 17 September 1998.

163 Remarks by Ann Thomson at 'Indonesia: The Social Cost of the Financial Crisis and International Aid', discussion hosted by the Asia Society, Washington, DC, 22 January 1999.

164 Sander Thoenes, 'Doubts Mount over Bank Rescue Plan', *Financial Times*, 12 December 1988. More than 40 Indonesian banks, including six of the seven state-owned banks, had capital-adequacy ratios of less than minus 25% in early 1999.

165 Noel Fung, 'Japan Ex-Im Bk Baffled by Lack of Indonesia Trade Loan Use', *Dow Jones Newswires*, 25 November 1998.

166 Two of Soeharto's sons, Bambang Trihatmodjo and Hutomo Mandala Putra, were said to be the two largest bad debtors to Bank Mandiri, the new institution created by the merger of four state-owned banks. See 'The Economic Standstill: On a Precipice?' *Van Zorge Report*, 9 April 1999.

167 Dan Murphy, 'Indonesia's Dangerous Delay on Bank Closures', *Far Eastern Economic Review*, 3 March 1999; Jay Solomon, 'Indonesia's Habibie-Tied Bank Manages to Stay Open', *Asian Wall Street Journal*, 3 March 1999; and Philip Bowring, 'Who Will Pick Up the Tab for Indonesia's Bad Debts?' *International Herald Tribune*, 10–11 April 1999.

168 Kevin Evans, 'The Economy: From Transition to Transformation', paper delivered at the Indonesia Update Conference, Australian National University, 25 September 1998.

169 Confidential interview, 2 September 1998. For details of the Frankfurt Agreement, see Michael Casey, Grainne McCarthy & I Made Sentana, 'Indonesia Debt Plan Modest Relief for Crippled Economy', *Dow Jones Newswires*, 4 June 1998; and *Indonesia in Crisis: A Macroeconomic Update*, World Bank, Washington, DC, 16 July 1998, p. 2.4.

170 Henny Sender, 'A Tale of Why Indonesia Never Got a Debt Deal', *The Wall Street Journal*, 4 November 1998.

171 Gde Anugrah Arke, 'Bankruptcy Verdicts Rattle Indonesia Reforms', *Reuter*, 1 April 1999,

172 See Margot Cohen, 'Million-Dollar Saliva', *Far Eastern Economic Review*, 21 January 1999; and Faith Keenan, 'Food for Thought', *Far Eastern Economic Review*, 21 January 1999.

173 Tom Bannikoff, 'A Company Copes in Post-Suharto Indonesia', *Asiaweek*, 13 November 1998; and 'Indorayon's Imbroglio', *Jakarta Post*, 30 November 1998. Indorayon executives rejected allegations of environmental damage and accused local trouble-makers of trying to extort money from the firm.

174 Peter Waldman & Jay Solomon, 'U.S. Power Deals in Indonesia Draw Flak', *Asian Wall Street Journal*, 24 December 1998.

175 Peter Waldman, 'Hand in Glove: How Suharto's Circle, Mining Firm Did so Well Together', *Wall Street Journal*, 29 September 1998; and Michael Shari, 'Indonesia: What Did Mobil Know?', *Business Week*, 29 December 1998.

176 It is often asserted, mistakenly, that the Chinese control up to three-quarters of Indonesia's economy. Although the Chinese play dominant roles in many private-sector industries, the government and agriculture account for a substantial share of national economic output. Even the share of private-sector activity attributed to the Chinese is often overstated. For example, the holdings of Indonesia's largest conglomerate, the Salim Group, are counted as Chinese wealth. In fact, non-Chinese partners hold considerable stakes in many of the Group's most profitable enterprises. As discussed in chapter 5, Soeharto relatives figure prominently in several Salim companies. See also Jusuf Wanandi, 'The Indonesian Crisis and Beyond', *Asia Pacific Review*, forthcoming.

177 The ethnic-Chinese community is not nearly as homogeneous as is often

portrayed in the press, domestic and foreign. Many poor and middle-class Chinese are resentful of the leading ethnic-Chinese tycoons, whom they blame for fuelling the stereotype of the 'greedy Chinese' and exacerbating ethnic tensions.

178 Interview, Abdurrahman Wahid, 27 August 1998.

179 Confidential interview, 1 September 1998. See also Aries Kelana, Ahmad Husein & Endang Sukendar, 'Tracking Down the Sins of the Bankers', *Gatra*, 5 September 1998.

180 Adam Schwarz, 'The Perils of Restructuring Indonesia', *Asian Wall Street Journal*, 13 October 1998; and S. Karene Witcher & Jay Solomon, 'Indonesia Takes Over Much of Country's Banking System', *Wall Street Journal*, 24 August 1998.

181 Interview, Aburizal Bakrie, 13 March 1998. See also 'Tycoon Wants Perks for Natives', *Straits Times*, 13 August 1998; and 'A Pribumi Tycoon on the New Indonesia', *Asiaweek*, 18 December 1998.

182 Interview, Suryo Sulistio, 2 March 1998.

183 Mahathir quoted in 'Mahathir on Ethnic Chinese', *Straits Times*, 10 February 1999; interview, Kusumo Martoredjo, 5 March 1998.

184 Jay Solomon, 'Habibie's Plan to Sell Off $15 billion in Assets Raises Concern with IMF', *Asian Wall Street Journal*, 27 October 1998.

185 'Indonesia Tells Timber Cos to Give 20% Stake to Cooperatives', *Dow Jones Newswires*, 18 October 1998.

186 Salil Tripathi & Dan Murphy, 'No Miracle Cure', *Far Eastern Economic Review*, 19 November 1998; and Jay Solomon, 'Indonesia Extends Time to Sell Companies for Loan Repayment', *Asian Wall Street Journal*, 10 November 1998.

187 Dan Murphy, 'Is Adi Sasono the Most Dangerous Man in Indonesia?', *Far Eastern Economic Review*, 3 December 1998. See also Raphael Pura, 'New Jakarta Minister Pushes Old Agenda', *Asian Wall Street Journal*, 2 December 1998; and Derwin Pereira, 'Adi Sasono: Can He Be Indonesia's Next President?', *Singapore Business Times*, 21 January 1999.

188 Quoted in 'Adi Sasono's People's Economy a Political Platform: Analyst', *Jakarta Post*, 18 February 1999.

189 See Ricklefs, *A History of Modern Indonesia since c. 1300*, Stanford University Press, Stanford, CA, 2nd edn, 1993, p. 189. Surjodiningrat's political organisation did not survive the Japanese occupation of the early 1940s. But it was revived in the early 1950s as a local Yogyakarta party known as Gerinda. Cooperatives were also promoted in the late 1950s by President Sukarno, who saw them as a politically popular alternative to Chinese-run businesses. See Richard Robison, *The Rise of Capital*, Allen & Unwin, Sydney, 1986.

190 Interview, Adi Sasono, 3 March 1998; and Murphy, 'Is Adi Sasono the Most Dangerous Man?'.

191 Interview, Adi Sasono, 3 March 1998.

192 Interview, Ahmad Soemargono, 26 August 1998.

193 Confidential interview, March 1998.

194 Lindsay Murdoch, 'Massacres at Dawn', *Sydney Morning Herald*, 14 November 1998; 'Indonesia: Human Rights and Pro-Independence

Actions in Irian Jaya', Human Rights Watch, New York, 28 December 1998; and Sander Thoenes, 'Indonesia's Urge to Break Up', *Christian Science Monitor*, 2 April 1999.

195 Interview, Xanana Gusmao, 30 August 1998.

196 John Martinkus, 'Timorese Flee from Marauding Militiamen', *Sydney Morning Herald*, 30 January 1999; and 'Church Speaks of "Almost Total Anarchy"', *BBC Summary of World Broadcasts*, 21 January 1999. For a longer account of the political debate inside East Timor, see Sidney Jones, 'Political Dynamics of the East Timor Issue in Post-Soeharto Indonesia', paper delivered at the conference 'Indonesia after Suharto', University of Auckland, 9–10 September 1998.

197 Greg Earl, 'Can Timor's fragments make a nation?', *Australian Financial Review*, 6 February 1999; and 'Indonesia to Propose East Timor Join ASEAN', *Agence France Presse*, 16 February 1999.

198 John McBeth & Dan Murphy, 'Sudden Impact', *Far Eastern Economic Review*, 11 February 1999. In the article, a senior Habibie aide, Dewi Fortuna Anwar, described East Timor as 'an appendix giving a fever to the rest of the country'.

199 Indonesian officials usually neglect to point out that the MPR decree making East Timor the 27th province of Indonesia in 1976 followed a highly manipulated 'vote' in the province.

200 Louise Williams, 'Now, Be Grateful . . . Or Be Cast Adrift', *Sydney Morning Herald*, 29 January 1999; and 'Indonesia Offers Integration or Civil War in Autonomy Message: Gusmao', *Agence France Presse*, 31 March 1999.

201 Dan Murphy, 'East Timor Up in Arms', *Far Eastern Economic Review*, 18 February 1999; and Lewa Pardomuan, 'E. Timor Loyalists say Ready to Die for Indonesia', *Reuter*, 4 February 1999.

202 Quoted in 'Forgiveness Requires Courage', *Asiaweek*, 26 February 1999; and 'Nobel Laureate Horta Says East Timor Talks Doomed', *Reuter*, 11 March 1999.

203 Interview, Xanana Gusmao, 30 August 1998. See also the interview with Xanana by Radio Australia, reprinted in *BBC Summary of World Broadcasts*, 17 February 1999.

204 See Michael Backman, 'Independent East Timor May Prove Pessimists Wrong', *Asian Wall Street Journal*, 10 March 1999; and Dan Murphy, John McBeth & Bertil Lintner, 'Economy of Scale', *Far Eastern Economic Review*, 11 February 1999.

205 Louise Williams, 'Timor's Lost Generation', *Sydney Morning Herald*, 20 February 1999; and Jenny Grant, 'East Timor: Medical Care in Tatters as Doctors Flee', *South China Morning Post*, 12 March 1999. For a longer account of East Timor's challenge, see Richard Tanter, 'Tomorrow, in Timor Lorosae', *Inside Indonesia*, April–June 1999.

206 Quoted in 'Forgiveness Requires Courage'.

207 See 'Indonesian Journalists Visit Falintel in the Bush', *Suara Pembaruan*, 20 February 1999. The article described the first-ever visit by Indonesian journalists to secret rebel positions in East Timor.

208 Andreas Harsono, 'Megawati's Stance May Hamper Timor Independence Move', *American Reporter*, 8 February 1999; and Karen Polglaze, 'East

Timor Should Remain Part of Indonesia, Says Megawati', *Australian Associated Press*, 16 March 1999.

209 Christopher Torchia, 'Veterans Angered by East Timor Talk', *Associated Press*, 20 February 1999; and 'Irian Jaya Wants Self-Determination Now Too: Church', *Australian Associated Press*, 23 February 1999.

210 Shoeb Kagda, 'Northern Sumatra Airs its Grievances', *Singapore Business Times*, 16 October 1998; John McBeth, 'Crisis, What Crisis?', *Far Eastern Economic Review*, 3 December 1998; 'Scholar Insists Riau Deserves Independence', *Jakarta Post*, 13 March 1999.

211 John McBeth & Margot Cohen, 'Loosening the Bonds', *Far Eastern Economic Review*, 21 January 1999. See also Margot Cohen, 'The More the Merrier', *Far Eastern Economic Review,* 21 January 1999; and Greg Earl, 'Indonesia's Separation Anxiety', *Australian Financial Review*, 26 February 1999. An economic ratio called the 'coefficient of vertical imbalance' measures the degree of central government fiscal control over lower levels of government. A score of zero represents total central control; a score of one represents total autonomy of sub-national governments. Indonesia's score in the early 1990s was 0.19. The equivalent score for Malaysia was 0.53 and for the USA it was 0.88. See 'Regional Development in Indonesia', World Bank, 27 February 1997.

212 Vaudine England, 'Break-Up Theories Ignore Years of Nation-Building and Strong Desire for Stability', *South China Morning Post*, 31 January 1999. See also 'Intellectuals, Go Home', *Indonesia Political Watch*, 25 January 1999; Gerry van Klinken, 'Is Indonesia Breaking Down?', *Far Eastern Economic Review*, 18 March 1999; and Jamie Mackie, 'Ethnic Violence in Indonesia', *Asian Wall Street Journal*, 21 March 1999. An opinion poll conducted in early 1999 found 75 per cent of Indonesians saying they were proud or content to be Indonesian citizens. See 'Preliminary Summary of Public Opinion Preceding the Parliamentary Elections in Indonesia—1999', a survey implemented by the International Foundation for Election Systems, March 1999.

213 'Much Ado about Autonomy', *Jakarta Post*, 15 February 1999. The laws on elections and party eligibility also ran counter to the decentralisation trend. In general, the laws discriminated against regional-based parties and effectively obliged all parties to have national constituencies. See 'The New Legal Framework for Elections in Indonesia', National Democratic Institute for International Affairs, Washington, DC, 23 February 1999; and Charlie Zenzie, 'Legislating Reformasi: Indonesia's New Political Laws and Parties', *USINDO Report*, no. 4, March 1999.

214 Atika Shubert, 'Separatism Revives in Indonesia', *Washington Post*, 12 January 1999; and 'Students in Aceh Province Press for Referendum', *Agence France Presse*, 8 March 1999.

215 See 'Enough with Politics, Food Please!', *Castle's Insight Indonesia*, 7 July 1998.

216 Greg Earl, 'Foreign Aid Need Gags Indonesia', *Australian Financial Review*, 22 January 1999; and Eduardo Lachica, 'Rais Urges U.S. to Aid Indonesia on Vote', *Asian Wall Street Journal*, 10 March 1999.

217 Quoted in 'Lawlessness Worse than Disintegration', *Jakarta Post*, 4 December 1998.
218 Interview, Amien Rais, 30 August 1998.
219 See John Colmey & David Liebhold, 'Suharto in the Shadows', *Time*, 8 February 1999; and Jenny Grant, 'Suharto Cash Linked to 12 Parties', *South China Morning Post*, 2 February 1999. An official of Amien Rais' National Mandate Party said a member of Soeharto's family offered the party Rp.11 billion in campaign finance support. The offer, which was intended to convince Rais to mute his criticisms of Soeharto, was rejected. Confidential interview, 28 January 1999.
220 Jeffrey Winters, 'Enemy of Progress', *Time*, 3 August 1998. See also Richard Robison, 'Economic and Political Liberalisation in Southeast Asia: Inexorable Force or Red Herring?', a paper delivered at the Southern California Workshop on Political and Economic Liberalization, University of Southern California, 21 March 1995. Speaking of the elite, Robison wrote 'the wealthy and powerful in Indonesia cannot be matched for their enthusiastic embrace of the free rider philosophy and rampant individualism in behaviour'.
221 In Habibie's first 10 months in office, 141 new political parties were formed and 106 of them applied for verification from the Ministry of Justice. Only 48 of the parties ultimately met the eligibility criteria to participate in the June 1999 elections. See 'Party Screening: A Difficult Test Passed with Surprising Ease', *Van Zorge Report*, 12 March 1999.
222 Lindsay Murdoch & Jenny Grant, 'Vote-Buying Fear in Poll', *Melbourne Age*, 31 March 1999.
223 For a comparative perspective on this problem, see Fareed Zakaria, 'The Rise of Illiberal Democracy', *Foreign Affairs*, November/December 1997. See also Vaudine England, 'Citizens "Have Poor Grasp of Democracy"', *South China Morning Post*, 16 March 1999. One poll conducted in early 1999 found that only about 50 per cent of Indonesians are tolerant of opposing political views. See 'Indonesia National Voter Education Survey', produced by Charney Research & ACNielsen, February 1999.
224 Quoted in Margot Cohen, 'Unguided Missiles', *Far Eastern Economic Review*, 26 November 1998.
225 Robin Madrid, 'Forces for Moderation: Islamic Students in the Indonesian Student Movement', *Bulletin of Concerned Asian Scholars*, forthcoming.
226 Dorodjatun Kuntjoro-jakti, comments at a seminar organised by the U.S.–Indonesia Society, 2 December 1998.
227 Confidential interview, 23 December 1998.
228 Interview, Amien Rais, 28 January 1999.
229 'Analysts Oppose Call for Only Male Moslem Presidents', *Jakarta Post*, 9 November 1998. See also Margot Cohen, 'Indonesia: A Women's Leader?', *Far Eastern Economic Review*, 4 February 1999.
230 Quoted in 'Kalau Status Quo Ini Menguntungkan Islam, Mengapa Tidak' (If the status quo is good to Islam, why not?), *Tempo Interaktif*, 23 November 1998.
231 See the summary of remarks by Laksamana Sukardi at an Open Forum of the US–Indonesia Society, Washington, DC, 11 January 1999.
232 Interview, Mochtar Buchori, 2 September 1998.

233 Jamie Mackie, 'In the Shadow of Sukarno', *Asian Wall Street Journal*, 4 November 1998; and Keith Richburg, 'Sukarno Heir Plans to Return to Presidential Palace', *Washington Post*, 4 February 1999. For a more favourable assessment, see Jusuf Wanandi, 'Megawati: RI's next president?', *Jakarta Post*, 11 November 1998.
234 Quoted in Keith Richburg, 'Riots Follow Peaceful Protest', *Washington Post*, 15 November 1998.
235 Interview, Mochtar Buchori, 2 September 1998.
236 See William Liddle, 'Indonesia's Unexpected Failure of Leadership', in *The Politics of Post-Suharto Indonesia*, eds Adam Schwarz & Jonathan Paris, Council on Foreign Relations, New York, 1999; and Hamish McDonald, 'Demokrasi!', *Sydney Morning Herald*, 27 March 1999.
237 A detailed party and provincial breakdown of the 1955 elections is in Herbert Feith, *The Indonesian Elections of 1955*, Modern Indonesia Project, Cornell University, 1957.
238 Interview, Jumhur Hidayat, 12 February 1999.
239 There are at least a half dozen smaller parties competing for the modernist Muslim vote as well.
240 Polls conducted in early 1999 found that rural residents in particular were worried that party politics will worsen conditions in Indonesia. See 'Preliminary Summary of Public Opinion Preceding the Parliamentary Elections in Indonesia—1999', a survey implemented by the International Foundation for Election Systems, March 1999.
241 The seminal work on the 1950s is Herbert Feith, *The Decline of Constitutional Democracy in Indonesia*, Cornell University Press, NY, 1962.
242 Interview, Amien Rais, 28 January 1999.

Index